Solaris 9:
The Complete Reference

About the Author

Dr. Paul A. Watters completed his Ph.D. in computer science at Macquarie University. He also has degrees from the University of Cambridge, the University of Tasmania, and the University of Newcastle. He has worked in both commercial and R&D organizations, designing systems and software on the Solaris platform. His commercial interests are focused on Java and e-commerce, while his research areas include neural networks, artificial intelligence, and natural language processing. He is a columnist for the trade journal *Inside Solaris*, and has previously written *Solaris 8: The Complete Reference*, *Solaris Administration: A Beginner's Guide*, and *All-In-One Sun Certified Solaris 8 System Administrator*, all published by McGraw Hill/Osborne. Watters is Managing Director of Cassowary Computing Pty Ltd, and lives with his wife Maya in Sydney, Australia.

Solaris 9:
The Complete Reference

Dr. Paul A. Watters

McGraw-Hill/Osborne

New York Chicago San Francisco
Lisbon London Madrid Mexico City
Milan New Delhi San Juan
Seoul Singapore Sydney Toronto

McGraw-Hill/Osborne
2600 Tenth Street
Berkeley, California 94710
U.S.A.

To arrange bulk purchase discounts for sales promotions, premiums, or fund-raisers, please contact **McGraw-Hill**/Osborne at the above address. For information on translations or book distributors outside the U.S.A., please see the International Contact Information page immediately following the index of this book.

Solaris 9: The Complete Reference

1234567890 CUS CUS 0198765432

ISBN 0-07-222305-7

Publisher
Brandon A. Nordin

Vice President & Associate Publisher
Scott Rogers

Acquisitions Editor
Jane Brownlow

Project Editor
Mark Karmendy

Acquisitions Coordinator
Emma Acker

Technical Editor
Nalneesh Gaur

Copy Editors
Darren Meiss, Lisa Theobald, and Dennis Weaver

Proofreader
Susie Elkind

Indexer
Claire Splan

Page Composition
Apollo Publishing Services and Osborne Production staff

Illustrators
Michael Mueller and Lyssa Wald

Series Design
Peter F. Hancik

This book was composed with Corel VENTURA™ Publisher.

This book is dedicated to my nephew
Matthew Watters.

Contents

Part I

Installation

Part II

System Essentials

Part III

Managing Users and Roles

Part IV

Managing File Systems and Printers

Part VI

Services and Directories

Part VII

Enterprise

Acknowledgments

I would like to acknowledge the inspiring professionalism and dedicated support of the team at McGraw Hill/Osborne. Jane Brownlow has worked tirelessly to ensure that this title arrived on the market in a timely fashion with a strict commitment to quality. Emma Acker and Mark Karmendy provided valuable insight and feedback on each chapter. Many thanks go to Darren Meiss, Lisa Theobald, and Dennis Weaver, who thoroughly worked the manuscript, ironing the creases and ensuring readability. The technical editor, Nalneesh Gaur, was as thorough as always. Thanks for your valuable input, Nalneesh.

To everyone at my agency, Studio B, thanks for your past and continued support. To Neil Salkind and Vicki Harding, my agents, thanks for your wisdom and pragmatic advice. To Kristen Pickens, Stacey Barone, and Jessica Richards, thanks for making sure everything works out. On the administrative front, thanks go to Craig Wiley, and Sherry and David Rogelberg.

To Bill Moffitt at Sun Microsystems, thanks for your support and valuable comments on this book.

Finally, thanks to my family, especially my wife Maya and my parents Wal and Judy Watters, for always being there, through good times and tough times.

Introduction

Today, Solaris is the most widely used UNIX operating system in the world. I can't quote figures (although the IDC reports I've read will back me up), but while other vendors have quietly slipped away, Sun has been at the forefront of advances in distributed and enterprise systems technology. Always putting stock in their catch cry, "The network is the computer!," Sun has fostered the development of Java 2 Enterprise Edition, Jiro, Jini, and other technologies that are removing some of the traditional barriers to highly available, loosely coupled but integrated systems.

Solaris 9 is the latest release in a long line of systems that go back for 20 years. Through the development of the SPARC and UltraSPARC chips, to the widespread deployment of 64-bit UNIX (even on the desktop with the Sun Blade!), innovation combined with stability continue to be the successes that drive Solaris. Although Solaris 9 introduces many new features, these build on existing strengths rather than completely changing the operating environment. I am constantly amazed at how much technical knowledge is learned then discarded two years later because vendors so often completely change directions. It's always comforting to know that by learning Solaris, you are developing skills that will be useful for many years to come.

Writing a reference book for an operating system that has a three-volume "basic" system administration set and has thousands of pages of reference material available, is a challenge. There will be some topics that you may expect to find here that are not present—this is either because (a) the reference manuals cover the topic adequately; (b) the topic is too complex for a general purpose reference and other books are available that can give more in-depth coverage; or (c) the topic has little relevance in a modern production environment. Please let me know by e-mail at **solaris9@cassowary.net** if there's something you believe is missing and you'd like to see covered in the future, or if you come across a typographical error. Complaints can be sent to **solaris9-complaints@cassowary.net** (no, this is not redirected to /dev/null....) ☺.

The basic approach I've taken in this book is to identify a core area—like LDAP—and write a chapter about it. The chapter aims to contain introductory material, as well as discussion of key topics, commonly used procedures, worked examples, and reference information for the commands covered. I know that some readers expect the book to contain 90 percent of material in the latter category, but my opinion is that man pages serve this purpose particularly well. Type **man man** for details, if you're new to Solaris.

A key issue for Solaris administrators is the future of Solaris on the Intel platform. While Sun has previously supported the concurrent release of Solaris on the SPARC and Intel platforms, they only released an early beta of Solaris 9 for Intel, and have not indicated when (if?) they will release Solaris 9 for Intel as a product. While support is still being provided for production systems running Solaris 8, the release of new low-cost Linux servers by Sun appears to indicate a shift away from Solaris for Intel. While I've covered the installation of Solaris for Intel, most examples in the book focus on commands that work on both platforms.

I hope you will find this book useful and that my material exceeds your needs and caters to your "wants".

The Complete Reference

Part I

Installation

The
Complete
Reference

Solaris 9

Chapter 1

Introduction to Solaris 9

Operating systems are the building blocks of computer systems, and provide the interface between user applications and computer hardware. Solaris 9 is a multi-user, multitasking operating system, developed and sold by Sun Microsystems (**http://www.sun.com/**), and is one implementation of the UNIX operating system that draws on both the System V (AT&T) and Berkeley (BSD) systems. It has risen from little more than a research project to become the dominant UNIX operating system in the international marketplace today. Solaris 9 is the latest in a long line of operating environment releases based around the SunOS operating system, which is currently in version 5.9. Solaris is commonly found in large corporations and educational institutions that require concurrent, multi-user access on individual hosts and between hosts connected via the Internet. However, it is also rapidly being adopted by small businesses and individual developers, through Sun's promotion of the "Free Solaris" program. In this book, when we refer to "Solaris 9," many of the commands and procedures will apply equally to earlier versions of Solaris 2.*x*. Commands for Solaris 1.*x* are specified only where relevant.

Many desktop computer users have never heard of the word "Sun" in the context of computing, nor are they usually familiar with the term "Solaris" as an operating environment. However, almost every time that an Internet user sends an e-mail message or opens a file from a networked server running Sun's Network File System (NFS) product, Solaris 9 is transparently supporting many of today's existing Internet applications. In the enterprise computing industry, Sun is synonymous with highly available, highly reliable performance hardware, while Solaris 9 is often the operating environment of choice to support database servers and application servers. Sun's hardware solutions are based around the SPARC and UltraSPARC integrated circuit technologies, which currently support more than 64 processors in a single E10000 server system.

In recent times, two of Sun's innovations have moved the spotlight from the server room to the desktop. First, Sun's development of the Java programming language, which promises "write once, read anywhere" application execution across any platform that supports the Java Virtual Machine, has revolutionized the development of networked applications. In addition, Java "applets" now appear on many Web pages, being small encapsulated applications that execute client-side, while "servlets" power the back end of many three-tier applications, such as CRM and complex HR applications.

Secondly, Sun is promoting a "free" version of Solaris 9 for the SPARC hardware platform. However, the release of a new version of Solaris for the Intel platform has been delayed. This means that organizations that have previously committed to using Microsoft Windows or Caldera/SCO OpenServer on the Intel platform, for example, can reuse the servers currently deployed with these operations by installing Solaris 8 for Intel, and upgrading when Solaris 9 becomes available. Sun has also made Solaris 9 more accessible for desktop users, offering the StarOffice productivity suite for free. StarOffice is a product that is competitive to Microsoft Office—it contains word processing, spreadsheet, presentation, and database components that are fully integrated. In addition, StarOffice runs on many different platforms, and in eight languages, meaning that a user on a Sun SPARCstation can share documents seamlessly with users on Linux and Microsoft

Windows. The combination of a solid operating system with a best of breed productivity suite has given Solaris new exposure in the desktop market.

This book is a "complete reference" for the Solaris 9 operating environment, and for the SunOS 5.9 operating system, meaning that we will try to cover, in detail, the operational aspects of Solaris and SunOS. If you simply need to look up a command's options, you can usually make use of Sun's own online "manual pages," which you can access by typing **man command**, where *command* is the command for which you require help. Or, you can retrieve the text of man pages and user manuals online by using the search facility at **http://docs.sun.com/**. This reference will be most useful when you need to implement a specific solution, and you need practical, tried-and-tested solutions. Although Solaris 9 comes with a set of remote access tools and servers by default, these are not always the best tools, in terms of security, that you should use in a production environment. For example, although FTP is fine for transferring files around a local area network, you should conduct remote exchanges of data using a secure file transfer system, such as sftp. In outlining a solution to a problem, we generally introduce Sun-supplied software first, and then discuss the installation and configuration of third-party alternatives. You can also use this book as a reference for previous versions of Solaris, since much of the command syntax remains unchanged across operating system releases. Command syntax is typically identical across different platforms as well (SPARC and Intel).

If you've been keeping track of recent press releases, you may be wondering why Solaris has a version number of "9," while SunOS has a revision level of 5.9. Since the release of Solaris 7 (SunOS 5.7), Sun has opted to number its releases sequentially with a single version number, based on the old minor revision number. This means that the release sequence for Solaris has been 2.5.1, 2.6, 7, 8, and now 9. Thus, many sites will still be running Solaris 2.6 without feeling too far left behind, especially if they don't require the 64-bit functionality for the UltraSPARC processors provided with Solaris 7 and beyond. Sun does provide "jumbo patches" for previous operating system releases, which should always be installed when released, to ensure that bugs (particularly security bugs) are resolved as soon as possible. Thus, most of the commands and topics covered in this book for Solaris 9 are equally applicable to Solaris 7, 8, and all previous releases of SunOS 5.*x*.

However, wherever possible, we have also included references to the SunOS 4.*x* operating system, which was retrospectively labeled the Solaris 1.*x* platform. This is because many installations have just started using SunOS 5.*x* in the past few years, and until Y2K problems emerged with SunOS 4.*x*, many sites still ran legacy applications on this platform (especially if they prefer the BSD-style SunOS 4.*x* to the System V–style SunOS 5.*x* operating system). Many Internet firewalls, mail servers, and news servers still run on SPARC architecture CPUs, and some of these models are not supported by the SunOS 5.*x* operating system. Making the decision to upgrade from SunOS 4.*x* to SunOS 5.*x* was tough for many Sun installations.

Fortunately, with the release of Solaris 7, 8, and 9, 64-bit computing has arrived, and a stable platform has been arrived at. Many of the changes between Solaris 7, 8, and 9 may appear cosmetic; for example, Larry Wall's Perl interpreter has been included since the Solaris 8 distribution, meaning that a new generation of system administrators will no longer have the pleasure of carrying out their first post-installation task. However, other quite important developments in the area of networking and administration may not affect all users, but which are particularly important for the enterprise.

In this chapter, we cover the background to the Solaris 9 operating environment, which really begins with the invention and widespread adoption of the UNIX operating system. In addition, we also cover the means by which Solaris 9 can run cross-platform applications; for example, Solaris for Intel is capable of running Linux binary applications by using an application called *Lxrun*, which is freely available from Sun. Although earlier attempts to emulate other operating systems were largely unsuccessful (e.g., WABI for emulating Microsoft Windows), Sun's development of Java can be seen as a strong commitment to cross-platform interoperability. In addition, Solaris 9 provides many network management features that allow a Solaris 9 server to act as a primary or backup domain controller to manage Windows NT clients using Samba—for example, if you want the reliability of Solaris 9 coupled with the widespread adoption of Microsoft Windows as a desktop operating system.

Finally, we review some of the many sites on the Internet that provide useful information, software packages, and further reading on many of the topics that we cover in this book.

What Is UNIX?

UNIX is not easily defined, since it is an "ideal" operating system that has been instantiated by different vendors over the years, in some quite nonstandard ways. However, there are a number of features of UNIX and UNIX-like systems (such as Linux) that can be readily described. UNIX systems have a core kernel that is responsible for managing core system operations—such as logical devices for input/output (such as /dev/pty, for pseudo-terminals)—and allocating resources to carry out user-specified and system-requisite tasks. In addition, UNIX systems have a hierarchical file system that allows both relative and absolute file path naming, and is extremely flexible. UNIX file systems can be mounted locally, or remotely from a central fileserver. All operations on a UNIX system are carried out by processes, which may spawn child processes or other lightweight processes to perform discrete tasks. Processes can be uniquely identified by their process ID (PID).

Originally designed as a text processing system, UNIX systems share many tools that manipulate and filter text in various ways. In addition, small, discrete utilities can be easily combined to form complete applications in rather sophisticated ways. These applications are executed from a user shell, which defines the user interface to the kernel. Although GUI environments can be constructed around the shell, they are not mandatory.

UNIX is multiprocess, multi-user, and multithreaded. This means that more than one user can execute a shell and applications concurrently, and that each user can execute applications concurrently from within a single shell. Each of these applications can then create and remove lightweight processes as required.

Because UNIX was created by active developers, rather than operating system gurus, there was always a strong focus on creating an operating system that suited programmer's needs. A Bell System Technical Journal article in 1978 lists the key guiding principles of UNIX development:

- *Create small, self-contained programs that perform a single task.* When a new task needs to be solved, either create a new program that performs it, or combine tools from the toolset that already exists, to arrive at a solution. This is a similar orientation to the current trend towards encapsulation and independent component building (such as Enterprise Java Beans), where complicated systems are built from smaller, interacting but logically independent modules.

- *Programs should accept data from standard input and write to standard input;* thus, programs can be "chained" to process each other's output sequentially. Avoid interactive input in favor of command-line options that specify a program's actions to be performed. Presentation should be separated from what a program is trying to achieve. These ideas are consistent with the concept of piping, which is still fundamental to the operation of user shells. For example, the output of the lst command to list all files in a directory can be "piped" using the | symbol to a program such as grep to perform pattern matching. The number of pipes on a single command-line instruction is not limited.

- *Creating a new operating system or program should be undertaken on a scale of weeks not years: the creative spirit that leads to cohesive design and implementation should be exploited.* If software doesn't work, don't be afraid to build something better. This process of iterative revisions of programs has resurfaced in recent years with the rise of object-oriented development.

- *Make best use of all the tools available, rather than asking for more help.* The motivation behind UNIX is to construct an operating system that supports the kinds of toolsets required for successful development.

This is not intended to be an exhaustive list of the characteristics that define UNIX, however, these features are central to understanding the importance that UNIX developers often ascribe to the operating system. It is designed to be a programmer-friendly system.

The History of UNIX

UNIX was originally developed at Bell Laboratories as a private research project by a small group of people starting in the late 1960s. This group had experience with a number of different operating systems research efforts in the previous decade, and their goals with the UNIX project were to design an operating system to satisfy the objectives of transparency, simplicity, and modifiability, with the use of a new third-generation programming language. At the time of conception, typical vendor-specific operating systems were extremely large, and all written in assembly language, making them difficult to maintain. Although the first attempts to write the UNIX kernel were based on assembly language, later versions were written in a high-level language called C, which was developed during the same era. Even today, most modern operating system kernels, such as the Linux kernel, are written in C. After the kernel was developed using the first C compiler, a complete operating environment was developed, including the many utilities associated with UNIX today (e.g., the visual editor, *vi*). In this section, we examine the timeline leading to the development of UNIX, and the origins of the two main "flavors" of UNIX: AT&T (System V) and BSD.

Origins of UNIX

In 1969, Ken Thompson from AT&T's Bell Telephone Labs wrote the first version of the UNIX operating system on a DEC PDP-7. Disillusioned with the inefficiency of the Multics (Multiplexed Information and Computing Service) project, Thompson decided to create a programmer-friendly operating system that limited the functions contained within the kernel and allowed greater flexibility in the design and implementation of applications. The PDP-7 was a modest system on which to build a new operating system— it only had an assembler and a loader, and it would allow only a single user login at any one time. It didn't even have a hard disk—the developers were forced to partition physical memory into an operating system segment and a RAM disk segment. Thus, the first UNIX file system was emulated entirely in RAM!

After successfully crafting a single user version of UNIX on the PDP-7, Thompson and his colleague Dennis Ritchie ported the system to a much larger DEC PDP-11/20 system in 1970. This project was funded with the requirement of building a text-processing system for patents, the descendents of which still exist in text filters such as `troff`. The need to create application programs ultimately led to the development of the first C compiler by Ritchie, which was based on the B language. C was written with portability in mind—thus, platform-specific libraries could be addressed using the same function call from source code that would also compile on another hardware platform. Although the PDP-11 was better than the PDP-7, it was still very modest compared to today's scientific calculators—it had 24K of addressable memory, with 12K reserved for the operating system. By 1972, the number of worldwide UNIX installations had grown to 10.

The next major milestone in the development of UNIX was the rewriting of the kernel in C, by Ritchie and Thompson, in 1973. This explains why C and UNIX are strongly related—even today, most UNIX applications are written in C, even though other programming languages have long been made available. Following the development of the C kernel, the owners of UNIX (being AT&T) began licensing the source code to educational institutions within the U.S. and abroad. However, these licenses were often restrictive, and the releases were not widely advertised. No support was offered, and no mechanism was available for officially fixing bugs. However, because users had access to the source code, the ingenuity in hacking code—whose legacy exists today in community projects like Linux—gathered steam, particularly in the University of

California at Berkeley. The issue of licensing and AT&T's control over UNIX would determine the future fragmentation of the operating system in years to come.

In 1975, the first distribution of UNIX software was made by the Berkeley group, and was known as the BSD. Berkeley was Ken Thompson's alma mater, and he teamed up with two graduate students (Bill Joy and Chuck Haley) who were later to become leading figures in the UNIX world. They worked on a UNIX Pascal compiler that was released as part of BSD, and Bill Joy also wrote the first version of vi, the visual editor, which continues to be popular even today.

In 1978, the seventh edition of the operating system was released, and it supported many different hardware architectures, including the IBM 360, Interdata 8/32, and an Interdata 7/32. The version 7 kernel was a mere 40K in size, and included the following system calls:

_exit	access	acct	alarm	brk	chdir
chmod	chown	chroot	close	creat	dup
dup2	exec*	exit	fork	fstat	ftime
getegid	geteuid	getgid	getpid	getuid	gtty
indir	ioctl	kill	link	lock	lseek
mknod	mount	mpxcall	nice	open	pause
phys	pipe	pkoff	pkon	profil	ptrace
read	sbrk	setgid	setuid	signal	stat
stime	stty	sync	tell	time	times
umask	umount	unlink	utime	wait	write

Indeed, the full manual for version 7 is now available online at **http://plan9.bell-labs .com/7thEdMan/index.html**.

With the worldwide popularity of UNIX version 7, AT&T began to realize that UNIX might be a valuable commercial product, and attempted to restrict the teaching of UNIX from source code in university courses, thereby protecting valuable intellectual property. In addition, AT&T began to charge license fees for access to the UNIX source for the first time. This prompted the UCB group to create their own variant of UNIX—the BSD distribution now contained a full operating system in addition to the traditional applications that originally formed the distribution. As a result, version 7 forms the basis for all the UNIX versions currently available. This version of UNIX also contained a full Brian Kernighan and Ritchie C compiler, and the Bourne shell. The branching of UNIX into AT&T and BSD "flavors" continues even today, although many commercial systems—such as SunOS, which are derived from BSD—have now adopted many System V features, as discussed below.

The most influential BSD versions of UNIX were 4.2, released in 1983, and 4.3, released in 1987. The DARPA-sponsored development of the Internet was largely undertaken on BSD UNIX, and most of the early commercial vendors of UNIX used BSD UNIX rather than paying license fees to AT&T. Indeed, many hardware platforms even today, right up to Cray super computers, can still run BSD out of the box. Other responses to the commercialization of UNIX included Andrew Tanenbaum's independent solution, which was to write a new UNIX-like operating system from scratch that would be compatible with UNIX, but without even one line of AT&T code. Tanenbaum called it Minix, and Minix is still taught in operating systems courses today. Minix was also to play a crucial role in Linus Torvalds' experiments with his UNIX-like operating system, known today as Linux.

Bill Joy left Berkeley prior to the release of 4.2BSD, and modified the 4.1c system to form SunOS. In the meantime, AT&T continued with their commercial development of the UNIX platform. In 1983, they released the first System V Release 1, which had worked its way up to Release 3 by 1987. This is the release that several of the older generation of mainframe hardware vendors, such as HP and IBM, based their HP-UX and AIX systems upon, respectively. At this time, Sun and AT&T also began planning a future merging of the BSD and System V distributions. In 1990, AT&T released System V Release 4, which formed the basis for the SunOS 5.*x* release in 1992—this differed substantially from the previous SunOS 4.*x* systems which were entirely based on BSD. Other vendors, such as IBM and DEC, eschewed this new cooperating and formed the Open Software Foundation (OSF).

In recent years, a new threat has emerged to the market dominance of UNIX systems: Microsoft's enterprise-level computing products, such as Windows NT and Windows 2000, are designed to deliver price-competitive alternatives to UNIX on inexpensive Intel hardware. In the same way that UNIX outgunned the dominant mainframe vendors with a faster, leaner operating system, Microsoft's strategy has also been based on arguments concerning total cost of ownership (TCO), and a worldwide support scheme for an enormous installed base of desktop Microsoft Windows clients. However, the increasing popularity of Linux and the release of Solaris for Intel has forced Microsoft to defend their platform publicly, and the future of enterprise operating systems is not clear. UNIX will have an important role to play in the future, however. As desktop computing systems rapidly become connected to the Internet, they will require the kinds of services typically available under operating systems such as Solaris 9. As part of their territorial defense of the UNIX environment, many former adversaries in the enterprise computing market, such as IBM, HP, and Sun, have agreed to work towards a Common Open Software Environment (COSE), which is designed to capitalize on the common features of UNIX provided by these vendors. By distributing common operating system elements such as the Common Desktop Environment, based on X11, these vendors will be looking to streamline their competing application APIs, and to support emerging enterprise data processing standards, such as the Object Management Group's CORBA object management service.

Features of BSD

Solaris was originally derived from the BSD distribution from the University of California. Thus, commands in SunOS 4.*x* were very similar to those found in other BSD distributions, although these changed significantly in SunOS 5.*x* when System V Release 4 was adopted. For example, many veteran system administrators would still find themselves typing `ps aux` to display a process list, which is BSD style, rather than the newer `ps -eaf`, which is correct for SVR4. Before AT&T commercialized UNIX, the BSD distribution required elements of the AT&T system to form a fully operational system. By the early 1990s, the UCB groups had removed all dependencies on the AT&T system. This led to the development of many of the existing BSD systems available today, including FreeBSD and NetBSD.

The innovations pioneered at UCB included the development of a virtual memory system for UNIX, a fast file system (which supported long filenames and symbolic links), and the basic elements of a TCP/IP networking system (including authentication with Kerberos). The TCP/IP package included support for services such as telnet and ftp, and the sendmail mail transport agent, which used the simple mail transfer protocol. In addition, alternate shells to the default Bourne shell—such as the C shell, which uses C-like constructs to process commands within an interpreted framework—were also first seen in the BSD distribution, as were extensions to process management, such as job control. Standard terminal management libraries such as termcap and curses also originated with BSD. Products from other vendors were also introduced into BSD, including NFS clients and servers from Sun Microsystems. Later releases also included support for symmetric multiprocessing, thread management, and shared libraries.

It is often said that the BSD group gave rise to the community-oriented free software movement, which underlies many successful software projects being conducted around the world today. However, BSD is not the only attempt to develop a "free" version UNIX. In 1984, Richard Stallman started developing the GNU (GNU's Not UNIX) system, which was intended to be a replacement for UNIX that was completely free. The GNU C and C++ compilers were some of the first to fully support industry standards (ANSI), and the GNU Bourne again shell has many more features than the original Bourne shell. You can find more information about the GNU project at **http://www.gnu.org/**. In addition, several versions of BSD are still freely distributed and available, such as FreeBSD.

Features of System V Release 4

Solaris 9 integrates many features from the AT&T System V releases, including support for interprocess communication, which were missing in the BSD distributions. As we discussed earlier, many legal battles were fought over the UNIX name and source. System V was developed by the UNIX System Laboratories (USL), which was still majority-owned by AT&T in the early 1980s. However, Novell bought USL in early 1993. Eventually, USL sold UNIX to Novell, which ultimately sold it to X/Open. In 1991, the OSF-1 specification was released, and although DEC is the only major manufacturer to fully implement the standard, there is much useful cross-fertilization between

System V and other operating systems. Since Sun joined OSF in 1994, there has been new hope of standardizing UNIX services and API's across platforms.

The major contributions of System V to the UNIX platform are as follows:

- Enhancement of the Bourne shell, including shell functions
- The STREAMS and TLI networking libraries
- Remote file sharing (RFS)
- Improved memory paging
- The Application Binary Interface (ABI)

The major differences between SVR4 and BSD UNIX can be summarized as follows:

- **Boot scripts** */etc/init.d* in System V, */etc/rc.d* in BSD
- **Default shell** Bourne shell in System V, C shell in BSD
- **File system mount database** */etc/mnttab* in System V, */etc/mtab* in BSD
- **Kernel name** */unix* in System V, */vmunix* in BSD
- **Printing system** *lp* in System V, *lpr* in BSD
- **String functions** *memcopy* in System V, *bcopy* in BSD
- **Terminal initialization** */etc/inittab* in System V, */etc/ttys* in BSD
- **Terminal control** *termio* in System V, *termios* in BSD

The Solaris Advantage

Sun Microsystems was formed by former graduate students from Stanford and Berkeley, who used Stanford hardware and Berkeley software to develop the workstation market in the enterprise. It aimed to compete directly with the mainframe vendors by offering CPU speed and a mature operating system on the desktop, which was unprecedented. For a given price, greater performance could be obtained from the Sun workstations than was ever possible using mainframes. From one perspective, this success destroyed the traditional client/server market, which used very dumb terminals to communicate with very clever but horrendously expensive mainframe systems. The vendors of some proprietary systems, such as HP and DEC, saw their market share rapidly decline in the enterprise market because Sun delivered more "bang per buck" in performance. By 1986, UNIX was the dominant force at the expense of operating systems like VAX/VMS, although VMS would later come back to haunt UNIX installations in the form of Windows NT. When users could have a workstation with graphics instead of a dumb terminal, there were few arguments about adopting Sun.

However, Sun's innovation enabled departments and workgroups to take control of their own computing environments and to develop productively with the C programming language. Sun took BSD and transformed it into a commercial product, adding some useful innovations, such as NFS, along the way. This was similar in some ways to the approach of Linux companies that create distributions of useful software packages and bundle them with the Linux kernel. However, one significant difference between Sun and Red Hat Linux is that Sun has always been a company with a hardware focus—its systems were designed with the SPARC chipset and, more recently, the UltraSPARC chipset in mind. This has enabled Sun to create very fast workstations and servers with typically lower CPU speeds than Intel, but faster and more efficient bus performance. Sun invests heavily in hardware design and implementation for an expected commercial reward, all the more so now that Sun gives away the Solaris 9 operating system.

The major innovations of SunOS 4.*x* can be summarized as follows:

- Implementation of the network file system (NFS version 2.0, running over UDP)
- The OpenWindows 2.0 graphical user environment, based on X11
- The OpenBoot monitor
- The DeskSet utilities
- Multiprocessing support

The major innovations of SunOS 5.*x* can be summarized as follows:

- Support for symmetric multiprocessing of up to 64 processors in a single server
- The OpenWindows 3.0 graphical user environment and OpenLook. Integration with MIT X11R5, Motif, PostScript, and the common desktop environment (CDE)
- The Network Information Service (NIS/NIS+)
- Kerberos integration for authentication
- Support for static and dynamic linking
- Full-moon clustering ensuring high availability
- The ability to serve NT clients as a primary domain controller
- Tooltalk
- Java
- POSIX-compliant development environment, including single threads, multithreading, shared memory, and semaphores
- Real-time kernel processing
- X/OPEN-compliant command environment
- Compliance with UNIX 95 and UNIX 98 standards
- Support for very large (>2G) files
- Microsoft Windows emulation on the desktop with WABI
- Advanced volume management (`vold`)

- Standardized package administration and deployment tools
- Standardized patch management and integration
- Software-based power management
- Access control lists for resource authorization
- Support for centralized management of user home directories using the automounter
- Improvements to NFS (Version 3), running over TCP
- Support for advanced networking, such as ATM, frame relay, and gigabyte Ethernet
- JumpStart customization of local site installation and deployment
- 64-bit kernel architecture with Solaris 7 and later
- Simplified backup and restore procedures
- Simplified site administration with the AdminSuite toolkit

Hardware Support (SPARC and x86)

The classic CPU for Sun systems is the SPARC chip. Many systems in deployment today, including SPARC 5, 10, and 20, use different versions of the SPARC chip, with processor speeds of around 40–60 MHz. However, later systems, which use the UltraSPARC chipset, have processor speeds of up to 400 MHz. Although this may not seem fast, the bus architectures of Sun systems are much faster than their PC counterparts, more than making up for apparently slower chip speeds. Many SPARC systems are still supported in Solaris 9, although it is advisable to check with Sun to determine whether older machines, such as IPCs and IPXs, will be supported in future releases. Sun 4 machines and older are no longer supported by Sun, but they may run one of the BSD releases or Linux. Some older machines, such as Classics, have a very loyal support base, and are still actively supported.

With the introduction of Solaris 2.1 came support for the Intel platform, supporting ISA, EISA, MCA, and PCI bus types. This performed adequately on high-end 486 systems. Given the significant variation in types and manufacturers of PC hardware, not all devices are currently supported. Indeed, although Sun has released Solaris 8 for Intel for production use, only one beta has been forthcoming for Solaris 9 for Intel. Sun has yet to announce whether they will continue to develop Solaris for Intel, and/or release Solaris 9 for Intel. Newer innovations, such as the Universal Serial Bus (USB), may be supported in later releases. Solaris for Intel runs very fast on modern Pentium-II and Pentium-III systems, meaning that Intel devotees now have a wider choice of operating system, if they don't want to buy Sun hardware. There was also a single port of Solaris to the PowerPC platform (with version 2.5.1), however, this failed to impress MacOS users, and was deprecated in Solaris 2.6.

Solaris for Intel users will require the Hardware Compatibility List (HCL) to determine whether their particular system or their peripheral devices are supported. You can find this list at **http://access1.sun.com/drivers/hcl/hcl.html**. The HCL lists all tested systems, components, and peripherals that are known to work with Solaris for Intel. Chances are, if your hardware is not listed, it won't be supported. However, many standards have been adopted by Sun, including the PCI bus, which is now integrated in the desktop Ultra workstations.

Cross-Platform Interoperability

Solaris supports several different kinds of cross-platform interoperability. For example, Sun recently released a product called *lxrun*, which allows Linux binaries to be run under Solaris for Intel. This is very handy, as many database vendors, for example, have given away free versions of their database management products for Linux, but not for Solaris. Being able to exploit a free offer for one platform, and make use of it on Solaris, is a very handy cost saver indeed.

Sun also includes a binary compatibility package in Solaris that allows Solaris 1.*x* applications to run without modification. However, success can depend on whether the application is statically or dynamically linked. It is not clear whether binary compatibility will continue to be supported in future releases of Solaris.

Of course, the greatest hope for the interoperability of different operating systems lies with the Java programming language developed by Sun. Starting life as the "Oak" project, Java promises a "write once, run anywhere" platform, which means that an application compiled on Windows NT, for example, can be copied to Solaris 9 and executed without modification and without recompilation. Even in the 1970s, when C was being implemented far and wide across different hardware platforms, it was often possible to transfer source and recompile it without modification, but binary compatibility was never achieved. The secret to Java's success is the two-stage compile and interpretation process, which differs from many other development environments. Java source is compiled on the source platform to an intermediary bytecode format, which can then be transferred to any other platform and interpreted by a Java Virtual Machine (JVM). Many software vendors, including SunSoft and Microsoft, have declared support for the Java platform, even though some vendors have failed to meet the specifications laid out by Sun. Until a standard is developed for Java, Sun will retain control over its direction, which is a risk for non-Solaris sites especially. However, Solaris 9 installations should have few qualms about integrating Java technology within their existing environments. With the release of free development tools, such as Borland's JBuilder Foundation (**http://www.borland.com/**), development in Java is becoming easier for C and experienced UNIX developers. Java is the best attempt yet at complete binary compatibility between operating systems and architectures.

Recent Solaris Innovations

Recent Solaris releases have contained many enhancements and new features compared to earlier versions, on both the client and server side, and specifically for Administrators. For example, StarOffice is now included with the operating system distribution, as well as providing support for integration between personal organization applications and the new generation of "Palm computing" devices. On the server side, Solaris now ships with the Apache Web server installed, and runs Linux applications through *lxrun*. Security is overhauled with the inclusion of Kerberos version 5, and IPSec for both IPv4 and IPv6, which are also supported, making it easy to create virtual private networks through improved tunneling and encryption technologies. Developers will appreciate the inclusion of a Perl interpreter, other popular tools released under the GNU license, and the Java 2 SDK.

New Client Tools

Solaris has always been known as a server-based operating system. Its history and involvement with powering the Internet and providing a reliable platform for database servers and client/server applications are the characteristics that most administrators would associate with Solaris. However, Solaris 9 has bought many improvements on the desktop as well, with further integration and support for standards-based, CDE-based applications (in contrast to the old proprietary OpenWindows system). Further support for multimedia is also provided, with facilities for MIDI audio, and streamed video supporting many popular formats. CDE support for interfacing with productivity applications hosted on mobile computing devices, such as Palm, is also provided in conjunction with CDE.

Of course, the biggest desktop announcement of 1999 was Sun's purchase of the StarOffice suite from Star Division, and their decision to both ship it for free to the general public, and to include it as an integral part of Solaris 8. In addition, Sun is promoting the Sun Ray client as a cost-effective alternative to desktop computing based around legacy PC architectures, with clients centrally managed by a departmental server (such as an E450). This approach promises to revolutionize the way that many organizations currently (and often inconsistently) manage software updates, patches, and distribution. With the security and reliability of Solaris on the server side, the Solaris desktop will continue to see innovation in Solaris 9 and beyond.

StarOffice

StarOffice is a complete office productivity suite, including integrated word processing, spreadsheet, database, presentation, formula rendering, image processing, and Web page design applications. A big advantage is the capability to import existing documents from office packages distributed by other vendors (including Microsoft Office products). The interoperability between StarOffice and competing products is also reflected in the cross-platform implementation of the product. In addition to running on Solaris, it is also available for OS/2, Linux, and Microsoft Windows computers. Reflecting its European roots, StarOffice natively supports many different languages, including Dutch, English, French, German, Italian, Portuguese, Spanish, and Swedish.

Creating a new "StarBase" database is easy: Just select the appropriate option from the menu, and a database design wizard appears. Using a wizard makes creating a database very easy for novice users, and although the StarOffice database is not an industrial strength server, it is perfectly adequate for routine administrative tasks, such as creating customer contact and product description tables.

StarOffice has some advantages over competing products. For example, it has the capability to render quite complex formulas through an innovative formula painter. You can simply select the appropriate function and enter the appropriate arguments. In addition, you can combine more than one predicate to form complex expressions. For example, you can construct a combined cubic-root and exponential function expression in just a few keystrokes.

StarOffice also has the capability to design and publish Web pages as new documents or to export existing documents. In fact, you can create an entire site by using the wizards that are supplied as part of the HTML editing package. The first Web site wizard screen demonstrates the wide variety of templates available through the program.

Although StarOffice comes with complete online documentation and help, you can find further information regarding StarOffice at the StarOffice Web center (**http://www.sun.com/staroffice**).

Mobile Computing

The Solaris Operating Environment includes a number of enhancements to the common desktop environment (CDE). Personal Digital Assistant (PDA) support synchronizes data (using PDASync) from most Palm computing devices with the CDE textpad, calendar, mail, and address book. This enables Palm users to transfer data seamlessly between the desktop and the palmtop, previously a feature of traditionally desktop-oriented operating systems. PDASync is based around 3Com's HotSync technology, making synchronization possible with a single click.

Sun has also released the "K" Java Virtual Machine (KVM), which will allow Java developers on Solaris to easily port their Java 2 applications to mobile computing platforms, including Palm. The KVM forms part of the Java 2 Micro Edition suite, and has a small memory and disk footprint (i.e., less than 128K RAM). For further information regarding interoperability between Solaris and mobile computing devices using Java, see the KVM home page at **http://java.sun.com/products/kvm/**.

PC Support

Although Solaris 8 was co-released for SPARC and Intel platforms at the same time, Sun has indicated that Solaris 9 for SPARC will be released on a different schedule than Solaris 9 for Intel. Sun has yet to commit to releasing Solaris 9 for Intel. Thus, Intel users may need to wait before they can upgrade from Solaris 8 to Solaris 9. However, PC networks that require a reliable server system for Web, database, file, and application serving can make use of proven Solaris reliability and high availability by using Solaris 9 on a SPARC server. In addition, Solaris for Intel provides a cost-effective alternative to SPARC hardware, and can act as a "drop in" replacement for other server operating systems that also use Intel hardware. For example, the Samba software, running on a Solaris server, provides many key networking services to PCs, which are normally provided by NT server systems. These services include the following:

- Primary and backup domain control, enabling centralized sharing of user and resource database for department-sized workgroups

- Security and authentication using security identifiers for generating genuinely unique accounts

- Support for legacy networking protocols, such as NetBIOS, and naming services such as WINS

- NT file and print services

With the reliability and scalability of Solaris providing these basic network services for existing PC networks, many organizations are centralizing their server software around Solaris, because the same server can provide Samba services to PCs while performing other tasks (such as database serving).

There are several good reasons for using Solaris 9 as a server platform for PCs. First, viruses written for a PC platform are both physically and logically ineffective against Solaris, because the compiled codebase is different for both operating systems. In addition, even if the same codebase was shared (e.g., a rogue Java application executed from a remote shell), the Solaris authentication and identification system does not permit unprivileged users to write to system areas, preventing any malicious damage from occurring to the server. Second, Solaris provides packet filtering technology that prevents network intruders from browsing internal networks, whereas PCs may freely broadcast and exchange information between each other.

One of the most exciting innovations in the new collaborative technology that accompanies Solaris 9 is WebNFS, literally "network file serving" through the Web. WebNFS provides a standard file system for the World Wide Web, making it easy for users within the same building, or across the globe, to exchange data in a secure way, using industry standard clients. In fact, existing applications can be "Webified" by gaining access to virtual remote file systems, by using an extension of Sun's original NFS system. Although many Web clients support FTP as a protocol, FTP is based around the unreliable UDP protocol, whereas NFS is strictly based on TCP, which guarantees transmission.

Server Tools

As always, Sun has released a new batch of server-side products to improve upon the existing functionality of Solaris. Of interest to those in the data center will be the new 3.0 release of Sun's "Cluster" product, which offers high system availability through management of hardware redundancy. This offering caters largely to the corporate world, however, developers who are more interested in championing open source technologies will also be pleased with the inclusion of *lxrun*, a platform for binary compatibility between Linux applications and the Solaris operating environment. Originally developed for UNIX systems distributed by the Santa Cruz Operation (SCO), *lxrun* allows applications developed for Linux, and released with a binary-only codebase, to be executed natively on the Solaris Intel platform, without recompilation or modification. This will ultimately lead to a greater exchange of technology and ideas between Solaris and Linux users.

Clustering Technology

Increased performance is often gained by the use of hardware redundancy, which can be achieved on a file system–by–file system basis, by using a software solution, such as DiskSuite, or a hardware-based solution, such as an A1000 or T3 RAID appliance. This allows partitions to be actively mirrored so that in the event of a hardware failure, you can rapidly resume service to restore missing data.

This approach is fine for single-server systems that do not require close to 100 percent uptime. However, for mission-critical applications, where the integrity of the whole server is at stake, it makes sense to invest in clustering technology. Quite simply, clusters are what the name suggests: groups of similar servers (or "nodes") that have similar functions, and that share responsibility for providing system and application services. Clustering is commonly found in the financial world, where downtime is measured in hundreds of thousands of dollars, and not in minutes. Large organizations need to undertake a cost-benefit analysis to determine whether clustering is an effective technology for their needs. However, Sun has made the transition to clustering easier by integrating the Cluster product with Solaris 9.

Solaris 9 ships with Cluster 3.0, which features a clustered virtual file system, and cluster-wide load balancing. For more information on introducing clustering technology using Sun Cluster 3.0, see Paul Korzeniowski's technical article at **http://www.sun.com/clusters/article/**.

lxrun

One of the advantages of Solaris for Intel over its SPARC companion is the greater interoperability between computers based on Intel architectures. This means that there is greater potential for cooperation between Linux, operating on Intel, and Solaris, also operating on Intel. This potential has been realized recently with the efforts of Steve Ginzburg and Solaris engineers, who developed *lxrun*, which remaps system calls embedded in Linux software binaries to those appropriate for the Solaris environment. This means that Linux binaries can run without recompilation or modification on Solaris. In some ways, *lxrun* is like the Java Virtual Machine in that Linux applications execute through a layer that separates the application from the operating system. This means that your favorite Linux applications are now directly available through Solaris, including the following:

- KDE
- Gnome
- WordPerfect 7 and 8
- Applix
- Quake 2
- GIMP

For more information on *lxrun*, see its home page at **http://www.ugcs.caltech.edu/ ~steven/lxrun/**.

Security Innovations

Security is a major concern for Solaris administrators. The Internet is rapidly expanding with the new IPv6 protocol set to completely supercede IPv4 sometime in the next few years. This will make many more addresses available for Internet hosts than are currently available. It also means that the number of crackers, thieves, and rogue users will also increase exponentially. Solaris 9 prepares your network for this "virtual onslaught" by embracing IPv6, not only for its autoconfiguration and network numbering features, but because of the built-in security measures that form part of the protocol. In particular, authentication is a key issue, after many highly-publicized IP-spoofing breaches reported in the popular press over the past few years. A second layer of authentication for internal networks and intranets is provided in Solaris 9 by the provision of Kerberos version 5 clients and daemons. Previous releases, such as Solaris 8, included support for Kerberos version 4 only.

Kerberos Version 5

Kerberos is the primary means of network authentication employed by many organizations to centralize authentication services. As a protocol, it is designed to provide strong authentication for client/server applications by using secret-key cryptography. Recall that Kerberos is designed to provide authentication to hosts inside and outside a firewall, as long as the appropriate realms have been created. The protocol requires a certificate granting and validation system based around "tickets," which are distributed between clients and the server. A connection request from a client to a server takes a convoluted but secure route from a centralized authentication server, before being forwarded to the target server. This ticket authorizes the client to request a specific service from a specific host, generally for a specific time period. A common analogy is a parking ticket machine that grants the drivers of motor vehicles permission to park in a specific street for one or two hours only.

Kerberos version 5 contains many enhancements over Kerberos version 4, including ticket renewal, removing some of the overhead involved in repetitive network requests. In addition, there is a pluggable authentication module, featuring support for RPC. The new version of Kerberos also provides both server- and user-level authentication, featuring a role-based access control feature that assigns access rights and permissions more stringently, ensuring system integrity. In addition to advances on the software front, Solaris 9 also provides integrated support for Kerberos and Smart card technology using the Open Card Framework (OCF) 1.1. More information concerning Kerberos is available from MIT at **http://web.mit.edu/network/kerberos-form.html**.

IPv6

IPv6, described in RFC 2471, is the replacement IP protocol for IPv4, which is currently deployed worldwide. The Internet relies on IP for negotiating many transport-related transactions on the Internet, including routing and the domain-name service. This means that host information is often stored locally (and inefficiently) at each network node. It is clearly important to establish a protocol that is more general in function, but more centralized for administration, and can deal with the expanding requirements of the Internet.

One of the growing areas of the Internet is obviously the number of hosts that need to be addressed; many subnets are already exhausted, and the situation is likely to get worse. In addition, every IP address needs to be manually allocated to each individual machine on the Internet, which makes the usage of addresses within a subnet sparse and less than optimal. Clearly, there is a need for a degree of centralization when organizing IP addresses that can be handled through local administration, and through protocols like Dynamic Host Configuration Protocol (DHCP). However, one of the key improvements of IPv6 over IPv4 is its auto-configuration capabilities, which make it easier to configure entire subnets and to renumber existing hosts. In addition, security is now included at the IP level, making host-to-host authentication more efficient and reliable, even allowing for data encryption.

One way that this is achieved is by authentication header extensions, which allows a target host to determine whether a packet actually originates from a source host. This prevents common attacks, such as IP spoofing and denial-of-service, and reduces reliance on a third-party firewall by locking in security at the packet level. Tools are also included with Solaris 9 to assist with IPv4 to IPv6 migration.

What's New in Solaris 9

Each new release of Solaris brings about changes at the client, server, and system level. These changes affect users, administrators, and developers in different ways. For example, Solaris 9 introduces a completely new multithreading library. This will affect users of multithreaded applications, such as Java servlets, by increasing response time and reducing errors. It will affect system administrators, who will need to update *LD_LIBRARY_PATH* variables and check the dependencies of existing libraries. It will also affect developers, who will need to recode some existing multithreaded applications, as well as adjust to coding with a new API.

The following sections discuss products and services released for the first time with Solaris 9.

Resource Manager

The Resource Manager extends a number of existing tools that provide for monitoring and allocation of system resources to various tasks and services. This is particularly useful in high-end systems, where a large pool of resources can be allocated to specific processes. Although the existing `nice` command allows priorities to be set on specific processes, and *top* displays the resources used by each process, the Resource Manager is an integrated toolkit, featuring a scheduler, accounting, and billing. Again, although accounting tools are supplied as part of the standard Solaris toolkit, they have never been integrated with useful real-time monitoring tools. The Resource Manager also features a command-line interface and optional GUI for configuring and monitoring resource allocation and usage.

Linux Compatibility Tools

In addition to the *lxrun* binary execution environment for Solaris Intel, a number of libraries are now provided as part of the standard Solaris distribution to ensure that Linux applications can be linked and executed under Solaris. These libraries include *glib*, *GTK+*, *JPEG*, *Tcl/Tk*, *libpng*, *libtif*, and *libxml12*. These enhancements will improve interoperability between Linux and Solaris SPARC systems.

iPlanet Directory Server

The iPlanet Directory Server (iDS) is a commercial-grade LDAP solution for providing directory storage and access for hundreds and thousands of users. LDAP extends traditional Solaris directory service tools, such as NIS+, by using the standard LDAP protocol. iDS provides developers with C and Java APIs to create LDAP-compatible applications so that they can maintain a single repository of authentication and identification data. In addition, iDS can be integrated with other iPlanet products, such as the proxy server, to ensure that Internet users have managed rather than unfettered access to the Internet during work hours.

Volume Manager

Although software RAID support has been previously provided in Solaris through Solstice Disk Suite (SDS), this product has now been superseded by Volume Manager (VM). VM supports RAID levels 0, 1, and 5, and allows a wide range of mirroring and striping facilities. Cross-grade and migration tools are also available to assist SDS users who are currently using metadevices as their primary virtual file systems for boot and nonboot disks and their associated slices.

Live Upgrade

Live Upgrade allows a Solaris system to continue running while components of its operating system are upgraded. This is particularly useful in production environments, where system downtime costs money and customers, particularly on shared platforms, like the StarFire. A separate boot environment is constructed during runtime, after which the system is rebooted with the new configuration, thereby minimizing downtime.

Smaller Installation Footprint

In a move that defies the trend towards bloatware, Sun has actually reduced the size of the minimal installation so that systems can be installed faster and with fewer of the optional features installed. This is particularly important where single- or limited-purpose servers are concerned, because they require only the base operating system packages, and one or two options, which may be installed at a later time.

Virtual Memory Sizing

Improvements have been made in the processes used to allocate virtual memory by swapping to disk. The previous 8K limit has now been removed—basically, any page size that is supported by your hardware will be supported under Solaris. This means that memory-intensive applications should see improved performance, particularly where they used virtual memory to support their operations.

New Multithreading Library

Solaris provides advanced lightweight process support in the form of threads. Threads are used by multithreaded applications, such as the Java Virtual Machine (JVM), to support many small, parallel operations being performed simultaneously, without requiring the spawning of multiple processes. The new *libthread* supersedes previous versions, improving speed, and making the most of modern multitasking CPUs.

Internet Key Exchange (IKE)

Virtual Private Network (VPN) technology is also provided with Solaris 9, using IPSec. IPSec is compatible with both IPv4 and IPv6, making it easier to connect hosts using both new and existing networking protocols. IPSec consists of a combination of IP tunneling and encryption technologies to create sessions across the Internet that are as secure as possible. IP tunneling makes it difficult for unauthorized users (such as intruders) to access data being transmitted between two hosts on different sites. This is supported by encryption technologies, and an improved method for exchanging keys, using the Internet key exchange (IKE) method. IKE facilitates inter-protocol negotiation and selection during host-to-host transactions, ensuring data integrity. By implementing encryption at the IP layer, it will be even more difficult for rogue users to "pretend" to be a target host, intercepting data with authorization.

Secure Shell (SSH)

Although secure shell (SSH) has been provided for several years at **www.ssh.com** for Solaris, Sun has finally released their own version, which is integrated into Solaris 9. SSH allows terminal sessions to be encrypted using public key cryptography to ensure that packets exchanged across the network cannot be easily be decrypted, even if they are intercepted by a hostile third party. SSH is a vast improvement over traditional remote access tools, such as telnet, and all sites should now switch off telnet in favor of SSH.

Web-Based Enterprise Management (WBEM)

Solaris provides WBEM tools to ease the administrative burden of managing multiple servers and networks in a production environment. WBEM tools make use of Internet protocols and data descriptors, like HTTP and XML, to ensure that networks and servers can be managed using a unified, single method.

Sources for Additional Information

In this chapter, we have so far examined the history of UNIX, and what distinguishes UNIX systems from other operating systems. We have also traced the integration of both "flavors" of UNIX into the current Solaris 9 release. With the ever rising popularity of Solaris 9, there are many Web sites, mailing lists, and documentation sets that new and experienced users will find useful when trying to capitalize on an investment in Sun equipment or the latest Solaris 9 operating environment. In this section, we present some pointers to the main Internet sites where you can find reliable information about Solaris 9.

Sun Documentation/SunSites

Unlike some operating systems, Solaris 9 comes with a complete set of online reference manuals and user guides on the AnswerBook CD-ROM, which is distributed with all Solaris 9 releases (Intel and SPARC). The AnswerBooks are in PDF format, and cover a wide range of system administration topics, including the following:

- Binary compatibility guide
- JumpStart guide
- Mail server guide
- Naming services guide
- NFS administration guide;
- NIS+ guide
- SunShield security guide
- System administration guides
- TCP/IP guide
- Troubleshooting guides

A set of user guides are also available on AnswerBook:

- OpenWindows user guide
- CDE user guide
- CDE transition guide
- Power management user guide

Developers will also be pleased with the AnswerBook coverage for development issues:

- 64-bit developer's guide
- Device drivers guide
- Internationalization guide
- SPARC assembly language guide (yes, it is still included for the adventurous)
- STREAMS guide
- Source compatibility guide
- WebNFS developer's guide

Hardware maintenance and technical staff will find the hardware reference guides invaluable.

The best things about the AnswerBook series is that they are available for download and interactive searching through **http://docs.sun.com/**. This means that if you are working in the field, and you need to consult a guide, you don't need to carry around a CD-ROM or a printed manual. Just connect through the Internet, and read the guide in HTML, or download and retrieve a PDF format chapter or two.

The two main Sun sites for Solaris 9 are at **http://www.sun.com/solaris** (for SPARC users) and **http://www.sun.com/intel** (for Intel users). Both of these pages contain internal and external links that will be useful in finding out more information about Solaris 9 and any current offerings. The Sun Developer Connection is a useful resource that users can join to obtain special pricing and to download many software components for free.

Web Sites

Many third-party Web sites are also available that deal exclusively with Sun and Solaris 9. For example, if you are looking for a Solaris 9 FAQ, or pointer to Sun information, try the Sun Help site (**http://www.sunhelp.org/**). If it's free, precompiled software that you're after, check the Sun Freeware site (**http://www.sunfreeware.com/**) or one of the many mirrors. Here you can find the GNU C compiler in a precompiled package (Sun dropped the compiler from Solaris 2.*x* to Solaris 8, leading to the most frequently asked question on many Solaris forums: "Why doesn't the Solaris C compiler work?"). For Solaris for

Intel users, there is also an archive of precompiled binaries available at **ftp://
x86.cs.duke.edu/pub/solaris-x86/bins/**.

In case you are interested in seeing what the pioneers of UNIX are doing these
days, check out the home pages of these famous UNIX developers:

- **Brian Kernighan**   http://cm.bell-labs.com/cm/cs/who/bwk/index.html
- **Dennis Ritchie**   http://cm.bell-labs.com/cm/cs/who/dmr/index.html
- **Ken Thompson**   http://cm.bell-labs.com/who/ken/

A list of Solaris resources for this book is maintained at **www.cassowary.net/solaris**.

USENET

USENET is a great resource for asking questions, finding answers, and contributing
your skills and expertise to help others in need. This is not necessarily a selfless act—
there will always be a Solaris 9 question that you can't answer, and if you've helped
others before, they will remember you. The **comp.unix.solaris** forum is the best USENET
group for Solaris 9 information and discussion. The best source of practical Solaris 9
information is contained in the Solaris FAQ, maintained by the legendary Casper Dik.
You can always find the latest version at **http://www.wins.uva.nl/pub/solaris/solaris2/**.
For Solaris for Intel users, there is the less formal **alt.solaris.x86** forum, where you won't
be flamed for asking questions about dual-booting with Microsoft Windows, or
mentioning non-SPARC hardware. For Solaris Intel, the best FAQ is at **http://sun
.pmbc.com/faq/**. For both SPARC and Intel platforms, there is a **comp.sys.sun.admin**
group that deals with system administration issues, which also has a FAQ available
at **ftp://thor.ece.uc.edu/pub/sun-faq/FAQs**.

Mailing Lists

Mailing lists are a good way of meeting colleagues and engaging in discussions in a
threaded format. The Sun Manager's List is the most famous Sun list, and contains
questions, answers, and most importantly, summaries of previous queries. All Solaris-
related topics are covered. Details are available at **ftp://ftp.cs.toronto.edu/pub/jdd/
sun-managers/faq**. In addition, there is a Solaris for x86 mailing list archived at
http://www.egroups.com/group/solarisonintel/, which has some great tips, tricks, and
advice for those who are new to Solaris 9, or who are having difficulties with specific
hardware configurations.

Summary

Solaris 9 is an exciting, innovative operating environment. It can provide more
functionality than existing desktop operating systems, however, there is an increased
administrative overhead that you must consider. In this book, we hope to convey sound

INSTALLATION

management practices and divulge practical techniques for solving many Solaris-related problems, and to implement the best-of-breed methods for all enterprise-level installations. By the end of this book, you should feel confident in managing all aspects of Solaris 9 system administration, and feel confident in transferring those skills to the management of related operating systems, such as Linux.

How to Find Out More

The main site for all Sun technologies is **http://www.sun.com/**. For further information on Java technologies, users should browse Sun's Java site at **http://java.sun.com/**. If you prefer an independent evaluation of Sun technologies, check out the Sun World site at **http://www.sunworld.com**, or Java technologies at **http://www.javaworld.com/**.

Chapter 2

System Concepts

nderstanding what makes Solaris different from other operating systems is critical to appreciating why it is the environment of choice for high-availability client-server environments. This chapter reviews the terms used to describe Solaris systems and major components, as well as networking terminology associated with Solaris networks. Understanding these terms will ensure that you understand some of the concepts discussed in later chapters. Many Solaris terminology is particular to the context of Solaris systems, and some generic terms may have one meaning in Solaris, but another meaning for other operating systems. For example, while the term *host* may be used generically to identify any system attached to a network, it may be used more specifically in Solaris, when referring to *multi-homed hosts*.

The Kernel

Operating systems are the building blocks of computer systems, and they provide the interface between user applications and computer hardware. Solaris is a multi-user, multi-tasking operating system developed and sold by Sun Microsystems (**http://www.sun.com/**), and it is one implementation of the UNIX operating system that draws on both the System V (AT&T) and Berkeley (BSD) systems. Solaris has evolved from little more than a research project to become the dominant UNIX operating system in the international marketplace.

Solaris 9 is the latest in a long line of operating environment releases that are based around the SunOS operating system, which is currently in version 5.9. Solaris is commonly found in large corporations and educational institutions that require concurrent, multi-user access on individual hosts and between hosts connected via the Internet.

Many desktop computer users have never heard of the word *Sun* in the context of computing, nor are they usually familiar with the term *Solaris* as an operating environment. However, almost every time that an Internet user sends an e-mail message or opens a file from a networked server running Sun's Network File System (NFS) product, Solaris is transparently supporting the Internet applications that allow these things to happen. In the enterprise computing industry, Sun is synonymous with highly available, highly reliable performance hardware, while Solaris is often the operating environment of choice to support database servers and application servers. Sun's hardware solutions are based around the SPARC and UltraSPARC integrated circuit technologies, which can currently support more than 64 processors in a single server system, such as the E10000 StarFire configuration.

UNIX is hard to define because different vendors have historically introduced different features to arrive at the entities that most users would think of as UNIX. However, it is easy enough to list the fundamental characteristics that are common to all UNIX and UNIX-like systems:

■ They have a *kernel*, written in the C programming language, which mainly manages input/output processing, rather than being a complete operating system. The kernel has ultimate responsibility for allocating system resources to complete various tasks.

- They have a hierarchical file system, which begins with a root directory, and from which the branches of all other directories (and file systems) are mounted.

- System hardware devices are represented logically on the file system as special files (such as */dev/pty*, for pseudo-terminals).

- They are process based, with all services and user shells being represented by a single identifying number (the process ID, or PID).

- They share a set of command-line utilities that can be used for text and numeric processing of various kinds, such as *troff*, *col*, *cat*, *head*, *tbl*, and so on.

- User processes can be spawned from a shell, such as the Bourne shell, which interactively executes application programs.

- Multiple processes can be executed concurrently by a single user and sent into the background by using the *&* operator.

- Multiple users can execute commands concurrently by logging in from pseudo-terminals.

Note that a graphical user interface (GUI) is not necessarily a defining feature of UNIX, unlike other desktop operating systems, which place much stock in "look and feel," even though most UNIX systems support X11 graphics and the common desktop environment (CDE). Although CDE remains the default desktop for Solaris 9, Sun plans to integrate the GNOME window manager (**http://www.gnome.org/**) into future maintenance releases. GNOME is currently the leading desktop of Linux users. Integrating GNOME into Solaris 9 will lead to greater interoperability between Solaris and Linux systems, particularly in terms of GUI application development. It will also make porting GUI applications between Solaris and Intel easier, because Linux back-end applications have been executed on Solaris Intel for some time by using *lxrun*.

The reasons for this distinction are largely historical and related to the UNIX design philosophy. For operating systems that are not layered, changing the window manager or even the "look and feel" involves rewriting significant portions of back-end code. In the Solaris environment, where the interface and display technologies are appropriately abstracted from the underlying kernel, moving from CDE to GNOME involves simply changing the command to initialize the X11 display manager; the kernel remains unmodified. The layering of the various components of a UNIX system is shown in Figure 2-1.

Broadly speaking, a UNIX system is layered according to applications that are invoked through user shells, which are managed by a kernel, which in turn uses file systems to create a persistent storage mechanism. Because the kernel provides the interface between shells and the file system, (and by extension, between applications and the file system), it is considered the central part of UNIX technology.

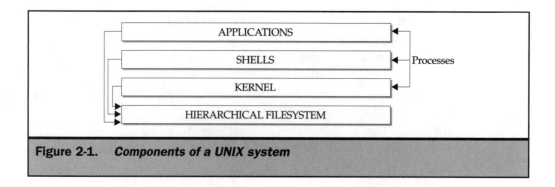

Figure 2-1.   *Components of a UNIX system*

Solaris kernels can trace their origins to both the System V and BSD variants of UNIX, while Microsoft NT was based on the Virtual Memory System (VMS) kernel originally developed for the high-end VAX systems. Most kernels during the 1960s were written using assembly language or machine (binary) code, so the development of a high-level language for writing kernels (the C language) was one of the founding ideas of UNIX. This level of abstraction from hardware meant that kernels could be ported to other hardware platforms without having to be completely rewritten. The tradition of writing kernels in C continues today, with the Linux kernel (for example) being written in C. Obviously, a kernel alone is not a complete operating environment, so many additional applications, such as the visual editor (vi), were later added to what UNIX users would recognize as the suite of standard UNIX tools.

All UNIX systems have a kernel, which is the central logical processor that provides an interface between the system hardware, the system services, and the user shells that directly enable applications. For example, support for network interfaces is provided in the form of a kernel module and a device file that logically represents the physical device. Services are defined in the services database, and network daemons provide the final layer for supporting applications that use the network to transmit data. Since UNIX kernels are typically written in the C programming language, many systems-level applications and daemons are also written in C.

Of course, UNIX systems share some common characteristics with other operating systems, including the use of a hierarchical file system, in which special files called *directories* are used to arrange related files logically. But UNIX has some distinctive features as well: explicit permissions to read, execute, and modify files on the UNIX file system can be granted to specific users or groups of users, making it easy to share work and collaborate with other users on the system.

Because UNIX was created by active developers, rather than by operating system gurus, the focus was on creating an operating system that suited a programmer's needs. A *Bell System Technical Journal* article in 1978 lists the following key guiding principles of UNIX development:

■ Create small, self-contained programs that perform a single task. When a new task needs to be solved, either create a new program that performs it, or combine tools from the toolset that already exists, to arrive at a solution. This is a similar orientation to the current trend toward encapsulation and independent component building (such as Enterprise JavaBeans), where complicated systems are built from smaller, interacting but logically independent modules.

■ Programs should accept data from standard input and write to standard output; thus, programs can be "chained" to process each other's output sequentially. Interactive input should be avoided in favor of command-line options that specify a program's actions to be performed. Presentation should be separated from what a program is trying to achieve. These ideas are consistent with the concept of piping, which is still fundamental to the operation of user shells. For example, the output of the ls command to list all files in a directory can be "piped" using the "|" symbol for a program such as *grep* to perform pattern matching. The number of pipes on a single command line instruction is not limited.

■ Creating a new operating system or program should be undertaken on a scale of weeks, not years: the creative spirit that leads to cohesive design and implementation should be exploited. If software doesn't work, don't be afraid to build something better. This process of iterative revisions of programs has resurfaced in recent years with the rise of object-oriented development.

■ Make best use of all the tools available, rather than asking for more help. The motivation behind UNIX is to construct an operating system that supports the kinds of toolsets that are required for successful development.

This is not intended to be an exhaustive list of the kernel-oriented characteristics that define UNIX; however, these features are central to understanding the importance that UNIX developers often ascribe to the operating system. It is designed to be a programmer-friendly system.

The Shell

A key Solaris concept is the functional separation between the user interface and the operating system. This distinction means that a user can access a Solaris system by using either a terminal-based character user interface (CUI), or a high-resolution graphical user interface (GUI), without modifying the underlying operating system.

With so much attention paid to GUI, why are CUI environments still important to Solaris? Are they just a historical hangover that Windows has managed to overcome? Or, are they simply the tools of choice for long-haired network administrators who have never used a mouse? In fact, mastering the Solaris command line is one of the effective tools available under any UNIX environment, and the good news is, it's not that difficult to learn. Using the command line (or *shell*) has several advantages over GUI environments.

The shell is essential for programming repetitive tasks that can be performed laboriously through a GUI. For example, searching a file system for all document files that have changed each day, and making a copy of all these files (with the extension .doc) to a backup directory (with the extension .bak), takes time.

The shell can be used to search for, modify, edit, and replace Solaris configuration files, which are typically stored in text format. This is much like the approach taken with Windows .ini configuration files, which were text based. However, after Windows 95, Windows versions store configuration information in the Registry in a binary format, making it impossible to edit manually. All Solaris configuration files, including the startup scripts, are text based.

The shell has a number of built-in commands that typically mirror those provided in the C programming language. This means that it is possible to write small programs as shell statements that are executed as sequential steps, without having to use a compiler (just like MS-DOS batch files are interpreted without requiring a compiler).

The shell can be used to launch applications that use a CUI, which is especially useful for logging onto a remote system and enabling access to the commands an administrator can use on the console, a valuable point in this era of global information systems. While Windows applications like Symantec's pcAnywhere can be used for remote access to the Windows Desktop, they don't easily support multi-user access (or multi-user access where one user requires a CUI and another a GUI).

The shell can be used to execute commands for which no equivalent GUI application exists. Although many operations could conceivably be performed using a GUI, it is usually easier to write a shell script than create a completely new GUI application.

Many applications in Solaris, Linux, and Windows are now available through a GUI interface. If you feel more comfortable using GUI interfaces, there is little reason to stop using them, as long as you can find the tools to perform all of the tasks you need to undertake regularly, such as monitoring resource usage, setting process alarms and diagnostics, and/or remote access. However, if you want to make the most of Solaris and competently administer the system, you will need to become familiar with the shell and command-line utilities.

In keeping with the philosophy that different administrators have different needs and styles, Solaris makes several different shells available:

- **Bourne shell (sh)**   The original UNIX shell used to write all system scripts by convention

- **Korn shell (ksh)**   Provides enhanced input/output features, including the `print` and `read` commands

- **C shell (csh)**   Offers a command syntax similar to the C programming language

- **The Cornell Shell (tcsh)**   Includes improved terminal handling compared to the original C Shell

- **Bourne Again Shell (bash)**   An open source, much improved version of the Bourne shell

The File System

UNIX also features a hierarchical file system that makes it easy for you to separate related files logically into directories, which are themselves special files. While MS-DOS and similar operating systems feature a hierarchical file system with simple file access permissions (such as read only), UNIX has a complete user-based file access permission system. Like process management, each file on the system is "owned" by a specific user, and by default, only that user can perform operations on that file. *Privileged* users can perform all operations on all files on the file system. Interestingly, a special file permission allows *unprivileged* users to execute certain commands and applications with *super-user* privileges (such as `setuid`).

The following file system types are supported by the kernel:

cachefs	The CacheFS cached file system
hsfs	The High Sierra file system
nfs	The Network File System (NFS)
pcfs	The MS-DOS file system
tmpfs	A file system that uses memory
ufs	The standard UNIX File System (UFS)

The default local file system type is contained in the */etc/default/fs* file, while the default remote file system type is contained in the */etc/default/fstypes* file.

Multi-user vs. Multitasking

Operating systems like MS-DOS are single-user, single-task systems; they are designed to be used by a single user who wishes to execute a single program from the shell. However, with advances in CPU technology, even the humble MS-DOS shell was expanded to allow multitasking, where more than one application can execute concurrently. This approach was extended with Microsoft Windows, which allows several applications to be executed concurrently in a GUI environment. In addition, Microsoft Windows has support for multiple users, although it is generally possible for only a single user to initiate a console session, limiting its concurrency—unless some third-party product (such as Symantec's pcAnywhere) is installed.

UNIX provides the best of both worlds, because it is designed from the ground up to permit multiple users to initiate multiple shells, which in turn can execute multiple applications. In addition, Solaris supports lightweight processes such as threads, which allow the traditional concept of multitasking to be generalized to execute multiple threads within a single process. Solaris also supports symmetric multiprocessing, meaning that the physical execution of processes, threads, and user applications may occur on one of many different supported processors.

Client/Server Networks

While PC operating systems were designed in response to the waning of client/server systems, Solaris and other UNIX systems are firmly designed as client/server systems. While a PC is designed to run many high-powered applications using the local CPU, a client/server network is designed around the concept of multiple *thin* clients that access data and execute applications on a *fat* centralized server, or on a number of servers that are dedicated to one particular purpose. For example, a typical Solaris network might consist of hundreds of Sun Ray thin client systems, which are supported on the front line by several E450 departmental servers, as well as a set of rack-mounted 420R systems that run database, Web server, and development systems.

The client/server topology is also reflected in the structure of UNIX services: client applications running on client systems are designed to connect through to server applications running on server systems. Sun was instrumental in initiating key distributed computing technologies, such as the Remote Procedure Call (RPC) technology used in the Network File System (NFS) protocol. In addition, the Remote Method Invocation (RMI) technology developed as part of the Java networking and distributed computing APIs allow objects to be passed around the network as seamlessly as RPC.

Basic Networking Terminology

A Solaris network consists of a number of different hosts that are interconnected using a switch or a hub. Solaris networks connect to one another via routers, which can be dedicated hardware systems or Solaris systems, which have more than one network interface. Each host on a Solaris network is identified by a unique hostname: these hostnames often reflect the function of the host in question. For example, a set of four FTP servers may have the hostnames *ftp1, ftp2, ftp3,* and *ftp4* .

Every host and network that is connected to the Internet uses the Internet Protocol (IP) to support higher level protocols such as Transmission Control Protocol (TCP) and User Datagram Protocol (UDP). Every interface of every host on the Internet has a unique IP address that is based on the network IP address block assigned to the local network. Networks are addressable by using an appropriate netmask that corresponds to a Class A (255.0.0.0), Class B (255.255.0.0), or Class C (255.255.255.0) network.

Solaris supports multiple Ethernet interfaces that can be installed on a single machine. These are usually designated as */etc/hostname.hmen*, where *n* is the interface number and *hme* is the interface type. Interface files contain a single unqualified domain name or IP address, with the primary network interface being designated with an interface number of zero. Thus, the primary interface of a machine called *ftp* would be defined by the file */etc/hostname.hme0*, which might contain the unqualified domain name "ftp," or the IP address *203.17.64.28*. A secondary network interface, connected to a different subnet, might be defined in the file */etc/hostname.hme1*. In this case, the file might contain the unqualified domain name "mail," or the IP address *10.17.65.28*.

The decision to use unqualified domain names or IP addresses rests largely with the naming service used by the system, which is defined by the *file /etc/nsswitch.conf.* If this file does not allow hostname resolution from the */etc/hosts* because the Domain Name System (DNS) is used exclusively, using unqualified domain names in */etc/hostname.** files can lead to a failure of local hostname resolution. However, because IP addresses can change from time to time (particularly if Dynamic Host Configuration Protocol, or DHCP, is used), some administrators may need to use unqualified domain names.

Enabling multiple interfaces is commonly used in organizations that have a provision for a failure of the primary network interface or to enable load balancing of server requests across multiple subnets (for example, for an intranet Web server processing HTTP requests). A system with a second network interface can act either as a router or as a multihomed host. Hostnames and IP addresses are locally administered through a naming service, which is usually DNS for companies connected to the Internet, and the Network Information Service (NIS/NIS+) for companies with large internal networks that require administrative functions beyond what DNS provides, including centralized authentication.

It is also worth mentioning at this point that it is possible for you to assign different IP addresses to the same network interface; this configuration can be useful for hosting "virtual" interfaces that require their own IP address, rather than relying on application-level support for multihoming (for example, when using the Apache Web server). You simply create a new */etc/hostname.hmeX:Y* file for each IP address required, where X represents the physical device interface and Y represents the virtual interface number.

The subnet mask used by each of these interfaces must also be defined in */etc/netmasks.* This is particularly important if the interfaces lie on different subnets, or if they serve different network classes. In addition, it might also be appropriate to assign a fully qualified domain name to each of the interfaces, although this will depend on the purpose to which each interface is assigned.

System Configuration

Solaris provides a simple way to view all the hardware devices on your system. This information can be used to configure your system. For example, by identifying the disk devices on your system, you can correctly select targets for formatting.

The `prtconf` command is used for displaying system information:

```
prtconf
System Configuration:   Sun Microsystems   sun4u
Memory size: 128 Megabytes
```

This section shows the hardware architecture (`sun4u`, which means that this is a Sun 4 system with an UltraSPARC CPU) and that it has 128MB of RAM.

The following section identifies the terminal emulator, keyboard, and UFS. These devices are necessary to boot a Solaris system:

```
System Peripherals (Software Nodes):
SUNW,Ultra-5_10
    packages (driver not attached)
        terminal-emulator (driver not attached)
     disk-label (driver not attached)
        SUNW,builtin-drivers (driver not attached)
        sun-keyboard (driver not attached)
        ufs-file-system (driver not attached)
```

The next section shows the OpenBoot PROM (programmable read-only memory), physical memory, and virtual memory monitor devices:

```
    chosen (driver not attached)
    openprom (driver not attached)
        client-services (driver not attached)
    options, instance #0
    aliases (driver not attached)
    memory (driver not attached)
    virtual-memory (driver not attached)
```

The final section displays devices attached to the first PCI local bus. This includes an Integrated Device Electronics (IDE) hard disk, IDE hard drive, and network interface:

```
pci, instance #0
        pci, instance #0
            ebus, instance #0
                auxio (driver not attached)
                power, instance #0
                SUNW,pll (driver not attached)
                se, instance #0
                su, instance #0
                su, instance #1
                ecpp (driver not attached)
                fdthree, instance #0
                eeprom (driver not attached)
                flashprom (driver not attached)
                SUNW,CS4231 (driver not attached)
          network, instance #0
```

```
SUNW,m64B (driver not attached)
ide, instance #0
    disk (driver not attached)
    cdrom (driver not attached)
    dad, instance #0
    sd, instance #30
```

Note   *Obviously, the specific devices installed on each system vary, and so will the configuration displayed when using* `prtconf`.

Processes

Processes lie at the heart of all modern multi-user operating systems. By dividing system tasks into small, discrete elements that are uniquely identified by a process identifier (PID), Solaris is able to manage all the applications that may be concurrently executed by many different users. In addition, individual users may execute more than one application at any time. Each Solaris process is associated with a UID and a GID, just like a standard file. This means that only users may send signals to their own processes (except for the super user, who may send signals to any process on the system). Signals are typically used to restart or terminate processes. The multi-user, multitasking process model in Solaris ensures that system resources can be shared equally among all competing processes or allocated preferentially to the most important applications. For example, a firewall application would probably take precedence over all other system processes. Individual users and the super user may allocate a priority level to active processes in real time.

Solaris provides a number of command-line tools that can be used to manage processes; these tools are discussed in Chapter 13. In addition, APIs are provided for C programmers to allow them to operate directly on processes—spawning, managing, and killing, as necessary. Solaris also provides lightweight processes (LWPs) that don't require as much overhead to operate as "normal" processes. The advantages of using LWPs are also discussed in Chapter 13.

Naming Services

Every computer connected to the Internet must have an IP address, which identifies it uniquely within the network. For example, *192.18.97.241* is the IP address of the Web server at Sun. IP addresses are difficult for humans to remember, and they don't adequately describe the network on which a host resides. Thus, by examining the Fully Qualified Domain Name (FQDN) of *192.18.97.241*—*www.sun.com*—it's immediately obvious that the host, *www*, lies within the *sun.com* domain. The mapping between human-friendly domain names and machine-friendly IP addresses is performed by a distributed naming service known as the *Domain Name Service* (DNS). DNS is the standard protocol used by UNIX systems (and other operating systems) for mapping IP addresses to hostnames, and vice versa.

Although Solaris provides complete support for DNS, it uses its own domain management and naming system, known as the Network Information Service (NIS). NIS is not only responsible for host naming and management, but it is a comprehensive resource management solution that can be used to structure and administer groups of local and remote users.

NIS uses a series of maps to create namespace structures. Sometimes administrators ask why this extra effort is required to manage hosts and naming, because DNS already provides this for Internet hosts by converting computer-friendly IP addresses to human-friendly "names." However, NIS does not just provide naming services; a NIS server also acts as a central repository of all information about users, hosts, Ethernet addresses, mail aliases, and supported Remote Procedure Call (RPC) services within a network. This information is physically stored in a set of maps that are intended to replace the network configuration files usually stored in a server's /etc directory, ensuring that configuration data within the local area network (LAN) is always synchronized. Many large organizations use NIS alongside DNS to manage both their Internet and LAN spaces effectively. Linux also supports NIS.

In the past, Sun introduced an enhanced version of NIS known as NIS+. Instead of a simple mapping system, it uses a complex series of tables to store configuration information and hierarchical naming data for all networks within an organization. Individual namespaces may contain up to 10,000 hosts, with individual NIS+ servers working together to support a completely distributed service. NIS+ also includes greater capabilities in the area of authentication, security (using DES encryption), and resource access control.

Recently, Solaris has begun a transition to Lightweight Directory Access Protocol (LDAP) directory services as an alternative source of authoritative information for naming, identification, and authentication. LDAP is based on the original Directory Access Protocol (DAP), which provided X.500-type services for centralized directory lookups. Like NIS and NIS+, LDAP performs lookups given a token and returns a result. However, the query is much more generalized than what can be returned from NIS or NIS+: text, sounds, and graphics can all be associated with an entry in the directory.

LDAP does not provide any kind of programmatic query language, like SQL, to query the directory, so its use is still limited. However, because it works directly over TCP/IP, and it can support directory services for clients on different operating systems, LDAP is often viewed as the future central naming and directory service for Solaris.

Server-Side Java

Java is a new programming language that is often used to create platform-independent GUIs that a user can interact with in complex and sophisticated ways. However, Java *applets*—the bits of code that are transmitted over the Internet and executed on the user's machine—are only one side of the whole Java story. This section will focus on the *server* side of Java.

Java applications that execute on the server are called *servlets*, and they have their own standard API specification that has now been widely implemented in Web server extension products known as servlet *runners* (such as Apache's Tomcat server). Servlets are useful in developing Web-enabled, Solaris-based enterprise applications.

Increasingly, applications in the enterprise are being implemented using Web interfaces, partly in response to the persistent heterogeneity of computing platforms within organizations that span cities, states, and even nations. Accepting platform diversity does not mean losing control of standards, however. Sun Microsystems has pioneered a platform-independent programming language in which applications run on top of a logical Java Virtual Machine (JVM) that presents a consistent API for developers. Most major hardware platforms and operating systems now have virtual machines implemented, including (obviously) Solaris. In fact, the Solaris JVM produced by Sun has been highly optimized in its production release series. JVMs have also been integrated into popular Web browsers, so that Java programs can be downloaded from a server and executed within these browsers. (HTML has an `<applet>` tag that facilitates this process.) Applets have increased the complexity of Web-based user interfaces from simple arrays of buttons and forms to dynamic interaction with the user in a way that is similar to a normal desktop application.

Although Java has been successful in improving the client side of Web-based computing, it has been slower to make an impact on the server-side (this is as much a result of the excitement surrounding applets as any deficit in the servlet API). However, many people believe that the server side is where Java has its greatest potential. The notion of having platform-independent enterprise applications that run through a standard Web interface promises to change the way that users, developers, and software interact. The "write once run anywhere" philosophy means that servers with totally different operating systems and hardware can be replaced with newer systems, without concern for application stability and porting. Commonly used Java classes can be bundled as *beans* that can provide rapid implementation for a client's business logic. Full access to the Java API and database servers is also provided for Java servlets, using the Java Database Classes (JDBC) supplied by Oracle and other major vendors. These features ensure that today's Java server-side programs will not become tomorrow's legacy applications.

How does server-side Java compare against Web-based client/server techniques such as the combination of a Common Gateway Interface (CGI) and a non–object-oriented language such as C? Although a compiled language like C is faster on a byte-per-byte basis than an interpreted language like Java, performance increases for Java can be gained by the combination of optimizing "just-in-time" (JIT) compilers for specific platforms and by reducing the process and memory overhead associated with the CGI. For example, if you wrote a search application in Perl that was accessed by 1000 Web users per hour, that would mean an extra 1000 invocations of Perl that the server has to deal with.

Of course, if you are running on an E10000, this would probably result in a negligible system strain. For other systems, invoking a Java servlet that occupies only a single process after being loaded into memory, and which *persists* across sessions, is both memory and process efficient. Servlets are therefore more appropriate for applications that are constantly being executed by multiple users, by taking advantage of Java's multithreading and synchronization capabilities.

On the flipside, CGI programs are often better suited to single-user, infrequently used, and numerically intensive applications that might only be invoked once per hour. In addition, CGI programs written in C are logically isolated from each other in the server's memory space: if Java servlets are executed using a single instance of a service manager (for example, Live Software's Jrun), an unhandled exception arising from malformed or unexpected input could potentially impact all servlets running through the manager, especially if the JVM crashes.

Chapter 3

Choosing Hardware

One of the main reasons for using Solaris is its SPARC-based hardware. While Intel-based systems have been supported for some time, many characteristics of SPARC-based systems make them appealing. For example, all new SPARC-based CPUs are capable of 64-bit processing, which has been available for several years on Solaris. This mature support is reflected in the current StarFire configurations that allow more than 64 CPUs to be combined into a single physical system that features completely redundant hardware devices, including power supplies and buses. This configuration enables high availability and hot swapping of failed components while the system is still running.

At the lower end of the market, 64-bit UltraSPARC workstations are now price comparable to many PC systems that offer only 32-bit CPU performance. While these systems generally have faster CPUs, they simply don't have the processing capacity of 64-bit CPUs. In addition, the UltraSPARC series features both Small Computer System Interface (SCSI) and PCI local buses, which allow a wide variety of third-party hardware devices to be attached to the workstations. (The PCI local bus is now the dominant bus technology in the PC market.)

You might be wondering what SPARC hardware can do, where it came from, and why you should (or shouldn't) use it. Some administrators may be concerned about the use of proprietary hardware, given the "vendor lock-in" they may have experienced in the past. However, Solaris complies with many open standards, and the SPARC platform is supported by multiple hardware vendors. Since a typical SPARC system can support graphical user interface (GUI) logons for hundreds of users, comparing SPARC with single-user operating systems like some versions of Microsoft Windows is like apples and oranges.

This chapter reviews some of the main hardware components used in building both SPARC- and Intel-based systems, and it reviews some of the common SPARC workstation and server systems currently available for Solaris 9. If you need to find out more about specific servers and workstations, Sun offers PDF and HTML versions of hardware manuals for all supported systems at **http://docs.sun.com/**.

SPARC Hardware

Sun has developed a wide range of hardware systems over the past few years, much of which are still supported by Solaris 9. These systems are based on the Scalable Processor ARChitecture (SPARC), which is managed by a SPARC member organization (**http://www.sparc.org/**). In addition to Sun Microsystems, Fujitsu (**http://www.fujitsu.com/**) and T.Sqware (**http://www.tsqware.com/**) also build SPARC-compliant CPU systems. System vendors that sell systems based on SPARC CPUs include Amdahl Corporation (**http://www.amdahl.com/**), Tatung (**http://www.tatung.com/**), Tadpole (**http://www.tadpole.com/**), and Toshiba (**http://www.toshiba.com/**). Vendors of system boards and peripherals for SPARC CPU–based systems include Hitachi (**http://www.hitachi.com/**), Seagate (**http://www.seagate.com/**), and Kingston Technology (**http://www.kingston.com/**).

Although media critics and competitors often paint SPARC systems from Sun as standalone, vendor-specific traps for the unwary, the reality is that a large number of hardware vendors also support the SPARC platform. It should also be noted that software vendors, such as Red Hat, also support SPARC versions of Linux, which proves that Solaris is not the only operating system that powers the SPARC platform. The SPARC standards can be downloaded free of charge from **http://www.sparc.org/standards.html**.

Often, administrators of Linux and Microsoft Windows systems who are used to "PC" hardware are incredulous to discover that some supported systems (such as the SPARCclassic) have CPUs that run below 100 MHz. This must seem like a slow CPU speed in the age of Intel CPUs, with their clones reaching the 1 GHz mark. However, CPU speed is only one component that contributes to the overall performance of a system—SPARC systems are renowned for their high-speed buses and very fast I/O performance. In addition, many SPARC systems were designed for continuous operation—it is not unheard of for systems to have several years of uptime, compared to several days for some operating systems. The many impressive features of the Solaris operating systems were developed with the SPARC hardware platform as a target, and these systems naturally have the best performance.

However, Sun has not ignored hardware developments and emerging standards— in recent years, Sun has created the Ultra series of workstations and servers that feature a PCI local bus and compatibility with Super Video Graphics Array (SVGA) multisync monitors commonly sold with PC systems. Of course, SPARC systems have always supported the SCSI standard, and all SCSI devices will work with Solaris. At the same time, Sun has proceeded with innovations, such as the 64-CPU Enterprise 10000 system, which can operate as a single system with massively parallel computational abilities, or it can be logically partitioned to act as up to 64 different systems. Imagine being able to control an entire Application Service Provider (ASP) with no apparent "shared hosting" to the client, which is actually being serviced by a single physical system. Although the up-front cost of an E10000 far exceeds that required for 64 systems running Linux or Microsoft Windows, only one administrator is required to manage an E10000, while 64 different systems might require more than one administrator.

Supported Platforms

SPARC systems have an application architecture and a kernel architecture: most modern Sun systems have an application architecture of type 4, while the latest UltraSPARC systems have a kernel architecture of type *u*. Thus, UltraSPARC systems are known as *sun4u* systems. One of the great advantages of SPARC is that systems with the same application architecture can run the same binaries; thus, the binary of an application compiled on an Ultra 1 should work on an E10000. However, the kernel architecture has changed significantly over the years so that systems with different kernel architectures cannot boot the same kernel. While an Ultra 1 and E-450 can boot from the same sun4u kernel, a SPARCstation 5 must boot from a sun4m kernel.

Table 3-1 shows a list of common application and kernel architectures for some type 4 Sun systems.

You will need a Sun-4 architecture system to run Solaris 9 or any kind of modern UNIX kernel for that matter. (Your old 3/60 really does belong in a museum!) Even

Application	Kernel	Architecture	System Name
4	c	sun4c	SPARCstation 1
4	c	sun4c	SPARCstation IPX
4	m	sun4m	SPARCstation 5
4	m	sun4m	SPARCstation 10
4	d	sun4d	SPARCserver 1000
4	d	sun4d	SPARCcenter 2000
4	u	sun4u	UltraSPARC 5
4	u	sun4u	Enterprise 220R

Table 3-1.   *Common Application and Kernel Architectures for Sun-4 Systems*

some Sun-4 architectures have had support deprecated in Solaris 9, mainly because of the requirement for a minimum of 96MB of RAM. The following SPARC systems are supported under Solaris 9:

SPARCclassic	SPARCstation LX	SPARCstation 4	SPARCstation 5
SPARCstation 10	SPARCstation 20	Ultra 1 (including Creator and Creator 3D models)	Enterprise 1
Ultra 2 (including Creator and Creator 3D models)	Ultra 5	Ultra 10	Ultra 30
Ultra 60	Ultra 450	Enterprise 2	Enterprise 150
Enterprise 250	Enterprise 450	Enterprise 3000	Enterprise 3500
Enterprise 4000	Enterprise 4500	Enterprise 5000	Enterprise 5500
Enterprise 6000	Enterprise 10000	SPARCserver 1000	SPARCcenter 2000

Some popular systems are no longer supported, particularly those in the sun4c family. Often, these systems can be upgraded with a firmware or CPU change to be compatible with Solaris 9. In addition, a minimum of 96MB of RAM is required to install Solaris 9—the Web Start Wizard will not let you proceed unless it can detect this amount of physical

INSTALLATION

RAM, so be sure to check that your system meets the basic requirements before attempting to install Solaris 9.

 Some machines listed in the table will support Solaris 9, but only in 32-bit mode.

System Components

A typical Solaris SPARC workstation consists of the following components:

- Base unit (aka "pizza box"), which contains the motherboard, SCSI controller, and SBUS cards
- Framebuffer or graphics card
- SCSI units connected by SCSI cables to the SCSI controller in the pizza box
- CD-ROM drive, internal or external (SCSI)
- DVD-ROM drive, internal on newer systems
- Speaker box and microphone, external
- Two serial ports (A and B)
- A parallel port
- A tape drive, internal or external (DAT/DDS/QIC and so on)
- Mouse (mechanical or infrared) and keyboard (Type 4 or Type 5)

As noted, most desktop workstations come in a "pizza box" chassis, although earlier Internetwork Packet Exchange (IPX) and similar systems had a "lunch box" chassis. Both of these designs were more compact than their PC counterparts. Servers generally come in two versions: standalone or rack-mountable. The version numbers on servers also differ with their chassis type. The 220R, for example, is the rack-mounted version of the standalone E-250, while the 420R is the rack-mounted version of the standalone 420. The 220R and E-250 have two CPUs each while the 420R and E-450 have four CPUs each.

Let's examine two SPARC systems in detail: a workstation (UltraSPARC 5) and a server (UltraSPARC E-450). The UltraSPARC 5 system is a popular, low-end desktop model. Although it has been replaced in this category by the new, lower cost Sun Blade 100 (available for around $1000), it remains a popular workstation for business and home use. It supports UltraSPARC-IIi CPUs with speeds ranging from 270 to 400 MHz. Internally, it features 16KB instruction and data caches, while it supports from 256KB to 2MB of external cache memory. In terms of memory and disk capacity, the system supports up to 512MB of physical RAM, a CD-ROM, a 1.44MB floppy disk, and two hard drives, making it possible to enable volume management. The system has three peripheral ports— two serial and one parallel—and it has a built-in Ethernet adapter and supports 10– 100 Mbps transmission rates. The system also features a PCMCIA bay, which allows a wide variety of PC-type hardware to be connected.

While the UltraSPARC 5 is comparable in performance to desktop PCs, the E-450 is a workgroup-level server that features symmetric multiprocessing, larger numbers of disks, fast buses, hot swapping, and more cache RAM per CPU. The E-450 supports up to four UltraSPARC-IIi CPUs, operating at 250–480 MHz. Internally, it features 16KB instruction and data caches per CPU, and up to 4MB of external cache per CPU—for a four-CPU system, that's a total of 16MB of external cache. The system also features two UPA buses operating at 100 MHz, supporting up to two CPUs on each bus. With respect to mass storage and memory, the system accepts up to 16 dual in-line memory modules (DIMMs), giving up to 4GB of physical RAM. Some 20 slots for hard disks provide a large pool of hot-swappable volumes on a fast SCSI-3 bus. A CD-ROM and floppy disk drive are also supplied, and a DDS-3 internal Digital Audio Tape (DAT) drive for backups. In addition, hot-swappable power supplies can be installed into the chassis, enabling two different power sources to be utilized.

Intel Hardware

If Solaris was originally designed to run on SPARC hardware, and if SPARC hardware is where Sun makes its money, why would Sun support an Intel version? For starters, many more Intel systems exist in the world than SPARC systems. Sun also has a historical relationship with Intel, which supported SunOS 4.x for several 80386 and 80486 systems. At this point, however, Sun introduced the SPARC range of CPUs, which were the forerunners of the current UltraSPARC series. Intel-based systems are also suitable for workstation environments, and were (until the recent release of the Sun Blade 100) much cheaper than SPARC systems. Since Sun is primarily in the server hardware business, it made sense to develop a reliable operating system for Intel workstations that was supported by its high-end servers.

For many potential Solaris users, SPARC systems are still prohibitively expensive, even though these users want the features of the UNIX operating system. Often, organizations need to make best use of their existing investment in PC hardware. However, some PC operating systems may not currently meet their needs. While PCs have become the de facto standard for desktop computers, investments in PC-based solutions have sometimes met with dissatisfaction from users because some PC operating systems lack stability—particularly regarding application-specific issues, although operating systems have also caused concern. Some of the problems included the perceived lack of reliability of operating systems that were prone to crash during important business operations. Although Intel CPUs featured modes that should logically isolate such failures to the operation that causes them (such as protected mode), this requires operating system support that was never fully perfected by some vendors. In other words, PC hardware is up to the task, but operating systems have not taken full advantage of its abilities.

Perhaps more frustrating is the fact that errors in existing PC operating systems could not be corrected by talented developers, because most PC operating systems are proprietary—in some instances, operating system vendors actually charged users to report operating system bugs, only refunding the charge if the bug was verified. In addition, frustration was often caused by so-called "standard" hardware, which often had incompatibilities with application and server software. For example, at the time when 80286 CPU systems were being touted as "IBM compatible," most were using an ISA bus, while IBMs were actually using the Micro Channel Architecture (MCA) as the bus on their PS/2 systems. However, PC hardware has converged on a number of standards, such as the PCI bus, which have vastly improved the performance figures for data throughput on PCs.

There are some key benefits to using Solaris for Intel over SPARC hardware. For a start, "plug and play" devices are supported, meaning that explicit device configuration is often not required. In addition, you can get access to modern bus architectures like PCI without having to purchase an UltraSPARC system. This point relates to overall system cost: If SPARC systems are going to use PCI for the foreseeable future, why use SPARC when PCI is supported by Intel systems at a smaller cost? In addition, Solaris for Intel supports multiple CPUs, each of which are much cheaper in cost than the equivalent SPARC CPUs.

There are, however, some limitations to using Solaris for Intel. These may be specific to Solaris, but some relate to the architecture itself. For example, while some versions of Microsoft Windows support up to four Enhanced Integrated Drive Electronics (EIDE) controllers, Solaris will see only the first two. Granted, IDE disks and controllers are generally less favorable than SCSI-3 drives, but they do exist and they are cheap. In addition, support for the Universal Serial Bus (USB) is still experimental, making it harder to add new devices that don't use the serial port for connection. Many new modems also won't work on anything but Windows (so-called "Winmodems") because they rely on Windows to control the modem hardware rather than having a built-in controller.

Because Sun makes no direct revenues from Solaris Intel, the bottom line is that, with the growing popularity of Linux for the Intel platform, continued development of the Solaris Intel edition may receive less attention than the SPARC edition. This doesn't mean that you shouldn't continue to use Solaris Intel, though, because it is a mature and stable product. In terms of contemplating future server purchases, however, it might be wiser to go with SPARC.

The Hardware Compatibility List (HCL), which is available at **http://soldc.sun.com/support/drivers/hcl/index.html**, is the definitive guide to all hardware devices supported by the Solaris Intel platform. If a device does not appear in the HCL, it is unlikely that it will be supported under Solaris Intel—with some exceptions: motherboards, for example, often follow fairly loose standards, with clone boards often working correctly under Solaris if they don't appear in the HCL. The most common compatibility issue occurs with video cards—many are not supported at all, or if they are, their full feature set is unsupported. For example, some video cards have hardware support for receiving TV signals. While their graphical rendering ability will be supported, the TV functions will generally not work with Solaris.

Fortunately, if your video card is not supported, it is possible to replace the X server provided by Solaris with the XFree-86 X server (**http://www.xfree.org/**). This server is functionally equivalent to any other server that supports the X11R6 standard, meaning that the common desktop environment (CDE) and all other Solaris GUI applications will run if you have installed XFree. The main advantage of using XFree-86 is that it supports a much larger array of hardware devices than the Solaris X server.

Devices Supported Under Solaris Intel

This section reviews some of the families of devices supported under Solaris Intel and examples of products that are likely to be supported. Most common motherboards are supported, including those developed by Acer, ASUS, EPoX, and Intel. Some examples are the Acer M9N MP, the ASUS A7V, and the EPoX EP-MVP3G. In addition, motherboard support has been established for many prebuilt systems, including the Acer AcerAcros T7000 MT, Bull Information Systems Express5800-HX4500, and Compaq Deskpro EN 6400. Many symmetric multiprocessing (SMP)-capable motherboards are also supported. No special configuration is required to support SMP devices—they are "plug and play"— and some popular models include the Dell PowerEdge 6300, the Fujitsu TeamSERVER-T890I, and the Gateway 8400.

Video cards from many different manufacturers are supported, including those operating from ISA, PCI, or AGP buses. Five display resolutions are supported:

- 800 × 600 pixels
- 1024 × 768 pixels
- 1152 × 900 pixels
- 1280 × 1024 pixels
- 1600 × 1200 pixels

Both 8- and 24-bit color are supported in all of these modes, depending on the chipset and onboard memory. Many cards are supported, including the ATI 3D RAGE, the Boca Voyager 64, and the Chips & Technology 65540. All multisync monitors are supported. However, the *kdmconfig* application used for setting up the display does not show 14-inch monitors in its selection list; in most cases, you will be able to use the 15-inch setting, as long as the frequency specified is supported by your monitor. Fixed-sync monitors should work as long as their frequency is supported by the video card at the resolution you require. Serial, bus, and PS/2 mouse devices are supported under Solaris. In addition, many third-party pointing devices are supported, including the MicroSpeed MicroTRAC trackball, the LogiTech MouseMan cordless, and the Kraft Systems MicroTrack.

In terms of SCSI host adapters, both standard and ultra-wide SCSI support is included for the most popular host adapters, including the Adaptec AHA-2940/2940W, AMD Pcscsi, and the Compaq 32-bit Fast-Wide SCSI-2. Many Iomega Jaz/Zip devices are supported under Solaris, including the SCSI devices 2250S Zip drive (250MB) and the V2008I Jaz drive (2GB), as well as the ATAPI and IDE Z100A Zip drives (100MB).

Many different types of network adapters are supported, including 10 Mbps and 100 Mbps data transfer rates. Supported adapters include the 3Com EtherLink III PCI Bus Master, the Adaptec ANA-6901, and the AMD PCnet-PCI.

For laptops, common PCMCIA devices are generally supported, such as modems and network adapters, including the ATI Technologies 14400 ETC-EXPRESS, the Compaq SpeedPaq 192, and the Hayes 5361US.

The
Complete
Reference

Chapter 4

Solaris 9 Installation

olaris 9 provides more installation methods than any previous version. These include the Web Start Wizard, JumpStart, *suninstall*, and Live Upgrade. The Web Start Wizard is the easiest method for installing Solaris 9: it uses a Java-based front end that presents a series of configuration choices. For those who prefer a command-line installation, the *suninstall* program is also available. This is particularly useful for installing servers that are attached to a simple terminal on the console port, using the `tip` command (see Chapter 23) rather than a high-resolution monitor. Large organizations are more likely to create a JumpStart configuration (as described in Chapter 30) to install a standard operating environment (SOE) on all Solaris 9 systems. Using JumpStart ensures that all systems have an identical installation base, which makes it easy for you to manage patches and maintain production systems. Live Upgrade is a new innovation that minimizes the downtime of production servers: a new boot environment is constructed while the server is still operating under its existing operating environment release. Once the second boot environment has been installed, the system is quickly rebooted into the new operating environment, and the previous version is uninstalled in the background.

In most cases, installing from a high-speed CD-ROM with a modern UltraSPARC will take one to two hours. However, JumpStart, Live Upgrade, and all network-based installations will be slower on a per-machine basis, since network bandwidth limits the data that can be transmitted from the install server to the install client.

Preinstallation Planning

The basic process of installing Solaris remains the same, regardless of the installation method selected. A number of planning tasks must be performed prior to installation:

- Choose the appropriate installation method from the Web Start Wizard, JumpStart, *suninstall*, and Live Upgrade.

- Decide whether you want to upgrade an existing installation or perform a clean install of the operating system. If your system is currently running Solaris 2.6, 7, or 8, an upgrade can be performed. If your system is running Solaris 2.5.1 or earlier, or if it is not running Solaris at all, you need to perform a clean installation. An upgrade preserves many of the system settings from the previous installation and generally takes less time to complete than a completely new installation. If an upgrade is being performed, the current system should first be backed up by using `ufsdump` or similar methods so that it can be restored in the event of an upgrade failure.

- Analyze your existing hardware devices to determine whether Solaris 9 will run on your system without an upgrade. For example, Solaris 8 on SPARC would run with only 64MB of RAM; however, at least 96MB of RAM is required to run Solaris 9. To perform an upgrade installation, you would need to add RAM to an existing Solaris 8 system with only 64MB of RAM.

■ Determine whether your storage devices have sufficient capacity to install Solaris 9 and all required third-party applications. A complete Solaris 9 installation requires 2.4GB of disk space if original equipment manufacturer (OEM) support is included, and 2.3GB if OEM support is not included. A developer installation requires at least 1.9GB, while the end-user installation requires 1.6GB. In addition, an amount of swap space equivalent to twice your physical memory should be factored into the sum, along with third-party and user disk space requirements.

■ Choose an appropriate installation medium. Possibilities include a JumpStart, CD-ROM, DVD-ROM, or net-based installation from a remotely mounted CD-ROM or DVD-ROM drive. For enterprises, it's often convenient to set up a single network server with a Network File System (NFS)-exported DVD-ROM or CD-ROM drive that is publicly available for mounting. In addition, enterprises might also choose a customized JumpStart installation, which also requires network access to a centralized boot server. Smaller organizations will almost certainly use a CD-ROM or DVD-ROM drive attached to the local system for installation.

■ Gather all of the necessary system configuration information. This includes the system hostname, IP address, subnet mask, name service type, name server IP address, default router IP address, time zone, locale, and proxy server IP address. These values, and when they are required, will be discussed in the "Configuration" section.

By undertaking a comprehensive preinstallation review, a successful installation can be assured. In addition to making decisions about the installation type and gathering basic system data, you need to understand the network context in which the system will operate. You can define the network context by answering several key questions:

■ Will the system be networked? If so, you will need an IP address, subnet mask, and default router (unless the system itself is intended to be a router).

■ Will the system use the Dynamic Host Configuration Protocol (DHCP)? If so, you will not need to supply an IP address, as a lease over an IP address will automatically be granted to you at boot time. However, you will need the IP address of the DHCP server to enable DHCP.

■ Will the system use IPv6, the newest version of the Internet Protocol?

■ Will the system form part of a Kerberos v5 realm to allow centralized authentication? If so, you will need the name of the realm, the administration server's IP address, and the address of the primary Key Distribution Center (KDC).

■ Will the system use the Domain Name Service (DNS)? If so, you will need the IP address of a primary and secondary DNS server that is authoritative for the local domain.

■ Will the system use Network Information Service (NIS) or NIS+? If so, the IP address of the local NIS or NIS+ server will need to be supplied.

■ Will the system make use of the Lightweight Directory Access Protocol (LDAP) for centralized authentication and authorization? If so, you will need to supply the profile server's IP address.

■ Will the system use a proxy server to access the Internet? If so, the IP address of the proxy server will be required.

Answers to these questions will be required before you can completely configure the system during installation.

Disk Space Planning

You can determine how much disk space you require to install Solaris 9 only by examining the purpose of the server. For a SPARC system, with 512MB of RAM, a complete installation will require 2.6GB of space for software, 1024MB for swap, and more space for user data and applications. Extra disk space must be set aside for special features such as internationalization, and you need to estimate the size of print and mail spooling directories that are located in */var*. Although the default size of */var* is usually small in the installation program, mail and print servers will require that you increase this amount by allowing for a reasonable allocation of spooling space per user. Since a full */var* file system caused by a large print job can affect other tasks such as mail, it's important that you overestimate rather than underestimate the size of */var*. In terms of applications, an Oracle database server, for example, will require at least 1–2GB of disk space for software packages, mount points, and table data. For a development system with multiple users, you should compute a projection based on the maximum quota for each user. For example, if each of 50 users is allowed 100MB of disk space, at least 5GB of disk space must be available for the users' exclusive use—as a rule, if users have quotas imposed on them, they should always be guaranteed access to that space. If data on a server is mission critical, consideration should be given to installing some volume management software, as described in Chapter 15.

In terms of specific layouts, the typical file system layout for a SPARC system follows a set of customary disk slice allocations. Slice 0 holds the root partition, while slice 1 is allocated to swap space. For systems with changing virtual memory requirements, it might be better to use a swap file on the file system, rather than allocating an entire slice for swap. Slice 2 often refers to the entire disk, while /export on slice 3 traditionally holds older versions of the operating system that are used by client systems with lower performance (for example, Classic or LX systems that use the trivial FTP daemon *tftpd* to download their operating system upon boot). These systems may also use slice 4 as exported swap space. Export may also be used for file sharing using NFS. Slice 5 holds the */opt* file system, which is the default location under Solaris 9 for local packages installed using the pkgadd command. Under earlier versions of Solaris, the */usr/local* file system held local packages, and this convention is still used by many sites. The system package file system */usr* is usually located on slice 6, while */export/home* usually contains user home directories on slice 7. Again, earlier systems located user home directories under */home,* but since /home is used by the *automounter* program in Solaris 9, some contention can be expected.

The typical file system layout for an Intel-based system also follows a set of customary disk slice allocations. Slice 0 again holds the root partition, while slice 1 is allocated to swap space. Slice 2 continues to refer to the entire disk, while */export* on slice 3 again holds older versions of the operating system that are used by client systems, and slice 4 contains exported swap space for these clients. The local package file system */opt* is still located on slice 5, and the system package file system */usr* is again located on slice 6. Slice 7 contains the user home directories on */export/home*. However, the two extra slices serve a different purposes: boot information for Solaris is located on slice 8 and is known as the *boot slice*, while slice 9 provides space for alternative disk blocks and is known as the Alternative Slice.

Device Names

Some of the most challenging aspects of understanding Solaris hardware are the device names and references used by Solaris to manage devices. Solaris uses a specific set of naming conventions to associate physical devices with instance names on the operating system. In addition, devices can also be referred to by their device name, which is associated with a device file created in the */dev* directory after configuration. For example, a hard disk may have the physical device name */pci@1f,0/pci@1,1/ide@3/dad@0,0*, which is associated with the device file */dev/dsk/c0t0d0*. The benefit of the more complex Solaris device names and physical device references is that it is easy to interpret the characteristics of each device by looking at its name, as discussed in Chapter 22. For the physical device name example given above, you can see that the Integrated Device Electronics (IDE) hard drive is located on a PCI local bus at target 0. When you view the amount of free disk space on the system, for example, it is easy to identify slices on the same disk by looking at the device name:

```
# df -k
Filesystem            kbytes     used    avail capacity  Mounted on
/proc                      0        0        0    0%     /proc
/dev/dsk/c0t0d0s0    1982988   615991  1307508   33%     /
fd                         0        0        0    0%     /dev/fd
/dev/dsk/c0t0d0s3    1487119   357511  1070124   26%     /usr
swap                  182040      416   181624    1%     /tmp
```

Here you can see that */dev/dsk/c0t0d0s0* and */dev/dsk/c0t0d0s3* are slice 0 and slice 3 of the disk I.

If you're ever unsure of which physical disk is associated with a specific disk device name, you can use the `format` command to find out:

```
# format
Searching for disks...done
AVAILABLE DISK SELECTIONS:
0. c1t3d0 <SUN2.1G cyl 2733 alt 2 hd 19 sec 80>
          /pci@1f,0/pci@1/scsi@1/sd@3,0
```

Here you can see that physical device */pci@1f,0/pci@1/scsi@1/sd@3,0* is matched with the disk device */dev/dsk/c1t3d0*. In addition, a list of mappings between physical devices to instance names is always kept in the */etc/path_to_inst* file. More information on device naming conventions can be found in Chapter 22.

SPARC Preinstallation

One of the main hardware differences between SPARC systems that run Solaris and PC systems that run Linux or Microsoft Windows is that SPARC systems have an OpenBoot PROM monitor program that can be used to modify firmware settings prior to booting. It is based on the Forth programming language and can be used to run Forth programs that perform the following functions:

- Booting the system using the `boot` command
- Performing diagnostics on hardware devices using the `diag` command
- Testing network connectivity using the `watch-net` command

Prior to installing or upgrading Solaris on a SPARC system, you should perform a few basic checks of the system to obtain the data necessary for installation (such as the device name of the boot disk), and also to verify that all system components are functional. The three most commonly performed tasks are checking network connectivity, checking the disks that have been detected on the SCSI bus, and reviewing how much memory is installed.

If you are booting over a network or if your system needs to access a DNS, NIS/NIS+, Kerberos, or LDAP server, and you want support for these services to be installed, your network connection will need to be operational. To ensure that packets are being sent and received to your system, you can use the `watch-net` command:

```
ok watch-net
Internal Loopback test - succeeded
External Loopback test - succeeded
Looking for Ethernet packets.
'.' is a good packet. 'X' is a bad packet.
Type any key to stop
......X.........XXXX.........XX............
```

If a large number of packets are showing as bad, you should check for hardware errors on your network cable, and/or use a packet analyzer to determine whether a structural fault exists on the local area network (LAN). To check whether all the disk devices attached to the system have been correctly detected, you can use the probe-scsi command to print a list of available devices:

```
ok probe-scsi
Target 1
Unit 0 Disk SUN0104 Copyright (C) 1995 Sun Microsystems All rights reserved
```

You can see the default boot disk at target 1 unit 0.

To check that sufficient memory is available on the local system for the installation of Solaris 9, you can use the banner command:

```
ok banner
SPARCstation 20, Type 5 Keyboard
ROM Rev. 2.4, 256 MB memory installed, Serial #456543
Ethernet address 5:2:12:c:ee:5a HostID 456543
```

In this case, 256MB of RAM is available, which is sufficient for installation.

Intel Preinstallation

To install Solaris Intel, first switch on the system and insert the Solaris Installation CD-ROM into the drive. If a high-resolution graphics monitor is attached to the system, the GUI-based Configuration Assistant will start. Alternatively, if you are using a low resolution terminal to connect, the Configuration Assistant will be text based.

After the BIOS messages have been displayed, the following message is displayed:

```
SunOS Secondary Boot
Solaris Intel Platform Edition Booting System
Running Configuration Assistant...
```

The Configuration Assistant is responsible for performing a number of preinstallation tasks and must be executed prior to starting the Web Start Wizard or any other installation program. At the opening screen, simply press F2 to proceed with the installation, unless you are performing an upgrade.

The first task performed by the Configuration Assistant is determining the bus types supported by your system and collecting data about the devices installed on your system. During this process, the following message will be displayed on your screen:

```
Determining bus types and gathering hardware configuration data ...
```

After all of the devices have been discovered by scanning, a list of identified devices is printed on the screen:

```
The following devices have been identified on this system. To identify
devices not on this list or to modify device characteristics, chose Device
Task. Platform types may be included in this list.

        ISA: Floppy disk controller
        ISA: IDE controller
        ISA: IDE controller
        ISA: Motherboard
        ISA: PS/2 Mouse
        ISA: PnP bios: 16550-compatible serial controller
        ISA: PnP bios: 8514-compatible display controller
        ISA: PnP bios: Audio device
        ISA: System keyboard (US-English)
```

If you are satisfied that the devices required for installation have been correctly detected (video card and RAM size, for example), press F2 again to proceed with booting. Alternatively, you may perform several other tasks on this screen, including the following:

- Viewing and editing devices
- Setting the keyboard type
- Saving the current configuration
- Deleting a saved configuration
- Setting the default console device

If your system does not already have a UNIX File System (UFS) installed, or if it is a completely new system, you will need to use *fdisk* to create new partitions at this point so that your system may be installed. However, if you have an existing Linux installation that you want to dual boot with Solaris, you must ensure that the Linux swap partition is not confused with a Solaris UFS device, because they have the same type within *fdisk*. You should be able to distinguish Linux swap partitions by their maximum size (127MB). The following page will be displayed during bootup and prior to the execution of *fdisk*:

```
<<< Current Boot Parameters >>>
Boot path: /pci@1,0/pci-ide@6,1/ide@2/sd@1,0:a
Boot args: kernel/unix
<<< Starting Installation >>>
SunOS Release 5.9 Version Generic 32-bit
Copyright 1983-2001 Sun Microsystems, Inc. All rights reserved.
Configuring /dev and /devices
Using RPC Bootparams for network configuration information.
Solaris Web Start installer
```

```
English has been selected as the language in which to perform the install.
Starting the Web Start Solaris installer
Solaris installer is searching the system's hard disks for a
location to place the Solaris installer software.
No suitable Solaris fdisk partition was found.
Solaris Installer needs to create a Solaris fdisk partition
on your root disk, c0d0, that is at least 395 MB.
WARNING: All information on the disk will be lost.
May the Solaris Installer create a Solaris fdisk [y,n,?]
```

Caution   *You should heed the warning that all data will be lost if you choose to overwrite it with fdisk.*

Disk Partitions

If you consent to using *fdisk*, you will see a screen similar to the following:

```
Total disk size is 2048 cylinders
Cylinder size is 4032 (512 byte) blocks
Cylinders
Partition  Status  Type   Start  End   Length  %
=========  ======  ====   =====  ====  ======  ===
1                  UNIX   0      1023  1024    50
2                  DOS    1024   2047  1024    50
SELECT ONE OF THE FOLLOWING:
1. Create a partition
2. Specify the active partition
3. Delete a partition
4. Exit (update disk configuration and exit)
5. Cancel (exit without updating disk configuration)
Enter Selection:
```

In this example, you can see that two existing partitions occupy 1204 cylinders each. Partition 1 is a UNIX partition (perhaps from SCO UNIX), while partition 2 is a MS-DOS partition. If you want to use the entire disk for Solaris, you would need to select option 3 on this menu, twice, to delete each existing partition in turn. Alternatively, if you wished to retain the UNIX partition but delete the MS-DOS partition, you would select option 3 only once, and then select partition 2 for deletion.

After you have freed up space (if necessary), you will be required to select option 1 to create a partition. You will then be required to select option A from the following menu to create a Solaris partition:

```
Select the partition type to create:
1=SOLARIS 2=UNIX 3=PCIXOS 4=Other
5=DOS12 6=DOS16 7=DOSEXT 8=DOSBIG
A=x86 Boot B=Diagnostic 0=Exit?
```

Note | *It is not possible to run Solaris from a non-UFS partition; however, it is possible to mount non-Solaris file systems after the system has been installed.*

Next, you need to specify the size of the partition, in either the number of cylinders or the percentage of the disk to be used. In this example, you enter either 100 percent or 2048 cylinders:

```
Specify the percentage of disk to use for this partition
(or type "c" to specify the size in cylinders).
```

Next, you need to indicate whether the target partition is going to be activated. This means that the system will attempt to boot the default operating system loader from this partition. If you are going to use the Solaris boot manager, you may activate this partition. However, if you are using Boot Magic or LILO to manage existing Microsoft Windows or Linux partitions, and you wish to continue using either of these systems, you should answer No.

After you have created the partition, the *fdisk* menu will be updated and displayed as follows:

```
2 Active x86 Boot 8 16 9 1
Total disk size is 2048 cylinders
Cylinder size is 4032 (512 byte) blocks
Cylinders
Partition  Status  Type        Start  End   Length  %
=========  ======  =========   =====  ====  ======  ===
2          Active  x86 Boot    0      2047  2048    100
SELECT ONE OF THE FOLLOWING:
1. Create a partition
2. Specify the active partition
3. Delete a partition
4. Exit (update disk configuration and exit)
5. Cancel (exit without updating disk configuration)
Enter Selection:
```

At this point, you should select option 4. You will then be prompted with the following message:

```
No suitable Solaris fdisk partition was found.
Solaris Installer needs to create a Solaris fdisk partition
on your root disk, c0d0, that is at least 395MB.
WARNING: All information on the disk will be lost.
May the Solaris Installer create a Solaris fdisk [y,n,?]
```

Since you've just created the appropriate partition using *fdisk*, you should type **n** here. You will then see this message:

```
To restart the installation, run /sbin/cd0_install.
```

After restarting the installer, you will see the formatting display shown in the next section.

Disk Formatting and Virtual Memory

If your system already has a UFS partition, or if you have just created one, you will see a screen containing text similar to the following:

```
<<< Current Boot Parameters >>>
Boot path: /pci@1,0/pci-ide@6,1/ide@2/sd@1,0:a
Boot args: kernel/unix
<<< Starting Installation >>>
SunOS Release 5.9 Version Generic 32-bit
Copyright 1983-2001 Sun Microsystems, Inc. All rights reserved.
Configuring /dev and /devices
Using RPC Bootparams for network configuration information.
Solaris Web Start installer
English has been selected as the language in which to perform the install.
Starting the Web Start Solaris installer
Solaris installer is searching the system's hard disks for a
location to place the Solaris installer software.
The default root disk is /dev/dsk/c0d0.
The Solaris installer needs to format
/dev/dsk/c0d0 to install Solaris.
WARNING: ALL INFORMATION ON THE DISK WILL BE ERASED!
Do you want to format /dev/dsk/c0d0? [y,n,?,q]
```

At this point, you simply type **y** and the disk will be formatted so that new partitions can be created. You will then be prompted to enter the size of the swap partition:

```
NOTE: The swap size cannot be changed during filesystem layout.
Enter a swap partition size between 384MB and 1865MB, default = 512MB [?]
```

You will then be asked to confirm that the swap slice can be installed at the beginning of the partition:

```
The Installer prefers that the swap slice is at the beginning of the
disk. This will allow the most flexible filesystem partitioning later
in the installation.
Can the swap slice start at the beginning of the disk [y,n,?,q]
```

After creating the swap partition, the other slices can be created on the target disk because the installation program requires a UFS to install correctly. However, the system must first be rebooted to perform the disk layout:

```
The Solaris installer will use disk slice, /dev/dsk/c0d0s1.
After files are copied, the system will automatically reboot, and
installation will continue.
Please Wait...
Copying mini-root to local disk....done.
Copying platform specific files....done.
Preparing to reboot and continue installation.
Need to reboot to continue the installation
Please remove the boot media (floppy or cdrom) and press Enter
Note: If the boot media is cdrom, you must wait for the system
to reset in order to eject.
```

After you press the ENTER key, you will see the standard Solaris shutdown messages, including this one:

```
Syncing file systems... 49 done
rebooting...
```

The Boot Manager

After ejecting the installation CD-ROM from your drive, the standard Solaris boot manager menu should appear:

```
SunOS - Intel Platform Edition Primary Boot Subsystem
Current Disk Partition Information
Part#    Status  Type      Start  Length
========================================
1        Active  X86 BOOT  0      2048
Please select the partition you wish to boot:
```

After you enter **1** and press the ENTER key, the following message appears:

```
SunOS Secondary Boot
Solaris Intel Platform Edition Booting System
Running Configuration Assistant...
Autobooting from boot path: /pci@1,0/pci-ide@6,1/ide@2/sd@1,0:a
If the system hardware has changed, or to boot from a different
device, interrupt the autoboot process by pressing ESC.
```

A few seconds later, the boot interpreter is initialized:

```
Initializing system
Please wait...
<<< Current Boot Parameters >>>
Boot path: /pci@0,0/pci-ide@7,1/ata@1/cmdk@0,0:b
Boot args:
Type b [file-name] [boot-flags] <ENTER> to boot with options
or i <ENTER> to enter boot interpreter
or <ENTER> to boot with defaults
<<< timeout in 5 seconds >>>
Select (b)oot or (i)nterpreter:
SunOS Release 5.9 Version Generic 32-bit
Copyright 1983-2001 Sun Microsystems, Inc. All rights reserved.
Configuring /dev and /devices
Using RPC Bootparams for network configuration information.
```

Next, you will need to use *kdmconfig* to set up your graphics card and monitor so that the Web Start Wizard can correctly display its windows. To start *kdmconfig*, press F2. Then you will be taken to the *kdmconfig* introduction screen. After pressing F2 again, you will be asked to perform the *kdmconfig* view/edit system operation. In the configuration window, you can make changes to the settings detected on your system. If your system is listed on the Hardware Compatibility List (HCL), you shouldn't have any problems with hardware detection.

Web Start Wizard Installation

To use the Web Start Wizard installer using a local DVD-ROM or CD-ROM drive, you need to bring the system to run level 0 so that commands can be entered into the PROM boot monitor (for more information about the boot monitor, see Chapter 5). The following command can be used from a root shell to bring the system to run level 0:

```
# sync; init 0
```

When the system has reached init level 0, the following prompt will be displayed:

```
ok
```

Next, place the Solaris 9 Installation CD-ROM or DVD-ROM into the local drive, and type the following command:

```
ok boot cdrom
```

This command is the same whether a DVD or CD-ROM is used as the source. If you are using a Solaris Intel system, you cannot upgrade from Solaris versions 2.6 or from versions 7 to 9 by using the Web Start Wizard from the CD-ROM: you must use a DVD-ROM or JumpStart, or you must perform a net-based installation. In addition, your BIOS and hard disk controller for the boot device must support Logical Block Addressing (LBA) to work with Solaris 9.

Soon after the system has started booting, you will then see output similar to the following:

```
Boot device: /sbus/espdma@e,8400000/esp@e,8800000/sd@6,0:f File and args:
SunOS Release 5.9 Version Generic 32-bit
Copyright 1983-2001 Sun Microsystems, Inc. All rights reserved.
Configuring /dev and /devices
Using RPC Bootparams for network configuration information.
Solaris Web Start installer
English has been selected as the language in which to perform the install.
Starting the Web Start Solaris installer
Solaris installer is searching the system's hard disks for a
location to place the Solaris installer software.
Your system appears to be upgradeable.
Do you want to do a Initial Install or Upgrade?
1) Initial Install
2) Upgrade
Please Enter 1 or 2 >
```

If the next message appears in the boot messages, you may elect to perform an upgrade of the existing Solaris installation. However, most administrators would back up their existing software, perform a fresh install, and then restore their data and applications after the system is operational. In this case, we will choose to perform an Initial Install, which will overwrite the existing operating system.

Type **1**, and then press ENTER. You will see a message like this:

```
The default root disk is /dev/dsk/c0t0d0.
The Solaris installer needs to format
/dev/dsk/c0t0d0 to install Solaris.
WARNING: ALL INFORMATION ON THE DISK WILL BE ERASED!
Do you want to format /dev/dsk/c0t0d0? [y,n,?,q]
```

Formatting the hard drive will overwrite all existing data on the drive—you must ensure that if you had previously installed an operating system on the target drive (*c0t0d0*), you have backed up all data that you will need in the future. This includes both user directories and application installations.

After you answer by typing **Y**, the following screen will appear:

```
NOTE: The swap size cannot be changed during filesystem layout.
Enter a swap slice size between 384MB and 2027MB, default = 512MB [?]
```

Press the ENTER key to accept the default of 512MB, if your system has 256MB of physical RAM, as this example system has. However, as a general rule, you should allocate twice the amount of physical RAM as swap space; otherwise, system performance will be impaired. The swap partition should be placed at the beginning of the drive, as the following message indicates, so that other slices are not dependent on its physical location:

```
The Installer prefers that the swap slice is at the beginning of the
disk. This will allow the most flexible filesystem partitioning later
in the installation.
Can the swap slice start at the beginning of the disk [y,n,?,q]
```

After you type **Y** to answer this question, you will be asked to confirm the formatting settings:

```
You have selected the following to be used by the Solaris installer:
Disk Slice : /dev/dsk/c0t0d0
Size : 1024 MB
Start Cyl. : 0
WARNING: ALL INFORMATION ON THE DISK WILL BE ERASED!
Is this OK [y,n,?,q]
```

If you answer by typing **Y**, the disk will be formatted and a mini-root file system will be copied to the disk. Then the system will reboot, and the Web Start Wizard installation process can begin:

```
The Solaris installer will use disk slice, /dev/dsk/c0t0d0s1.
After files are copied, the system will automatically reboot, and
installation will continue.
Please Wait...
Copying mini-root to local disk....done.
Copying platform specific files....done.
Preparing to reboot and continue installation.
Rebooting to continue the installation.
Syncing file systems... 41 done
rebooting...
Resetting ...
SPARCstation 20 (1 X 390Z50), Keyboard Present
```

```
ROM Rev. 2.4, 256 MB memory installed, Serial #456543
Ethernet address 5:2:12:c:ee:5a HostID 456543
Rebooting with command: boot /sbus@1f,0/espdma@e,8400000/
esp@e,8800000/sd@0,0:b
Boot device: /sbus@1f,0/espdma@e,8400000/esp@e,8800000/
sd@0,0:b File and args:
SunOS Release 5.9 Version Generic 32-bit
Copyright 1983-2001 Sun Microsystems, Inc. All rights reserved.
Configuring /dev and /devices
Using RPC Bootparams for network configuration information.
```

Configuration

The Web Start Wizard asks a number of configuration questions that are used to determine which files are copied to the target drive and how the new system's key parameters will be set. Many of these questions involve network and software configuration, because these are the two foundations of the Solaris installation. The following sections will review each of the configuration options and will provide examples of appropriate settings.

Network Support

The Network Support screen gives users the option of selecting a networked or non-networked system. Some examples of non-networked systems include standalone workstations and offline archives. If you don't want or need to install network support, however, you will still need a unique hostname to identify the localhost.

DHCP Server

Network users must first identify how their system is identified using the IP. One possibility is that the system will use DHCP, which is useful when IP addresses are becoming scarce on a Class C network. DHCP allows individual systems to be allocated only for the period during which they are "up." Thus, if a client machine is operated only between 9 A.M. and 5 P.M. every day, for example, it is only "leased" an IP address for that period of time. When an IP address is not leased to a specific host, it can be reused by another host. Solaris DHCP servers can service Solaris clients as well as Microsoft Windows and Linux clients.

Hostname

A hostname is used to uniquely identify a host on the local network; when combined with a domain name, the hostname allows a host to be uniquely identified on the Internet. Solaris administrators often devise related sets of hostnames that form part of a single domain. Alternatively, a descriptive name can be used to describe systems with a single purpose, such as "mail" for mail servers.

IP Address

If your network does not provide DHCP, you will need to enter the IP address assigned to this system by the network administrator. It is important that the IP address is not currently being used by another host, because packets may be misrouted if identical IP addresses exist. Like a hostname, the IP address needs to be unique to the local system.

Netmask

You will next need to enter the netmask for the system: *255.0.0.0* (Class A), *255.255.0.0* (Class B), or *255.255.255.0* (Class C). If you're not sure, ask your network administrator.

IPv6 Support

Next, you need to indicate whether IPv6 needs to be supported by this system. The decision to use or not to use DHCP will depend on whether your network is part of MBone, the IPv6-enabled version of the Internet. As proposed in RFC 2471, IPv6 will replace IPv4 in the years to come, as version 6 provides for many more IP addresses than IPv4. Once IPv6 is adopted worldwide, less reliance on DHCP will be necessary.

However, IPv6 also incorporates a number of innovations above and beyond the addition of more IP addresses for the Internet. Enhanced security provided by authenticating header information, for example, will reduce the risk of IP spoofing and denial of service (DoS) attacks. Since IPv6 support does not interfere with existing IPv4 support, most administrators will want to support version 6.

Kerberos Server

Kerberos is a network authentication protocol that is designed to provide centralized authentication for client/server applications by using secret-key cryptography, which is based around ticketing. Once a ticket has expired, the trust relationship between two hosts is broken. To use Kerberos, you'll need to identify the name of the local KDC.

Name Services

A name service allows your system to find other hosts on the Internet or on the LAN. Solaris supports several different naming servers, including NIS/NIS+, the DNS, and file-based name resolution. Solaris supports the concurrent operation of various naming services, so it's possible to select NIS/NIS+ and set up DNS manually later. However, because most hosts are now connected to the Internet, it may be more appropriate for you to install DNS first and then install NIS/NIS+.

DNS Server

The DNS maps IP addresses to hostnames. If you select DNS, you will be asked to enter a domain name for the local system. This should be the fully qualified domain name (for example, *cassowary.net*). You will either need to search the local subnet for a DNS server or enter the IP address of the primary DNS server for your domain. You may also enter up to two secondary DNS servers that have records of your domain, which can be a useful backup if your primary DNS server goes down. It is also possible that when searching for hosts with a hostname rather than a fully qualified domain name, you would want to search multiple local domains. For example, the host **www.buychapters.com** belongs to the *buychapters.com* domain. However, your users may wish to locate other hosts within the broader *cassowary.net* domain by using the simple hostname, in which case, you can add the *cassowary.net* domain to a list of domains to be searched for hosts.

NIS/NIS+ Server

NIS/NIS+ is used to manage large domains by creating maps or tables of hosts, services, and resources that are shared between hosts. NIS/NIS+ centrally manages the naming and logical organization of these entities. If you choose NIS or NIS+ as a naming service, you will need to enter the IP address of the local NIS or NIS+.

LDAP Server

LDAP provides a "white pages" service that supersedes existing X.500 systems and runs directly over TCP/IP. The LDAP server is used for managing directory information for entire organizations, using a centralized repository. If you want to use a LDAP server, you will need to provide both the name of your profile and the IP address of the LDAP server. If the machine that you're installing will be the LDAP server, you shouldn't set up the system as a LDAP client.

Router

To access the LAN and the Internet, you will need to supply the IP address of the default router for the system. A router is a multihomed host that is responsible for passing packets between subnets. More information about routers is provided in Chapters 19 and 20.

Timezone and Locale

The next section requires that you enter your time zone as specified by geographic region— the number of hours beyond or before Greenwich Mean Time (GMT) or by timezone file. Using the geographic region is the easiest method, although if you already know the GMT offset and/or the name of the timezone file, you may enter that instead. Next, you are required to enter the current time and date, with a four-digit year, a month, day, hour, and minute. In addition, you will need to specify support for a specific geographic region in terms of locales, if required.

Power Management

Do you want your system to switch off automatically after 30 minutes of inactivity? If you can honestly answer yes to this question (e.g., because you have a workstation that does not run services), then you should enable power management, as it can save costly power bills. However, if you're administering a server, you'll definitely want to turn power management off. A case in point: Once your server shuts down in the middle of the night, and your clients cannot access data, you'll understand why disabling power management is so important.

Proxy Server

A proxy server acts as a buffer between hosts on a local network and the rest of the Internet. A proxy server passes connections between local hosts and any other host on the Internet. It sometimes acts in conjunction with a firewall to block access to internal systems, thereby protecting sensitive data. One of the most popular proxy servers is squid, which also acts as a caching server. To enable access to the Internet through a proxy server, you need to enter the hostname of the proxy server, and the port on which the proxy operates.

64-Bit Support

Solaris 9 provides support for 64-bit kernels for the SPARC platform. By default, only a 32-bit kernel will be installed. For superior performance, a 64-bit kernel is preferred, because it can natively compute much larger numbers than the 32-bit kernel. In the 64-bit environment, 32-bit applications run in compatibility mode. However, only some UltraSPARC systems support the 64-bit kernel (see Chapter 3 for details).

Disk Selection and Layout

If you are performing an upgrade or installing a new system, you will need to decide whether you want to preserve any preexisting data on your target drives. For example, you may have five SCSI disks attached, only one of which contains slices used for a previous version of Solaris. Obviously, you will want to preserve the data on the four nonboot disks. However, partitions on the boot disk will be overwritten during installation, so it's important that you back up and/or relocate files that need to be preserved. Fortunately, if you choose to perform an upgrade rather than a fresh installation, many system configuration files will be preserved.

The Web Start Wizard will also ask if you want to "auto-layout" the boot disk slices or if you want to configure them manually. You should be aware that the settings supplied by the installation program are conservative, and trying to recover a system that has a full root file system can be time-consuming, especially given the low cost of disk space. It's usually necessary to increase the size of the / and /var partitions by at least 50 percent over what the installer recommends. If you have two identical disks installed, and you have more space than you need, you can always set up volume management to ensure high availability through root partition mirroring; thus, if your primary boot disk fails, the system can continue to work uninterrupted until the hardware issue is resolved.

Finally, some client systems use NFS to mount disks remotely on central servers. While this can be a useful way of accessing a centralized home directory from a number of remote clients (by using the automounter), database partitions should never be mounted remotely. If you need to access a remote partition via NFS, you can nominate these partitions during the installation program.

Root Password

An important stage of the installation process involves selecting the root password for the super-user. The root user has the same powers as the root user on Linux or the Administrator account on Windows NT. If an intruder gains root access, he or she is free to roam the system, deleting or stealing data, removing or adding user accounts, or installing Trojan horses that can transparently modify the way your system operates.

One way to protect against an authorized user gaining root access is to use a difficult-to-guess root password, which makes it difficult for a cracker to use a password cracking program to guess your password successfully. The optimal password is a completely random string of alphanumeric and punctuation characters. Some applications, which are discussed in Chapter 15, can be used to generate passwords that are easy to remember but that contain almost random combinations of characters.

In addition, you should never write down the root password, unless it is locked in the company safe; nor should this password be known by anyone who doesn't need to know it. If users require levels of access that are typically privileged (such as mounting CD-ROMs), it is better to use the *sudo* utility to limit the access of each user to specific applications for execution as the super-user, rather than giving out the root password to everyone who asks for it.

The root password must be entered twice—just in case you should happen to make a typographical error, as the characters that you type are masked on the screen.

Software Selection

After all the configuration settings have been entered, the following message will appear:

```
Please wait while the system is configured with your settings...
```

The installation Kiosk will then appear on the screen. In the Kiosk, you select the type of installation that you want to perform. To begin the software selection process, you need to eject the Web Start CD-ROM and insert the Software (1) CD-ROM. Next, you have the option of installing all Solaris software using the default options or customizing your selection before copying the files from the CD-ROM. Obviously, if you have a lot of disk space and a fast system, you may prefer to install the entire distribution and delete packages after installation that you no longer require. This is definitely the fastest method. Alternatively, you can elect to perform a custom installation.

You are then presented with a list of all the available software groups. You can select or deselect individual package groups, or package clusters, depending on your requirements. For example, you may decide to install the Netscape Navigator software, but not install the NIS/NIS+ server for Solaris.

After choosing the packages that you want to install, you are required to enter your locale based on geographic region (the U.S. entry is selected by default). You may also elect to install third-party software during the Solaris installation process—this is particularly useful if you have a standard operating environment that consists of using the Oracle database server in conjunction with the Solaris operating environment, for example. You would need to insert the product CD-ROM at this point so that it could be identified.

After selecting your software, you will need to lay out the disks, which involves defining disk slices that will store the different kinds of data on your system. The fastest configuration option involves selecting the boot disk and allowing the installer to lay out the partitions automatically according to your software selections. For example, you may want to expand the size of the */var* partition to allow for large print jobs to be spooled or Web server logs to be recorded.

Finally, you will be asked to confirm your software selections and proceed with installation. All the packages will then be installed to your system. A progress bar indicates which packages have been installed at any particular point, and how many remain to be installed. After you have installed the software, you must reboot the system. After restarting, your system should boot directly into Solaris unless you have a dual-booting system—in which case, you will need to select the Solaris boot partition from the Solaris boot manager.

Upon reboot, a status message is printed on the console, looking something like this:

```
ok boot
Resetting ...
SPARCstation 20 (1 X 390Z50), Keyboard Present
ROM Rev. 2.4, 256 MB memory installed, Serial #456543
Ethernet address 5:2:12:c:ee:5a HostID 456543
Boot device: /iommu/sbus/espdma@f,400000/esp@f,800000/sd@1,0
File and args:
SunOS Release 5.9 Version generic [UNIX(R) System V Release 4.0]
Copyright (c) 1983-2001, Sun Microsystems, Inc.
configuring network interfaces: le0.
Hostname: server
The system is coming up. Please wait.
add net default: gateway 204.58.62.33
NIS domainname is paulwatters.net
starting rpc services: rpcbind keyserv ypbind done.
Setting netmask of le0 to 255.255.255.0
Setting default interface for multicast: add net 224.0.0.0: gateway client
syslog service starting.
Print services started.
volume management starting.
The system is ready.
client console login:
```

By default, the common desktop environment (CDE) login screen is displayed.

Network Installation

Although we've looked in detail at CD-ROM and DVD-ROM installation from a local drive, it's actually possible to set up a single install server from which installation clients read all their data. This approach is useful when a number of clients will be installing from the same disk and/or if installation is concurrent. Thus, it's possible for a number of users to install Solaris from a single server, which can be very useful when a new release of Solaris is made. For example, the Solaris 9 beta was distributed in a form suitable for network installation, allowing multiple developers to get their systems running as quickly as possible. For existing install servers, this reduces administration overhead, since different versions of Solaris (Solaris 8 and 9, for example) can be distributed from the same server.

The install server reads copies of the installation CD-ROMs and DVD-ROMs and creates a distributable image that can then be downloaded by remote clients. In addition, you can create images for both SPARC and Intel versions that can be distributed from a single system; thus, a high-end SPARC install server could distribute images to many Intel clients. The install server uses DHCP to allocate IP addresses dynamically to all install clients. Alternatively, a name server can be installed and used for allocating permanent IP addresses to install clients.

To create SPARC disk images on the install server, you use the `setup_install_server` command. For a SPARC DVD-ROM or CD-ROM, this command is located in */cdrom/cdrom0/s0/Solaris_9/Tools*. For an Intel DVD-ROM or CD-ROM, this command is located in */cdrom/cdrom0/Solaris_9/Tools*. The only parameter that needs to be supplied to the command is the path where the disk images should be installed. You should ensure that the path can be exported to clients and that the partition selected has sufficient disk space to store the images.

The same command is used for creating Intel disk images, but the path is different: for a SPARC DVD-ROM or CD-ROM, the command is located in */cdrom/cdrom0/Solaris_9/Tools*, while for an Intel DVD-ROM or CD-ROM, the command is located in */cdrom/cdrom0/s2/Solaris_9/Tools*.

To set up individual clients, execute the `add_install_client` command on the install server—once for each client. You need to specify the name of the client to be installed, as well as its architecture. For a sun4m system named pink, for example, you would use the following command:

```
# /export/install/boot/Solaris_9/Tools/add_install_client pink sun4m
```

On the client side, instead of typing **boot cdrom** at the OK prompt, you would need to enter the following command:

```
ok boot net
```

suninstall Installation

To boot with the *suninstall* program, you don't use the Solaris 9 Installation CD-ROM; rather, the Solaris 9 Software 1 CD-ROM, which is bootable, should be employed. *suninstall* has the advantage of not requiring high-resolution graphics to complete installation, so a low-resolution monitor or terminal can be used. It requires a minimal amount of RAM and allows you flexibility in configuring your system prior to installation (including internationalization). The order of questions and procedures followed are generally the same as those used in the Web Start Wizard. However, *suninstall* does not allow you to install third-party software as part of the installation process.

Using the *suninstall* method is more reliable than the Web Start Wizard when installing Solaris Intel, because *suninstall* relies less on graphic cards and displays, which may not be compatible with the Solaris X11 server.

JumpStart

JumpStart is an installation technology that allows a group of systems to be installed concurrently, using a standard file system layout and software package selection. For sites with hundreds of systems that are maintained by a small staff, JumpStart is the ideal tool for upgrading or reinstalling systems.

For example, when a staff member leaves, her workstation can be simply reinstalled using JumpStart. By enforcing a standard operating environment (SOE), there is no need to configure individually every system that needs to be installed, greatly reducing the administrative burden on system administrators.

When using JumpStart on a large number of clients, installation can be expedited by using a *sysidcfg* file, which defines a number of standard parameters for installation. The *sysidcfg* file can contain configuration entries for the following properties:

Current date and time	DHCP server IP address	Local domain name
Graphics card	Local hostname	Local IP address
IPv6 support	Locale	Security policy
Monitor type	DNS server	NIS/NIS+ server
LDAP server	Netmask	Network interface
Pointing device	Power management	Root password
Security policy	Terminal type	Time zone

The following is a sample *sysidcfg* file:

```
system_locale=en_US
timezone=US/Eastern
timeserver=192.168.34.3
network_interface=le0 {netmask=255.255.255.0 protocol_ipv6=yes}
security_policy=NONE
terminal=dtterm
name_service=NONE
root_password=5fg48;r3f
name_service=NIS {domain_name=cassowary.net name_server=nis(192.168.44.53)}
```

Here, you can see that the system locale has been set to standard U.S. English, the time zone set to the U.S. East Coast, the timeserver set to *192.168.34.3*, and the network interface running *IPv6 to /dev/le0*. While the default terminal and root password are also set, the name service and security policy have not been set because these might change from system to system. In addition, the name service selected is NIS, with the NIS server set to *nis.cassowary.net* (*192.168.44.53*). More details on JumpStart are provided in Chapter 32.

Live Upgrade

All the installation methods reviewed so far require that an existing system be acquired to run level 0 to start the installation process. In addition, any system undergoing upgrade can expect to be in single-user mode for a matter of hours while distribution files are copied and third-party software is reinstalled. This kind of downtime may be unacceptable for a production server. While many departmental servers will no doubt have a backup server that can take their place during upgrading and installation testing, many high-end servers, such as the StarFire, are logically divided into domains that run on a single system. A second standby system may not be available to replace a high-end server, just for the purpose of an upgrade. While it's possible to configure each domain individually, many sites would prefer to keep all servers at the same release level.

In such cases, Solaris now offers a Live Upgrade facility that allows a separate boot environment to be created, with the distribution of the new operating system files installed to an alternative location. Once the installation of the new boot environment has been completed, the system needs to be rebooted only once to allow it to run the new operating environment. If the new boot environment fails for some reason, the old boot environment can be reinstated as the default and the system can be rebooted to its previous state. This allows operations to resume as quickly as possible in the event of a failure.

One of the nice features of Live Upgrade is that the file system layout and configuration can be different from your existing installation. This allows you to fine tune your existing settings before upgrading. For example, if print and mail jobs have continually caused the */var* partition to overfill on a regular basis, you can increase the size of the */var* partition in the new boot environment. Changes can be made to the */, /usr, /var,* and */opt* partitions. Other file systems continue to be shared between the existing and new boot environments, unless otherwise specified.

To create a new boot environment, you must identify and format a separate partition before the procedure can begin. This partition must have sufficient disk space to install the new boot environment. The current contents of */, /usr,* and */opt* are then copied to the new partition prior to upgrade. Alternatively, if you have a second disk installed on the system, you can copy the existing files to the appropriate slices on the new disk. Once these files are in place, the new boot environment is ready to be upgraded. All these processes can occur without interfering with the current boot environment.

Upgrading typically involves overwriting the files stored on the new boot environment in */, /usr,* and */opt*. After this has been completed, you can activate the new boot environment and boot the system into the new environment.

Live Upgrade operates through a terminal-based menu that allows the following operations to be performed:

Operation	Description
Activate	Activates a newly installed boot environment
Cancel	Cancels a file transfer operation
Compare	Checks for differences between the new and current boot environments
Copy	Begins a file transfer operation
Create	Initializes a new boot environment
Current	Prints the name of the current boot environment
Delete	Uninstalls a boot environment
List	Displays the file systems in a boot environment
Rename	Modifies the name of a new or existing boot environment
Status	Prints the condition of any boot environment
Upgrade	Begins the upgrade process on the new boot environment
Help	Prints the Help menu
Exit	Quits the program

The Complete Reference

Solaris 9

Chapter 5

The OpenBoot PROM

One of the main hardware differences between SPARC systems that run Solaris and PC systems that run Linux or Microsoft Windows is that SPARC systems have an OpenBoot PROM monitor program, which can be used to modify firmware settings prior to booting. In this chapter, we'll examine how to use the OpenBoot PROM monitor to manage SPARC system firmware.

Key Concepts

The OpenBoot PROM monitor is based on the Forth programming language, and can be used to run Forth programs that perform the following functions:

- Booting the system, by using the `boot` command.
- Performing diagnostics on hardware devices by using the `diag` command.
- Testing network connectivity by using the `watch-net` command.

The OpenBoot monitor has two prompts from which you can issue commands: the `ok` prompt and the `>` prompt. In order to switch from the `>` prompt to the `ok` prompt, you simply need to type **n**:

```
> n
ok
```

Commands are typically issued from the `ok` prompt. These commands include `boot`, which boots a system from the default system boot device, or from an optional device specified at the prompt. Thus, if a system is at run level 0 and needs to be booted, the `boot` command with no options specified will boot the system:

```
ok boot
SPARCstation 20, Type 5 Keyboard
ROM Rev. 3.2, 256 MB memory installed, Serial #456543
Ethernet address 5:2:12:c:ee:5a HostID 456543
Rebooting with command:
Boot device: /iommu@f,e0000000/sbus@f,e0001000/espdma@f,400000/esp@f,8...
SunOS Release 5.9 Version Generic 32-bit
Copyright (c) 1983-2001 by Sun Microsystems, Inc.
configuring IPv4 interfaces: hme0.
Hostname: winston
The system is coming up. Please wait.
checking ufs filesystems
/dev/rdsk/c0t0d0s1: is clean.
NIS domainname is Cassowary.Net.
starting rpc services: rpcbind keyserv ypbind done.
Setting netmask of hme0 to 255.255.255.0
```

```
Setting default IPv4 interface for multicast: add net 224.0/
4: gateway winston
syslog service starting.
Print services started.
volume management starting.
The system is ready.
winston console login:
```

Or, if you have modified your hardware configuration since the last boot, and you want the new devices to be recognized, you should always reboot using this command:

```
ok boot -r
```

This is equivalent to performing a reconfiguration boot using the following command sequence in a shell as the super-user:

```
# touch /reconfigure; sync; init 6
```

So far, we've looked at automatic booting. However, sometimes performing a manual boot is desirable, using the command boot -a, where you can specify parameters at each stage of the booting process. These parameters include the following:

- The path to the kernel that you wish to boot
- The path to the kernel's modules directory
- The path to the system file
- The type of the root file system
- The name of the root device

For example, if you wished to use a different kernel, such as an experimental kernel, you would enter the following parameters during a manual boot:

```
Rebooting with command: boot -a
Boot device: /pci@1f,0/pci@1,2/ide@1/disk@0,1:a File and args: -a
Enter filename [kernel/sparcv9/unix]: kernel/experimental/unix
Enter default directory for modules [/platform/SUNW,Sparc-20/kernel
/platform/sun4m/kernel /kernel /usr/kernel]:
Name of system file [etc/system]:
SunOS Release 5.9 Version Generic 64-bit
Copyright (c) 1983-2001 by Sun Microsystems, Inc.
root filesystem type [ufs]:
Enter physical name of root device
[/pci@1f,0/pci@1,2/ide@1/disk@0,1:a]:
```

To accept the default parameters, simply press ENTER when prompted. Thus, to change only the path to the experimental kernel, you would enter **kernel/experimental/unix** at the Enter Filename prompt.

Procedures

The following procedures can be used to interact with the OpenBoot PROM monitor.

Viewing Release Information

To view the OpenBoot release information for your firmware and the system configuration, use this command:

```
ok banner
SPARCstation 20, Type 5 Keyboard
ROM Rev. 3.2, 256 MB memory installed, Serial #456543
Ethernet address 5:2:12:c:ee:5a HostID 456543
```

Here, you can see that the system is a SPARCstation 20, with a standard keyboard, and that the OpenBoot release level is 3.2. There is 256MB of RAM installed on the system, which has a hostid of 456543. Finally, the Ethernet address of the primary Ethernet device is 5:2:12:c:ee:5a.

Changing the Default Boot Device

To boot from the default boot device (usually the primary hard drive), you would type this:

```
ok boot
```

However, you can also boot using the CD-ROM by using this command:

```
ok boot cdrom
```

You may boot the system from a host on the network by using this command:

```
ok boot net
```

Or, if you have a boot floppy, you may use the following command:

```
ok boot floppy
```

Because many early Solaris distributions were made on magnetic tape, you can also boot using a tape drive with the following command:

```
ok boot tape
```

Instead of specifying a different boot device each time you want to reboot, you can set an environment variable within the OpenBoot monitor so that a specific device is booted by default. For example, to set the default boot device to be the primary hard disk, you would use the following command:

```
ok setenv boot-device disk
boot-device = disk
```

To verify that the boot device has been set correctly to disk, you can use the following command:

```
ok printenv boot-device
boot-device disk disk
```

In order to reset the system to use the new settings, you simply use the reset command:

```
ok reset
```

To set the default boot device to be the primary network device, you would use the following command:

```
ok setenv boot-device net
boot-device = net
```

This configuration is commonly used for diskless clients, such as Sun Rays, which use RARP and NFS to boot across the network. To verify that the boot device has been set correctly to net, you can use the following command:

```
ok printenv boot-device
boot-device net disk
```

To set the default boot device to be the primary CD-ROM device, you would use the following command:

```
ok setenv boot-device cdrom
boot-device = cdrom
```

This is often useful when installing or upgrading the operating system. To verify that the boot device has been set correctly to *cdrom*, you can use the following command:

```
ok printenv boot-device
boot-device cdrom disk
```

To set the default boot device to be the primary floppy drive, you would use the following command:

```
ok setenv boot-device floppy
boot-device = floppy
```

To verify that the boot device has been set correctly to floppy, you can use the following command:

```
ok printenv boot-device
boot-device floppy disk
```

To set the default boot device to be the primary tape drive, you would use the following command:

```
ok setenv boot-device tape
boot-device = tape
```

To verify that the boot device has been set correctly to tape, you can use the following command:

```
ok printenv boot-device
boot-device tape disk
```

Testing System Hardware

The test command is used to test specific hardware devices, such as the loopback network device. You could test this device by using this command:

```
ok test net
Internal Loopback test - (OK)
External Loopback test - (OK)
```

This indicates that the loopback device is operating correctly. Or, you could use the watch-clock command to test the clock device.

```
ok watch-clock
Watching the 'seconds' register of the real time clock chip.
 It should be ticking once a second.
 Type any key to stop.
1
2
3
```

You can cross-check these results against a reliable timing device for accuracy.

If the system is meant to boot across the network, but a boot attempt does not succeed, you can test network connectivity by using the watch-net program. This determines whether the system's primary network interface is able to read packets from the network it is connected to. The output from watch-net program looks like this:

```
Internal Loopback test - succeeded
External Loopback test - succeeded
Looking for Ethernet packets.
'.' is a good packet. 'X' is a bad packet.
Type any key to stop
......X.........XXXX........….XX............
```

In this case, a number of packets are marked as bad, even though the system has been connected successfully to the network. This can occur because of network congestion.

In addition to the watch-net command, the OpenBoot monitor can perform a number of other diagnostic tests. For example, you can detect all of the SCSI devices attached to the system by using the probe-scsi command. The probe-scsi command displays all of the SCSI devices attached to the system. The output of probe-scsi looks like this:

```
ok probe-scsi
Target 1
Unit 0 Disk SUN0104 Copyright (C) 1995 Sun Microsystems All rights
reserved
Target 1
Unit 0 Disk SUN0207 Copyright (C) 1995 Sun Microsystems All rights
reserved
```

Here, you can see that two SCSI disks have been detected. If any other disks or SCSI devices were attached to the chain, they have not been detected, indicating a misconfiguration or hardware error. Because most modern SPARC systems also ship with a PCI bus, you can display the appropriate PCI devices by using the `probe-pci` and `probe-pci-slot` commands.

Creating and Removing Device Aliases

The OpenBoot monitor is able to store certain environment variables in nonvolatile RAM (NVRAM) so that they can be used from boot to boot by using the `nvalias` command. For example, to set the network device to use RARP for booting, you would use the following command:

```
ok nvalias net /pci@1f,4000/network@1,1:rarp
```

This means that booting using the net device, as shown in the following example, would use the */pci@1f,4000/network@1,1* device to boot the system across the network:

```
ok boot net
```

However, if you wanted to use the Dynamic Host Configuration Protocol (DHCP) to retrieve the host's IP address when booting, instead of using RARP, you would use the following command:

```
ok boot net:dhcp
```

To remove the alias from NVRAM, you simply use the `nvunalias` command:

```
ok nvunalias net
```

This would restore the default value of *net*.

Examples

The following examples demonstrate how to use the OpenBoot PROM monitor effectively.

Single-User Mode

If a system fails to start correctly in multi-user mode, it's likely that one of the scripts being run in */etc/rc2.d* is the cause. In order to prevent the system from going into multi-user mode, you can boot directly into single-user mode from the ok prompt:

```
INIT: SINGLE USER MODE
Type Ctrl-d to proceed with normal startup,
(or give root password for system maintenance):
```

At this point, you can enter the root password, and the user will be given a root shell. However, not all file systems will be mounted, although you can then check individual scripts for misbehaving applications.

Recovering the System

If the system will not boot into single-user mode, the solution is more complicated, because you cannot use the default boot device. For example, if an invalid entry has been in the */etc/passwd* file for the root user, the system will not boot into single- or multi-user mode. To recover the installed system, you need to boot the host needs from the installation CD-ROM into single-user mode. At this point, you can mount the default root file system on a separate mount point, edit the */etc/passwd* file, and reboot the system with the default boot device. This sequence of steps is shown here, assuming that */etc* is located on */dev/dsk/c0t0d0s1*:

```
ok boot cdrom
...
INIT: SINGLE USER MODE
Type Ctrl-d to proceed with normal startup,
(or give root password for system maintenance):
# mkdir /temp
# mount /dev/dsk/c0t0d0s1 /temp
# vi /temp/etc/passwd
# sync; init 6
```

If a system is hung, and you cannot enter commands into a shell on the console, you can use the key combination STOP-A to halt the system and access the OpenBoot PROM monitor. If you halt and reboot the system in this way, all data that has not been written to disk will be lost, unless you use the go command to resume the system's normal operation. Another method of accessing a system if the console is locked is to telnet to the system as an unprivileged user, use the su command to obtain super-user status, and kill whatever process is hanging the system. You can then resume normal operation.

Command Reference

The following commands can be used within the OpenBoot PROM monitor to manage the SPARC firmware.

STOP Commands

The STOP commands are executed on the SPARC platform by holding down the special STOP key located on the left-hand side of the keyboard, and another key, which specifies the operation to be performed. The following functions are available:

STOP	Enters the POST environment
STOP-A	Enters the PROM monitor environment
STOP-D	Performs diagnostic tests
STOP-F	Enters a program in the Forth language
STOP-N	Initializes the nonvolatile RAM settings to their factory defaults

Boot Commands

You can use the `boot` command with any one of the following options:

net	Boots from a network interface
cdrom	Boots from a local CD-ROM drive
disk	Boots from a local hard disk
tape	Boots from a local tape drive

In addition, you can specify the name of the kernel to boot by including its relative path after the device specifier. Or, you can pass the *–a* option on the command line to force the operator to enter the path to the kernel on the boot device.

The Complete Reference

Part II

System Essentials

The Complete Reference

Solaris 9

Chapter 6

System Run Levels

Solaris 9 uses a flexible boot process that is based on the System V Release 4.0 specification for UNIX systems. The System V approach makes it easier to create and customize startup and shutdown procedures that are consistent across sites and systems. This is in contrast to the simpler BSD-style boot process used by Solaris 1.x, which lacked a differentiated organization of startup scripts corresponding to distinct system states. The aim of this chapter is to introduce readers to the basic terminology and initialization elements that play an important role in bringing a Solaris system to single- and multi-user *run levels* or *init states*. Each run level is a mutually exclusive mode of operation. Transitions between run levels are managed by the *init* process. After reading this chapter, Solaris 9 administrators should feel confident in tailoring the startup and shutdown of their own systems, and should have a clear understanding of the boot sequence dependencies when upgrading legacy Solaris 1.x systems.

In many respects, Solaris startup and shutdown is similar to many other systems. However, recognizing and appreciating the distinguishing features of the Solaris operating system from other servers is important. One of the outstanding facilities for SPARC hardware is the firmware monitoring system (OpenBoot PROM), discussed in Chapter 5, which is responsible for key prebooting tasks:

- Starting the Solaris operating system by typing ok boot at the OpenBoot prompt, which boots the Solaris kernel (on Solaris x86, the boot command must be issued through the Primary Boot Subsystem menu)

- Setting system configuration parameters, such as the boot device, which could be one of the hard disks (specified by a full device path name), another host on the network, or a CD-ROM

- Watching network traffic by issuing the command ok watch-net at the OpenBoot prompt

- Performing simple diagnostic tests on system devices (e.g., testing the termination status of a SCSI bus, or the Power-On Self-Test [POST] tests)

Rather than just being a simple operating system loader, like the LILO Linux Loader supplied with many Linux distributions, OpenBoot also permits programs written in the stack-based Forth programming language to be written, loaded, and run before booting commences. This is very useful for customizing servers in large organizations, where a corporate logo must be displayed on boot, rather than the default Sun logo. You can achieve this task by creating a Forth array with the appropriate pixel values, and executing the oem-logo command. You can also set variables post-boot during single- and multi-user init states by using the eeprom command as super-user.

For example, you can use `eeprom` to change the amount of RAM self-tested at boot to 64MB:

```
# eeprom selftest-#megs=64
```

On Solaris x86 systems, the firmware does not directly support this kind of *eeprom* functionality; every PC manufacturer has a different "BIOS" system, making it difficult. Instead, storage is simulated by variables set in the *bootenv.rc* file.

To view the OpenBoot release information for your firmware, use the following command:

```
ok banner
SPARCstation 20, Type 5 Keyboard
ROM Rev. 2.4, 128 MB memory installed, Serial #6745644
Ethernet address 6:3:10:a:cc:4a HostID 5767686
```

If the prompt for OpenBoot is not `ok` (for example, it is displayed as >), simply type **n** to return to the `ok` prompt:

```
>
n
ok
```

A second distinguishing feature of the Solaris operating system is the aim of maximized uptime, through efficient kernel design and the user application model. In some non-Solaris server environments, the system must be rebooted every time a new application is installed. Or, a kernel rebuild might be required to change a configuration. Fortunately, rebooting is rarely required for Solaris systems, because applications are logically isolated from system configuration options, and you can set many system-level configuration options in a super-user shell. For example, you can set many TCP/IP options dynamically using the following command:

```
# ndd /dev/tcp
```

In some newer hardware configurations, you don't even need to reboot to install new hardware. These are the kinds of benefits that will be a welcome relief to new Solaris Administrators.

SYSTEM ESSENTIALS

 Key Concepts

The following concepts are required knowledge for starting up and shutting down a system.

/sbin/init

Upon booting from OpenBoot, Solaris has several different modes of operation, which are known as *run levels* or *init states*, so called because the init command is often used to change run levels, although init-wrapper scripts (such as shutdown) are also used. These *init* states can be single- or multi-user, and often serve a different administrative purpose, and are mutually exclusive (i.e., a system can only ever be in one *init* state). Typically, a Solaris system designed to "stay up" indefinitely, will cycle through a predefined series of steps in order to start all the software daemons necessary for the provision of basic system services, primary user services, and optional application services. These services are often provided only during the time a Solaris system operates in a multi-user run state, with services being initialized by run control (*rc*) shell scripts. Usually, one run control script is created to start each system, user, or application service. Fortunately, many of these scripts are created automatically for Administrators during the Solaris installation process. However, if you intend to install third-party software (such as a database server), you will need to create your own run control scripts in the */etc/init.d* directory to start up these services automatically at boot time. This process is fully described in the "Writing Control Scripts" section.

If the system needs to be powered off for any reason (e.g., a scheduled power outage), or switched into a special maintenance mode to perform diagnostic tests, there is also a cycle of iterating through a predefined series of run control scripts to kill services and preserve user data. It is essential that this sequence of events is preserved so that data integrity is maintained. For example, operating a database server typically involves communication between a server-side, data-writing process and a daemon listener process, which accepts new requests for storing information. If the daemon process is not stopped prior to the data-writing process, it could accept data from network clients and store it in a cache, while the database has already been closed. This could lead to the database being shut down in an inconsistent state, potentially resulting in data corruption and/or record loss. It is essential that Solaris administrators apply their knowledge of shell scripting to rigorously managing system shutdowns as well as startups using run control scripts.

Run Levels

In terms of system startup, Solaris has some similarities to Microsoft Windows and Linux. Although it doesn't have an *autoexec.bat* or *config.sys* file, Solaris does have a number of script files that are executed in a specific order to start services, just like Linux. These scripts are typically created in the *etc/init.d* directory as Bourne shell scripts, and are then symbolically linked into the "run level" directories. Just like Microsoft Windows has "Safe Modes," Solaris supports a number of different modes of operation, from restricted single-user modes to full multi-user run levels. The complete set of run levels, with their respective run control script directories, is displayed in Table 6-1.

Each run level is associated with a run-level script, as shown in Table 6-2. The run-level script is responsible for the orderly execution of all run-level scripts within a specific run-level directory. The script name matches the run level and directory name.

Run Level	Description	User Status	Run Control Script Directory
0	Hardware maintenance mode	Console Access	*etc/rc0.d*
1	Administrative state; only root file system is available	Single User	*etc/rc1.d*
2	First multi-user state; NFS resources unavailable	Multi-User	*etc/rc2.d*
3	NFS resources available	Multi-User	*etc/rc3.d*
4	User-defined state	Not Specified	N/A
5	Power down firmware state	Console Access	*etc/rc5.d*
6	Operating system halted for reboot	Single User	*etc/rc6.d*
S	Administrative tasks and repair of corrupted file systems	Console Access	*etc/rcS.d*

Table 6-1.   *Solaris Run Levels and Their Functions*

Run Level	Run Control Script
0	/etc/rc0
1	/etc/rc1
2	/etc/rc2
3	/etc/rc3
4	N/A
5	/etc/rc5
6	/etc/rc6
S	/etc/rcS

Table 6-2.   *Solaris Run-Level Scripts*

When a Solaris system starts, the `init` process is spawned, which is responsible for managing processes and the transitions between run levels. You can actually switch manually between run levels yourself by using the `init` command; to halt the operating system and reboot (run-level 6), you can simply type the following command:

```
# init 6
```

Control Scripts and Directories

Every Solaris *init* state (such as *init* state 6) has its own run-level script directory (e.g., */etc/rc6.d*). This contains a set of symbolic links (like shortcuts in Microsoft Windows) that are associated with the service startup files in the */etc/init.d* directory. Each linked script starts with a letter *S* ("start") or the letter *K* ("kill"), and are used to start or kill processes, respectively. When a system is booted, processes are started. When a system is shut down, processes are killed. The start and kill links are typically made to the same script file, which interprets two parameters: *start* and *stop*. The scripts are executed in numerical order, so a script like */etc/rc3.d/ S20dhcp* is executed before */etc/rc3.d/ S21sshd*. If you're curious about what kind of scripts are started or killed in Solaris during startup and shutdown, Table 6-3 shows the startup scripts in */etc/rc2.d*, and Table 6-4 shows the kill scripts found in */etc/rc0.d*. You need to realize that these will change from system to system.

Script	Description
S05RMTMPFILES	Removes temporary files in the */tmp* directory.
S20sysetup	Establishes system setup requirements, and checks */var/crash* to determine whether the system is recovering from a crash.
S21perf	Enables system accounting using */usr/lib/sa/sadc* and /var/adm/sa/sa.
S30sysid.net	Executes */usr/sbin/sysidnet*, */usr/sbin/sysidconfig* and */sbin/ifconfig*, which are responsible for configuring network services.
S69inet	Initiates second phase of TCP/IP configuration, following the basic services established during single-user mode (*rcS*). Setting up IP routing (if */etc/defaultrouter* exists), performing TCP/IP parameter tuning (using *ndd*), and setting the NIS domain name (if required), are all performed here.
S70uucp	Initializes the UNIX to UNIX copy program (*UUCP*), by removing locks and other unnecessary files.
S71sysid.sys	Executes */usr/sbin/sysidsys* and */usr/sbin/sysidroot*.
S72autoinstall	Script to execute JumpStart installation if appropriate.
S72inetsvc	Final network configuration using */usr/sbin/ifconfig* after NIS/NIS+ have been initialized. Also initializes Internet Domain Name System (DNS) if appropriate.
S80PRESERVE	Preserves editing files by executing */usr/lib/expreserve*.
S91leoconfig	Configuration for ZX graphics cards (if installed).
S92rtvc-config	Configuration for SunVideo cards (if installed).
S92volmgt	Starts volume management for removable media using */usr/sbin/vold*.

Table 6-3.   *Typical Multi-User Startup Scripts under Solaris 9*

SYSTEM ESSENTIALS

Script	Description
K00ANNOUNCE	Announces that "System services are now being stopped"
K10dtlogin	Initializes tasks for the CDE (common desktop environment), including killing the *dtlogin* process
K20lp	Stops printing services using */usr/lib/lpshut*
K22acct	Terminates process accounting using */usr/lib/acct/shutacct*
K42audit	Kills the auditing daemon (*/usr/sbin/audit*)
K47asppp	Stops the asynchronous PPP daemon (*/usr/sbin/aspppd*)
K50utmpd	Kills the *utmp* daemon (*/usr/lib/utmpd*)
K55syslog	Terminates the system logging service (*/usr/sbin/syslogd*)
K57sendmail	Halts the sendmail mail service (*/usr/lib/sendmail*)
K66nfs.server	Kills all processes required for the NFS server (*/usr/lib/nfs/nfsd*)
K69autofs	Stops the automounter (*/usr/sbin/automount*)
K70cron	Terminates the *cron* daemon (*/usr/bin/cron*)
K75nfs.client	Disables client NFS
K76nscd	Kills the name service cache daemon (*/usr/sbin/nscd*)
K85rpc	Disables remote procedure call (*rpc*) services (*/usr/sbin/rpcbind*)

Table 6-4.   *Typical Single-User Kill Scripts under Solaris 9*

Boot Sequence

Booting the kernel is a straightforward process, once the operating system has been successfully installed. You can identify the Solaris kernel by the pathname */platform/ PLATFORM_NAME/kernel/unix*, where *PLATFORM_NAME* is the name of the current architecture. For example, sun4u systems boot with the kernel */platform/sun4u/kernel/*. Kernels can also be booted from a CD-ROM drive or through a network connection (by using the `boot cdrom` and `boot net` commands from the OpenBoot PROM monitor, respectively).

When a SPARC system is powered on, the system executes a series of basic hardware tests before attempting to boot the kernel. These Power-On Self-Tests (POSTs) ensure that your system hardware is operating correctly. If the POST tests fail, you will not be able to boot the system.

Once the POST tests are complete, the system will attempt to boot the default kernel using the path specified in the firmware. Or, if you wish to boot a different kernel, you can press STOP-A, enter **boot kernel/name**, and boot the kernel specified by *kernel/name*. For example, to boot a kernel called newunix, you would use the command boot kernel/newunix.

Systems either boot from a UFS file system (whether on the local hard disk or a local CD-ROM drive) or across the network. Two applications facilitate these different boot types: ufsboot is responsible for booting kernels from disk devices, and inetboot is responsible for booting kernels using a network device. Although servers typically boot themselves using ufsboot, diskless clients must use inetboot.

The ufsboot application reads the bootblock on the active partition of the boot device, and inetboot performs a broadcast on the local subnet, searching for a trivial FTP (TFTP) server. Once located, the kernel is downloaded using NFS and booted.

SYSTEM ESSENTIALS

Procedures

The following procedures are commonly used for starting up and shutting down a Solaris system.

Startup

Administrators should be aware of three kinds of boots. In addition to a normal reboot, which is initiated by the command # shutdown from a super-user shell, a reconfiguration boot involves reconstructing device information in the */dev* and */devices* directories, and a recovery boot involves saving and analyzing crash dump files if a system does not respond to commands issued on the console. A reconfiguration boot is commonly undertaken in older SPARC systems when new hard disks are added to the system, although this may not be necessary with newer systems, such as the E450, which have hot-swapping facilities. You can initiate this kind of boot by typing **# boot –r** at the OpenBoot monitor prompt, or by issuing the command # touch /reconfigure prior to issuing a shutdown command from a super-user shell. A recovery boot is a rare event on a Solaris system— although hardware failures, kernel module crashes, and incorrect kernel parameters can sometimes result in a hung system. A stack trace is usually provided if a system crash occurs, which can provide vital clues to tracking the source of any system problems using the kernel debugger (kadb).

Although Solaris has eight *init* states, only five are commonly encountered by Administrators during normal operations: run level S, which is a single-user *init* state used for administrative tasks and the repair of corrupted file systems, using the following command:

```
# /usr/sbin/fsck
```

Also encountered are run-level 2, where the *init* state changes to multi-user mode for the first time, with the exception of NFS exported network resources; run-level 3, where all users can log in, and all system and NFS network resources are available; run-level 6, which halts the operating system and initiates a reboot; and run-level 0, during which the operating system is shut down, ensuring that it is safe to power down. In older SPARC systems, you need to bring the system down to run-level 0 to install new hardware, such as disk drives, peripheral devices, and memory modules. However, newer systems, such as the E450, are able to continue to operate in multi-user *init* states while disks are "hot swapped" into special drive bays. This means that these machines may not have a need to enter the run-level 6. Further, uptimes of many months are not uncommon.

The Solaris software environment provides a detailed series of run control (*rc*) scripts to control run-level changes. In this section, we examine each of the control scripts in turn, and highlight the improvements and innovations from the old BSD-style Solaris 1.*x* control scripts. Each run level has an associated *rc* script located in the */sbin* directory, which is also symbolically linked into the */etc* directory: *rc0*, *rc1*, *rc2*, *rc3*, *rc5*, *rc6*, and *rcS*. */sbin/rc0* is responsible for the following:

- Executing all scripts in */etc/rc0.d*, if the directory exists
- Terminating all system services and active processes, initially using */usr/sbin/killall* and */usr/sbin/killall 9* for stubborn processes
- Syncing all mounted file systems, using */sbin/sync*
- Unmounting all mounted file systems, using */sbin/umountall*

/sbin/rc5 and */sbin/rc6* are just symbolic links to */sbin/rc0*, and do not need to be maintained separately; */sbin/rc1* is responsible for executing all scripts in the */etc/rc1.d* directory, if it exists. This terminates all system services and active processes, initially using */usr/sbin/killall* and */usr/sbin/killall 9* for stubborn processes. The differences between */etc/rc0* and */etc/rc1* are that the latter brings up the system into single-user mode after shutting down all processes in multi-user mode, and does not unmount any file systems.

In run-level 2 state, */sbin/rc2* executes all scripts in the */etc/rc2.d* directory, bringing the system into its first multi-user state. Thus, all local file systems listed in */etc/vfstab* are mounted, disk quotas and file system logging are switched on if configured, temporary editor files are saved, the */tmp* directory is cleared, system accounting is enabled, and many network services are initialized. Table 6-2 describes these services in more detail.

In run-level 3 state, */sbin/rc3* executes all scripts in the */etc/rc3.d* directory, bringing the system into its final multi-user state. These services are mainly concerned with shared network resources, such as NFS, but Solstice Enterprise Agents and other SNMP-based systems may also be started here. */sbin/rcS* executes all scripts in the */sbin/rcS.d* directory, to bring the system up to the single-user run level. A minimal network configuration is established if a network can be found, otherwise an interface error is reported. Essential system file systems (such as */*, */usr*, and */proc*) are mounted if they are available, and the system name is set.

Solaris 1.*x* had two main BSD-style control scripts: */etc/rc* and */etc/rc.local*. Typically, vendor-provided daemons were initialized from */etc/rc*; customized and locally installed daemons were executed from */etc/rc.local*. For example, */etc/rc* was responsible for mounting file systems, enabling quotas, adding swap space, and starting the Internet super daemon (inetd). Alternatively, */etc/rc.local* was responsible for later innovations, such as Web servers and authentication services, as well as printer drivers. A general rule of thumb when upgrading legacy systems from Solaris 1.*x* to Solaris 2.*x* is to cross-check all of the required services in */etc/rc*, and ensure that they are enabled in either */etc/rc1.d* or */etc/rc2.d*, and to add any local customizations from */etc/rc.local* to a System V–style startup script in */etc/rc2.d*. You can also add shared network resource scripts to */etc/rc3.d*. Many Solaris 1.*x* applications will run in binary compatibility mode under Solaris 2.*x*, but you should contact your software vendor for the latest versions of third-party software.

To the super-user on the console, the transition between run levels is virtually invisible: most daemons, whether starting in a single-user or multi-user *init* state, display a status message when starting up, which is echoed to the console. A sample console display during booting will look something like this:

```
ok boot
Resetting ...
SPARCstation 20 (2 X 390Z50), Keyboard Present
ROM Rev. 2.4, 128 MB memory installed, Serial #6745644
Ethernet address 6:3:10:a:cc:4a HostID 5767686
Boot device: /iommu/sbus/espdma@f,400000/esp@f,800000/sd@1,0
File and args:
SunOS Release 5.9 Version generic [UNIX(R) System V Release 4.0]
Copyright (c) 1983-2001, Sun Microsystems, Inc.
configuring network interfaces: le0.
Hostname: server
The system is coming up. Please wait.
add net default: gateway 10.16.27.1
NIS domainname is www.cassowary.net
starting rpc services: rpcbind keyserv ypbind done.
Setting netmask of le0 to 255.255.255.0
Setting default interface for multicast: add net 224.0.0.0: gateway server
syslog service starting.
Print services started.
volume management starting.
Starting Apache webserver...done.
The system is ready.
server console login:
```

Obviously, when booting into single-user mode, fewer messages will appear on the console, because multi-user *init* state processes are not started. The single-user run-level messages will appear as something like this:

```
ok boot -s
SunOS Release 5.9 Version [UNIX(R) System V Release 4.0]
Copyright (c) 1983-2001, Sun Microsystems, Inc.
configuring network interfaces: le0.
Hostname: server
INIT: SINGLE USER MODE
Type Ctrl-d to proceed with normal startup,
(or give root password for system maintenance):
```

At this point, you enter the password for the super-user account (it will not be echoed to the display). Assuming that you enter the correct password, the display will then proceed with another banner and a Bourne shell prompt:

```
Sun Microsystems Inc. SunOS 5.9 November 2001
#
```

After maintenance is complete, simply exit the shell by using CTRL-D, and the system will then proceed with a normal multi-user boot.

The */sbin/init* daemon is responsible for process control initialization, and is a key component of the booting process. Although it is not significant in many day-to-day operations after booting, its configuration for special purposes can be confusing for first-time users. In this section, we examine the initialization of *init* using the */etc/inittab* file, and explain in detail what each entry means. The primary function of init is to spawn processes, usually daemon processes, from configuration information specified in the file */etc/inittab* in ASCII format. Process spawning always takes place in a specific software context, which is determined by the current run level.

After booting the kernel from the OpenBoot monitor, *init* reads the system environment variables stored in */etc/default/init* (e.g., the time zone variable *TZ*), and sets them for the current run level. *init* then reads the */etc/inittab* file (described more completely in the next section), setting the *init* level specified in that file by the *initdefault* entry. In most multi-user systems, this entry will correspond to run-level 3, and the entry will look like this:

```
is:3:initdefault:
```

If the file */etc/inittab* does not exist during booting, the super-user will be asked to manually enter the desired run-level for the system. If this event ever occurs unexpectedly for a multi-user system, it is a good strategy to enter single-user mode (by typing **s**) to perform maintenance on the */etc/inittab* file. Another potential problem that is discussed later is if */etc/inittab* does contain an empty *rstate* value in the *initdefault* entry: The system will go to firmware and continuously reboot! If this occurs, exit from the operating system into the OpenBoot monitor by holding down the STOP key and pressing A. You can now boot directly into single-user mode, and add an appropriate *rstate* entry to the */etc/inittab* file. Safeguards are built into *init*; however, if the system discovers that any entry in */etc/inittab* is respawning rapidly (i.e., more than five times per minute), *init* assumes that a typographical error has been made in the entry, and a warning message is printed on the system console. *init* will then not respawn the affected entry until at least five minutes has elapsed since the problem was identified.

After entering a multi-user run level for the first time since booting from the OpenBoot monitor, *init* reads any appropriate *boot* and *bootwait* entries in */etc/inittab*. This provides for basic initialization of the operating system, such as mounting file systems, which are generally performed before users are allowed to operate on the system.

In order to spawn processes specified in */etc/inittab*, *init* reads each entry and determines the process requirements for the commands to be executed. For example, for entries that must be respawned in the future, a child process is created using `fork()`. After reading all entries, and spawning all processes, *init* simply waits until it receives a signal to change the system's *init* state (this explains why *init* is always visible in the process list). */etc/inittab* is always reread at this point to ensure that any modifications to its specified behavior are used. In addition, *init* can be initialized at any time by passing a special parameter to force rereading of */etc/inittab*:

```
# init q
```

When *init* receives a valid request to change run levels, a warning signal is sent to all affected processes, and waits five seconds before forcibly terminating any processes which do not behave well and exit by sending a kill signal. Affected processes are those that will be invalid under the target *init* state (e.g., when going from multi-user to single-user mode, daemons started in multi-user mode will be invalid). Because five seconds may not be sufficient to shut down an entire database server and close all open files, it is best to ensure that such activities precede any change of state that affects the main applications running on your system (e.g., by executing the appropriate command in */etc/init.d* with the *stop* parameter).

/sbin/init can be executed only by a super-user, because changes in the system's *init* state executed by a normal user could have serious consequences (e.g., using *init* to power down a live server). Thus, it is always wise to ensure that file permissions are correctly set on the */sbin/init* binary.

Shutdown

A Solaris system is designed to stay up continuously, with as few disruptions to service through rebooting as possible. This design is facilitated by a number of key high-availability and redundancy features in Solaris, including the following:

- **Dual power supplies**, where a secondary supply can continue to power the system if the primary power supply fails.

- **Mirroring of disk data**, meaning that the system can generally continue to operate, even in the face of multiple disk failure.

- **Hot-swappable disks**, meaning that you can remove a faulty disk and replace it while the system is still online. You can format and use the new disk immediately, especially when you use DiskSuite.

- **The use of domains on E10000 systems**, where you can perform maintenance on one "virtual" host while a second domain acts in its place.

However, there are two situations where a Solaris system must be halted by the super-user:

- Performing a reconfiguration boot
- Powering down the system

Note that you can use the `drvconfig` command to recognize most new hardware devices, further reducing the need for rebooting. A number of different commands are available to shut down and halt a system, and which one is used depends on the specific situation at hand. For example, some commands cycle through a series of shutdown scripts, which ensure that key applications and services, such as databases, are cleanly shut down. Others are designed to ensure that a system is powered down as rapidly as possible. For example, if a storm strikes out the main power system, and you're left with only a few minutes of battery backup, it might be wise to perform a rapid powerdown, to protect equipment from further damage. We investigate the following commands: `init`, `shutdown`, `poweroff`, `halt`, and `reboot`.

Shutting Down the System

The `shutdown` command is used to change a system's state, performing a similar function to `init`, as described earlier. However, `shutdown` has several advantages over `init`:

- You can specify a grace period so that the system can be shut down at some future time, rather than immediately.

- A confirmation message requires the super-user to confirm the shutdown before it proceeds. If an automated shutdown is to be executed at some future time, you can avoid the confirmation message by using the –*y* option.

- Only *init* states 0, 1, 5, 6, and S can be reached using `shutdown`.

For example, to shut down the system to run-level 5 so that you can move the system, you would use the following command, giving 60 seconds notice:

```
# shutdown -i 5 -g 60 "System will be powered off for
maintenance. LOGOUT NOW."
```

This will print the following messages at 60 and 30 seconds, respectively:

```
Shutdown started.   Tue Feb   12  12:00:00 EST   2002
Broadcast Message from root (pts/1) on cassowary Tue Feb    12
  12:00:00 EST  2002...
          The system will be shut down in 1 minute
System will be powered off for maintenance. LOGOUT NOW.
Shutdown started.   Tue Feb   12  12:00:30 EST   2002
Broadcast Message from root (pts/1) on cassowary Tue Feb    12
  12:00:30 EST  2002...
          The system will be shut down in 30 seconds
System will be powered off for maintenance. LOGOUT NOW.
```

Once the countdown has been completed, the following message will appear:

```
Do you want to continue? (y or n):
```

If you type **Y**, the shutdown will proceed. If you type **N**, the shutdown will be cancelled, and the system will remain at the current run level.

Rebooting

The reboot command is used to reboot the system, from the current run level to the default run level, and not to change to any other run level. The reboot command has several options: you can use the *–l* flag to prevent the recording of the system halt in the system log, which it normally attempts before halting the CPU; the *–n* option prevents the refreshing of the superblock, which is performed by default, to prevent damage to mounted file systems. The most extreme option is *–q*, which does not attempt any kind of fancy actions before shutting down the system and rebooting.

In addition, reboot accepts the standard parameters passed to the boot command if they are preceded by two dashes, and are placed after the reboot parameters (described in the preceding paragraph) on the command line.

For example, to perform a configuration reboot, without recording an entry in the system log, you could use the following command:

```
# reboot -l -- -r
```

Reconfiguration Boot

Performing a reconfiguration boot involves updating the hardware configuration for the system. If you add new hardware to the system, other than a disk, you must bring the system down to the hardware maintenance state (level 0) before you can insert the new device. In addition, you must notify the system of a reconfiguration reboot by either booting from the OpenBoot PROM monitor with the command boot -r, or by creating an empty file called */reconfigure* before changing to run-level 0. You can achieve this by using the command touch /reconfigure. Be sure to remove the */reconfigure* file after the system has been reconfigured, if necessary.

Powering Down

The poweroff command is used to rapidly shut down the system and switch off power (like switching to run-level 5), without cycling through any intermediate run levels and executing the kill scripts specified for those run levels. This ensures that you can achieve a very fast shutdown when emergency situations dictate that the system cannot remain live, even with the risk of data loss. For example, if a system is under a denial of service attack, and the decision is made to pull the plug on the service, poweroff will be so much faster than init or shutdown. The CPU is halted as quickly as possible, no matter what the run level.

The poweroff command has several options: you can use the *–l* flag to prevent the recording of the system halt in the system log, which it normally attempts before halting the CPU; the *–n* option prevents the refreshing of the superblock, which is performed by default, to prevent damage to mounted file systems. The most extreme option is *–q*, which does not attempt any kind of fancy actions before shutting down.

Halting the System

You can use the halt command to rapidly shut down the system to the OpenBoot PROM monitor, without cycling through any intermediate run levels and executing the kill scripts specified for those run levels. This ensures that you can achieve a very fast shutdown when emergency situations dictate that the system cannot remain live, even with the risk of data loss. For example, if a system is under a denial of service attack, and the decision is made to pull the plug on the service, halt will be so much faster than init or shutdown. The CPU is halted as quickly as possible, no matter what the run level.

The halt command has several options: you can use the *–l* flag to prevent the recording of the system halt in the system log, which it normally attempts before halting the CPU; the *–n* option prevents the refreshing of the superblock, which is performed by default, to prevent damage to mounted file systems. The most extreme option is *–q*, which does not attempt any kind of fancy actions before halting.

Examples

The following examples provide some real-world cases for starting up and shutting down a Solaris system.

Writing Control Scripts

For a multi-user system, the most important control scripts reside in the */etc/rc2.d* and */etc/rc3.d* directories, which are responsible for enabling multi-user services and NFS network resource sharing, respectively. A basic script for starting up a Web server looks like this:

```
#!/bin/sh
# Sample webserver startup script
# Should be placed in /etc/rc2.d/S99webserver
case "$1" in
    'start')
            echo "Starting webserver...\c"
            if [ -f /usr/local/sbin/webserver ]; then
                    /usr/local/sbin/webserver start
            fi
            echo ""
            ;;
    'stop')
            echo "Stopping webserver...\c"
            if [ -f /usr/local/sbin/webserver ]; then
                    /usr/local/sbin/webserver stop
            fi
            echo ""
    ;;
    *)
            echo "Usage: /etc/rc2.d/S99webserver { start | stop }"
            ;;
    esac
```

This file should be created by root (with the group sys) and placed in the file /etc/rc2.d/S99webserver, and should have executable permissions.

```
# chmod 0744 /etc/rc2.d/S99webserver
 # chgrp sys /etc/rc2.d/S99webserver
```

This location of the file is a matter of preference. Many admins treat the Web server similar to a NFS server. In this regard, the system's run-level 3 represents a "share" state.

Note that because a Web server is a shared service, you could also start it from a script in */etc/rc3.d*. When called with the argument *start* (represented in the script by *$1*), the script prints a status message that the Web server daemon is starting, and proceeds to execute the command if the Web server binary exists. The script can also act as a kill script, because it has a provision to be called with a *stop* argument. Of course, a more complete script would provide more elaborate status information if the Web server binary did not exist, and may further process any output from the Web server by using a pipe (e.g., mailing error messages to the super-user).

One of the advantages of the flexible boot system is that you can execute these scripts to start and stop specific daemons without changing the *init* state. For example, if you were going to update a Web site and needed to switch off the Web server for a few minutes, the command:

```
# /etc/rc2.d/S99webserver stop
```

would halt the Web server process, but would not force the system back into a single-user state. You could restart the Web server after all content was uploaded by typing the following command:

```
# /etc/rc2.d/S99webserver start
```

In order to conform to System V standards, it is actually more appropriate to create all the run control scripts in the */etc/init.d* directory, and create symbolic links back to the appropriate *rc2.d* and *rc3.d* directories. This means that all scripts executed by init through different run levels are centrally located and can be easily maintained. With the Web server example, you could create a file in */etc/init.d* with a descriptive filename:

```
# vi /etc/init.d/webserver
```

After adding the appropriate contents, you could save the file and create the appropriate symbolic link by using the symbolic link command ln:

```
# ln -s /etc/init.d/webserver /etc/rc2.d/S99webserver
```

Using this convention, kill and startup scripts for each service can literally coexist in the same script, with the capability to process a *start* argument for startup scripts, and a stop argument for kill scripts. In this example, you would also need to create a symbolic link to */etc/init.d/webserver* for *K99webserver*.

Writing Kill Scripts

Under System V, kill scripts follow the same convention as startup scripts, in that a `stop` argument is passed to the script to indicate that a kill rather than a startup is required, in which a *start* argument would be passed. A common approach to killing off processes is to find them by name in the process list. The following script kills the asynchronous PPP daemon, which is the link manager for the asynchronous data link protocol. This daemon is started using `aspppd`—thus, the script generates a process list which is piped through a *grep* to identify any entries containing *aspppd*, and the process number is extracted using awk. This value is assigned to a variable (*$procid*), which is then used by the `kill` command to terminate the appropriate process. Alternatively, you could use `pgrep` or `pkill`.

```
procid=`ps -e | grep aspppd | awk '{print $1}'`
if test -n "$procid"
then
     kill $procid
fi
```

Alternatively, you could use `sed` to match the process name:

```
procid=`/usr/bin/ps -e |
   /usr/bin/grep aspppd |
   /usr/bin/sed -e 's/^  *//' -e 's/ .*//'`
```

When multiple processes are to be terminated using a single script (for example, when the NFS server terminates), you can write a shell function, `killprocid()`, which takes an argument and searches for it in the process list, terminating the named process if its exists:

```
killprocid() {
procid=`/usr/bin/ps -e |
        /usr/bin/grep -w $1 |
        /usr/bin/sed -e 's/^  *//' -e 's/ .*//'`
   [ "$procid" != "" ] && kill $procid
}
```

You can then terminate individual processes by using the same function:

```
killproc nfsd
killproc mountd
```

```
killproc rpc.boot
killproc in.rarpd
killproc rpld
```

There are two problems with these approaches to process termination. First, there is an ambiguity problem in that different daemons and applications can be identified by the same name. For example, a system may be running the Apache Web server, which is identified by the process name *httpd*, as well as a Web server from another vendor (such as iPlanet), which is also identified by *httpd*. If you wrote a script to kill the Apache Web server, but the first process identified actually belonged to the iPlanet Web server, the iPlanet Web server process would be terminated. One solution to this problem is to ensure that all applications are launched with a unique name, or from a wrapper script with a unique name. The second problem is that for a system with even a moderately heavy process load (e.g., 500 active processes), executing the ps command to kill each process is going to generate a large CPU overhead, leading to excessively slow shutdown times. Alternative solutions to this problem are provided in the previous section.

Displaying eeprom *Variables*

To examine the default values used by your system for booting the kernel, and the default boot devices, simply use the */usr/sbin/eeprom* command:

```
$ /usr/sbin/eeprom
tpe-link-test?=true
scsi-initiator-id=7
keyboard-click?=false
keymap: data not available.
ttyb-rts-dtr-off=false
ttyb-ignore-cd=true
ttya-rts-dtr-off=false
ttya-ignore-cd=true
ttyb-mode=9600,8,n,1,-
ttya-mode=9600,8,n,1,-
pcia-probe-list=1,2,3,4
pcib-probe-list=1,2,3
mfg-mode=off
diag-level=max
#power-cycles=50
system-board-serial#: data not available.
system-board-date: data not available.
fcode-debug?=false
output-device=screen
```

```
input-device=keyboard
load-base=16384
boot-command=boot
auto-boot?=true
watchdog-reboot?=false
diag-file: data not available.
diag-device=net
boot-file: data not available.
boot-device=disk net
local-mac-address?=false
ansi-terminal?=true
screen-#columns=80
screen-#rows=34
silent-mode?=false
use-nvramrc?=false
nvramrc: data not available.
security-mode=none
security-password: data not available.
security-#badlogins=0
oem-logo: data not available.
oem-logo?=false
oem-banner: data not available.
oem-banner?=false
hardware-revision: data not available.
last-hardware-update: data not available.
diag-switch?=false
```

You can also change the values of the boot device and boot command from within Solaris by using the eeprom command, rather than having to reboot, jump into the OpenBoot monitor, and set the values directly.

Shutting Down the System

In order to manually change run levels, the desired *init* state is used as an argument to */sbin/init*. For example, to bring the system down to a single-user mode for maintenance, you could use the following command:

```
# init s
INIT: New run level: S
The system is coming down for administration. Please wait.
Print services stopped.
```

```
syslogd: going down on signal 15
Killing user processes: done.
INIT: SINGLE USER MODE
Type Ctrl-d to proceed with normal startup,
(or give root password for system maintenance):
Entering System Maintenance Mode ...
#
```

The system is most easily shut down by using the new */usr/sbin/shutdown* command (not the old BSD-style */usr/ucb/shutdown* command discussed later). This command is issued with the form

```
# shutdown -i run-level -g grace-period -y
```

where "run-level" is an *init* state different from the default *init* state S (i.e., one of the run levels 0, 1 2, 5, or 6). However, most Administrators will typically be interested in using *shutdown* with respect to the reboot or powerdown run levels. The *grace-period* is the number of seconds before the shutdown process is initiated. On single-user machines, the super-user will easily know who is logged in, and what processes need to be terminated gracefully. On a multi-user machine, however, it is more useful to warn users in advance of a powerdown or reboot. If the change of *init* state is to proceed without user intervention, including the –*y* flag at the end of the shutdown command is useful; otherwise, the message

```
Do you want to continue? (y or n):
```

will be displayed, and you must type **Y** in order for the shutdown to proceed. The default grace-period on Solaris is 60 seconds, so if the Administrators wanted to reboot with 2 minutes warning given to all users, without user intervention, the command would be as follows:

```
# shutdown -i 5 -g 120 -y
```

The system will then periodically display a message warning all users of the imminent *init* state change:

```
Shutdown started. Tue Feb 12 10:22:00 EST 2002
Broadcast Message from root (console) on server Tue Feb 12 10:22:00...
The system server will be shut down in 2 minutes
```

The system will then reboot without user intervention, and does not enter the OpenBoot monitor. If you need to issue commands using the monitor (i.e., an *init* state of 0 is desired), you can use the following command:

```
# shutdown -i0 -g180 -y
Shutdown started. Tue Feb 12 11:15:00 EST 2002
Broadcast Message from root (console) on server Tue Feb 12 11:15:00...
The system will be shut down in 3 minutes

.

.

.

INIT: New run level: 0
The system is coming down. Please wait.

.

.

.

The system is down.
syncing file systems... [1] [2] [3] done
Program terminated
Type help for more information
ok
```

There are many ways to warn users in advance of a shutdown. One way is to edit the "message of the day" file (*/etc/motd*) to contain a warning that the server will be "down" and/or rebooted for a specific time. This message will be displayed every time a user successfully logs in with an interactive shell. The following message gives the date and time of the shutdown, expected duration, and a contact address for inquiries:

```
System server will be shutdown at 5 p.m. 2/12/2002.
Expected downtime: 1 hour.
E-mail root@system for further details.
```

At least 24 hours notice is usually required for users on a large system, because long jobs need to be rescheduled. In practice, many Administrators will shut down or reboot only outside business hours to minimize inconvenience; however, power failure and hardware problems can necessitate unexpected downtime.

This method works well in advance, but because many users are continuously logged in from remote terminals, they won't always read the new "message of the day." Another approach is to use the "write all" command (wall), which sends a message to all terminals of all logged-in users. You can send this command manually at hourly intervals prior to shutdown, or you could establish a `cron` job to perform this task automatically. An example command would be

```
# wall
System server will be shutdown at 5 p.m. 2/12/2001.
Expected downtime: 1 hour.
E-mail root@system for further details.
^d
```

After sending the *wall* message, you can perform a final check of logged-in users prior to shutdown by using the who command:

```
# who
root          console     Feb 12 10:15
pwatters      pts/0       Feb 12 10:15       (client)
```

You can send a message to the user *pwatters* on *pts/0* directly to notify him of the imminent shutdown:

```
# write pwatters
Dear pwatters,
Please logout immediately as the system server is going down.
If you do not logout now, your unsaved work may be lost.
Yours Sincerely,
System Administrator (root@system)
CTRL+d
```

Depending on the status of the user, you may also want to request a talk session, by using the following command:

```
# talk pwatters
```

If all these strategies fail to convince the user *pwatters* to log out, you have no choice but to proceed with the shutdown.

Command Reference

The following commands are used to manage *init* states.

/sbin/init

In addition to being the process spawner, init can be used to switch run levels at any time. For example, to perform hardware maintenance, you can use the following command:

```
# init 0
```

To enter the administrative state, you can use the following command:

```
# init 1
```

To enter the first multi-user state, you can use the following command:

```
# init 2
```

To enter the second multi-user state, you can use the following command:

```
# init 3
```

To enter a user-defined state, you can use the following command:

```
# init 4
```

To power down the system, you can use the following command:

```
# init 5
```

To halt the operating system, you can use the following command:

```
# init 6
```

To enter the administrative state, with all of the file systems available, you can use the following command:

```
# init S
```

Before using init in this way, preceding its execution with a call to sync is often advisable. The sync command renews the disk superblock, which ensures that all outstanding data operations are flushed, and the file system is stable before shutting down.

/etc/inittab

After the kernel is loaded into memory, the */sbin/init* process is initialized, and the system is brought up to the default *init* state, which is determined by the *initdefault* value contained in */etc/inittab*, which controls the behavior of the *init* process. Each entry has the form

```
identifier:runlevel:action:command
```

where *identifier* is a unique two-character identifier, *runlevel* specifies the run level to be entered, *action* specifies the process characteristics of the command to be executed, and *command* is the name of the program to be run. The program can be an application or a script file. The run level must be one of S, A, B, C, 1, 2, 3, 4, 5, or 6. If the process is to be executed by all run levels, no run level should be specified.

The following is a standard *inittab* file:

```
ap::sysinit:/sbin/autopush -f /etc/iu.ap
ap::sysinit:/sbin/soconfig -f /etc/sock2path
fs::sysinit:/sbin/rcS sysinit              >/dev/msglog 2<>/dev/msglog \
   </dev/console
is:3:initdefault:
p3:s1234:powerfail:/usr/sbin/shutdown -y -i5 -g0 >/dev/msglog 2<>/dev/msglog
sS:s:wait:/sbin/rcS                        >/dev/msglog 2<>/dev/msglog \
   </dev/console
s0:0:wait:/sbin/rc0                        >/dev/msglog 2<>/dev/msglog \
   </dev/console
s1:1:respawn:/sbin/rc1                     >/dev/msglog 2<>/dev/msglog \
   </dev/console
s2:23:wait:/sbin/rc2                       >/dev/msglog 2<>/dev/msglog \
   </dev/console
s3:3:wait:/sbin/rc3                        >/dev/msglog 2<>/dev/msglog \
   </dev/console
s5:5:wait:/sbin/rc5                        >/dev/msglog 2<>/dev/msglog \
   </dev/console
s6:6:wait:/sbin/rc6                        >/dev/msglog 2<>/dev/msglog \
   </dev/console
fw:0:wait:/sbin/uadmin 2 0                 >/dev/msglog 2<>/dev/msglog \
   </dev/console

of:5:wait:/sbin/uadmin 2 6                 >/dev/msglog 2<>/dev/msglog \
   </dev/console
rb:6:wait:/sbin/uadmin 2 1                 >/dev/msglog 2<>/dev/msglog \
   </dev/console
sc:234:respawn:/usr/lib/saf/sac -t 300
co:234:respawn:/usr/lib/saf/ttymon -g -h -p "`uname -n` console login: "\
   -T sun -d /dev/console -l console -m ldterm,ttcompat
```

This */etc/inittab* file contains only entries for the actions `sysinit`, `respawn`, `initdefault`, `wait`, and `powerfail`. These are the common actions found on most systems. However, Solaris provides a wide variety of actions that may be useful in special situations (e.g., when `powerwait` is more appropriate then `powerfail`). Potential actions are identified by any one of the following:

- **`initdefault`**   This is a mandatory entry found on all systems, and it is used to configure the default run level for the system. This is specified by the highest *init* state specified in the *rstate* field. If this field is empty, `init` interprets the *rstate* as the highest possible run level (run-level 6), which will force a continuous reboot of the system. In addition, if the entry is missing, the Administrator must supply one manually on the console for booting to proceed.

- **`sysinit`**   This entry is provided as a safeguard for asking which run level is required at boot time if the *initdefault* entry is missing. Only devices required to ask the question are affected.

- **`boot`**   This entry is parsed only at boot time, and is mainly used for initialization following a full reboot of the system after powerdown.

- **`off`**   This entry ensures that a process is terminated upon entering a particular run level. A warning signal is sent, followed by a kill signal, again with a five-second interval.

- **`once`**   This entry is similar to `boot`, but more flexible, in that the named process runs only once, and is not respawned.

- **`ondemand`**   This entry is similar to the `respawn` action.

- **`powerfail`**   Runs the process associated with the entry when a power fail signal is received.

- **`powerwait`**   Similar to `powerfail`, except that *init* waits until the process terminates before further processing entries in */etc/inittab*. This is especially useful for enforcing sequential shutdown of services that are prioritized.

- **`bootwait`**   This entry is parsed only on the first occasion that the transition from single-user to multi-user run levels occur after a system boot.

- **`wait`**   This entry starts a process and waits for its completion on entering the specified run level, however, the entry is ignored if */etc/inittab* is reread during the same run level.

- **`respawn`**   This entry ensures that if a process that should be running is not, it should be respawned.

The */etc/inittab* file follows conventions for text layout used by the Bourne shell: A long entry can be continued on the following line by using a backslash "\", and comments can only be inserted into the process field by using a has character "#". There is a limitation of 512 characters for each entry imposed on */etc/inittab*; however, there is no limit on the number of entries which may be inserted.

The Complete Reference

Solaris 9

Chapter 7

Installing Software

All Solaris software installed as part of the operating environment is included in an archive known as a *package*. Solaris packages provide an easy way to bring together application binaries, configuration files, and documentation for distribution to other systems. In addition to the Solaris packaging system, Solaris also supports standard UNIX archiving and compression tools, such as *tar* (tape archive) and *compress*. In this chapter, we examine how you can manage packages using the standard Solaris packaging tools, CLI (Command Line Interface), and admintool. Operations reviewed include installing packages, displaying information about packages, and removing packages using both the CLI tools and the admintool GUI utility.

Key Concepts

Packages are text files that contain archives of binary applications, configuration files, documentation, and even source code. All files in the Solaris operating environment are supplied as part of a package, making it easy for you to group files associated with different applications. If files are installed without packaging, it can become difficult over the years for administrators to remember which files were installed with particular applications. Packaging makes it easy to recognize application dependencies, because all files required by a specific application can be included within the archive.

Getting Information About Packages

Administrators can use the pkgchk command to examine the package properties of a file that has already been installed:

```
# pkgchk -l -p /usr/bin/mkdir
Pathname: /usr/bin/mkdir
Type: regular file
Expected mode: 0555
Expected owner: bin
Expected group: bin
Expected file size (bytes): 9876
Expected sum(1) of contents: 38188
Expected last modification: Oct 06 05:47:55 PM 1998
Referenced by the following packages:
        SUNWcsu
Current status: installed
```

Another advantage of using packages is that they make use of the standard installation interface provided to install Solaris packages. This means that all Solaris applications are installed using one of two standard installation applications (pkgadd or the admintool), rather than each application having its own installation program.

This reduces coding time and makes it easier for administrators to install software, because only a single interface with standard options, such as overwriting existing files, needs to be learned. Using packages reduces the administrative overhead of software management on Solaris 9.

In this chapter, we will examine how to install new packages, display information about downloaded packages, and remove packages that have been previously installed on the system, by using both admintool and the command-line package tools.

Procedures

Here are procedures for viewing, installing, and uninstalling packages.

Viewing Package Information with pkginfo

At any time, you can examine which packages have been installed on a system using the pkginfo command:

```
# pkginfo
application GNUlstdc        libstdc++
application GNUmake         make
system      NCRos86r        NCR Platform Support,
                            OS Functionality (Root)
system      SFWaalib        ASCII Art Library
system      SFWaconf        GNU autoconf
system      SFWamake        GNU automake
system      SFWbison        GNU bison
system      SFWemacs        GNU Emacs
system      SFWflex         GNU flex
system      SFWfvwm         fvwm virtual window manager
system      SFWgcc          GNU compilers
system      SFWgdb          GNU source-level debugger
system      SFWgimp         GNU Image Manipulation Program
system      SFWglib         GLIB - Library of useful routines
                            for C programming
system      SFWgm4          GNU m4
system      SFWgmake        GNU make
system      SFWgs           GNU Ghostscript
system      SFWgsfot        GNU Ghostscript Other Fonts
system      SFWgsfst        GNU Ghostscript Standard Fonts
system      SFWgtk          GTK - The GIMP Toolkit
system      SFWjpg          The Independent JPEG Groups JPEG
software
system      SFWlxrun        lxrun
```

```
system        SFWmpage        mpage - print multiple pages per sheet
system        SFWmpeg         The MPEG Library
system        SFWncur         ncurses library
system        SFWolvwm        OPEN LOOK Virtual Window Manager
system        SFWpng          PNG reference library
```

As you can see, this system has quite a few packages installed in both the system and application categories, including lxrun, the application that allows Linux binaries to be executed on Solaris Intel, and the Gimp, a graphics manipulation program. There are no restrictions on the kinds of files and applications that can be installed with packages.

Viewing Package Information with admintool

Viewing information about installed packages is easy using the admintool utility's graphical user interface (GUI). You execute admintool by using the command */usr/ bin/admintool*. After choosing Browse | Software from admintool's menu bar, you can view all the installed software packages. Many packages will have already been installed on the system, including PC File Viewer Help in Swedish, Italian, French, and German, as well as support files for the ShowTV multimedia software suite.

Using admintool, you can also display only files that have been installed as packages in the system category by deselecting All Software from the software selection drop-down menu, and selecting System Software. Here, several key system packages will have been installed, including operating system (OS), Common Desktop Environment (CDE), Open Windows (OW), and 64-bit architecture support for Eastern European, Central European, Southern European, and German locales.

It is also possible to display only files that have been installed as application packages by deselecting System Software from the software selection drop-down menu and selecting Application Software. Several key application packages will have been installed, including many support packages for the ShowTV multimedia software suite.

Installing a Solaris Package Using the CLI

The best way to learn about adding packages is to use an example. In this section, you'll download a package from **http://www.sunfreeware.com** called *gpw-6.94-sol8-intel-local.gz*, which is Tom Van Vleck's random password creation application. Let's look more closely at the package name to determine what software this package contains:

■ The *.gz* extension indicates that the package file has been compressed using gzip after it was created. Other possible extensions include .Z, which indicates compression with the compress program, while a .z extension suggests compression by the *pack* program.

- The *local* string indicates that the package contents will be installed under the directory */usr/local*. Other typical installation targets include the */opt* directory, where optional packages from the Solaris distribution are installed.
- The *intel* string states that the package is intended for use on Solaris Intel and not Solaris Sparc.
- The *6.94* string indicates the current software revision level.
- The *gpw* string states the application's name.

To use the package file, you first need to decompress it using the `gzip` command:

```
# gzip -d gpw-6.94-sol8-intel-local
```

You can then examine the contents of the file by using the `head` command:

```
# head gpw-6.94-sol8-intel-local
# PaCkAgE DaTaStReAm
TVVgpw 1 150
# end of header
NAME=gwp
ARCH=intel
VERSION=6.94
CATEGORY=application
VENDOR=Tom Van Vleck
EMAIL=steve@smc.vnet.net
```

This kind of header exists for all Solaris packages and makes it easy to understand what platform a package is designed for, who the vendor was, and who to contact for more information.

Now that the package is decompressed and ready, you can begin the installation process by using the `pkgadd` command. To install the *gpw-6.94-sol8-intel-local* package, use the following command:

```
# pkgadd -d gpw-6.94-sol8-intel-local
```

You'll see the following output:

```
The following packages are available:
  1  TVVgpw     gwp
                (sparc) 6.94
```

```
Select package(s) you wish to process (or 'all' to process
all packages). (default: all) [?,??,q]:   all
```

Press ENTER at this point to proceed with the installation:

```
Processing package instance <TVVgpw> from </tmp/gpw-6.94-sol8-intel-local>

gwp
(sparc) 6.94
Tom Van Vleck
Using </usr/local> as the package base directory.
## Processing package information.
## Processing system information.
   2 package pathnames are already properly installed.
## Verifying disk space requirements.
## Checking for conflicts with packages already installed.
## Checking for setuid/setgid programs.

Installing gwp as <TVVgpw>

## Installing part 1 of 1.
/usr/local/bin/gpw
/usr/local/doc/gpw/README.gpw
[ verifying class <none> ]

Installation of <TVVgpw> was successful.
```

After processing package and system information and checking that the required amount of disk space is available, the pkgadd command copies only two files from the archive to the local file system: */usr/local/bin/gpw* and */usr/local/doc/gpw/README.gpw*.

Uninstalling a Solaris Package Using the CLI

After a package has been installed on the system, it can easily be removed by using the pkgrm command. For example, if you wanted to remove the gpw program after it was installed in the */usr/local* directory, you would use this command,

```
# pkgrm TVVgpw
```

and respond to the following information:

```
The following package is currently installed:
```

```
    TVVgpw              gwp
                        (sparc) 6.94

Do you want to remove this package? y

## Removing installed package instance <TVVgpw>
## Verifying package dependencies.
## Processing package information.
## Removing pathnames in class <none>
/usr/local/doc/gpw/README.gpw
/usr/local/doc/gpw
/usr/local/doc <shared pathname not removed>
/usr/local/bin/gpw
/usr/local/bin <shared pathname not removed>
## Updating system information.

Removal of <TVVgpw> was successful.
```

The pkgrm command also operates in an interactive mode, in which multiple
packages can be removed using the same interface:

```
# pkgrm

The following packages are available:
    1  GNUlstdc        libstdc++
                       (i86pc) 2.8.1.1
    2  GNUmake         make
                       (i86pc) 3.77
    3  NCRos86r        NCR Platform Support, OS Functionality (Root)
                       (i386) 1.1.0,REV=1998.08.07.12.41
    4  SFWaalib        ASCII Art Library
                       (i386) 1.2,REV=1999.11.25.13.32
    5  SFWaconf        GNU autoconf
                       (i386) 2.13,REV=1999.11.25.13.32
    6  SFWamake        GNU automake
                       (i386) 1.4,REV=1999.11.25.13.32
    7  SFWbison        GNU bison
                       (i386) 1.28,REV=1999.11.25.13.32
    8  SFWemacs        GNU Emacs
                       (i386) 20.4,REV=1999.11.25.13.32
    9  SFWflex         GNU flex
```

```
                    (i386) 2.5.4,REV=1999.11.25.13.32
 10   SFWfvwm       fvwm virtual window manager
                    (i386) 2.2.2,REV=1999.11.25.13.32

... 288 more menu choices to follow;
<RETURN> for more choices, <CTRL-D> to stop display:
```

At this point, you can enter the number of the package that you wish to remove.

Examples

In the following examples, we'll examine how to use admintool's GUI to manage packages. The flexible package format is independent of the interface used to install specific packages. This means that while administrators from a Linux background may prefer to use the `pkgadd` command to manage packages, administrators from a Windows background might find the package administration features of admintool easier to use.

Installing a Solaris Package with admintool

admintool provides an easy-to-use interface for installing packages, in which the following options may be selected from drop-down boxes:

- Check for existing files.
- Check for existing packages.
- Check for existing partial installations.
- Allow *setuid/setgid* files to be installed.
- Allow *setuid/setgid* scripts to be run.
- Check that installation dependencies have been met.
- Check that removal dependencies have been met.
- Check for correct run level.
- Check for sufficient space.
- Display copyrights.
- Run the installation interactively.

admintool also allows the administrator to specify an installation source so that packages may be installed directly from a CD-ROM.

Once a valid CD-ROM directory containing packages has been selected, the Add Software interface is displayed. Here, you'll see a left-hand pane showing the full titles for the packages that have been located in the specified directory. The right-hand pane shows the description of the last selected software package. For example, you may see the package SUNWcesh, which is the Sun Management Center Simplified Chinese Help package distributed by Sun Microsystems and is less than 1MB in size when installed.

You should always verify that sufficient space is available in the indicated partitions by checking the Space Meter. Here you can verify that more than sufficient space is available for installing the required files for the SUNWcesh package.

After checking the boxes associated with every package that you wish to install, you can proceed with installation by clicking the Add button. A separate installation window then appears. As an example, let's say the SUNWescon software package (the Sun Management Center console package) is being installed. After setting the installation target directory (/opt), package and system information is processed. After disk space requirements have been verified, any conflicts with existing packages are identified. Next, all *setuid* and *setgid* applications are identified, and assent must be granted to install any *setuid* or *setgid* files that are found in the package. Finally, the files are installed into their appropriate target directories.

Packages may also be installed from a special package spooling directory, at */var/spool/pkg*, using the admintool utility, or from any directory that contains a valid package file. The */var/spool/pkg* folder has an important role in upgrading machines in an automated fashion, since it can be mounted automatically using the Network File System (NFS) and the automounter from another server. It is possible to use a script or a `cron` job to then noninteractively install or upgrade new software.

After a valid spooling directory containing packages has been selected, the Add Software interface is displayed. The left-hand pane will show all the full titles for the packages that have been located in the specified directory. The right-hand pane will show the description of the last selected software package. For our example the only package shown will be SUNWcesh. After checking the boxes associated with the SUNWcesh package, you can proceed with installation by clicking the Add button. A separate installation window appears, and the software is installed.

Uninstalling a Solaris Package Using admintool

After a package has been installed on the system, it can easily be removed by using admintool. Choose Browse | Software, highlight the package that you wish to remove, and then choose Edit | Delete. A popup window then appears, asking for confirmation of the deletion instruction.

After you click OK, a separate window will show the output of the package removal:

```
The following package is currently installed:
   SUNWdesmt          ShowMe TV German Localization Files
                      (sparc) 1.1,REV=1999.04.30

Do you want to remove this package? y
```

```
## Removing installed package instance <SUNWdesmt>
## Verifying package dependencies.
## Processing package information.
## Removing pathnames in class <none>
/opt/SUNWsmtv/lib/locale/de/share/showmetv-defaults
/opt/SUNWsmtv/lib/locale/de/share
/opt/SUNWsmtv/lib/locale/de/help/xdh_saveFile.html
/opt/SUNWsmtv/lib/locale/de/help/xdh_printItem.html
/opt/SUNWsmtv/lib/locale/de/help/xdh_openFile.html
/opt/SUNWsmtv/lib/locale/de/help/xdh_historyDialog.html
/opt/SUNWsmtv/lib/locale/de/help/xdh_findText.html
/opt/SUNWsmtv/lib/locale/de/help/xdh_entry.html
/opt/SUNWsmtv/lib/locale/de/help/watchtimer.html
/opt/SUNWsmtv/lib/locale/de/help/videosettings.html
/opt/SUNWsmtv/lib/locale/de/help/undelete.html
/opt/SUNWsmtv/lib/locale/de/help/transmitterproperties.html
/opt/SUNWsmtv/lib/locale/de/help/transmitter.html
/opt/SUNWsmtv/lib/locale/de/help/statistics.html
/opt/SUNWsmtv/lib/locale/de/help/showcards.html
/opt/SUNWsmtv/lib/locale/de/help/recordtimer.html
/opt/SUNWsmtv/lib/locale/de/help/record.html
/opt/SUNWsmtv/lib/locale/de/help/receiver.html
/opt/SUNWsmtv/lib/locale/de/help/properties.html
/opt/SUNWsmtv/lib/locale/de/help/programinfo.html
/opt/SUNWsmtv/lib/locale/de/help/printsnap.html
/opt/SUNWsmtv/lib/locale/de/help/printformat.html
/opt/SUNWsmtv/lib/locale/de/help/print.html
/opt/SUNWsmtv/lib/locale/de/help/preview.html
/opt/SUNWsmtv/lib/locale/de/help/preferences.html
/opt/SUNWsmtv/lib/locale/de/help/open.html
/opt/SUNWsmtv/lib/locale/de/help/new.html
/opt/SUNWsmtv/lib/locale/de/help/mail.html
/opt/SUNWsmtv/lib/locale/de/help/import.html
/opt/SUNWsmtv/lib/locale/de/help/group.html
/opt/SUNWsmtv/lib/locale/de/help/findres.html
/opt/SUNWsmtv/lib/locale/de/help/filewindow.html
/opt/SUNWsmtv/lib/locale/de/help/exportcards.html
/opt/SUNWsmtv/lib/locale/de/help/broadcast.html
/opt/SUNWsmtv/lib/locale/de/help/addrbook.html
/opt/SUNWsmtv/lib/locale/de/help/addfields.html
/opt/SUNWsmtv/lib/locale/de/help
```

```
/opt/SUNWsmtv/lib/locale/de/LC_MESSAGES/splitmov.cat
/opt/SUNWsmtv/lib/locale/de/LC_MESSAGES/showmetvt.cat
/opt/SUNWsmtv/lib/locale/de/LC_MESSAGES/showmetvh.cat
/opt/SUNWsmtv/lib/locale/de/LC_MESSAGES/showmetvd.cat
/opt/SUNWsmtv/lib/locale/de/LC_MESSAGES/showmetvab.cat
/opt/SUNWsmtv/lib/locale/de/LC_MESSAGES/showmetv.cat
/opt/SUNWsmtv/lib/locale/de/LC_MESSAGES/pic.cat
/opt/SUNWsmtv/lib/locale/de/LC_MESSAGES/mpext.cat
/opt/SUNWsmtv/lib/locale/de/LC_MESSAGES/libvid.cat
/opt/SUNWsmtv/lib/locale/de/LC_MESSAGES/libvcr.cat
/opt/SUNWsmtv/lib/locale/de/LC_MESSAGES/libtv.cat
/opt/SUNWsmtv/lib/locale/de/LC_MESSAGES/libsunsolxt.cat
/opt/SUNWsmtv/lib/locale/de/LC_MESSAGES/libsunsol.cat
/opt/SUNWsmtv/lib/locale/de/LC_MESSAGES/libsnmp.cat
/opt/SUNWsmtv/lib/locale/de/LC_MESSAGES/librtp.cat
/opt/SUNWsmtv/lib/locale/de/LC_MESSAGES/libregserv.cat
/opt/SUNWsmtv/lib/locale/de/LC_MESSAGES/libpdb.cat
/opt/SUNWsmtv/lib/locale/de/LC_MESSAGES/libh261.cat
/opt/SUNWsmtv/lib/locale/de/LC_MESSAGES/libavdata.cat
/opt/SUNWsmtv/lib/locale/de/LC_MESSAGES/libaud.cat
/opt/SUNWsmtv/lib/locale/de/LC_MESSAGES/libab.cat
/opt/SUNWsmtv/lib/locale/de/LC_MESSAGES/h261vis.cat
/opt/SUNWsmtv/lib/locale/de/LC_MESSAGES/devthr.cat
/opt/SUNWsmtv/lib/locale/de/LC_MESSAGES
/opt/SUNWsmtv/lib/locale/de
/opt/SUNWsmtv/lib/locale <shared pathname not removed>
/opt/SUNWsmtv/lib <shared pathname not removed>
/opt/SUNWsmtv/app-defaults/de/showmetvh
/opt/SUNWsmtv/app-defaults/de/help.mesgs
/opt/SUNWsmtv/app-defaults/de
/opt/SUNWsmtv/app-defaults <shared pathname not removed>
/opt/SUNWsmtv <shared pathname not removed>
## Updating system information.

Removal of <SUNWdesmt> was successful.
press <Return> to continue
```

Solstice Launcher

The Solstice Launcher is part of an integrated suite of system administration tools that are an alternative to admintool and the command-line toolset. Solstice maintains a separate application registry that determines which applications are displayed in the Launcher, in addition to Sun's own tools. Thus, it is possible to customize the interface to suit local requirements. Note that the application package must have been already installed prior to registry addition.

To add an application to the registry, the */usr/snadm/bin/soladdapp* command is used. For example, to add an application called Database Query, the following command could be used:

```
# soladdapp -r /opt/SUNWadm/etc/.solstice_registry \
  -n "Database Query" \
  -i /usr/local/CSWdbquery/dbquery.xpm \
  -e /usr/local/CSWdbquery/bin/dbquery
```

This would add an item for "Database Query" with the path to the application set to */usr/local/CSWdbquery/bin/dbquery*, an icon located in */usr/local/CSWdbquery/dbquery.xpm*, and the default registry path of */opt/SUNWadm/etc/.solstice_registry*.

In a similar fashion, an application can be removed from the registry by using the */usr/snadm/bin/soldelapp* command. In this case, the name of the package must be supplied along with the registry path:

```
# /usr/snadm/bin/soldelapp \
  -r /opt/SUNWadm/etc/.solstice_registry \
  -n "Database Query"
```

Note *This does not delete the application package from the system.*

Command Reference

The following commands are commonly used to install packages and files on Solaris.

Package Commands

This table summarizes the various commands used to create, install, and remove packages.

Command	Description
pkgproto	Creates a prototype file that specifies the files contained in a package
pkgmk	Creates a package directory
pkgadd	Installs a package from a package file

Command	Description
pkgtrans	Converts a package directory into a file
pkgrm	Uninstalls a package
pkgchk	Verifies that a package is valid
pkginfo	Prints the contents of a package

install

The install command is not part of the standard package tools, but is often used in scripts to copy files from a source to destination directory, as part of an installation process. It does not require super-user privileges to execute, and will not overwrite files unless the effective user has permission. However, if the super-user is executing the command, then files can be written with a specific username, group membership, and octal permissions code. This allows a super-user to install multiple files with different permissions, and ownership different to root.

The three ownership and permission options are specified by:

−m	Octal permissions code
−u	File owner
−g	Group membership

There are four options that indicate which operations are to be performed:

−c	Copies a source file to a target directory
−f	Overwrites the target file with a source file if the former exists
−n	Copies a source file to a target directory if and only if it does not exist in any of a specified set of directories
−d	Creates a directory

To install the file */tmp/setup_server.sh* to the directory */opt/scripts*, as the user *bin* and group *sysadmin*, the following command would be used:

```
# install -c /opt/scripts -m 0755 -u bin -g sysadmin /tmp/setup_script
```

The Complete Reference

Solaris 9

Chapter 8

Installing Patches

One of the most important aspects of system maintenance involves identifying, downloading, and installing patches that have been released for a specific revision level. *Patches* are binary code modifications that generally fix bugs but may also introduce new, urgently required features into existing applications and system services. In this chapter, we'll look at the process of patch installation and backing out of patches that have already been applied.

Key Concepts

Patches are binary code modifications that affect the way that Sun-supplied software operates. They are released by Sun when previously identified bugs have been fixed, or because a security exploit has been discovered in a piece of software and a simple workaround is inadequate to prevent intrusion or disruption of normal system activity.

For example, until recently, many of the older Solaris daemons suffered from buffer overflow vulnerabilities, in which the fixed boundaries on an array are deliberately overwritten by a rogue client to "crash" the system. Many of the system daemons, such as Web servers, may be crashed because memory is overwritten with arbitrary values outside the declared size of an array. Without appropriate bounds checking, passing a GET request to a Web server of 1025 bytes when the array size is 1024 would clearly result in unpredictable behavior, as the C language does not prevent a program from doing this.

Since Solaris daemons are typically written in C, a number of them have been fixed in recent years to prevent this problem from occurring (but you may be surprised at just how often new weaknesses are exposed). Sendmail, Internet Message Access Protocol (IMAP), and Post Office Protocol (POP) daemons for Solaris have all experienced buffer overflow vulnerabilities in the past, which have required the urgent installation of security patches. Any "first release" of an operating system inevitably contains bugs that are not identified until the system has been tested across hundreds and thousands of sites. This is because no one test site has access to the entire range of software, hardware, and peripheral devices that can form part of a system. For example, a bug that might affect a certain type of mouse when installed on a non-standard port might cause a kernel panic because an unexpected instruction is received. This situation may not have been anticipated in the code, and a patch may need to be released to fix the bug. For this reason, production systems are rarely upgraded until at least the first maintenance release has been issued. Let's look at some past examples of bugs, and how they might affect system security. In past Solaris releases, two critical problems were identified, both associated with gaining root access via buffer overflow:

- The Common Desktop Environment (CDE) based Calendar Manager service was vulnerable to a buffer overflow attack, as identified in Common

Vulnerabilities and Exposures (CVE) report 1999-0320 and 1999-0696. The Calendar Manager is used to manage appointments and other date/time based functions.

■ The remote administration daemon (sadmind) was vulnerable to a buffer overflow attack, as described in CVE 1999-0977. The remote administration daemon is used to manage system administration activities across a number of different hosts.

| Note | *The CVE number matches descriptions of each security issue from the Common Vulnerabilities and Exposures database (**http://cve.mitre.org/**). Each identified vulnerability will contain a hyperlink back to the CVE database so that information displayed about every issue is updated directly from the source. New patches and bug fixes are also listed.* |

Patches for these bugs were released by Sun, and once installed, the issues were resolved.

Retrieving Patches Online

To find out information about current patches, system administrators can check out SunSolve Online at **http://www.sunsolve.sun.com/**. Here, details about current patches for each operating system release can be found.

Two basic types of patches are available from SunSolve: *single* patches and *jumbo* patches. A single patch has a single patch number associated with it and is generally aimed at resolving a single outstanding issue and usually insert, delete, or update data in a small number of files. Single patches are also targeted at resolving specific security issues. Each patch is associated with an internal bug number from Sun's bug database. For example, patch number 108435-01 aims to fix BugId 4318566, involving a shared library issue with the 64-bit C++ compiler.

In contrast, a jumbo patch consists of many single patches that have been bundled together, on the basis of operating system release levels, to ensure that the most common issues for a particular platform are resolved by the installation of the jumbo patch. It's standard practice to install the current jumbo patch for Solaris 9 after it has been installed from scratch or if the system has been upgraded from Solaris 8, for example.

Some of the current patches released for Solaris include the following:

Patch Number	Description
110322-01	Patch for /usr/lib/netsvc/yp/ypbind
110853-01	Patch for Sun-Fire-880

Patch Number	Description
110856-01	Patch for /etc/inet/services
110888-01	Patch for figgs
110894-01	Patch for country name
110927-01	Patch for SUNW_PKGLIST
111078-01	Patch Solaris Resource Manager
111295-01	Patch for /usr/bin/sparcv7/pstack and /usr/bin/sparcv9/pstack
111297-01	Patch for /usr/lib/libsendfile.so.1
111337-01	Patch for /usr/sbin/ocfserv
111400-01	Patch for KCMS configure tool
111402-01	Patch for crontab
111431-01	Patch for /usr/lib/libldap.so.4
111439-01	Patch for /kernel/fs/tmpfs
111473-01	Patch for PCI Host Adapter
111562-01	Patch for /usr/lib/librt.so.1
111564-01	Patch for SunPCi 2.2.1
111570-01	Patch for uucp
111588-01	Patch for /kernel/drv/wc
111606-01	Patch for /usr/sbin/in.ftpd
111624-01	Patch for /usr/sbin/inetd
111648-01	Patch for env3test, cpupmtest, ifbtest and rsctest
111656-01	Patch for socal and sf drivers
111762-01	Patch for Expert3D and SunVTS

One of the most useful guides to the currently available patches for Solaris 9 is the Patch Report (**http://sunsolve.sun.com/sunalert_patches.html**). This report provides a quick reference to all the newly released patches for the platform, as well as updates on previous patches that have now been modified. A list of suggested patches for the platform is also contained in the report, while recommended security patches are listed separately. Finally, a list of obsolete patches is provided. Some of the currently listed security patches available include the following:

Patch Number	Description
108528-09	Patch for kernel update
108869-06	Patch for snmpdx/mibiisa/libssasnmp/snmplib
108875-09	Patch for c2audit
108968-05	Patch for vol/vold/rmmount
108975-04	Patch for /usr/bin/rmformat and /usr/sbin/format
108985-03	Patch for /usr/sbin/in.rshd
108991-13	Patch for /usr/lib/libc.so.1
109091-04	Patch for /usr/lib/fs/ufs/ufsrestore
109134-19	Patch for WBEM
109234-04	Patch for Apache and NCA
109279-13	Patch for /kernel/drv/ip
109320-03	Patch for LP
109322-07	Patch for libnsl
109326-05	Patch for libresolv.so.2 and in.named
109354-09	Patch for dtsession
109783-01	Patch for /usr/lib/nfs/nfsd
109805-03	Patch for pam_krb5.so.1
109887-08	Patch for smartcard
109888-05	Patch for platform drivers
109892-03	Patch for /kernel/drv/ecpp driver
109894-01	Patch for /kernel/drv/sparcv9/bpp driver
109896-04	Patch for USB driver
109951-01	Patch for jserver buffer overflow

Figure 8-1 shows the Patch Finder screen on SunSolve, where you can search for all the available jumbo patches and recommended clusters for Solaris 9.

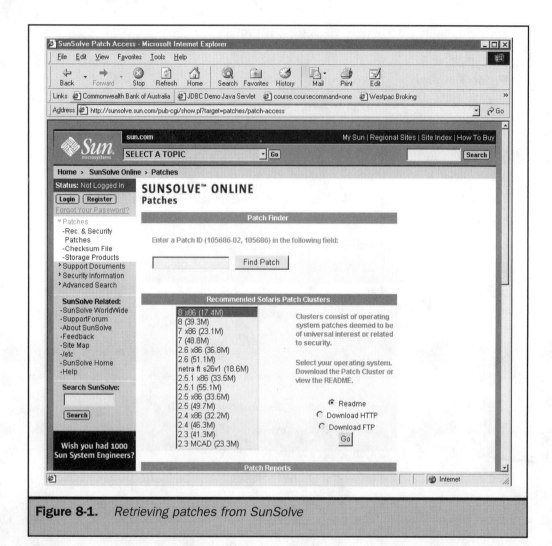

Figure 8-1. Retrieving patches from SunSolve

Determining Which Patches Are Installed

To determine which patches are currently installed on your system, use the `showrev` command as follows:

```
# showrev -p
Patch: 107430-01 Obsoletes:  Requires:  Incompatibles:  Packages: SUNWwsr
Patch: 108029-01 Obsoletes:  Requires:  Incompatibles:  Packages: SUNWwsr
Patch: 107437-03 Obsoletes:  Requires:  Incompatibles:  Packages: SUNWtiu8
```

```
Patch: 107316-01 Obsoletes:  Requires:  Incompatibles:  Packages: SUNWploc
Patch: 106541-15 Obsoletes: 106832-03, 106976-01, 107029-01, 107030-01,
107334-01, 107031-01, 107117-05, 107899-01, 108752-01, 107147-08,
109104-04 Requires: 107544-02 Incompatibles:  Packages: SUNWkvm,
SUNWcsu, SUNWcsr, SUNWcsl, SUNWcar, SUNWesu, SUNWarc, SUNWatfsr,
SUNWscpu, SUNWcpr, SUNWdpl, SUNWhea, SUNWipc, SUNWtoo, SUNWnisu,
SUNWpcmci, SUNWpcmcu, SUNWtnfc, SUNWvolu, SUNWvolr
```

From the example shown here, you can see that showrev reports several different properties of each patch installed:

- The patch number.
- Whether the patch makes a previously released patch (or patches) obsolete, and which version numbers.
- Whether any prerequisite patches (and their version numbers) exist on which the current patch depends.
- Whether the patch is incompatible with any other patches.
- What standard Solaris packages are affected by installation of the patch.

If you look at one of the examples above (106541-15), you can see that it obsoletes a large number of other patches, including 106832-03, 106976-01, 107029-01, 107030-01, 107334-01, 107031-01, 107117-05, 107899-01, 108752-01, 107147-08, and 109104-04. In addition, it depends on patch 107544-02 and is compatible with all other known patches. Finally, it affects a large number of different packages, including SUNWkvm, SUNWcsu, SUNWcsr, SUNWcsl, SUNWcar, SUNWesu, SUNWarc, SUNWatfsr, SUNWscpu, SUNWcpr, SUNWdpl, SUNWhea, SUNWipc, SUNWtoo, SUNWnisu, SUNWpcmci, SUNWpcmcu, SUNWtnfc, SUNWvolu, and SUNWvolr.

Command Reference

The following commands are commonly used to add and delete patches in Solaris 9.

patchadd

To install single patches, use the patchadd command:

```
# patchadd /patches/106541-15
```

where /patches is the directory in which your patches are downloaded, and 106541-15 is the patch filename (it should be the same as the patch number).

To add multiple patches from the same directory, use the following command:

```
# patchadd /patches/106541-15 106541-10 107453-01
```

where 106541-15, 106541-10, and 107453-01 are the patches to be installed. Once the patches have been successfully installed, they can be verified using the showrev command. For example, to check that patch 106541-15 has been successfully installed, the following command could be used:

```
# showrev -p | grep 106541-15
```

patchadd has a large number of options that can be used for non-standard patch installations. For example, if you need to patch a net install image, then you will need to specify the path to the image. Alternatively, if you don't want to have the ability to back out of a patch, then you can flag this. As a strategy, this is not recommended, because you won't be able to revert your system to a pre-patched state. The options for patchadd are shown here:

–B	Specifies a directory for storing back out information other than the default
–C	Specifies the path to the net install image that is to be patched, if required
–d	Disallows backing out of patch installations
–M	Specifies an alternative directory where patches are located
–p	Prints a list of all installed patches
–u	Does not validate file installations
–R	Specifies an alternative root directory for client installations
–S	Patches a client from a server, where clients share the server's operating system directories

Let's look at how some of these options can be used in practice. In order to patch a client system called mars, with its root directory mapped to */export/mars*, the following command could be used:

```
# patchadd -d -R /export/mars /var/spool/patch/106541-15
```

Note that this command would disallow backing out of the patch installation. To add the patch to a net install image, located in */export/Solaris_2.9/Tools/boot*, the following command would be used:

```
# patchadd -C /export/Solaris_2.9/Tools/boot /var/spool/patch/106541-15
```

Since patches overwrite system files, there are some potential pitfalls that may be experienced when applying patches. The most common problem is running out of disk space on the */var* partition. If this occurs during patch installation, then the following error message will be observed:

```
Insufficient space in /var/sadm/pkg/106541-15/save to save old files
```

In this situation, there are several possible courses of actions, listed in order of desirability:

- Increase the available space on */var* by removing unnecessary files, even temporarily, until the patch can be applied.
- Specify an alternative backout directory that is located on a different filesystem.
- Create a symbolic link from */var/sadm/pkg/106541-15/save* to a directory on another filesystem, such as */usr/local/var/sadm/pkg/106541-15/save*.
- Switch off backing out of the patch installation.

Any error messages for the patch installation will generally be logged in */tmp/log.106541-15*, which may indicate other reasons for installation failure. For example, if a patch is applied twice to a system, then the following entry will appear in the log:

```
This appears to be an attempt to install the same architecture
and version of a package which is already installed. This
installation will attempt to overwrite this package.
```

patchrm

Patches can be easily removed using the patchrm command. For example, to remove the patch 106541-15, the following command would be used:

```
# patchrm 106541-15
```

If the patch was previously installed, it would now be removed.

However, if the patch was not previously installed, the following errors message would be displayed:

```
Checking installed packages and patches...
Patch 106541-15 has not been applied to this system.
patchrm is terminating.
```

Like `patchadd`, `patchrm` has a number of options which may be passed on the command line:

–B	Specifies a directory for storing back out information for the patch removal, other than the default
–C	Specifies the path to the net install image from which a patch is to be removed, if required
–f	Forces a package to be removed
–R	Specifies an alternative root directory for patch removal from client installations
–S	Removes a patch from a client system, executed from the server

For example, to remove patch 106541-15 from the client system jupiter, the following command could be used:

```
# patchrm -C /export/Solaris_2.9/Tools/boot 106541-15
```

Chapter 9

System Security

ecurity is a central concern of system administrators of all network operating systems, because all services may potentially have inherent flaws or weaknesses revealed through undetected bugs that can compromise a system. Solaris is no exception, and new Solaris administrators will find themselves visiting issues that they may have encountered with other operating systems. For example, Linux, Microsoft Windows, and Solaris all run database systems that have daemons that listen for connections arriving through the Internet. These servers may be shipped with default user accounts with well-known passwords that are not inactivated by local administrators after configuration and administration. Consequently, exploits involving such services are often broadcast on Usenet newsgroups, cracking mailing lists, and Web sites.

Some security issues are specific to Solaris. For example, username and password sniffing while a remote user is using Telnet to spawn a local shell is unique to Solaris and other UNIX systems, because PC-based products that provide remote access (such as Symantec's pcAnywhere product) encrypt the exchange of authentication credentials by default.

This chapter will lay the groundwork to help you understand the vulnerabilities of the Solaris operating system, as well as detail the techniques used by Solaris managers to reduce the risk of a successful attack by a rogue user. Our starting point will be the single host, which can be secured from both internal and externals threats by strict administration of user accounts and groups and their corresponding entries within standard password and shadowed password files.

It is critical that you maintain access to various files and directories by setting user and group ownership on those files. Once a user and group have been assigned ownership of a file or directory, they are free to determine which other users (if any) are able to read or write to that file—or for a directory, whether any files can be created under that directory. An exception to user- and group-based access control is the special *super-user* account (also known as the *root* user), who has global read, write, and create access on all files on a Solaris system. This includes normal files as well as directories and device files.

Finally, we'll examine how to keep tabs on all active users on a Solaris system so that their behavior and activities can be monitored to ensure that only authorized activities are being conducted at all times.

Key Concepts

The following key concepts are important for understanding system security in the context of Solaris.

Checking User and Group Identification

The concept of the user is central to Solaris—all processes and files on a Solaris system are "owned" by a particular user and are assigned to a specific user group. No data or activities on the system may exist without first establishing a valid user or group. Managing users and groups as a Solaris administrator can be a challenging activity—

you will be responsible for assigning all the privileges granted or denied to a user or group of users, and many of these permissions carry great risk. For example, a user with an inappropriate privilege level may execute inappropriate commands as the super user, causing damage to your system.

You can determine which user is currently logged in from a terminal session by using the id command:

```
$ id
uid=1001(natashia) gid=10(dialup)
```

The output shows that the currently logged-in user is natashia, with UID=1001. In addition, the current group of natashia is a dialup group with GID=10. It is possible for the user and group credentials to change during a single terminal session. For example, if the *su* facility is used effectively to "become" the super user, the UID and GID associated with the current terminal session will also change:

```
$ su root
Password:
# id
uid=0(root) gid=1(other)
```

Here, the root user (UID=0) belonging to the other group (GID=1) has spawned a new shell with full super-user privileges.

You can obtain a list of all groups that a user belongs to using the groups command. For example, to view all the groups that the root user belongs to, we use the following command:

```
# groups root
other root bin sys adm uucp mail tty lp nuucp daemon
```

Protecting the Super-User Account

We've just examined how to use the *su* facility to invoke super-user privileges from an unprivileged account. The user with UID=0 (typically the root user) has unlimited powers to act on a Solaris system. The root user can perform the following potentially dangerous functions:

- Add, delete, or modify all other user accounts
- Read and write all files, and create new ones
- Add or delete devices to the system
- Install new system software

- Read everyone's e-mail

- Snoop network traffic for usernames and passwords of other systems on the local area network (LAN)

- Modify all system logs to remove all traces of super-user access

- Pretend to be an unprivileged user and access their accounts on other systems where login access is authenticated against a username

These powers combine to make the root account sound rather sinister; however, many of these activities are legitimate and necessary system administration routines that are undertaken daily. For example, network traffic can be snooped to determine where network outages are occurring, and copying user files to backup tapes every night is generally in everyone's best interest. However, if an intruder gains root access, he/she is free to roam the system, deleting or stealing data, removing or adding user accounts, or installing Trojan horses that can transparently modify the way that your system operates.

One way to protect against an authorized user gaining root access is to use a hard-to-guess root password. This makes it difficult for a cracker to use a password cracking program to guess your password successfully. The optimal password is a completely random string of alphanumeric and punctuation characters.

In addition, the root password should never be written down unless it is locked in the company safe, nor should it be told to anyone who doesn't need to know it. The root password must usually be entered twice—just in case you should happen to make a typographic error, as the characters that you type are masked on the screen.

The root user should never be able to log in using telnet; instead, the *su* facility should be used by individual users to gain root privileges where necessary. This protects the root account since at least one other password is required to log in, unless the root user has access to the console. In addition, the su command should be owned by a sysadmin group (or similar) so that only those users who need access to the root account should be able to obtain it. Once su has been used to gain root access, the root user can use su to spawn a shell with the effective ID of any other user on the system. This is a security weakness because the root user could pretend to be another user and perform actions or modify data, which would be traceable to the effective user, and not to root.

The /etc/passwd and /etc/shadow Password Files

Each Solaris user has a username and password associated with his account, except when a user account has been explicitly locked (designated *LK*), or when a system account has been specified not to have a password at all (*NP*). Many early exploits of Solaris systems were associated with default passwords used on some system accounts; the most common method of gaining unauthorized access to a Solaris system remains password cracking and/or guessing. In this section, we examine the password database (*/etc/passwd*) and its more secure counterpart the shadow database (*/etc/shadow*), and we examine strategies for making passwords safer.

The standard password database is stored in the file */etc/passwd*, and looks like this:

```
# cat /etc/passwd
root:x:0:1:Super-User:/:/sbin/sh
daemon:x:1:1::/:
bin:x:2:2::/usr/bin:
sys:x:3:3::/:
adm:x:4:4:Admin:/var/adm:
lp:x:71:8:Line Printer Admin:/usr/spool/lp:
uucp:x:5:5:uucp Admin:/usr/lib/uucp:
nuucp:x:9:9:uucp Admin:/var/spool/uucppublic:/usr/lib/uucp/uucico
listen:x:37:4:Network Admin:/usr/net/nls:
nobody:x:60001:60001:Nobody:/:
noaccess:x:60002:60002:No Access User:/:
nobody4:x:65534:65534:SunOS 4.x Nobody:/:
security:x:1898:600:Security User:/security:/bin/ksh
natashia:x:1001:10::/dialup/natashia:/bin/sh
```

These fields have the following meaning:

- The username field, which has a maximum of eight characters
- The encrypted password field, which in a system using shadow passwords is crossed with an *x*
- The user ID field, which contains the numeric and unique UID
- The primary group ID field, which contains the numeric GID
- The user comment, which contains a description of the user
- The path to the user's home directory
- The user's default shell

In older versions of Solaris, the encrypted password field would have contained an encrypted password string such as "X14oLaiYg7bO2." However, this presented a security problem, because the login program required all users to have read access to the password file:

```
# ls -l /etc/passwd
-rw-r--r--   1 root      sys            605 Jul 24 11:04 /etc/passwd
```

Thus, any user with the lowest form privilege would be able to access the encrypted password field for the root user and could attempt to gain root access by guessing the password. A number of programs were specifically developed for this purpose, such as *crack*, which takes a standard Solaris password file and uses a dictionary and some clever lexical rules to guess passwords. Once a root password has been obtained, a rogue user may perform any operation on a Solaris system, including formatting hard disks, installing Trojan horses, and launching attacks on other systems.

The cryptographic algorithm used by Solaris is not easy to crack; indeed, a brute force guess of a password composed of a completely random set of characters would take many CPU years to compute. The task would be made even more difficult (if not impossible) if the root password was changed weekly, again with a random set of characters. However, the reality is that most users enter passwords that are easily guessed from a dictionary or from some knowledge about the user. Raise your hand if you've entered the name of a spouse, parent, child, or pet as a password—or a password like root, sun, windows, or linux. Since we are constantly required to use personal identification number (PINs) and passwords for access to our various bank accounts, computer accounts, and other sources of information, we tend to choose passwords that are easy to remember. However, easily remembered passwords are also the easiest to crack.

Solaris has reduced the chances of a rogue user obtaining the password file in the first place by implementing a *shadow* password facility. This creates a file called */etc/shadow* that is similar to the password file (*/etc/passwd*) but is readable only by root and contains the encrypted password fields for each UID. Thus, if a rogue user cannot obtain the encrypted password entries, it is impossible to use them as the basis for a crack attack.

A shadow password file corresponding to the password file (shown previously) looks like this:

```
# cat /etc/shadow
root:YTS88sd7fSS:10528:::::::
daemon:NP:6445:::::::
bin:NP:6445:::::::
sys:NP:6445:::::::
adm:NP:6445:::::::
lp:NP:6445:::::::
uucp:NP:6445:::::::
nuucp:NP:6445:::::::
listen:*LK*:::::::
nobody:NP:6445:::::::
noaccess:NP:6445:::::::
nobody4:NP:6445:::::::
security:*LK*:::::::
natashia:hY72er3Ascc:::::::
```

If a system is correctly installed, the */etc/passwd* file should be readable by all users, but it should contain no passwords. Conversely, the */etc/shadow* file should be readable only by root and should contain the encrypted password strings traditionally stored in */etc/passwd*.

Remote Access Tools

Remote access is the hallmark of modern multiple-user operating systems such as Solaris and its antecedents, such as VAX/VMS. Unlike the single-user Windows NT system, users can concurrently log into and interactively execute commands on Solaris server systems from any client that supports Transmission Control Protocol/Internet Protocol (TCP/IP), such as Solaris, NT, and Macintosh. Single-user remote access has now been made possible on Windows NT Server also using TCP/IP through products like Symantec's pcAnywhere; however, remote logins prevent concurrent console logins on NT. This is not the case with Solaris, which can support hundreds and thousands of interactive user shells at any one time, constrained only by memory and CPU availability.

In this section, we will examine several popular methods of remote access, such as Telnet, which have been popular historically. We will also outline the much-publicized security holes and bugs that have led to the innovation of secure remote access systems, such as Secure Shell (SSH). These "safer" systems facilitate the encryption of the contents of user sessions and/or authentication sequences and provide an important level of protection for sensitive data. Although remote access is useful, the administrative overhead in securing a Solaris system can be significant, reflecting the increased functionality that remote access services provide.

Telnet

Telnet is the standard remote access tool for logging into a Solaris machine from a client using the original DARPA TELNET protocol. A client can be executed on most operating systems that support TCP/IP. Alternatively, a Java Telnet client is available (**http:// srp.stanford.edu/~tjw/telnet.html**), which is supported on any operating system that has a browser that runs Java natively or as a plug-in. Telnet is a terminal-like program that gives users interactive access to a login shell of their choice (for example, the C-shell, or csh). Most Telnet clients support VT100 or VT220 terminal emulations. The login shell can be used to execute scripts, develop applications, and read e-mail and news—in short, everything a Solaris environment should provide to its users, with the exception of X11 graphics and Open Windows, or more recently, the common desktop environment (CDE). A common arrangement in many organizations is for a Solaris server to be located in a secure area of a building with Telnet-only access allowed. This arrangement is shown in Figure 9-1.

The sequence of events that occur during a Telnet session begins with a request for a connection from the client to the server. The server either responds (or times out) with a connection being explicitly accepted or rejected. A rejection may occur because the port that normally accepts Telnet client connections on the server has been blocked by a packet filter or firewall. If the connection is accepted, the client is asked to enter a username followed by a password. If the username and password combination is valid, a shell is spawned, and the user is logged in. This sequence of events in shown in Figure 9-2.

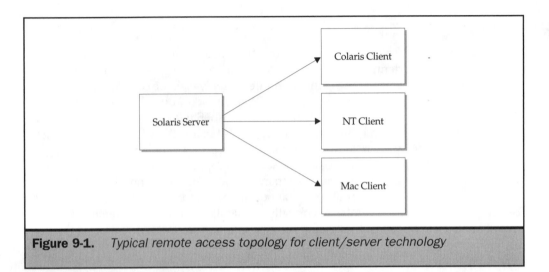

Figure 9-1. *Typical remote access topology for client/server technology*

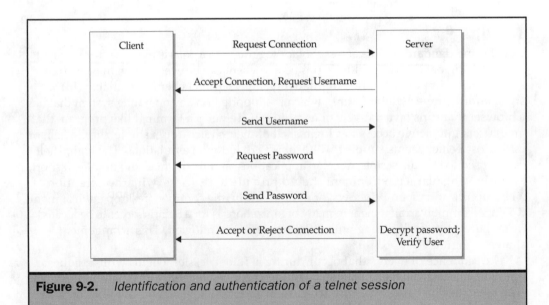

Figure 9-2. *Identification and authentication of a telnet session*

The standard port for Telnet connections is 23. Thus, a command like this,

```
$ telnet server
```

is expanded to give the effective command:

```
$ telnet server 25
```

This means that Telnet can be used as a tool to access a service on virtually any port. Telnet is controlled by the super Internet daemon (*inetd*), which invokes the in.telnetd server. An entry is made in */etc/services* that defines the port number for the Telnet service, which looks like this:

```
telnet    23/tcp
```

The configuration file */etc/inetd.conf* also contains important details of the services provided by *inetd*. The telnet daemon's location and properties are identified here:

```
telnet stream tcp nowait root /pkgs/tcpwrapper/bin/tcpd in.telnetd
```

In this case, we can see that *in.telnetd* is protected by the use of TCP *wrappers*, which facilitate the logging of Telnet accesses through the Solaris *syslog* facility. TCP wrappers are discussed in Chapter 30. In addition, *inetd* has some significant historical security holes and performance issues that, although mostly fixed in recent years, have caused administrators to shy away from servers invoked by *inetd*. The Apache Web server (**http://www.apache.org**), for example, runs as a standalone daemon process and does not use *inetd*.

inetd also controls many other standard remote access clients, including the so-called *r-commands*, including the remote login (*rlogin*) and remote shell (*rsh*) applications. The *rlogin* application is similar to Telnet in that it establishes a remote connection through TCP/IP to a server, spawning an interactive login shell. For example, the command

```
$ rlogin server
```

by default produces the response,

```
password:
```

after which the password is entered, authenticated by the server, and access denied or granted. If the target user account has a different name than your current user account, you can try this:

```
$ rlogin server -l user
```

There are two main differences between Telnet and *rlogin*, which are significant, however. The first is that *rlogin* attempts to use the username on your current system as the account name to connect to on the remote service, whereas Telnet always prompts for a separate username. This makes remotely logging into machines on a single logical network with *rlogin* much faster than with Telnet. Second, on a trusted, secure network, it is possible to set up a remote authentication mechanism by which the remote host allows a direct, no-username/no-password login from authorized clients. This automated authentication can be performed on a system-wide level by defining an "equivalent" host for authentication purposes on the server in */etc/hosts.equiv*, or on a user-by-user basis with the file *.rhosts*. If the file */etc/hosts.equiv* contains the client machine name and your username, you will be permitted to automatically execute a remote login. For example, if the */etc/hosts.equiv* file on the server contains this line,

```
client
```

any user from the machine client may log into a corresponding account on the server without entering a username and password. Similarly, if your username and client machine name appear in the *.rhosts* in the home directory of the user with the same name on the server, you will also be permitted to remotely log in without an identification/ authentication challenge. This means that a user on the remote system may log in with all the privileges of the user on the local system, without being asked to enter a username or password—clearly a dangerous security risk. The sequence of identification and authentication for rlogin is shown in Figure 9-3.

Remote-shell (*rsh*) connects to a specified hostname and executes a command. *rsh* is equivalent to *rlogin* when no command arguments are specified. *rsh* copies its standard input to the `remote` command, the standard output of the `remote` command to its standard output, and the standard error of the `remote` command to its standard error. Interrupt, quit, and terminate signals are propagated to the `remote` command. In contrast to commands issued interactively through *rlogin*, *rsh* normally terminates when the `remote` command does.

As an example, the following command executes the command df -k on the server, returning information about disk slices and creating the local file server.*df.txt* that contains the output of the command:

```
$ rsh server df -k > server.df.txt
```

Clearly, *rsh* has the potential to be useful in scripts and automated command processing.

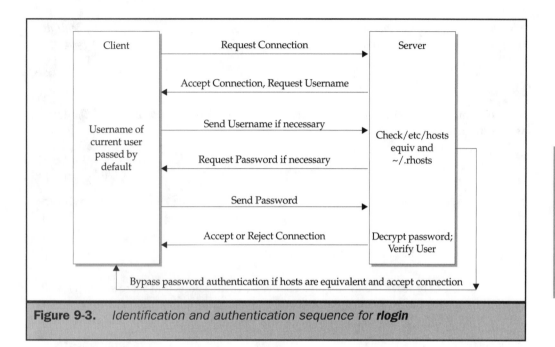

Figure 9-3. *Identification and authentication sequence for rlogin*

Procedures

The following procedures can be used to implement basic Solaris security measures.

Checking File and Directory Ownership

One of the most confusing issues for novice users of Solaris is understanding the Solaris file access permissions system. The basic approach to setting and interpreting relative file permissions involves a set of symbolic codes that represent users and permission types. However, even advanced users may find it difficult to understand the *octal* permissions codes used to set *absolute* permissions. When combined with a default permission mask set in the user's shell (the umask), octal permission codes are more powerful than symbolic permission codes. In this section, we review only relative file permissions using symbolic codes.

The Solaris UNIX File System (UFS) permits three basic kinds of file access—the ability to read (*r*), to write (*w*), and to execute (*x*) a file or directory. These permissions can be granted exclusively or nonexclusively on individual files or on a group of files specified by a wildcard character (*). These permissions can be set using the chmod command, in combination with a plus (+) operator. Permissions can be easily removed with the chmod command using the minus (–) operator.

For example, to set read permissions (for the current user) on the file */usr/local/lib/ libproxy.a*, we would use this command:

```
$ chmod +r /usr/local/lib/libproxy.a
```

Alternatively, to set read permissions for all users on the file */usr/local/lib/libproxy.a*, we would use this command:

```
$ chmod a+r /usr/local/lib/libproxy.a
```

To remove read permissions on the file */usr/local/lib/libproxy.a* for all users who are not members of the current user's default group, we would use this command:

```
$ chmod o-r /usr/local/lib/libproxy.a
```

This does not remove the group and user read permissions that were set previously. Similarly, execute and write permissions can be set. For example, to set execute permissions on the */usr/local/bin/gcc files* for each class of user (current user, group, and world), we would use these commands:

```
$ chmod u+x /usr/local/bin/gcc
$ chmod g+x /usr/local/bin/gcc
$ chmod o+x /usr/local/bin/gcc
```

To explicitly remove write permissions on the */usr/local/bin/gcc* files for each class of user (current user, group, and world), we would use these commands:

```
$ chmod u-w /usr/local/bin/gcc
$ chmod g-w /usr/local/bin/gcc
$ chmod o-w /usr/local/bin/gcc
```

The rationale behind using read and write permissions should be clear: permitting read access on a file allows an identified user to access the text of a file by reading it byte-by-byte, while write access permits the user to modify or delete any file upon which the write permission is granted, regardless of who originally created the file. Thus, individual users can create files that are readable and writeable by any other user on the system.

The permission to execute a file must be granted on scripts (such as shell scripts or Perl scripts) to be executed, while compiled and linked applications must also have the execute bit set on a specific application. The executable permission must also be granted on the special files that represent directories on the file system if the directory's contents are to be accessed by a specific class of user.

The various options available for granting file access permissions can sometimes lead to interesting but confusing scenarios; for example, permissions can be set to allow a group to delete a file but not execute it. More usefully, a group might be given execute permission on an application but be unable to write over it. In addition, setting file permissions using relative permission strings (rather than absolute octal permission codes) means that permissions set by a previous chmod change of permission command are not revoked by any subsequent chmod command.

However, the permissions themselves are only half the story: unlike those on single-user file systems, permissions on Solaris are associated with different file owners (that is, all files and processes on a Solaris system are "owned" by a specific user). In addition, groups of users can be granted read, write, and execute permissions on a file or set of files stored in a directory.

Alternatively, file permissions can be granted on a system-wide basis, effectively granting file access without respect to file ownership. Since file systems can be exported using NFS and/or Samba, it's bad practice to grant system-wide read, write, and execute permissions on any file, unless every user needs access to that file. For example, all users need to read the password database (*/etc/passwd*), but only the root user should have read access to the shadow password database (*/etc/shadow*). Blindly exporting all files with global read, write, or execute permissions on a NFS-shared volume is inviting trouble!

The three file system categories of ownership are defined by three permission setting categories: the user (*u*) who owns the file, group members (*g*) who have access to the file, and all other users (*o*) on the system. The group specified by *g* can be the user's primary group (as defined in */etc/passwd*) or a secondary group to which the file has been assigned (as defined in */etc/group*). It is important to remember that there are ultimately few secrets on a Solaris file system: the root user has full access at all times (read, write, and execute) on all files on the file system, so even if a user removes all permissions on a file, the rule of root is absolute. If the contents of a file really need to be hidden, it is best to encrypt a file's contents using Pretty Good Privacy (PGP), *crypt*, or a similar utility. A root user can also change the ownership of a file—thus, a user's files do not absolutely belong to a specific user. The chown command can only be used by the super-user for this purpose.

Policies regarding default file permissions need to be set selectively in different environments. For example, in a production Web server system that processes credit card data, access should be denied by default to all users except those who are required to conduct online transactions (such as the apache user for the Apache Web server). On a system that supports team-based development, obviously permissions will need to be set that allow the exchange of data among team partners, but that prevent the access to development files by others. There are few Solaris systems that would allow a default world-writeable policy on any file system, except for the temporary swap (I) file system.

It is possible to enforce system-wide permissions by using a default umask, which sets the read, write, and execute permissions on all new files created by a specific user. If a user wishes to use a umask other than the default system-wide setting, this can be achieved by setting umask on the command line when required by using the umask command, or in the user's shell start-up file (for example .kshrc for the Korn shell).

Access Control Lists

One problem with assigning file access permissions is that users other than oneself fall into two categories: group members or nongroup members. Thus, if you want to make some files available to one group of users, and not another, you will need to ask the system administrator to create a group for you. Of course, the main problem with the random group creation approach is group sprawl—administrators are generally unwilling to create groups at the request of users because of the overhead in administering potentially hundreds of different groups on each system.

The best solution to the problem is to leave group members to reflect organizational divisions, but to use access control lists (ACLs) to manage file access. While it may seem like creating more work to have two sets of file access permissions operating, in reality, it's the simplest solution for users that doesn't require super-user permission.

To grant the user charles read-only access to the file secret.doc that is owned by the user ainsley and has read-write permissions only for ainsley, the following command would be executed by ainsley:

```
$ setfacl -m user:charles:r--secret.doc
```

Alternatively, to allow charles to have read-write access to the file, the following command can be used:

```
$ setfacl -m user:charles:rw-secret.doc
```

When an ACL has been set, the file listing shows a + symbol at the end of the permissions string:

```
# ls -l /home/charles/secret.doc
-rw-------+   1 charles     admin          105433   Jan 24 12:07
     /home/charles/secret.doc
```

The `getfacl` command can be used to display the ACLs for any file on the file system, displaying the real and effective access permissions on files as determined by file permissions and ACLs.

Monitoring User Activity

System access can be monitored interactively using a number of measures. For example, *syslog* entries can be automatically viewed in real time using this command:

```
$ tail -f /var/adm/messages
```

However, most administrators want to view interactively what remote users are doing on a system at any time. We will examine two methods here for viewing remote user activity. The command who displays who is currently logged into the system. The output of who displays the username, connecting line, date of login, idle time, process id, and a comment. Here's an example output:

```
$ who
root           console       Nov 22 12:39
natashia    pts/0          Nov 19 21:05      (client.site.com)
```

This command can be automated to update the list of active users. An alternative to who is the w command, which displays a more detailed summary of the current activity on the system, including the current process name for each user. The header output from w shows the current time, the uptime of the current system, and the number of users actively logged into the system. The average system load is also displayed as a series of three numbers at the end of the w header, indicating the average number of jobs in the run queue for the previous 1, 5, and 15 minutes. In addition to the output generated by who, the w command displays the current foreground process for each user, which is usually a shell. For example, the following command shows that the root user has an active *shelltool* running under Open Windows, while the user natashia is running the Cornell shell:

```
7:15pm  up 1 day(s),  5:11,  2 users,  load average: 1.00, 1.00, 1.01
User      tty            login@ idle   JCPU   PCPU  what
root    console      Thu12pm 3days     6      6    shelltool
natashia   pts/12        Thu11am  8:45     9            /usr/local/bin/tcsh
```

The w and who commands are useful tools for getting an overview of current usage patterns on any Solaris system. Another useful command is last, which displays historical usage patterns for the current system in a sequential format:

```
$ last
natashia   pts/4        hp               Wed Apr 11 19:00    still logged in
root       console      :0               Tue Apr 10 20:11    still logged in
natashia   pts/2        nec              Tue Apr 10 19:17 - 19:24  (00:06)
natashia   pts/6        austin           Tue Apr 10 15:53 - 15:53  (00:00)
root       console      :0               Tue Apr 10 14:24 - 16:25  (02:01)
reboot     system boot                   Tue Apr 10 14:04
natashia   pts/5        hp               Thu Apr  5 21:38 - 21:40  (00:01)
natashia   pts/5        hp               Thu Apr  5 21:22 - 21:37  (00:15)
natashia   pts/5        10.64.18.1       Thu Apr  5 19:30 - 20:00  (00:30)
natashia   pts/5        hp               Thu Apr  5 19:18 - 19:29  (00:11)
root       console      :0               Thu Apr  5 19:17 - 22:05  (4+02:48)
```

```
reboot     system boot              Thu Apr  5 19:14
natashia   pts/5         hp         Tue Apr  3 16:14 - 18:26  (02:11)
natashia   pts/5         hp         Tue Apr  3 08:48 - 10:35  (01:47)
root       console       :0         Tue Apr  3 08:45 - 22:01  (13:15)
reboot     system boot              Tue Apr  3 08:43
root       console       :0         Fri Mar 30 18:54 - 19:27  (00:32)
reboot     system boot              Fri Mar 30 18:46
natashia   pts/6         hp         Tue Mar 27 20:46 - 21:51  (01:04)
root       console       :0         Tue Mar 27 19:50 - 21:51  (02:01)
reboot     system boot              Tue Mar 27 19:48
root       console       :0         Mon Mar 26 17:43 - 17:47  (00:04)
```

Testing Service Connectivity

Since a port number can be specified on the command line, Telnet clients can be used to connect to arbitrary ports on Solaris servers. This makes a Telnet client a useful tool for testing whether services that should have been disconnected are actually active. For example, you can interactively issue commands to an FTP server on port 21,

```
$ telnet server 21
Trying 172.16.1.1...
Connected to server.
Escape character is '^]'.
220 server FTP server (UNIX(r) System V Release 4.0) ready.
```

and on a sendmail server on port 25:

```
$ telnet server 25
Trying 172.16.1.1...
Connected to server.
Escape character is '^]'.
220 server ESMTP Sendmail 8.9.1a/8.9.1; Mon, 22 Nov 1999
    14:31:36 +1100 (EST)
```

Interactive testing of this kind has many uses. For example, if we Telnet to port 80 on a server, we are usually connected to a Web server, where we can issue interactive commands using the Hypertext Transfer Protocol (HTTP). For example, to GET the default index page on a server, we could type **GET index.html**:

```
Trying 172.16.1.1...
Connected to server.
Escape character is '^]'.
```

```
GET index.html
<!DOCTYPE HTML PUBLIC "-//IETF//DTD HTML 2.0//EN">
<HTML><HEAD>
<TITLE>Server</TITLE></HEAD>
<h1>Welcome to server!</h1>
...
```

This technique is useful when testing proxy server configurations for new kinds of HTTP clients (for example, a HotJava browser), or it can be executed during a script to check whether the Web server is active and serving expected content.

Securing Remote Access

One of the unfortunate drawbacks of the Telnet system is that usernames, and especially unencrypted passwords, are transmitted in *cleartext* around the network. Thus, if you were using a Telnet client to connect from a cyber café in Paris to a server in New York, your traffic might pass through 20 or 30 routers and computers, all of which can be programmed to "sniff" the contents of network packets. A sample *traceroute* of the path taken by packets from AT&T to Sun's Web page looks like this:

```
$ traceroute www.sun.com
Tracing route to wwwwseast.usec.sun.com [192.9.49.30]
over a maximum of 30 hops:
  1    184 ms    142 ms    138 ms   202.10.4.131
  2    147 ms    144 ms    138 ms   202.10.4.129
  3    150 ms    142 ms    144 ms   202.10.1.73
  4    150 ms    144 ms    141 ms   ia4.optus.net.au [202.139.32.17]
  5    148 ms    143 ms    139 ms   202.139.1.197
  6    490 ms    489 ms    474 ms   sf1.optus.net.au [192.65.89.246]
  7    526 ms    480 ms    485 ms   gn.cwix.net [207.124.109.57]
  8    494 ms    482 ms    485 ms   core7.SanFrancisco.cw.net [204.70.10.9]
  9    483 ms    489 ms    484 ms   core2.SanFrancisco.cw.net [204.70.9.132]
 10    557 ms    552 ms    561 ms   xcore3.Boston.cw.net [204.70.150.81]
 11    566 ms    572 ms    554 ms   sun.Boston.cw.net [204.70.179.102]
 12    577 ms    574 ms    558 ms   wwwwseast.usec.sun.com [192.9.49.30]
Trace complete.
```

That's a lot of intermediate hosts, any of which could potentially be sniffing passwords and other sensitive data. If the network packet that contains the username and password is sniffed in this way, a rogue user could easily log into the target account using a Telnet client. This risk has led to the development of Secure Shell (SSH) and similar products that encrypt the exchange of username and password information between client and server, making it difficult for sniffers to extract useful information from network packets. OpenSSH is now supplied with Solaris for the first time with the release of Solaris 9.

Although *rlogin* is the fastest kind of remote login possible, it can be easily exploited on systems that are not trusted and secure. Systems that are directly connected to the Internet, or those that form part of a subnet that is not firewalled, should never be considered secure. These kinds of configurations can be dangerous in some circumstances, even if they are convenient for remotely administering many different machines.

The most dangerous use of */etc/hosts.equiv* occurs, for example, when the file contains the single line

```
+
```

This allows any users from any host that has equivalent usernames to remotely log in.

The *.rhosts* file is also considered dangerous in some situations. For example, it is common practice in some organizations to allow the root and privileged users to permit automatic logins by root users from other machines by creating a */.rhosts* file. A more insidious problem can occur when users define their own *.rhosts* files in their own home directories. These files are not directly controlled by the system administrator and may be exploited by malicious remote users. One way to remove this threat is to enforce a policy of disallowing user *.rhosts* files and activating a nightly cron job to search for and remove any files named *.rhosts* in the user directories. A cron entry for a root like this

```
0 2 * * * find /staff -name .rhosts -print -exec rm{} \;
```

should execute this simple find and remove command every morning at 2 A.M. for all user accounts whose home directories lie within the */staff* partition.

Examples

The following examples show how to implement basic security measures for Solaris.

File Permissions

We start our examination of Solaris file permissions by examining how to create files, set permissions, change ownership and group membership, and use the ls command to examine existing file permissions. All these commands can be used by nonprivileged users, except for the chown command.

The ls command is the main directory and file permission listing program used in Solaris. When displaying a long listing, it prints file access permissions, user and group ownership, file size and creation date, and the filename. For example, for the password file */etc/passwd*, the output from ls would look like this:

```
$ ls -l /etc/passwd
-r--r--r--   1 root     other         256 Sep  18 00:40 passwd
```

This directory entry can be read from left to right in the following way:

- The password file is not a directory, indicated by the first "-"
- The password file has read-only permissions for the owner *r*— (but not execute or write permissions)
- The password file has read-only permissions for group members *r*—
- The password file has read-only permissions for other dialup *r*—
- The password file is owned by the root user
- The password file has other group permissions
- The password file size is 256K
- The password file was created on September 18 at 00:40 A.M.
- The name of the password file is *passwd*

The permissions string shown changes depending on the permissions that have been set by the owner. For example, if the password file had execute and write permissions for the root user, the permissions string would read *–rwxr—r—* rather than just *–r—r—r—*. Each of the permissions can be set using symbolic or octal permissions codes by using the chmod command.

We've seen how a normal file looks under ls, but let's compare this with a directory entry, which is a special kind of file that is usually created with the mkdir command:

```
$ mkdir samples
```

We can check the permissions of the directory entry by using the ls command:

```
$ ls -l
total 8
drwxrwxr-x   2 root     other         512 Sep  5 13:41 samples
```

The directory entry for the directory samples can be read from left to right in the following way:

- The directory entry is a special file denoted by a leading *d*
- The directory entry has read, write, and execute permissions for the owner *rwx*
- The directory entry has read, write, and execute permissions for group members *rwx*

- The directory entry has read and execute permissions for other dialup *r-x*
- The directory entry is owned by the root user
- The directory entry has other group permissions
- The directory entry size is 512K
- The directory entry was created on September 5 at 1:41 P.M.
- The name of the directory is *samples*

For a directory to be accessible to a particular class of user, the executable bit must be set using the chmod command.

Using Remote Access Tools

With the increased use of the Internet for business-to-business and consumer-to-business transactions, securing remote access has become a major issue in the provision of Solaris services. Fortunately, solutions based around the encryption of sessions and authentication of clients have improved the reliability of remote access facilities in a security-conscious operating environment.

Secure Shell (SSH)

Open Secure Shell OpenSSH or just plain SSH is a secure client and server solution that facilitates the symmetric and asymmetric encryption of identification and authentication sequences for remote access. It is designed to replace the Telnet and *rlogin* applications on the client side, with clients available for Solaris, Windows, and many other operating systems. On the server side, it improves upon the nonsecure services supported by *inetd*, such as the r-commands. Figure 9-4 shows a typical SSH client session for vpn.cassowary.net from a Windows client.

SSH makes use of a generic transport layer encryption mechanism over TCP/IP, which uses the popular Blowfish or government-endorsed triple-DES (Data Encryption Standard) algorithms for the encryption engine. This is used to transmit encrypted packets whose contents can still be sniffed like all traffic on the network by using public key cryptography, implementing the Deffie-Helman algorithm for key exchange. Thus, the contents of encrypted packets appears to be random without the appropriate "key" to decrypt them.

The use of encryption technology makes it extremely unlikely that the contents of the interactive session will ever be known to anyone except the client and the server. In addition to the encryption of session data, identification and authentication sequences are also encrypted using RSA encryption technology. This means that username and password combinations also cannot be sniffed by a third party. SSH also provides automatic forwarding for graphics applications, based around the X11 windowing system, which is a substantial improvement over the text-only Telnet client.

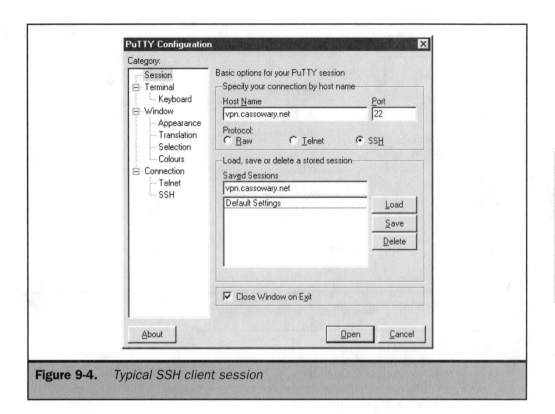

Figure 9-4.   *Typical SSH client session*

The sequence of events for establishing a SSH client connection to a server is demonstrated in Figure 9-5, and proceeds as follows:

1. The client connects to a server port requesting a connection (usually port 22, but this can be adapted to suit local conditions).

2. The server replies with its standard public RSA host key (1024 bits), as well as another RSA server key (768 bits) that changes hourly. Since the server key changes hourly, even if the keys for the traffic of one session was cracked, historic data would still remain encrypted, limiting the utility of any such attack.

3. The server can be configured to reject connections from hosts that it doesn't know about, but by default, it will accept connections from any client.

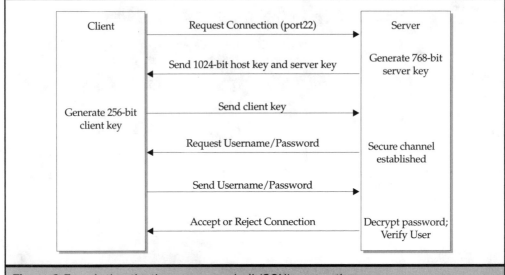

Figure 9-5. *Authenticating a secure shell (SSH) connection*

4. If the connection is accepted, the client generates a session key composed of a 256-bit random number and chooses an encryption algorithm that the server supports (triple-DES or Blowfish).

5. The client then encrypts the session key using RSA, using both the host and server key, and returns the encrypted key to the server.

6. The server decrypts the session key and encryption is enabled between the client and server.

7. If the default authentication mechanism is selected, the client passes the username and password for the server across the secure channel.

It is possible to disable the username/password authentication sequence by permitting logins to clients that have an appropriate private RSA key, as long as the server has a list of accepted public keys. However, if a client computer is stolen, and the private key is retrieved by a rogue user, access to the server can be obtained without a valid username and password combination.

On the client side, a *knwnhsts.txt* file is created and server keys are recorded there. Entries look like this:

```
server 1024 35 07448318855220650928863459182148090008748760313126632026365561406995692291726767198155252016701986067549820423736393736593998729350847306606972263971147429524250769197415119584295606317662645984226922061878553598043326806246000016982513757260
```

```
2927556592987704211810142126175715452796748871506131894685401576
4183
```

In addition, a private key for the client is stored in *Identity*, and a public key for the client is stored in *Identity.pub*. Entries in this file are similar to the server key file:

```
1024 37 2590984202231997581736656902901504139087369478896425656721464229667226227437398365816534529060328087939018802894227642524259614636549518998450524923811481002360439473852363542223359868114619253961948185309446681933562979774158070860950587770774247373117735318506922304377996946111769127284747352249217710411151
Paul Watters
```

It is sensible in a commercial context to enforce a policy of SSH-only remote access for interactive logins. This can easily be enforced by enabling the SSH daemon on the server side and removing entries for the Telnet and *rlogin* services in */etc/services* and */etc/inetd.conf*. Now that OpenSSH is supplied with Solaris, there is no excuse for not deploying SSH across all hosts in your local network.

Kerberos

While SSH is an excellent tool for remote access between a single client and multiple servers, maintaining local databases of keys on every client machine is costly in terms of disk space and network traffic. Although some argue that such information should always be distributed across the network, the level of redundancy that SSH requires for installations of 1000 or more clients is inefficient.

One alternative to using SSH servers as the primary means of authentication across a network is to use a centralized authentication system such as Kerberos, which grew out of the Athena Project at the Massachusetts Institute of Technology (MIT). Kerberos is a network authentication protocol that is designed to provide strong authentication for client/server applications by using secret-key cryptography, which is similar to that provided by SSH. However, the main difference between the two systems is that while authentication is performed by the target server when using SSH, a Kerberos authentication server can provide services to many different servers for a large number of clients. Thus, The Many Relationships Realized In The Kerberos Authentication Database Makes The network authentication process more streamlined and efficient.

Kerberos is also designed to provide authentication to hosts inside and outside a firewall, since many attacks may originate in internal networks that are normally considered trusted. In addition, Release 5 introduced the notion of *realms*, which are external but trusted networks with authentication being extended beyond the firewall. Another advantage of the Kerberos system is that the protocol has been published and widely publicized. Of course, the greatest advantage for Solaris users is that it's no longer necessary to download the free implementation from MIT. While Solaris 8 supplied client tools for Kerberos, Solaris 9 now supports Kerberos servers and clients that are compliant with Kerberos Release 5 v1.1. The Kerberos daemon in Solaris is kadmind, which is responsible for running the primary Key Distribution Center (KDC).

Kerberos is based on a certificate granting and validation system called tickets. If a client machine wants to make a connection to a target server, it requests a ticket from a centralized authentication server, which can be physically the same machine as the target server but is logically quite separate. An encrypted ticket is produced by the authentication server that authorizes the client to request a specific service from a specific host, generally for a specific time period. This is similar to a parking ticket machine that grants the drivers of motor vehicles permission to park on a specific street for one or two hours only. Release 5 of Kerberos supports tickets that can be renewed.

When authentication is requested from the authentication server, a session key is created by that server that is based on your password, which it retrieves from your username—a random value that represents the requested service. The session key is like a voucher that the client then sends to a ticket-granting server, which then returns a ticket that can be used to access the target server. Clearly, some overhead is involved in making a request to an authentication server, a ticket-granting server, and a target server. However, the overhead is well worth the effort if important data is at risk of interception. The sequence of events leading to authentication is shown in Figure 9-6.

A significant limitation of Kerberos is that all applications that make use of its authentication services must be "kerberized"—that is, significant changes must be made to the application's source code for it to make use of Kerberos services.

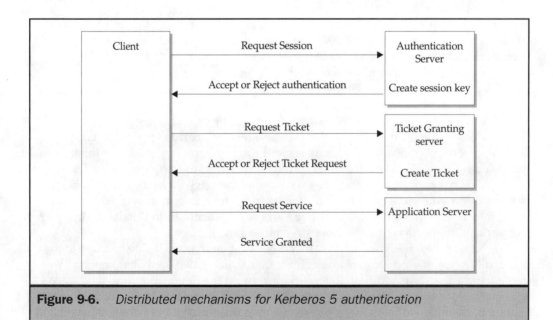

Figure 9-6. *Distributed mechanisms for Kerberos 5 authentication*

Kerberos configuration is reasonably straightforward given appropriate network resources. A configuration file (*/etc/krb5/krb5.conf*) contains entries like this:

```
[libdefaults]
        default_realm = site.com

[realms]
        site.com = {
                kdc = kerberos1.site.com
                kdc = kerberos2.site.com
                admin_server = kerberos1.site.com
        }
```

This configuration is for a domain called *site.com*, which has a primary KDC called *kerberos1.site.com* and a backup server called *kerberos2.site.com*. In addition to *krb5.conf*, several other configuration files are maintained by Kerberos:

- */var/krb5/principal.db*   Database of principals
- */var/krb5/principal.kadm5*   Principal management database
- */etc/krb5/kadm5.acl*   Access Control List for principals
- */etc/krb5/kadm5.keytab*   Local keytab

Secure Remote Password Protocol

The Secure Remote Password (SRP) protocol is the core technology behind the Stanford SRP Authentication Project. The project is an open source initiative that integrates secure password authentication into existing networked applications. The project's primary purpose is to improve network security from the ground up by integrating secure password authentication into widely used protocols instead of adding security as an afterthought. SRP makes these objectives possible because it offers a unique combination of password security and user convenience, and because it is free of intellectual property encumbrances.

First and foremost, SRP is a strong password authentication protocol. It was designed as a solution to the age-old problem of deploying logins and passwords in a distributed system across networks that may be monitored or compromised by adversaries. While the strongest version of SRP, known as SRP-3, performs well in such a role, it is also versatile enough to serve in other capacities, namely as a *zero-knowledge identification* protocol, which is highly desirable as these protocols do not leak information about the password even to a legitimate host, and which provides protection against both passive snooping and active host impersonation. SRP also provides an asymmetric key-exchange protocol (secure key exchange is provided but does not require both parties to share secrets before the exchange takes place).

SRP is the newest addition to a new class of strong authentication protocols that resist all the well-known passive and active attacks over the network. It generates keys that are cryptographically strong. It is also safe against snooping, since the password is never passed over the network, either in the clear or encrypted. This is in contrast to SSH, which enables an encrypted exchange of passwords across the network. By use of a session key similar to Kerberos, a compromised password will not allow an intruder to decrypt past sessions because it is time-locked.

Technically, SRP is quite simple, because it based on exponentiation, addition, multiplication, and hashing, all of which are easily understood and implemented. SRP is also fast, and typical unoptimized implementations have been shown to take under a second to complete authentication.

SRP addresses a fairly specific class of hard password authentication problems, namely that of authenticating a network user to a server host, both of which reside on a network susceptible to both passive and active attacks and subject to several constraints. Unlike Kerberos, no third party is involved in the authentication process. The system supports only password authentication, unlike SSH, which supports either passwords or certificate-based authentication.

The current SRP distribution can be downloaded from **http://srp.stanford.edu/**.

Command Reference

The following commands are commonly used to secure Solaris systems.

kadmin

The `kadmin` command is used to manage local Kerberos services, by administering keytabs, principals, and policies. There are two versions of `kadmin` available; `kadmin.local` is used only on the master KDC and does not require authentication, and `lkadmin`, when executed on any other server, requires Kerberos authentication across a secure link. Once logged in, the following prompt is displayed, ready for commands to be entered:

```
kadmin:
```

When `kadmin` starts up, it checks the value of the USER environment variable to determine the principal name. For example, if USER=pwatters, then the principal name would be pwatters/admin. Alternatively, the *–p* option can be passed to `kadmin` when starting up followed by the principal name. In addition, if a realm other than the default is to be administered, the realm name must be supplied on the command line after the *-r* option is passed. The user will be prompted for a password, unless one has been passed on the command line with the *-w* option. Thus, to start `kadmin` for the *realm site.com* with the principal pwatters/admin and the password 6fgj4gsd, the following command would be used:

```
# kadmin -p pwatters/admin -r site.com -w 6fgj4gsd
```

The following commands are supported by `kadmin`:

`list_requests`	Displays all kadmin commands
`add_principal`	Adds a new principal
`get_privs`	Displays the Access Control Lists (ACLs) for the current principal
`-expire`	Sets the principal's effective end date
`-pwexpire`	Sets the principal's password effective end date
`-maxlife`	Specifies an upper time limit for tickets
`-maxrenewlife`	Specifies an upper time limit for ticket renewal
`-policy`	Sets the policy name
`-pw`	Sets the principal's password
`delete_principal`	Completely removes a principal
`modify_principal`	Updates principal's characteristics
`get_principal`	Displays the principal's characteristics
`list_principals`	Prints all known principal names
`add_policy`	Attaches a new policy
`delete_policy`	Completely removes a policy
`get_policy`	Displays the characteristics of a policy
`list_policy`	Displays policy names
`ktadd`	Attaches a principal to a keytab
`ktadd`	Removes a principal from a keytab

kdb5_util

The kdb5_util program is used to manage the Kerberos database files. It accepts the database name as an argument on the command line after the -d option has been passed. One of the following options must also be included to perform a specific action:

create	Creates a new database
destroy	Deletes an existing database
stash	Initializes a stash file to store the master key for the database
dump	Exports the database to ASCII format
load	Imports the database from ASCII format

The Complete Reference

Solaris 9

Part III

Managing Users and Roles

The
Complete
Reference

Solaris

Chapter 10

User and Group Management

The concept of the user is central to Solaris—all processes and files on a Solaris system are "owned" by a particular user and are assigned to a specific user group. No data or activities on the system may exist without a valid user or group. Managing users and groups as a Solaris administrator can be a challenging activity—you will be responsible for assigning all of the privileges granted or denied to a user or group of users, and many of these permissions carry great risk. For example, a user with an inappropriate privilege level may execute commands as the super-user, causing damage to your system. In this chapter, you will learn how to add users to the system and add and modify groups. In addition, the contents and structure of key user databases, including the password, shadow password, and group files, are examined in detail. Finally, we introduce the *admintool*, which is a GUI-based user-administration tool designed to make user management easier under Solaris.

Key Concepts

The following concepts are required knowledge for managing users and groups.

Users

All users on a Solaris system have a number of unique identifiers and characteristics that can be used to distinguish individual users from each other, and also to logically group related users. Most physical users of a Solaris system will have a unique "login" assigned to them, which is identified by a username with a maximum of eight characters. Once a user account is created, it can be used for the following purposes:

- Spawning a shell
- Executing applications interactively
- Scheduling applications to run on specific times and dates
- Access database applications and other system services

In addition to user accounts, Solaris also uses a number of predefined system accounts (such as *root*, *daemon*, *bin*, *sys*, *lp*, *adm*, and *uucp*) to perform various kinds of routine maintenance, including the following:

- Allocation of system resources to perform specific tasks
- Running a mail server
- Running a Web server
- Process management

Users may access a Solaris system by accessing the console, or through a remote terminal, in either graphical or text mode. In each case, a set of authentication credentials is presented to the system, including the username and password. When entered, a user's password is compared to an encrypted string stored in the password database (*/etc/passwd*) or the shadow password database (*/etc/shadow*). Once the string entered by the user has been encrypted, it is matched against the already encrypted entry in the password database. If a match is made, authentication occurs, and the user may spawn a shell. A Solaris username may have a maximum of eight characters, as may a Solaris password. Because the security of a Solaris system relies heavily on the difficulty of guessing passwords, user policies should be developed to either recommend or enforce the use of passwords containing random or semirandom character strings. The specific characteristics of the password can be defined in the */etc/default/passwd* file.

A number of other user characteristics are associated with each user, in addition to a username and password. These features include the following:

- **The User ID (UID)**, which is a unique integer that begins with the *root* user (UID=0), with other UIDs typically (but not necessarily) being allocated sequentially. Some administrators will reserve all UIDs below 1023 for system accounts (e.g., the "apache" user for managing the Apache Web server); those UIDs above 1024 are designated for ordinary users. The UID of 0 designates the super-user account, which is typically called "root."

- **A flexible mechanism for distinguishing different classes of users, known as groups.** Groups are not just sets of related users: The Solaris file system allows for group-designated read, write, and execute file access for groups, in addition to permissions granted to the individual user and to all users. Every UID is associated with a primary group ID (GID), however, UIDs may also be associated with more than one secondary group.

- **A home directory**, which is the default file storage location for all files created by a particular user. If the automounter is used, then home directories may be exported using NFS on */home*, as discussed in Chapter 24. When a user spawns a login shell, the current working directory will always be the home directory.

- **A login shell**, which can be used to issue commands interactively or to write simple programs. A number of different shells are available under Solaris, including the Bourne shell (*sh*), C shell (*csh*), the Bourne again shell (*bash*), and the Cornell shell (*tcsh*). The choice of shell depends largely on personal preference, user experience with C-like programming constructs, and terminal handling.

- **A comment**, which is typically the user's full name, such as "Paul Watters." However, system accounts may use names that describe their purpose (e.g., the command "Web Server" might be associated with the apache user).

Groups

Solaris provides a facility for identifying sets of related users into groups. Each user is associated with a primary group ID (GID), which is associated with a name. The group name and GID can be used interchangeably. In addition, users can also be associated with one or more secondary groups. This flexibility means that although a user might have a primary group membership based on their employment or organizational status (e.g., "staff" or "managers"), they can actively share data and system privileges with other groups based on their workgroup needs (e.g., "sales" or "engineer").

All information about groups in Solaris is stored in the groups database (*/etc/group*). Let's examine a typical set of groups:

```
# cat /etc/group
root::0:root
other::1:
bin::2:root,bin,daemon
sys::3:root,bin,sys,adm
adm::4:root,adm,daemon
uucp::5:root,uucp
mail::6:root
tty::7:root,tty,adm
lp::8:root,lp,adm
nuucp::9:root,nuucp
staff::10:paul,maya,brad,natashia
postgres:a.mBzQnr1ei2D.:100:postgres, paul
daemon::12:root,daemon
sysadmin::14:
nobody::60001:
noaccess::60002:
nogroup::65534:
```

You can see that the lower group numbers are associated with all of the system functions and accounts, such as the *bin* group, which has the members *root*, *bin*, and *daemon*, and the *sys* group, which has the members *root*, *bin*, *sys*, and *adm*. Higher numbered groups, such as staff, contain several different users, such as paul, maya, brad, and natashia. Notice also that paul has a secondary group membership in the *postgres* group, giving him database access privileges. A group password can also be set for each group to restrict access, although most groups don't use this facility. In this group database, you can see that the *postgres* group is the only group that has an encrypted password (*a.mBzQnr1ei2D.*).

You can obtain a list of all groups that a user belongs to by using the groups command. For example, to view all of the groups that the *root* users belongs to, use this command:

```
# groups root
other root bin sys adm uucp mail tty lp nuucp daemon
```

Passwords

All Solaris users have a username and password associated with their account, except where a user account has been explicitly locked (designated *LK*), or where a system account has been specified not to have a password at all (NP). Many early exploits of Solaris systems were associated with default passwords used on some system accounts, and the most common method of gaining unauthorized access to a Solaris system remains password cracking and/or guessing. In this section, we examine the password database (*/etc/passwd*) and its more secure counterpart the shadow database (*/etc/shadow*), and we examine strategies for making passwords safer.

The standard password database is stored in the file */etc/passwd*, and it looks like this:

```
# cat /etc/passwd
root:x:0:1:Super-User:/:/sbin/sh
daemon:x:1:1::/:
bin:x:2:2::/usr/bin:
sys:x:3:3::/:
adm:x:4:4:Admin:/var/adm:
lp:x:71:8:Line Printer Admin:/usr/spool/lp:
uucp:x:5:5:uucp Admin:/usr/lib/uucp:
nuucp:x:9:9:uucp Admin:/var/spool/uucppublic:/usr/lib/uucp/uucico
listen:x:37:4:Network Admin:/usr/net/nls:
nobody:x:60001:60001:Nobody:/:
noaccess:x:60002:60002:No Access User:/:
nobody4:x:65534:65534:SunOS 4.x Nobody:/:
postgres:x:1001:100:Postgres User:/usr/local/postgres:/bin/sh
htdig:x:1002:10:htdig:/opt/www:/usr/local/bin/bash
apache:x:1003:10:apache user:/usr/local/apache:/bin/sh
```

We have already seen some of the fields shown here when adding users to the system:

- The username field, which has a maximum of eight characters.
- The encrypted password field, which in a system using shadow passwords is crossed with an "x."
- The user ID field, which contains the numeric and unique UID.
- The primary group ID field, which contains the numeric GID.
- The user comment, which contains a description of the user.
- The path to the user's home directory.
- The user's default shell.

In older versions of Solaris, the encrypted password field would have contained an encrypted password string like *X14oLaiYg7bO2*. However, this presented a security problem, because the login program required all users to have *read* access to the password file:

```
# ls -l /etc/passwd
-rw-r--r--   1 root       sys            605 Jul 24 11:04 /etc/passwd
```

Thus, any user with the lowest form privilege would be able to access the encrypted password field for the *root* user, and attempt to gain root access by guessing the password. A number of programs were specifically developed for this purpose, such as *crack*, which takes a standard Solaris password file and uses a dictionary and some clever lexical rules to guess passwords. Once a rogue user obtains a root password, he or she may perform any operation on a Solaris system, including formatting hard disks, installing Trojan horses, launching attacks on other systems, and so on.

The cryptographic algorithm used by Solaris is not easy to crack; indeed, a brute force guess of a password composed of a completely random set of characters would take many CPU years to compute. The task would be made even more difficult (if not impossible) if the root password was changed weekly, again with a random set of characters. However, the reality is that most users enter passwords that are easily guessed from a dictionary or from some knowledge about the user. Because users are constantly required to use PINs and passwords, they generally choose passwords that are easy to remember. However, easily remembered passwords are also the easiest to crack.

Solaris has reduced the chances of a rogue user obtaining the password file in the first place by implementing a shadow password facility. This creates a file called */etc/shadow*, which is similar to the password file (*/etc/passwd*), but is readable only by root and contains the encrypted password fields for each UID. Thus, if a rogue user cannot obtain the encrypted password entries, using them as the basis for a "crack" attack is very difficult.

UNIX passwords are created by calling the *crypt* function, which requires salt and the password to create an encrypted string. Because the crypt function is one way (i.e., it is not mathematically reversible), then there is no corresponding function called *decrypt*. Thus, the only way to obtain a password from an encrypted string is by passing the salt plus a "guess string" containing what you think the password might be and seeing if the encrypted string generated matches the one stored in the shadow password file. In this case, "guess strings" are often generated by reading a dictionary file containing thousands of possible passwords or by using a list of commonly used passwords (such as "root," "system," "manager," "tiger," and so on).

Procedures

The following procedures must be performed to add users and groups to the system.

Adding Users

Adding a user to a Solaris system is easy, however, this operation may be performed only by the *root* user. There are two options. The first option is to edit the */etc/passwd* file directly, incrementing the UID, adding the appropriate GID, adding a home directory (and remembering to physically create it on the file system), inserting a comment, and choosing a login name. In addition, a password for the user must be set using the `passwd` command.

Does this sound difficult? If so, you should consider using the second option: the automated `useradd` command, which will do all of the hard work for you, as long as you supply the correct information. The `useradd` command has the following format:

```
# useradd -u uid -g gid -d home_directory -s path_to_shell
-c comment login_name
```

Let's add a user to the system and examine the results:

```
# useradd -u 1004 -g 10 -d /opt/www -s /bin/sh -c
"Web User" www
```

Here, you are adding a Web user called "www" with the UID 1004, GID 10, with the home directory */opt/www*, and the Bourne shell as their login shell. At the end of the `useradd` script, an appropriate line should appear in the */etc/passwd file*:

```
# grep www /etc/passwd
www:x:1004:10:Web User:/opt/www:/bin/sh
```

However, the `useradd` command may fail under the following conditions:

- The UID that you specified has already been taken by another user. UIDs may be recycled, as long as precautions are taken to ensure that a previous owner of the UID no longer owns files on the file system.

- The GID that you specified does not exist. Verify its entry in the groups database (*/etc/group*).

- The comment contains special characters, such as double quotes (""), exclamation marks (!), or slashes (/).

- The shell that you specified does not exist. Check that the shell actually exists in the path specified and that the shell has an entry in the shells database (*/etc/shells*).

Modifying User Attributes

Once you have created a user account, you can change any of its characteristics by directly editing the password database (*/etc/passwd*) or by using the usermod command. For example, if you wanted to modify the UID of the www account from 1004 to 1005, you would use the command:

```
# usermod -u 1005 www
```

Again, you can verify that the change has been made correctly by examining the entry for www in the password database:

```
# grep www /etc/passwd
www:x:1005:10:Web User:/opt/www:/bin/sh
```

Remember that if you change a UID or GID, you must manually update existing directory and file ownerships manually by using the chmod, chgrp, and chown commands where appropriate.

Once a user account has been created, the next step is to set a password, which you can perform using the passwd command:

```
# passwd user
```

where *user* is the login name for the account whose password you want to change. In all cases, you will be required to enter the new password twice—if you happen to make a typing error, the password will not be changed, and you will be warned that the two password strings entered did not match. Here's an example for the user www:

```
# passwd www
New password:
Re-enter new password:
passwd(SYSTEM): They don't match; try again.
New password:
Re-enter new password:
passwd (SYSTEM): passwd successfully changed for www
```

After a password has been entered for a user, such as the www user, it should appear as an encrypted string in the shadow password database (*/etc/shadow*):

```
# grep www /etc/shadow
www:C4dMH8As4bGTM:::::::
```

Once a user has been granted an initial password, he or she may then enter a new password by using the `passwd` command with no options.

Deleting Users

Now imagine that one of your prized employees has moved into greener pastures unexpectedly—although you will eventually be able to change the ownership on all of his or her files, you cannot immediately restart some production applications. In this case, you can temporarily disable logins to a specific account by using a command like this:

```
# passwd -l natashia
```

This command would lock natashia's account until the *root* user once again used the `passwd` command on this account to set a new password. A locked account can be identified in the password database by the characters *LK*:

```
# grep natashia /etc/shadow
natashia:*LK*:::::::
```

Once all of the user's files have been backed up, and any active processes have been killed by the super-user, the user account may be permanently deleted by using the `userdel` command. For example, to delete the user account natashia and remove that user's home directory and all of the files underneath that directory, you would use this command:

```
# userdel -r natashia
```

Or, you could edit both the password and shadow password databases and remove the appropriate lines containing the entries for the user natashia. You would also need to manually remove the user's home directory and all of her files underneath that directory.

There are also several system accounts, including *adm*, *bin*, *listen*, *nobody*, *lp*, *sys*, and *uucp*, that should remain locked at all times to prevent interactive logins.

Adding Groups

To add a new group to the system, you may either manually edit the */etc/group* file or use the `groupadd` command, which has the following syntax:

```
/usr/sbin/groupadd -g gid  group_name
```

Thus, to add a group called managers to the system, with a GID of 500, you would use the command:

```
# groupadd -g 500 managers
```

You would then be able to verify the new group's existence by searching the groups database:

```
# grep management /etc/group
managers::500:
```

The groupadd command will fail if the GID that you specify has already been allocated to an existing group or if the *group_name* is greater than eight characters.

Managing Groups

If you want to change your group from the primary to secondary during an interactive session to ensure that all of the files that you create are associated with the correct GID, you need to use the newgrp command. For example, the *root* user has the following primary group membership:

```
# id
uid=0(root) gid=0(root)
```

However, if the *root* user wishes to act as a member of another group, such as *sys*, you would have to use the following command:

```
# newgrp sys
```

The effective GID would then change to *sys*:

```
# id
uid=0(root) gid=3(sys)
```

Note that if a password is set on the target group, a non-*root* user would have to enter that password to change the effective group.

Any operations (such as creating files) that the root user performs after using newgrp will be associated with the GID of 3 (sys) rather than 0 (root). For example, if you created a new file with the primary group, the group associated with the new file would be GID 0:

```
# touch root.txt
 # ls -l root.txt
-rw-r--r--   1 root       root      0 Oct 12 11:17 root.txt
```

However, if the *root* user then changes groups to *sys* and creates a new file, the group associated with the file will be *sys*, rather than *root*:

```
# newgrp sys
# touch sys.txt
# ls -l sys.txt
-rw-r--r--   1 root       sys       0 Oct 12 11:18 sys.txt
```

Command Reference

The following commands are used to manage users on Solaris systems.

admintool

So far, we have examined only user and group administration by using command-line tools, such as *useradd* and *groupadd*. Fortunately, Solaris also provides an easy to use administrative interface for adding users and groups to the system called *admintool*. The *admintool* interface is shown in Figure 10-1. The interface shown is for user management, displaying the username, UID, and user comment. In addition to managing users and

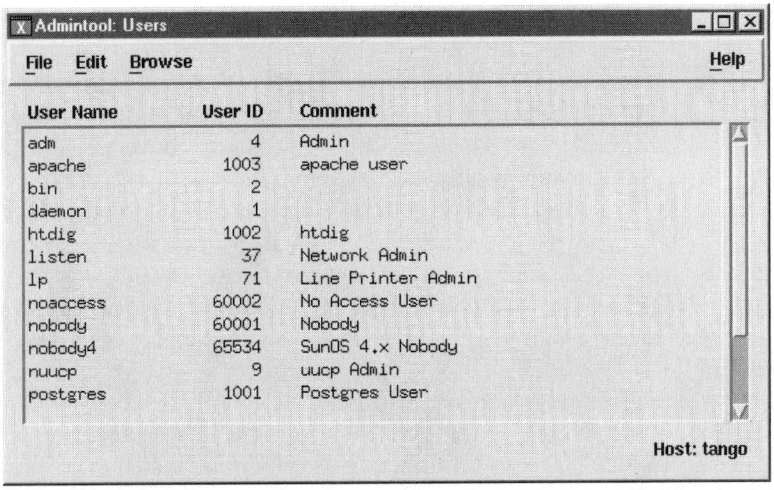

Figure 10-1.   *The Solaris **admintool***

groups, *admintool* is also useful for managing hosts, printers, serial ports, and software. Each management option has its own interface, which is accessible from the Browse menu. When an interface is selected, such as the printers interface, administrators may then add, modify, or delete the entries that exist in the current database (in this case, administrators may add, delete, or modify the entries for printers).

Let's examine how to modify existing user information using the *admintool*, as shown in Figure 10-1. First, select the user whose data you wish to modify (e.g., the *adm* user, one of the preconfigured system accounts that is created during Solaris installation). Next, select Edit | Modify. The user entry modification window is shown in Figure 10-2 for the *adm* user. Here, you can modify the following options:

- The username
- The primary group
- All secondary groups
- The user comment
- The login shell, which you can select from a drop-down containing all valid shells defined in the shells database (*/etc/shells*)
- The minimum and maximum days required before a password change
- The maximum number of inactive days for an account
- An expiration date for the user's account
- The number of days warning to give a user before their password must be changed
- The path to the user's home directory

Of course, you can set all of this information on the command line by using the `passwd` command. However, the *admintool* interface is easier to use and provides some additional functionality. For example, entering an invalid expiration date is impossible, because the day, month, and year are selected from drop-down boxes. In addition, if you encounter any problems during modification, no changes will be recorded.

Adding a user to the system involves entering data into the same interface used for modifying user details, as shown in Figure 10-3. The UID is sequentially generated, as is a default primary group, user shell, password option (not set until first login), and the option to create a new directory for the user as his or her home directory. Again, *admintool* has advanced error-checking facilities that make it difficult to damage or overwrite system files with invalid data.

You can also use *admintool* as a group administration tool. You can create groups and add users to specific groups, or remove users from groups. In addition, you can delete groups using *admintool*. The group administration interface is shown in Figure 10-4, which shows five groups; the *adm* group (GID 4) has three members: *root*, *adm*, and *daemon*. To add a user to the group, simply select the *adm* group and Edit | Add.

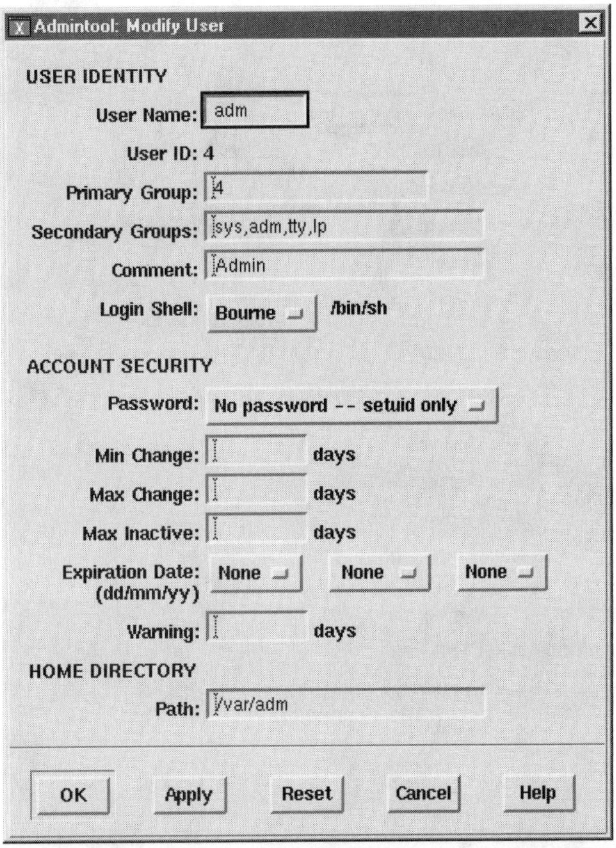

Figure 10-2. *Modifying user details with **admintool***

A comma-delimited list of users in the group would then be displayed. You could add the *bin* user to the *adm* group by inserting a comma after the last entry and adding the name "bin" to the list.

pwck

The pwck command is used to verify the accuracy of the password file. It reads */etc/passwd*, and it verifies that the expected number of fields exist for each entry in the file and validates the contents of the username, UID, and GID fields. It also checks whether the home directory exists and whether the default shell noted is a valid shell.

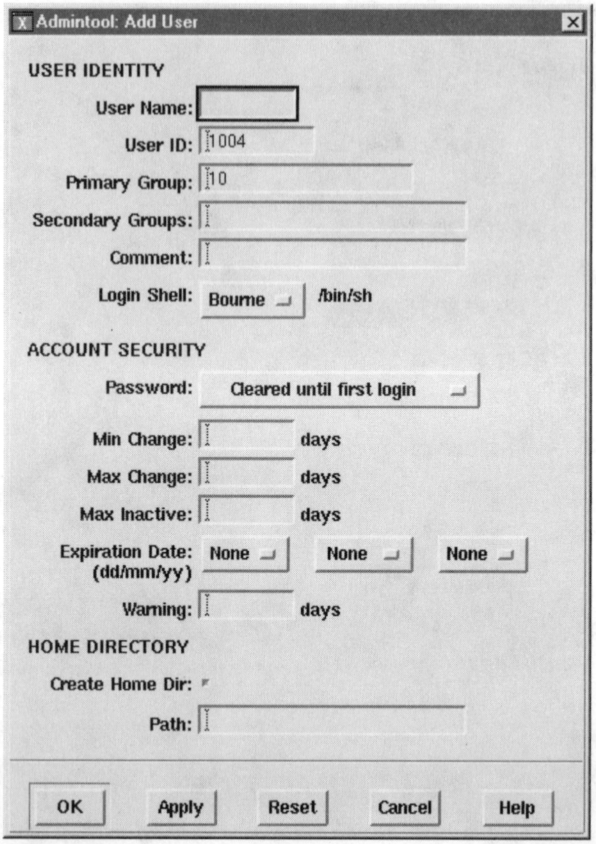

Figure 10-3. *Adding user details with **admintool***

grpck

The grpck command is similar to the pwck command; you can use it to verify the accuracy of the group file. It reads */etc/group* and verifies that the expected number of fields exist for each entry in the file, and it validates the contents of the group name and GID fields. It also creates a list of usernames defined in the group and checks that these are contained in the */etc/passwd* file. If not, an error is reported, because an old user account may have been deleted from */etc/passwd* but may still be listed in a group.

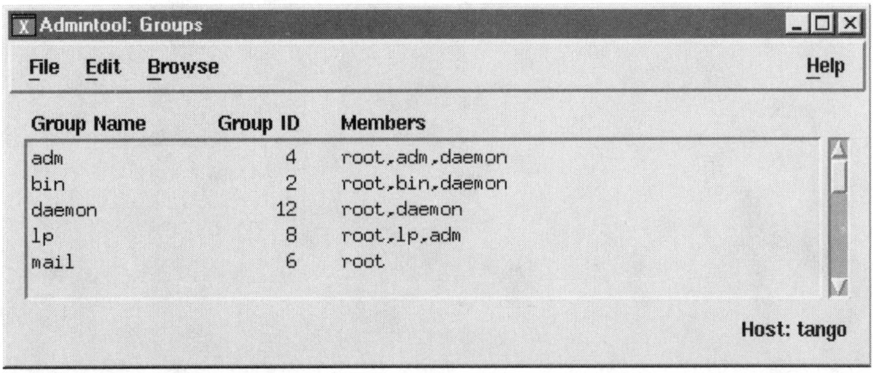

Figure 10-4. *Managing groups with **admintool***

pwconv

You can use the pwconv command to convert systems that do not have a shadow password file to use password shadowing. Most (if not all) modern systems would use password shadowing. However, if the */etc/shadow* file does not exist, the encrypted password is stripped from */etc/passwd* and replaced by "x," indicating that the password for each user is shadowed. A shadow password file would then be created using the encrypted passwords extracted from the password file.

However, a more common use of *pwconv* is to update the shadow password file with entries that have been created manually in */etc/passwd*. Although this is not the recommended method of adding users to the system, some sites have scripts that create blocks of new user accounts by generating sequential usernames with generic group and password information. In such cases, it would be necessary to run *pwconv* after the script has been executed to ensure that entries created in */etc/passwd* are correctly transferred to */etc/shadow*.

The
Complete
Reference

Chapter 11

Shells and File Permissions

A lthough graphical user environments (GUIs) are an increasingly popular metaphor for interacting with computer systems, character user interfaces (CUIs) are a core feature of Solaris 9, because they provide a programmatic environment in which commands can be executed. Many operations on Solaris systems are performed in the context of a script, whether starting services at boot time or processing text to produce a report. Indeed, one of the key advantages of UNIX and UNIX-like environments over non-UNIX systems is the capability to combine large numbers of small commands in a CUI, in conjunction with pipes and filters, to create complex command sets that perform repetitive tasks.

Key Concepts

The following key concepts are required knowledge for understanding the shell and file permissions.

The Shell

All shells have a command prompt—the prompt usually tells the user which shell is currently being used, the user who owns the shell, and/or the current working directory. For example, the following prompt

```
#
```

usually indicates that the current user has super-user privileges. Shell prompts are completely customizable—the default for Bash is just the name of the shell:

```
bash-2.04$
```

When you start a new terminal window from within the CDE, a shell is automatically spawned for you. This will be the same shell that is specified in your */etc/passwd* entry:

```
apache:x:1003:10:apache user:/usr/local/apache:/usr/local/bin/bash
```

In this case, the apache user has the Bash shell set as default. To be a valid login shell, */usr/local/bin/bash* must also be included in the shells database (stored in the file */etc/shells*). If the default shell prompt is not to your liking, you can easily change its format by setting two environment variables—*PS1* and *PS2*. We cover environment variables in the "Setting Environment Variables" section; however, the Solaris environment is equivalent to that found in Linux and Windows NT. For example, to set the prompt to display the username and host, you would use the following command:

```
PS1='\u@\H> '; export PS1
```

The prompt displayed by the shell would then look like this:

```
oracle@db>
```

Many users like to display their current username, hostname, and current working directory, which can be set using the following command:

```
PS1='\u@\H:\w> '; export PS1
```

When executed, this shell prompt is changed to the following:

```
oracle@db:/usr/local>
```

where *oracle* is the current user, *db* is the hostname, and */usr/local* is the current working directory. A list of different customization options for shell prompts is given in Table 11-1.

Setting	Description	Output
\a	ASCII beep character	"beep"
\d	Date string	Wed Sep 6
\h	Short hostname	www
\H	Full hostname	www.paulwatters.com
\s	Shell name	bash
\t	Current time (12-hour format)	10:53:44
\T	Current time (24-hour format)	10:53:55
\@	Current time (A.M./P.M. format)	10:54 A.M.
\u	Username	root
\v	Shell version	2.03
\W	Shell version with revision	2.03.0
\!	Command history number	223

Table 11-1. *Environment Variable Setting for Different Command Prompts Under Bash*

Setting	Description	Output
\$	Privilege indicator	#
\u\$	Username and privilege indicator	root#
\u:\!:\$	Username, command history number, and privilege indicator	root:173:#

Table 11-1.   *Environment Variable Setting for Different Command Prompts Under Bash* (Continued)

At the shell prompt, you enter commands in the order in which you intend for them to be executed. For example, to execute the *admintool* from the command prompt, you would type this command:

```
oracle@db:/usr/sbin> ./admintool
```

The ./ in this example indicates that the *admintool* application resides in the current directory—you could also execute the application using this command:

```
oracle@db:/usr/sbin> /usr/sbin/admintool
```

The *admintool* window would then appear on the desktop, assuming that you're using a terminal window to execute a shell. Once the shell is executing a command in the "foreground" (like *admintool*), no other commands can be executed. However, by sending a command process into the "background," you can execute more than one command in the shell. You can send a process into the background immediately by adding an ampersand (&) to the end of the command line:

```
oracle@db:/usr/sbin> ./admintool &
```

Or, once a command has been executed, you can suspend it by pressing CTRL-Z, and then send it into the background by using the command bg:

```
oracle@db:/usr/sbin> ./admintool
^Z[1] + Stopped (SIGTSTP)         admintool
oracle@db:/usr/sbin> bg
[1] admintool&
oracle@db:/usr/sbin>
```

The application name is displayed along with the job number. You can bring an application back into the foreground by using the following command:

```
oracle@db:/usr/sbin> fg
admintool
```

This will bring job number 1 back into the foreground by default. However, if you had multiple jobs suspended, you would need to specify a job number with the `fg` command:

```
oracle@db:/usr/local/bin> ./netscape
^Z[2] + Stopped (SIGTSTP)          netscape
oracle@db:/usr/sbin> bg
[2] netscape&
oracle@db:/usr/sbin> fg
netscape
```

You can obtain a list of all running jobs in the current shell by typing the following command:

```
$ jobs
[2] +  Running                  ./netscape&
[1] -  Running                  admintool&
```

Procedures

The following procedures are required knowledge for understanding the shell and file permissions.

Symbolic *File Permissions*

One of the most confusing issues for novice users of Solaris is understanding the Solaris file access permissions system. The basic approach to setting and interpreting relative file permissions is using a set of symbolic codes to represent users and permission types. However, even advanced users may find it difficult to understand the octal permissions codes that are used to set absolute permissions. When combined with a default permission mask set in the user's shell (the *umask*), octal permission codes are more powerful than symbolic permission codes.

The Solaris file system permits three basic kinds of file access—the ability to read ("r"), to write ("w"), and to execute ("x") a file or directory. These permissions can be granted exclusively or nonexclusively on individual files, or on a group of files specified by a wildcard ("*"). These permissions can be set by using the chmod command, in combination with a "+" operator. Permissions can be easily removed with the chmod command by using the "-" operator.

For example, to set read permissions (for the current user) on the file */usr/local/lib/libproxy.a*, you would use this command:

```
$ chmod +r /usr/local/lib/libproxy.a
```

Or, to set read permissions for all users on the file */usr/local/lib/libproxy.a*, you would use this command:

```
$ chmod a+r /usr/local/lib/libproxy.a
```

To remove read permissions on the file */usr/local/lib/libproxy.a* for all users who are not members of the current user's default group, you would use this command:

```
$ chmod o-r /usr/local/lib/libproxy.a
```

This does not remove the group and user read permissions that were set previously. Similarly, you can set execute and write permissions. For example, to set execute permissions on the */usr/local/bin/gcc* files, for each class of user (current user, group, and world), you would use the commands:

```
$ chmod u+x /usr/local/bin/gcc
$ chmod g+x /usr/local/bin/gcc
$ chmod o+x /usr/local/bin/gcc
```

To explicitly remove write permissions on the */usr/local/bin/gcc* files for each class of user (current user, group, and world), you would use the commands:

```
$ chmod u-w /usr/local/bin/gcc
$ chmod g-w /usr/local/bin/gcc
$ chmod o-w /usr/local/bin/gcc
```

It makes sense to combine these settings into a single command:

```
$ chmod oug-w /usr/local/bin/gcc
```

The rationale behind using read and write permissions should be clear: permitting read access on a file allows an identified user to access the text of a file by reading it byte-by-byte; write access permits the user to modify or delete any file on which the write permission is granted, regardless of who originally created the file. Thus, individual users can create files that are readable and writeable by any other user on the system.

The permission to execute a file must be granted on scripts (such as shell scripts or Perl scripts) in order for them to be executed; compiled and linked applications must also have the execute bit set on a specific application. The executable permission must also be granted on the special files that represent directories on the file system, if the directory's contents are to be accessed by a specific class of user.

The different options available for granting file access permissions can sometimes lead to interesting but confusing scenarios: For example, permissions can be set to allow a group to delete a file, but not to execute it. More usefully, a group might be given execute permission on an application, but be unable to write over it. In addition, setting file permissions using relative permission strings (rather than absolute octal permission codes) means that permissions set by a previous change of permission command (chmod) are not revoked by any subsequent chmod commands.

However, the permissions themselves are only half the story. Unlike single-user file systems, permissions on Solaris are associated with different file owners (all files and processes on a Solaris system are "owned" by a specific user). In addition, groups of users can be granted read, write, and execute permissions on a file or set of files stored in a directory. Or, file permissions can be granted on a system-wide basis, effectively granting file access without respect to file ownership. Because file systems can be exported using NFS and/or Samba, it's bad practice to grant system-wide read, write, and execute permissions on any file, unless every user needs access to that file. For example, all users need to read the password database (*/etc/passwd*), but only the root user should have read access to the shadow password database (*/etc/shadow*). Blindly exporting all files with world read, write, or execute permissions on a NFS-shared volume is inviting trouble.

The three file system categories of ownership are defined by three permission setting categories: the user ("u"), who owns the file; group members ("g"), who have access to the file; and all other users ("o") on the system. The group specified by "g" can be the user's primary group (as defined in */etc/passwd*), or a secondary group to which the file has been assigned (defined in */etc/group*). Remember that there are ultimately few secrets on a Solaris file system: The root user has full access at all times (read, write, and execute) on all files on the file system; even if a user removes all permissions on a file, the rule of root is absolute. If the contents of a file really need to be hidden, encrypting a file's contents using PGP, crypt, or similar is best. A root user can also change the ownership of a file— thus, a user's files do not absolutely belong to a specific user. The chown command can be used only by the super-user for this purpose.

Policies regarding default file permissions need to be set selectively in different environments. For example, in a production Web server system that processes credit card data, access should be denied by default to all users except those required to conduct online transactions (e.g., the "apache" user for the Apache Web server). On a system that supports team-based development, permissions will obviously need to be set that allow the exchange of data between team partners, but which prevent the access to development files by others. Very few Solaris systems would allow a default world-writeable policy on any file system, except for the temporary swap (*/tmp*) file system.

Enforcing system-wide permissions is possible by using a default umask, which sets the read, write, and execute permissions on all new files created by a specific user. If a user wishes to use a umask other than the default system-wide setting, he or she can achieve this by setting it on the command-line when required, or in the user's shell startup file (e.g., .kshrc for Korn shell).

We start our examination of Solaris file permissions by examining how to create files, set permissions, change ownerships, group memberships, and how to use the `ls` command to examine existing file permissions. All of these commands can be used by nonprivileged users, except for the `chown` command.

The `ls` command is the main directory and file permission listing program used in Solaris. When displaying a long listing, it prints file access permissions, user and group ownerships, file size and creation date, and the filename. For example, for the password file */etc/passwd*, the output from `ls` would look like this:

```
$ ls -l /etc/passwd
-r--r--r--   1 root      other        256 Sep  18 00:40 passwd
```

This directory entry can be read from left to right in the following way:

- The password file is not a directory, indicated by the first "–". This could also indicate a character or block special device
- The password file has read-only permissions for the owner *r--* (but not execute or write permissions)
- The password file has read-only permissions for group members *r--*
- The password file has read-only permissions for other staff *r--*
- The password file is owned by the root user
- The password file has other group permissions
- The password file size is 256 kilobytes
- The password file was created on September 18th, at 00:40 A.M.
- The name of the password file is *passwd*

The permissions string shown changes depending on the permissions that have been set by the owner. For example, if the password file had execute and write permissions for the root user, then the permissions string would read *–rwxr—r—*, rather than just *–r—r—r—*. Each of the permissions can be set using symbolic or octal permissions codes, by using the `chmod` command.

You've seen how a normal file looks under `ls`, but let's compare this with a directory entry, which is a special kind of file that is usually created by the `mkdir` command:

```
# mkdir samples
```

You can check the permissions of the directory entry by using the `ls` command:

```
# ls -l
total 8
drwxrwxr-x   2 root      other          512 Sep  5 13:41 samples
```

The directory entry for the directory samples can be read from left to right in the following way:

- The directory entry is a special file denoted by a leading "d"
- The directory entry has read, write, and execute permissions for the owner "rwx"
- The directory entry has read, write, and execute permissions for group members "rwx"
- The directory entry has read and execute permissions for other staff "r-x"
- The directory entry is owned by the root user
- The directory entry has other group permissions
- The directory entry size is 512 kilobytes
- The directory entry was created on September 5th, at 1:41 P.M.
- The name of the directory is samples

For a directory to be accessible to a particular class of user, the executable bit must be set using the `chmod` command.

Octal *File Permissions*

Some expert users prefer not to separate user and permission information by using the user symbols (o, u, g) and the permission symbols (r, w, x). Instead, a numeric code can be used to combine both user and permission information. If you use a lot of common permissions settings, it may be easier for you to remember a single octal code than to work out the permissions string symbolically. The octal code consists of three numbers, which represent owner permissions, group permissions, and other user permissions, respectively (from left to right). The higher the number, the greater the permissions for each user. For example, to set a file to have read, write, and execute permissions for the file owner, you can use the octal code 700 with the `chmod` command:

```
$ chmod 700 *
```

MANAGING USERS
AND ROLES

You can now check to see if the correct permissions have been granted:

```
$ ls -l
total 4
drwx------   2 root      users        4096 Jun  8 20:10 test
-rwx------   1 root      users           0 Jun  8 20:10 test.txt
```

You can also grant read, write, and execute permissions to members of the group users by changing the middle number from 0 to 7:

```
$ chmod 770 *
```

Again, the changes are reflected in the symbolic permissions string displayed by ls:

```
$ ls -l
total 4
drwxrwx---   2 root      users        4096 Jun  8 20:10 test
-rwxrwx---   1 root      users           0 Jun  8 20:10 test.txt
```

If you want to grant read, write, and execute permissions to all users, simply change the third permissions number from 0 to 7:

```
$ chmod 777 *
```

Now, all users on the system have read, write, and execute permissions on all files in the directory:

```
$ ls -l
total 4
drwxrwxrwx   2 root      users        4096 Jun  8 20:10 test
-rwxrwxrwx   1 root      users           0 Jun  8 20:10 test.txt
```

Of course, the codes that can be used to specify permissions are usually not just 0 or 7. For example, the code 5 gives read and execute access, but not write access. So, if you wanted to grant read and execute access to members of the group, but deny write access, you could use the code 750:

```
$ chmod 750 *
```

This produces the following result:

```
$ ls -l
total 4
drwxr-x---   2 root      users          4096 Jun  8 20:10 test
-rwxr-x---   1 root      users             0 Jun  8 20:10 test.txt
```

If you wanted to remove all access permissions from the files in the current directory, you could use the code 000 (you should not normally need to do this):

```
$ chmod 000 *
```

Let's examine the result of the command:

```
$ ls -l
total 4
d---------   2 root      users          4096 Jun  8 20:10 test
----------   1 root      users             0 Jun  8 20:10 test.txt
```

All access permissions have been removed, except for the directory indicator on the special file test. Note the main difference between setting files using symbolic codes rather than octal codes: Symbolic codes are relative; numeric codes are absolute. This means that unless you explicitly revoke a file permission when setting another using symbolic codes, it will persist. Thus, if a file already has group write access, and you grant group execute access (or remove group execute access), the write access permission is not removed. However, if you specify only group execute access using an octal code, the group write access will automatically be removed if it has been previously set. You may well find that in startup scripts and situations where the permissions are unknown in advance, using octal codes is wiser.

Setting Default Permissions (umask)

You can enforce system-wide permissions by using a default "user mask" (umask), which sets the read, write, and execute permissions on all new files created by a specific user. If a user wants to use a umask other than the default system-wide setting, he or she can achieve this by setting it on the command line when required, or in the user's shell startup file (e.g., .kshrc for Korn shell), or in the global system default file */etc/default/login*. In addition, the mask that is set for the current user can be displayed by using the umask command by itself.

Like file permissions, the umask is set using octal codes (symbolic codes cannot be used). There are two different strategies for computing umasks: For directories, you must subtract the octal value of the default permission you want to set from octal 777; for files, you must subtract the octal value of the default permission you want to set from octal 666. For example, to set the default permission to 444 (all read-only), you would subtract 444 from 666 for files, to derive the umask of 222. For the default permission 600 (user read/write, no other access), you would subtract 600 from 666, leaving a umask of 066 (which will often be displayed as 66).

If you want all users to have full access permissions on all files that you create, you would set the umask to 000 (666-000=666):

```
$ umask 000
```

Let's examine the results, after creating a file called *data.txt*, after setting the umask to 000:

```
$ touch data.txt
 $ ls -l
total 4
-rwxrwxrwx   1 root      users          0 Jun  8 20:20 data.txt
```

Everyone now has full access permissions. However, you are more likely to set a umask like 022, which would give new files the permissions 755 (777 – 022=755). This would give the file owner read, write, and execute access, but only read permissions for group members and other users:

```
$ umask 022
```

If you now create a new file called *newdata.txt* with the new umask, you should see that the default permissions have changed:

```
$ touch newtest.txt
 $ ls -l
total 4
-rw-r--r--   1 root      root           0 Jun  8 20:21 newdata.txt
-rwxrwxrwx   1 root      users          0 Jun  8 20:20 data.txt
```

If you're more conservative, and you don't want to grant any access permissions to other users (including group members), you can set the umask to 077, which still gives the file owner full access permissions:

```
$ umask 077
```

Let's see what happens when you create a new file called *lastminute.txt*:

```
$ touch lastminute.txt
$ ls -l
total 4
-rw-r--r--    1 root      root             0 Jun  8 20:21 newdata.txt
-rw-------    1 root      root             0 Jun  8 20:22
lastminute.txt
-rwxrwxrwx    1 root      users            0 Jun  8 20:20 data.txt
```

The new file has full access permissions for the owner, but no access permissions for other users. Resetting the umask does not affect the permissions of other files that have already been created.

setuid *and* setgid *Permissions*

The file permissions we've covered so far are used by users in their day-to-day file management strategies. However, administrators can make use of a different set of file permissions, which allow files to be executed as a particular user (*setuid*), and/or as a member of a particular group (*setgid*). These facilities are very powerful, because they allow unprivileged users to gain access to limited super-user privileges in many cases, without requiring super-user authentication. For example, the volume daemon (*vold*) allows unprivileged users logged into the console to mount and unmount CD-ROMs and floppy disks, an operation which required super-user privileges in previous Solaris releases. Here, the effective user ID is set to 0, meaning that unprivileged users can effectively run processes as root. The downside to this is obvious: *setgid* and *setuid* permissions open up a Pandora's box in terms of security, because normal authentication procedures are bypassed. For example, imagine a device management tool that needed to run as *setuid* 0, in order to read and write device files. If the tool had a standard feature of many UNIX program (the ability to spawn a shell), the shell spawned would have full root privileges, rather than the privileges of the original user. For this reason, some administrators refuse to allow *setgid* and *setuid* permissions to be set. The find command, for example, can be used to scan all file systems and automatically remove any files with *setuid* or *setgid* privileges.

You can determine whether a file is *setuid* by root by (a) checking for files that are owned by root and (b) checking whether these files have the "s" flag assigned to the user's permissions. For example, if a file management tool called *filetool* was *setuid* root, the following directory listing would clearly indicate this property:

```
-r-sr-sr-x 3 root sys 1220334 Jul 18 11:01 /usr/local/bin/filetool
```

The first "s" in the permissions table refers to *setuid* root. In addition, this file is also *setgid* for the *sys* group, which is indicated by the second "s" in the permissions table.

The *setuid* bit can be set by using a command like this

```
# chmod u+s file.txt
```

where *file.txt* is the file that requires *setuid* to be set. The *setgid* bit can be set by using a command like this

```
# chmod g+s file.txt
```

where *file.txt* is the file that requires *setgid* to be set.

Sticky Bit Permissions

A network administrator once explained to me that sticky bits were those bits that slowed down network transmission rates, because they were highly attracted to magnetic qualities of the Ethernet. This is not true! A sticky bit is a special permission that prevents files in common file areas from being deleted by other users. For example, a download area consisting of a large 10GB partition may be set aside for user downloads, which are not counted against individual user quotas. This means that users could download up to 10GB of data without infringing on their allocated directory space. However, although a shared public file area sounds like a great idea, it would be unwise to allow users to overwrite one another's files. In this case, the sticky bit can be set on the top-level directory of the public file area, allowing only users who created individual files to delete them.

You can set the sticky bit by using a command like this

```
# chmod +t somedir
```

where *somedir* is the directory that requires the sticky bit to be set.

Examples

The following examples demonstrate how to use the shell.

Setting Environment Variables

Environment variables are used to store information in a form that is accessible to commands within the shell and other applications that are spawned from the shell. You can obtain a list of all environment variables that have been set in a shell by using the following command:

```
bash-2.03$ set
BASH=/usr/local/bin/bash
BASH_VERSINFO=([0]="2" [1]="03" [2]="0" [3]="1" [4]="release" \
```

```
   [5]="i386-pc-solaris2.7")
BASH_VERSION='2.03.0(1)-release'
COLUMNS=80
DIRSTACK=()
DISPLAY=cassowary:0.0
EDITOR=/usr/bin/vi
ENV=/.kshrc
EUID=0
GROUPS=()
HELPPATH=/usr/openwin/lib/locale:/usr/openwin/lib/help
HISTFILE=/.sh_history
HISTFILESIZE=500
HISTSIZE=500
HOME=/
HOSTNAME=cassowary
HOSTTYPE=i386
IFS=' '
LANG=en_AU
LC_COLLATE=en_AU
LC_CTYPE=en_AU
LC_MESSAGES=C
LC_MONETARY=en_AU
LC_NUMERIC=en_AU
LC_TIME=en_AU
LD_LIBRARY_PATH=/usr/local/lib:/usr/openwin/lib:/usr/dt/lib
LINES=24
LOGNAME=root
MACHTYPE=i386-pc-solaris2.8
MAIL=/var/mail/root
MAILCHECK=60
MANPATH=/usr/dt/man:/usr/man:/usr/openwin/share/man
OPENWINHOME=/usr/openwin
OPTERR=1
OPTIND=1
OSTYPE=solaris2.7
PATH=/usr/sbin:/usr/bin:/bin:/usr/ucb:/usr/local/bin::/usr/ccs/bin
PIPESTATUS=([0]="1")
PPID=1584
PS1='\s-\v\$ '
PS2='> '
PS4='+ '
PWD=/etc
SESSION_SVR=tango
SHELL=/bin/ksh
```

```
SHLVL=1
TERM=dtterm
TERMINAL_EMULATOR=dtterm
TZ=Australia/NSW
UID=0
USER=root
WINDOWID=58720265
```

Although there seem to be a lot of shell variables, the most significant ones include the following:

BASH	The path to the shell on the file system
COLUMNS	The columns width for the terminal
DISPLAY	The display variable that is used for X11 graphics
HOME	The default home directory for the user
HOSTNAME	The hostname of the current system
LD_LIBRARY_PATH	The path to system and user libraries
LOGNAME	The username of the shell owner
MANPATH	The path to the system manuals
NNTPSERVER	The hostname of the NNTP server
PATH	The path that is searched to find applications where no absolute path is specified on the command line
PPID	The parent process ID
TERM	The terminal type (usually VT100)
UID	The user ID
WINDOWMANAGER	The name of the X11 window manager

The values of all shell variables can be set on the command-line by using the export command. For example, if you wanted to set the terminal type to VT220, you would use this command:

```
$ TERM=vt220; export TERM
```

Command Reference

The following commands are commonly used to get the most from the shell. Help for each of these commands is usually available through the *man* facility or the *GNU info* command.

Source (.)

The `source` command reads in and executes the lines of a shell script. The format of this command is

```
. file
```

where *file* is a valid filename that contains a Bourne shell script. The first line should contain a directive that points to the absolute location of the shell:

```
#!/bin/sh
```

Or, you can execute Bourne shell scripts by calling them with a new shell invocation, or calling them directly if the executable bit is set for the executing user. For example, the following three commands would each execute the script file *myscript.sh*:

```
$ . myscript.sh
$ sh myscript.sh
$ ./myscript.sh
```

However, only the source command (.) preserves any environment variable settings made in the script.

basename

The `basename` command strips a filename of its extension. The format of this command is

```
basename filename.ext
```

where *filename.ext* is a valid filename like *mydata.dat*. The `basename` command parses *mydata.dat* and extracts *mydata*. Because file extensions are not mandatory in Solaris, this command is very useful for processing files copied from Windows or MS-DOS.

cat

The `cat` command prints out the contents of the file, without any special screen control features like scrolling backwards or forwards in a file. The format of this command is as follows:

```
cat filename
```

To display the groups database, for example, you could run the command:

```
$ cat /etc/group
root::0:root
other::1:
bin::2:root,bin,daemon
sys::3:root,bin,sys,adm
adm::4:root,adm,daemon
uucp::5:root,uucp
mail::6:root
tty::7:root,tty,adm
lp::8:root,lp,adm
nuucp::9:root,nuucp
staff::10:
```

cd

The `cd` command changes the current working directory to a new directory location, which you can specify in both absolute or relative terms. The format of this command is as follows:

```
cd directory
```

For example, if the current working directory is */usr/local*, and you type the command,

```
cd bin
```

the new working directory would be */usr/local/bin*. However, if you type the command,

```
cd /bin
```

the new working directory would be */bin*. For interactive use, relative directory names are often used; however, scripts should always contain absolute directory references.

chgrp

The chgrp command modifies the default group membership of a file. The format of this command is

```
chgrp group file
```

where *group* is a valid group name, defined in the groups database (*/etc/groups*), and *file* is a valid filename. Because permissions can be assigned to individual users or groups of users, assigning a nondefault group membership can be useful for users who need to exchange data with members of different organizational units (e.g., the Web master who swaps configuration files with the database administrator, and also exchanges HTML files with Web developers). Only the file owner or the super-user can modify the group membership of a file.

date

This command prints the current system date and time. The format of this command is as follows:

```
date
```

The default output for the command output is of this form:

```
Tuesday February  12 13:43:23 EST 2002
```

You can also modify the output format by using a number of parameters corresponding to days, months, hours, minutes, and so on. For example, the command,

```
date '+Current Date: %d/%m/%y%nCurrent Time:%H:%M:%S'
```

produces the following output:

```
Current Date: 06/09/00
Current Time:13:45:43
```

grep

The grep command searches a file for a string (specified by string) and prints the line wherever a match is found. The format of this command is as follows:

```
grep string file
```

The `grep` command is very useful for interpreting log files, where you just want to display a line that contains a particular code (e.g., a Web server logfile can be *grep*ped for the string 404, which indicates a page not found).

head

The `head` command displays the first page of a file. The format of this command is as follows:

```
head filename
```

The `head` command is very useful for examining the first few lines of a very long file. For example, to display the first page of the name service switch configuration file (*/etc/nsswitch.conf*), you could use this command:

```
$ head /etc/nsswitch.conf
# /etc/nsswitch.nisplus:
# An example file that could be copied over to /etc/nsswitch.conf; it
# uses NIS+ (NIS Version 3) in conjunction with files.
# "hosts:" and "services:" in this file are used only if the
# /etc/netconfig file has a "-" for nametoaddr_libs of "inet" transports.
# the following two lines obviate the "+" entry in /etc/passwd and
# /etc/group.
```

less

The `less` command prints a file "file" on the screen, and it allows searching backwards and forwards through the file. The format of this command is as follows:

```
less filename
```

To scroll through the contents of the system log configuration file (*/etc/syslog.conf*), you would use the following command:

```
less /etc/syslog.conf
#ident  "@(#)syslog.conf      1.4      96/10/11 SMI"   /* SunOS 5.0 */
# Copyright (c) 1991-1993, by Sun Microsystems, Inc.
# syslog configuration file.
# This file is processed by m4 so be careful to quote (`') names
# that match m4 reserved words.  Also, within ifdef's, arguments
# containing commas must be quoted.
*.notice                                    @loghost
*.err;kern.notice;auth.notice               /dev/console
```

```
*.err;kern.debug;daemon.notice;mail.crit;daemon.info    /var/adm/messages
*.alert;kern.err;daemon.err                             operator
*.alert                                                 root
```

The `less` command has a number of commands that can be issued interactively. For example, to move forward one window, just type **F**, or to move back one window, just type **B**. *Less* also supports searching with the */pattern* command.

ls

The `ls` command prints the names of files contained in the directory *dir* (by default, the contents of the current working directory are displayed). The format of the command is

```
ls directory
```

where *directory* is the name of the directory whose contents you wish to list. For example, to list the contents of the */var/adm* directory, which contains a number of system logs, you could use the command:

```
$ ls /var/adm
aculog        log           messages.1    passwd     utmp     wtmp
ftpmessages   messages      messages.2    spellhist  utmpx    wtmpx
lastlog       messages.0    messages.3    sulog      vold.log
```

mkdir

The `mkdir` command makes new directory entries. The format of this command is as follows:

```
mkdir directory
```

For example, if the current working directory is */sbin*, and you type the command,

```
mkdir oracle
```

the new directory would be */sbin/oracle*. However, if you type the command,

```
mkdir /oracle
```

the new directory would be */oracle*. For interactive use, relative directory names are often used; however, scripts should always contain absolute directory references.

more

The more command prints the contents of a file, like the less command, but just permits the scrolling forward through a file. The format of this command is as follows:

```
more filename
```

To scroll through the contents of the disk device configuration file (*/etc/format.dat*), you would use the following command:

```
more /etc/format.dat
#pragma ident    "@(#)format.dat 1.21     98/01/24 SMI"
# Copyright (c) 1991,1998 by Sun Microsystems, Inc.
# All rights reserved.
# Data file for the 'format' program.  This file defines the known
# disks, disk types, and partition maps.
# This is the list of supported disks for the Emulex MD21 controller.
disk_type = "Micropolis 1355" \
        : ctlr = MD21 \
        : ncyl = 1018 : acyl = 2 : pcyl = 1024 : nhead = 8 : nsect = 34 \
        : rpm = 3600 : bpt = 20832
```

The more command has a number of commands that can be issued interactively. For example, to move forward one window, just press the SPACEBAR, or to move forward one line, just press ENTER. *More* also supports searching with the */pattern* command.

pwd

The pwd command prints the current working directory in absolute terms. The format of the command is as follows:

```
pwd
```

For example, if you change directory to */etc* and issue the pwd command, you would see the following result:

```
$ cd /etc
 $ pwd
/etc
```

rmdir

The `rmdir` command deletes a directory. However, the directory concerned must be empty for the `rmdir` command to be successful. The format of this command is as follows:

```
rmdir directory
```

For example, if the current working directory is */usr/local*, and you want to remove the directory *oldstuff*, you would use this command:

```
rmdir oldstuff
```

However, you could use the command,

```
rmdir /usr/local/oldstuff
```

to remove the directory as well. For interactive use, relative directory names are often used; however, scripts should always contain absolute directory references.

tail

The `tail` command displays the last page of a file. The format of this command is as follows:

```
tail filename
```

The `tail` command is very useful for examining the last few lines of a very long file. For example, to display the first page of a Web log file (*/usr/local/apache/logs/access_log*), you could use the command:

```
$ tail /usr/local/apache/logs/access_log
192.168.205.238 - - [12/Feb/2002:09:35:59 +1000]
  "GET /images/picture10.gif HTTP/1.1" 200 53
192.168.205.238 - - [12/Feb/2002:09:35:59 +1000]
  "GET /images/ picture1.gif HTTP/1.1" 200 712
192.168.205.238 - - [12/Feb/2002:09:35:59 +1000]
  "GET /images/ picture5.gif HTTP/1.1" 200 7090
192.168.205.238 - - [12/Feb/2002:09:35:59 +1000]
  "GET /images/ picture66.gif HTTP/1.1" 200 997
```

MANAGING USERS
AND ROLES

```
192.168.205.238 - - [12/Feb/2002:09:35:59 +1000]
  "GET /images/ picture49.gif HTTP/1.1" 200 2386
192.168.205.238 - - [12/Feb/2002:09:36:09 +1000]
  "GET /servlet/SimpleServlet HTTP/1.1" 200 10497
```

The tail command also has an option that allows you to continuously monitor all new entries made to a file. This is very useful for monitoring a live service such as Apache, where you need to observe any error made in real time. The format for this command is as follows:

```
tail -f filename
```

Chapter 12

Role-Based
Access Control

One of the most frustrating aspects of setting a strict security policy is that some actions that require a form of access privilege must occasionally be undertaken by nonprivileged users. Although you don't want normal users to have all of root's privileges for obvious reasons, there are occasions when normal users could conveniently and securely perform certain actions without jeopardizing system integrity. In other words, a number of specific roles require super-user privileges, which you may need to grant to users who should not have complete root access.

In Solaris 1.*x*, the solution to this problem was to prevent normal users from having any kind of privileged access. Normal users, for example, could not eject a floppy disk or CD-ROM drive without root access! However, this draconian solution just led to the root password being shared around to every user who needed to eject a floppy (not very security-conscious!). Alternatively, applications can be compiled as *setuid* root, allowing an unprivileged user to execute specific commands as the root user, without requiring a password. This approach is fine, as long as the scope of the application is restricted. For example, any application that allows the effective user to spawn a shell is not suited to be *setuid* root, because an unprivileged user could then spawn a root shell without a password. Relying on a single super-user to protect a system's resources is one of the great strengths and weaknesses of UNIX and UNIX-like systems.

More often than not, operations on a system can be classified as being associated with a specific role. For example, a network administrator who is responsible for backups really needs only write access to tape devices, but not to any local file systems, other than for spooling. Thus, a backup "role" can have its scope limited in a way that doesn't overlap with a printer administrator, who needs to be able to manage print jobs and write to spooling areas, while being denied write access to tape drives. Identifying tasks and roles is the first step in ensuring that privileges are granted only to those who need them.

Three approaches are commonly used to provide "role-based" access to Solaris systems: installing Trusted Solaris, installing *sudo*, or using the Role-Based Access Control (RBAC) features built into Solaris. We cover Trusted Solaris in Chapter 30, however, it requires a new operating system installation to take advantage of its role-based features, which build on top of RBAC by introducing security labels, ranging from "top secret" to "unclassified." In contrast, *sudo* is a small utility that you can download and install, providing a simple role-based access system. However, RBAC provides a system for role-based access that is integrated into the operating system, providing a superior solution to *sudo*.

Key Concepts

The following key concepts will assist you to understand RBAC.

sudo

sudo allows privileged roles to be assigned to various users by maintaining a database of privileges mapped to usernames. These privileges are identified by sets of different commands listed in the database. In order to access a privileged item, qualified users simply need to reenter their own passwords (not the root password) after the command name has been entered on the command line. *sudo* permits a user to format disks, for instance, but have no other root privileges.

One of the most useful features of *sudo* is its logging. By maintaining a logfile of all operations performed using the *sudo* facility, system administrators can audit the logfile and trace any actions that may have had unintended consequences. This is something that the normal *su* facility does not provide. Alternatively, patterns of malicious behavior can also be identified: *sudo* logs all successful and unsuccessful attempts to perform privileged actions. This can be very important in a security context, because brute force attacks against weak passwords of unprivileged accounts might now be able to access some super-user functions through *sudo*. Thus, if the user nobody is given access via *sudo* to format disks, and the password for the user nobody is guessed, an intruder would be able to format disks on the system without requiring the root password. In addition, because the effective user ID of a user executing a privileged application through *sudo* is set to zero (i.e., the super-user), then such applications should not allow shells to be spawned.

All of the roles in *sudo* are independent. Thus, granting one or more roles to one user and one or more roles to another is possible. User roles can be shared, or they may be completely separate. For example, the user harry may have the privilege to format disks, and the user butler may have the privilege to both format disks and write to tape drives. To access these privileges, harry and butler do not need to know the root password.

RBAC

Role-Based Access Control (RBAC) was first introduced in Solaris 8 as a means of defining roles for managing a specific task or set of tasks, based on a set of administrator-defined profiles. Although the RBAC implementation supplied with Solaris is a Sun-specific product, it is based on a standard developed by NIST (see **http://csrc.nist.gov/ rbac/** for more information). Broadly defined, access control extends beyond the notion of administrative access: It can be defined as the ability to create, read, update, and delete data from a system. Standard file system permissions are based on this principle: various users and groups have access permissions to data stored in files based on a permission string that is associated with every file on the file system. However, although file access can be easily demarcated along organizational lines, deciding who should and who should not have administrative access to execute applications can be a more complex issue. What if a secretary needs to have "root access" to a system to add or delete users as they join an organization? Data entry of this kind seems like a reasonable task for a secretary, but it is usually assigned to system administrators, because it requires root access. *RBAC* allows tasks like these to be separated from other tasks that do require a high level of technical knowledge, such as managing metadevices.

Roles

The first stage of implementing *RBAC* is to define roles, which are then assigned to individual users. Access rights to various resources can then be associated with a specific role name. As with any organization, change to roles and the users who are associated with roles is inevitable, so the process for reflecting these changes in the list of roles and users needs to be as easy to implement as possible. In addition, individual tasks are not always easy to associate with a single role: indeed, in a large organization, some tasks will be performed by a number of different employees. It's also possible to assign specific authorizations to specific users, bypassing roles, but this defeats the whole "role-based" purpose of RBAC, and is not recommended.

One way of dealing with task overlap is to introduce the notion of hierarchies: Profiles and authorizations at the bottom of a conceptual hierarchy are "inherited" by the assignment of a role at a higher level. For example, a role defined as "backup maintainer" involves running *ufsdump*, which in turn requires write access to the tape device. Thus, the backup role inherently requires access to lower level profiles for which new roles do not need to be separately defined. Another role, such as "device manager," may also require write access to the tape device, through the `tapes` command. Again, no separate role is required to be created for those tasks that form part of the role by inference. However, although Solaris RBAC does support hierarchies of profiles and authorizations, it does not support hierarchies of roles. When a user assumes a role, the effect is all-or-nothing: No inheritance of roles is allowed.

By default, Solaris 9 supports three different system management roles:

- A *Primary Administrator (PA)*, who assigns rights to other users and is responsible for security

- A *System Administrator (SA)*, who is responsible for day-to-day administration that is not security-related

- An *Operator*, who performs backups and device maintenance

Figure 12-1 shows the hierarchy of rights associated with the different roles. The distinction between PA and SA will depend on the local security policy. For example, whereas the default PA role permits both adding users and changing passwords, the default SA role does not permit password modifications. However, for many sites, denying SA's access to passwords would be impractical. One of the great benefits of RBAC is that the rights granted to different profiles can be easily modified and customized to suit local requirements. Parallels can be drawn with Trusted Solaris and the assignment of tasks with different levels of authority to completely different roles.

Profiles

Associated with the concept of overlapping roles are the notions of authority and operational responsibility. Two individuals may carry out operations using similar roles but for entirely different purposes. For example, a clerk in a supermarket may be allowed to enter cash transactions into the cash register, but only a supervisor can void transactions already entered. Conversely, a supervisor cannot enter cash transactions,

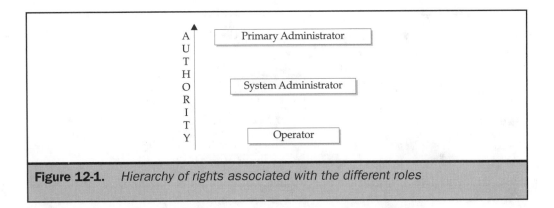

Figure 12-1.   *Hierarchy of rights associated with the different roles*

because the organizational requirements mandate a separation of supervisory and procedural roles, even though both operate on the same set of data and devices. Clearly, these roles and their associated operations must be defined "offline" before being implemented using the Solaris RBAC facility.

A profile is a specific command or set of commands for which an authorization can be granted. These authorizations are linked together to form a role, which is in turn associated with a single user, or a number of different users, as shown in Figure 12-2. Profiles can be executed several ways:

- The new `pfexec` command can be used to execute a single command contained in a profile.

- Commands in profiles can be executed through new, restricted versions of the standard shells, such as `pfsh` (profile Bourne shell) and `pfcsh` (profile C shell).

- A new user account for each role can be created, with its own home directory and password. To execute commands contained in a profile, users who have access to the role can just *su* to the new account—they are not allowed to log in directly. Note that if two users *su* to the same role account, they will both be operating on the same files and could potentially overwrite each other's data. The same is true for the normal root account. However, one difference between using *su* to access a role and using *su* to access a normal account is auditing—all of the operations carried out when using *su* to access a role are logged with the user's original UID. Thus, the operations of individual users who access roles can be logged (and audited) distinctively.

Authorizations

Let's look more closely at authorizations before examining how they are assigned to different roles. An authorization is a privilege that is granted to a role to allow operations

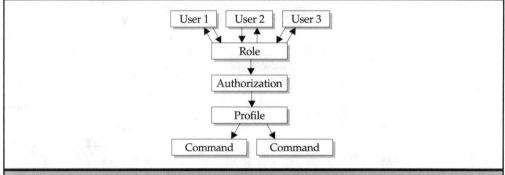

Figure 12-2.   *Profiles and authorizations are associated with roles that are granted to individual users.*

to be performed, and that is defined in the file */etc/security/auth_attr*. Some applications allow RBAC authorizations to be checked before allowing an action to be performed, including the device management commands (e.g., `allocate` and `deallocate`), as well as the batch processing commands (e.g., `at`, `crontab`). Authorizations have a form similar to Internet domain names: reading from left to right, the company name is followed by more specific package and function information. For example, *net.cassowary.** is an authorization that pertains to any function supplied by the vendor *cassowary.net*. By default, all Solaris packages are identified by the prefix "solaris." Thus, the authorization for changing passwords is identified as *solaris.admin.usermgr.pswd* rather than the longer *com.sun.solaris.admin.usermgr.pswd*. Many authorizations are fine-grained, allowing read access but not write access, and vice versa. For example, a Primary Administrator may have the *solaris.admin.usermgr.read* and *solaris.admin.usermgr.write* authorizations that allow read and write access to user configuration files, respectively. However, an SA may only be granted the *solaris.admin.usermgr.read* authorization but not the *solaris.admin.usermgr.write* authorization, effectively preventing him or her from changing the contents of user configuration files, even if they have read access to the same files. The following examples show some of the common *solaris.admin* authorizations currently defined:

```
solaris.admin.fsmgr.:::Mounts and Shares::
solaris.admin.fsmgr.read:::View Mounts and Shares::help=AuthFsmgrRead.html
solaris.admin.fsmgr.write:::Mount and Share Files::help=AuthFsmgrWrite.html
solaris.admin.logsvc.:::Log Viewer::
solaris.admin.logsvc.purge:::Remove Log Files::help=AuthLogsvcPurge.html
solaris.admin.logsvc.read:::View Log Files::help=AuthLogsvcRead.html
```

```
solaris.admin.logsvc.write:::Manage Log Settings::help=AuthLogsvcWrite.html
solaris.admin.serialmgr.:::Serial Port Manager::
solaris.admin.usermgr.:::User Accounts::
solaris.admin.usermgr.pswd:::Change Password::help=AuthUserMgrPswd.html
solaris.admin.usermgr.read:::View Users and Roles::
  help=AuthUsermgrRead.html
solaris.admin.usermgr.write:::Manage Users::help=AuthUsermgrWrite.html
```

We can see that several authorizations have been defined for *solaris.admin*, including file system management (*fsmgr*), logging system management (*logsvc*), port management (*serialmgr*), and user management (*userxmgr*). The corresponding help files are also listed.

An important aspect of authorizations is the capability to transfer permissions to other users by using the *grant* keyword. Once *grant* is attached to the end of an authorization string, it enables the delegation of authorizations to other users. For example, the *solaris.admin.usermgr.grant* authorization, in conjunction with *solaris.admin.usermgr.pswd*, allows password changing to be performed by a delegated user.

How do roles, profiles, and authorizations fit together? Figure 12-3 attempts to show the flow of data from the definition of authorizations and command definition, through to the association of authorizations to specific profiles, which are in turn utilized by users who have been assigned various roles. The sense in which RBAC abstracts users from directly using commands and authorizations is shown by the dotted lines in the diagram. In this diagram, it is easy to see how central roles are in systems where profiles for different tasks are well defined.

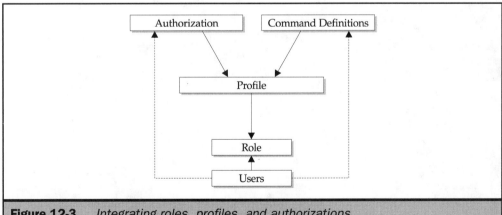

Figure 12-3. *Integrating roles, profiles, and authorizations*

MANAGING USERS
AND ROLES

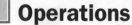

Operations

The following operations are commonly performed when implementing role-based access control.

sudo

The *sudo* facility is configured by the file */etc/sudoers*. This file contains a list of all users who have access to the *sudo* facility and defines their privileges. A typical entry in */etc/sudoers* looks like this:

```
jdoe     ALL=(ALL) ALL
```

This entry gives the user *jdoe* access to all applications as the super-user. For the user *jdoe* to run commands as the super-user, she simply needs to prefix the command string with *sudo*. Thus, to execute the `format` command as root, *jdoe* would enter the following command string:

```
$ sudo format
```

The following output will then be displayed:

```
We trust you have received the usual lecture from the local System
Administrator. It usually boils down to these two things:

        #1) Respect the privacy of others.
        #2) Think before you type.

Password:
```

If *jdoe* correctly types in her normal password, the `format` command will execute with root privileges. If *jdoe* incorrectly types her password up to three times, the following messages appear after each prompt:

```
Take a stress pill and think things over.
Password:
You silly, twisted boy you.
Password:
He has fallen in the water!
Password not entered correctly
```

At this point, an alert is e-mailed to the super-user, informing him or her of the potential security breach—repeated login attempts of this kind may signal a password-guessing attack by a rogue user. Equally, it could indicate that someone is incorrectly typing his or her password (perhaps the CAPS LOCK key is on) or that he or she is entering the root password rather than his or her own.

In order to list all of the privileges currently allowed for a user, that user simply needs to run *sudo* with the *–l* option:

```
$ sudo -l
You may run the following commands on this host:
    (ALL) ALL
```

In addition to granting full super-user access, *sudo* can more usefully delegate authority to specific individuals. For example, you can create command aliases that correspond to the limited set of commands that *sudo*ers can execute:

```
Cmnd_Alias   TCPD=/usr/sbin/tcpd
```

In this case, you are giving users control over the TCP daemon. You can also specify a group of users other than *ALL*, which share the ability to execute different classes of commands:

```
User_Alias   DEVELOPERS=pwatters,tgibbs
User_Alias   ADMINS=maya,natashia
```

Thus, the *DEVELOPERS* group can be assigned access to specific facilities that are not available to *ADMINS*. Putting it all together, you can create complex user specifications like this:

```
ADMINS ALL=(ALL) NOPASSWD: ALL
DEVELOPERS    ALL=TCPD
```

This specification allows admins to perform operations without a password, while giving developers privileges to operate on the TCP daemon. Notice that we've included administrators in the user specification, even though these users probably know the root password. This is because *sudo* leaves an audit trail for every command executed, meaning that you can trace actions to a specific user account. This makes it easy to find out which individual is responsible for system problems. Of course, these administrators can just use the *su* facility to bypass the *sudo* facility, if they know the root password.

MANAGING USERS AND ROLES

This is the main drawback of using *sudo* on Solaris—it is not integrated into the operating system, rather, it is just an application.

RBAC

Common operations performed in the context of *RBAC* including setting up profiles and defining roles. The following commands are commonly used:

- **smexec** is used to create, read, update, and delete rows in the *exec*_attr database.
- **smmultiuser** is used to perform batch functions.
- **smuser** is used to perform operations on user accounts.
- **smprofile** is used to create, read, update, and delete profiles in the *prof*_attr database.
- **smrole** is used to create, read, update, and delete role accounts.
- **rolemod** is used to modify roles.
- **roledel** is used to delete roles.
- **roleadd** is used to add roles.

The *prof_attr* database contains all of the profile definitions for the system. For example, profiles might be created for the Primary Administrator, System Administrator, Operator, Basic Solaris User, and Printer Manager. A special profile is the All Rights profile, which is associated with all commands that have no security restrictions enforced on their use. This is the default profile, which covers all commands not designated as requiring specific authorization. In contrast, the Primary Administrator is granted explicit rights over all security-related commands and operations, as defined by the *solaris.** authorization. The Primary Administrator can then delegate tasks to other users where appropriate if the *solaris.grant* authorization is granted. The scope of the Primary Administrator can be limited if this role is considered too close in power to the super-user.

The System Administrator, in contrast, has a much more limited role. Specific authorizations are granted to the System Administrator, rather than using wildcards to allow complete access. Typical commands defined in this profile allow auditing and accounting, printer administration, batch processing, device installation and configuration, file system repairs, e-mail administration, name and directory service configuration, process administration, and setting up new software. The Operator profile has very few privileges at all: Only printer and backup administration is permitted. Note that the Operator is not allowed to restore data: This privilege is reserved for the System Administrator or Primary Administrator. As an alternative to the Operator, the Printer Manager profile allows only printer administration tasks to be performed. Typical authorizations that are permitted include *solaris.admin.printer.delete*, *solaris.admin.printer.modify*, and *solaris.admin.printer.read*, encompassing commands like lpsched, lpstat, and lpq.

A slightly different approach is taken for the definition of the Basic Solaris User: This policy is contained within the *policy.conf* file. Typical authorizations permitted for the Basic Solaris User include the following:

solaris.admin.dcmgr.read	*solaris.admin.diskmgr.read*	*solaris.admin.fsmgr.read*
solaris.admin.logsvc.read	*solaris.admin.printer.read*	*solaris.admin.procmgr.user*
solaris.admin.prodreg.read	*solaris.admin.serialmgr.read*	*solaris.admin.usermgr.read*
solaris.compsys.read	*solaris.jobs.user*	*solaris.profmgr.read*

Database Reference

The following reference provides details on the different databases that are used with RBAC.

user_attr

The *user_attr* file is the RBAC user database. It contains a single entry by default, which defines the security information for every user that has access to RBAC. The following entry gives the root user permission to do everything on the system:

```
root::::type=normal;auths=solaris.*,solaris.grant;profiles=All
```

Clearly, if the power of root was to be reduced, *solaris.** would need to be replaced with something more restricted in scope, such as *solaris.admin.**.

auth_attr

The *auth_attr* file is the RBAC authorization database. It contains lists of all authorizations defined on the system. Some sample entries are shown here:

```
solaris.admin.fsmgr.:::Mounts and Shares::
solaris.admin.fsmgr.read:::View Mounts and Shares::help=AuthFsmgrRead.html
solaris.admin.fsmgr.write:::Mount and Share Files::help=AuthFsmgrWrite.html
solaris.admin.logsvc.:::Log Viewer::
solaris.admin.logsvc.purge:::Remove Log Files::help=AuthLogsvcPurge.html
solaris.admin.logsvc.read:::View Log Files::help=AuthLogsvcRead.html
solaris.admin.logsvc.write:::Manage Log Settings::help=AuthLogsvcWrite.html
solaris.admin.serialmgr.:::Serial Port Manager::
solaris.admin.usermgr.:::User Accounts::
solaris.admin.usermgr.pswd:::Change Password::help=AuthUserMgrPswd.html
solaris.admin.usermgr.read:::View Users and Roles::
help=AuthUsermgrRead.html
solaris.admin.usermgr.write:::Manage Users::help=AuthUsermgrWrite.html
```

prof_attr

The *prof_attr* file is the RBAC profile database. Sample *prof_attr* entries for the Basic Solaris User, User Management, and User Security are shown here:

```
Basic Solaris User:::Automatically assigned rights:
auths=solaris.profmgr.read,solaris.jobs.users,
solaris.admin.usermgr.read,solaris.admin.logsvc.read,
solaris.admin.fsmgr.read,solaris.admin.serialmgr.read,
solaris.admin.diskmgr.read,solaris.admin.procmgr.user,
solaris.compsys.read,solaris.admin.printer.read,
solaris.admin.prodreg.read,solaris.admin.dcmgr.read;
profiles=All;help=RtDefault.html
User Management:::Manage users, groups, home directory:
auths=profmgr.read,solaris.admin.usermgr.write,
solaris.admin.usermgr.read;help=RtUserMngmnt.html
User Security:::Manage passwords, clearances:
auths=solaris.role.*,solaris.profmgr.*,solaris.admin.usermgr.*;
help=RtUserSecurity.html
```

exec_attr

The *exec_attr* file is the RBAC command database. It contains lists of commands associated with a specific profile. For example, a set of entries for the User Manager profile would look like this:

```
User Management:suser:cmd::::/etc/init.d/utmpd:uid=0;gid=sys
User Management:suser:cmd::::/usr/sbin/grpck:euid=0
User Management:suser:cmd::::/usr/sbin/pwck:euid=0
```

Command Reference

The following reference provides details on the different databases that are used with RBAC.

smexec

The smexec command is used to create, update, and delete rows in the *exec_attr* database. One of three options must be passed to the command upon execution: *add*, which adds an entry; *delete*, which deletes an entry; and *modify*, which updates an entry. In order to use smexec, the user must have the *solaris.profmgr.execattr.write* authorization. There are two sets of parameters that can be passed to smexec (depending on which option has been selected): authorization parameters and specific parameters for each option.

The authorization parameters are common to each option, and they specify the following characteristics:

–domain	The domain to be administered
–hostname:port	The hostname and port on which operations are to be performed (default port is 898)
–rolepassword	The password for role authentication
–password	The password for the user rather than the role
–rolename	The name of the role
–username	The name of the user

For adding entries using `smexec add`, the following parameters can be passed on the command line:

–c	Specifies the full path to the new command name to be added
–g	Specifies the effective GID for executing the new command
–G	Specifies the actual GID for executing the new command
–n	Specifies the profile name with which the command is associated
–t cmd	Specifies that the operation is a command
–u	Specifies the effective UID for executing the new command
–U	Specifies the actual UID for executing the new command

An example `smexec add` operation looks like this:

```
# smexec add -hostname localhost -password xyz123 -username root -- -n
"Print Manager" -t cmd -c /usr/sbin/lpsched -u 0 -g 0
```

This entry adds the capability to start the printing service to the Printer Manager profile, with the effective UID and GID of 0 (i.e., root).

For removing entries using `smexec delete`, the following parameters can be passed on the command line:

–c	Specifies the full path to the command name to be deleted
–n	Specifies the profile name with which the command is currently associated
–t cmd	Specifies that the operation is a command

To remove the entry for lpsched, you would use the following command:

```
# smexec delete -hostname localhost -password xyz123 -username root -- -n
"Print Manager" -t cmd -c /usr/sbin/lpsched
```

For changing entries using smexec modify, the following parameters can be passed on the command line:

–c	Specifies the full path to the command name to be modified
–g	Specifies the modified effective GID for executing the new command
–G	Specifies the modified actual GID for executing the new command
–n	Specifies the modified profile name with which the command is associated
–t cmd	Specifies that the operation is a command
–u	Specifies the modified effective UID for executing the new command
–U	Specifies the modified actual UID for executing the new command

An example smexec modify operation looks like this:

```
# smexec modify -hostname localhost -password xyz123 -username root -- -n
"Print Manager" -t cmd -c /usr/some/new/path/lpsched -u 0 -g 0
```

This entry modifies the command to start the printing service for the Printer Manager profile from the path */usr/sbin/lpsched* to */usr/some/new/path/lpsched*.

smmultiuser

The smmultiuser command is used to perform batch functions, such as adding or deleting a large number of users. This is particularly useful when a file already exists that specifies all of the required user data. For instance, a backup system may need a setup that is similar to a current production system. Rather than just copying the file systems directly, all of the operations associated with new account creation can be performed, such as creating home directories. In addition, the file that specifies the user data can be updated to include path name changes. For example, if the original system's home directories were exported using NFS, they could be mounted under the */export* mount point on the new system, and the data in the user specification file could be updated accordingly before being processed. Or, if mount points changed at a later time, user data on the system could be modified by using the smmultiuser command as well.

Like smexec, smmultiuser has three options that must be passed to the command upon execution: *add*, which adds multiple user entries; *delete*, which deletes one or more user entries; and *modify*, which modifies a set of existing entries. In order to use `smmultiuser` to change passwords, the user must have the *solaris.admin.usermgr.pswd authorization*. Two sets of parameters—authorization parameters and operation parameters—can be passed to `smmultiuser`, depending on which option has been selected.

The authorization parameters are common to each option, and they specify the following characteristics:

–domain	The domain to be administered
–hostname:port	The hostname and port on which operations are to be performed (default port is 898)
–password	The password for the user rather than the role
–rolename	The name of the role
–rolepassword	The password for role authentication
–trust	Required when operating in batch mode
–username	The name of the user

For add, delete, and modify operations using `smmultiuser`, the following parameters can be passed on the command line:

–i	Specifies the input file to be read. This contains data for all entries to be added, modified, or deleted.
–L	Specifies the name of the logfile that records whether individual operations in the batch job were a success or failure.

In the following example, a set of records is read in from */home/paul/newaccounts.txt* and added to the system:

```
# smmultiuser add -hostname localhost -p xyz123 -username root -- -I
/home/paul/newaccounts.txt
```

smuser

The `smuser` command is used to perform operations on user accounts, whether the data is retrieved from the local user databases or from NIS/NIS+. It is similar to `smmultiuser`, however, it is generally used only to add single users, rather than a set of users in batch mode. In addition to adding, deleting, and modifying user records, existing user data can be retrieved and listed. One of four options must be passed to the command upon execution: *add*, which adds an entry; *delete*, which deletes an entry; *list*, which lists all existing entries; and *modify*, which updates an entry. In order to use `smuser add`,

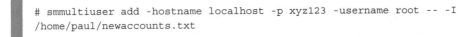

delete, or modify, the user must have the *solaris.profmgr.execattr.write* authorization. However, only the *solaris.admin.usermgr.write* authorization is required to list entries.

There are two sets of parameters that can be passed to smuser (depending on which option has been selected): authorization parameters and specific parameters for each option. The authorization parameters are common to each option, and they specify the following characteristics:

–domain	The domain to be administered. This can be the local databases (file), NIS (nis), NIS+ (nisplus), DNS (dns), or LDAP (ldap). To administer the host *foxtrot.cassowary.net* using LDAP, you would specify the domain as *ldap://foxtrot/cassowary.net*.
–hostname:port	The hostname and port on which operations are to be performed. The default port is 898.
–password	The password for the user rather than the role.
–rolename	The name of the role.
–rolepassword	The password for role authentication.
–username	The name of the user.

For adding entries using smuser add, the parameters are similar to those discussed for adding users using useradd, as described in Chapter 10. The following parameters can be passed on the command line:

–c	Specifies an account description, such as "Joe Bloggs"
–d	Specifies the user's home directory
–e	Specifies the account expiration date
–f	Specifies a limit on the number of inactive days before an account is expired
–F	Specifies a full name for the account, which must not be used by another account within the domain
–g	Specifies the account GID
–n	Specifies the account name
–P	Specifies the account password
–s	Specifies the default shell
–u	Specifies the account UID

An example `smuser add` command is shown here:

```
# smuser add -H localhost -p xyz123 -u root -- -F "Paul Watters"
  -n walrus -c "Paul A Watters Director" -P jimmy123 -g 10 -u 1025
```

This command adds an account called *walrus* to the system for *Paul Watters*, with the password *jimmy123*. The UID for the account is 1025, and the GID is 10.

For removing entries using `smuser delete`, only the *–n* parameter, specifying the account name, needs to be passed on the command line. The following command would remove the account for *walrus* on the localhost:

```
# smuser delete -H localhost -p xyz123 -u root -- -n walrus
```

The `smuser list` command can display a list of users without any parameters, by using a command like this:

```
# smuser list -H localhost -p xyz123 -u root --
```

For modifying entries using `smuser modify`, the same parameters can be passed on the command line as for `smuser add`, with any new supplied values resulting in the appropriate fields being updated. For example, to modify the default shell for a user to the Korn shell, the following command would be used:

```
# smuser update -H localhost -p xyz123 -u root -- -n walrus -s /bin/ksh
```

smprofile

The `smprofile` command is used to create, list, update, and delete profiles in the *prof_attr* database, using `smprofile add`, `smprofile list`, `smprofile modify`, and `smprofile delete`, respectively. The authorization arguments are similar to those used for `smuser` and `smexec`. For adding entries using `smprofile add`, the following parameters can be passed on the command line:

–a	Adds a single authorization or a set of authorizations
–d	Adds a description for the new profile
–m	Specifies the path to the HTML help file associated with the profile
–n	Specifies a name for the profile

An example `smprofile add` command is shown here:

```
# smprofile add -H localhost -p xyz123 -u root -- -n "Password Manager" \
  -d "Change user passwords" -a solaris.admin.usermgr.pswd \
  -m PasswordManager.html
```

This command adds a profile for the Password Manager, who has the authorization *solaris.admin.usermgr.pswd* to change passwords.

For listing entries using `smprofile list`, only the *–n* parameter can be passed on the command line, which optionally specifies the name of the profile to list. An example `smprofile list` command is shown here:

```
# smprofile list -H localhost -p xyz123 -u root --
```

For modifying entries using `smprofile modify`, the same parameters can be passed on the command line as for `smprofile add`. Any parameters specified will result in the corresponding field being updated. An example `smprofile modify` command is shown here:

```
# smprofile modify -H localhost -p xyz123 -u root -- \
  -n "Password Manager" -d "Modify user passwords
```

This example changes the description for the profile Password Manager.

For deleting entries using `smprofile delete`, only the *–n* parameter can be passed on the command line, which specifies the name of the profile to delete. An example `smprofile delete` command is shown here:

```
# smprofile delete -H localhost -p xyz123 -u root -- \
  -n "Password Manager"
```

smrole

The `smrole` command is used to perform operations on role accounts. It is generally used to add single roles rather than a set of roles in batch mode. In addition to adding, deleting, and modifying role account records, existing role data can be retrieved and listed. One of four options must be passed to the command upon execution: *add*, which adds an entry; *delete*, which deletes an entry; *list*, which lists all existing entries; and *modify*, which updates an entry. In order to use `smrole add`, `delete`, or `modify`, the user must have the *solaris.role.write* authorization. However, only the *solaris.admin.usermgr.read* authorization is required to list entries. There are two sets of parameters that can be passed to `smrole` (depending on which option has been selected): authorization parameters and specific parameters for each option. The authorization parameters are similar to those used for `smuser`.

For adding entries using `smrole add`, the following parameters can be passed on the command line:

–c	Specifies a role account description, such as "System Manager"
–d	Specifies the role account's home directory
–G	Specifies any secondary GIDs for the role account, because the primary GID is always *sysadmin*
–n	Specifies the role name
–P	Specifies the account password
–s	Specifies the default shell
–u	Specifies the account UID

An example `smrole add` command is shown here:

```
# smrole add -H localhost -p xyz123 -u root -- -F "System Manager" \
  -n bofh -P abc123 -G 10 -u 666
```

This command adds an account called *bofh* to the system for System Manager, with the password *jimmy123*. The UID for the account is 666, and the secondary GID is 10.

For removing entries using `smrole delete`, only the *–n* parameter, specifying the role account name, needs to be passed on the command line. The following command would remove the account for *bofh* on the localhost:

```
# smrole delete -H localhost -p xyz123 -u root -- -n bofh
```

The `smrole list` command can display a list of roles without any parameters, by using a command like this:

```
# smrole list -H localhost -p xyz123 -u root --
```

For modifying entries using `smrole modify`, the same parameters can be passed on the command line as for `smrole add`, with any new supplied values resulting in the appropriate fields being updated. For example, to modify the default shell for a role to the Bourne shell, the following command would be used:

```
# smrole update -H localhost -p xyz123 -u root -- -n walrus -s /bin/sh
```

MANAGING USERS
AND ROLES

Chapter 13

Process Management

Processes lie at the heart of modern multi-user operating systems, providing the ability to run multiple applications and services concurrently on top of the kernel. In user terms, process management is a central feature of using a single login shell to start and stop multiple jobs running concurrently, often suspending their execution while waiting for input. Solaris 9 provides many tools for process management, which have changed significantly during the transition from Solaris 1. This chapter highlights the new process management tools and command formats, and it discusses the innovative /proc file systems and associated tools that allow administrators to deal with "zombie" processes. This chapter will also talk about automating tasks and using the scheduling facility.

Key Concepts

One of the appealing characteristics of Solaris and other UNIX-like systems is that applications can execute (or *spawn*) other applications; after all, user shells are nothing more than applications themselves. A shell can spawn another shell or application, which can spawn another shell or application, and so on. Instances of applications, such as the Sendmail mail transport agent or the Telnet remote access application, can be uniquely identified as individual processes and are associated with a unique process identifier (PID), which is an integer.

You may be wondering why process identifiers are not content addressable—that is, why the Sendmail process cannot be identified as simply Sendmail. Such a scheme would be quite sensible if it were impossible to execute multiple, independent instances of the same application (like early versions of the MacOS). However, Solaris allows the same user or different users to concurrently execute the same application independently, which means that an independent identifier is required for each process. This also means that each PID is related to a user identifier (UID) and to that user's group identifier (GID). The UID in this case can be either the *real* UID of the user who executed the process or the *effective* UID if the file executed is setUID. Similarly, the GID in this case can either be the *real* GID, which the user who executed the process belongs to, or the *effective* GID if the file executed is setGID. When an application can be executed as setUID and setGID, other users can execute such a program as the user who owns the file. This means that setting a file as setGID for root can be dangerous in some situations, although necessary in others.

An application, such as a shell, can spawn another application by using the system call system() in a C program. This is expensive performance-wise, however, because a new shell process is spawned in addition to the target application. However, an alternative is to use the fork() system call, which spawns child processes directly, with applications executed using exec(). Each child process is linked back to its parent process; if the parent process exits, the parent process automatically reverts to PID 1, which exits when the system is shut down or rebooted.

In this section, you'll look at ways to determine which processes are currently running on your system and how to examine process lists and tables to determine what system resources are being used by specific processes.

The main command used to list commands is ps, which is highly configurable and has many command-line options. These options, and the command format, changed substantially from Solaris 1 to Solaris 9: the former used BSD-style options, like ps aux, while the latter uses System V–style parameters, like ps -eaf.

However, ps takes a snapshot of the current process list; many administrators find that they need to interactively monitor processes on systems that have a high load, so they kill processes that are consuming too much memory or at least assign them a lower execution priority. One popular process monitoring tool is *top*, which is described later in this chapter in the section "Using the *top* Program."

As shown in Figure 13-1, the CDE (Common Desktop Environment) also has its own graphical "process finder," which also lists currently active processes. It is possible to

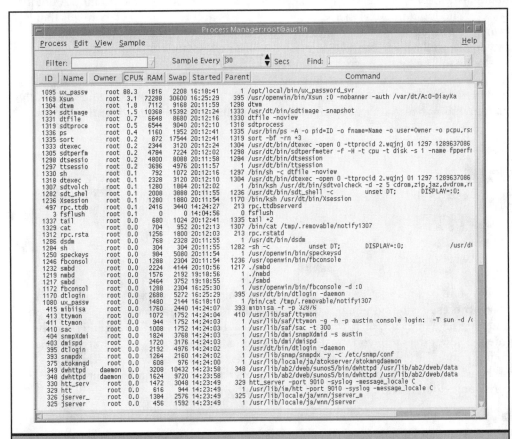

Figure 13-1. *CDE's graphical process finder*

list processes here by PID, name, owner, percentage of CPU time consumed, physical memory used, virtual memory used, date started, parent PID, and the actual command executed. This does not provide as much information as *top*, but it is a useful tool within the CDE.

Sending Signals

Since all processes are identifiable by a single PID, the PID can be used to manage that process, by means of a *signal*. Signals can be sent to other processes in C programs using the signal() function, or they can be sent directly from within the shell. Solaris supports a number of standard signal types that can be used as a means of interprocess communication.

A common use for signals is to manage user applications that are launched from a shell. A "suspend" signal, for example, can be sent to an application running in the foreground by pressing CTRL-Z at any time. To run this application in the background in the C-shell, for example, you would need to type **bg** at the command prompt. A unique background job number is then assigned to the job, and typing **fg** *n*, where *n* is that job number, brings the process back to the foreground. You can run as many applications as you like in the background.

In the following example, httpd is run in the foreground. When you press CTRL-Z, the process is suspended, and when you type **bg**, it is assigned the background process number 1. You can then execute other commands, such as ls, while httpd runs in the background. When you then type **fg**, the process is brought once again into the foreground.

```
client 1% httpd
^z
Suspended
client 2% bg
[1] httpd&
client 3% ls
httpd.conf   access.conf   srm.conf
client 4% fg
```

A useful command is the kill command, which is used to send signals directly to any process on the system. It is usually called with two parameters—the signal type and the *PID*. For example, if you have made changes to the configuration file for the Internet super daemon, you must send a signal to the daemon to tell it to re-read its configuration file. Note that you don't need to restart the daemon itself: This is one of the advantages of a process-based operating system that facilitates interprocess communication. If inetd had the PID 167, typing

```
# kill -1 167
```

would force `inetd` to re-read its configuration file and update its internal settings. The *–1* parameter stands for the *SIGHUP* signal, which means "hang up." However, imagine a situation in which you wanted to switch off `inetd` temporarily to perform a security check. You can send a `kill` signal to the process by using the "*–9* parameter (the *SIGKILL* signal):

```
# kill -1 167
```

Although *SIGHUP* and *SIGKILL* are the most commonly used signals in the shell, several others are used by programmers and are defined in the signal.h header file. Another potential consequence of sending a signal to a process is that instead of "hanging up" or "being killed," the process could exit and dump a *core file*, which is a memory image of the process to which the message was sent. This result is useful for debugging, although too many core files will quickly fill up your file system! You can always obtain a list of available signals to the `kill` command by passing the *–l* option:

```
$ kill -l
HUP INT QUIT ILL TRAP ABRT EMT FPE KILL BUS SEGV SYS PIPE
ALRM TERM USR1 USR2 CLD PWR WINCH URG POLL STOP TSTP CONT
TTIN TTOU VTALRM PROF XCPU XFSZ WAITING LWP FREEZE THAW
RTMIN RTMIN+1 RTMIN+2 RTMIN+3 RTMAX-3 RTMAX-2 RTMAX-1
RTMAX
```

Procedures

The following procedures are commonly used to manage processes.

Listing Processes

You can use the `ps` command to list all currently active processes on the local system. By default, `ps` prints the processes belonging to the user who issues the `ps` command:

```
$ ps
PID TTY        TIME CMD
 29081 pts/8     0:00 ksh
```

The columns in the default `ps` list are the process identifier (PID), the terminal from which the command was executed (TTY), the CPU time consumed by the process (TIME), and the actual command that was executed (CMD), including any command-line options passed to the program.

Alternatively, if you would like more information about the current user's processes, you can add the *–f* parameter:

```
$ ps -f
     UID     PID    PPID   C STIME      TTY         TIME CMD
   pwatters 29081  29079   0 10:40:30 pts/8       0:00 /bin/ksh
```

Again, the PID, TTY, CPU time, and command are displayed. However, the UID is also displayed, as is the PID of the parent process (PPID), along with the starting time of the process (STIME). In addition, a deprecated column (C) is used to display processor utilization. To obtain the maximum detail possible, you can also use the *–l* option, which means "long"—and long it certainly is, as shown in this example:

```
$ ps -l
 F S  UID    PID  PPID C PRI NI    ADDR  SZ    WCHAN TTY    TIME CMD
 8 S 6049 29081 29079 0  51 20 e11b4830 372 e11b489c pts/8  0:00 ksh
 8 R 6049 29085 29081 0  51 20 e101b0d0 512          pts/8  0:00 bash
```

Here, you can see the following:

- The flags (F) associated with the processes

- The state (S) of the processes (29081 is sleeping "S", 29085 is running "R")

- The process identifier (29081 and 29085)

- Parent process identifier (29079 and 29081)

- Processor utilization (deprecated)

- Process priority (PRI), which is 51

- Nice value (NI), which is 20

- Memory address (ADDR), which is expressed in hex (e11b4830 and e101b0d0)

- Size (SZ), in kilobytes, which is 372K and 512K

- The memory address for sleeping process events (WCHAN), which is e11b489c for PID 29081

- CPU time used (TIME)

- The command executed (CMD)

If you're a system administrator, you're probably not interested in the status of just your own processes; you probably want details about all or some of the processes actively running on the system, and you can do this in many ways. You can generate a process list using the *–A* or the *–e* option, for example, and either of these lists information for all processes currently running on the machine:

```
# ps -A
    PID TTY         TIME CMD
      0 ?          0:00 sched
      1 ?          0:01 init
      2 ?          0:01 pageout
      3 ?          9:49 fsflush
    258 ?          0:00 ttymon
    108 ?          0:00 rpcbind
    255 ?          0:00 sac
     60 ?          0:00 devfseve
     62 ?          0:00 devfsadm
    157 ?          0:03 automount
    110 ?          0:01 keyserv
    112 ?          0:04 nis_cache
    165 ?          0:00 syslogd
```

Again, the default display of PID, TTY, CPU time, and command is generated. The processes listed relate to the scheduler, *init*, the system logging facility, the NIS cache, and several other standard applications and services.

It is good practice for you to become familiar with the main processes on your system and the relative CPU times they usually consume. This can be useful information when troubleshooting or when evaluating security. One of the nice features of the ps command is the ability to combine multiple flags to print out a more elaborate process list. For example, we can combine the *–A* option (all processes) with the *–f* option (full details) to produce a process list with full details. Here are the full details for the same process list:

```
# ps -Af
     UID   PID  PPID  C    STIME TTY   TIME CMD
    root     0     0  0   Mar 20 ?    0:00 sched
    root     1     0  0   Mar 20 ?    0:01 /etc/init -
    root     2     0  0   Mar 20 ?    0:01 pageout
    root     3     0  0   Mar 20 ?    9:51 fsflush
    root   258   255  0   Mar 20 ?    0:00 /usr/lib/saf/ttymon
    root   108     1  0   Mar 20 ?    0:00 /usr/sbin/rpcbind
    root   255     1  0   Mar 20 ?    0:00 /usr/lib/saf/sac -t 300
    root    60     1  0   Mar 20 ?    0:00 /usr/lib/devfsadm/devfseventd
    root    62     1  0   Mar 20 ?    0:00 /usr/lib/devfsadm/devfsadmd
    root   157     1  0   Mar 20 ?    0:03 /usr/lib/autofs/automountd
    root   110     1  0   Mar 20 ?    0:01 /usr/sbin/keyserv
```

```
root    112    1  0   Mar 20 ?    0:05 /usr/sbin/nis_cachemgr
root    165    1  0   Mar 20 ?    0:00 /usr/sbin/syslogd
```

Another common use for ps is to print process information in a format that is suitable for the scheduler:

```
% ps -c
   PID  CLS PRI TTY       TIME CMD
 29081   TS  48 pts/8    0:00 ksh
 29085   TS  48 pts/8    0:00 bash
```

Doing this can be useful when used in conjunction with the priocntl command, which displays the parameters used for process scheduling. This allows administrators, in particular, to determine the process classes currently available on the system, or to set the class of a specific process to interactive or time-sharing. You can obtain a list of all the supported classes by passing the –*l* parameter to priocntl:

```
# priocntl -l
CONFIGURED CLASSES
==================
SYS (System Class)
TS (Time Sharing)
        Configured TS User Priority Range: -60 through 60
IA (Interactive)
        Configured IA User Priority Range: -60 through 60
```

You can combine this with a –*f* full display flag to ps –c to obtain more information:

```
$ ps -cf
     UID    PID   PPID  CLS PRI     STIME TTY       TIME CMD
    paul  29081  29079   TS  48 10:40:30 pts/8    0:00 /bin/ksh
    paul  29085  29081   TS  48 10:40:51 pts/8    0:00
/usr/local/bin/bash
```

If you want to obtain information about processes being executed by a particular group of users, this can be specified on the command line by using the –*g* option, followed by the GID of the target group. In this example, all processes from users in group 0 will be printed:

```
$ ps -g 0
   PID TTY        TIME CMD
     0 ?          0:00 sched
     1 ?          0:01 init
     2 ?          0:01 pageout
     3 ?          9:51 fsflush
```

Another common configuration option used with ps is *–j*, which displays the session identifier (SID) and the process group identifier (PGID), as shown here:

```
$ ps -j
   PID   PGID   SID TTY        TIME CMD
 29081 29081 29081 pts/8      0:00 ksh
 29085 29085 29081 pts/8      0:00 bash
```

Finally, you can print out the status of lightweight processes (LWP) in your system. These are virtual CPU or execution resources, which are designed to make the best use of available CPU resources based on their priority and scheduling class. Here is an example:

```
$ ps -L
   PID   LWP TTY      LTIME CMD
 29081     1 pts/8    0:00 ksh
 29085     1 pts/8    0:00 bash
```

Using the top Program

If you're an administrator, you probably want to keep an eye on all processes running on a system, particularly if the system is in production use. This is because buggy programs can consume large amounts of CPU time, preventing operational applications from carrying out their duties efficiently. Monitoring the process list almost constantly is necessary, especially if performance begins to suffer on a system. Although you could keep typing **ps –eaf** every 5 minutes or so, a much more efficient method is to use the *top* program to monitor the processes in your system interactively, and to use its "vital statistics," such as CPU activity states, real and virtual memory status, and the load average. In addition, *top* displays the details of the leading processes which consume the greatest amount of CPU time during each sampling period.

The display of *top* can be customized to include any number of these leading processes at any one time, but displaying the top 10 or 20 processes is usually sufficient to keep an eye on rogue processes. The latest version of *top* can always be downloaded from **ftp://ftp.groupsys.com/pub/top**.

top reads the /proc file system to generate its process statistics. This usually means that *top* runs as a setUID process, unless you remove the read and execute permissions for non root users and run it only as root. Paradoxically, doing this may be just as dangerous, because any errors in *top* may impact the system at large if executed by the root user. Again, setUID processes are dangerous, and you should evaluate whether the tradeoff between accessibility and security is worthwhile in this case.

One of the main problems with *top* running on Solaris is that top is very sensitive to changes in architecture and/or operating system version. This is particularly the case if the GNU gcc compiler is used to build *top*, as it has its own set of include files. These must exactly match the version of the current operating system, otherwise, *top* will not work properly; the CPU state percentages may be wrong, indicating that processes are consuming all CPU time, when the system is actually idle. The solution is to rebuild gcc so that it generates header files that are appropriate for your current operating system version.

Let's examine a printout from *top*:

```
last PID: 16630;  load averages:  0.17,  0.08,  0.06     09:33:29
72 processes:  71 sleeping, 1 on cpu
CPU states: 87.6% idle, 4.8% user, 7.5% kernel, 0.1% iowait, 0.0% swap
Memory: 128M real, 3188K free, 72M swap in use, 172M swap free
```

This summary tells us that the system has 72 processes, with only 1 running actively and 71 sleeping. The system was 87.6 percent idle in the previous sampling epoch, and there was little swapping or iowait activity, ensuring fast performance. The load average for the previous 1, 5, and 15 minutes was 0.17, 0.08, and 0.06, respectively—this is not a machine that is taxed by its workload. The last PID to be issued to an application, 16630, is also displayed.

```
  PID USERNAME THR PRI NICE  SIZE   RES STATE   TIME    CPU COMMAND
  259 root       1  59    0   18M 4044K sleep  58:49  1.40% Xsun
16630 pwatters   1  59    0 1956K 1536K cpu     0:00  1.19% top
  345 pwatters 8  33    0 7704K 4372K sleep   0:21  0.83% dtwm
16580 pwatters 1  59    0 5984K 2608K sleep   0:00  0.24% dtterm
 9196 pwatters 1  48    0   17M 1164K sleep   0:28  0.01% netscape
13818 pwatters 1  59    0 5992K  872K sleep   0:01  0.00% dtterm
  338 pwatters 1  48    0 7508K   0K sleep   0:04  0.00% dtsession
  112 pwatters 3  59    0 1808K  732K sleep   0:03  0.00% nis_cachemgr
  157 pwatters 5  58    0 2576K  576K sleep   0:02  0.00% automountd
  422 pwatters 1  48    0 4096K  672K sleep   0:01  0.00% textedit
 2295 pwatters 1  48    0 7168K   0K sleep   0:01  0.00% dtfile
 8350 root      10  51    0 3000K 2028K sleep   0:01  0.00% nscd
 8757 pwatters 1  48   10 5992K 1340K sleep   0:01  0.00% dtterm
 4910 nobody    1   0    0 1916K   0K sleep   0:00  0.00% httpd
  366 pwatters 1  28    0 1500K   0K sleep   0:00  0.00% sdtvolcheck
```

This *top* listing shows a lot of information about each process running on the system, including the PID, the user who owns the process, the nice value (priority), the size of the application, the amount resident in memory, its current state (active or sleeping), the CPU time consumed, and the command name. For example, the Apache Web server runs as the httpd process (PID=4910) by the user nobody and is 1916K in size.

Changing the nice value of a process ensures that it receives more or less priority from the process scheduler. Reducing the nice value ensures that the process priority is decreased, while increasing the nice value increases the process priority. Unfortunately, while ordinary users can decrease their nice value, only the super-user can increase the nice value for a process. In the preceding example for top, the dtterm process is running with a nice value of 10, which is low. If the root user wanted to increase the priority of the process by 20, he /she would issue the command:

```
# nice --20 dtterm
```

Reducing the nice value can be performed by any user. To reduce the nice value of the top process, the following command would be used:

```
$ nice -20 ps
```

Now, if you execute an application that requires a lot of CPU power, you will be able to monitor the impact on the system as a whole by examining the changes in the processes displayed by *top*. If you execute the command

```
$ find . -name apache -print
```

the impact on the process distribution is immediately apparent:

```
last PID: 16631;  load averages: 0.10, 0.07, 0.06   09:34:08
73 processes:  71 sleeping, 1 running, 1 on cpu
CPU states:  2.2% idle,  0.6% user, 11.6% kernel, 85.6% iowait,
0.0% swap
Memory: 128M real, 1896K free, 72M swap in use, 172M swap free
```

This summary tells you that the system now has 73 processes, with only 1 running actively, 1 on the CPU, and 71 sleeping. The new process is the find command, which is actively running. The system is now only 2.2 percent idle, a large increase on the previous sampling epoch. There is still no swapping activity, but iowait activity has risen to 85.6 percent, slowing system performance. The load average for the previous 1, 5, and 15 minutes was 0.10, 0.07, and 0.06, respectively—on the average, this machine is still not taxed by its workload and wouldn't be unless the load averages grew to greater than 1. The last PID to be issued to an application, 16631, is also displayed, and in this case it again refers to the `find` command.

```
  PID USERNAME THR PRI NICE  SIZE    RES STATE   TIME    CPU COMMAND
16631 pwatters 1   54    0   788K   668K run      0:00  1.10% find
  259 root         1   59    0    18M  4288K sleep   58:49  0.74% Xsun
16630 pwatters 1   59    0  1956K 1536K cpu      0:00  0.50% top
 9196 pwatters 1   48    0    17M  3584K sleep    0:28  0.13% netscape
 8456 pwatters 1   59    0  5984K    0K sleep    0:00  0.12% dtpad
  345 pwatters 8   59    0  7708K    0K sleep    0:21  0.11% dtwm
16580 pwatters 1   59    0  5992K 2748K sleep    0:00  0.11% dtterm
13838 pwatters 1   38    0  2056K  652K sleep    0:00  0.06% bash
13818 pwatters 1   59    0  5992K 1884K sleep    0:01  0.06% dtterm
  112 root         3   59    0  1808K  732K sleep    0:03  0.02% nis_cachemgr
  337 pwatters 4   59    0  4004K    0K sleep    0:00  0.01% ttsession
  338 pwatters 1   48    0  7508K    0K sleep    0:04  0.00% dtsession
  157 root         5   58    0  2576K  604K sleep    0:02  0.00% automountd
 2295 pwatters 1   48    0  7168K    0K sleep    0:01  0.00% dtfile
  422 pwatters 1   48    0  4096K    0K sleep    0:01  0.00% textedit
```

`find` now uses 1.1 percent of CPU power, which is the highest of any active process (i.e., in the "run" state) on the system. It uses 788K of RAM, less than most other processes; however, most other processes are in the "sleep" state, and do not occupy much resident memory.

Using the truss Program

If you've identified a process that appears to be having problems, and you suspect it's an application bug, it's not just a matter of going back to the source to debug the program or making an educated guess about what's going wrong. In fact, one of the great features of Solaris is the ability to trace system calls for every process running on the system. This means that if a program is hanging, for example, because it can't find its initialization file, the failed system call revealed using *truss* would display this information. *truss* prints out each system call, line by line, as it is executed by the system. The syntax is rather like a C program, making it easy for C programmers to interpret the output. The arguments are displayed by retrieving information from the appropriate headers, and any file information is also displayed.

As an example, let's look at the output from the `cat` command, which we can use to display the contents of /etc/resolv.conf, which is used by the Domain Name Service (DNS) to identify domains and name servers. Let's look at the operations involved in this running this application:

```
# truss cat /etc/resolv.conf
execve("/usr/bin/cat", 0xEFFFF740, 0xEFFFF74C)  argc = 2
open("/dev/zero", O_RDONLY)                      = 3
```

```
mmap(0x00000000, 8192, PROT_READ|PROT_WRITE|PROT_EXEC, MAP_PRIVATE, 3, 0) =
 0xEF7B0000
open("/usr/lib/libc.so.1", O_RDONLY)              = 4
fstat(4, 0xEFFFF2DC)                              = 0
mmap(0x00000000, 8192, PROT_READ|PROT_EXEC, MAP_PRIVATE, 4, 0) = 0xEF7A0000
mmap(0x00000000, 704512, PROT_READ|PROT_EXEC, MAP_PRIVATE, 4, 0) =
 0xEF680000
munmap(0xEF714000, 57344)
              = 0
mmap(0xEF722000, 28368, PROT_READ|PROT_WRITE|PROT_EXEC, MAP_PRIVATE|
MAP_FIXED, 4, 598016) = 0xEF722000
mmap(0xEF72A000, 2528, PROT_READ|PROT_WRITE|PROT_EXEC, MAP_PRIVATE|
MAP_FIXED, 3, 0) = 0xEF72A000
close(4)                                          = 0
open("/usr/lib/libdl.so.1", O_RDONLY)             = 4
fstat(4, 0xEFFFF2DC)                              = 0
mmap(0xEF7A0000, 8192, PROT_READ|PROT_EXEC, MAP_PRIVATE|
MAP_FIXED, 4, 0) = 0xEF7A0000
close(4)                                          = 0
open("/usr/platform/SUNW,Ultra-2/lib/libc_psr.so.1", O_RDONLY) = 4
fstat(4, 0xEFFFF0BC)                              = 0
mmap(0x00000000, 8192, PROT_READ|PROT_EXEC, MAP_PRIVATE, 4, 0) = 0xEF790000
mmap(0x00000000, 16384, PROT_READ|PROT_EXEC, MAP_PRIVATE, 4, 0) =
 0xEF780000
close(4)                                          = 0
close(3)                                          = 0
munmap(0xEF790000, 8192)                          = 0
fstat64(1, 0xEFFFF648)                            = 0
open64("resolv.conf", O_RDONLY)                   = 3
fstat64(3, 0xEFFFF5B0)                            = 0
llseek(3, 0, SEEK_CUR)                            = 0
mmap64(0x00000000, 98, PROT_READ, MAP_SHARED, 3, 0) = 0xEF790000
read(3, " d", 1)                                  = 1
memcntl(0xEF790000, 98, MC_ADVISE, 0x0002, 0, 0) = 0
domain paulwatters.com
nameserver 192.56.67.16
nameserver 192.56.67.32
nameserver 192.56.68.16
write(1, " d o m a i n   p a u l w a t t e r s .".., 98)    = 98
llseek(3, 98, SEEK_SET)                           = 98
munmap(0xEF790000, 98)                            = 0
llseek(3, 0, SEEK_CUR)                            = 98
close(3)                                          = 0
close(1)                                          = 0
llseek(0, 0, SEEK_CUR)                            = 57655
_exit(0)
```

First, `cat` is called using *execve()*, with two arguments (i.e., the application name, *cat*, and the file to be displayed, */etc/resolv.conf*). The arguments to *execve* include the name of the application (*/usr/bin/cat*), a pointer to the argument list (0xEFFFF740), and a pointer to the environment (0xEFFFF74C). Next, library files such as */usr/lib/libc.so.1* are read. Memory operations (such as *mmap()*) are performed continuously. The resolv .conf is opened as read-only, after which the contents are literally printed to standard output. Then the file is closed. *truss* can be used in this way to trace the system calls for any process running on your system.

Automating Jobs

Many system administration tasks need to be performed on a regular basis. For example, log files for various applications need to be archived nightly and a new log file created. Often, a short script is created to perform this, by following these steps:

1. Kill the daemon affected, using the `kill` command.

2. Compress the logfile using the `gzip` or `compress` command.

3. Change the log filename to include a timestamp so that it can be distinguished from other logfiles by using the `time` command.

4. Move it to an archive directory, using the `mv` command.

5. Create a new logfile by using the `touch` command.

6. Restart the daemon by calling the appropriate */etc/init.d* script.

Instead of the administrator having to execute these commands interactively at midnight, they can be scheduled to run daily using the `cron` scheduling command. Alternatively, if a job needs to be run only once at a particular time, like bringing a new Web site online at 7 A.M. one particular morning, the `at` scheduler can be used. The next section looks at the advantages and disadvantages of each scheduling method.

Using at

You can schedule a single system event for execution at a specified time by using the `at` command. The jobs are specified by files in the */var/spool/cron/atjobs*, while configuration is managed by the file */etc/cron.d/at.deny*. The job can be a single command, or it can refer to a script that contains a set of commands.

Suppose, for example, that you want to start up Sendmail at a particular time because some scheduled maintenance of the network infrastructure is scheduled to occur until 8:30 A.M tomorrow morning, but you really don't feel like logging in early and starting up Sendmail (you've switched it off completely during an outage to prevent users from filling the queue). You can add a job to the queue, which is scheduled to run at 8:40 A.M., giving the network guys a 10-minute window to do their work:

```
$ at 0840
at> /usr/lib/sendmail -bd
```

```
at> <EOT>
commands will be executed using /bin/ksh
job 954715200.a at Mon Apr  3 08:40:00 2000
```

After submitting a job using at, check that the job is properly scheduled by checking to see whether an *atjob* has been created:

```
$ cd /var/spool/cron/atjobs
client% ls -l
total 8
-r-Sr--r--   1 paul     other       3701 Apr  3 08:35 954715200.a
```

The file exists, which is a good start. Now check that it contains the appropriate commands to run the job:

```
$ cat 954715200.a
: at job
: jobname: stdin
: notify by mail: no
export PWD; PWD='/home/paul'
export _; _='/usr/bin/at'
cd /home/paul
umask 22
ulimit unlimited
/usr/lib/sendmail -bd
```

This looks good. After 8:40 A.M. the next morning, the command should have executed at the appropriate time, and some output should have been generated and sent to you as an e-mail message.

Here's what the message contains:

```
From paul Sat Apr  1 08:40:00 2000
Date: Sat Apr  1 2000 08:40:00 +1000 (EST)
From: paul <paul>
To: paul
Subject: Output from "at" job
Your "at" job on austin
"/var/spool/cron/atjobs/954715200.a"
produced the following output:
/bin/ksh[5]: sendmail: 501 Permission denied
```

Oops! You forgot to submit the job as root: normal users don't have permission to start Sendmail in the background daemon mode. You would need to submit this job as root to be successful.

Scheduling with cron

An at job executes only once at a particular time. However, cron is much more flexible because you can schedule system events to execute repetitively at regular intervals by using the crontab command.

Each user on the system can have a crontab file, which allows them to schedule multiple events at multiple times on multiple dates. The jobs are specified by files in the */var/spool/cron/cronjobs*, while configuration information is managed by the files */etc/cron.d/cron.allow* and */etc/cron.d/cron.deny*.

To check your own crontab file, you can use the crontab -l command:

```
# crontab -l root
10 3 * * 0,4 /etc/cron.d/logchecker
10 3 * * 0   /usr/lib/newsyslog
15 3 * * 0 /usr/lib/fs/nfs/nfsfind
1 2 * * * [ -x /usr/sbin/rtc ] && /usr/sbin/rtc -c > /dev/null 2>&1
30 3 * * * [ -x /usr/lib/gss/gsscred_clean ] && /usr/lib/gss/gsscred_clean
```

This is the standard crontab command generated by Solaris for root, and it performs tasks like checking whether the cron logfile is approaching the system limit at 3:10 A.M. on Sundays and Thursdays, creating a new system log at 3:10 A.M. only on Sundays, and reconciling time differences at 2:01 A.M. every day of the year.

The six fields in the crontab file stand for the following:

- Minutes, in the range 0–59
- Hours, in the range 0–23
- Days of the month, in the range 1–31
- Months of the year, in the range 1–12
- Days of the week, in the range 0–6, starting with Sundays
- The command to execute

If you want to add or delete an entry from your crontab file, you can use the crontab -e command. This will start up your default editor (*vi* on the command line, *textedit* in CDE, or as defined by the *EDITOR* environment variable), and you can make changes interactively. After saving your job, you need to run crontab by itself to make the changes.

Examples

Now that you have examined what processes are, you will now look at some special features of processes as implemented in Solaris. One of the most innovative characteristics of processes under Solaris is the process file system (PROCFS), which is mounted as the /proc file system. Images of all currently active processes are stored in the /proc file system by their PID.

Here's an example: firs, a process is identified—in this example, the current Korn shell for the user pwatters:

```
# ps -eaf | grep pwatters
 pwatters 310   291   0  Mar 20 ?        0:04 /usr/openwin/bin/Xsun

 pwatters 11959 11934  0 09:21:42 pts/1   0:00 grep pwatters
 pwatters 11934 11932  1 09:20:50 pts/1   0:00 -ksh
```

Now that you have a target PID (11934), you can change to the /proc/11934 directory and you will be able to view the image of this process:

```
# cd /proc/11934
 # ls -l
total 3497
-rw-------   1 pwatters   other    1769472 Mar 30 09:20 as
-r--------   1 pwatters   other        152 Mar 30 09:20 auxv
-r--------   1 pwatters   other         32 Mar 30 09:20 cred
--w-------   1 pwatters   other          0 Mar 30 09:20 ctl
lr-x------   1 pwatters   other          0 Mar 30 09:20 cwd ->
dr-x------   2 pwatters   other       1184 Mar 30 09:20 fd
-r--r--r--   1 pwatters   other        120 Mar 30 09:20 lpsinfo
-r--------   1 pwatters   other        912 Mar 30 09:20 lstatus
-r--r--r--   1 pwatters   other        536 Mar 30 09:20 lusage
dr-xr-xr-x   3 pwatters   other         48 Mar 30 09:20 lwp
-r--------   1 pwatters   other       2016 Mar 30 09:20 map
dr-x------   2 pwatters   other        544 Mar 30 09:20 object
-r--------   1 pwatters   other       2552 Mar 30 09:20 pagedata
-r--r--r--   1 pwatters   other        336 Mar 30 09:20 psinfo
-r--------   1 pwatters   other       2016 Mar 30 09:20 rmap
lr-x------   1 pwatters   other          0 Mar 30 09:20 root ->
-r--------   1 pwatters   other       1440 Mar 30 09:20 sigact
-r--------   1 pwatters   other       1232 Mar 30 09:20 status
-r--r--r--   1 pwatters   other        256 Mar 30 09:20 usage
```

MANAGING USERS
AND ROLES

```
-r--------   1 pwatters     other              0 Mar 30 09:20 watch
-r--------   1 pwatters     other           3192 Mar 30 09:20 xmap
```

Each of the directories with the name associated with the PID contains additional subdirectories, which contain state information, and related control functions. In addition, a watchpoint facility is provided, which is responsible for controlling memory access. A series of *proc* tools interpret the information contained in the /proc subdirectories, which display the characteristics of each process.

Using proc tools

The *proc* tools are designed to operate on data contained within the */proc* filesystem. Each utility takes a PID as its argument and performs operations associated with the PID. For example, the `pflags` command prints the flags and data model details for the PID in question.

For the preceding Korn shell example, you can easily print out this status information:

```
# /usr/proc/bin/pflags 29081
29081:   /bin/ksh
        data model = _ILP32   flags = PR_ORPHAN
  /1:    flags = PR_PCINVAL|PR_ASLEEP [ waitid(0x7,0x0,0x804714c,0x7) ]
```

You can also print the credential information for this process, including the effective and real UID and GID of the process owner, by using the `pcred` command:

```
$ /usr/proc/bin/pcred 29081
29081:   e/r/sUID=100   e/r/sGID=10
```

Here, both the effective and the real UID is 100 (user pwatters), and the effective and real GID is 10 (group staff).

To examine the address space map of the target process, you can use the `pmap` command and all of the libraries it requires to execute:

```
# /usr/proc/bin/pmap 29081
29081:   /bin/ksh
08046000       8K read/write/exec      [ stack ]
08048000     160K read/exec            /usr/bin/ksh
08070000       8K read/write/exec      /usr/bin/ksh
08072000      28K read/write/exec      [ heap ]
DFAB4000      16K read/exec            /usr/lib/locale/en_AU/en_AU.so.2
DFAB8000       8K read/write/exec      /usr/lib/locale/en_AU/en_AU.so.2
```

```
DFABB000      4K read/write/exec      [ anon ]
DFABD000     12K read/exec            /usr/lib/libmp.so.2
DFAC0000      4K read/write/exec      /usr/lib/libmp.so.2
DFAC4000    552K read/exec            /usr/lib/libc.so.1
DFB4E000     24K read/write/exec      /usr/lib/libc.so.1
DFB54000      8K read/write/exec      [ anon ]
DFB57000    444K read/exec            /usr/lib/libnsl.so.1
DFBC6000     20K read/write/exec      /usr/lib/libnsl.so.1
DFBCB000     32K read/write/exec      [ anon ]
DFBD4000     32K read/exec            /usr/lib/libsocket.so.1
DFBDC000      8K read/write/exec      /usr/lib/libsocket.so.1
DFBDF000      4K read/exec            /usr/lib/libdl.so.1
DFBE1000      4K read/write/exec      [ anon ]
DFBE3000    100K read/exec            /usr/lib/ld.so.1
DFBFC000     12K read/write/exec      /usr/lib/ld.so.1
 total     1488K
```

It's always surprising to see how many libraries are loaded when an application is executed, especially something as complicated as a shell, leading to a total of 1488K memory used. You can obtain a list of the dynamic libraries linked to each process by using the pldd command:

```
# /usr/proc/bin/pldd 29081
29081:   /bin/ksh
/usr/lib/libsocket.so.1
/usr/lib/libnsl.so.1
/usr/lib/libc.so.1
/usr/lib/libdl.so.1
/usr/lib/libmp.so.2
/usr/lib/locale/en_AU/en_AU.so.2
```

As discussed in the section "Sending Signals," *signals* are the way in which processes communicate with each other, and they can also be used from shells to communicate with spawned processes (usually to suspend or kill them).

By using the psig command, it is possible to list the signals associated with each process:

```
$ /usr/proc/bin/psig 29081
29081:   /bin/ksh
HUP     caught   RESTART
INT     caught   RESTART
QUIT    ignored
ILL     caught   RESTART
```

```
TRAP      caught   RESTART
ABRT      caught   RESTART
EMT       caught   RESTART
FPE       caught   RESTART
KILL      default
BUS       caught   RESTART
SEGV      default
SYS       caught   RESTART
PIPE      caught   RESTART
ALRM      caught   RESTART
TERM      ignored
USR1      caught   RESTART
USR2      caught   RESTART
CLD       default  NOCLDSTOP
PWR       default
WINCH     default
URG       default
POLL      default
STOP      default
TSTP      ignored
CONT      default
TTIN      ignored
TTOU      ignored
VTALRM    default
PROF      default
XCPU      caught   RESTART
XFSZ      ignored
WAITING   default
LWP       default
FREEZE    default
THAW      default
CANCEL    default
LOST      default
RTMIN     default
RTMIN+1   default
RTMIN+2   default
RTMIN+3   default
RTMAX-3   default
RTMAX-2   default
RTMAX-1   default
RTMAX     default
```

It is also possible to print a hexadecimal format stack trace for the LWP (Light Weight Process) in each process by using the pstack command. This can be useful in the same way that the truss command was used:

```
$ /usr/proc/bin/pstack 29081
29081:   /bin/ksh
 dfaf5347 waitid    (7, 0, 804714c, 7)
 dfb0d9db _waitPID  (ffffffff, 8047224, 4) + 63
 dfb40617 waitPID   (ffffffff, 8047224, 4) + 1f
 0805b792 job_wait  (719d) + 1ae
 08064be8 sh_exec   (8077270, 14) + af0
 0805e3a1 ???????? ()
 0805decd main      (1, 8047624, 804762c) + 705
  0804fa78 ???????? ()
```

Perhaps the most commonly used *proc* tool is the pfiles command, which displays all of the open files for each process. This is useful for determining operational dependencies between data files and applications:

```
$ /usr/proc/bin/pfiles 29081
29081:   /bin/ksh
  Current rlimit: 64 file descriptors
   0: S_IFCHR mode:0620 dev:102,0 ino:319009 UID:6049 GID:7 rdev:24,8
      O_RDWR|O_LARGEFILE
   1: S_IFCHR mode:0620 dev:102,0 ino:319009 UID:6049 GID:7 rdev:24,8
      O_RDWR|O_LARGEFILE
   2: S_IFCHR mode:0620 dev:102,0 ino:319009 UID:6049 GID:7 rdev:24,8
      O_RDWR|O_LARGEFILE
  63: S_IFREG mode:0600 dev:174,2 ino:990890 UID:6049 GID:1 size:3210
      O_RDWR|O_APPEND|O_LARGEFILE FD_CLOEXEC
```

In addition, it is possible to obtain the current working directory of the target process by using the pwdx command:

```
$ /usr/proc/bin/pwdx 29081
29081:   /home/paul
```

If you need to examine the process tree for all parent and child processes containing the target PID, you can use the ptree command. This is useful for determining dependencies between processes that are not apparent by consulting the process list:

```
$ /usr/proc/bin/ptree 29081
247   /usr/dt/bin/dtlogin -daemon
```

```
    28950 /usr/dt/bin/dtlogin -daemon
      28972 /bin/ksh /usr/dt/bin/Xsession
        29012 /usr/dt/bin/sdt_shell -c        unset DT;
DISPLAY=lion:0;
          29015 ksh -c         unset DT;      DISPLAY=lion:0;
                /usr/dt/bin/dt
          29026 /usr/dt/bin/dtsession
            29032 dtwm
              29079 /usr/dt/bin/dtterm
                29081 /bin/ksh
                  29085 /usr/local/bin/bash
                    29230 /usr/proc/bin/ptree 29081
```

Here, `ptree` has been executed from the Bourne again shell (`bash`), which was started from the Korn shell (`ksh`), spawned from the `dtterm` terminal window, which was spawned from the `dtwm` window manager, and so on. Although many of these proc tools will seem obscure, they are often very useful when trying to debug process-related application errors, especially in large applications like database management systems.

Using the lsof Command

lsof stands for "list open files" and lists information about files that are currently opened by the active processes running on Solaris. It is not included in the Solaris distribution; however, the current version can always be downloaded from **ftp://vic.cc.purdue.edu/ pub/tools/unix/lsof**.

What can you use `lsof` for? The answer largely depends on how many problems you encounter that relate to processes and files. Often, administrators are interested in knowing which processes are currently using a target file or files from a particular directory. This can occur when a file is locked by one application, for example, but is required by another application (again, a database system's data files are one example where this might happen if two database instances attempt to write to the files at once). If you know the path to a file of interest, you can use `lsof` to determine which processes are using files in that directory.

To examine the processes that are using files in the /tmp file system, use this:

```
$ lsof /tmp
COMMAND     PID USER      FD    TYPE DEVICE SIZE/OFF      NODE NAME
ssion       338 pwatters  txt   VREG  0,1   271596 471638794 /tmp (swap)
(unknown)   345 pwatters  txt   VREG  0,1   271596 471638794 /tmp (swap)
le         2295 pwatters  txt   VREG  0,1   271596 471638794 /tmp (swap)
le         2299 pwatters  txt   VREG  0,1   271596 471638794 /tmp (swap)
```

Obviously, there's a bug in the routines that obtain the command name (the first four characters are missing!), but since the PID is correct, this is enough information to identify the four applications that are currently using files in /tmp. For example, dtsession (PID 338) manages the CDE session for the user pwatters, who is using a temporary text file in the /tmp directory.

Another common problem that lsof is used for, with respect to the */tmp* file system, is the identification of processes that continue to write to unlinked files; thus, space is being consumed, but it may appear that no files are growing any larger! This confusing activity can be traced back to a process by using lsof. However, rather than using lsof on the */tmp* directory directly, you would need to examine the root directory ("/") on which /tmp is mounted. After finding the process that is writing to an open file, the process can be killed. If the size of a file is changing across several different sampling epochs (e.g., by running the command once a minute), you've probably found the culprit:

```
# lsof /
COMMAND     PID    USER   FD    TYPE DEVICE SIZE/OFF   NODE NAME
(unknown)     1    root   txt   VREG  102,0  446144 118299 / (/dev/dsk/c0d0s0)
(unknown)     1    root   txt   VREG  102,0    4372 293504 / (/dev/dsk/c0d0s0)
(unknown)     1    root   txt   VREG  102,0  173272 293503 / (/dev/dsk/c0d0s0)
sadm         62    root   txt   VREG  102,0  954804 101535 / (/dev/dsk/c0d0s0)
sadm         62    root   txt   VREG  102,0  165948 101569 / (/dev/dsk/c0d0s0)
sadm         62    root   txt   VREG  102,0   16132 100766 / (/dev/dsk/c0d0s0)
sadm         62    root   txt   VREG  102,0    8772 100765 / (/dev/dsk/c0d0s0)
sadm         62    root   txt   VREG  102,0  142652 101571 / (/dev/dsk/c0d0s0)
```

One of the restrictions on mounting a file system is that you can't unmount that file system if files are open on it; if files are open on a file system and it is dismounted, any changes made to the files may not be saved, resulting in data loss. Looking at a process list may not always reveal which processes are opening which files, and this can be very frustrating if Solaris refuses to unmount a file system because some files are open. Again, lsof can be used to identify the processes that are opening files on a specific file system.

The first step is to consult the output of the df command to obtain the names of currently mounted file systems:

```
$ df -k
Filesystem            kbytes      used    avail capacity  Mounted on
/proc                      0         0        0     0%    /proc
/dev/dsk/c0d0s0      2510214    929292  1530718    38%    /
fd                         0         0        0     0%    /dev/fd
/dev/dsk/c0d0s3     5347552    183471  5110606     4%    /usr/local
swap                  185524     12120   173404     7%    /tmp
```

If you wanted to unmount the /dev/dsk/c0d0s3 file system, but you were prevented from doing so because of open files, you can obtain a list of all open files under /usr/local by using this command:

```
$ lsof /dev/dsk/c0d0s3
COMMAND PID     USER  FD TYPE DEVICE SIZE/OFF    NODE NAME
postgres    423 pwatters txt VREG   102,3  1747168 457895 /usr/local
(/dev/dsk/c0d0s3)
d  4905    root txt VREG  102,3   333692   56455 /usr/local (/dev/dsk/c0d0s3)
d  4906  nobody txt VREG  102,3   333692   56455 /usr/local (/dev/dsk/c0d0s3)
d  4907  nobody txt VREG  102,3   333692   56455 /usr/local (/dev/dsk/c0d0s3)
d  4908  nobody txt VREG  102,3   333692   56455 /usr/local (/dev/dsk/c0d0s3)
d  4909  nobody txt VREG  102,3   333692   56455 /usr/local (/dev/dsk/c0d0s3)
d  4910  nobody txt VREG  102,3   333692   56455 /usr/local (/dev/dsk/c0d0s3)
d  4911  nobody txt VREG  102,3   333692   56455 /usr/local (/dev/dsk/c0d0s3)
d  4912  nobody txt VREG  102,3   333692   56455 /usr/local (/dev/dsk/c0d0s3)
d  4913  nobody txt VREG  102,3   333692   56455 /usr/local (/dev/dsk/c0d0s3)
```

Obviously, all of these processes will need to stop using the open files before the file system can be unmounted. If you're not sure where a particular command is running from, or on which file system its data files are stored, you can also use lsof to check open files by passing the PID on the command line. First, you need to identify a PID by using the ps command:

```
$ ps -eaf | grep apache
  nobody 4911 4905 0  Mar 22 ?       0:00 /usr/local/apache/bin/httpd
  nobody 4910 4905 0  Mar 22 ?       0:00 /usr/local/apache/bin/httpd
  nobody 4912 4905 0  Mar 22 ?       0:00 /usr/local/apache/bin/httpd
  nobody 4905    1 0  Mar 22 ?       0:00 /usr/local/apache/bin/httpd
  nobody 4907 4905 0  Mar 22 ?       0:00 /usr/local/apache/bin/httpd
  nobody 4908 4905 0  Mar 22 ?       0:00 /usr/local/apache/bin/httpd
  nobody 4913 4905 0  Mar 22 ?       0:00 /usr/local/apache/bin/httpd
  nobody 4909 4905 0  Mar 22 ?       0:00 /usr/local/apache/bin/httpd
  nobody 4906 4905 0  Mar 22 ?       0:00 /usr/local/apache/bin/httpd
```

Now, examine the process 4905 for Apache to see what files are currently being opened by it:

```
$ lsof -p 4905
COMMAND  PID USER   FD  TYPE DEVICE  SIZE/OFF      NODE NAME
d        4905 nobody txt  VREG  102,3   333692   56455 /usr/local
(/dev/dsk/c0d0s3)
d        4905 nobody txt  VREG  102,0    17388  100789 / (/dev/dsk/c0d0s0)
d        4905 nobody txt  VREG  102,0   954804  101535 / (/dev/dsk/c0d0s0)
d        4905 nobody txt  VREG  102,0   693900  101573 / (/dev/dsk/c0d0s0)
```

```
d        4905 nobody txt    VREG   102,0    52988 100807 / (/dev/dsk/c0d0s0)
d        4905 nobody txt    VREG   102,0     4396 100752 / (/dev/dsk/c0d0s0)
d        4905 nobody txt    VREG   102,0   175736 100804 / (/dev/dsk/c0d0s0)
```

Apache obviously has a number of open files!

Command Reference

The following commands are commonly used to manage processes.

ps

The following table summarizes the main options used with ps.

−a	Lists most frequently requested processes
−A, −e	Lists all processes
−c	Lists processes in scheduler format
−d	Lists all processes
−f	Prints comprehensive process information
−g	Prints process information on a group basis for a single group
−G	Prints process information on a group basis for a list of groups
−j	Includes SID and PGID in printout
−l	Prints complete process information
−L	Displays LWP details
−p	Lists process details for list of specified process
−P	Lists the CPU ID to which a process is bound
−s	Lists session leaders
−t	Lists all processes associated with a specific terminal
−u	Lists all processes for a specific user

kill

The following table summarizes the main signals used to communicate with processes using kill.

MANAGING USERS
AND ROLES

Signal	Code	Action	Description
SIGHUP	1	Exit	Hangup
SIGINT	2	Exit	Interrupt
SIGQUIT	3	Core	Quit
SIGILL	4	Core	Illegal Instruction
SIGTRAP	5	Core	Trace
SIGABRT	6	Core	Abort
SIGEMT	7	Core	Emulation Trap
SIGFPE	8	Core	Arithmetic Exception
SIGKILL	9	Exit	Killed
SIGBUS	10	Core	Bus Error
SIGSEGV	11	Core	Segmentation Fault
SIGSYS	12	Core	Bad System Call
SIGPIPE	13	Exit	Broken Pipe
SIGALRM	14	Exit	Alarm Clock
SIGTERM	15	Exit	Terminate

pgrep

The pgrep command is used to search for a list of processes whose names match a pattern specified on the command line. The command returns a list of corresponding PIDs. This list can then be piped to another command, such as kill, to perform some action on the processes or send them a signal.

For example, to kill all processes associated with the name "java," the following command would be used:

```
$ kill -9 `pgrep java`
```

pkill

The pkill command can be used to send signals to processes that have the same name. It is a more specific version of pgrep, since it can be used only to send signals, and the list of PIDs cannot be piped to another program.

To kill all processes associated with the name "java," the following command would be used:

```
$ pkill -9 java
```

killall

The `killall` command is used to kill all processes running on a system. It is called by shutdown when the system is being bought to run level 0. However, since a signal can be passed to the `killall` command, it is possible for a super-user to send a different signal (other than 9) to all processes. For example, to send a SIGHUP signal to all processes, the following command could be used:

```
# killall 1
```

The Complete Reference

Part IV

Managing File Systems and Printers

The
Complete
Reference

Chapter 14

Installing Disks and
File Systems

D isks are the most commonly used persistent storage devices attached to Solaris 9 systems. A wide variety of disks and disks types are available, including those using the Small Computer System Interface (SCSI) and Integrated Device Electronics (IDE) interfaces, with a variety of sustained data transfer rates (exceeding 10,000 RPM in some cases). This chapter will examine how to install disks and create file systems using standard Solaris 9 commands.

Key Concepts

The following concepts are required knowledge for installing disks and file systems.

File System Structure

Solaris file systems are generally of the type UFS (for UNIX File System), although other file system types can be defined in */etc/default/fs*. UFS file systems are found on hard disks that have both a raw and block device interface on Solaris, as found in the */dev/rdsk* and */dev/dsk* directories, respectively. Every partition created on a Solaris file system will have its own entry in */dev/dsk* and */dev/rdsk*.

A UFS file system contains the following elements:

- A boot block, which contains booting data if the file system is bootable
- A super block, which contains the location of inodes, size of the file system, number of blocks, and status
- Inodes, which store the details of files on the file system
- Data blocks, which store the files

Physical and Logical Device Names

One of the most challenging aspects of Solaris hardware to understand is the device names used by Solaris to refer to devices. Solaris uses a specific set of naming conventions to associate physical devices with instance names on the operating system. For administrators who are new to Solaris, these conventions can be incredibly confusing.

In addition, devices can also be referred to by their device name, which is associated with a device file created in the */dev* directory after configuration. For example, a hard disk may have the physical device name */pci@1f,0/pci@1,1/ide@3/dad@0,0*, which is associated with the device file */dev/dsk/c0t0d0*. In some versions of Microsoft Windows, disks are simply labeled by their drive letter (C:, D:, E:, and so on), while in Linux, device files are more simplified (for example, */dev/hda* for an IDE hard disk or */dev/sda* for a SCSI hard disk).

The benefit of the more complex Solaris logical device names and physical device references is that they make it easy to interpret the characteristics of each device by looking at its name. For the disk example above (*/pci@1f,0/pci@1,1/ide@3/dad@0,0*), we can see that the IDE hard drive is located on a PCI bus at target 0. When we view the amount of free disk space on the system, for example, it is easy to identify slices on the same disk by looking at the device name:

```
# df -k
Filesystem            kbytes     used   avail capacity  Mounted on
/proc                      0        0       0     0%    /proc
/dev/dsk/c0t0d0s0    1982988   615991 1307508    33%    /
fd                         0        0       0     0%    /dev/fd
/dev/dsk/c0t0d0s3    1487119   357511 1070124    26%    /usr
swap                  182040      416  181624     1%    /tmp
```

Here, we can see that */dev/dsk/c0t0d0s0* and */dev/dsk/c0t0d0s3* are slice 0 and slice 3 of the disk */dev/dsk/c0t0d0*.

Hard Disk Layout

When formatted for operation with the Solaris 9 operating system, hard disks are logically divided into one or more "slices" (or *partitions*) on which a single file system resides. File systems contains sets of files, which are hierarchically organized around a number of directories. The Solaris 9 system contains a number of predefined directories that often form the top level of a file system hierarchy. Many of these directories lie one level below the *root* directory (often indicated by the forward slash, /), which exists on the primary system disk of any Solaris 9 system.

In addition to a primary disk, many Solaris 9 systems have additional disks that provide storage space for user and daemon files. Each file system has a *mount point* that is usually created in the top level of the root file system. For example, the */export* file system is mounted in the top level of root file system (indicated by the /). The mount point is created by using the `mkdir` command:

```
# mkdir /export
```

In contrast, the */export/home* file system, which usually holds the home directories of users and user files, is mounted in the top level of the */export* file system. Thus, the mount point is created using this command:

```
# mkdir /export/home
```

A single logical file system can be created on a single slice, but it cannot exist on more than one slice unless an extra level of abstraction lies between the logical and physical file systems. (For example, a metadevice can be created using DiskSuite, providing *striping* across many physical disks, as described in Chapter 15.) A physical disk can also contain more than one slice. On SPARC architecture systems, eight slices can be used, numbered 0 through 7. On Intel architecture systems, however, 10 slices are available, numbered 0 through 9.

The actual assignment of logical file systems to physical slices is a matter of discretion for the individual administrator, and while Sun and other hardware vendors recommend some customary assignments, it is possible that a specific site policy, or an application's requirements, will necessitate the development of a local policy. For example, database servers often make specific requirements about the allocation of disk slices to improve performance. However, with modern high-performance RAID systems in use, these recommendations are often redundant. Since many organization will deploy many different kinds of systems, it is useful to maintain compatibility among systems as much as possible.

Figure 14-1 shows the typical file system layout for a SPARC system architecture following customary disk slice allocations.

Slice 0 holds the root partition, while Slice 1 is allocated to swap space. For systems with changing virtual memory requirements, it might be better to use a swap file on the file system rather than allocating an entire slice for swap. Slice 2 often refers to the entire disk, while */export* on Slice 3 traditionally holds older versions of the operating system that are used by client systems with lower performance (for example, Classic or LX systems, which use the trivial FTP daemon, `tftpd`, to download their operating system upon boot). These systems may also use Slice 4 as exported swap space. In addition,

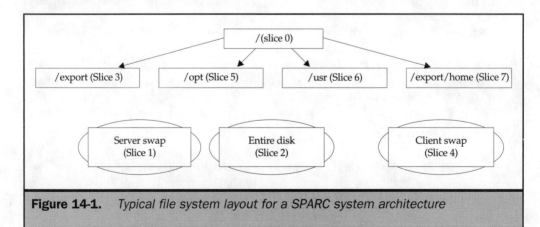

Figure 14-1.   *Typical file system layout for a SPARC system architecture*

/export may also be used for file sharing using the networked file system, Network File System (NFS). Slice 5 holds the */opt* file system, which is the default location under Solaris 9 for local packages installed using the pkgadd command. In earlier versions of Solaris, the */usr/local* file system held local packages, and this convention is still used by many sites. The system package file system */usr* is usually located on Slice 6, while */export/home* usually contains user home directories on Slice 7. Again, earlier systems located user home directories under */home,* but since this used the automounter program in Solaris 9, some contention can be expected.

Figure 14-2 shows the typical file system layout for an Intel system architecture following customary disk slice allocations. Slice 0 again holds the root partition, while Slice 1 is also allocated to swap space. Slice 2 continues to refer to the entire disk, while */export* on Slice 3 again holds older versions of the operating system that are used by client systems, and Slice 4 contains exported swap space for these clients. The local package file system */opt* is still located on Slice 5, and the system package file system */usr* is again located on Slice 6. Slice 7 contains the user home directories on */export/home.* However, the two extra slices serve different purposes: boot information for Solaris is located on Slice 8, which is known as the *boot slice*, while Slice 9 provides space for alternative disk blocks, and is known as the *alternative slice*.

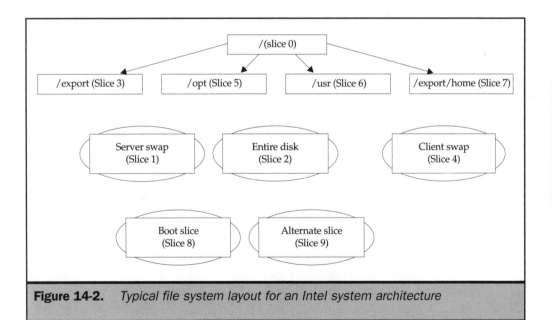

Figure 14-2.   *Typical file system layout for an Intel system architecture*

Procedures

The following procedures are commonly used for installing disks and file systems.

Creating a File System

To create a new UNIX File System, a disk must first be partitioned into different slices. These slices can then be used for creating new file systems using the mkfs or newfs command. For example, the following two commands are equivalent for the purposes of creating a new file system on the partition *c0t0d0s1*:

```
# newfs /dev/rdsk/c0t0d0s1
# mkfs -F ufs /dev/rdsk/c0t0d0s1
```

Examples: Installing Disks and File Systems

The following provides some real-world examples for installing disks and file systems.

Monitoring Disk Usage

The most commonly used command for monitoring disk space usage is /usr/bin/df, which by default displays the number of free blocks and files on all currently mounted volumes. Alternatively, many administrators create an alias for df in their shell initialization script (e.g., ~/.cshrc for C-shell) like df -k, which displays the amount of free disk space in kilobytes. The basic output for df for a SPARC system looks like this:

```
# df
Filesystem              kbytes      used    avail  capacity   Mounted on
/dev/dsk/c0t0d0s0       245911     30754   190566     14%     /
/dev/dsk/c0t0d0s4      1015679    430787   523952     46%     /usr
/proc                        0         0        0      0%     /proc
fd                           0         0        0      0%     /dev/fd
/dev/dsk/c0t0d0s3       492871    226184   217400     51%     /var
/dev/md/dsk/d1         4119256   3599121   478943     89%     /opt
swap                    256000     43480   212520     17%     /tmp
/dev/dsk/c0t2d0s3      4119256   3684920   393144     91%     /disks/vol1
/dev/md/dsk/d0        17398449  12889927  4334538     75%      /disks/vol2
/dev/md/dsk/d3         6162349   5990984   109742     99%     /disks/vol3
/dev/dsk/c1t1d0s0      8574909   5868862  1848557     77%     /disks/vol4
/dev/dsk/c2t3d0s2      1820189   1551628   177552     90%     /disks/vol5
/dev/dsk/c1t2d0s0      4124422   3548988   575434     87%     /disks/vol6
/dev/dsk/c2t2d0s3      8737664   8281113   456551     95%     /disks/vol7
/dev/md/dsk/d2         8181953   6803556  1296578     84%     /disks/vol8
client:/disks/junior_developers
                       4124560   3469376   613944     85%
                                                             /disks/junior_developers
```

For an Intel system, the output is similar, although disk slices have a different naming convention:

```
# df
Filesystem             kbytes     used    avail capacity  Mounted on
/proc                       0        0        0    0%     /proc
/dev/dsk/c0d0s0         73684    22104    44212   34%     /
/dev/dsk/c0d0s6        618904   401877   161326   72%     /usr
fd                          0        0        0    0%     /dev/fd
/dev/dsk/c0d0s1         29905     4388    22527   17%     /var
/dev/dsk/c0d0s7       7111598        9  7040474    1%     /export/home
swap                   222516      272   222244    1%     /tmp
/vol/dev/diskette0/unnamed_floppy
                         1423      131     1292   10%
                                                          /floppy/unnamed_floppy
```

df has a number of command line options that can used to customize the collection and display of information. For example, this code prints usage data for all file systems:

```
# df -a
Filesystem             kbytes     used    avail capacity  Mounted on
/dev/dsk/c0t0d0s0      245911    30754   190566   14%     /
/dev/dsk/c0t0d0s4     1015679   430787   523952   46%     /usr
/proc                       0        0        0    0%     /proc
fd                          0        0        0    0%     /dev/fd
/dev/dsk/c0t0d0s3      492871   226185   217399   51%     /var
/dev/md/dsk/d1        4119256  3599121   478943   89%     /opt
swap                   256000    43480   212520   17%     /tmp
/dev/dsk/c0t2d0s3     4119256  3684920   393144   91%     /disks/vol1
/dev/md/dsk/d0       17398449 12889927  4334538   75%     /disks/vol2
/dev/md/dsk/d3        6162349  5990984   109742   99%     /disks/vol3
/dev/dsk/c1t1d0s0     8574909  5868862  1848557   77%     /disks/vol4
/dev/dsk/c2t3d0s2     1820189  1551628   177552   90%     /disks/vol5
/dev/dsk/c1t2d0s0     4124422  3548988   575434   87%     /disks/vol6
auto_direct           4124560  3469376   613944   85%     /disks/www
auto_direct                 0        0        0    0%     /disks/ftp
server:vold(pid329)
                            0        0        0    0%     /vol
/dev/dsk/c2t2d0s3     8737664  8281113   456551   95%     /disks/vol7
/dev/md/dsk/d2        8181953  6803556  1296578   84%     /disks/vol8
client:/disks/junior_developers
                      4124560  3469376   613944   85%
                                                          /disks/junior_developers
```

It prints even those file systems that have their "ignore" option set in their entries in
/etc/mnttab:

```
# cat /etc/mnttab
/dev/dsk/c0t0d0s0          /        ufs      rw,suid,dev=800000,
                                             largefiles   944543087
/dev/dsk/c0t0d0s4          /usr     ufs      rw,suid,dev=800004,
                                             largefiles   944543087
/proc    /proc    proc    rw,suid,dev=29c0000     944543087
fd       /dev/fd fd       rw,suid,dev=2a80000     944543087
/dev/dsk/c0t0d0s3          /var     ufs      rw,suid,dev=800003,
                                             largefiles   944543087
/dev/md/dsk/d1   /opt     ufs      suid,rw,largefiles,dev=1540001  944543105
swap     /tmp     tmpfs   ,dev=1 944543105
/dev/dsk/c0t2d0s3          /disks/vol1ufs       suid,rw,
                                             largefiles,dev=800013    944543105
/dev/md/dsk/d0   /disks/vol2      ufs      nosuid,rw,
                                             largefiles, dev=1540000  944543105
/dev/md/dsk/d3   /disks/vol3      ufs      nosuid,rw,
                                             largefiles,dev=1540003   944543106
/dev/dsk/c1t1d0s0          /disks/vol4 ufs      nosuid,rw,
                                             largefiles,dev=800080 944543105
/dev/dsk/c2t3d0s2          /disks/vol5      ufs      nosuid,rw,
                                             largefiles,dev=80010a 944543106
/dev/dsk/c1t2d0s0          /disks/vol6 ufs      suid,rw,
                                             largefiles,dev=800088    944543106
auto_direct     /disks/www       autofs ignore,direct,
                                         nosuid,dev=2c00001           944543181
auto_direct     /disks/ftp autofs ignore,direct,
                                         nosuid,dev=2c00002           944543181
server:vold(pid329)   /vol     nfs      ignore,
                                         dev=2bc0002      944543192
/dev/dsk/c2t2d0s3          /disks/vol7 ufs      nosuid,rw,
                                             largefiles,dev=800103 944548661
/dev/md/dsk/d2   /disks/vol8 ufs      nosuid,rw,
                                             largefiles, dev=1540002   944553321
client:/disks/junior_developers   /disks/junior_developers         nfs
                                         nosuid,dev=2bc0040           944604066
```

To avoid delays in printing resource information on NFS-mounted volumes, it is
also possible to check local file systems with this command:

```
# df -l
Filesystem            kbytes   used    avail capacity  Mounted on
/dev/dsk/c0t0d0s0     245911   30754   190566   14%      /
```

```
/dev/dsk/c0t0d0s4    1015679    430787    523952     46%    /usr
/proc                      0         0         0      0%    /proc
fd                         0         0         0      0%    /dev/fd
/dev/dsk/c0t0d0s3     492871    226184    217400     51%    /var
/dev/md/dsk/d1       4119256   3599121    478943     89%    /opt
swap                  256000     43488    212512     17%    /tmp
/dev/dsk/c0t2d0s3    4119256   3684920    393144     91%    /disks/vol1
/dev/md/dsk/d0      17398449  12889901   4334564     75%    /disks/vol2
/dev/md/dsk/d3       6162349   5990984    109742     99%    /disks/vol3
/dev/dsk/c1t1d0s0    8574909   5868862   1848557     77%    /disks/vol4
/dev/dsk/c2t3d0s2    1820189   1551628    177552     90%    /disks/vol5
/dev/dsk/c1t2d0s0    4124422   3548988    575434     87%    /disks/vol6
/dev/dsk/c2t2d0s3    8737664   8281113    456551     95%    /disks/vol7
/dev/md/dsk/d2       8181953   6803556   1296578     84%    /disks/vol8
```

A block device can be specified on the command line, and its individual usage measured; for example, consider this code for a slice on controller 1:

```
# df /dev/dsk/c1d0d2
Filesystem           kbytes    used  avail capacity  Mounted on
/dev/dsk/c1t1d0s0   8574909 5868862 1848557    77%   /disks/vol4
```

Users can also check the status of the disks holding their individual user directories and files by using df. For example, this code will display the disk space usage for the disk on which the home directory exists for user pwatters:

```
# df /staff/pwatters
Filesystem           kbytes    used  avail capacity  Mounted on
/dev/md/dsk/d0     17398449 12889146 4335319    75%   /disks/vol2
```

This code checks the size of the partition on which the temporary mailbox for the user pwatters was created by the elm mail-reading program. This is a good thing to check if you intend to send a lot of e-mail messages!

```
# df /tmp/mbox.pwatters
Filesystem           kbytes    used  avail capacity  Mounted on
swap                  256000   45392  210608    18%   /tmp
```

Another way of obtaining disk space usage information with more directory-by-directory detail is by using the /usr/bin/du command. This command prints the sum of the sizes of every file in the current directory and performs the same task recursively for any subdirectories. The size is calculated by summing all of the file sizes in the directory, where the size for each file is rounded up to the nearest 512-byte block. For example, taking a du of the */etc* directory looks like this:

```
# cd /etc
 # du
14         ./default
7          ./cron.d
6          ./dfs
8          ./dhcp
201        ./fs/hsfs
681        ./fs/nfs
1          ./fs/proc
209        ./fs/ufs
1093       ./fs
26         ./inet
127        ./init.d
339        ./lib
37         ./mail
4          ./net/ticlts
4          ./net/ticots
4          ./net/ticotsord
13         ./net
3          ./opt/SUNWleo/bin
4          ./opt/SUNWleo
92         ./opt/licenses/from-zoul
118        ./opt/licenses
13         ./opt/SUNWmd
1          ./opt/SUNWimap/license_dir
2          ./opt/SUNWimap
1          ./opt/SUNWicg
32         ./opt/totalnet/httpd/conf
33         ./opt/totalnet/httpd
37         ./opt/totalnet
7          ./opt/ssh
2          ./opt/SUNWneo
13         ./opt/SUNWsymon
198        ./opt
3          ./rc0.d
2          ./rc1.d
13         ./rc2.d
14         ./rc3.d
5          ./rcS.d
3          ./saf/zsmon
6          ./saf
2          ./security/audit/localhost
3          ./security/audit
1          ./security/dev
18         ./security/lib
```

```
1          ./security/spool
53         ./security
5          ./skel
1          ./tm
2          ./acct
32         ./uucp
2          ./fn
1          ./openwin/devdata/profiles
2          ./openwin/devdata
3          ./openwin
9          ./lp/alerts
1          ./lp/classes
15         ./lp/fd
1          ./lp/forms
1          ./lp/interfaces
1          ./lp/printers
1          ./lp/pwheels
36         ./lp
2          ./dmi/ciagent
3          ./dmi/conf
6          ./dmi
42         ./snmp/conf
43         ./snmp
7          ./http
2          ./ski
2          ./totalnet
2429       .
```

Thus, */etc* and all its subdirectories contain a total of 2429 kilobytes of data. Of course, this kind of output is fairly verbose and is probably not much use in its current form.

Installing and Configuring a Hard Disk

Hard disk installation and configuration on Solaris is often more complicated than it is for other UNIX systems. Such complexity is required to support the sophisticated hardware operations typically undertaken by Solaris systems. For example, Linux refers to hard disks using a simple Berkeley Software Distribution (BSD)–style scheme: */dev/hd*n are the IDE hard disks on a system, and */dev/sd*n are the SCSI hard disks on a system, where *n* refers to the hard disk number. A system with two IDE hard disks and two SCSI hard disks will therefore have the following device files configured:

```
/dev/hda
/dev/hdb
/dev/sda
/dev/sdb
```

Partitions created on each drive are also sequentially numbered: if */dev/hda* is the boot disk, it may contain several partitions, reflecting the basic UNIX system directories:

```
/dev/hda1 (/ partition)
/dev/hda2 (/usr)
/dev/hda3 (/var)
/dev/hda4 (swap)
```

Instead of simply referring to the disk type, disk number, and partition number, the device file name for each partition (the "slice") on a Solaris disk contains four identifiers: controller (c), target (t), disk (d), and slice (s). Thus, the device file

```
/dev/dsk/c0t3d0s0
```

identifies slice 0 of disk 0, controller 0 at SCSI target ID 3. To complicate matters further, disk device files exist in both the */dev/dsk* and */dev/rdsk* directories, which correspond to block device and raw device entries, respectively. Raw and block devices refer to the same physical partition, but they are used in different contexts; using raw devices allows operations only of small amounts of data, whereas a buffer can be used with a block device to increase the data read size. It is not always clear whether a block or raw device interface should be used, however, as a rule of thumb, low-level system commands (like the `fsck` command, which performs disk maintenance) typically use raw device interfaces, whereas commands that operate on the entire disk (such as `df`, which reports disk usage) will most likely use block devices.

To install a new hard drive on a Solaris system, just follow these steps:

1. Prepare the system for a reconfiguration boot by issuing the command

   ```
   # touch /reconfigure
   ```

2. Synchronize disk data and power-down the system using the commands

   ```
   # sync; init 0
   ```

3. Switch off power to the system and attach the new hard disk to the external SCSI chain, or install it internally into an appropriate disk bay.

4. Check that the SCSI device ID does not conflict with any existing SCSI devices. If a conflict exists, simply change the ID using the switch.

5. Power-on the system and use the `boot` command to load the kernel if the OpenBoot monitor appears:

   ```
   ok boot
   ```

6. The next step, assuming that you have decided which partitions you wish to create on your drive, and using the information supplied above, is to run the *format* program. In addition to creating slices, *format* also displays information

about existing disks and slices, and it can be used to repair a faulty disk. When *format* is invoked without a command line argument, like so:

```
# format
```

it displays the current disks and asks the administrator to enter the number of the disk to format. Selecting a disk for formatting at this point is nondestructive, so even if you make a mistake, you can always exit the *format* program without damaging data. For example, on a SPARC-20 system with three 1.05G SCSI disks, *format* opens with the following onscreen:

```
Searching for disks...done
AVAILABLE DISK SELECTIONS:
0. c0t1d0 <SUN1.05 cyl 2036 alt 2 hd 14 sec 72>
/iommu@f,e0000000/sbus@f,e0001000/espdma@f,400000/esp@f,800000/
sd@1,0
1. c0t2d0 <SUN1.05 cyl 2036 alt 2 hd 14 sec 72>
/iommu@f,e0000000/sbus@f,e0001000/espdma@f,400000/esp@f,800000/
sd@2,0
2. c0t3d0 <SUN1.05 cyl 2036 alt 2 hd 14 sec 72>
/iommu@f,e0000000/sbus@f,e0001000/espdma@f,400000/esp@f,800000/
sd@3,0
Specify disk (enter its number):
```

7. It is also possible to pass a command line option to *format*, comprising the disk (or disks) to be formatted; for example:

```
# format /dev/rdsk/c0t2d0
```

8. After selecting the appropriate disk message, this code will appear if the disk has previously been formatted:

```
[disk formatted]
```

This is an important message, as it is a common mistake to misidentify a target disk from the available selection of both formatted and unformatted disks. The menu looks like this:

```
FORMAT MENU:
        disk       - select a disk
        type       - select (define) a disk type
        partition  - select (define) a partition table
        current    - describe the current disk
        format     - format and analyze the disk
        fdisk      - run the fdisk program
        repair     - repair a defective sector
        show       - translate a disk address
        label      - write label to the disk
```

```
        analyze    - surface analysis
        defect     - defect list management
        backup     - search for backup labels
        verify     - read and display labels
        save       - save new disk/partition definitions
        volname    - set 8-character volume name
        !<cmd>     - execute <cmd>, then return
        quit
format>
```

9. If the disk has not been formatted, you need to prepare the disk to contain slices and file systems by formatting the disk. Issue the command `format`:

```
format> format
Ready to format. Formatting cannot be interrupted
and takes 15 minutes (estimated). Continue? yes
```

10. The purpose of formatting is to identify defective blocks, mark them as bad, and generally verify that the disk is operational from a hardware perspective. Once this has been completed, new slices can be created and sized by using the *partition* option at the main menu:

```
format> partition
```

In this case, we want to create a new Slice 5 on disk 0 at target 3, which will be used to store user files when mounted as */export/home* and corresponding to block device */dev/dsk/c0t3d0s5*.

11. After determining the maximum amount of space available, enter that size in gigabytes (in this case, 1.05GB) when requested to do so by the format program for Slice 5 (enter **0** for the other slices). If the disk is not labeled, you will also be prompted to enter a label that contains details of the disk's current slices, which is useful for recovering data. This is an important step, as the operating system will not be able to find any newly created slices unless the volume is labeled.

12. To view the disk label, use the `prtvtoc` command. Here's the output from the primary drive in an x86 system:

```
# prtvtoc /dev/dsk/c0d0s2
* /dev/dsk/c0d0s2 partition map
*
* Dimensions:
*       512 bytes/sector
*        63 sectors/track
*       255 tracks/cylinder
*     16065 sectors/cylinder
*      1020 cylinders
*      1018 accessible cylinders
*
* Flags:
```

```
*    1: unmountable
*   10: read-only
*
*                            First      Sector     Last
* Partition   Tag   Flags    Sector     Count      Sector     Directory
        0      2     00      48195      160650     208844     /
        1      7     00      208845     64260      273104     /var
        2      5     00          0      16354170   16354169
        3      3     01      273105     321300     594404
        6      4     00      594405     1317330    1911734    /usr
        7      8     00      1911735    14442435   16354169
                                                              /export/home
        8      1     01          0      16065      16064
        9      9     01      16065      32130      48194
```

13. The disk label contains a full partition table, which can be printed for each disk using the print command:

```
format> print
```

For your 1.05GB disk, the partition table will look like this:

```
Part Tag Flag Cylinders Size Blocks
0 root wm 0 0 (0/0/0) 0
1 swap wu 0 0 (0/0/0) 0
2 backup wm 0 - 3732 (3732/0/0) 2089920
3 unassigned wm 0 0 (0/0/0) 0
4 unassigned wm 0 0 (0/0/0) 0
5 home wm 0 - 3732 1075MB (3732/0/0) 2089920
6 usr wm 0 0 (0/0/0) 0
7 unassigned wm 0 0 (0/0/0) 0
```

14. After saving the changes to the disk's partition table, exit the *format* program and create a new UFS file system on the target slice using the newfs command:

```
# newfs /dev/rdsk/c0t3d0s5
```

15. After a new file system is constructed, it is ready to be mounted. First, create a mount point

```
# mkdir /export/home
```

followed by the appropriate mount command:

```
# mount /dev/dsk/c0t3d0s5 /export/home
```

16. At this point, the disk is available to the system for the current session. However, if you want the disk to be available after reboot, you must create an entry in the virtual file systems table from */etc/vfstab* file. An entry like this

```
/dev/dsk/c0t3d0s5 /dev/rdsk/c0t3d0s5 /export/home ufs 2 yes -
```

MANAGING FILESYSTEMS
AND PRINTERS

contains details of the slice's block and raw devices, the mount point, the file system type, instructions for `fsck`, and most important a flag to force a mount at boot.

For an x86 system, the output of *format* looks slightly different, given the differences in the way that devices are denoted:

```
AVAILABLE DISK SELECTIONS:
       0. c0d0 <DEFAULT cyl 1018 alt 2 hd 255 sec 63>
          /pci@0,0/pci-ide@7,1/ata@0/cmdk@0,0
Specify disk (enter its number):
```

The partition table is similar to that for the SPARC architecture systems:

```
partition> print
Current partition table (original):
Total disk cylinders available: 1018 + 2 (reserved cylinders)

Part        Tag    Flag     Cylinders        Size            Blocks
  0        root    wm       3 -    12       78.44MB    (10/0/0)       160650
  1         var    wm      13 -    16       31.38MB    (4/0/0)         64260
  2      backup    wm       0 -  1017        7.80GB    (1018/0/0)   16354170
  3        swap    wu      17 -    36      156.88MB    (20/0/0)       321300
  4  unassigned    wm       0                    0     (0/0/0)             0
  5  unassigned    wm       0                    0     (0/0/0)             0
  6         usr    wm      37 -   118      643.23MB    (82/0/0)      1317330
  7        home    wm     119 -  1017        6.89GB    (899/0/0)    14442435
  8        boot    wu       0 -     0        7.84MB    (1/0/0)         16065
  9  alternates    wu       1 -     2       15.69MB    (2/0/0)         32130
```

Command Reference

The following commands are commonly used for managing and installing file systems.

format

If you're ever unsure which physical disk is associated with a specific disk device name, you can use the `format` command to find out:

```
# format
Searching for disks...done
AVAILABLE DISK SELECTIONS:
0. c1t3d0 <SUN2.1G cyl 2733 alt 2 hd 19 sec 80>
 /pci@1f,0/pci@1/scsi@1/sd@3,0
```

You can see that physical device */pci@1f,0/pci@1/scsi@1/sd@3,0* is matched with the disk device */dev/dsk/c1t3d0* from the df output.

The /etc/path_to_inst File

A list of mappings between physical devices to instance names is always kept in the */etc/path_to_inst* file. The following example reviews the device to instance name mapping for a SCSI-based SPARC system:

```
"/sbus@1f,0" 0 "sbus"
"/sbus@1f,0/sbusmem@2,0" 2 "sbusmem"
"/sbus@1f,0/sbusmem@3,0" 3 "sbusmem"
"/sbus@1f,0/sbusmem@0,0" 0 "sbusmem"
"/sbus@1f,0/sbusmem@1,0" 1 "sbusmem"
"/sbus@1f,0/SUNW,fas@2,8800000" 1 "fas"
"/sbus@1f,0/SUNW,fas@2,8800000/ses@f,0" 1 "ses"
"/sbus@1f,0/SUNW,fas@2,8800000/sd@1,0" 16 "sd"
"/sbus@1f,0/SUNW,fas@2,8800000/sd@0,0" 15 "sd"
"/sbus@1f,0/SUNW,fas@2,8800000/sd@3,0" 18 "sd"
"/sbus@1f,0/SUNW,fas@2,8800000/sd@2,0" 17 "sd"
"/sbus@1f,0/SUNW,fas@2,8800000/sd@5,0" 20 "sd"
"/sbus@1f,0/SUNW,fas@2,8800000/sd@4,0" 19 "sd"
"/sbus@1f,0/SUNW,fas@2,8800000/sd@6,0" 21 "sd"
"/sbus@1f,0/SUNW,fas@2,8800000/sd@9,0" 23 "sd"
"/sbus@1f,0/SUNW,fas@2,8800000/sd@8,0" 22 "sd"
"/sbus@1f,0/SUNW,fas@2,8800000/sd@a,0" 24 "sd"
"/sbus@1f,0/SUNW,fas@2,8800000/st@1,0" 8 "st"
"/sbus@1f,0/SUNW,fas@2,8800000/st@0,0" 7 "st"
"/sbus@1f,0/SUNW,fas@2,8800000/sd@c,0" 26 "sd"
"/sbus@1f,0/SUNW,fas@2,8800000/st@3,0" 10 "st"
"/sbus@1f,0/SUNW,fas@2,8800000/sd@b,0" 25 "sd"
"/sbus@1f,0/SUNW,fas@2,8800000/st@2,0" 9 "st"
"/sbus@1f,0/SUNW,fas@2,8800000/sd@e,0" 28 "sd"
"/sbus@1f,0/SUNW,fas@2,8800000/st@5,0" 12 "st"
"/sbus@1f,0/SUNW,fas@2,8800000/sd@d,0" 27 "sd"
"/sbus@1f,0/SUNW,fas@2,8800000/st@4,0" 11 "st"
"/sbus@1f,0/SUNW,fas@2,8800000/sd@f,0" 29 "sd"
"/sbus@1f,0/SUNW,fas@2,8800000/st@6,0" 13 "st"
"/sbus@1f,0/SUNW,CS4231@d,c000000" 0 "audiocs"
"/sbus@1f,0/dma@0,81000" 0 "dma"
"/sbus@1f,0/dma@0,81000/esp@0,80000" 0 "esp"
"/sbus@1f,0/dma@0,81000/esp@0,80000/sd@0,0" 30 "sd"
"/sbus@1f,0/dma@0,81000/esp@0,80000/sd@1,0" 31 "sd"
"/sbus@1f,0/dma@0,81000/esp@0,80000/sd@2,0" 32 "sd"
"/sbus@1f,0/dma@0,81000/esp@0,80000/sd@3,0" 33 "sd"
"/sbus@1f,0/dma@0,81000/esp@0,80000/sd@4,0" 34 "sd"
"/sbus@1f,0/dma@0,81000/esp@0,80000/sd@5,0" 35 "sd"
"/sbus@1f,0/dma@0,81000/esp@0,80000/sd@6,0" 36 "sd"
"/sbus@1f,0/dma@0,81000/esp@0,80000/st@0,0" 14 "st"
```

```
"/sbus@1f,0/dma@0,81000/esp@0,80000/st@1,0" 15 "st"
"/sbus@1f,0/dma@0,81000/esp@0,80000/st@2,0" 16 "st"
"/sbus@1f,0/dma@0,81000/esp@0,80000/st@3,0" 17 "st"
"/sbus@1f,0/dma@0,81000/esp@0,80000/st@4,0" 18 "st"
"/sbus@1f,0/dma@0,81000/esp@0,80000/st@5,0" 19 "st"
"/sbus@1f,0/dma@0,81000/esp@0,80000/st@6,0" 20 "st"
"/sbus@1f,0/sbusmem@f,0" 15 "sbusmem"
"/sbus@1f,0/sbusmem@d,0" 13 "sbusmem"
"/sbus@1f,0/sbusmem@e,0" 14 "sbusmem"
"/sbus@1f,0/cgthree@1,0" 0 "cgthree"
"/sbus@1f,0/SUNW,hme@e,8c00000" 0 "hme"
"/sbus@1f,0/zs@f,1000000" 1 "zs"
"/sbus@1f,0/zs@f,1100000" 0 "zs"
"/sbus@1f,0/SUNW,bpp@e,c800000" 0 "bpp"
"/sbus@1f,0/lebuffer@0,40000" 0 "lebuffer"
"/sbus@1f,0/lebuffer@0,40000/le@0,60000" 0 "le"
"/sbus@1f,0/SUNW,hme@2,8c00000" 1 "hme"
"/sbus@1f,0/SUNW,fdtwo@f,1400000" 0 "fd"
"/options" 0 "options"
"/pseudo" 0 "pseudo"
```

You can see entries for the network interface */sbus@1f,0/SUNW,hme@2,8c00000*, as well as the floppy disk */sbus@1f,0/SUNW,fdtwo@f,1400000* and the SBUS *sbus@1f,0*.

For a Peripheral Component Interconnect (PCI) local bus–based system such as a Sun Blade 100, the output would look like this:

```
"/pci@1f,0" 0 "pcipsy"
"/pci@1f,0/isa@7" 0 "ebus"
"/pci@1f,0/isa@7/power@0,800" 0 "power"
"/pci@1f,0/isa@7/dma@0,0" 0 "isadma"
"/pci@1f,0/isa@7/dma@0,0/parallel@0,378" 0 "ecpp"
"/pci@1f,0/isa@7/dma@0,0/floppy@0,3f0" 0 "fd"
"/pci@1f,0/isa@7/serial@0,2e8" 1 "su"
"/pci@1f,0/isa@7/serial@0,3f8" 0 "su"
"/pci@1f,0/pmu@3" 0 "pmubus"
"/pci@1f,0/pmu@3/i2c@0" 0 "smbus"
"/pci@1f,0/pmu@3/i2c@0/temperature@30" 0 "max1617"
"/pci@1f,0/pmu@3/i2c@0/card-reader@40" 0 "scmi2c"
"/pci@1f,0/pmu@3/i2c@0/dimm@a0" 0 "seeprom"
"/pci@1f,0/pmu@3/fan-control@0" 0 "grfans"
"/pci@1f,0/pmu@3/ppm@0" 0 "grppm"
"/pci@1f,0/pmu@3/beep@0" 0 "grbeep"
"/pci@1f,0/ebus@c" 1 "ebus"
"/pci@1f,0/usb@c,3" 0 "ohci"
"/pci@1f,0/usb@c,3/mouse@2" 0 "hid"
"/pci@1f,0/usb@c,3/keyboard@4" 1 "hid"
"/pci@1f,0/firewire@c,2" 0 "hci1394"
"/pci@1f,0/ide@d" 0 "uata"
```

```
"/pci@1f,0/ide@d/dad@0,0" 0 "dad"
"/pci@1f,0/ide@d/sd@1,0" 0 "sd"
"/pci@1f,0/sound@8" 0 "audiots"
"/pci@1f,0/SUNW,m64B@13" 0 "m64"
"/pci@1f,0/network@c,1" 0 "eri"
"/pci@1f,0/pci@5" 0 "pci_pci"
"/options" 0 "options"
"/SUNW,UltraSPARC-IIe@0,0" 0 "us"
"/pseudo" 0 "pseudo"
```

You can see that all of the sbus entries have been replaced by the pci entries and that the network interface is no longer a hme, but an eri (*"/pci@1f,0/network@c,1" 0 "eri"*). In addition, some completely new types of hardware, such as a smart-card reader (*"/pci@1f,0/pmu@3/i2c@0/card-reader@40" 0 "scmi2c"*), are also available.

dmesg

The dmesg command is often used to determine whether specific device drivers for network interfaces and mass storage devices have been correctly loaded at boot time. While its functions have largely been taken over by the *syslog* daemon (*syslogd*), dmesg provides a useful record of error and status messages printed by the kernel.

When the system boots, several status messages of log level *kern.notice* will be recorded and can be subsequently retrieved by using dmesg:

```
Jan 15 14:23:16 austin genunix: [ID 540533 kern.notice] SunOS Release
        5.9 Version Generic_108528-06 64-bit
Jan 15 14:23:16 austin genunix: [ID 784649 kern.notice] Copyright
        1983-2001 Sun Microsystems, Inc.  All rights reserved.
Jan 15 14:23:16 austin genunix: [ID 678236 kern.info] Ethernet
        address = 0:3:ba:4:a4:e8
Jan 15 14:23:16 austin unix: [ID 389951 kern.info] mem =
        131072K (0x8000000)
Jan 15 14:23:16 austin unix: [ID 930857 kern.info] avail mem = 121085952
```

You can see that a 64-bit kernel has been loaded successfully for SunOS 5.9 (Solaris 9). Sun's copyright banner is also recorded, along with the Ethernet address of the primary network interface card (*0:3:ba:4:a4:e8*), the amount of installed RAM, and the amount of currently available RAM after the kernel has been loaded.

Before the kernel begins loading device drivers, it performs an integrity check to determine whether any naming conflicts exist. If a conflict is found, it is logged for future reference and action:

```
May 15 14:23:16 austin genunix: [ID 723599 kern.warning]
        WARNING: Driver alias "cal" conflicts with an existing
        driver name or alias.
```

You can see that the device driver alias *cal* has been used more than once, giving rise to a naming conflict. Next, details about the system architecture and its main bus type are displayed:

```
Jan 15 14:23:16 austin rootnex: [ID 466748 kern.info]
       root nexus = Sun Blade 100 (UltraSPARC-IIe)
Jan 15 14:23:16 austin rootnex: [ID 349649 kern.info]
       pcipsy0 at root: UPA 0x1f 0x0
Jan 15 14:23:16 austin genunix: [ID 936769 kern.info] pcipsy0 is /pci@1f,0
Jan 15 14:23:16 austin pcipsy: [ID 370704 kern.info]
       PCI-device: pmu@3, pmubus0
Jan 15 14:23:16 austin pcipsy: [ID 370704 kern.info]
       PCI-device: ppm@0, grppm0
Jan 15 14:23:16 austin genunix: [ID 936769 kern.info]
       grppm0 is /pci@1f,0/pmu@3/ppm@0
```

You can see that the system is a Sun Blade 100 and that its PCI bus architecture has been correctly identified. The next stage involves identifying the hard drives attached to the system, as follows:

```
Jan 15 14:23:27 austin pcipsy: [ID 370704 kern.info]
       PCI-device: ide@d, uata0
Jan 15 14:23:27 austin genunix: [ID 936769 kern.info]
       uata0 is /pci@1f,0/ide@d
Jan 15 14:23:28 austin uata: [ID 114370 kern.info] dad0 at pci10b9,52290
Jan 15 14:23:28 austin uata: [ID 347839 kern.info]  target 0 lun 0
Jan 15 14:23:28 austin genunix: [ID 936769 kern.info]
       dad0 is /pci@1f,0/ide@d/dad@0,0
Jan 15 14:23:28 austin dada: [ID 365881 kern.info]
       <ST315320A cyl 29649 alt 2 hd 16 sec 63>
Jan 15 14:23:29 austin swapgeneric: [ID 308332 kern.info]
       root on /pci@1f,0/ide@d/disk@0,0:a fstype ufs
```

The IDE hard drive installed on the system has been correctly detected (*/pci@1f,0/ide@d/ dad@0,0*) and has the label *ST315320A cyl 29649 alt 2 hd 16 sec 63*. In addition, the file system type has been identified as native UFS.

The status of every device on the system is logged during device driver loading, so it's possible to use the `dmesg` command to determine whether drivers have been correctly loaded. In the following entry, the Fiber Distributed Data Interface (FDDI) cannot be activated because it is not correctly installed:

```
Jan 15 14:26:38 austin smt: [ID 272566 kern.notice]
       smt0: nf FDDI driver is not active.
       Initialization of this driver cannot be completed.
```

prtconf

If you're ever been confused about the devices that have been detected on a system and are currently active, you can use the prtconf command to display their configuration details:

```
# prtconf
System Configuration:  Sun Microsystems  sun4u
Memory size: 128 Megabytes
```

Initially, the system architecture is displayed (*sun4u* in the case of an Ultra 5 workstation), along with the amount of physical RAM. What follows is a hierarchical list of all system peripherals and attached drivers (where appropriate), arranged in logical order. For example, all PCI devices are listed under the *pci* node, being associated with either *pci* instance #0 or *pci* instance #1:

```
pci, instance #0
        pci, instance #0
            ebus, instance #0
                auxio (driver not attached)
                power, instance #0
                SUNW,pll (driver not attached)
                se, instance #0
                su, instance #0
                su, instance #1
                ecpp (driver not attached)
                fdthree, instance #0
                eeprom (driver not attached)
                flashprom (driver not attached)
                SUNW,CS4231 (driver not attached)
            network, instance #0
            SUNW,m64B (driver not attached)
            ide, instance #0
                disk (driver not attached)
                cdrom (driver not attached)
                dad, instance #0
                sd, instance #30
        pci, instance #1
            scsi, instance #0
                disk (driver not attached)
                tape (driver not attached)
                sd, instance #0 (driver not attached)
                sd, instance #1 (driver not attached)
                sd, instance #2 (driver not attached)
                sd, instance #3
                sd, instance #4 (driver not attached)
```

MANAGING FILESYSTEMS
AND PRINTERS

```
sd, instance #5 (driver not attached)
sd, instance #6 (driver not attached)
sd, instance #7 (driver not attached)
sd, instance #8 (driver not attached)
sd, instance #9 (driver not attached)
sd, instance #10 (driver not attached)
sd, instance #11 (driver not attached)
sd, instance #12 (driver not attached)
sd, instance #13 (driver not attached)
sd, instance #14 (driver not attached)
```

mkfile

The mkfile command creates a file of a specified size, which is padded with zeros. File sizes can be specified in gigabytes 'g', megabytes 'm', bytes 'b', or kilobytes 'k'. For example, to create a 1 gigabyte file in /tmp/newfile, the following command would be used:

```
# newfile 1g /tmp/newfile
```

If disk blocks should not be allocated until a request from an application, then the -n option should be passed on the command line. This conserves disk space while ensuring that the file created does not exceed its maximum flagged size.

mkfs

The mkfs command creates a new file system on the raw disk device specified on the command line. The file system type is determined by the contents of the file */etc/default/fs*. In most Solaris systems, the contents of this file are "LOCAL=ufs," indicating that UFS file systems are default. If a different file system type is to be created, then the -F option can be passed on the command line, followed by the file system type. For example, to create a file system of type *pcfs* that uses a standard FAT type on a floppy disk, the following command would be used:

```
# mkfs -F pcfs /dev/rdiskette
```

A number of aliases to the mkfs command are also available, which can be used to create file systems of different types directly. These commands include:

■ mkfs_udfs creates a Universal Disk File System (UDFS) format file system.

■ mkfs_pcfs creates a FAT format file system.

■ mkfs_udfs creates a UFS format file system.

In addition, passing the -m option displays the complete command string that was used to create the file system. This is useful for extracting and storing in a script to re-create the file system on another disk.

newfs

The newfs command uses the mkfs command to create UFS file systems. The main difference is the number of parameters that can be passed to newfs to tune the file system during creation. The following parameters can be used to specify file system parameters:

–a n	Specifies n blocks to be held in reserve to replace bad blocks
–b n	Sets the block size on the file system to be n bytes
–c n	Indicates that n cylinders should be allocated to each cylinder group
–C n	Specifies n as the maximum number of contiguous disk blocks per file
–d n	Sets the rotational delay to n milliseconds
–f n	Sets the smallest disk fragment for a single file to n bytes
–i n	Specifies that n bytes should be allocated to each inode
–m n	Specifies that n% of the physical file system should be reserved as free
–n n	Sets the number of different group cylinder rotations to n
–r n	Sets the disk speed to n revolutions per minute
–s n	Sets the disk size to n sectors
–t n	Specifies that n tracks be allocated to each cylinder

For most applications, the defaults selected by newfs will provide adequate performance. However, some specialized applications do require smaller or larger disk minimum fragments or block size for their file systems, and these can easily be set during file system creation.

lofiadm

The lofiadm command is used to initialize a file on an existing partition that is labelled as a raw device, by making use of the loopback file device driver. A new file system can then be created on the device by using newfs or mkfs as if it was a separate partition. This can be useful if a new partition needs to be created, but the disk cannot be easily reformatted, particularly if it's only required temporarily.

To create a file system on a file, the mkfile command should be used to create a file to be a specific size. Next, the association between the file and the loopback file device driver needs to be made. For example, if the file */tmp/datafile* was created with mkfile, the following command would create the association:

```
# lofiadm -a /tmp/datafile /dev/lofi/2
```

Finally, a new file system can be created by using the newfs command:

```
# newfs /dev/rlofi/2
newfs: construct a new file system /dev/rlofi/2: (y/n)? y
```

The file system can then be mounted on a mount point (such as */testdata*) as required:

```
# mount /dev/lofi/2 /testdata
```

When the file system is no longer required, the umount command can be used to remove the file system from operation, and the lofiadm command can be used to remove the association between the file and the loopback file device driver:

```
# umount /testdata
# lofiadm -d /tmp/datafile
```

swap

The swap command is used to add virtual RAM to a system. Virtual RAM is typically used to provide memory for process execution when physical memory has been exhausted. Disk blocks are used to simulate physical memory locations using an interface that is invisible to the user. Thus, users never need to be concerned about the type of RAM that their process is addressing. While virtual memory allows a system's effective capacity to be increased to many times its physical capacity, it is much slower than physical RAM. When a system experiences peak demands for memory causing virtual memory to be used, the CPU must work harder to support virtual memory operations. Coupled with the relatively slow speed of disk writing, this can have a significant impact on performance. When virtual memory is being utilized, and many new memory access calls are made along with normal file reading and writing, so-called "disk thrashing" can occur, since the number of disk operations requested far exceeds the capacity of the disk to read and write. If this is a common occurrence, then extra physical RAM should be installed into the system, and/or the file system may need to be tuned with tunefs.

Virtual memory should generally be added to the system at twice the physical RAM installed. Thus, for a 256MB system, 512MB of virtual memory should be initialized. In order to add virtual memory, an empty file of the required size should be created with the mkfile command. Next, the swap command must be used to add the file into the pool of available disk space. For example, if two swap files are created on different file systems for redundancy (such as *u1/swap* and *u2/swap*), they can be added to the swap space pool by using the following commands:

```
# swap -a /u1/swap
# swap -a /u2/swap
```

To verify that the swap has been correctly added to the pool, the following command can be used:

```
# swap -l
```

If you have a dedicated slice set aside for swap, then the block device name can simply be passed on the command line:

```
# swap -a /dev/dsk/c1t1d2s1
```

To remove a file (or device) from the swap pool, the –*d* option needs to be passed on the command line. Thus, to remove */u1/swap* and */dev/dsk/c1t1d2s1* from the swap pool, the following commands would be used:

```
# swap -d /u1/swap
# swap -d /dev/dsk/c1t1d2s1
```

The file */u1/swap* can now be safely deleted, and the slice */dev/dsk/c1t1d2s1* can be safely used for other purposes.

sync

The sync command is generally executed prior to a shutdown or halt to flush all disk buffers, and to write the super block. This ensures that data integrity is preserved when the system is either rebooted or when the run level is modified. It is simply executed without options, as shown here:

```
# sync
```

MANAGING FILESYSTEMS
AND PRINTERS

tunefs

The tunefs command allows a file system's performance to be tuned to specific requirements. The key setting that can be modified is optimization for speed of execution or amount of disk space required. Generally, unless a system is critically low on disk space, it is best to optimize for speed. The following options are supported:

-a n	Specifies that n blocks be written before a pause in rotation
-e n	Specifies n as the maximum number of contiguous disk blocks per file
-d n	Sets the rotational delay to n milliseconds
-m n	Specifies that n% of the physical file system should be reserved as free
-o *key*	Optimizes the file system for a *key* with either "time" or "space"

The
Complete
Reference

Solaris 9

Chapter 15

File System and Volume Management

Once disks have been installed and formatted, a number of further operations must be performed to allow them to be used. For a start, disks must be manually mounted by the super-user and an entry created for each partition created in */etc/vfstab*. Alternatively, disks may need to be unmounted for maintenance using the *fsck* program. However, if file system journalling is enabled in */etc/vfstab*, then the need for *fsck* is reduced. Finally, setting up volume management is critical to the enterprise, since the logical sizes of disks can be extended and/or redundancy can be implemented. All of these topics are examined in this chapter.

Key Concepts

The following concepts are required knowledge for managing disk file systems and volumes.

Mounting Local File Systems

Solaris (UNIX File System, or UFS) file systems are mapped in a one-to-one relationship to physical slices, which makes it easy for you to associate file systems with partitions, even if the physical and logical device references are complex. For example, the slice */dev/dsk/c0t3d0s5* may be mounted on the mount point */export/home*.

Mount points are simply empty directories that have been created using the mkdir command. One of the nice features of the UFS is that it has a one-to-many mapping to potential mount points; this means that a file system can be mounted, and its files and directories can be manipulated, unmounted, and then remounted on a different mount point. All of the data that was modified when the file system was mounted using a different mount point are retained. For example, if you mount */dev/dsk/c0t3d0s5* on */export/ home*, create a directory called *pwatters* (that is, */export/home/pwatters*), unmount the file system, and then remount it on */usr/local*, the content of the folder *pwatters* will still be available, albeit with a new absolute path (*/usr/local/pwatters*).

Unmounting Local File Systems

In normal operations, a file system is mounted at boot time if its mount point and options are specified in the virtual file systems table (*/etc/vfstab*). The file system is unmounted before the system is shut down. However, at times, you may find it necessary to unmount a file system manually. For example, if the file system's integrity needs to be checked using the fsck command, the target file system must be unmounted. Alternatively, if the mount point of a file system is going to be modified, the file system needs to be unmounted from its current mount point and remounted on the new mount point. You cannot mount a file system on two different mount points.

Creating Entries in /etc/vfstab

Although we've used the mount command to manually mount file systems, it's preferable to simply create an entry in */etc/vfstab* to mount the file system automatically after boot. Alternatively, if a number of entries are to be made in */etc/vfstab* and the system is not going to be rebooted for some time, then the following command can be used to mount any entries in */etc/vfstab* that have not already been mounted:

```
# mountall
```

Let's look at an example entry in */etc/vfstab*:

```
#device             device          mount  FS   fsck  mount   mount
#to mount           to fsck         point  type pass  at boot options
/dev/dsk/c0t0d0s5 /dev/rdsk/c0t0d0s5 /usr   ufs  2     yes     -
```

This example shows an entry for the raw disk device */dev/rdsk/c0t0d0s5*, mounted on */usr*, standard UFS file system, mounted at boot time, with no options. In addition, the raw device on which *fsck* operates is */dev/rdsk/c0t0d0s5*, with a *fsck* file system check being required. The options field contains a comma-delimited list of mounting options, which are equivalent to those used for the mount command (see "Command Reference" for the mount command for details). In addition to UFS file systems, file systems of other types can be mounted, including special types such as swap space or NFS-mounted volumes.

Fixing Problems with fsck

/usr/sbin/fsck is a file system checking and repair program that's commonly found on Solaris and other UNIX platforms. The program is usually executed by the super-user while the system is in a single-user mode state (for example, after you enter run level S), but it can also be executed on individual volumes during multiple-user run levels.

There is one "golden rule" of which you must be aware while using *fsck*: Never apply *fsck* to a mounted file system. Doing so could leave the file system in an inconsistent state and cause a kernel panic, at which point you need to head for the backup tape locker! Any fixes to potential problems on a mounted file system could end up creating more damage than the original problem. This section examines the output of *fsck* and some examples of common problems. It also investigates how *fsck* repairs corrupt and inconsistent disk data.

Although Solaris 9 still retains *fsck*, the program is necessary only for Solaris 2.6 and previous releases because with later releases, logging is provided for UNIX file systems. Thus, before any changes are made to a file system, details of the change are recorded in a log prior to their physical application. While this consumes some extra

CPU and disk overhead (approximately 1 percent of disk space on each volume with logging enabled is required), it does ensure that the file system is never left in an inconsistent state. In addition, boot time is reduced, because *fsck* does not need to be executed.

Why do inconsistencies occur in the first place? In theory, they shouldn't, but they can occur under three common scenarios:

- If the Solaris server has been switched off like an old MS-DOS machine, without powering down first

- If a system is halted without synchronizing disk data (it is advisable that you explicitly use `sync` before shutting down using `halt`)

- If hardware defects are encountered, including damage to disk blocks and heads, which can be caused by moving the system and/or by power surges

These problems are realized as corruption to the internal set of tables that every UNIX file system keeps to manage free disk blocks and inodes, which leads to blocks that are free being reported as already allocated, and conversely, to some blocks occupied by a program being recorded as free. This is obviously problematic for mission-critical data, which is a good reason to add RAID storage (or at least reliable backups). If physical damage is suspected, then surface analysis of the hard disk should be performed by using the `diskscan` command.

The first step to running *fsck* is to enable file system checking during bootup. To do this, you need to specify an integer value in the *fsck* field in the virtual file system configuration file */etc/vfstab*. Entering a *1* in this field ensures sequential *fsck* checking, while entering 2 does not ensure sequential checking, as shown in the following example:

```
#device device mount FS fsck mount mount
#to mount to fsck point type pass at boot options
#
/dev/dsk/c1t2d1s3 /dev/rdsk/c1t2d1s3 /usr ufs 2 yes -/
-
```

After being enabled for a particular file system, *fsck* can be executed. *fsck* checks the integrity of several features of the file system. Most significant is the superblock that stores summary information for the volume. Since the superblock is the most modified item on the file system being written and rewritten when data is changed on a disk, it is the most commonly corrupted feature. However, copies of the superblock are stored in many different locations to ensure that it can be reliably retrieved. Checks on the superblock include the following:

- A check of the file system size, which obviously must be greater than the size computed from the number of blocks identified in the superblock

- The total number of inodes, which must be less than the maximum number of inodes
- A tally of reported free blocks and inodes

If any of these values are identified as corrupt by *fsck*, the super-user can select one of the many superblock backups that were created during initial file system creation as a replacement for the current superblock. We will examine superblock corruption and how to fix it in the next section.

In addition to superblock, the number and status of cylinder group blocks, inodes, indirect blocks, and data blocks are also checked. Since free blocks are located by maps stored in the cylinder group, *fsck* verifies that all the blocks marked as free are not actually being used by any files—if they are, files could be corrupted. If all blocks are correctly accounted for, *fsck* determines whether the number of free blocks plus the number of used blocks equals the total number of blocks in the file system. If *fsck* detects any incongruity, the maps of unallocated blocks are rebuilt, although there is obviously a risk of data loss whenever a disagreement over the actual state of the file system is encountered. *fsck* always uses the actual count of inodes and/or blocks if the superblock information is wrong, and it replaces the incorrect value if this is verified by the super-user. This issue is revisited in the next section.

When inodes are examined by *fsck*, the process is sequential in nature and aims to identify inconsistencies in format and type, link count, duplicate blocks, bad block numbers, and inode size. Inodes should always be in one of three states: allocated (used by a file), unallocated (not used by a file), and partially allocated. (This means that during an allocation or unallocation procedure, data has been left behind that should have been deleted or completed. Alternatively, partial allocation could result from a physical hardware failure. In all of these cases, *fsck* will attempt to clear the inode.)

The link count is the number of directory entries that are linked to a particular inode. *fsck* always checks that the number of directory entries listed is correct by examining the entire directory structure, beginning with the root directory, and tallying the number of links for every inode. Clearly, the stored link count and the actual link count should agree; however, the stored link count can occasionally be different to the actual link count. This could result from a disk not being synchronized before a shutdown, for example, and while changes to the file system have been saved, the link count has not been correctly updated. If the stored count is not zero, but the actual count is zero, disconnected files are placed in the *lost+found* directory found in the top-level of the file system concerned. In other cases, the actual count replaces the stored count.

An indirect block is a pointer to a list of every block claimed by an inode. *fsck* checks every block number against a list of allocated blocks: if two inodes claim the same block number, that block number is added to a list of duplicate block numbers. The administrator may be asked to choose which inode is correct—obviously a difficult decision that usually indicates that it's time to verify files against backups. *fsck* also checks the integrity of the actual block numbers that can also become corrupt—block numbers should always lie in the interval between the first data block and the last data block. If a bad block number is detected, the inode is cleared.

Directories are also checked for integrity by *fsck*. Directory entries are equivalent to other files on the file system, except they have a different mode entry in the inode. *fsck* checks the validity of directory data blocks, checking for the following problems: unallocated nodes associated with inode numbers; inode numbers exceeding the maximum number of inodes for a particular file system; incorrect inode numbers for the standard directory entries "." and ".."; and directories being accidentally disconnected from the file system. We will examine some of these errors and how they are rectified in the next section.

fsck examines each disk volume in five distinct stages:

1. Blocks and sizes are checked.

2. Path names are verified.

3. Connectivity is examined.

4. An investigation of reference counts is undertaken.

5. The cylinder groups are checked.

What Is RAID?

Solaris servers are often set up to be *highly available*, which means that the databases, application servers, and distributed applications that they host must be accessible to clients at all times. Such applications and services are often deployed on Solaris because of the failover technologies provided by Sun's hardware offerings; for example, many high-end SPARC systems feature dual power supplies and allow for the installation of many hard disks in a single cabinet. The E-450, for example, can house up to 20 high speed, high capacity disks (e.g., 18G @ 10,000 RPM).

Production systems of this kind invariably experience two kinds of capacity problems: first, even though the E-450 system may have a total capacity of 360GB, the largest file size that can be supported by the system is the size of an individual hard drive. This means, for example, that database servers that require multiple mount points must be located on a single file system for storing extremely large data files. Having 20 hard disks in this context is only as useful as having one. One solution is to wait until hard disks with higher capacities are manufactured; however, relying on future hardware updates is not feasible for systems that have immediate deployment requirements. What is required is some way of splitting physical data storage across several physical disk volumes, while providing a single logical interface for access.

The second problem that arises is that hard disks and other physical media inevitably fail after periods of heavy use. Even if quality hard drives have mean time between failures (MTBFs) of several years, this is an average figure; some drives last ten years, others only last one. Again, Sun Microsystems' hardware provides some relief here; it is possible to "hot swap" hard drives in an E-450, for example, without having to shut down the system and reboot. The faulty drive is simply removed and replaced by the new drive. Once backups have been loaded, the system will be available again. However, this is an idealistic scenario, and the success of hot swapping ultimately depends on the RAID configuration.

However, to restore disk contents from backups might take several hours, and customers often complain of downtime counted in minutes. While restoring from backups is an excellent strategy for countering catastrophic failure, it is simply not an option for production systems experiencing single disk failures. What is required is some level of content redundancy that retains more than one copy of a system's data across different disks.

To solve the capacity and redundancy problem, Solaris provides support for the redundant array of independent disks (RAID) standard. RAID defines a number of different *levels* that provide various types of *striping* and *mirroring*. In this context, *striping* is the process of spreading data across different physical disks while presenting a single logical interface for the logical volume. Thus, a striped disk set containing four 18GB drives would have a total logical capacity of 72GB. This configuration is shown in Figure 15-1.

A different approach is offered by mirroring, with which a logical volume's contents are copied in real time to more than one physical device. Thus, four 18GB drives could be mirrored to provide two completely redundant 18GB volumes. This means that if one disk failed, its mirror would automatically be used to continue create, read, update, and delete operations on the file system, while the disk was physically replaced (again, with no reboot required). This kind of seamless operation requires no downtime. This configuration is shown in Figure 15-2.

Alternatively, the four disks could be configured so that a 36GB striped volume could be created, combining the capacities of two disks, while the remaining two disks could be used to mirror this striped volume. Thus, the system is provided with a logical 36GB volume that also features complete redundancy. This configuration is shown in Figure 15-3.

Six major RAID levels are supported by DiskSuite, the tool used to set up mirrored and striped virtual file systems on Solaris. RAID Level 0 is the primary striping level, and it allows a virtual file system to be constructed of several physical disks. Their

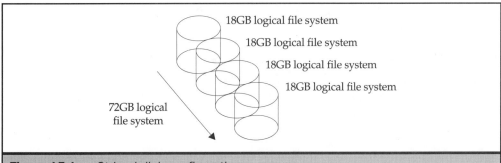

Figure 15-1. *Striped disk configuration*

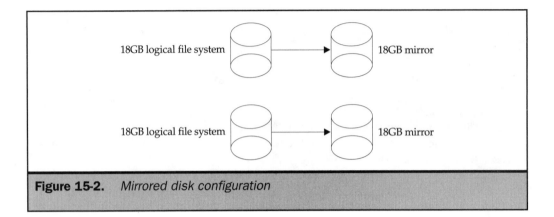

Figure 15-2. *Mirrored disk configuration*

capacities are effectively combined to produce a single disk with a large capacity. In contrast, RAID Level 1 is the primary mirroring level; all data that is written to the virtual file system is also copied in real time to a separate physical disk that has the same capacity as the original. This level has the slowest performance for writes, because all data must be written twice to two different disks; it also costs the most, because each drive to be mirrored makes use of a second drive that cannot be used for any other purpose. However, full redundancy can be achieved using RAID Level 1, and read performance is very good.

The remaining RAID levels are variations on these two themes. RAID Level 2 is a secondary mirroring level that uses Hamming codes for error correction. RAID Levels 3 and 4 are secondary striping levels, writing parity information to a single drive, but writing all other data to multiple physical disks.

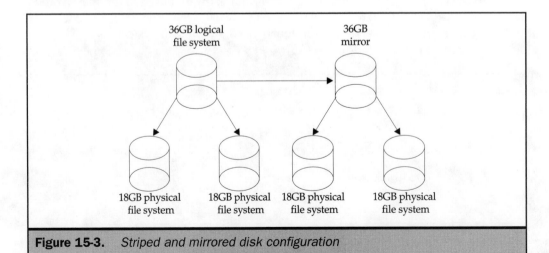

Figure 15-3. *Striped and mirrored disk configuration*

In contrast, RAID Level 5 is a striping and mirroring level that allows data, including parity information, to be written to different disks. RAID 5 offers the best solution for systems that require both mirroring and striping. These levels are summarized in Table 15-1. The following procedures are commonly used for installing disks and file systems.

Mounting a File System

The following procedure can be used to mount a local file system:

```
# mkdir /export/home
# mount  /dev/dsk/c0t3d0s5 /export/home
# cd /export/home
# mkdir pwatters
# ls
pwatters
# umount /export/home
# mkdir /usr/local
# mount  /dev/dsk/c0t3d0s5 /usr/local
# cd /usr/local
# ls
pwatters
```

Level	Description
0	Primary striping level, allowing a single virtual file system to be constructed of multiple physical disks
1	Primary mirroring level, where all data written to a virtual file system is copied in real time to a separate mirroring disk
2	A secondary mirroring level, which uses Hamming codes for error correction
3	A secondary striping level, which writes parity information to a single drive, but writes all other data to multiple drives
4	A secondary striping level, which writes parity information to a single drive, but writes all other data to multiple drives
5	A striping and mirroring level which allows data to be written to different disks, including parity information

Table 15-1.   *Commonly Used RAID Levels (1)Procedures*

The mkdir command is used to create mount points, which are equivalent to directories. If you wish to make a mount point one level below an existing directory, you can use the mkdir command with no options. However, if you want to make a mount point several directory levels below an existing directory, you will need to pass the option–p to the mkdir command. For example, the following command will create the mount point */staff*, since the parent / directory already exists:

```
# mkdir /staff
```

However, to create the mount point */staff/nfs/pwatters*, you would use the –p option, if the directory */staff/nfs* did not already exist:

```
# mkdir -p /staff/nfs/pwatters
```

Once a mount point has been created, the mount command is used to attach the file system to the mount point. For example, to mount the file system */dev/dsk/c0t3d0s5* on the mount point */export/home*, you would use the following command:

```
# mount  /dev/dsk/c0t3d0s5 /export/home
```

The mount command assumes a UFS will be mounted. If the target file system is non-UFS, an option specifying the file system type will need to be passed on the command-line using the –F options. Supported file system types include

nfs   Network File System (NFS)

pcf   MS DOS formatted file system

s5fs   System V compliant file system

Details of all currently mounted files are kept in the */etc/mnttab* file. This file should never be directly edited by the super-user. The */etc/mnttab* file will contain entries similar to the following:

```
# cat /etc/mnttab
/dev/dsk/c0t0d0s0 / ufs rw,intr,largefiles,suid,dev=1100000 921334412
/proc /proc proc dev=2280000 922234443
fd /dev/fd fd rw,suid,dev=2240000 922234448
mnttab /etc/mnttab mntfs dev=2340000 922234442
swap /tmp tmpfs dev=1 922234451
/dev/dsk/c0t0d0s5 /usr ufs rw,intr,onerror=panic,suid,dev=1100005 922234441
```

Configuring /etc/vfstab

If you want a disk to be available after reboot, you must create an entry in the virtual file systems table (*/etc/vfstab*). An entry like this,

```
/dev/dsk/c0t3d0s5 /dev/rdsk/c0t3d0s5 /export/home ufs 2 yes -
```

contains details of the slice's block and raw devices, the mount point, the file system type, instructions for *fsck*, and most importantly, a flag to force mount at boot. These options are largely equivalent to those used with the `mount` command.

All file systems, including floppy disks, can be listed in the virtual file systems table. The mount point configuration for the floppy drive is typically similar to the following:

```
fd  -  /dev/fd  fd  -  no  -
```

Instead of mounting file systems individually using the `mount` command, all file systems defined in */etc/vfstab* can be mounted by using the `mountall` command:

```
# mountall
mount: /tmp already mounted
mount: /dev/dsk/c0t0d0s5 is already mounted
```

This attempts to mount all listed file systems, and reports file systems that have previously been mounted. Obviously, file systems that are currently mounted cannot be mounted twice.

Setting Up RAID

The first step in setting up any kind of RAID system is to install the DiskSuite packages and prepare the disks for mirroring or striping by formatting them. Primary disks and their mirrors must be set up with exactly the same partition structure to ensure that virtual file systems can be created that are compatible with both primary and mirror.

Once the DiskSuite packages have been installed, you need to prepare disks that will be used with DiskSuite. This preparation includes creating state database replicas for virtual file systems used on the system. Ideally, these state database replicas will be distributed across each controller and/or disk so that maximum redundancy can be achieved. A small partition must be created on each disk that will contain the state database (typically around 5MB).

For example, to create a state database replica on the file system */dev/dsk/c1t0d0s7*, you would use the following command:

```
# metadb -c 3 -a -f /dev/dsk/c1t0d0s7 /dev/dsk/c0t0d0s7
```

This creates three replicas on each of the two disks specified (*/dev/dsk/c1t0d0s7* and */dev/dsk/c0t0d0s7*). Note that two controllers are used rather than one.

If no existing state database replicas can be found, the following message will be displayed:

```
metadb: There are no existing databases
```

Striping

Next, you need to create configurations for the virtual file systems that you want to use. These can be permanently recorded in the DiskSuite configuration file (*md.tab*). For example, the striping configuration mentioned above involving four 18GB disks could have its configuration recorded with the following entry, if the virtual file system (*s5*) had the path */dev/md/dsk/d5*:

```
d5 4 1 c1t1d0s5 1 c1t2d0s5 1 c2t1d0s5 1 c2t2d0s5
```

Here, the four physical disks involved are */dev/dsk/c1t1d0s5*, */dev/dsk/c1t2d0s5*, */dev/dsk/c2t1d0s5*, and */dev/dsk/c2t2d0s5*. To ensure that the virtual file system is mounted at boot time, it could be included in the */etc/vfstab* file, just like a normal file system. Indeed, only an entry for */dev/md/dsk/d5* should appear in */etc/vfstab* after striping is complete, and the entries for */dev/dsk/c1t1d0s5*, */dev/dsk/c1t2d0s5*, */dev/dsk/c2t1d0s5*, and */dev/dsk/c2t2d0s5* should be commented out.

To initialize the *d5* metadevice, use this command:

```
# metainit d5
```

If this command succeeds, you simply treat the new metadevice as if it were a new file system and initialize a UFS on it:

```
# newfs /dev/md/rdsk/d5
```

Next, you create an appropriate mount point for the device (such as */staff*) and mount the metadevice:

```
# mkdir /staff
# mount /dev/md/dsk/d5 /staff
```

The striped volume *d5* is now ready for use.

Mirroring

To create a mirror between two file systems, you follow a procedure similar to creating an entry in the *md.tab* file. For example, if you want to create a mirror of */dev/dsk/c1t1d0s5* with */dev/dsk/c0t1d0s5* (note the different controller), you would need to create a virtual file system (*d50*) that mirrored the primary file system (*d52*) to its mirror (*d53*). The following entries would need to be made in *md.tab*:

```
d50 -m /dev/md/dsk/d52 /dev/md/dsk/d53
d52 1 1 /dev/dsk/c1t1d0s5
d53 1 1 /dev/dsk/c0t1d0s5
```

To initialize the *d5* metadevice, you would use this command:

```
# metainit d50
# metainit d52
# metainit d53
```

If this command succeeds, you simply treat the new metadevice as if it were a new file system and initialize a UFS on it:

```
# newfs /dev/md/rdsk/d50
# newfs /dev/md/rdsk/d52
# newfs /dev/md/rdsk/d53
```

Next, you create an appropriate mount point for the device (such as */work*), and mount the metadevice:

```
# mkdir /work
# mount /dev/md/dsk/d50 /work
```

The mirrored volume *d50* is now ready for use.

Examples

The following examples provide some real-world cases for installing disks and file systems.

umount

Unmounting local file systems is easy using the umount command. The file system to be unmounted is specified on the command line. For example, to unmount the file system mounted on */export/home*, the following command would be used:

```
# umount /export/home
```

However, if there are open files on the file system, or users logging into their home directories on the target file system, it's obviously a bad idea to unmount the file system without giving users some kind of notice. It's also important to determine whether other processes are using files on the file system. In fact, umount requires that no processes have files open on the target file system. The fuser command can be used to determine which users are accessing a particular file system. For example, to determine whether any processes have open files on the */export/home* partition, the following command could be used:

```
# fuser -c /export/home
```

To give a listing of the UIDs associated with each process, the following command could be used:

```
# fuser -c -u /export/home
```

To warn users about the impending unmounting of the file system, the wall command can be used to send a message to all logged in users. For example, the following message could be sent:

```
# wall
Attention all users
/export/home is going down for maintenance at 6:00 p.m.
Please kill all processes accessing this file system (or I will)
```

At 6 P.M., a fuser check should show that no processes are accessing the file system. However, if some users did not heed the warning, the fuser command can be used to kill all processes that are still active:

```
# fuser -c -k /export/home
```

This is obviously a drastic step, but it may be necessary in emergency or urgent repair situations.

To save time, if you wish to unmount all user file systems (excluding /, /proc, /usr, and /var), you could use the `umountall` command:

```
# umountall
```

This command unmounts only file systems that are listed in the virtual file system table, subject to the aforementioned exclusions.

fsck

This section examines a full run of *fsck*, outlining the most common problems and how they are rectified. It also presents some examples of less-commonly encountered problems. On a SPARC 20 system, *fsck* for the / file system looks like this:

```
** /dev/rdsk/c0d0s0
** Currently Mounted on /
** Phase 1 - Check Blocks and Sizes
** Phase 2 - Check Pathnames
** Phase 3 - Check Connectivity
** Phase 4 - Check Reference Counts
** Phase 5 - Check Cyl groups
FREE BLK COUNT(S) WRONG IN SUPERBLK
SALVAGE?
```

Clearly, the actual block count and the block count recorded in the superblock are at odds with each other. At this point, *fsck* requires super-user permission to install the actual block count in the superblock, which the administrator indicates by pressing Y. The scan continues with the /usr partition:

```
1731 files, 22100 used, 51584 free (24 frags, 6445 blocks,
  0.0% fragmentation)
** /dev/rdsk/c0d0s6
** Currently Mounted on /usr
** Phase 1 - Check Blocks and Sizes
** Phase 2 - Check Pathnames
** Phase 3 - Check Connectivity
** Phase 4 - Check Reference Counts
** Phase 5 - Check Cyl groups

FILE SYSTEM STATE IN SUPERBLOCK IS WRONG; FIX?
```

MANAGING FILESYSTEMS
AND PRINTERS

In this case, the file system state in the superblock records is incorrect, and again, the administrator is required to give consent for it to be repaired. The scan then continues with the */var* and */export/home* partitions:

```
26266 files, 401877 used, 217027 free (283 frags, 27093 blocks,
  0.0% fragmentation)
** /dev/rdsk/c0d0s1
** Currently Mounted on /var
** Phase 1 - Check Blocks and Sizes
** Phase 2 - Check Pathnames
** Phase 3 - Check Connectivity
** Phase 4 - Check Reference Counts
** Phase 5 - Check Cyl groups
1581 files, 4360 used, 25545 free (41 frags, 3188 blocks,
  0.1% fragmentation)
** /dev/rdsk/c0d0s7
** Currently Mounted on /export/home
** Phase 1 - Check Blocks and Sizes
** Phase 2 - Check Pathnames
** Phase 3 - Check Connectivity
** Phase 4 - Check Reference Counts
** Phase 5 - Check Cyl groups
2 files, 9 used, 7111589 free (13 frags, 888947 blocks,
  0.0% fragmentation)
```

Obviously, the */var* and */export/home* partitions have passed examination by *fsck* and are intact. However, the fact that the / and */usr* file systems were in an inconsistent state suggests that the file systems were not cleanly unmounted, perhaps during the last reboot. Fortunately, the superblock itself was intact. However, this is not always the case. In this example, the superblock of */dev/dsk/c0t0d0s2* has a bad "magic number," indicating that it is damaged beyond repair:

```
# fsck /dev/dsk/c0t0d0s2
 BAD SUPER BLOCK: MAGIC NUMBER WRONG
 USE ALTERNATE SUPER-BLOCK TO SUPPLY NEEDED INFORMATION
eg. fsck [-F ufs] -o b=# [special ...]
where # is the alternate super block. SEE fsck_ufs(1M).
```

In this case, you need to specify one of the alternative superblocks that were created by the newfs command. When a file system is created, a message appears about the creation of superblock backups, as shown next.

```
super-block backups (for fsck -b #) at:
32, 5264, 10496, 15728, 20960, 26192, 31424, 36656, 41888,
47120, 52352, 57584, 62816, 68048, 73280, 78512, 82976, 88208,
93440, 98672, 103904, 109136, 114368, 119600, 124832, 130064,
135296, 140528, 145760, 150992, 156224, 161456.
```

In this example, you may need to specify one of these alternative superblocks so that the disk contents are once again readable. If you didn't record the superblock backups during the creation of the file system, you can easily retrieve them by using the newfs command (and using *–N* to prevent the creation of a new file system):

```
# newfs -Nv /dev/dsk/c0t0d0s2
```

Once you have determined an appropriate superblock replacement number (such as 32), use *fsck* again to replace the older superblock with the new one:

```
# fsck -o b=32 /dev/dsk/c0t0d0s2
```

Disks that have physical hardware errors often report being unable to read inodes beyond a particular point. For example, this error message

```
Error reading block 31821 (Attempt to read from file system
resulted in short read) while doing inode scan. Ignore error
<y> ?
```

stops the user from continuing with the *fsck* scan and correcting the problem. This is probably a good time to replace a disk, rather than attempting any corrective action. Never be tempted to ignore these errors and hope for the best—especially in commercial organizations; you will ultimately have to take responsibility for lost and damaged data. Users will be particularly unforgiving if you had advance warning of a problem.

Here is an example of what can happen if a link count problem exists:

```
# fsck /
** /dev/rdsk/c0t1d0s0
** Currently Mounted on /
** Phase 1 - Check Blocks and Sizes
** Phase 2 - Check Pathnames
** Phase 3 - Check Connectivity
** Phase 4 - Check Reference Counts
LINK COUNT DIR I=4  OWNER=root MODE=40700
```

```
SIZE=4096 MTIME=Nov  1 11:56 1999   COUNT 2 SHOULD BE 4
ADJUST? y
```

If the adjustment does not fix the error, use find to track down the problem file and delete it:

```
# find / -mount -inum 4 -ls
```

The problem file should be in the *lost+found* directory for the partition in question (in this case, */lost+found*).

As outlined, having duplicate inodes can also create a problem:

```
** Phase 1 - Check Blocks and Sizes
 314415 DUP I=5009
 345504 DUP I=12011
 345505 DUP I=12011
 854711 DUP I=91040
 856134 DUP I=93474
 856135 DUP I=93474
```

This problem is often encountered in systems using Solaris 2.5 and 2.6, although the problem is not usually seen in systems running Solaris 7, 8, or 9; an upgrade may correct the problem.

Command Reference

The following command is commonly used to mount file systems.

mount

The mount command, executed without any options, provides a list of all mounted file systems:

```
# mount
/ on /dev/dsk/c0t0d0s0 read/write/setuid/intr/largefiles/onerror=
    panic on Tue Jul 10 09:10:01 2001
/usr on /dev/dsk/c0t0d0s6 read/write/setuid/intr/largefiles/
    onerror=panic on Tue Jul 10 09:10:02 2001
/proc on /proc read/write/setuid on Tue Jul 10 09:10:03 2001
/etc/mnttab on mnttab read/write/setuid on Tue Jul 10 09:10:04 2001
```

```
/tmp on swap read/write/setuid on Tue Jul 10 09:10:05 2001
/export/home on /dev/dsk/c0t0d0s7 read/write/setuid/intr/largefiles
    /onerror=panic on Tue Jul 10 09:10:06 2001
```

The mount command has several options, which are described below. These can also be used to specify mounting options in */etc/vfstab*:

bg	If mounting initially fails, continue to attempt mounting in the background. Useful for mounting NFS volumes where the server is temporarily unavailable. The default is *fg*, which attempts to mount in the foreground.
hard	Specifies that hard mounting is attempted, where requests to mount are continually sent. The alternative is soft, which just returns an error message.
intr	Allows keyboard commands to be used during mounting. To switch this off, use *nointr*.
largefiles	Enables support for large file systems (those greater than 2GB in size). To remove support for large file systems, the *nolargefiles* option is used.
logging	Allows a log of all UFS transactions to be maintained. In the event of a system crash, the log can be consulted and all transactions verified. This virtually eliminates the need to run lengthy *fsck* passes on file systems at boot. The default option is *nologging* since logs occupy around 1 percent of file system space.
noatime	Prevents access timestamps from being touched on files. This significantly speeds up access times on large file systems with many small files.
remount	Permits a file system's properties to be modified while it is still mounted, reducing downtime.
retry	Specifies the number of attempts to remount a file system.
rw	Specifies that the file system is to be mounted as read-write. Some file systems, however, are read-only (such as CD-ROMs). In this case, the *ro* option should be specified. Note that it is not physically possible to write to a read-only file system.
suid	Permits set user ID applications to be executed from the file system, while *nosuid* prevents set user ID applications from executing.

The Complete Reference

Chapter 16

Shell Scripts
and Utilities

A key feature of Solaris 9 shells is the ability to write complex scripts that perform repetitive actions and can process various kinds of decision logic. There are many more commands available for the Bourne Again shell than for MS-DOS batch files, which makes them very powerful. However, Microsoft Windows Script is evolving to provide some of the advanced functionality featured by Solaris shell scripts. Script files are more dependent on understanding file permissions than just using the shell to enter commands, which makes them more complex. In this chapter, we review how to create executable scripts that can be used with the Bourne Again shell. In addition, we examine how to schedule shell scripts to run at regular intervals using the *cron* and *at* facilities. Finally, we focus on the advanced text processing features of the Solaris shell, and how these can be used when developing scripts.

Key Concepts

The following concepts are required knowledge for working with the shell and utilities.

Text-Processing Utilities

Solaris has many user commands available to perform tasks ranging from text processing, file manipulation, and terminal management. In this section, we look at some standard UNIX utilities that are the core of using a shell in Solaris. However, readers are urged to obtain an up-to-date list of the utilities supplied with Solaris by typing this command:

```
$ man intro
```

The cat command displays the contents of a file to standard output, without any kind of pagination or screen control. It is most useful for viewing small files, or for passing the contents of a text file through another filter or utility (e.g., the grep command, which searches for strings). To examine the contents of the groups database, for example, you would use the following command:

```
$ cat /etc/group
root::0:root
other::1:
bin::2:root,bin,daemon
sys::3:root,bin,sys,adm
adm::4:root,adm,daemon
uucp::5:root,uucp
mail::6:root
tty::7:root,tty,adm
lp::8:root,lp,adm
```

```
nuucp::9:root,nuucp
staff::10:
postgres::100:
daemon::12:root,daemon
sysadmin::14:
nobody::60001:
noaccess::60002:
nogroup::65534:
```

The `cat` command is not very useful for examining specific sections of a file. For example, if you need to examine the first few lines of a Web server's log files, using `cat` would display them, but they would quickly scroll off the screen out of sight. However, you can use the `head` command to display only the first few lines of a file. This example extracts the lines from the log file of the Inprise Application Server:

```
$ head access_log
203.16.206.43 - - [31/Jan/2002:14:32:52 +1000]
  "GET /index.jsp HTTP/1.0" 200 24077
203.16.206.43 - - [31/Jan/2002:14:32:52 +1000]
  "GET /data.jsp HTTP/1.0" 200 13056
203.16.206.43 - - [31/Jan/2002:14:32:52 +1000]
  "GET /names.jsp HTTP/1.0" 200 15666
203.16.206.43 - - [31/Jan/2002:14:32:52 +1000]
  "GET /database.jsp HTTP/1.0" 200 56444
203.16.206.43 - - [31/Jan/2002:14:32:52 +1000]
  "GET /index.jsp HTTP/1.0" 200 24077
203.16.206.43 - - [31/Jan/2002:14:32:52 +1000]
  "GET /index.jsp HTTP/1.0" 200 24077
203.16.206.43 - - [31/Jan/2002:14:32:52 +1000]
  "GET /names.jsp HTTP/1.0" 200 15666
203.16.206.43 - - [31/Jan/2002:14:32:53 +1000]
  "GET /database.jsp HTTP/1.0" 200 56444
203.16.206.43 - - [31/Jan/2002:14:32:53 +1000]
  "GET /index.jsp HTTP/1.0" 200 24077
203.16.206.43 - - [31/Jan/2002:14:32:53 +1000]
  "GET /search.jsp HTTP/1.0" 200 45333
```

Or, if you just want to examine the last few lines of a file, you could use the `cat` command to display the entire file ending with the last few lines, or you could use the `tail` command to specifically display these lines. If the file is large (e.g., an Inprise Application Server log file of 2MB), displaying the whole file using `cat` would be a large waste of system resources, whereas tail is very efficient. Here's an example of using tail to display the last few lines of a file:

```
$ tail access_log
203.16.206.43 - - [31/Aug/2000:14:32:52 +1000]
   "GET /index.jsp HTTP/1.0" 200 24077
203.16.206.43 - - [31/Aug/2000:14:32:52 +1000]
   "GET /index.jsp HTTP/1.0" 200 24077
203.16.206.43 - - [31/Aug/2000:14:32:52 +1000]
   "GET /index.jsp HTTP/1.0" 200 24077
203.16.206.43 - - [31/Aug/2000:14:32:52 +1000]
   "GET /index.jsp HTTP/1.0" 200 24077
203.16.206.43 - - [31/Aug/2000:14:32:52 +1000]
   "GET /index.jsp HTTP/1.0" 200 24077
203.16.206.43 - - [31/Aug/2000:14:32:52 +1000]
   "GET /index.jsp HTTP/1.0" 200 24077
203.16.206.43 - - [31/Aug/2000:14:32:52 +1000]
   "GET /index.jsp HTTP/1.0" 200 24077
203.16.206.43 - - [31/Aug/2000:14:32:53 +1000]
   "GET /index.jsp HTTP/1.0" 200 24077
203.16.206.43 - - [31/Aug/2000:14:32:53 +1000]
   "GET /index.jsp HTTP/1.0" 200 24077
203.16.206.43 - - [31/Aug/2000:14:32:53 +1000]
   "GET /index.jsp HTTP/1.0" 200 24077
```

Now, imagine that you were searching for a particular string within the *access_log* file, such as a 404 error code, which indicates that a page has been requested that does not exist. Webmasters regularly check log files for this error code to create a list of links that need to be checked. To view this list, you can use the grep command to search the file for a specific string (in this case, "404"); you can use the more command to display the results page by page:

```
$ grep 404 access_log | more
203.16.206.56 - - [31/Aug/2000:15:42:54 +1000]
   "GET /servlet/LibraryCatalog?command=mainmenu HTTP/1.1" 200 21404
203.16.206.56 - - [01/Sep/2000:08:32:12 +1000]
   "GET /servlet/LibraryCatalog?command=searchbyname HTTP/1.1" 200 14041
203.16.206.237 - - [01/Sep/2000:09:20:35 +1000]
   "GET /images/LINE.gif HTTP/1.1" 404 1204
203.16.206.236 - - [01/Sep/2000:10:10:35 +1000]
   "GET /images/black.gif HTTP/1.1" 404 1204
203.16.206.236 - - [01/Sep/2000:10:10:40 +1000]
   "GET /images/white.gif HTTP/1.1" 404 1204
```

```
203.16.206.236 - - [01/Sep/2000:10:10:47 +1000]
  "GET /images/red.gif HTTP/1.1" 404 1204
203.16.206.236 - - [01/Sep/2000:10:11:09 +1000]
  "GET /images/yellow.gif HTTP/1.1" 404 1204
203.16.206.236 - - [01/Sep/2000:10:11:40 +1000]
  "GET /images/LINE.gif HTTP/1.1" 404 1204
203.16.206.236 - - [01/Sep/2000:10:11:44 +1000]
  "GET /images/LINE.gif HTTP/1.1" 404 1204
203.16.206.236 - - [01/Sep/2000:10:12:03 +1000]
  "GET /images/LINE.gif HTTP/1.1" 404 1204
203.16.206.41 - - [01/Sep/2000:12:04:22 +1000]
  "GET /data/books/576586955.pdf HTTP/1.0" 404 1204
--More--
```

These log files contain a line for each access to the Web server, with entries relating to the source IP address, date and time of access, the HTTP request string sent, the protocol used, and the success/error code. When you see the *--More—* prompt, you can press the SPACEBAR to advance to the next screen, or you can press ENTER to advance by a single line in the results. As you have probably guessed, the pipeline operator | was used to pass the results of the grep command through to the more command.

In addition to the pipeline, you can use four other operators on the command line to direct or append input streams to standard output, or output streams to standard input. Although that sounds convoluted, it can be very useful when working with files to direct the output of a command into a new file (or append it to an existing file). Or, you can generate the input to a command from the output of another command. These operations are performed by the following operators:

>	Redirect standard output to a file
>>	Append standard output to a file
<	Redirect file contents to standard input
<<	Append file contents to standard input

Bash also has logical operators, including the "less than" (*lt*) operator, which uses the test facility to make numerical comparisons between two operands. Other commonly used operators include the following:

a –eq b	a equals b
a –ne b	a not equal to b
a –gt b	a greater than b
a –ge b	a greater than or equal to b
a –le b	a less than or equal to b

Let's look at an example with the `cat` command, which displays the contents of files, and the `echo` command, which echoes the contents of a string or an environment variable that has been previously specified. For example, imagine if you wanted to maintain a database of endangered species in a text file called animals.txt. If we wanted to add the first animal "zebra" to an empty file, you could use this command:

```
$ echo "zebra" > animals.txt
```

You could then check the contents of the file *animals.txt* with this command:

```
$ cat animals.txt
zebra
```

Thus, the insertion was successful. Now, imagine that you want to add a second entry (the animal "emu") to the animals.txt file. You could try using this command:

```
$ echo "emu" > animals.txt
```

However, the result may not be what you expected:

```
$ cat animals.txt
emu
```

This is because the > operator always overwrites the contents of an existing file, whereas the >> operator always appends to the contents of an existing file. Let's run that command again with the correct operators:

```
$ echo "zebra" > animals.txt
$ echo "emu" >> animals.txt
```

This time, the output is just what we expected:

```
$ cat animals.txt
zebra
emu
```

Once you have a file containing a list of all the animals, you would probably want to sort it alphabetically, which simplifies searching for specific entries. To do this, you can use the sort command:

```
$ sort animals.txt
emu
zebra
```

The sorted entries are then displayed on the screen in alphabetical order. You can also redirect the sorted list into another file (called *sorted_animals.txt*) by using this command:

```
$ sort animals.txt > animals_sorted.txt
```

If you wanted to check that the sorting process actually worked, you could compare the contents of the animals.txt file line-by-line with the *sorted_animals.txt* file by using the diff command:

```
$ diff animals.txt sorted_animals.txt
1d0
< zebra
2a2
> zebra
```

This result indicates that the first and second lines of the *animals.txt* and *sorted_animals.txt* files are different, as expected. If the sorting process had failed, the two files would have been identical, and no differences would have been reported by diff.

A related facility is the basename facility, which is designed to remove file extensions from a filename specified as an argument. This is commonly used to convert files with one extension to another extension. For example, imagine that you had a graphics file–conversion program which took as its first argument the name of a source JPEG file, and took the name of a target bitmap file. Somehow, you'd need to convert a filename of the form *filename.jpg* to a file of the form *filename.bmp*. You can do this with the basename command. In order to strip a file extension from an argument, you need to pass the filename and the extension as separate arguments to basename. For example, the command

```
$ basename maya.gif .gif
```

will produce this output:

```
maya
```

If you want the .gif extension to be replaced by a .bmp extension, you could use the command

```
$ echo `basename maya.gif`.bmp
```

to produce the following output:

```
maya.bmp
```

Of course, you are not limited to extensions like .gif and .bmp. Also, keep in mind that the basename technique is entirely general—and because Solaris does not have mandatory filename extensions, you can use the basename technique for other purposes, such as generating a set of strings based on filenames.

Procedures

The following procedures are required to program the shell effectively.

sed *and* awk

So far, we've looked at some fairly simple examples of text processing. However, the power of Solaris-style text processing lies with advanced tools like *sed* and *awk*. *sed* is a command-line editing program that can be used to perform search-and-replace operations on very large files, as well as other kinds of noninteractive editing. *awk*, on the other hand, is a complete text-processing programming language that has a C-like syntax and which can be used in conjunction with *sed* to program repetitive text-processing and editing operations on large files. These combined operations include double and triple spacing files, printing line numbers, left and right justifying text, performing field extraction and field substitution, and filtering on specific strings and pattern specifications. We examine some of these applications shortly.

To start this example, create a set of customer address records stored in a flat text, tab-delimited database file called *test.dat*:

```
$ cat test.dat
Bloggs  Joe     24 City Rd      Richmond        VA      23227
Lee     Yat Sen 72 King St      Amherst MA      01002
```

```
Rowe      Sarah    3454 Capitol St Los Angeles      CA      90074
Sakura    Akira    1 Madison Ave   New York         NY      10017
```

This is a fairly common type of record, storing a customer's surname, first name, street address, city, state, and zip code. For presentation, we can double space the records in this file by redirecting the contents of the *test.dat* file through sed, with the *G* option:

```
$ sed G < test.dat
Bloggs  Joe      24 City Rd       Richmond       VA      23227

Lee     Yat Sen  72 King St       Amherst MA     01002

Rowe    Sarah    3454 Capitol St  Los Angeles    CA      90074

Sakura  Akira    1 Madison Ave    New York       NY      10017
```

The power of sed lies in its ability to be used in pipelines; thus, an action can literally be performed in conjunction with many other operations. For example, to insert double spacing and then remove it, simply invoke sed twice with the appropriate commands:

```
$ sed G < test.dat | sed 'n;d'
Bloggs  Joe      24 City Rd       Richmond       VA      23227
Lee     Yat Sen  72 King St       Amherst MA     01002
Rowe    Sarah    3454 Capitol St  Los Angeles    CA      90074
Sakura  Akira    1 Madison Ave    New York       NY      10017
```

If printing reports, you'll probably be using line numbering at some point to uniquely identify records. You can generate line numbers dynamically for display by using sed:

```
$ sed '/./=' test.dat | sed '/./N; s/\n/ /'
1 Bloggs          Joe      24 City Rd       Richmond       VA      23227
2 Lee    Yat Sen 72 King St         Amherst MA     01002
3 Rowe    Sarah    3454 Capitol St Los Angeles    CA      90074
4 Sakura           Akira    1 Madison Ave   New York        NY      10017
```

Or, you could use *nl*. For large files, counting the number of lines is often useful. Although you can use the wc command for this purpose, you can also use sed in situations where wc is not available in the *PATH* environment variable:

```
$ cat test.dat | sed -n '$='
4
```

When you're printing databases for display, you might want comments and titles left-justified, but all records being displayed with two blank spaces before each line. You can achieve this by using sed:

```
$ cat test.dat | sed 's/^/  /'
  Bloggs       Joe     24 City Rd       Richmond        VA      23227
  Lee    Yat Sen 72 King St       Amherst MA      01002
  Rowe   Sarah   3454 Capitol St Los Angeles      CA      90074
  Sakura       Akira   1 Madison Ave   New York        NY      10017
```

Imagine that due to some municipal reorganization, all cities currently located in CT were being reassigned to MA. sed would be the perfect tool to identify all instances of *CT* in the data file and replace them with *MA*:

```
$ cat test.dat | sed 's/MA/CT/g'
Bloggs  Joe     24 City Rd      Richmond        VA      23227
Lee     Yat Sen 72 King St      Amherst CT      01002
Rowe    Sarah   3454 Capitol St Los Angeles     CA      90074
Sakura  Akira   1 Madison Ave   New York        NY      10017
```

If a data file has been entered as a First-In Last-Out (FILO) stack, you'll generally be reading records from the file from top to bottom. However, if the data file is to be treated as a Last-In First-Out (LIFO) stack, reordering the records from the last to the first would be useful:

```
$ cat test.dat | sed '1!G;h;$!d'
Sakura  Akira   1 Madison Ave   New York        NY      10017
Rowe    Sarah   3454 Capitol St Los Angeles     CA      90074
Lee     Yat Sen 72 King St      Amherst MA      01002
Bloggs  Joe     24 City Rd      Richmond        VA      23227
```

Some data-hiding applications require that data be encoded in some way that is nontrivial for another application to detect a file's contents. One way to foil such programs is to reverse the character strings that comprise each record, which you can achieve by using sed:

```
$ cat test.dat | sed '/\n/!G;s/\(.\)\(.*\n\)/&\2\1/;//D;s/.//'
72232   AV      dnomhciR        dR ytiC 42      eoJ     sggolB
20010   AM      tsrehmA tS gniK 27      neS taY eeL
47009   AC      selegnA soL     tS lotipaC 4543 haraS   ewoR
71001   YN      kroY weN        evA nosidaM 1   arikA   arukaS
```

Some reporting applications might require that the first line of a file be processed before deletion. Although you can use the head command for this purpose, you can also use sed:

```
$ sed q < test.dat
Bloggs  Joe     24 City Rd      Richmond        VA      23227
```

Or, if you want to print a certain number of lines, you can use sed to extract the first *q* lines:

```
$ sed 2q < test.dat
Bloggs  Joe     24 City Rd      Richmond        VA      23227
Lee     Yat Sen 72 King St      Amherst MA      01002
```

The grep command is often used to detect strings within files. However, you can also use sed for this purpose, as shown in the following example, where the string *CA* (representing California) is searched for:

```
$ cat test.dat | sed '/CA/!d'
Rowe    Sarah   3454 Capitol St Los Angeles     CA      90074
```

However, this is a fairly gross and inaccurate method, because *CA* might match a street address like "1 CALGARY Rd," or "23 Green CAPE." Thus, you need to use the field extraction features of awk. In the following example, use awk to extract and print the fifth column in the data file representing the state:

```
$ cat test.dat | awk 'BEGIN {FS = "\t"}{print $5}'
VA
MA
CA
NY
```

Note that the tab character (\t) is specified as the field delimiter. Now, if you combine the field extraction capability of awk with the string searching facility of sed, you should be able to print out a list of all occurrences of the state *CA*:

```
$ cat test.dat | awk 'BEGIN {FS = "\t"}{print $5}' | sed '/CA/!d'
CA
```

Or, you could simply count the number of records that contained *CA* in the state field:

```
$ cat test.dat | awk 'BEGIN {FS = "\t"}{print $5}' | sed '/CA/!d' \
  | sed -n '$='
1
```

When producing reports, selectively displaying fields in a different order is useful. For example, although surname is typically used as a primary key, and is generally the first field, most reports would display the first name before the surname, which you can achieve by using awk:

```
$ cat test.dat | awk 'BEGIN {FS = "\t"}{print $2,$1}'
Joe Bloggs
Yat Sen Lee
Sarah Rowe
Akira Sakura
```

You can also split such reordered fields across different lines, and using different format specifiers. For example, the following script prints the first name and surname on one line, and the state on the following line. Such code is the basis of many mail merge and bulk printing programs:

```
$ cat test.dat | awk 'BEGIN {FS = "\t"}{print $2,$1,"\n"$5}'
Joe Bloggs
VA
Yat Sen Lee
MA
Sarah Rowe
CA
Akira Sakura
NY
```

Because awk is a complete programming language, it contains many common constructs, like *if/then/else* evaluations of logical states. These states can be used to test business logic cases. For example, in a mailing program, you could check the bounds of valid zip codes by determining whether the zip code lay within a valid range. For example, the following routine checks to see whether a zip code is less than 9999, and rejects it as invalid if it is greater than 999:

```
$ cat test.dat | awk 'BEGIN {FS = "\t"}{print $2,$1}{if($6<9999) \
   {print "Valid zipcode"} else {print "Invalid zipcode"}}'
Joe Bloggs
Invalid zipcode
Yat Sen Lee
Valid zipcode
Sarah Rowe
Invalid zipcode
Akira Sakura
Invalid zipcode
```

Examples

The following show how to write effective shell scripts.

Writing Shell Scripts

Shell scripts are combinations of shell and user commands that are executed in noninteractive mode for a wide variety of purposes. Whether you require a script that converts a set of filename extensions, or whether you need to alert the system administrator by e-mail that disk space is running low, you can use shell scripts. The commands that you place inside a shell script should normally execute in the interactive shell mode as well, making it easy to take apart large scripts and debug them line by line in your normal login shell. In this section, we examine only shell scripts that run under the Bourne Again shell (Bash). Although many of the scripts will work without modification using other shells, it is always best to check the syntax chart of your own shell before attempting to run the scripts on a non-Bash shell.

Processing Shell Arguments

A common goal of writing shell scripts is to make them as general as possible so that you can use them with many different kinds of input. For example, in the *cat* examples presented in previous sections, you wouldn't want to have to create an entirely new script for every file that you wanted to insert data into. Fortunately, shell scripts are able to make use of command-line parameters, which are numerically ordered arguments that are accessible from within a shell script. For example, a shell script to move files from one computer to another computer might require parameters for the source host, the destination host, and the name of the file to be moved. Obviously, you want to be able to pass these arguments to the script, rather than "hard wiring" them into the code. This is one advantage of shell scripts (and Perl programs) over compiled languages like C: scripts are easy to modify, and their operation is completely transparent to the user.

Arguments to shell scripts can be identified by a simple scheme—the command executed is referred to with the argument $0, with the first parameter identified as $1, the second parameter identified by $2, and so on, up to a maximum of nine parameters.

Thus, a script executed with these parameters

```
$ display_hardware.sh cdrom scsi ide
```

would refer internally to *cdrom* as $1, *scsi* as $2, and *ide* as $3.

Let's see how arguments can be used effectively within a script to process input parameters. The first script simply counts the number of lines in a file (using the wc command), specified by a single command-line argument ($1). To begin with, create an empty script file:

```
$ touch count_lines.sh
```

Next, set the permissions on the file to be executable:

```
$ chmod +x count_lines.sh
```

Next, edit the file

```
$ vi count_lines.sh
```

and add the appropriate code:

```
#!/bin/bash
echo "Number of lines in file " $1
wc -l $1
```

The script will take the first command-line argument, then print the number of lines, and then exit. Run the script with the command

```
$ ./count_lines.sh /etc/group
```

which gives the following output:

```
Number of lines in file /etc/group
43
```

Although the individual activity of scripts is quite variable, the procedure of creating the script file, setting its permissions, editing its contents, and executing it on the command-line remains the same across scripts. Of course, you may want to make the script available only to certain users or groups for execution. You can enable this by using the chmod command and explicitly adding or removing permissions when necessary.

Testing File Properties

One of the assumptions that we made in the previous script was that the file specified by *$1* actually existed; if it didn't exist, we obviously would not be able to count the number of lines it contained. If the script is running from the command-line, we can safely debug it, and interpret any error conditions that arise (such as a file not existing or having incorrect permissions). However, if a script is intended to run as a scheduled job (using the *cron* or *at* facility), debugging it in real time is impossible. Thus, writing scripts that can handle error conditions gracefully and intelligently is often useful, rather than leaving administrators wondering why a job didn't produce any output when it was scheduled to run.

The number one cause of run-time execution errors is the incorrect setting of file permissions. Although most users remember to set the executable bit on the script file itself, they often neglect to include error checking for the existence of data files that are used by the script. For example, if you wanted to write a script that checked the syntax of a configuration file (like the Apache configuration file, *httpd.conf*), you need to check that the file actually exists before performing the check—otherwise, the script may not return an error message, and you may erroneously assume that the script file is correctly configured.

Fortunately, Bash makes it easy to test for the existence of files by using the (conveniently named) test facility. In addition to testing for file existence, files that exist can also be tested for read, write, and execute permissions, prior to any read, write, or execute file access being attempted by the script. The following example revises the previous script that counted the number of lines in a file by first verifying that the target file (specified by *$1*) exists, and then by printing the result; otherwise, an error message will be displayed:

```
#!/bin/bash
if test -a $1 then
echo "Number of lines in file " $1
wc -l $1
else
        echo "The file" $1 "does not exist"
fi
```

When you run this command, if a file exists, it should count the number of lines in the target file as before, otherwise, an error message will be printed. If the */etc/group* file did not exist, for example, you'd really want to know about it:

```
$ ./count_lines.sh /etc/group
The file /etc/group does not exist
```

There may be some situations where you want to test another file property. For example, the */etc/shadow* password database must be readable only by the super-user. Thus, if you execute a script to check whether the */etc/shadow* file is readable by a nonprivileged user, it should not return a positive result. You can check file readability by using the –*r* option rather than the –*a* option. Here's the revised script:

```
#!/bin/bash
if test -r $1 then
echo "I can read the file " $1
else
        echo "I can't read the file" $1
fi
```

You can also test the following file permissions using the *test* facility:

–*b*	File is a special block file
–*c*	File is a special character file
–*d*	File is a directory
–*f*	File is a normal file
–*h*	File is a symbolic link
–*p*	File is a named piped
–*s*	File has nonzero size
–*w*	File is writeable by the current user
–*x*	File is executable by the current user

Looping

All programming languages have the capability to repeat blocks of code for a specified number of iterations. This makes performing repetitive actions very easy for a well-written program. The Bourne shell is no exception. It features a *for* loop, which repeats the actions of a code block for a specified number of iterations, as defined by a set of consecutive arguments to the `for` command. It also features a *while* and *until* loop. In addition, an iterator is available within the code block to indicate which of the sequence of iterations that will be performed is currently being performed. If that sounds a little complicated, let's have a look at a concrete example that uses a *for* loop to generate a set of filenames. These filenames are then tested using the *test* facility to determine whether they exist:

```
#!/bin/bash
for i in apple orange lemon kiwi guava
do
        DATAFILE=$i".dat"
        echo "Checking" $DATAFILE
        if test -s $FILENAME
        then
                echo "$DATAFILE "has zero-length"
        else
                echo $FILENAME "is OK"
        fi
done
```

The *for* loop is repeated nine times, with the variable *$i* taking on the values *apple*, *orange*, *lemon*, *kiwi*, and *guava*. Thus, on the first iteration, when *$i=apple*, the shell interprets the *for* loop in the following way:

```
FILENAME="apple.dat"
echo "Checking apple.dat"
if test -s apple.dat
then
echo "apple.dat has zero-length"
else
echo "apple.dat is OK"
fi
```

If you run this script in a directory with files of zero-length, you would expect to see the following output:

```
$ ./zero_length_check.sh
Checking apple.dat
apple.dat is zero-length
Checking orange.dat
orange.dat is zero-length
```

```
Checking lemon.dat
lemon.dat is zero-length
Checking kiwi.dat
kiwi.dat is zero-length
Checking guava.dat
guava.dat is zero-length
```

However, if you entered data into each of the files, you should see them receive the OK message:

```
$ ./zero_length_check.sh
Checking apple.dat
apple.dat is OK
Checking orange.dat
orange.dat is OK
Checking lemon.dat
lemon.dat is OK
Checking kiwi.dat
kiwi.dat is OK
Checking guava.dat
guava.dat is OK
```

Using Shell Variables

In the previous example, you assigned different values to a shell variable, which was used to generate filenames for checking. It is common to modify variables within scripts by using export, and to attach error codes to instances where variables are not defined within a script. This is particularly useful if a variable that is available within a user's interactive shell is not available in their noninteractive shell. For example, you can create a script called *show_errors.sh* that returns an error message if the *PATH* variable is not set:

```
#!/bin/bash
echo ${PATH:?PATH_NOT_SET}
```

Of course, because the *PATH* variable is usually set, you should see output similar to the following:

```
$ ./path_set.sh
/sbin:/bin:/usr/games/bin:/usr/sbin:/root/bin:/usr/local/bin:
/usr/local/sbin/:/usr/bin:
/usr/X11R6/bin: /usr/games:/opt/gnome/bin:/opt/kde/bin
```

However, if the *PATH* was not set, you would see the following error message:

```
./show_errors.sh: PATH_NOT_SET
```

You can use system-supplied error messages as well by not specifying the optional error string:

```
$ ./path_set.sh
#!/bin/bash
echo ${PATH:?}
```

Thus, if the *PATH* variable is not set, you would see the following error message:

```
$ ./path_set.sh
./showargs: PATH: parameter null or not set
```

You can also use the numbered shell variables (*$1, $2, $3,* and so on) to capture the space-delimited output of certain commands, and perform actions based on the value of these variables using the set command. For example, the command

```
$ set `ls`
```

will sequentially assign each of the fields within the returned directory listing to a numbered shell variable. For example, if the directory listing contained the entries,

```
apple.dat    guava.dat    kiwi.dat    lemon.dat    orange.dat
```

you could retrieve the values of these filenames by using the echo command:

```
$ echo $1
apple.dat
$ echo $2
guava.dat
$ echo $3
kiwi.dat
$ echo $4
lemon.dat
$ echo $5
orange.dat
```

This approach is very useful if your script needs to perform some action based on only one component of the date. For example, if you wanted to create a unique filename to assign to a compressed file, you could combine the values of each variable with a .Z extension to produce a set of strings like *orange.dat.Z*.

Command Reference

The following commands are used to write to shell scripts.

sed

The standard options for sed are shown here:

–n	Prevents display of pattern space
–e filename	Executes the script contained in the file filename
–V	Displays the version number

awk

The standard POSIX options for awk are shown here:

- *–f filename*, where *filename* is the name of the awk file to process
- *–F field*, where *field* is the field separator
- *–v x=y*, where *x* is a variable and *y* is a value
- *–W lint* turns on lint checking
- *–W lint-old* uses old-style lint checking
- *–W traditional* enforces traditional usage
- *–W version* displays the version number

The Complete Reference

Solaris 9

Chapter 17

Backup and Recovery

oftware and hardware failures are an unfortunate fact of life in the IT industry, and panic can result when missing or corrupt data is revealed during a peak service period. However, a system crash or a disk failure should not be a cause for alarm; instead, it should be the signal to a well-armed and well-prepared administrator to determine the cause of the problem, rectify any hardware faults, and restore any lost data by using a recovery procedure. This general procedure can be followed regardless of whether user files or database tables have been lost or corrupted.

Fortunately, Solaris provides a wide variety of backup and restore software that can be used in conjunction with any number of media—for example, magnetic and digital audio tapes, writeable CD-ROMs, Zip drives, and redundant hard drives. This chapter will examine the development and implementation of backup and recovery procedures with Solaris and review some of the popular backup and recovery freeware and commercial tools.

Key Concepts

The following concepts are required knowledge for implementing efficient backup and recovery services.

Understanding Backups

In many company networks, valuable data is stored on Solaris server systems in user files and database tables. The variety of information stored is endless: personnel files, supplier invoices, receipts, and all kinds of intellectual property. In addition, many organizations provide some kind of service that relies on server uptime and information availability to generate income, or maintain prestige. For example, if a major business-to-consumer Web site like *amazon.com* or business-to-business hub like *office.com* experiences downtime, every minute that the system is unavailable costs money in lost sales, frustrated consumers, and reduced customer confidence. On the other hand, a government site such as the Government Accounting Office (**http://www.gao.gov/**) provides valuable advice to government, business, and consumers, and is expected to be available continuously. The reputation of online service providers can suffer greatly if servers go down. It is not enough, however, to ensure that a service is highly available; the data it provides also needs to be valid, which is why regular data backup needs to occur.

On a smaller scale, but just as significant, is a department server, which might provide file serving, authentication services, and print access for several hundred PC systems or Sun Rays. If the server hard disk crashes, the affected users who can't read their mail or retrieve their files are going to be inconvenienced if system data cannot be restored in a timely fashion.

This chapter examines the background and rationale for providing a reliable backup and restore service that will ensure a high level of service provision, even in the event of hardware failure.

Analyzing Backup Requirements

The first requirement of a backup service is the ability to restore a dysfunctional system to a functional state as quickly as possible. The relationship between time of restoration and user satisfaction is inverse, as shown in Figure 17-1: The longer a restore takes, the faster users will become angry, while the rapid restoration of service will give users confidence. For this reason, many sites take incremental backups of their complete file systems each night but may take a weekly "full dump" snapshot that can be used to rapidly rebuild an entire system from a single tape or disk.

The second requirement for a backup service is data integrity: It is not sufficient just to restore some data and hope that it's close enough to the original. It is essential that all restored data can actually be used by applications as if no break in service had occurred. This is particularly important for database applications that may have several kinds of files associated with them. Table indices, data files, and rollback segments must all be synchronized if the database is to operate correctly, and user data must be consistent with the internal structure and table ownership rights. If files are simply backed up onto disk while the database is open, these files can be restored, but the database system may not be able to use them.

It is essential that you understand the restoration and data integrity requirements for all key applications on your system and identify any risks to service provision associated with data corruption. Thus, a comprehensive backup and restore plan should include provision for regular cold and warm dumps of databases to a file system that is regularly backed up.

A third requirement for a backup and restore service is flexibility: Data should be recorded and compressed on media that can potentially be read on a different machine,

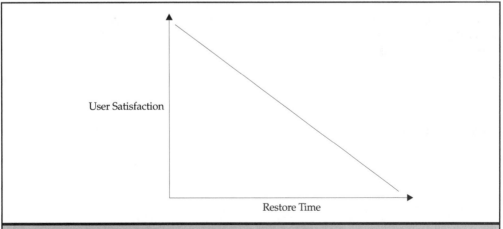

Figure 17-1.   *The relationship between time to restore and user satisfaction*

User Satisfaction

Restore Time

using a different operating system. In addition, using alternative media for concurrent backups is also useful for ensuring availability in case of hardware failure of a backup device. For example, you may use a DDS-3 DAT tape drive as your main backup device for nightly incremental backups, but you may also decide to burn a weekly CD-ROM containing a full dump of the database. If your server was affected by a power surge, the DAT drive was damaged, and a replacement would take one week to arrive, the CD-ROM dump can be used as a fallback, even though it may not be completely up-to-date.

Determining a Backup Strategy

Typical backup and restore strategies employ two related methods for recording data to any medium:

- Full dumps
- Incremental dumps

A full dump involves taking a copy of an entire file system, or set of file systems, and copying it to a backup medium. Historically, large file systems take a long time to back up because of slow tape speeds and poor I/O performance, which can be improved by using the incremental method.

An incremental dump is an iterative method that involves taking a baseline dump on a regular basis (usually once every week) and then taking another dump of only those files that have changed since the previous full dump. Although this approach can require the maintenance of complex lists of files and file sizes, it reduces the overall time to back up a file system because on most file systems, only a small proportion of the total number of files changes from week to week. This reduces the overall load on the backup server and improves tape performance by minimizing friction on drive heads. However, using incremental backups can increase the time to restore a system, as up to seven (one for each day of the week) backup tapes must be processed to restore data files fully. Seven tapes are required so that a single tape can be assigned to each day. A balance can therefore be struck between convenience and the requirement for a speedy restore in the event of an emergency. Many sites use a combination of incremental and full daily dumps on multiple media to ensure that full restores can be performed rapidly and to ensure redundant recording of key data.

After deciding on an incremental or full dump backup strategy, you need to plan how backups can be integrated into an existing network. There are four possible configurations which can be considered The simplest approach is to attach a single backup device to each server so that the server acts as its own backup host. This configuration is shown here:

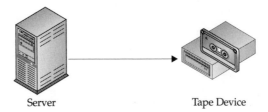

Server   Tape Device

This approach is appealing because it allows data to be backed up and restored using the same device, without any requirement for network connectivity. However, this architecture has poor scaling capacity, and it does not provide for redundancy through the use of multiple backup devices. This can be rectified by including multiple backup devices for a single host, as shown in here:

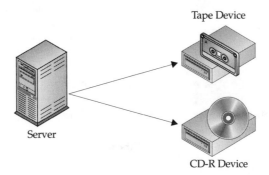

Tape Device

Server

CD-R Device

The cost of maintaining single or multiple backup devices for each server in an organization can be expensive. To reduce cost, many organizations centralize the management and storage of data for entire departments or sites on a single server. This approach is shown in Figure 17-2.

In this configuration, multiple client machines' hard drives are backed up to a central Solaris server, which can also be attached to multiple backup devices to provide various levels of redundancy for more- or less-significant data. For example, data from user PCs may not require the double or triple redundancy that financial records need. The

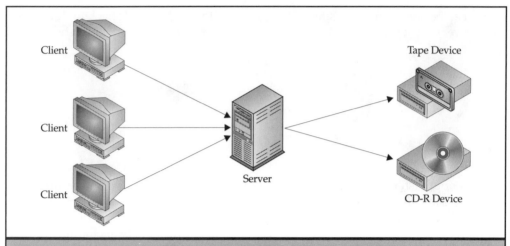

Figure 17-2. *Centralized backup server with multiple storage devices*

freeware software product AMANDA, reviewed later in this chapter, is ideal for backing up multiple clients through a single server.

In recent years, storage area networks (SANs) have been employed. In a SAN, backup management and data storage is distributed across multiple backup hosts and devices. Thus, a client's data could potentially be stored on many different backup servers, and management of that data could be performed from a remote manager running on the client. This configuration is shown in Figure 17-3.

For example, a Veritas client for Windows called Backup Exec can connect to many different Solaris servers through an SMB, backing up data to multiple mediums. Other server-side packages, such as Legato Networker, offer distributed management of all backup services. Both products are reviewed later in this chapter. New to the game is Sun's Java-based Jiro technology, which implements the proposed Federated Management Architecture (FMA) standard. FMA is a proposal for implementing distributed storage across networks in a standard way, and it is receiving support from major hardware manufacturers such as Hitachi, Quantum, Veritas, and Fujitsu for future integration with their products. More information on Jiro and FMA can be found at **http://www .jiro.com/**.

Selecting Backup Tools

If you want to use anything other than the standard UNIX backup tools, many freeware and commercial packages are available, depending on what facilities you require. For example, the AMANDA freeware program centralizes the storage and control for backup and restore of remote machines. However, it does not support

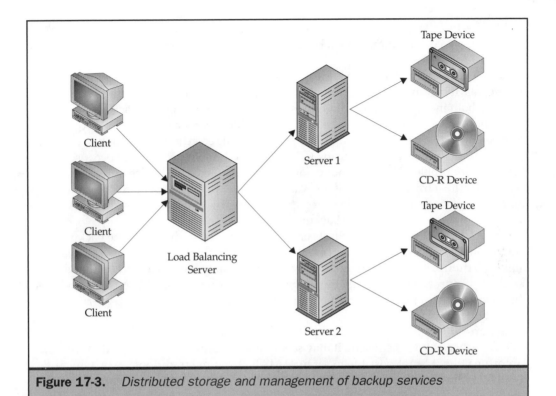

Figure 17-3.   *Distributed storage and management of backup services*

distributed storage, in which the two commercial vendors (Veritas and Legato) specialize. Veritas Software and Legato Systems are far and away the leading vendors in the automated enterprise-wide backup and restore application arena, since they provide failover and clustering capabilities along with backup and restore.

AMANDA

AMANDA, the Advanced Maryland Automatic Network Disk Archiver, is a backup system that follows the centralized backup server for the multiple clients scheme shown in Figure 17-2. It can back up client drives from any operating system that supports SMB, including Solaris, Linux, and Windows NT clients. Although AMANDA was designed to operate with a single tape drive, it can be configured to use multiple tape drives and other backup devices.

One advantage of AMANDA over other backup systems is that it provides management of native Solaris backup and restore commands; this means that AMANDA backup files are *tar* files that can be manually extracted and viewed without using the AMANDA system if it is not available for some reason. This is particularly significant for full dumps that must be restored to a "green fields" server that does not yet have

AMANDA installed. AMANDA can be downloaded from **http://www.amanda.org**, and answers to questions are available at **http://www.ic.unicamp.br/~oliva/snapshots/ amanda/FAQ**.

The AMANDA approach to backups is a solution based on `cron` scheduling of `tar` commands: It has an efficient scheduling and storage management system that involves spooling both incremental and full dumps to a "holding disk" on the backup server. The data is not written directly to the backup device so that there is a better logical separation between the preparation of backup files and the actual recording process. This separation is particularly important when using CD-R (CD-recordable) technology because of the *buffer overrun* problem: If data is not made available to the CD-R device quickly enough, it fails to write a track, and the disc is wasted because data cannot be rewritten to it. If the backup file is prepared in advance on the holding disk, most of the overhead involved in copying the backup file to the backup device is removed.

AMANDA's other advantage is its efficient scheduling of dumps to the backup device. Simply performing an incremental dump each night, followed by a Sunday night full dump, is wasteful because only a few files may have changed on the server. While this approach is standard among many backup programs, AMANDA introduces the concept of a dump *cycle*, which minimizes the total number of dumps performed by estimating the time taken to dump any particular file. It attempts to balance total backup times across different days, based on past performance of a particular device.

While this feature is efficient, it may seem initially confusing to many administrators. Unfortunately, it is not possible to set up AMANDA in the traditional way, whereby a full dump is performed on weekends and incremental dumps are performed each week night, and this may be inappropriate for organizations that have a strict policy regarding backup scheduling. In addition, AMANDA has a further limitation in that it cannot backup a file system that is larger than the size of a single backup medium; for large disks (18GB and larger), AMANDA may be used only with the latest Digital Audio Tapes (DATs) and Digital Linear Tapes (DLTs), and not with Quarter Inch Cartridge (QIC) tapes or CD-R technology. While small drives and partitions can be backed up using these devices, it is obviously a limitation for organizations with large data-handling requirements.

Legato Networker

Legato's Networker storage management product is a commercial product that is often supplied with database server packages like Oracle. It is similar to AMANDA in that it prefers centralized over distributed control of all backup resources, in contrast to the Veritas product, which is reviewed next. However, unlike AMANDA, multiple backup servers can exist as long as they are controlled by a central backup server. This approach is outlined in Figure 17-5. Networker is well known for its ability to back up data from and restore data to different clients, even those running different operating systems. This feature can be useful, for example, when you're upgrading client operating systems migrating from Linux to Solaris, because a complete reinstall of user packages and files is not necessary; they can be simply retrieved from a central Networker server.

To make it easy for Windows and other PC users to integrate neatly within an enterprise server environment, Legato also supplies a NT client, which is shown in Figure 17-4.

For more information about Legato products, visit **http://www.legato.com/**.

Veritas NetBackup

While AMANDA is focussed on a single backup server providing services to many clients, Veritas provides a distributed backup management system, known as NetBackup, which can be used to process terabytes of data from many different clients across many different backup servers and multiple devices. This is similar to the approach outlined in Figure 17-5 and is aimed at maximizing the utilization of existing resources, such as tape drives and CD-R devices, no matter where they are located on a corporate intranet or even across the Internet. In addition, NetBackup provides the greatest amount of choices for clients, who can seamlessly manage their own backups across multiple hosts and devices.

NetBackup also includes support for many server-side database systems, such as Oracle, dispensing with the need for performing separate warm dumps to backed-up

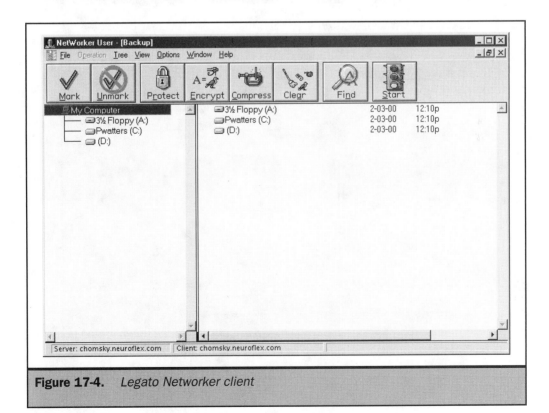

Figure 17-4. *Legato Networker client*

files. NetBackup uses a set of storage rules on the server side to determine how files and data sources of various types are managed. These can be configured remotely by network administrators from any client that has access to the backup servers. Veritas, like Legato, supplies several clients, which make it easier for PC clients to operate within a larger storage management framework.

Backup Exec is the Veritas Windows NT client that can be used to back up local files to a remote server running NetBackup. Figure 17-5 shows the easy-to-use interface for the Backup Exec client.

Similar to RAID, backup devices can be used concurrently to store data from different clients transparently through multiplexing; there is a logical separation between the client and what storage may be optimal with respect to the particular strengths and weaknesses of any one server. In addition, load can be balanced much more evenly across backup devices without concern for the capacity of any one particular drive. Thus, unlike AMANDA, it is easy to back up a single large partition using NetBackup.

Further information about NetBackup can be found at **http://www.veritas.com/**.

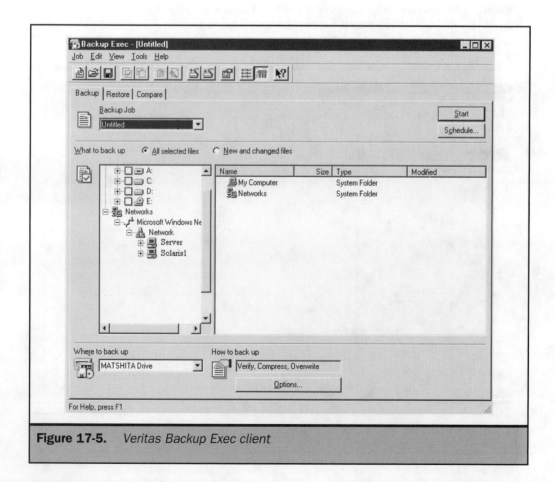

Figure 17-5.   *Veritas Backup Exec client*

 Procedures

The following procedures should be followed to perform backup and restore operations.

Selecting a Backup Medium

When selecting a backup medium, you should always attempt to best meet the requirements of rapid restoration, data integrity, and flexibility. The four main media currently in use include tapes, disk drives, Zip and Jaz drives, and CD writing and rewriting technologies. Capacity and reliability criteria must also considered; for example, while tapes are generally considered reliable for bulk storage, tape drives are much slower than a hard drive. However, a 20GB tape is much cheaper than an equivalent capacity hard drive; the cost of any backup solutions must be weighed against the value of the data being stored. It is also important to consider the size of the data being backed up, and how often data changes on a hard disk. This affects how large tapes need to be to store incremental dumps. For more information on choosing a bulk storage device, see the FAQ for the USENET forum **comp.arch.storage** at **http://alumni.caltech.edu/ ~rdv/comp-arch-storage/FAQ-1.html**.

Tape

Solaris supports tape drives from the old Archive (QIC) 150 1/4-inch tape drives (with a maximum 250MB capacity), up to modern digital audio tape (DAT) and DLT systems. The QIC is a low-end drive that takes a two-reel cassette; QIC was used widely in many early Sun workstations. DAT tapes for DDS-2 drives have a capacity of 4 to 8GB, while tapes for the newer DDS-3 standard have 12 to 24GB capacity, depending on compression ratios. DDS-2 drives can typically record between 400KB and 800KB per second, again depending on compression ratios. The transition from analog to digital encoding methods has increased the performance and reliability of tape-based backup methods, and they are still the most commonly used methods today. On the other hand, DLT drives are becoming more popular in the enterprise because of their very large storage capacities; for example, a Compaq 1624 DLT drive can store from 35 to 70GB, depending on compression, which is much more than the DAT drives. They also feature much higher transfer rates of from 1.25 to 2.5 Mbps. Of course, DLT drives are more expensive than DAT drives, and DAT drives have always been more costly than a QIC, although a QIC is generally much too small to be useful for most systems today.

Hard Drives

Because hard drives have the fastest seek times of all backup media, they are often used to store archives of user files that are copied from client drives using a Server Message Block (SMB) protocol service. In addition, hard drives form the basis of RAID systems. Thus, an array of RAID drives can work together as a single, logical storage device, collectively acting as a single storage system that can withstand the loss of one or more of its constituent devices. For example, if a single drive is damaged by a power surge, depending on the level of RAID protection, your system may be able to continue its functions with a minimum of administrator interference, with no impact on functionality until the drive is replaced.

Many systems now support hot-swapping of drives so that the faulty drive could be removed and replaced, with the new drive coming seamlessly online. You may be wondering, in the days of RAID, why would anybody consider still using backups: the answer is that entire RAID arrays are just as vulnerable to power surges as a single drive, so in the event of a full hardware failure, all your data could still be lost unless it is stored safely offsite on a tape or CD-ROM. To circumvent concurrent drive corruption at the end of a disk's life, many administrators use drives of equivalent capacities from different manufacturers, some new and some used, in a RAID array. This ensures that drives are least likely to fail concurrently.

RAID Levels 0 and 1 are most commonly used. RAID Level 0 involves parallelizing data transfer between disks, spreading data across multiple drives, thereby improving overall data transmission rates. This technique is known as *striping*. However, while RAID Level 0 can write multiple disks concurrently, it does not support redundancy, which is provided with RAID Level 1. This Level makes an identical copy of a primary disk onto a secondary disk. This kind of *mirroring* provides complete redundancy: if the primary disk fails, the secondary disk is able to provide all data contained on the primary disk. Because striping and mirroring consume large amounts of disk space, they are costly to maintain per megabyte of actual data. Thus, higher RAID levels attempt to use heuristic techniques to provide similar functionality to the lower RAID levels, while reducing the overall cost. For example, RAID Level 4 stores parity information on a single drive, which reduces the overall amount of disk space required but is more risky than RAID Level 1. For further information about new innovations in RAID technology, see **http://www.raid.org/**.

Software RAID solutions typically support both striping and mirroring. This speeds up data writing and makes provisions for automating the transfer of control from the primary disk to the secondary disk in the event of a primary disk failure. In addition, many software solutions support different RAID levels on different partitions on a disk, which may also be useful in reducing the overall amount of disk space required to store data safely. For example, while users might require access to a fast partition using RAID Level 0, another partition may be dedicated to a financial database, which requires mirroring (thus RAID Level 1). Sun's DiskSuite product is currently one of the most popular software RAID solutions.

Alternatively, custom hardware RAID solutions are also proving popular because of the minimal administrative overhead involved with installing and configuring such systems. While not exactly "plug and play," external RAID arrays such as the StorEdge A1000 include many individual disks that can be used to support both mirroring and striping, with data transfer rates of up to 40 Mbps. In addition, banks of fast caching memory (up to 80MB) speed up disk writes by temporarily storing them in RAM before writing them to one or more disks in the array. This makes the RAID solution not only safe but significantly faster than a normal disk drive.

Zip/Jaz Disks

Zip and Jaz disks are portable, magnetic storage media that are ideal as a backup medium. Only Small Computer System Interfaces (SCSIs) are fully supported under Solaris, although it may be possible to use ATAPI interfaces on Solaris x86. USB and parallel port interfaces are presently unsupported under Solaris. Zip drives come in two storage capacities: the standard 100MB drive and the expanded 250MB drive, which is backward compatible with the 100MB drive. 100MB and 250MB drives are not going to get you very far with backups, even though Zip drives have relatively fast write speeds compared with tape drives. Zip drives are most useful for dumps of database tables and/or user files that need to be interchanged with PCs and other client systems.

Jaz drives offer several improvements over Zip technology, the most distinguishing characteristic being increased storage capacity. Jaz drives also come in two flavors: the standard 1GB drive and a newer 2GB version, which is backward compatible with the standard drive. The Jaz drive is also much faster than the Zip drive, with reported average seek times of around 10ms. This makes Jaz drives comparable in speed terms to many Integrated Device Electronics (IDE) hard drives and provides the flexibility of easily sharing data between server and client systems.

Zip drive technology has improved in recent years, however, early versions of the 100MB suffered from a problem known as the "click of death," where a drive would fail to read or write and a number of repetitive clicks were heard from inside the drive. This problem has now completely disappeared with new models, and users should feel confident in using Zip as a storage medium. For historical information on the "click of death" problem, see Steve Gibson's Web page at **http://grc.com/clickdeath.htm**. Further discussion of Zip and Jaz drives can be found on the **alt.iomega.zip.jazz** USENET forum.

CD-Rs and CD-RWs

CD writing and rewriting devices are rapidly gaining momentum as desktop backup systems, which are cheap, fast, and, in the case of CD-RW (CD rewriteable), reusable. CD-R and CD-RW devices are reviewed in Chapter 7. These devices serve two distinct purposes in backup systems: while CD-RW discs are useful for day-to-day backup operations because they can be reused, CD-R technology is more useful for archiving and auditing purposes. For example, many organizations outsource their development projects to third-party contractors; in such a case, it is useful for both the contractor and the client to have an archival copy of what has been developed, in case there is some later disagreement concerning developmental goals and milestones. On the other hand, contracts involved with government organizations may require regular snapshots to satisfy auditing requirements. Since CD-R is a write-once, read-only technology, it is best suited to this purpose. CD-R is wasteful as a normal backup medium, because writeable CDs can be used only once. CD-RWs can be rewritten hundreds of times, and with more than 600MBs of storage capacity, they are competitive with Zip disks and are much cheaper per unit than Jaz disks.

Backup and Restore

Backup and restore software falls into three categories:

- Standard Solaris tools like *tar*, *dd*, *cpio*, *ufsdump*, and *ufsrestore*. These tools are quite adequate for backing up single machines with multiple backup devices.
- Centralized backup tools like AMANDA and Legato Networker, which are useful for backing up multiple machines through a single backup server.
- Distributed backup tools like Veritas NetBackup, which are capable of remotely managing storage for multiple machines.

This section will examine the standard Solaris backup and restore tools that are generally used for single machines with one or two backup devices. In addition, these tools are often useful for normal users to manage their own accounts on the server. For example, users can create tape archives using the `tar` command, whose output can be written to a single disk file. This is a standard way of distributing source trees in the Solaris and broader UNIX community. Users can also make copies of disks and tapes using the `dd` command. It is also possible to back up database files in combination with standard Solaris tools. For example, Oracle server is supplied with an *exp* utility, which can be used to archive the database while it is still running:

```
exp system/manager FULL=Y
```

Here, `system` is the user name for an administrator with DBA privileges, and `manager` is the password. This will create a file called *expat.dmp*, which can then be scheduled to be backed up every night using a `cron` job, like so:

```
0 3 * * * exp system/manager FULL=Y
```

Some sites take full data dumps every night, which involves transferring an entire file to a backup medium. This involves a small amount of system overhead if the archive is only a few megabytes in size, but for a database with a tablespace of 50GB, this would place a great strain on a backup server, especially if it was being used for other purposes. Thus, it might be more appropriate to take an incremental dump that records only data that has changed. Incremental dumps will be discussed later in the "Using *ufsdump* and *ufsrestore*" section.

Using tar

The `tar` command is used to create a tape archive or to extract the files contained on a tape archive. Although `tar` was originally conceived with a tape device in mind, any device can hold a *tar* file, including a normal disk file system. This is why many users have adopted *tar* as their standard archiving utility, even though it does not perform compression like the Zip tools for PCs. Tape archives are easy to transport between systems using FTP or secure-copy in binary transfer mode, and they are the standard means of exchanging data between Solaris systems.

As an example, the following script creates a *tar* file of the */opt/totalnet* package. First, it checks the potential size of the tape archive by using the du command:

```
$ cd /opt/totalnet
$ du
4395     ./bin
367      ./lib/charset
744      ./lib/drv
434      ./lib/pcbin
777      ./lib/tds
5731     ./lib
5373     ./sbin
145      ./man/man1
135      ./man/man1m
281      ./man
53       ./docs/images
56       ./docs
15837    .
```

The estimated size of the archive is therefore 15,387 blocks. This could also have been achieved by using the command du –s, which just computes the size, without printing details of directory sizes. To create a tape archive in the */tmp* directory for the whole package, including subdirectories, you would execute the following command:

```
# tar cvf /tmp/totalnet.tar *
a bin/ 0K
a bin/atattr 54K
a bin/atconvert 58K
a bin/atkprobe 27K
a bin/csr.tn 6K
a bin/ddpinfo 10K
a bin/desk 17K
a bin/ipxprobe 35K
a bin/m2u 4K
a bin/maccp 3K
a bin/macfsck 3K
a bin/macmd 3K
a bin/macmv 3K
a bin/macrd 3K
```

```
a bin/macrm 3K
a bin/nbmessage 141K
a bin/nbq 33K
a bin/nbucheck 8K
a bin/ncget 65K
a bin/ncprint 66K
a bin/ncput 65K
a bin/nctime 32K
a bin/nwmessage 239K
a bin/nwq 26K
a bin/pfinfo 70K
a bin/ruattr 122K
a bin/rucopy 129K
a bin/rudel 121K
a bin/rudir 121K
a bin/ruhelp 9K
a bin/u2m 4K
a bin/rumd 120K
a bin/rumessage 192K
a bin/ruprint 124K
a bin/rurd 120K
a bin/ruren 121K
...
```

To extract the *tar* file's contents to disks, execute the following command:

```
# cd /tmp
 # tar xvf totalnet.tar
x bin, 0 bytes, 0 tape blocks
x bin/atattr, 54676 bytes, 107 tape blocks
x bin/atconvert, 58972 bytes, 116 tape blocks
x bin/atkprobe, 27524 bytes, 54 tape blocks
x bin/csr.tn, 5422 bytes, 11 tape blocks
x bin/ddpinfo, 9800 bytes, 20 tape blocks
x bin/desk, 16456 bytes, 33 tape blocks
x bin/ipxprobe, 35284 bytes, 69 tape blocks
x bin/m2u, 3125 bytes, 7 tape blocks
x bin/maccp, 2882 bytes, 6 tape blocks
x bin/macfsck, 2592 bytes, 6 tape blocks
x bin/macmd, 2255 bytes, 5 tape blocks
x bin/macmv, 2866 bytes, 6 tape blocks
```

```
x bin/macrd, 2633 bytes, 6 tape blocks
x bin/macrm, 2509 bytes, 5 tape blocks
x bin/nbmessage, 143796 bytes, 281 tape blocks
x bin/nbq, 33068 bytes, 65 tape blocks
x bin/nbucheck, 7572 bytes, 15 tape blocks
x bin/ncget, 66532 bytes, 130 tape blocks
x bin/ncprint, 67204 bytes, 132 tape blocks
x bin/ncput, 65868 bytes, 129 tape blocks
x bin/nctime, 32596 bytes, 64 tape blocks
x bin/nwmessage, 244076 bytes, 477 tape blocks
x bin/nwq, 26076 bytes, 51 tape blocks
x bin/pfinfo, 71192 bytes, 140 tape blocks
x bin/ruattr, 123988 bytes, 243 tape blocks
x bin/rucopy, 131636 bytes, 258 tape blocks
x bin/rudel, 122940 bytes, 241 tape blocks
x bin/rudir, 123220 bytes, 241 tape blocks
x bin/ruhelp, 8356 bytes, 17 tape blocks
x bin/u2m, 3140 bytes, 7 tape blocks
x bin/rumd, 122572 bytes, 240 tape blocks
x bin/rumessage, 195772 bytes, 383 tape blocks
x bin/ruprint, 126532 bytes, 248 tape blocks
x bin/rurd, 122572 bytes, 240 tape blocks
x bin/ruren, 123484 bytes, 242 tape blocks
...
```

Tape archives are not compressed by default in Solaris. However, they could be compressed with the normal Solaris *compress* utility:

```
$ compress file.tar
```

This will create a compressed file called *file.tar.Z*. Alternatively, the GNU *gzip* utility often achieves better compression ratios than a standard *compress*, so it should be downloaded and installed. When executed, the gzip command creates a file call *file.tar.gz*:

```
$ gzip file.tar
```

Although Solaris does come with *tar* installed, it is advisable to download, compile, and install GNU *tar*, because of the increased functionality that it includes with respect to compression. For example, to create a compressed tape archive *file.tar.gz*, use the *z* flag in addition to the normal *cvf* flags:

```
$ tar zcvf file.tar *
```

Using cpio

cpio is used for copying file archives and is much more flexible than *tar*, because a *cpio* archive can span multiple volumes. *cpio* can be used in three different modes:

- Copy in mode, executed with `cpio -i`, extracts files from standard input, from a stream created by `cat` or similar
- Copy out mode, denoted by `cpio -o`, obtains a list of files from standard input and creates an archive from these files, including their path name
- Copy pass mode, performed by `cpio -p`, is equivalent to copy out mode, except that no archive is actually created

The basic idea behind using *cpio* for archiving is to generate a list of files to be archived, print it to standard output, and then pipe it through *cpio* in copy out mode. For example, to archive all the text files in your home directory and store them in an archive called *myarchive* in the */staff/pwatters* directory, you would use this command:

```
$ find . -name '*.txt' -print | cpio -oc > \
   /staff/pwatters/myarchive
```

Recording headers in ASCII is portable and is achieved by using the –c option. When the command completes, the number of blocks required to store the files is reported:

```
8048 blocks
```

The files themselves are stored in text format with an identifying header, which we can examine with `cat` or `head`:

```
$ head myarchive
0707010009298a00008180000011fc0000005400000001380bb9b600001e9b0
000005500000000000000000000000000000001f00000003Directory/file.
txtThe quick brown fox jumps over the lazy dog.
```

Since recording headers in ASCII is portable, files can actually be extracted from the archive by using the `cat` command:

```
$ cat myarchive | cpio -icd "*"
```

This extracts all files and directories as required (specified by using the–*d* option). It is just as easy to extract a single file. To extract *Directory/file.txt*, we use this command:

```
$ cat myarchive | cpio -ic "Directory/file.txt"
```

If you are copying files directly to tape, it is important that you use the same blocking factor when you retrieve or copy files from the tape to the hard disk that you used when you copied files from the hard disk to the tape. If you use the defaults, there should be no problems, although you can specify a particular blocking factor by using the *–B* directive.

Using dd

The *dd* program copies raw disk or tape slices block-by-block to other disk or tape slices; it is like *cp* for slices. It is often used for backing up disk slices to other disk slices and/ or to a tape drive, and for copying tapes. To use *dd*, you must specify an input file *if*, an output file *of*, and a block size. For example, to copy the root partition (/) on */dev/rdsk/c1t0d0s0* to */dev/rdsk/c1t4d0s0*, you can use this command:

```
# dd if=/dev/rdsk/c1t0d0s0 of=/dev/rdsk/c1t4d0s0 bs=128k
```

To make the new partition bootable, you will also need to use the `installboot` command after dd. Another use for *dd* is to back up tape data from one tape to another tape. This is particularly useful for re-creating archival backup tapes that may be aging. For example, to copy from tape drive 0 (*/devrmt/0*) to tape drive 2 (*/dev/rmt/2*), use this command:

```
# dd if=/dev/rmt/0h  of=/dev/rmt/1h
```

It is also possible to copy the contents of a floppy drive by redirecting the contents of the floppy disk and piping it through dd:

```
# dd < /floppy/floppy0 > /tmp/floppy.disk
```

Examples

The following examples show how to perform backup and restore operations.

Using ufsdump and ufsrestore

ufsdump and *ufsrestore* are standard backup and restore applications for UNIX file systems. *ufsdump* often set to run from `cron` jobs late at night to minimize load on server systems. *ufsrestore* is normally run in single-user mode after a system crash. *ufsdump* can be run on a mounted file system; however, it may be wise to unmount it first, perform a file system check (using *fsck*), remount it, and then perform the backup.

The key concept in planning *ufsdump*s is the dump level of any particular backup. The dump level determines whether or not *ufsdump* performs a full or incremental dump. A full dump is represented by a dump level of 0, while the numbers 1 through 9 can be arbitrarily assigned to incremental dump levels. The only restriction on the assignment of dump level numbers for incremental backups is their numerical relationship to each other: a high number should be used for normal daily incremental dumps, followed once a week by a lower number that specifies that the process should be restarted. This approach uses the same set of tapes for all files, regardless of which day they were recorded on. For example, Monday through Saturday would have a dump level of 9, while Sunday would have a dump level of 1. After cycling through incremental backups during the weekdays and Saturday, the process starts again on Sunday.

Some organizations like to separate each day's archive in a single tape. This makes it easier to recover work from an incremental dump, where speed is important, and/or whether or not backups from a particular day need to be retrieved. For example, someone may want to retrieve a version of a file that was edited on a Wednesday and the following Thursday, but the user wants only the version prior to the latest (Wednesday). The Wednesday tape can then be used in conjunction with *ufsdump* to retrieve the file. A weekly full dump is scheduled to occur on Sunday, when few people are using the system. Thus, Sunday would have a dump level of 0, followed by Monday, Tuesday, Wednesday, Thursday, and Friday with dump levels of 5, 6, 7, 8, and 9, respectively. To signal the end of a backup cycle, Saturday then has a lower dump level than Monday, which could be 1, 2, 3, or 4.

Prior to beginning a *ufsdump*, it is often useful to estimate the size of a dump to determine how many storage tapes will be required. This estimate can be obtained by dividing the size of the partition by the capacity of the tape. For example, to determine how many tapes would be required to back up the */dev/rdsk/c0t0d0s4* file system, use this:

```
# ufsdump S /dev/rdsk/c0t0d0s4
50765536
```

The approximately 49MB on the drive will therefore easily fit onto a QIC, DAT, or DLT tape. To perform a full dump of a x86 partition (*/dev/rdsk/c0d0s0*) at Level 0, you can use the following approach:

```
# ufsdump 0cu /dev/rmt/0 /dev/rdsk/c0d0s0
  DUMP: Writing 63 Kilobyte records
  DUMP: Date of this level 0 dump: Mon Feb 03 13:26:33 1997
  DUMP: Date of last level 0 dump: the epoch
  DUMP: Dumping /dev/rdsk/c0d0s0 (solaris:/) to /dev/rmt/0.
  DUMP: Mapping (Pass I) [regular files]
  DUMP: Mapping (Pass II) [directories]
  DUMP: Estimated 46998 blocks (22.95MB).
  DUMP: Dumping (Pass III) [directories]
  DUMP: Dumping (Pass IV) [regular files]
  DUMP: 46996 blocks (22.95MB) on 1 volume at 1167 KB/sec
  DUMP: DUMP IS DONE
  DUMP: Level 0 dump on Mon Feb 03 13:26:33 1997
```

The parameters passed to ufsdump include *0* (dump level), *c* (cartridge: blocking factor 126), and *u* (updates the dump record */etc/dumpdates*). The dump record is used by *ufsdump* and *ufsrestore* to track the last dump of each individual file system:

```
# cat /etc/dumpdates
/dev/rdsk/c0t0d0s0        0 Wed Feb  2 20:23:31 2000
/dev/md/rdsk/d0          0 Tue Feb  1 20:23:31 2000
/dev/md/rdsk/d2          0 Tue Feb  1 22:19:19 2000
/dev/md/rdsk/d3          0 Wed Feb  2 22:55:16 2000
/dev/rdsk/c0t0d0s3        0 Wed Feb  2 20:29:21 2000
/dev/md/rdsk/d1          0 Wed Feb  2 21:20:04 2000
/dev/rdsk/c0t0d0s4        0 Wed Feb  2 20:24:56 2000
/dev/rdsk/c2t3d0s2        0 Wed Feb  2 20:57:34 2000
/dev/rdsk/c0t2d0s3        0 Wed Feb  2 20:32:00 2000
/dev/rdsk/c1t1d0s0        0 Wed Feb  2 21:46:23 2000
/dev/rdsk/c0t0d0s0        3 Fri Feb  4 01:10:03 2000
/dev/rdsk/c0t0d0s3        3 Fri Feb  4 01:10:12 2000
```

ufsdump is flexible because it can be used in conjunction with *rsh* (remote shell) and remote access authorization files (*.rhosts* and */etc/hosts.equiv*) to log on remotely to another server and dump the files to one of the remote server's backup devices. However, the problem with this approach is that using *.rhosts* leaves the host system vulnerable to attack: If an intruder gains access to the client, he can remotely log onto a remote backup server without a user name and password. The severity of the issue is compounded by the fact that a backup server that serves many clients has access to most of those clients' information in the form of tape archives. Thus, a concerted attack on a single client, leading to an unchallenged remote logon to a backup server, can greatly expose an organization's data. The problems associated with remote access and authorization are covered in depth in Chapter 16; however, a secure shell (SSH) tool can be used to overcome the need for using the remote commands. By combining SSH and *ufsdump*, you can create a full dump of a file system from a client, transfer it securely to the backup server, and then copy it to the backup server's remote devices:

```
# ufsdump 0f - / | ssh server "dd of=/dev/rmt/0 bs=24b conv=sync"
```

A handy trick often used by administrators is to use *ufsdump* to move directories across file systems. A *ufsdump* is taken of a particular file system, which is then piped through *ufsrestore* to a different destination directory. For example, to move existing staff files to a larger file system, use these commands:

```
# mkdir /newstaff
# cd /staff
# ufsdump 0f - /dev/rdsk/c0t0d0s2 | (cd /newstaff; ufsrestore xf -)
```

Users of *ufsdump* should be aware of the buffer overflow vulnerability that exists in some versions of *ufsdump* supplied with Solaris 2.6 and Solaris 7. A vulnerability exists that permits rogue local users to obtain root access under some conditions. A patch is available from SunSolve (**http://www.sunsolve.com**), and a full explanation of the problem can be found at **http://www.securityfocus.com/bid/680**.

After backing up data using *ufsdump*, it easy to restore the same data using the *ufsrestore* program. To extract data from a tape volume on */dev/rmt/0*, use this command:

```
# ufsrestore xf /dev/rmt/0
You have not read any volumes yet.
Unless you know which volume your file(s) are on you should start
with the last volume and work towards the first.
Specify next volume #: 1
set owner/mode for '.'? [yn] y
```

ufsrestore then extracts all the files on that volume. However, you can also list the table of contents of the volume to standard output, if you are not sure of the contents of a particular tape:

```
# ufsrestore tf /dev/rmt/0
1         ./openwin/devdata/profiles
```

```
2          ./openwin/devdata
3          ./openwin
9          ./lp/alerts
1          ./lp/classes
15         ./lp/fd
1          ./lp/forms
1          ./lp/interfaces
1          ./lp/printers
1          ./lp/pwheels
36         ./lp
2          ./dmi/ciagent
3          ./dmi/conf
6          ./dmi
42         ./snmp/conf
```

Command Reference

The following commands can be used to back up and restore Solaris file systems.

ufsrestore

ufsrestore supports an interactive mode, which has online help to assist you in finding the correct volume from which you can restore:

```
# ufsrestore i
ufsrestore > help
Available commands are:
        ls [arg] - list directory
        cd arg - change directory
        pwd - print current directory
        add [arg] - add `arg' to list of files to be extracted
        delete [arg] - delete `arg' from list of files to be
            extracted
        extract - extract requested files
        setmodes - set modes of requested directories
        quit - immediately exit program
        what - list dump header information
        verbose - toggle verbose flag (useful with ``ls'')
        help or `?' - print this list
If no `arg' is supplied, the current directory is used
ufsrestore >
```

The
Complete
Reference

Solaris 9

Chapter 18

Printer Management

olaris supports a wide variety of printers, whose details are stored in the *terminfo* database (*/usr/share/lib/terminfo*). Most plaintext and PostScript printers are supported. However, some older SPARC-specific printing hardware, which relied on the proprietary NeWSPrint software, is no longer supported in Solaris 9. To install a printer for Solaris correctly, you must verify that a driver exists in the *terminfo* database, as this defines printer interface data.

Key Concepts

This chapter examines printing using the `lp` command, checking printer status with `lpstat`, setting up printer classes, and using `lpadmin` to manage a printer. In addition, it explores supported Solaris printers and the *terminfo* database, configuring name services for printing, setting printer environment variables, and using *admintool* to add and configure printers. Most commands used to manage print services are located in the */usr/lib/lp* and */usr/sbin* directories, while user print commands can be found in */usr/bin*.

You need to keep several important system configuration in mind when you're planning to set up printing services on a Solaris system. First, you must ensure that plenty of disk space is available in the */var* partition so that print jobs may be spooled in */var/spool* (spool is an acronym for "system peripheral operation off-line"). This is particularly important when your system is spooling PostScript print jobs that may be several megabytes in size. When several PostScript jobs are submitted concurrently, the system will require 10 to 20MB of disk space. In addition, you need to ensure that sufficient physical RAM is available; otherwise, spooling will be slowed down by the use of virtual RAM. If you must use virtual RAM for spooling, you need to ensure that enough virtual RAM is available (more can be added by using the `swap` command). In addition, when print jobs are spooling, it pays to have invested in fast Small Computer System Interface (SCSI) disks for the */var* partition; 10,000 RPM disks are now available as standard in all new UltraSPARC systems, and these give excellent print spooling performance.

A large set of configuration files for printing are located underneath the */etc/lp* directory. These files specify how print services are to be executed for all installed printers. The */etc/lp/classes* directory may contain files that define printer classes, while the */etc/lp/fd* directory may contain files that define print filters. A list of these filters is maintained in the file */etc/lp/filter.table*, while locally developed forms are stored in */etc/lp/forms*. Print cartridge data is located underneath the */etc/lp/pwheels* directory, while configuration data for supported printers is stored in the */etc/lp/printers* directory.

Procedures

The following procedures will allow you to install and configure a printer for Solaris.

Determining Whether a Printer Is Supported

The *terminfo* database is just a set of hierarchical directories that contain files that define communication settings for each printer type. Printers from different vendors are defined in files that sit in a subdirectory whose name is defined by the first letter of the vendor's name. Thus, the directory */usr/share/lib/terminfo* contains the following entries:

```
# ls /usr/share/lib/terminfo
1  3  5  7  9  a  b  d  f  g  h  j  l  m  o  p  r  s  u  w  y
2  4  6  8  A  B  c  e  G  H  i  k  M  n  P  q  S  t  v  x  z
```

For example, if you wanted to see which Epson printers are supported under Solaris 8, you would change to the root directory of the *terminfo* database and then to the subdirectory in which Epson drivers are found (*/usr/share/lib/terminfo/e*). This directory contains drivers for the following printers:

```
$ ls -l
total 80
-rw-r--r--   2 bin    bin       1424 Sep  1  1998 emots
-rw-r--r--   2 bin    bin       1505 Sep  1  1998 env230
-rw-r--r--   2 bin    bin       1505 Sep  1  1998 envision230
-rw-r--r--   1 bin    bin       1717 Sep  1  1998 ep2500+basic
-rw-r--r--   1 bin    bin       1221 Sep  1  1998 ep2500+color
-rw-r--r--   1 bin    bin       1093 Sep  1  1998 ep2500+high
-rw-r--r--   1 bin    bin       1040 Sep  1  1998 ep2500+low
-rw-r--r--   2 bin    bin        971 Sep  1  1998 ep40
-rw-r--r--   2 bin    bin        971 Sep  1  1998 ep4000
-rw-r--r--   2 bin    bin        971 Sep  1  1998 ep4080
-rw-r--r--   2 bin    bin        971 Sep  1  1998 ep48
-rw-r--r--   1 bin    bin       2179 Sep  1  1998 epson2500
-rw-r--r--   1 bin    bin       2200 Sep  1  1998 epson2500-80
-rw-r--r--   1 bin    bin       2237 Sep  1  1998 epson2500-hi
-rw-r--r--   1 bin    bin       2257 Sep  1  1998 epson2500-hi80
-rw-r--r--   2 bin    bin       1209 Sep  1  1998 ergo4000
```

```
-rw-r--r--    1 bin    bin        1095 Sep   1   1998 esprit
-rw-r--r--    1 bin    bin         929 Sep   1   1998 ethernet
-rw-r--r--    1 bin    bin         927 Sep   1   1998 ex3000
-rw-r--r--    2 bin    bin        1053 Sep   1   1998 exidy
-rw-r--r--    2 bin    bin        1053 Sep   1   1998 exidy2500
```

You can see that the Epson 2500, for example, has its settings contained within the file *ep2500+basic*. However, several other versions of the printer driver are available, including *ep2500+color*, *ep2500+high*, and i.

Adding a Printer with Admintool

The easiest way to add printers to a Solaris system is by using *admintool*, as shown in Figure 18-1. *Admintool* can also be used to modify all current settings for installed printers when necessary.

Several fields can be used to define a printer entry:

- A printer name, such as hp1, must be set and should uniquely identify a printer with respect to the local host so that there is no confusion about which printer a job should be sent

- The name of the server on which the printer is attached, such as "admin" or "finance"

- A description of the printer, which could refer to its physical location, such as "Building C Level 2 Room 143"

- A printer port, such as */dev/term/a*, which identifies the parallel port

- The printer type, such as a Hewlett Packard (HP) Printer

- The file types that will be accepted for printing, usually both PostScript and ASCII for supported printers

- Who should be notified in case of faults, such as sending an e-mail message to the super-user

- Several optional settings, such as whether the current printer is the default printer, and whether a banner should always be printed

- A list of users who can submit jobs to the printer queue; many printers have no user restrictions on printing, so **all** can be entered into the user access list

Setting Up Printer Classes

A set of printers can be grouped together to form a *class*. When you set up a printer class, users can specify the class (rather than individual printers) as the destination for a print

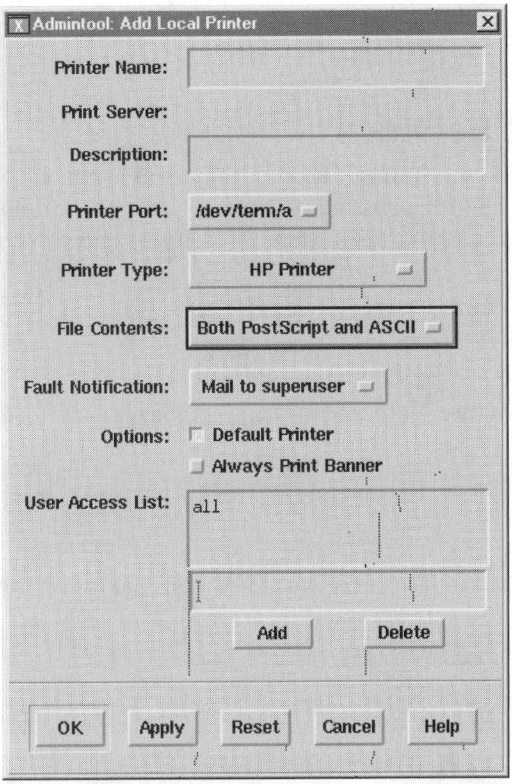

Figure 18-1.   *Using **admintool** to add a printer*

request. This can be useful, for example, when the printers are located in different buildings, or where printing load needs to balanced across multiple printers. These class definitions are stored in the directory */etc/lp/classes*. A file is created for each printer class, with the file name set to the name of the class. The file contains a list of all printers belonging to the class. To add a printer to the class, you can either manually edit the appropriate class file or use the lpadmin command. For example, either of the following commands would add the printer hp2 to the class bubblejets:

```
# cat "hp2" >> /etc/lp/classes/bubblejets
# lpadmin -p hp2 -c bubblejets
```

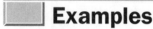

Examples

The following examples demonstrate how to set up print services for Solaris.

Configuring Print Services

The first place to start is the configuration of the printers entry in the */etc/nsswitch.conf* file, where your local naming service is used to resolve printer names. For example, if you use only file-based naming resolution, the printers entry in */etc/nsswitch.conf* would look like this:

```
printers: files
```

Alternatively, if you use Network Information Service (NIS), the entry would look like this:

```
printers: files nis
```

Finally, if you use NIS+, the entry would contain the following:

```
printers: nisplus files xfn
```

It is also possible that individual users will define printers in the file *~/.printers*, in which case, the entry user can also be added to the */etc/nsswitch.conf* printer configuration entry in the order in which the *~/.printers* file should be consulted.

For individual users, the environment variables *LPDEST* and *PRINTER* can be set to indicate which printer should be used as the default. For example, the following command will set the default printer for the current user to be the local hp1 printer:

```
$ PRINTER=hp1; export PRINTER
```

The *LPDEST* environment variable can be set in the same manner:

```
$ LPDEST=hp1; export LPDEST
```

Next, you need to examine entries within the */etc/printers.conf* file, which determines, for file-based name resolution, which printers are available to users of the local system. The printers concerned may be connected locally through the parallel port, or they could be mounted remotely by using the Network File System (NFS) or Samba. A typical */etc/printers.conf* file looks like this:

```
$ cat /etc/printers.conf
hp1:\
        :bsdaddr=pserver,hp1,Solaris:\
        :description=HP Primary:
hp2:\
        :bsdaddr=pserver,hp2,Solaris:\
        :description=HP Secondary:
_default:\
        :use=hp1:
```

There are two printers defined in the *printers.conf file*: hp1 (default) and hp2. Each entry in the */etc/printers.conf* file should have its own directory created underneath the */etc/lp/printers* directory. A number of files can exist in this directory for each printer, including the following:

- *alert.sh*   Shell script that responds to alerts
- *alert.var*   Contains alert variables
- *comment*   Name of printer
- *configuration*   Individual printer configuration file
- *users.deny*   List of users who are denied access to the printer
- *users.deny*   List of users who are granted access to the printer

A sample configuration file (*/etc/lp/printers/hp1*) for the printer *hp1* is shown here:

```
Banner: on: always
Content types: PS
Device: /dev/term/a
Interface: /usr/lib/lp/model/standard
Modules: default
Printer type: PS
```

This configuration states that banners are always printed, PostScript and ASCII files are supported, the device */dev/term/a* is used to send print output, and that the standard interface (*/usr/lib/lp/model/standard*) will be used with default modules.

Accessing Remote Printers

In order to access a central print service from a client, the lpadmin command can be used to set up an association. To allow local access to a printer called *samuel* on the host *mason*, the following command would be executed from the client:

```
# lpadmin -p samuel -s mason
```

Optionally, a description can be associated with the printer *samuel*:

```
# lpadmin -p samuel -D "epson 2500 on mason"
```

Users on the local system should now be able to obtain status information for the printer *samuel*:

```
# lpstat -p samuel
printer samuel is idle. enabled since Jan 24 14:28 2002. available.
```

Forms and Filters

Many businesses deal with form letters as a matter of course. These are predesigned templates for creating bulk copies of letters and other types of forms. Users are responsible for creating their own forms by defining characteristics such as character size, ink color, page length, and page width. Forms can be set up to support preprinted stationery, inserting text between predefined areas where necessary. The following form can be used to print a standard two-page financial summary, 48 lines long and 80 characters wide. The character pitch size is 12, with characters being printed in black courier:

```
Page length: 48
Page width: 60
Number of pages: 2
Line pitch: 6
Character pitch: 12
Character set choice: courier
Ribbon color: black
Comment:
Financial summary form
```

If the form was stored in the file */etc/lp/forms/financial.fmd*, then the lpforms command can be used to make the form available for use:

```
# lpforms -f financial -F /etc/lp/forms/financial.fmd
```

To use the form, any existing forms must first be unmounted and any jobs sent to the printer rejected. This allows customized stationery to be loaded. Once the form has been loaded into the system, print requests can be accepted once again. The following example shows the command sequence for loading the form *financial.fmd* for the printer *ainsley*, after first unmounting the *bank.fmd* form:

```
# reject ainsley
# lpadmin -p ainsley -M -f bank
# lpadmin -p ainsley -M -f financial
# accept ainsley
```

Print filters extend the concept of a UNIX filter, since output from a print request is piped through a print filter as standard input to produce a modified version of the original text. Typically, some kind of transposition or interpretation occurs between input and output. Commonly used filters include those that convert ditroff, dmd, plot, and tek files to PostScript. New filters can be added to the system by using the `lpfilter` command. For example, if you developed a new image processing system that prepared documents in a format called "fract," a new filter to convert these files to PostScript could be installed by using the following command:

```
# lpfilter -f fract -F /etc/lp/fd/fract.fd
```

This filter could be deleted, when no longer required, by using the following command:

```
# lpfilter -f fract -x
```

Command Reference

The following commands are commonly used for printing in Solaris.

Solaris Print Manager

The Solaris Print Manager provides a more sophisticated view of current printer settings by displaying a list of all printers that are known to the local system, as well as their configuration settings. You can set display options for the Print Manager that make it easy to customize views based on local site preferences. Figure 18-2, for example, shows the default view on a network that has three printers available: *yasimov, henryov,* and *prova*. The entry [Empty] appears next to the icon for each printer because no jobs are currently being processed by any of the printers. The details of print jobs can be minimized for each printer by clicking the minus (–) symbol next to the appropriate icon.

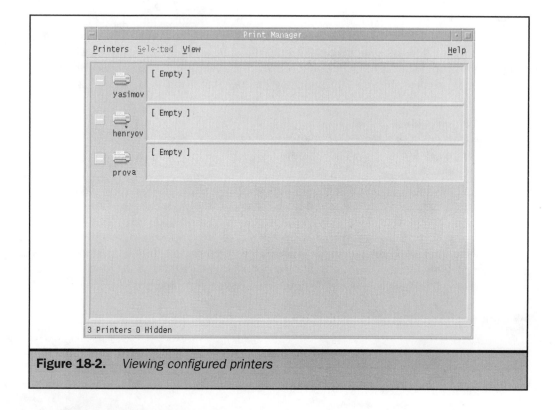

Figure 18-2. *Viewing configured printers*

The printer Properties window can be opened for each printer defined on the system. For the printer *yasimov*, the current properties are shown in Figure 18-3. Several key characteristics are noted in the Properties window:

- The icon label, which is usually the name of the printer (*yasimov*)
- The icon set to be used for the printer
- A description of the printer
- The name of the printer queue
- The status of the printer queue
- The name of the printer device
- The status of the printer device

It is possible to further modify the display of printer sets in Print Manager by selecting View | Set Options, as shown in Figure 18-4.

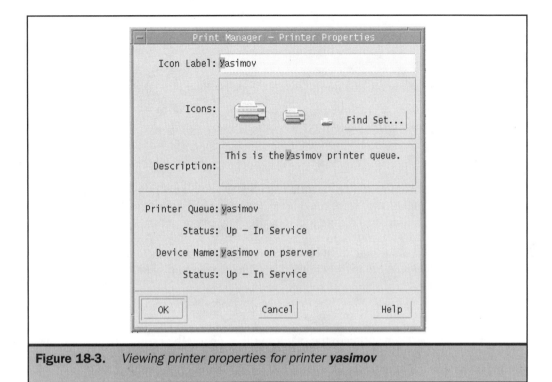

Figure 18-3.   *Viewing printer properties for printer* ***yasimov***

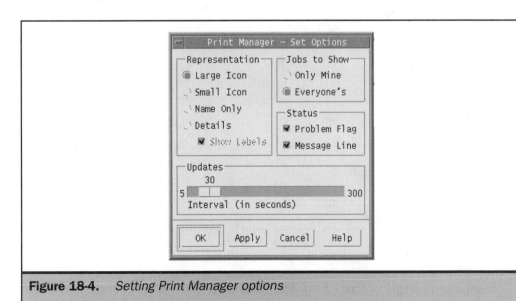

Figure 18-4.   *Setting Print Manager options*

The following options can be displayed:

- Representation of printers by using large or small icons, names only, or full details
- Whether to show all jobs on the printer or only the jobs of the current user
- Whether to display various flags when errors are encountered
- How often to update the display of printers on the system

lp

The lp (line printer) commands predate the *admintool* and Solaris Print Manager interfaces and are most likely to be used by experienced Solaris administrators. They are typically used to add and delete local and remote printer entries and to perform a number of other administrative tasks.

After a printer is configured, it's then easy to submit jobs. Let's look at some examples. To submit a PostScript job to the printer *hp1* on the local server, use the command:

```
$ lp -d hp1 file.ps
```

After the job has been spooled, the printer will interpret the PostScript commands embedded in the file correctly. If your printer does not support PostScript, you will be printing the embedded PostScript codes and not the rendered document. The *–d* flag is used to specify the name of the printer (hp1). If a printer is not specified, the job will be sent to the default printer.

A similar command can be used to spool a text file to the same printer:

```
$ lp file.txt
```

A large number of options can be passed to lp for various purposes. For example, instead of issuing the lp command 50 times to print 50 copies of a report, the following command could be used:

```
$ lp -n 50 report.txt
```

Alternatively, if you are printing a large job, you can be notified by e-mail when the job has finished printing by using the *–m* option:

```
$ lp -m bigjob.ps
```

As an alternative to lp, the POSIX-style of printing can be used to submit jobs. This involves specifying both the print server and printer name, rather than just the printer name. This ensures that no conflict exists between printers of the same names that are attached to different hosts. For example, the server admin could have a printer called *hp1*, as could the server finance; if you pass "*–d hp1* on the command line with lp, which printer would be selected for our job? To make sure the correct printer is used, you need to specify both the server and printer on the command line.

For the host admin, let's revisit our PostScript example, using the POSIX-compliant format:

```
$ lpr -P admin:hp1 file.ps
```

If you want to print to the hp1 server attached to the server finance, you could use the following command instead:

```
$ lpr -P finance:hp1 file.ps
```

cancel

A print job can be easily cancelled by using the cancel command and passing the job's ID to the command. For example, to cancel the job hp1-212, you would use the following command:

```
# cancel hp1-212
```

lpadmin

lpadmin is a printing administration utility that is used to add and configure printers. Adding a printer or modifying its operating characteristics is usually performed with a number of *lpadmin* commands.

To set a printer name and port, use the following command:

```
# lpadmin -p hp2 -v /dev/null
```

This command sets the port to */dev/null* for the printer *hp2*.

To specify the printer software type to be used, use the following command:

```
# lpadmin -p hp2 -m netstandard
```

This command would force the hp2 printer to use the netstandard printing software.

To set the protocol and timeout parameters, use the following command:

```
#  lpadmin -p hp2 -o dest=montana:hp2 -o protocol=tcp -o timeout=5
```

This command specifies that hp2 (being mounted from the server *montana*) would use the TCP protocol and would have a timeout of 5 seconds.

If the hp2 printer was no longer attached to the system, its data could be removed with the following command:

```
# lpadmin -x hp2
```

If a printer is temporarily unavailable due to maintenance, the `reject` command can be used to prevent new jobs being sent to a local printer. In the following example, the hp2 printer is temporarily removed from access:

```
# reject hp2
```

The `disable` command is used to stop all print jobs from proceeding. Thus, to disable all print jobs on the printer *hp2*, use the following command:

```
# disable hp2
```

To add a more meaningful description to a printer entry, an optional description string can be included. For example, to add the description "HP printer on montana" to the hp2 printer, use the following command:

```
# lpadmin -p hp2 -D "HP printer on montana"
```

By default, a banner page is printed when using the `lp` print commands. However, to disable the banner page from printing to conserve paper, the *-nobanner* option can be set. For example, to set the *nobanner* option on hp2, use this command:

```
# lpadmin -p hp2 -o nobanner=never
```

Alternatively, to make banner printing optional on hp2, the following command would be used:

```
# lpadmin -p hp2 -o nobanner=optional
```

If you want to refer to a remote printer as if it were a locally attached printer, you can do so by using `lpadmin`. In the following example, the server montana has the printer *wyoming* attached, so you can add it using this command:

```
# lpadmin -p wyoming -s montana
```

lpstat

The `lpstat` command can be used to verify that a printer is available for printing. The following example verifies whether the printer *wyoming* is available for printing:

```
$ lpstat -D -p wyoming
printer wyoming is idle. enabled since Dec 07 17:23 2001. available.
```

The `lpstat` command returns a description of any error conditions that exist for the printer. For example, if there is a paper misfeed in the printer, the following error message will be displayed:

```
# lpstat -D -p wyoming
printer wyoming faulted. enabled since Dec 07 17:23 2001.
available.
unable to print: paper misfeed jam
```

The Complete Reference

Part V

Networking

The Complete Reference

Solaris 9

Chapter 19

Network Concepts and Services

M
ost Solaris networks are comprised of class A, B, and C subnets interconnected by routers, since this is the default supported by all versions of Solaris using IPv4. The simplest Solaris network consists of two hosts connected using a hub or crossover cable to form a single physical network segment. However, many larger Solaris networks are comprised of many class C subnets that are connected to each other, perhaps as part of a large class B network. In this chapter, we'll examine some networking basics that are essential for understanding more complex topics, such as routing. We'll also look at a typical network service—the File Transfer Protocol (FTP) daemon—to examine how low-level networking is used to implement high-level system services. Finally, we'll review how IP addresses are leased using DHCP, and examine the security implications of transmitting data in the clear across the network.

Key Concepts

The following concepts are required knowledge for understanding more advanced concepts like routing.

Hostnames and Interfaces

A Solaris network consists of a number of different hosts that are interconnected using a switch or a hub. Solaris networks connect through to each other by using routers, which can be dedicated hardware systems or Solaris systems that have more than one network interface. Each host on a Solaris network is identified by a unique hostname: these hostnames often reflect the function of the host in question. For example, a set of four Web servers may have the hostnames www1, www2, www3, and www4, respectively.

Every host and network that is connected to the Internet uses the Internet Protocol (IP) to support higher-level protocols such as TCP and UDP. Every interface of every host on the Internet has a unique IP address, which is based on the network IP address block assigned to the local network. Networks are addressable by using an appropriate netmask, which corresponds to a class A (255.0.0.0), class B (255.255.0.0), or class C (255.255.255.0) network, respectively.

Solaris supports multiple Ethernet interfaces, which can be installed on a single machine. These are usually designated by files like this:

    /etc/hostname.hme*n*

or this:

    /etc/hostname.le*n*

where *n* is the interface number, and le and hme are interface types. The network interface device name can be determined by using the sysdef or prtconf command. Interface files contain a single name, with the primary network interface being designated with an interface number of zero. Thus, the primary interface of a machine called "helium" would be defined by the file */etc/hostname.hme0*, which would contain the name `helium.` A secondary network interface, connected to a different subnet, might be defined in the file */etc/hostname.hme1*. In this case, the file might contain the name "helium1." This setup is commonly used in organizations that have a provision for a failure of the primary network interface, or to enable load balancing of server requests across multiple subnets (for example, for an intranet Web server processing HTTP requests). Alternatively, IP addresses may be stored in */etc/hostname.** files, depending on whether **/etc/nsswitch.conf** permits name-based lookups in the */etc/hosts file*, and whether or not your DNS service is reliable.

A system with a second network interface can either act as a router or as a multihomed host. Hostnames and IP addresses are locally administered through a naming service, which is usually the Domain Name Service (DNS) for companies connected to the Internet, and the Network Information Service (NIS/NIS+) for companies with large internal networks that require administrative functions beyond what DNS provides, including centralized authentication.

It is also worth mentioning, at this point, that it is quite possible to assign different IP addresses to the same network interface, which can be useful for hosting "virtual" domains that require their own IP address, rather than relying on application-level support for multihoming (for example, when using the Apache Web server). Simply create a new */etc/hostname.hmeX:Y* file for each IP address required, where X represents the physical device interface, and Y represents the virtual interface number.

The subnet mask used by each of these interfaces must also be defined in */etc/netmasks*. This is particularly important if the interfaces lie on different subnets, or if they serve different network classes. In addition, it might also be appropriate to assign a fully qualified domain name to each of the interfaces, although this will depend on the purpose to which each interface is assigned.

Subnets are visible to each other by means of a mask. Class A subnets use the mask 255.0.0.0. Class B networks use the mask 255.255.0.0. Class C networks use the mask 255.255.255.0. These masks are used when broadcasts are made to specific subnets. A class C subnet 134.132.23.0, for example, can have 255 hosts associated with it, starting with 134.132.23.1 and ending with 134.132.23.255. Class A and B subnets have their own distinctive enumeration schemes.

Internet Daemon

`inetd` is the "super" Internet daemon that is responsible for centrally managing many of the standard Internet services provided by Solaris through the application layer. For example, telnet, ftp, finger, talk, and uucp are all run from the `inetd`. Even third-party Web servers can often be run through `inetd`. Both UDP and TCP transport layers are supported with `inetd`. The main benefit of managing all services centrally through `inetd` is reduced administrative overhead, since all services use a standard configuration format from a single file. Just like Microsoft Internet Information Server (IIS), `inetd` is able to manage many network services with a single application.

There are also several drawbacks with using `inetd` to run all of your services: there is now a single point of failure, meaning that if `inetd` crashes because of one service that fails, all of the other `inetd` services may be affected. In addition, connection pooling for services like the Apache Web server is not supported under inetd: high-performance applications, where there are many concurrent client requests, should use a standalone daemon.

The Internet daemon relies on two files for configuration: the */etc/inetd.conf* file is the primary configuration file, consisting of a list of all services currently supported, and their runtime parameters, such as the file system path to the daemon that is executed. In addition, the */etc/services* file maintains a list of mappings between service names and port numbers, which is used to ensure that services are activated on the correct port.

FTP Administration

FTP is one of the oldest and most commonly used protocols for transferring files between hosts on the Internet. Although it has been avoided in recent years for security reasons, anonymous FTP is still the most popular method for organizing and serving publicly available data. In this section, we will examine the FTP protocol, and demonstrate how to set up an FTP site with the tools that are supplied with Solaris. We will also cover the popular topic of anonymous FTP, GUI FTP clients, and explain some of the alternative FTP servers designed to handle large amounts of anonymous FTP traffic.

After the UNIX-to-UNIX Copy Program (UUCP) was beginning to show its age, in the era of Fast Ethernet and the globalization of the Internet, the File Transfer Protocol (FTP) was destined to become the de facto standard for transferring files between computers connected to each other using a TCP/IP network. FTP is simple, transparent, and has a rich number of client commands and server features that are very powerful in the hands of an experienced user. In addition, there are a variety of clients available on all platforms with a TCP/IP stack, which assist with transferring entire directory trees, for example, rather than performing transfers file by file.

Although originally designed to provide remote file access for users with an account on the target system, the practice of providing "anonymous FTP" file areas has become very common in recent years, allowing remote users without an account to download (and in some cases upload) data to and from their favorite servers. This allowed the easy dissemination of data and applications before the widespread adoption of more sophisticated systems for locating and identifying networked information sources (such as gopher and HTTP, the Hypertext Transfer Protocol). Anonymous FTP servers typically contain archives of application software, device drivers, and configuration files. In addition, many electronic mailing lists keep their archives on anonymous FTP sites so that an entire year's worth of discussion can be retrieved rapidly. However, relying on anonymous FTP can be precarious, because sites are subject to change and there is no guarantee that what is available today will still be there tomorrow.

FTP is a TCP/IP protocol specified in RFC 959. On Solaris, it is invoked as a daemon through the Internet super daemon (inetd), thus, many of the options that are used to configure an FTP server can be entered directly into the configuration file for `inetd` (*/etc/inetd.conf*). For example, `in.ftpd` can be invoked with a debugging option (–*d*), or a logging options (–*l*), in which case, all transactions will be logged to the */var/adm/messages* file by default.

The objectives of providing an FTP server are to permit the sharing of files between hosts across a TCP/IP network reliably and without concern for the underlying exchanges, which must take place to facilitate the transfer of data. A user need only be concerned with identifying which files he or she wishes to download or upload, and whether or not binary or ASCII transfer is required. The most common file types, and the recommended transfer mode, are shown in Table 19-1. A general rule of thumb is that text-only files should be transferred using ASCII, but applications and binary files should be transferred using binary mode. Many clients have a simple interface that makes it very easy for users to learn to send and retrieve data using FTP.

FTP has evolved through the years, although many of its basic characteristics remain unchanged. The first RFC for FTP was published in 1971, with a targeted implementation

Extension	Transfer Type	Description
.arc	Binary	ARChive compression
.arj	Binary	Arj compression
.gif	Binary	Image file
.gz	Binary	GNU Zip compression
.hqx	ASCII	HQX (Mac OS version of uuencode)
.jpg	Binary	Image file
.lzh	Binary	LH compression
.shar	ASCII	Bourne shell archive
.sit	Binary	Stuff-It compression
.tar	Binary	Tape archive
.tgz	Binary	Gzip compressed tape archive
.txt	ASCII	Plaintext file
.uu	ASCII	Uuencoded file
.Z	Binary	Standard UNIX compression
.zip	Binary	Standard zip compression
.zoo	Binary	Zoo compression

Table 19-1.   *Common File Types for Binary vs. ASCII Transfer Mode*

NETWORKING

on hosts at M.I.T. (RFC 114), by A. K. Bhushan. Since that time, enhancements to the original RFC have been suggested, including the following:

- RFC 2640: Internationalization of the File Transfer Protocol
- RFC 2389: Feature negotiation mechanism for the File Transfer Protocol
- RFC 1986: Experiments with a Simple File Transfer Protocol for Radio Links Using Enhanced Trivial File Transfer Protocol (ETFTP)
- RFC 1440: SIFT/UFT: Sender-Initiated/Unsolicited File Transfer
- RFC 1068: Background File Transfer Program (BFTP)
- RFC 2585: Internet X.509 Public Key Infrastructure Operational Protocols: FTP and HTTP
- RFC 2428: FTP Extensions for IPv6 and NATs
- RFC 2228: FTP Security Extensions
- RFC 1639: FTP Operation Over Big Address Records (FOOBAR)

Some of these RFCs are informational only; however, many suggest concrete improvements to FTP that have been implemented as standards. For example, many changes will be required to fully implement IPv6 at the network level—including support for IP addresses, which are much longer than standard. Despite these changes and enhancements, however, the basic procedures for initiating, conducting, and terminating a FTP session have remained unchanged for many years. FTP is a client/server process: a client attempts to make a connection to a server by using a command, like this:

```
$ ftp server
```

If there is an FTP server active on the host server, the FTP process proper can begin. After a user initiates the FTP session through the user interface or client program, the client program requests a session through the client protocol interpreter (client PI), such as "DIR" for a directory listing. The client PI then issues the appropriate command to the server PI, which replies with the appropriate response number (for example, "200 Command OK," if the command is accepted by the server PI). FTP commands must reflect the desired nature of the transaction (for example, port number and data transfer mode, whether binary or ASCII), and the type of operating to be performed (for example, file retrieval with GET, file deletion with DELE, and so forth). The actual data transfer process (DTP) is conducted by the server DTP agent, which connects to the client DTP agent, transferring the data packet by packet. After transmitting the data, both the client and server DTP agents then communicate the end of a transaction, successful or otherwise, to their respective PIs. A message is then sent back to the user interface, and ultimately the user finds out whether or not their request has been processed. This process is shown in Figure 19-1.

Anonymous FTP allows an arbitrary remote user to make an FTP connection to a remote host. The permissible usernames for anonymous FTP are usually "anonymous"

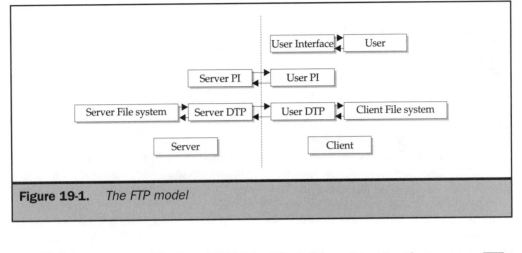

Figure 19-1. *The FTP model*

or "ftp." Not all servers offer FTP; often, it is only possible to determine if anonymous FTP is supported by trying to login as "ftp" or "anonymous." Sites that support anonymous FTP usually allow the downloading of files from an archive of publicly available files. However, some servers also support an upload facility where remote, unauthenticated, and unidentified users can upload files of arbitrary size. If this sounds dangerous, it is: if you don't apply quotas to the ftp users' directories on each file system that the ftp user has write access to, it is possible for a malicious user to completely fill up the disk with large files. This is a kind of "denial of service" attack, since a completely filled file system cannot be written to by other users or system processes. If a remote user really does need to upload files, it is best to give them a temporary account by which they can be authenticated and identified at login time.

Solaris 9 provides the `ftpconfig` command to install anonymous FTP.

Allocating IP Addresses

The Internet is a worldwide, networked environment through which information can be exchanged by using a number of well-defined network protocols, such as TCP and UDP. Each host on the Internet can be identified by a single machine-friendly number (e.g., 128.43.22.1), which is mapped to a human-friendly, fully-qualified domain name (e.g., **www.paulwatters.com**). This mapping is provided by a globally distributed database, known as the Domain Name Service (DNS), allowing local networks to statically assign IP address ranges to all their local hosts.

When DNS was first introduced, the exponential growth of networks and hosts connected to the Internet was not anticipated. This means that IP addresses allocations initially reserved for Class A, B, and C networks were rather generous in hindsight— many address ranges were not used to their full capacity. Nowadays, there is a critical shortage of available IP address space using the current IPv4 standard. Although the new IPv6 protocol (supported by Solaris 9) will provide many more potential addresses, organizations worldwide are seeking solutions to use their existing resources more efficiently. While IPv6 is currently being adopted by many organizations, widespread deployment is not anticipated in the near future. In addition, while IPv6 is expected to solve the IP allocation dilemma in the short term, once the forecast billions of Internet-enabled devices are connected to the mbone (**http://www.mbone.com/**), the IP address allocation dilemma will come to the fore once again.

As an alternative to static IP address allocation, a practical alternative IP address management strategy is to use the Dynamic Host Configuration Protocol (DHCP). This protocol allows a server to dynamically allocate IP addresses from a central DHCP server, to all configured DHCP clients on the local network. DHCP provides a mechanism by which computers using TCP/IP can obtain protocol configuration parameters automatically—by using a lease mechanism—without having to rely on static addresses, which could be incorrect or outdated. This means that only hosts that are "up" will be taking an IP address from the pool of existing addresses assigned to a particular network, by requesting and accepting an IP address lease from the DHCP server. For a Class C network, the pool of available addresses is (at most) 254, excluding the broadcast address, which is insufficient for many growing organizations. In addition, if an organization changes ISP, they ordinarily need to change the network configuration parameters for each client system, a manual and inefficient process that consumes the valuable time of network administrators.

DHCP is not the only protocol to lease out IP addresses in this way. Previously, Solaris clients used the Reverse Address Resolution Protocol (RARP) to obtain an IP address dynamically from a RARP server. This protocol is particularly important for diskless clients who cannot store their IP address locally. However, DHCP is better than RARP because it supports clients from Solaris, Linux, and Microsoft Windows, as well as being able to serve more parameters than just an IP address. In addition, RARP servers can only provide addresses to a single network, while DHCP is capable of serving multiple networks from a single server, provided that routing is correctly set up. On the other hand, Microsoft Windows administrators will be familiar with the Bootstrap Protocol (BOOTP), which provided IP addresses dynamically in the same way that DHCP does. In fact, DHCP can be considered a superset of BOOTP, and DHCP servers are generally backwards compatible with BOOTP. The relationship between DHCP and BOOTP is historical: the BOOTP protocol is the foundation on which DHCP was built. Many similarities remain: the packet formats for DHCP and BOOTP are the same, although BOOTP packets are fixed length and DHCP packets are variable length. The DHCP packet length is negotiated between the client and the server.

Another advantage of DHCP over proprietary protocols is that it is an open network standard, developed through the Internet Engineering Task Force (IETF). It is based on a client/server paradigm, in which the DHCP client (e.g., a PC running Microsoft Windows), contacts a DHCP server (e.g., a server running Solaris) for its network configuration parameters. Typically, the DHCP server is centrally located and is under the control of the network administrator. Since the server is secure, DHCP clients can obtain reliable information for dynamic configuration, with parameters that reflect up-to-date changes in the current network architecture. For example, if a client is moved to a new network, it must be assigned a new IP address for that new network. DHCP can be used to manage these assignments automatically. Readers interested in finding out more about how DHCP works can refer to RFC 2131. There is also a reference implementation of both a DHCP server, client, and relay agent available from ISC (**http://www.isc.org/**). While unsuitable for production purposes, the ISC implementation uses a modular API, which is designed to work with both POSIX-compliant and non–POSIX-compliant operating systems. It also includes source code, making it useful for understanding how DHCP works behind the scenes.

In addition to dynamically allocating IP addresses, DHCP also serves other key network configuration parameters, such as the subnet mask, default router, and Domain Name System (DNS) server. Again, this goes beyond the capabilities of competing protocols like RARP. By deploying a DHCP server, network administrators can reduce repetitive client-based configuration of individual computers, often requiring the use of confusing operating system specific setup applications. Instead, clients can obtain all their required network configuration parameters automatically, without manual intervention, from a centrally managed DHCP server.

Both commercial and freeware versions of DHCP clients and servers are available for all platforms. For example, Checkpoint's DHCP server can be integrated with its firewall product Firewall-1 to maximize the security potential of centralized network configuration management. Advanced network management protocols are supported by DHCP, like the Simple Network Management Protocol (SNMP). In addition, configuration change management issues, like IP mobility, and managing addresses for multiple subnets, can all be handled from a single DHCP server. Implementation of DHCP should always be evaluated in the context of other network management protocols, like SNMP, and other directory services, like the Lightweight Directory Access Protocol (LDAP). Both LDAP and SNMP are crucial to the management of hosts and users in large and distributed networks. Since DHCP is responsible for the allocation of network configuration parameters, it is essential that SNMP agents obtain the correct information about hosts which they manage. In addition, LDAP servers need to be aware that host IP addresses will change over time.

Procedures

The following procedures must be used to configure a system's networking and basic services.

Network Configuration Files

Independent of DNS is the local hosts file (*/etc/hosts*), which is used to list local hostnames and IP addresses. For a network with large numbers of hosts, using the */etc/hosts* file is problematic, since its values must be updated on every host on the network each time a change is made. This is why DNS or NIS/NIS+ are better solutions for managing distributed host data.

However, the */etc/hosts* file contains entries for some key services, such as logging, so it usually contains at least the following entries:

■ The loopback address, 127.0.0.1, which is associated with the generic hostname "localhost." This allows applications to be tested locally using the IP address 127.0.0.1 or the hostname localhost.

■ The IP address, hostname, and fully qualified domain name of the localhost, since it requires this data before establishing a connection to a DNS server or NIS/NIS server when booting.

■ An entry for a loghost so that syslog data can be redirected to the appropriate host on the local network.

A sample */etc/hosts* file is shown here:

```
127.0.0.1       localhost
192.68.16.1     emu       emu.cassowary.net
192.68.16.2     hawk      hawk.cassowary.net        loghost
192.68.16.3     eagle     eagle.cassowary.net
```

In this configuration, the localhost entry is defined, followed by the name and IP address of the localhost (hostname *emu*, with an IP address *192.68.16.1*). In this case, *emu* redirects all of its syslog logging data to the host *hawk* (*192.68.16.2*), while another host *eagle* (*192.68.16.3*) is also defined.

Configuring Network Interfaces

The `ifconfig` command is responsible for configuring each network interface at boot time. `ifconfig` can also be used to check the status of active network interfaces by passing the *–a* parameter:

```
# ifconfig -a
lo0: flags=849<UP,LOOPBACK,RUNNING,MULTICAST> mtu 8232
        inet 127.0.0.1 netmask ff000000
hme0: flags=863<UP,BROADCAST,NOTRAILERS,RUNNING,MULTICAST> mtu 1500
        inet 10.17.65.16 netmask ffffff00 broadcast 10.17.65.255
hme1: flags=863<UP,BROADCAST,NOTRAILERS,RUNNING,MULTICAST> mtu 1500
        inet 204.17.65.16 netmask ffffff00 broadcast 204.17.65.255
```

In this case, the primary interface hme0 is running on the internal network, while the secondary interface hme1 is visible to the external network. The netmask for a class C network is used on both interfaces, while both have a distinct broadcast address. This ensures that information broadcast on the internal network is not visible to the external network. There are several parameters shown with `ifconfig -a`, including whether or not the interface is UP or DOWN (that is, active or inactive). In the following example, the interface has not been enabled at boot time:

```
# ifconfig hme1
hme1: flags=863<DOWN,BROADCAST,NOTRAILERS,RUNNING,MULTICAST>
      mtu 1500 inet 204.17.64.16 netmask ffffff00        broadcast
204.17.64.255
```

If the /etc/ethers database has been updated by the administrator to include details of the Ethernet addresses of hosts on the local network, there is also an entry displayed about the corresponding interface when using `ifconfig`:

```
# cat /etc/ethers
8:0:19:7:f2:a1 server
server# ifconfig hme1
hme1: flags=863<UP,BROADCAST,NOTRAILERS,RUNNING,MULTICAST>
      mtu 1500 inet 204.17.128.16 netmask ffffff00
      broadcast 204.17.128.255 ether 8:0:19:7:f2:a1
```

It can also be useful in detecting problems with a routing network interface to examine the address resolution protocol results for the local area network. This will determine whether or not the interface is visible to its clients:

```
# arp -a
Net to Media Table
Device   IP Address                Mask            Flags    Phys Addr
------   -------------------       ---------------  ----    ----------------
hme0     server1.cassowary.net 255.255.255.255         00:c0:ff:19:48:d8
hme0     server2.cassowary.net 255.255.255.255         c2:d4:78:00:15:56
hme0     server3.cassowary.net 255.255.255.255         87:b3:9a:c2:e9:ea
```

Modifying Interface Parameters

There are two methods for modifying network interface parameters. First, the `ifconfig` command can be used to modify operational parameters, and to bring an interface online ("up"), or shut it down ("down"). Second, one can use /usr/sbin/ndd to set parameters for TCP/IP transmission, which will affect all network interfaces. In this section, we will examine both of these methods, and how they may be used to manage interfaces and improve performance.

It is sometimes necessary to shut down and start up a network interface in order to upgrade drivers or install patches affecting network service. To shut down a network interface, for example, one can use the command:

```
# ifconfig hme1 down
 # ifconfig hme1
hme1: flags=863<DOWN,BROADCAST,NOTRAILERS,RUNNING,MULTICAST>
      mtu 1500 inet 204.17.64.16 netmask ffffff00
      broadcast 204.17.64.255
```

It is also possible to bring this interface back "up" by using `ifconfig`:

```
# ifconfig hme1 up
 # ifconfig hme1
hme1: flags=863<UP,BROADCAST,NOTRAILERS,RUNNING,MULTICAST>
      mtu 1500 inet 204.17.64.16 netmask ffffff00
      broadcast 204.17.64.255
```

To ensure that this configuration is preserved from boot to boot, it is possible to edit the networking startup file */etc/rc2.d/S69inet* and to add this line to any others that configure the network interfaces.

It may be necessary to set several of these parameters in a production environment to ensure optimal performance, especially when application servers and Web servers are in use. For example, when a Web server makes a request to port 80 using TCP, a connection is opened and closed. However, the connection is kept open for a default time of two minutes to ensure that all packets are correctly received. For a system with a large number of clients, this can lead to a bottleneck of stale TCP connections, which can significantly impact on the performance of the Web server. Fortunately, the parameter that controls this behavior (*tcp_close_wait_interval*) can be set using ndd to something more sensible (like 30 seconds):

```
# ndd -set /dev/tcp tcp_close_wait_interval 30000
```

However, administrators should be aware that altering this parameter will affect all TCP services, so while a Web server might perform optimally with *tcp_close_wait_interval* equal to 30 seconds, a database listener that handles large datasets may require a much wider time window. The best way to determine optimal values is to perform experiments with low, moderate, and peak levels of traffic for both the Web server and the database listener to determine a value that will provide reasonable performance for both applications. It is also important to check SunSolve for the latest patches and updates for recently discovered kernel bugs.

Checking Logged-In Users

The command who displays who is currently logged into the system. The output of who displays the username, connecting line, date of login, idle time, process ID, and a comment. An example output is

```
$ who
root        console      Nov 22 12:39
pwatters    pts/0        Nov 19 21:05     (client.site.com)
```

This command can be automated to update the list of active users. An alternative to who is the w command, which displays a more detailed summary of the current activity on the system, including the current process name for each user. The header output from w shows the current time, the uptime of the current system, and the number of users actively logged into the system. The average system load is also displayed as a series of three numbers at the end of the w header, indicating the average number of jobs in the run queue for the previous one, five, and fifteen minutes. In addition to the output generated by who, the w command displays the current foreground process for each user, which is usually a shell. For example, the output

```
root        console      Thu12pm 3days     6       6   /usr/openwin/bin/shelltool
pwatters    pts/12        Thu11am  8:45     9           /usr/local/bin/tcsh
```

shows that the root user has an active shell tool running under Open Windows, while the user pwatters is running the Cornell shell. The w and who commands are very useful tools for getting an overview of current and historical usage patterns on any Solaris system.

Configuring inetd

Services for inetd are defined in */etc/inetd.conf*. Every time you make a change to inetd.conf, you will need to send a HUP signal to the inetd process. You can identify the process ID (PID) of inetd by using the ps command and then sending a kill SIGHUP signal to that PID from the shell. In addition, commenting an entry in the */etc/services* file will not necessarily prevent a service from running: strictly speaking, only services that make the getprotobyname() call to retrieve their port number require the */etc/services* file. So, for applications like Sendmail, removing their entry in */etc/services* has no effect. To prevent Sendmail from running, you would need to comment out its entry in */etc/inetd.conf*, and send a SIGHUP to the inetd process.

A service definition in */etc/inetd.conf* has the following format:

```
service socket protocol flags user server_name arguments
```

where the service uses either datagrams or streams, uses UDP or TCP on the transport layer, with the server_name being executed by the user. An example entry is the UDP talk service:

```
talk dgram udp wait root /usr/sbin/in.talkd in.talkd
```

The talk service uses datagrams over UDP and is executed by the root user, with the talk daemon being physically located in */usr/sbin/in.talkd*. Once the talk daemon is running through inetd, it is used for interactive screen-based communication between two users (with at least one user "talking" on the local system).

In order to prevent users from using (or abusing) the talk facility, you would need to comment out the definition for the talk daemon in the */etc/inetd.conf* file. Thus, the line shown earlier would be changed to this:

```
#talk dgram udp wait root /usr/sbin/in.talkd in.talkd
```

In order for inetd to register the change, it needs to be restarted by using the kill command. To identify the PID for inetd, the following command may be used:

```
# ps -eaf | grep inetd
    root    206    1  0   May 16 ?        30:19 /usr/sbin/inetd -s
```

To restart the process, the following command would be used:

```
kill -1 206
```

The daemon would then restart after reading in the modified inetd.conf file.

Configuring DHCP

The basic DHCP configuration procedure is a straightforward, two-phase process involving a single DHCP client and at least one DHCP server. When the DHCP client (dhcpagent) is started on a client, it broadcasts a DHCPDISCOVER request for an IP address on the local network, which is received by all available servers running a DHCP server (in.dhcpd). Next, all DHCP servers that have spare IP addresses answer the client's request through a DHCPOFFER message, which contains an IP address, subnet mask, default router name, and DNS server IP address. If there are multiple DHCP servers that have IP addresses available, it is possible that multiple servers will respond to the client request. The client simply accepts the first DHCPOFFER that it receives, upon which it broadcasts a DHCPREQUEST message, indicating that a lease has been obtained.

Once the server has received this second request, it confirms the lease with a DHCPACK message. After a client has finished using the IP address, a DHCPRELEASE message is sent to the server.

In the situation where a server has proposed a lease in the first phase that it is unable to fulfill in the second phase, it must respond with a DHCPNACK message. This means that the client will then broadcast a DHCPDISCOVER message, and the process will start again. A DHCPNACK message is usually sent if a timeout has occurred between the original DHCPDISCOVER request, and the subsequent reception at the server side of a DHCPREQUEST message. This is often due to network outages or congestion. The list of all possible DHCP messages is shown in Table 19-2.

The DHCPOFFER message specifies the lease period, after which the lease will be deemed to have expired, and it will be made available to other clients. However, clients also have the option of renewing an existing lease so that their existing IP address can be retained. The DHCP protocol defines fixed intervals prior to actual lease expiry, at which time a client should indicate whether or not it wishes to extend the lease. If these renewals are not made in time, a DHCPRELEASE message will be broadcast and the lease will be invalid.

DHCP has three ways to allocate leases to client. Automatic allocation grants an IP address permanently to a client. This is useful for granting IP addresses to servers that require a static IP address. A DNS server typically requires a static IP address that can be registered in host records lodged with InterNIC. The majority of clients will have addresses assigned dynamically by the server, which allows the greatest reuse of addresses. Alternatively, an administrator may manually assign an address to a specific client.

The process of allocating DHCP lease is shown in Figure 19-2.

Code	Description
DHCPDISCOVER	Broadcast from client to all reachable servers
DHCPOFFER	Server responds to DHCPDISCOVER requests
DHCPREQUEST	Client accepts lease proposal from only one server
DHCPACK	Server acknowledges lease
DHCPNAK	Server refuses to accept DHCPREQUEST
DHCPRELEASE	Lease no longer required

Table 19-2.   *DHCP Codes and Their Meanings*

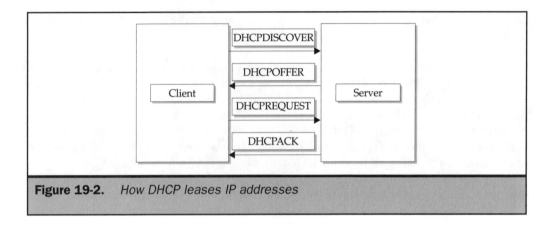

Figure 19-2. *How DHCP leases IP addresses*

Examples

The following examples show how to configure network services.

/etc/inetd.conf

A sample *inetd.conf* file is shown here. It contains entries for the most commonly used Internet services.

```
ftp       stream  tcp   nowait  root    /usr/sbin/in.ftpd      in.ftpd -l
telnet    stream  tcp   nowait  root    /usr/sbin/in.telnetd   in.telnetd
name      dgram   udp   wait    root    /usr/sbin/in.tnamed    in.tnamed
shell     stream  tcp   nowait  root    /usr/sbin/in.rshd      in.rshd
login     stream  tcp   nowait  root    /usr/sbin/in.rlogind   in.rlogind
exec      stream  tcp   nowait  root    /usr/sbin/in.rexecd    in.rexecd
comsat    dgram   udp   wait    root    /usr/sbin/in.comsat    in.comsat
talk      dgram   udp   wait    root    /usr/sbin/in.talkd     in.talkd
uucp      stream  tcp   nowait  root    /usr/sbin/in.uucpd     in.uucpd
tftp      dgram   udp   wait    root    /usr/sbin/in.tftpd     in.tftpd -s
          /tftpboot
finger    stream  tcp   nowait  nobody  /usr/sbin/in.fingerd   in.fingerd
systat    stream  tcp   nowait  root    /usr/bin/ps            ps -ef
netstat         stream  tcp   nowait  root    /usr/bin/netstat
          netstat -f inet
time      stream  tcp   nowait  root    internal
time      dgram   udp   wait    root    internal
echo      stream  tcp   nowait  root    internal
echo      dgram   udp   wait    root    internal
discard   stream  tcp   nowait  root    internal
discard   dgram   udp   wait    root    internal
```

```
daytime stream  tcp     nowait  root    internal
daytime dgram   udp     wait    root    internal
chargen stream  tcp     nowait  root    internal
chargen dgram   udp     wait    root    internal
100232/10       tli     rpc/udp wait root /usr/sbin/sadmind      sadmind
```

Some of these services are described here:

fingerd	Checks to see who is logged into a system
rdisc	Allows routes to be discovered on the network
rexecd	Permits commands to be executed remotely
rlogind	Allows a remote login to another server
rshd	Spawns a shell on a remote system
rwhod	Checks to see who is running processes
telnetd	Connects to a remote host
tftpd	Supports Trivial FTP for diskless clients
uucpd	Implements the Unix-to-Unix Copy Program
pcmciad	Manages PCMCIA operations
rstatd	Allows system resources to be monitored remotely
rwalld	Permits a message to be written to all logged in users on a network
statd	Allows system resources to be monitored locally
syslogd	Configurable system log
talkd	Allows remote users to chat in real time

/etc/services

Many `inetd` services must be mapped to a specific port number: a sample */etc/services* file, shown here, defines port numbers for most of the commonly used services:

```
tcpmux          1/tcp
echo            7/tcp
echo            7/udp
discard         9/tcp           sink null
discard         9/udp           sink null
systat          11/tcp          users
```

NETWORKING

```
daytime        13/tcp
daytime        13/udp
netstat        15/tcp
chargen        19/tcp        ttytst source
chargen        19/udp        ttytst source
ftp-data       20/tcp
ftp            21/tcp
telnet         23/tcp
smtp           25/tcp        mail
time           37/tcp        timserver
time           37/udp        timserver
name           42/udp        nameserver
whois          43/tcp        nicname
domain         53/udp
domain         53/tcp
bootps         67/udp
bootpc         68/udp
hostnames      101/tcp       hostname
pop2           109/tcp       pop-2
pop3           110/tcp
sunrpc         111/udp       rpcbind
sunrpc         111/tcp       rpcbind
imap           143/tcp       imap2
ldap           389/tcp
ldap           389/udp
ldaps          636/tcp
ldaps          636/udp
tftp           69/udp
rje            77/tcp
finger         79/tcp
link           87/tcp        ttylink
supdup         95/tcp
iso-tsap       102/tcp
x400           103/tcp
x400-snd       104/tcp
csnet-ns       105/tcp
pop-2          109/tcp
uucp-path      117/tcp
nntp           119/tcp       usenet
```

```
ntp              123/tcp
ntp              123/udp
NeWS             144/tcp           news
cvc_hostd        442/tcp
exec             512/tcp
login            513/tcp
shell            514/tcp           cmd
printer          515/tcp           spooler
courier          530/tcp           rpc
uucp             540/tcp           uucpd
biff             512/udp           comsat
who              513/udp           whod
syslog           514/udp
talk             517/udp
route            520/udp           router routed
klogin           543/tcp
new-rwho         550/udp           new-who
rmonitor         560/udp           rmonitord
monitor          561/udp
pcserver         600/tcp
kerberos-adm     749/tcp
kerberos-adm     749/udp
kerberos         750/udp           kdc
kerberos         750/tcp           kdc
krb5_prop        754/tcp
ufsd             1008/tcp          ufsd
ufsd             1008/udp          ufsd
cvc              1495/tcp
www-ldap-gw      1760/tcp
www-ldap-gw      1760/udp
listen           2766/tcp
nfsd             2049/udp          nfs
nfsd             2049/tcp          nfs
eklogin          2105/tcp
lockd            4045/udp
lockd            4045/tcp
dtspc            6112/tcp
fs               7100/tcp
```

An Example FTP Transaction

After examining the possible client FTP commands and server response codes, let's see how this transactional system actually works in practice on Solaris. The first step is to make a connection to a remote host from the local system by using the standard client:

```
$ ftp server
Connected to server.
220 server FTP server (SunOS 5.9) ready.
Name (server:pwatters): pwatters
331 Password required for pwatters.
Password:
230 User pwatters logged in.
ftp>
```

In this simple transaction, a user logs in, enters their password, and a session is established. This involves the client program sending a session request, receiving a 220 response, sending a USER command ("USER pwatters"), receiving back a 331 response requesting a password, and sending the password ("PASS password"). If the username and password combination is correct, the session is established and a 230 response is generated by the server. Let's look at what happens when the incorrect password is typed:

```
$ ftp server
Connected to server.
220 server FTP server (SunOS 5.9) ready.
Name (server:pwatters): pwatters
331 Password required for pwatters.
Password:
530 Login incorrect.
Login failed.
ftp>
```

In this transaction, the user logs in as before, entering their password and establishing a session. This client program then sends a session request, receives a 220 response, then sends a USER command ("USER pwatters") and receives back a 331 response requesting a password. The client then sends the password ("PASS password"), which in this example is incorrect; a 530 response is then sent back from the server to the client, and the user is left in their local client without establishing a session. However, the connect is still open, so mistyping your password can be remedied by using the following combination:

```
ftp> user pwatters
331 Password required for pwatters.
Password:
230 User pwatters logged in.
ftp>
```

Thus, the session is established and we can proceed with retrieving or uploading files. Let's look at an example:

```
ftp> dir
200 PORT command successful.
150 ASCII data connection for /bin/ls (192.58.64.22,34754)
     (0 bytes).
total 72573
drwxr-xr-x  13 pwatters staff 2048 Mar 27 08:43 .
dr-xr-xr-x  2 root      root  2 Mar 21 18:55 ..
-rw-r--r--  1 pwatters staff 0 Jan 27 15:42 .addressbook
-rw-r--r--  1 pwatters staff 2285 Jan 27 15:42 .addressbook.lu
-rw-r--r--  1 pwatters staff 5989 Mar 27 08:42 .bash_history
lrwxrwxrwx  1 pwatters staff 8 Mar 27 08:43 .bash_profile ->
     .profile
drwxr-xr-x  16 pwatters staff 512 Mar 21 10:10 .dt
-rwxr-xr-x  1 pwatters staff 5113 Jan 27 15:59 .dtprofile
-rw-------  1 pwatters staff 10 Feb 23 13:18 .hist10161
-rw-------  1 pwatters staff 28 Feb 23 16:17 .hist11931
-rw-------  1 pwatters staff 20 Mar  7 15:30 .hist12717
-rw-------  1 pwatters staff 30 Feb 21 08:11 .hist1298
-rw-------  1 pwatters staff 24 Mar  7 16:05 .hist13069
-rw-------  1 pwatters staff 18 Feb 21 15:16 .hist1370
-rw-------  1 pwatters staff 8 Feb 21 15:21 .hist1395
-rw-------  1 pwatters staff 8 Feb 22 08:43 .hist15962
-rw-------  1 pwatters staff 100 Feb 28 11:15 .hist17367
-rw-------  1 pwatters staff 24 Feb 28 11:16 .hist17371
-rw-------  1 pwatters staff 16 Feb 22 11:14 .hist19318
-rw-------  1 paul staff 68 Mar  7 14:38 .hist1954
226 ASCII Transfer complete.
6162 bytes received in 0.092 seconds (65.34 Kbytes/s)
ftp>
```

This is the content of the current directory. Let's say we wanted to examine the contents of the subdirectory "packages":

```
cd packages
250 CWD command successful.
ftp> dir
200 PORT command successful.
150 ASCII data connection for /bin/ls (192.58.64.22,34755)
    (0 bytes).
total 224056
drwxr-xr-x   3 pwatters staff 1024 Mar 27 08:37 .
drwxr-xr-x  13 pwatters staff 2048 Mar 27 08:43 ..
-rw-r--r--   1 pwatters staff 2457088 Mar 17 14:37
    apache-1.3.6-sol7-intel-local
-rw-r--r--   1 pwatters staff 3912704 Mar 17 14:38
    bash-2.03-sol7-intel-local
-rw-r--r--   1 pwatters staff 12154880 Mar 27 08:18
    communicator-v472-export.sparc-sun-solaris2.5.1.tar
drwxr-xr-x   2 pwatters staff 512 Feb  1 07:11
    communicator-v472.sparc-sun-solaris2.5.1
-rw-r--r--   1 pwatters staff 597504 Mar 17 16:18
    flex-2.5.4a-sol7-intel-local
-rw-r--r--   1 pwatters staff 59280384 Mar 17 14:42
    gcc-2.95.2-sol7-intel-local
226 ASCII Transfer complete.
1389 bytes received in 0.051 seconds (26.51 Kbytes/s)
ftp>
```

Now, let's look at the situation where we want to retrieve a binary and an ASCII file. An example would be a Java source file (with a `.java` extension), which must be transferred in ASCII mode, and a Java class file (with a `.class` extension), which must be transferred in binary mode:

```
ftp> ascii
200 Type set to A.
ftp> get test.java
200 PORT command successful.
150 ASCII data connection for test.java (192.168.205.48,34759)
    (117 bytes).
```

```
226 ASCII Transfer complete.
local: test.java remote: test.java
127 bytes received in 0.02 seconds (6.25 Kbytes/s)
ftp> bin
200 Type set to I.
ftp> get test.class
200 PORT command successful.
150 Binary data connection for test.class (192.168.205.48,34760)
    (431 bytes).
226 Binary Transfer complete.
local: test.class remote: test.class
431 bytes received in 0.0031 seconds (137.10 Kbytes/s)
ftp>
```

Although there are many more commands available in FTP, as discussed above, these are the most commonly used commands and the responses associated with each kind of transfer.

Troubleshooting FTP

The most common mistake in configuring FTP is not to have a valid shells database (*/etc/shells*) on your system. Although you can insert any shell you like into the */etc/passwd* file, if the shell is not registered in the database, users will not be able to log in. This is a security measure, and prevents arbitrary shells with hidden features from being used on the system.

One of the nice features of FTP is that you can test it by telnetting to the FTP port. This will allow you to issue FTP commands interactively and examine the results. It is possible to determine, using this method, whether there is a problem with the remote server or a problem with your local client. For example, if you receive a 421 response, you know that the remote FTP server is not running, in which case you can advise the administrator of the remote machine to check the status of inetd.

If your client attempts to connect to a host for a long time without receiving an acknowledgement, it's often worthwhile to check that the host is actually known through DNS. You can use the nslookup command to achieve this; if a host is not registered using DNS, you won't be able to make a connection.

If the host has a resolvable hostname, you can use any one of the network troubleshooting tools like ping or traceroute to determine whether a path exists between your local client and the remote server. If no valid path exists, you can contact the administrator of the intermediate site where the connection fails.

NETWORKING

Checking if a Host Is "Up"

The easiest way to check if a remote host is accessible is to use the `ping` command. The following example checks whether the host *emu* is accessible from the host *dingo*:

```
$ ping emu
```

If *emu* is accessible, the following output will be generated:

```
emu is alive
```

However, if *emu* is not accessible, an error message similar to the following will be seen:

```
Request timed out
```

If you need to determine at what point in the network the connection is failing, the `traceroute` command can be used to display the path taken by packets between the two hosts as they travel across the network. For example, to observe the route of the path taken by packets from AT&T to Sun's Web server, we would use the following command:

```
$ traceroute www.sun.com
Tracing route to wwwwseast.usec.sun.com [192.9.49.30]
over a maximum of 30 hops:
  1    184 ms    142 ms    138 ms   202.10.4.131
  2    147 ms    144 ms    138 ms   202.10.4.129
  3    150 ms    142 ms    144 ms   202.10.1.73
  4    150 ms    144 ms    141 ms   atm11-0-0-11.ia4.optus.net.au
             [202.139.32.17]
  5    148 ms    143 ms    139 ms   202.139.1.197
  6    490 ms    489 ms    474 ms   hssi9-0-0.sf1.optus.net.au
             [192.65.89.246]
  7    526 ms    480 ms    485 ms   g-sfd-br-02-f12-0.gn.cwix.net
             [207.124.109.57]
  8    494 ms    482 ms    485 ms   core7-hssi6-0-0.SanFrancisco.cw.net
             [204.70.10.9]
  9    483 ms    489 ms    484 ms   corerouter2.SanFrancisco.cw.net
             [204.70.9.132]
 10    557 ms    552 ms    561 ms   xcore3.Boston.cw.net [204.70.150.81]
 11    566 ms    572 ms    554 ms   sun-micro-system.Boston.cw.net
             [204.70.179.102]
 12    577 ms    574 ms    558 ms   wwwwseast.usec.sun.com [192.9.49.30]
Trace complete.
```

If the connection was broken at any point, then "*" or "!" would be displayed in place of the average connection times displayed. An asterisk would also appear if the router concerned was blocking connections for traceroute packets.

Enabling FTP Access

Now that we have examined the most common uses for FTP, we will investigate how to configure the FTP daemon. The FTP server in Solaris is installed by default during configuration and package copying, during the initial installation or upgrade process. By default, the FTP server and protocol will also be active after installation. You can check the status of the FTP server on the local system by checking whether the FTP service is enabled in the `services` database, and in the configuration file for the inetd superdaemon:

```
# grep ftp /etc/services
ftp-data        20/tcp
ftp             21/tcp
tftp            69/udp


 # grep ftp /etc/inetd.conf
ftp      stream  tcp     nowait  root   /usr/sbin/in.ftpd   in.ftpd
```

We can see that FTP is both defined as a service (ftp 21/tcp), and as a daemon that runs from within the Internet superdaemon (*/usr/sbin/in.ftpd*). As long as the Internet superdaemon is started up during one of the single- or multiple-user init states, the FTP service will start. If you ever want to disable the FTP service, you need to comment out the appropriate line in both */etc/services* and */etc/inetd.conf*. You can do this by entering a hash character "#" in front of the appropriate line:

```
#ftp             21/tcp
#ftp  stream  tcp  nowait  root  /usr/sbin/in.ftpd  in.ftpd
```

You can also check the process list by using the command ps –eaf | grep inetd to verify that the Internet superdaemon is running at any point in time.

Setting Up DHCP

The Solaris client (dhcpagent) and server (in.dhcpd) solution features backward compatibility with other methods already in use, particularly the Reverse Address Resolution Protocol (RARP) and static configurations. In addition, the address of any workstation's network interfaces can be changed after the system has been booted. The dhcpagent client for Solaris features caching and automated lease renewal, and is fully integrated with IP configuration (ifconfig). The in.dhcpd server for Solaris can provide both primary and secondary DHCP services, and is fully integrated with the NIS+ Network Information Service. The Solaris DHCP server has the ability to handle hundreds of concurrent requests, and also has the ability to boot diskless clients. Multiple DHCP support is provided through the Network File System (NFS). Although we won't cover these advanced features in this chapter, it's worthwhile considering them when making a decision to use RARP or DHCP (or some other competing dynamic IP allocation method).

The main program used to configure DHCP under Solaris is */usr/sbin/dhcpconfig*, which is a shell script that performs the entire configuration for you. Alternatively, you can use the *dhtadm* or *pntadm* applications to manage the DHCP configuration table (*/var/dhcp/dhcptab*). The *dhcpconfig* program is menu-based, making it easy to use. The first menu displayed when you start the program looks like this:

```
***                    DHCP Configuration                 ***
    Would you like to:
    1)         Configure DHCP Service
    2)         Configure BOOTP Relay Agent
    3)         Unconfigure DHCP or Relay Service
    4)         Exit
    Choice:
```

The first menu option allows the DHCP service to be configured for initial use. If your system has never used DHCP before, then you must start with the option. You will be asked to confirm DHCP startup options, such as the timeout periods made on lease offers (i.e., between sending DHCPOFFER and receiving a DHCPREQUEST), and whether or not to support legacy BOOTP clients. You will also be asked about bootstrapping configuration, including the following settings:

- Timezone
- DNS server
- NIS server
- NIS+ server
- Default router
- Subnet mask
- Broadcast address

These settings can all be offered to the client as part of the DHCPOFFER message. The second menu option allows the DHCP server to act simply as a relay agent. After entering a list of BOOTP or DHCP servers to which requests can be forwarded, the relay agent should be operational. Finally, you may choose to unconfigure either the full DHCP service or the relay service, which will revert all configuration files.

If you selected option 1, you will first be asked if you want to stop any current DHCP services:

```
Would you like to stop the DHCP service? (recommended) ([Y]/N)
```

Obviously, if you are supporting live clients, then you should not shut down the service. This is why DHCP configuration needs to take place outside normal business hours so that normal service is not disrupted. If you have ensured that no clients are depending on the in.dhcpd service, you can answer yes to this question and proceed. Next, you will be asked to identify the datastore for the DHCP database:

```
### DHCP Service Configuration ###
### Configure DHCP Database Type and Location ###
Enter datastore (files or nisplus) [nisplus]:
```

The default value is the NIS+ network information service. However, if you are not using NIS+ to manage network information, then you may choose the *files* option. If you choose the *files* option, you will need to identify the path to the DHCP datastore directory:

```
Enter absolute path to datastore directory [/var/dhcp]:
```

The default path is the */var/dhcp* directory. However, if your */var* partition is small or running on low on space, and you have a large network to manage, you may wish to locate the datastore directory somewhere else. You will then be asked if you wish to enter any nondefault DHCP options:

```
Would you like to specify nondefault daemon options (Y/[N]):
```

Most users will choose the standard options. However, if you wish to enable additional facilities like BOOTP support, then you will need to answer yes to this question. You will then be asked whether you want to have transaction logging enabled:

```
Do you want to enable transaction logging? (Y/[N]):Y
```

Transaction logs are very useful for debugging but grow rapidly in size over time, especially on a busy network. The size of the file will depend on the syslog level that you wish to enable as well:

```
Which syslog local facility [0-7] do you wish to log to? [0]:
```

NETWORKING

Next, you will be asked to enter expiry times for leases that have been offered to client:

```
How long (in seconds) should the DHCP server keep outstanding OFFERs? [10]:
```

The default is ten seconds, which is satisfactory for a fast network. However, if you are operating on a slow network or expect to be servicing slow clients (like 486 PCs and below), then you may wish to increase the timeout. In addition, you can also specify that the dhcptab file be reread during a specified interval, which is useful only if you have made manual changes using dhtadm:

```
How often (in minutes) should the DHCP server rescan the dhcptab?
[Never]:
```

If you wish to support BOOTP clients, you should indicate this at the next prompt:

```
Do you want to enable BOOTP compatibility mode? (Y/[N]):
```

After configuring these nondefault options, you will be asked to configure the standard DHCP options. The first option is the default lease time, which is specified in days:

```
Enter default DHCP lease policy (in days) [3]:
```

This value is largely subjective, although it can be estimated from the address congestion of your network. If you are only using an average of 50 percent of the address on your network, then you can probably set this value to 7 days without concern. If you are at the 75 percent level, then you may wish to use the default value of 3 days. If you are approaching saturation, then you should select daily lease renewal. Finally, if the number of hosts exceeds the number of available IP addresses, you may need to enter a fractional value to ensure the most equitable distribution of addresses.

Most sites will wish to allow clients to renegotiate their existing leases:

```
Do you want to allow clients to renegotiate their leases? ([Y]/N):
```

However, just like a normal landlord, you may sometimes be compelled to reject requests for lease renewal, especially if your network is saturated. You must now enable DHCP support for at least one network for DHCP to operate:

```
Enable DHCP/BOOTP support of networks you select? ([Y]/N):
```

For an example local network of 192.65.34.0, you will be asked the following questions:

```
Configure BOOTP/DHCP on local LAN network: 192.65.34.0? ([Y]/N):
```

You should (of course!) answer Yes if this is the network that you wish to configure DHCP for. Next, you will need to determine whether you wish DHCP to insert hostnames into the hosts file for you, based on the DHCP data:

```
Do you want hostnames generated and inserted in the files hosts
  table? (Y/[N]):
```

Most sites will use DNS or similar for name resolution, rather than the hosts file, so this option is not recommended. One situation where you may wish to generate hostnames is a terminal server or Web server pool, where the hostnames are arbitrary and frequently change in number. In this case, you simply need to enter a sensible basename for the hostnames to generate from:

```
What rootname do you want to use for generated names?
[yourserver-]:
```

For a Web server bank, you could use a descriptive name like *www-*. Next, you will be asked to define the IP address range that you want the DHCP server to manage, beginning with the starting address:

```
Enter starting IP address [192.65.34.0]:
```

Next, you must specify the number of clients. In our Class C network, this will be 254:

```
Enter the number of clients you want to add (x < 65535):
```

Once you have defined the network that you wish to support, you're ready to start using DHCP.

Once the DHCP server has been configured, it is then very easy to configure a Solaris client. When installing the client, you will be asked whether you wish to install DHCP support. At this point, you should answer Yes. You will then not be asked to enter a static IP address as per a normal installation, as this will be supplied by the DHCP server with DHCPOFFER message.

If you wish to enable support for DHCP on a client that has already been installed, you will need to use the `sys-unconfig` command, which can be used on all systems to reconfigure network and system settings without having to manually edit configuration files. The `sys-unconfig` command reboots the system in order to perform this task, so users should be given plenty of warning before reconfiguration commences. Again, you will be asked during configuration to install DHCP support, to which you should answer Yes.

Setting up support for a Microsoft Windows client is easy—you simply select the DHCP support option in the TCP/IP section of the Network Control Panel, which can be found in most versions of Windows. Once DHCP support is enabled, it is no longer necessary to enter any static IP address information.

NETWORKING

r-Commands

So far, we've focused on the FTP command to perform remote access operations; however, there is another set of remote access commands known as the *r-commands*. These can be used to spawn remote shells, using the rsh command, and execute commands remotely using the rlogin command. The *rsh* application is used to execute commands remotely on a server that has the remote shell daemon running. The command that is to be executed can be specified on the command line—for example, run the who command on a remote server to see who is currently logged in:

```
$ rsh server who
```

The output from the command is piped to standard output, meaning that it can be redirected to a file on the client system. For example, if the command was run once hourly as a security measure to log all active users every hour, the output could be redirected to a running logfile like the following:

```
$ rsh server who >> /var/log/server.who.log
```

The */var/log/server.who.log* file would then contain all of the entries for the command every time it is executed. A cron job could be created that schedules this command to run hourly, in which case, all logged entries will appear sequentially in the file. Once the application has been executed on the remote server, terminal control returns to the client.

The rlogin command is different from rsh in that the client is remotely logged into a server after spawning a remote shell. Thus, the rlogin command does not terminate once a connection has been established and a shell has been spawned. To make a connection to a server running the rlogin daemon, you would need to use the following command:

```
$ rlogin server
```

You would then be prompted to enter your password:

```
password:
```

If the username and password can be authenticated, then a shell will be spawned, and you will be able to enter commands directly. Alternatively, if your remote username is different to your local username, you may pass it on the command line by using the –l parameter. For example, the local user *bill* may have an account called *william* on the remote server, in which case, the following command could be used:

```
$ rlogin server -l william
```

The r-commands are used as alternatives to telnet in a number of different situations. Using `rlogin` is typically faster than using telnet, and in some networks, the telnet service may be completely disabled. Authentication in this case may rely on kerberos or another distributed authentication mechanism. This means that each user would have a single password in the domain; that is, if the user authenticated at one server, he or she can `rlogin` to another without authentication. This is a very useful feature for managing large networks of hosts that have similar configurations and can be set by defining hosts as equivalent in the *sl /etc/hosts.equiv* file.

Another nice trick for servers running X11 is that it is possible to telnet from one system to another, and to remotely execute applications whose display is set to the current system's console. For example, if we logged into the host *chile* on the console but wished to run a statistical analysis package on the host *ecuador*, then we would simply telnet to *ecuador* from *chile* and execute the application. The application would run on the remote system, but all input and output would be redirected to the current terminal. However, two steps are usually required to get this process working properly. First, you must set the DISPLAY environment variable on the server *ecuador* to be *chile* with the following command:

```
ecuador$ DISPLAY=chile:0.0; export DISPLAY
```

In addition, if you get a message like this,

```
Error: Can't open display: chile:0
```

then you will need to explicitly allow connections from *ecuador* to *chile*'s display by executing the following command:

```
chile$ xhost + ecuador
```

This procedure is very useful when a central server has many CPUs, lots of RAM, and all of the major applications installed, and also when your local client system is not powerful. An example is the Sun Ray thin client, which is the size of a small book and which executes all processes on a central workgroup server, such as an Enterprise 450.

snoop

If you want to make a remote connection across the Internet, there is a possibility that someone is intercepting your telnet, rlogin, rsh, or ftp packets on an intermediate host. You can obtain an idea of how many potential sniffers could be capturing your data packets by examining a list of all intermediate hosts between the client and server, using the `traceroute` command, as shown earlier.

NETWORKING

If your username and password are sent "in the clear" (i.e, not encrypted), as rlogin, rsh, telnet, and ftp all do, then these two authentication credentials could be intercepted by using the snoop command. You can see for yourself the power of the snoop command by running it on your local system to intercept all packets generated by telnet running on port 23:

```
# snoop tcp port 23
Using device /dev/hme0 (promiscuous mode)
moppet.paulwatters.com -> miki.paulwatters.com TELNET C port=62421
miki.paulwatters.com -> moppet.paulwatters.com TELNET R port=62421
Using device /dev/hme0
moppet.paulwatters.com -> miki.paulwatters.com TELNET C port=62421
miki.paulwatters.com -> moppet.paulwatters.com TELNET R port=62421
moppet.paulwatters.com ->
moppet.paulwatters.com -> miki.paulwatters.com TELNET C port=62421
miki.paulwatters.com -> moppet.paulwatters.com TELNET R port=62421
miki.paulwatters.com ->
moppet.paulwatters.com -> miki.paulwatters.com TELNET C port=62421
miki.paulwatters.com -> moppet.paulwatters.com TELNET R port=62421
miki.paulwatters.com ->
moppet.paulwatters.com -> miki.paulwatters.com TELNET C port=62421
miki.paulwatters.com -> moppet.paulwatters.com TELNET R port=62421
moppet.paulwatters.com ->
moppet.paulwatters.com -> miki.paulwatters.com TELNET C port=62421
miki.paulwatters.com -> moppet.paulwatters.com TELNET R port=62421
miki.paulwatters.com ->
moppet.paulwatters.com -> miki.paulwatters.com TELNET C port=62421
miki.paulwatters.com -> moppet.paulwatters.com TELNET R port=62421
moppet.paulwatters.com ->
moppet.paulwatters.com -> miki.paulwatters.com TELNET C port=62421
```

Here, we can see that telnet data is being transferred between the hosts *miki* and *moppet*. To actually see what data is being transmitted, such as a username and password, you simply switch to verbose mode by specifying the *–v* option on the command-line:

```
# snoop -v tcp port 23
Using device /dev/hme0 (promiscuous mode)
ETHER:  ----- Ether Header -----
ETHER:
ETHER:  Packet 1 arrived at 14:13:22.14
ETHER:  Packet size = 60 bytes
ETHER:  Destination = 1:58:4:16:8a:34,
```

```
ETHER:   Source     = 2:60:5:12:6b:35, Sun
ETHER:   Ethertype = 0800 (IP)
ETHER:
IP:    ----- IP Header -----
IP:
IP:    Version = 4
IP:    Header length = 20 bytes
IP:    Type of service = 0x00
IP:         xxx. .... = 0 (precedence)
IP:         ...0 .... = normal delay
IP:         .... 0... = normal throughput
IP:         .... .0.. = normal reliability
IP:    Total length = 40 bytes
IP:    Identification = 46864
IP:    Flags = 0x4
IP:         .1.. .... = do not fragment
IP:         ..0. .... = last fragment
IP:    Fragment offset = 0 bytes
IP:    Time to live = 255 seconds/hops
IP:    Protocol = 6 (TCP)
IP:    Header checksum = 11a9
IP:    Source address = 64.23.168.76, moppet.paulwatters.com
IP:    Destination address = 64.23.168.48, miki.paulwatters.com
IP:    No options
IP:
TCP:   ----- TCP Header -----
TCP:
TCP:   Source port = 62421
TCP:   Destination port = 23 (TELNET)
TCP:   Sequence number = 796159562
TCP:   Acknowledgement number = 105859685
TCP:   Data offset = 20 bytes
TCP:   Flags = 0x10
TCP:         ..0. .... = No urgent pointer
TCP:         ...1 .... = Acknowledgement
TCP:         .... 0... = No push
TCP:         .... .0.. = No reset
TCP:         .... ..0. = No Syn
TCP:         .... ...0 = No Fin
TCP:   Window = 8760
TCP:   Checksum = 0x8f8f
TCP:   Urgent pointer = 0
```

```
TCP:   No options
TCP:
TELNET:  ----- TELNET:    -----
TELNET:
TELNET:   ""
TELNET:
```

The details just listed are only for a single packet, which is a lot of information being made available to all who are listening. One method for reducing the risk of exposing authentication credentials to public scrutiny is to use a remote access client that encrypts the exchange of username and password data between the client and the server. This means that, although the username and password strings can still be captured, their contents would need to be "cracked" by using a brute force method. Such a method is extremely unlikely to succeed if a password is selected that is difficult to crack (e.g., a password composed of eight random numbers and characters). Alternatively, the entire session may be encrypted making it ever more difficult for an eavesdropper to determine what data is being exchanged.

Note that while the r-commands have been widely used historically, they are deprecated in Solaris 9 because of the introduction of the secure shell (SSH) and secure FTP (SFTP). Both of these services can be configured in such a way that they can securely replace the existing r-commands, while preserving the security and integrity of data being transmitted across the network. SSH and SFTP are discussed in Chapter 9.

Command Reference

The following commands are commonly used for service provision and tuning under Solaris 9.

ndd

ndd is used to set parameters for network protocols, including TCP, IP, UDP, and ARP. It can be used to modify the parameters associated with IP forwarding and routing. For example, let's look at the set of configurable parameters for TCP transmission:

```
server# ndd /dev/tcp \?
?                          (read only)
tcp_close_wait_interval    (read and write)
tcp_conn_req_max_q         (read and write)
tcp_conn_req_max_q0        (read and write)
tcp_conn_req_min           (read and write)
tcp_conn_grace_period      (read and write)
```

```
tcp_cwnd_max                    (read and write)
tcp_debug                      (read and write)
tcp_smallest_nonpriv_port      (read and write)
tcp_ip_abort_cinterval         (read and write)
tcp_ip_abort_linterval         (read and write)
tcp_ip_abort_interval          (read and write)
tcp_ip_notify_cinterval        (read and write)
tcp_ip_notify_interval         (read and write)
tcp_ip_ttl                     (read and write)
tcp_keepalive_interval         (read and write)
tcp_maxpsz_multiplier          (read and write)
tcp_mss_def                    (read and write)
tcp_mss_max                    (read and write)
tcp_mss_min                    (read and write)
tcp_naglim_def                 (read and write)
tcp_rexmit_interval_initial    (read and write)
tcp_rexmit_interval_max        (read and write)
tcp_rexmit_interval_min        (read and write)
tcp_wroff_xtra                 (read and write)
tcp_deferred_ack_interval      (read and write)
tcp_snd_lowat_fraction         (read and write)
tcp_sth_rcv_hiwat              (read and write)
tcp_sth_rcv_lowat              (read and write)
tcp_dupack_fast_retransmit     (read and write)
tcp_ignore_path_mtu            (read and write)
tcp_rcv_push_wait              (read and write)
tcp_smallest_anon_port         (read and write)
tcp_largest_anon_port          (read and write)
tcp_xmit_hiwat                 (read and write)
tcp_xmit_lowat                 (read and write)
tcp_recv_hiwat                 (read and write)
tcp_recv_hiwat_minmss          (read and write)
tcp_fin_wait_2_flush_interval  (read and write)
tcp_co_min                     (read and write)
tcp_max_buf                    (read and write)
tcp_zero_win_probesize         (read and write)
tcp_strong_iss                 (read and write)
tcp_rtt_updates                (read and write)
tcp_wscale_always              (read and write)
tcp_tstamp_always              (read and write)
tcp_tstamp_if_wscale           (read and write)
tcp_rexmit_interval_extra      (read and write)
```

```
tcp_deferred_acks_max          (read and write)
tcp_slow_start_after_idle      (read and write)
tcp_slow_start_initial         (read and write)
tcp_co_timer_interval          (read and write)
tcp_extra_priv_ports           (read only)
tcp_extra_priv_ports_add       (write only)
tcp_extra_priv_ports_del       (write only)
tcp_status                     (read only)
tcp_bind_hash                  (read only)
tcp_listen_hash                (read only)
tcp_conn_hash                  (read only)
tcp_queue_hash                 (read only)
tcp_host_param                 (read and write)
tcp_1948_phrase                (write only)
```

Parameters can also be set for IP as well as TCP. For example, if the parameter `ip_forwarding` has a value of 2 (the default), it will only perform routing when two or more interfaces are active. However, if this parameter is set to zero, `ip_forwarding` will never be performed (that is, to ensure that multihoming is enabled rather than routing). This can be set by using the command:

```
# ndd -set /dev/ip ip_forwarding 0
```

in.ftpd

As we mentioned in the previous section, FTP commands are associated with specific operations that are to be performed on the server. Most FTP clients and the Solaris FTP server support the following case-insensitive commands:

Command	Function
!	Escapes to the default shell
$	Executes a predefined macro
account	Sends account information to the remote server
append	Appends server output to a file
ascii	Sets ASCII transfer type. ASCII mode is the default transfer mode, and is used for transferring text files.
bell	Beeps when the specified command is completed
binary	Sets binary transfer type. Typically used for transferring binary files like *.zip*, *.gif*, and *.z* files.

Command	Function
bye	Terminates the FTP session, and exit from the client
case	Toggles mget upper/lowercase mapping
cd	Changes remote working directory; changes the directory to the one named. If the directory named is not a subdirectory of the current directory, the path (for example, *cd /pub/library*) must be specified.
cdup	Changes remote working directory to parent directory
close	Terminates FTP session, but do not exit from the client
cd	Changes remote working directory
delete	Deletes the remote file specified
debug	Toggles/sets debugging mode on server
dir	Lists the contents of a remote director
disconnect	Terminates the current FTP session
form	Sets file transfer format to be binary or ASCII
get	Downloads file from the server to the local client
glob	Toggles metacharacter expansion of local filenames
hash	Toggles printing '#' for each buffer transferred. Prints a hash "#" on the screen for every 1,024 bytes transferred. This is useful for keeping track of an FTP transfer interactively.
help	Gives local help on the use of commands within the FTP client
lcd	Changes local working directory to that specified
ls	Lists contents of current remote directory
macdef	Defines a macro interactively
mdelete	Deletes multiple files as determined by a file specification (for example, "mdelete *.txt")
mdir	Lists contents of multiple remote directories in one request
mget	Downloads multiple files, as specified by using a wildcard character * in the file specification
mkdir	Creates a directory on the remote machine as a subdirectory relative to the current directory
mls	Lists contents of multiple remote directories in a single request

Command	Function
mode	Sets file transfer mode to be ASCII or binary
mput	Uploads multiple files from your local file system to the remote server
nmap	Sets templates for default filename mapping
ntrans	Sets translation table for default filename mapping
open	Connects to remote server
prompt	Forces interactive prompting on multiple commands
proxy	Issues command on alternate connection
sendport	Toggles use of PORT cmd for each data connection
put	Uploads one file at a time
pwd	Prints working directory on remote machine
quit	Terminates FTP session and exit
quote	Sends arbitrary FTP command
recv	Receives file
remotehelp	Gets help from remote server
rename	Renames file
reset	Clears queued command replies
rmdir	Removes directory on the remote machine
runique	Toggles store unique for local files
send	Uploads a single file
status	Shows current status
struct	Sets file transfer structure
sunique	Toggles store unique on remote machine
tenex	Sets tenex file transfer type
trace	Toggles packet tracing
type	Sets file transfer type
user	Sends new user information
verbose	Toggles verbose mode
?	Prints local help information

The following is a list of possible response codes that the server generates in response to each command issued from the client:

110	Restart marker reply
120	Service ready in *nnn* minutes
125	Data connection already open; transfer starting
150	File status okay; about to open data connection
200	Command okay
202	Command not implemented, superfluous at this site
211	System status, or system help reply
212	Directory status
213	File status
214	Help message
215	NAME system type
220	Service ready for new user
221	Service closing control connection
225	Data connection open; no transfer in progress
226	Closing data connection
227	Entering passive mode (h1, h2, h3, h4, p1, p2)
230	User logged in, proceed
250	Requested file action okay, completed
257	"PATHNAME" created
331	User name okay, need password
332	Need account for login
350	Requested file action pending further information
421	Service not available, closing control connection
425	Can't open data connection
426	Connection closed; transfer aborted
450	Requested file action not taken
451	Requested action aborted: local error in processing

452	Requested action not taken
500	Syntax error, command unrecognized
501	Syntax error in parameters or arguments
502	Command not implemented
503	Bad sequence of commands
504	Command not implemented for that parameter
530	Not logged in
532	Need account for storing files
550	Requested action not taken
551	Requested action aborted: page type unknown
552	Requested file action aborted
553	Requested action not taken

Chapter 20

Network Interfaces, Routing, and Firewalls

In this chapter, we examine how to connect multiple machines in subnets and how to connect subnets to form local area networks (LANs) through routers. Inter-router connection allows the formation of wide area networks (WANs), and ultimately the Internet. Communication between different machines, through the transmission of data packets, can take place only through the process of routing. Routing involves finding a route between two hosts, whether they exist on the same network or are separated by thousands of miles and hundreds of intermediate hosts. Fortunately, the basic principles are the same in both cases. However, for security reasons, many sites on the Internet have installed packet filters, which deny certain packet transmissions on a host or port basis. In this chapter, we examine static and dynamic methods for configuring routes between hosts and examine the mechanisms of IP filtering and firewalls.

Key Concepts

This section introduces key concepts for understanding network interfaces, routing, and firewalls.

Network Interfaces

Solaris supports many different kinds of network interfaces, for local-area and wide-area transmission. Ethernet and FDDI are commonly used for creating networks of two or more systems at a single site through a LAN, while supporting high-speed, wide-area connections through T1 and X.25 lines, and most recently, ATM (Asynchronous Transfer Mode) networks. A switch is a device that can interconnect many devices so that they can be channeled directly to a router for wide-area connection. For example, each physical floor of a building may have a switch, and each of these switches then connects to a single switch for the whole building. This switch is connected to an Internet Service Provider (ISP) through a router (*router.buychapters.com*) and a dedicated ISDN service. A general rule of thumb for connecting routable networks is not to have more than three levels of connection between a server and a router; otherwise, the number of errors increases dramatically. Figure 20-1 shows a possible "Class C" network configuration for this building.

This configuration is fine if a single company (*buychapters.com*) owns and occupies this building, and both use the same ISP. However, let's imagine that *buychapters.com* downsizes, and leases the second floor to a government department (*department.gov*). The government department wants to make use of the existing ISP arrangements, and is happy to share the cost of the ISDN connection. However, they want to logically isolate their network from that of *buychapters.com* for security purposes. They intend to install a packet filter on their own router, which explicitly denies or allows packets to cross into the government department's network.

They can easily achieve this logical separation by separating the existing network into two subnets, allowing the government department to install its own router, and connecting the two networks through that router. Traffic to the ISP can still flow through

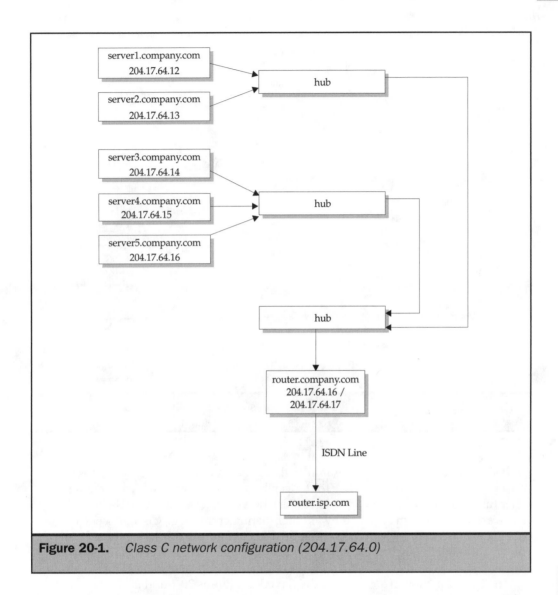

Figure 20-1.   *Class C network configuration (204.17.64.0)*

the existing connection, even though from the hosts on the second floor, they are now separated from the router. The way that the department's traffic can "find" the ISP is the kind of problem that routing can solve. More generally, routing allows one host to find a path to any other host on the Internet. Figure 20-2 shows the revised configuration for this building, incorporating the changes required by the government department, forming two Class C networks whose routers are connected to each other.

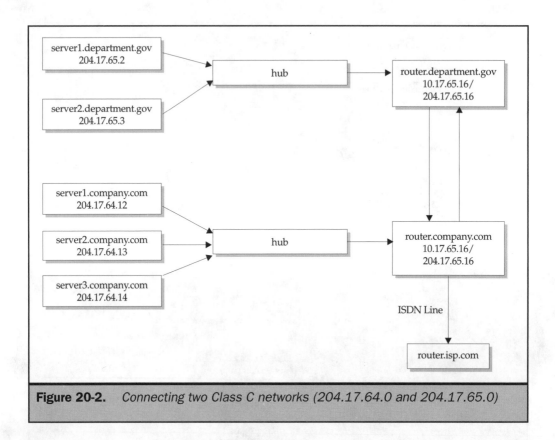

Figure 20-2. *Connecting two Class C networks (204.17.64.0 and 204.17.65.0)*

It should be clear from these examples that from a network perspective, a system must either be a router or a host. A router can be a Solaris server, which performs other functions (e.g., DNS server, NIS server); however, it can also be a dedicated, hardware-based system supplied by another manufacturer (e.g., Cisco, Ascend). In this chapter, we examine ways of setting up and configuring a Solaris host to be a router, although it may be that your organization prefers to use a dedicated system for routing.

The basic function of a router, as displayed in Figures 20-1 and 20-2, is to pass information from one network to another. In the examples, information is passed from one Class C network to another, but also to the router of an ISP. The ISP's router then connects with many other ISP's routers, eventually giving global coverage. The information passed between networks is contained in discrete packets, and because the router passes this information along, it follows that the router can potentially make a copy of the data and save it to a local disk. This is the basis of many security-related problems on the Internet, because usernames and passwords are also transmitted as packets, and can be intercepted by any intermediate router between client and server.

To be a router, a system must have multiple physical network interfaces. This is distinct from a system having one or more virtual interfaces defined for a single physical interface card. Thus, the router for *buychapters.com* has the interfaces 204.17.64.16 and 204.17.64.17. The first interface accepts traffic from the internal network and passes it to the second interface; the second interface accepts traffic from the other routers and passes it to the internal network, or to other routers as appropriate. Having two network interfaces allows data to be passed through the machine and exchanged across different networks. In the preceding example, the *buychapters.com* router was able to exchange information between the *department.gov* router and the ISP's router. Thus, many routers can be interconnected to form networks, in which packets can be passed from a source to a destination host transparently.

Because the *department.gov* router servers as a packet-filtering firewall, it is likely that the network has a nonroutable, internal structure, which is not directly accessible to the external network, but is visible from the router (the 10.17.65.0 network). Thus, a rogue user from *buychapters.com* will be able to "see" the external interface for the *department.gov* router, but will not be able to see the internal interface, or any of the hosts beyond, unless she manages to break into the router through the external interface. This adds a second layer of protection against intrusion. A packet filter can then be used to explicitly deny connections to machines in the internal network, except for very specific system or network services. For example, a departmental mail server may reside on server1.*department.gov*, and external machines will ultimately need access to the *sendmail* ports on this server. This can be achieved by port forwarding, or the ability of the router to map a port on its external interface to a port on a machine on the internal network. For example, a Web server on *server1.department.gov:80* could be accessed from the external network by connecting to *router.department.gov:8080* if the mapping was enabled. These techniques can achieve the necessary logical isolation between external users and actual network configuration, which can be useful for security planning. Packet filtering, port forwarding, and nonroutable networks are discussed later in the chapter.

A machine with more than one network interface may not be configured to act as a router, in which case, it is referred to a multihomed host. Multihoming can be useful for performing such functions as load balancing and directly serving different Class C networks, without passing information between them.

IP Routing

Now that we have discussed how to install, configure, and tune network interfaces, we turn our attention to setting up routing by explaining how packets are transferred from hosts to routers and exchanged between routers. We also examine how to troubleshoot routing problems with *traceroute*, and introduce the different routing protocols that are currently being used on the Internet.

There are two kinds of routing. The first type is *static routing*, which is common in simple networks with only a few hosts and networks interconnected. Static routing is much simpler to implement than dynamic routing, which is suitable for large networks,

NETWORKING

where the routes between networks cannot be readily specified. For example, if your organizational network has only two routers connecting three networks, the number of routes that need to be installed statically is four (i.e., the square of the number of routers). In contrast, for a building with 5 routers, the number of routes that need to specified statically is 25.

If a router configuration changes, all of the static configuration files on all of the routers need to be changed (i.e., there is no mechanism for the "discovery" of routes). Or, if a router fails because of a hardware fault, packets may not be able to be correctly routed. *Dynamic routing* solves all of these problems, but it requires more processing overhead on each router. There are two related dynamic routing daemons—`in.rdisc`, the router discovery daemon, and `in.routed`, the route daemon—whose configuration is discussed at length in this section.

Overview of Packet Delivery

Before we examine the differences between static and dynamic routing in detail, let's take a step back and consider how information is passed between two systems, whether the exchange is host–host, host–router, or router–router. All information is exchanged in the form of discrete packets, which is the smallest unit of information that is transmitted between hosts using TCP/IP. A packet contains both a header and a message component, as shown in Figure 20-3. In order to deliver packets from one host to another host successfully, each packet contains information in the header that is similar to an envelope: Among many other fields, it contains the address of the destination machine and the address of the source machine. The message section of the packet contains the actual data to be transferred. Packets are often transferred on the transport layer using the Transmission Control Protocol (TCP), which guarantees the delivery of packets, whereas some applications use User Datagram Protocol (UDP), where the continuity of a connection cannot be guaranteed. In normal TCP transmission mode, only 64KB of data can be transferred in a single session, unless large window support is enabled, in which case, up to 1GB of data may be transmitted. The header may also have information inserted by the source machine, which is referred to as data encapsulation. The action of passing a packet is referred to as a *hop*, so routing involves enabling packets to hop from a source host to any arbitrary host on the Internet.

In order for packets to be delivered correctly between two hosts, all intermediate routers must be able to determine where the packets have come from and where they must be delivered to. This can be achieved by referring to a host by using its IP address (e.g., 203.16.42.58) or its fully qualified domain name (e.g., server.*buychapters.com*). Although it is also possible to refer to a machine by its Ethernet (hardware) address, a logical rather than a physical representation of a machine's network interface card must be used in TCP/IP.

Sending a packet across a network makes full use of all network layers. For example, if a telnet session is to be established between two machines, the application protocol specifies how the message and header are to be constructed, information which is then passed to the transport layer protocol. For a telnet session, the transport layer protocol is TCP, which proceeds with encapsulation of the packet's data, which is split into

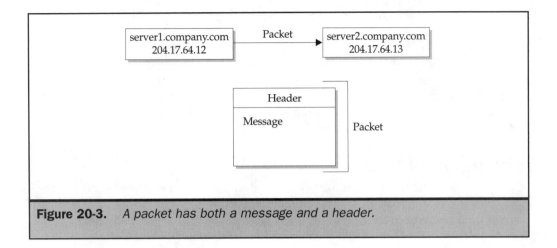

Figure 20-3. *A packet has both a message and a header.*

segments. The data is divided depending on the size of the TCP window allowed by the system. Each segment has a header and a checksum, which is used by the destination host to determine whether a received packet is likely to be free of corruption. When a segment is due to be transmitted from the source host, a three-way handshake occurs between source and destination: a SYN segment is sent to the destination host requesting a connection, and an acknowledgement (ACK) is returned to the source when the destination host is ready to receive. When the ACK is received by the source host, its receipt is acknowledged back to the destination, and transmission proceeds with data being passed to the IP layer, where segments are realized as IP datagrams. IP also adds a header to the segment and passes it to the physical networking layer for transport. A common method of enacting a denial of service attack on a remote host involves sending many SYN requests to a remote host, without completing the "three-way handshake." Solaris now limits the maximum number of connections with an incomplete handshake to reduce the impact of the problem. When a packet finally arrives at the destination host, it travels through the TCP/IP protocol stack in the reverse order from that which it took on the sender—just like a deck of cards that has been dealt onto a playing table and retrieved from the top of the pack.

The story becomes more complicated when packets need to be passed through several hosts to reach their ultimate destination. Although the method of passing data from source to destination is the same, the next hop along the route needs to be determined somehow. The path that a packet takes across the network depends on the IP address of the destination host as specified in the packet header. If the destination host is on the local network, it can be delivered immediately without intervention of a separate router. For example, a source host 204.12.60.24 on the Class C network 204.12.60.0 can directly pass a packet to a destination 204.12.60.32. However, once a packet needs to be delivered beyond the local network, the process becomes more complicated. The packet is passed to the router on the local network (which may be defined in */etc/defaultrouter*), and a router table is consulted. The router table contains a list of the hosts on the local network and other routers to which the router has a connection. For example, the router for the 204.12.60.0 network might be 204.12.60.64. Thus, a packet from 204.12.60.24 would be passed to 204.12.60.64 if the destination host was not on the 204.12.60.0 network. The router 204.12.60.64 may have a second interface 204.12.61.64 that connects the 204.12.60.0 and 204.12.59.0 networks. If the destination host was 204.12.59.28, the packet could now be delivered directly to the host because the router bridges the two networks. However, if the packet is not deliverable to a host on the 204.12.59.0 network, it must be passed to another router defined in the current router's tables.

IP Filtering and Firewalls

After going to all the trouble of making routing easy to use and semi-automated with the dynamic routing protocols, some situations require that the smooth transfer of packets from one host to another via a router be prevented. This is usually because of security concerns about data that is contained on hosts on a particular network. For example, Windows networks broadcast all kinds of information about workgroups and domains that is visible to any computer that can connect through the network's router. However, if the network's router prevents a computer from another network from listening to this information, it can still be broadcast internally, but is not visible to the outside world. Fortunately, this kind of "packet filtering" is selective: Only specific ports are blocked at the router level, and they can also be blocked in only one direction. For example, a database listener operating on a router could accept connections from machines internal to the network, but external access would be blocked. For large organizations that have direct connections to the Internet, setting up a corporate firewall at the router level has become a priority to protect sensitive data while providing employees with the access to the Internet that they require. In this section, we examine the basics of packet filtering. In the examples section, we review the installation and configuration of the popular *ipfilter* package for Solaris 9.

IP filtering involves the selective restriction and permission of access to TCP and UDP ports on a system. IP filtering is commonly used for two purposes: to secure a network from attacks and intrusion from rogue users on outside hosts, and to prevent the broadcast and transmission of unauthorized data from an internal network to the rest of the Internet. In the former case, an attacker may attempt to gain entry to your system by using an application such as telnet, or he may try to insert or retrieve data from a database by connecting to a database listener and issuing SQL commands from a client application. Both of these scenarios are common enough to motivate many sites to restrict all incoming traffic to their networks, except on a very small number of specific ports. Commonly allowed ports include the following:

- Secure shell (*ssh*) on port 22
- Secure copy (*scp*) on port 24
- Mail server (*sendmail*) on port 25
- WWW server (apache) on port 80

This may seem like a very minimal list to many Administrators, but the fact is that almost every UNIX daemon has been discovered to suffer from "buffer overflow" problems in recent years, leaving systems open to exploitation. A rule of thumb is to allow only services that users definitely need to be productive and have been approved by management. Some users might argue that allowing the *finger* service is useful, but it also gives away a lot of information about home directories and valid usernames that can be exploited by rogue users. In addition, some users may set up Web and FTP servers without permission. Because Solaris restricts only ports less than 1024 for the super-user and system accounts, all ports above 1024 are available for users to engage in unauthorized activities for which your company may be held responsible. For example, a user might run a Web server on port 8080 that distributes pirate software. If a software manufacturer discovers this operation, they will most likely sue your company rather than the individual involved. Blocking access to all ports unless they are specifically required or sanctioned limits these kinds of problems.

What is less intuitive than restricting incoming traffic is the notion of also restricting outgoing traffic. Firewalls are able to manage both because a firewall may also act as a router (and recall that routers always have at least two network interfaces). One good reason to consider blocking outgoing network on some ports is that users may engage in leisure activities, such as playing networked adventure games and *talk*, which are nonproductive activities. Because you don't really want to be the policeman "patrolling" the system for violators, it is best just to restrict any access in the first place to avoid any problems. You can also use a firewall to accept or deny connections based on IP address; obviously, a machine making a connection from the external network, but pretending to have an address from inside the network, should be identified and their attempts rejected (this is known as *IP spoofing*). Figure 20-4 summarizes the functions of a router that acts as a packet filtering "firewall." Permitted ports are shown with the label "OK," whereas denied ports are shown with "NO." All connections for *sendmail (25)* are accepted, as are *ssh* connections. However, external connections to a database listener are rejected (port 1521), and a machine on the external network spoofing an internal network IP address has all its connections rejected.

The Kernel Routing Table

The routing table maintains an index of routes to networks and routers that are available to the local host. Routes can be determined dynamically by using RDISC, for example, or can be added manually by using *route* or *ifconfig*. These commands are normally used at boot time to initialize network services. There are three kinds of routes:

- **Host routes** Map a path from the local host to another host on the local network
- **Network routes** Allow packets to be transferred from the local hosts to other hosts on the local network
- **Default routes** Pass the task of finding a route to a router

NETWORKING

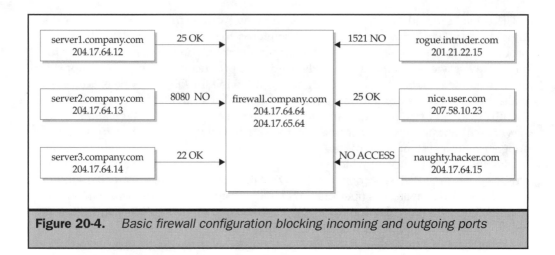

Figure 20-4. *Basic firewall configuration blocking incoming and outgoing ports*

Both RIP and RDISC daemons can use default routes. Dynamic routing often causes changes in the routing table after booting, when a minimal routing table is configured by `ifconfig` when initializing each network interface, as the daemons manage changes in the network configuration and router availability.

Procedures

The following procedures are commonly used to configure network interfaces, routing, and firewalls.

Configuring a Router

In order to configure routing, you need to enable the appropriate network interfaces. In this chapter, we assume that an Ethernet network is being used, thus, each system that acts as a router must have at least two Ethernet interfaces installed. In addition, Solaris also supports multiple Ethernet interfaces to be installed on a single machine. These are usually designated by files like

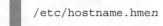

```
/etc/hostname.hmen
```

or

```
/etc/hostname.len
```

where *n* is the interface number, and *hme* and *le* represent the network devices */etc/hme0* and */etc/le0*, respectively. Interface files can contain a single IP address, or a hostname, with the primary network interface being designated with an interface number of zero. Thus, the primary interface of a machine called *server* would be defined by the file */etc/hostname.hme0*, which might contain the IP address 203.17.64.28, or the domain name.*server*. A secondary network interface, connected to a different subnet, might be defined in the file */etc/hostname..hme1*. In this case, the file might contain the IP address 10.17.65.28, or *internal*. Note that it in some cases it is preferable to use domain names to IP addresses, because the latter may be dynamically allocated using DHCP or a similar protocol. Alternatively, if you mistrust naming services and choose not to run DHCP, then an IP address may be used in lieu of a hostname.

A multihomed network interface configuration is commonly used in organizations that have a provision for a failure of the primary network interface, or it is used to enable load balancing of server requests across multiple subnets (e.g., for an intranet Web server processing HTTP requests). However, the practice of assigning dynamic addresses to router interfaces is not recommended.

A system with a second network interface can either act as a router, or as a multihomed host. Hostnames and IP addresses are locally administered through a naming service, which is usually the Domain Name Service (DNS) for companies connected to the Internet, and the Network Information Service (NIS/NIS+) for companies with large internal networks that require administrative functions beyond what DNS provides, including centralized authentication. It is also worth mentioning at this point that it is quite possible to assign different IP addresses to the same network interface, which can be useful for hosting "virtual" domains that require their own IP addresses, rather than relying on application-level support for multihoming (e.g., when using the Apache Web server). Simply create a new */etc/hostname.hmeX:Y* file for each IP address required, where X represents the physical device interface, and Y represents the virtual interface number.

In the examples presented in the "Network Interfaces" section, each of the routers had two interfaces, one for the internal network, and one for the external Internet. The subnet mask used by each of these interfaces must also be defined in */etc/netmasks*. This is particularly important if the interfaces lie on different subnets, or if they serve different network classes. In addition, it might also be appropriate to assign a fully qualified domain name to each of the interfaces, although this will depend on the purpose to which each interface is assigned. For the system *router.department.gov*, there will be two hostname files created in the */etc* directory. The */etc/hostname.hme0* file will contain the entry *internal*; the */etc/hostname.hme0* file will contain the entry *router*.

When installing a system as a router, you need to determine which network interface to use as the external interface for passing information between networks. This interface must be defined in the file */etc/defaultrouter* by including that interface's IP address. These addresses can be matched to hostnames if appropriate. For example, the interfaces for *router.department.gov* will be defined in */etc/hosts* as:

```
127.0.0.1      localhost     loghost
10.17.65.16      internal
204.17.65.16      router      router.department.gov
```

If the server is to be multihomed instead of being a router, ensure that */etc/defaultrouter* does not exist, and create an */etc/notrouter* file:

```
# rm /etc/defaultrouter
# touch /etc/notrouter
```

Viewing Router Configuration

The `ifconfig` command is responsible for configuring each network interface at boot time. You can also use `ifconfig` to check the status of active network interfaces by passing the *–a* parameter:

```
# ifconfig -a
lo0: flags=849<UP,LOOPBACK,RUNNING,MULTICAST> mtu 8232
        inet 127.0.0.1 netmask ff000000
hme0: flags=863<UP,BROADCAST,NOTRAILERS,RUNNING,MULTICAST> mtu 1500
        inet 10.17.65.16 netmask ffffff00 broadcast 10.17.65.255
hme1: flags=863<UP,BROADCAST,NOTRAILERS,RUNNING,MULTICAST> mtu 1500
        inet 204.17.65.16 netmask ffffff00 broadcast 204.17.65.255
```

In this case, the primary interface *hme0* is running on the internal network, while the secondary interface *hme1* is visible to the external network. The netmask for a Class C network is used on both interfaces, while both have a distinct broadcast address. This ensures that information broadcast on the internal network is not visible to the external network. There are several parameters shown with `ifconfig –a`, including whether the interface is "up" or "down" (i.e., active or inactive). In the following example, the interface has not been enabled at boot time:

```
# ifconfig hme1
hme1: flags=863<DOWN,BROADCAST,NOTRAILERS,RUNNING,MULTICAST> mtu 1500
        inet 204.17.64.16 netmask ffffff00 broadcast 204.17.64.255
```

If the */etc/ethers* database has been updated by the Administrator to include details of the Ethernet addresses of hosts on the local network, an entry is also displayed about the corresponding interface when using `ifconfig`:

```
# cat /etc/ethers
8:0:19:7:f2:a1 server
# ifconfig hme1
hme1: flags=863<UP,BROADCAST,NOTRAILERS,RUNNING,MULTICAST> mtu 1500
        inet 204.17.128.16 netmask ffffff00 broadcast 204.17.128.255
ether 8:0:19:7:f2:a1
```

It can also be useful in detecting problems with a routing network interface to examine the address resolution protocol results for the local area network. This will determine whether the interface is visible to its clients:

```
# arp -a
Net to Media Table
Device   IP Address              Mask            Flags Phys Addr
------   ------------------      ---------------  ----- ---------------
hme0     server1.buychapters.com 255.255.255.255        00:c0:ff:19:48:d8
hme0     server2.buychapters.com 255.255.255.255        c2:d4:78:00:15:56
hme0     server3.buychapters.com 255.255.255.255        87:b3:9a:c2:e9:ea
```

Modifying Interface Parameters

There are two methods for modifying network interface parameters. First, you can use the ifconfig command to modify operational parameters and to bring an interface on-line ("up"), or shut it down ("down"). Second, you can use ndd to set parameters for TCP/IP transmission that will affect all network interfaces. In this section, we examine both of these methods, and how you can use them to manage interfaces and improve performance.

Sometimes, you need to shut down and start up a network interface in order to upgrade drivers or install patches affecting network service. To shut down a network interface, for example, you can use this command:

```
# ifconfig hme1 down
 # ifconfig hme1
hme1: flags=863<DOWN,BROADCAST,NOTRAILERS,RUNNING,MULTICAST> mtu 1500
      inet 204.17.64.16 netmask ffffff00 broadcast 204.17.64.255
```

You can also bring this interface back "up" by using ifconfig:

```
# ifconfig hme1 up
 # ifconfig hme1
hme1: flags=863<UP,BROADCAST,NOTRAILERS,RUNNING,MULTICAST> mtu 1500
      inet 204.17.64.16 netmask ffffff00 broadcast 204.17.64.255
```

To ensure that this configuration is preserved from boot to boot, you can edit the networking startup file */etc/rc2.d/S69inet* and add this line to any others that configure the network interfaces. Or, creating a separate startup file that contains the nondefault settings (e.g., /etc/rc2.d/S69spNet) may be wiser, so that you can easily reverse these changes by typing:

```
# /etc/rc2.d/S69spNet stop
 # /etc/rc2.d/S69inet start
```

You may need to set several of these parameters in a production environment to ensure optimal performance, especially when application servers and Web servers are in use. For example, when a Web server makes a request to port 80 using TCP, a connection is opened and closed. However, the connection is kept open for a default time of two minutes to ensure that all packets are correctly received. For a system with a large number of clients, this can lead to a bottleneck of stale TCP connections, which can significantly impact the performance of the Web server. Fortunately, you can set the parameter that controls this behavior (*tcp_close_wait_interval*) using ndd to something more sensible (like 30 seconds):

```
# ndd -set /dev/tcp tcp_close_wait_interval 30000
```

However, Administrators should be aware that altering this parameter will affect all TCP services, so although a Web server might perform optimally with *tcp_close_wait_interval* equal to 30 seconds, a database listener that handles large datasets may require a much wider time window. The best way to determine optimal values is to perform experiments with low, moderate, and peak levels of traffic for both the Web server and the database listener to determine a value that will provide reasonable performance for both applications. It is also important to check SunSolve for the latest patches and updates for recently discovered kernel bugs.

Static Routes

On hosts, routing information can be extracted in two ways, by building a full routing table, exactly as it does on a router, or by creating a minimal kernel table, containing a single default route for each available router (i.e., static routing). The most common static route is from a host to a local router, as specified in the */etc/defaultrouter* file. For example, for the host 204.12.60.24, the entry in */etc/defaultrouter* might be

```
204.12.60.64
```

This places a single route in the local routing table. Responsibility for determining the next hop for the message is then passed to the router. You can also add static routes for servers using *in.routed* by defining them in the */etc/gateways* file. When using static routing, routing tables in the kernel are defined when the system boots and do not normally change, unless modified by using the route or ifconfig command. When a local network has a single gateway to the rest of the Internet, static routing is the most appropriate choice.

Routing Protocols

The Routing Information Protocol (RIP) and the Router Discovery Protocol (RDISC) are some of the standard routing protocols for TCP/IP networks, and Solaris supports both. RIP is implemented by in.routed, the routing daemon, and is usually configured to start during multi-user mode startup (see Chapter 4 for more information). The route daemon always populates the routing table with a route to every reachable network, but whether or not it advertises its routing availability to other systems is optional.

Hosts use the RDISC daemon (*in.rdisc*) to collect information about routing availability from routers. The daemon should run on both routers and hosts. *in.rdisc* typically creates a default route for each router that responds to requests. This "discovery" is central to the ability of RDISC-enabled hosts to dynamically adjust to network changes. Routers that run only *in.routed* cannot be discovered by RDISC-enabled hosts. For hosts running both *in.rdisc* and *in.routed*, the latter will operate until an RDISC-enabled router is discovered on the network, in which case, RDISC will take over routing.

Viewing the Routing Table (netstat –r)

The command `netstat -r` shows the current routing table. Routes are always specified as a connection between the local server and a remote machine, via some kind of gateway. The output from the `netstat -r` command contains several different flags. Flag *U* indicates that the route between the destination and gateway is up; flag *G* shows that the route passes through a gateway. Flag *H* indicates that the route connects to a host; the *D* flag signifies that the route was dynamically created using a redirect. Three other columns are shown in the routing table: *Ref* indicates the number of concurrent routes occupying the same link layer; *Use* indicates the number of packets transmitted along the route (on a specific *Interface*, the final column).

The following example shows an example server (*server.buychapters.com*) that has four routes. The first is for the loopback address (*lo0*), which is up and is connected through a host, and the second route is for the local Class C network (204.16.64.0), through the gateway *gateway.buychapters.com*, which is also up. The third route is the special multicast route, which is also up; the fourth route is the default route, pointing to the local network router, which is also up.

```
$ netstat -r

Routing Table:
Destination             Gateway                 Flags Ref   Use    Interface
--------------------    --------------------    ----- ----- ------ ---------
127.0.0.1               localhost               UH    0     877    lo0
204.17.64.0             gateway.buychapters.com U     3     85     hme0
BASE-ADDRESS.MCAST.NET  host.buychapters.com    U     3     0      hme0
default                 router.buychapters.com  UG    0     303
```

Manipulating the Routing Table (route)

The `route` command is used to manually manipulate the routing tables. If dynamic routing is working correctly, it should not normally be necessary to do this. However, if static is being used, or the RDISC daemon does not discover any routes, it may be necessary to add routes manually. In addition, it may also be necessary to delete routes explicitly for security purposes. You should be aware, though, that except for interface changes, the routing daemon may not respond to any modifications to the routing table that may have been enacted manually. It is best to shut down the routing daemon first before making changes, and then restart it after all changes have been initiated.

Adding Host Routes

To add a direct route to another host, you can use the route command with the following syntax:

```
# route add -host destination_ip local_ip -interface interface
```

Thus, if you wanted to add a route between the local host (e.g., 204.12.17.1) and a host on a neighboring Class C network (204.12.16.100), for the primary interface *hme0*, you would use this command:

```
# add -host 204.12.16.100 204.12.17.1 -interface hme0
```

Adding Network Routes

To add a direct route to another network, use the route command with the following syntax:

```
# route add -net destination_network_ip local_ip" -netmask mask
```

If you wanted to add a route between the local host (e.g., 204.12.17.1) and the same network as the host specified in the preceding section (i.e., the 204.12.16.0 network), for the Class C netmask (255.255.255.0), you would use the following command:

```
# route add -net 204.12.16.0 204.12.17.1 -netmask 255.255.255.0
```

Adding a Default Route

To add a default route, use the route command with the following syntax:

```
# route add default hostname -interface interface
```

For example, to add a default route to a local router (204.54.56.1) for a secondary interface *hme1*, you can use the command:

```
# route add default 204.54.56.1 -interface hme1
```

Dynamic Routing

In this section, we look more closely at the RIP and RDISC dynamic routing protocols. A prerequisite for dynamic routing to operate is that the */etc/defaultrouter* file should be empty.

routed

in.routed is the network routing daemon, and it is responsible for dynamically managing entries in the kernel routing tables. It is usually started from a line during multi-user boot (*/etc/rc2.d/S69inet*) using the following command:

```
# /usr/sbin/in.routed -q
```

The routing daemon uses port 520 to route packets and to establish which interfaces are currently up and which are down. *in.routed* listens for requests for packets and for known routes from remote hosts. This supplies hosts on a network with the information they need to determine how many hops to a host. When it is initialized, the routing daemon checks both gateways specified in */etc/gateways*. You can also run the routing daemon in a special memory saving mode that retains only the default routes in the routing table. Although this may leave a system at the mercy of a faulty router, it does save memory and reduces the resources that *in.routed* requires to maintain lists of active routes that are periodically updated. You can enable this by initializing *in.routed* with the *–S* parameter.

rdisc

The RDISC daemon uses the ICMP router discovery protocol, and it is usually executed on both hosts and routers at boot time, at which time routers broadcast their availability, and hosts start listening for available routers. Routers broadcast their availability using the 224.0.0.1 multicast address. Routers that share a network with a host are selected first as the default route, if one is found. Another approach is for the host to send out a broadcast on the 224.0.0.2 multicast address to solicit any available routers. In either case, if a router is available, it will accept packet forwarding requests from the host concerned.

Configuring the IPFilter Firewall

IPFilter is a popular freeware packet filtering package for Solaris—it is a kernel-loadable module that is attached at boot time. This makes IPFilter very secure, because it cannot be tampered with by user applications. However, as you will see shortly, there are also problems with this approach because loading unstable modules into the kernel can cause a Solaris system to crash. The IPFilter distribution is available from **http://coombs.anu.edu.au/~avalon/**.

The first step in creating an IPFilter configuration file is to consult with users and managers to determine a list of acceptable services. Many companies will already have an acceptable use policy that will govern which ports should be available and what permissions should be given for user-initiated services. After you determine a list of ingoing and outgoing port requirements, it is best to write a rule that first denies all packets and then to write additional rules that explicitly allow the services you have identified. You must also enable allowed services in both directions. For example, it is usually necessary for users to both receive and send electronic mail, so you need to include an inbound and outbound rule for *sendmail* (port 25).

IPFilter rules are processed in the order that they are specified in the configuration file. Every rule is processed, which means that more general rules (like blocking all connections) should precede specific rules (like allowing bidirectional *sendmail* connections) in the configuration file. If you have a very complicated configuration, you can also specify that processing terminate at any point in the file, if a condition is met, by using the `quick` keyword. Other important keywords include `block`, `to`, and `from` to construct rules for limiting packet transmission. The `block` command blocks packets from a particular source to a particular destination. The `from` command specifies the source of these packets; the `to` command specifies the destination of these packets. The following example prevents any packets from the Class B network 178.222.0.0:

```
block in quick from 178.222.0.0/16 to any
```

The `pass` command allows packets to pass the firewall. For example, the rule

```
pass in all
```

allows all packets to pass. Because routers by definition have more than two interfaces, you can also specify a network interface to which a specific rule applies. For example, the rule

```
block in quick on hme2 all
```

prevents all transmissions on the *hme2* interface. You can mix an interface specification with a normal rule so that one interface accepts traffic from one Class C network (178.222.1.0), but another interface may accept traffic only from a different Class C network (178.221.2.0):

```
block in quick on hme2 from 178.222.1.0/24 to any
block in quick on hme1 from 178.222.2.0/24 to any
```

All of the examples so far have focused on inbound traffic using the `in` command. As we mentioned earlier, you can also restrict outbound traffic in the same way, by using the `out` command. The following example prevents traffic from the internal, nonroutable network (10.222.1.0) to pass through:

```
block out quick on hme0 from 10.222.1.0/24 to any
```

That rule would be applied only to organizations that didn't want its employees using the Internet. Perhaps it could be combined with a `cron` job, which would reconfigure the firewall to allow access during lunchtime and after work. You can also limit particular protocols so that TCP applications (like *SSH*) would be allowed, but UDP applications (like some streamed audio applications) would be banned by specifying *proto udp* in the rule:

```
block in quick on hme0 proto udp from 10.222.1.0/24 to any
```

The most complicated rule comes in the form of a port-by-port specification of what is allowed and disallowed on a protocol-by-protocol basis. For example, the following rule blocks all Web server requests from the internal network from reaching their destination:

```
block in quick on hme0 proto tcp from any to 10.222.1.0/24 port = 80
```

This would allow Telnet and FTP connections to proceed freely, because TCP is only restricted on port 80.

Although this technology is very comprehensive and is very useful in placing very specific restrictions on network transmission, there are some drawbacks with configuring firewalls in general, and IPFilter in particular. Because firewall configuration involves writing rules, the syntax of the commonly used rule languages is often difficult to understand, thus packet filters can be difficult to configure correctly. Once you've created a configuration, there is also no testbed provided that determines that your configuration is satisfactory. There may be contention between one or more rules that is incorrectly resolved. There are also bugs in packet filtering packages, which means that Administrators should not just rely on them to protect their networks. Other measures, such as disabling unrequired services in */etc/services* and commenting out all unwanted daemons in */etc/inetd.conf*, go a long way towards protecting a system. Bugs are more serious in IPFilter because it is a kernel-loadable module. Thus, instead of an application-level filtering program crashing and dumping core, IPFilter will sometimes crash the kernel and cause a panic. Be aware that some versions of IPFilter will cause panics on Solaris kernels, while others work happily. The output from a crash looks like this:

```
BAD TRAP: cpu=1 type=0x31 rp=0x3b103003 addr=0xe1 mmu_fsr=0x0
BAD TRAP occurred in module "ipf" due to an illegal access to a user
address.
sched: trap type = 0x31
addr=0x1e
pid=0, pc=0x60bc8607, sp=0x33ba0300, tstate=0x1e02f000, context=0x0
g1-g7: 1c, 13578104, 0, 0, 0, 0, 333e8000
Begin traceback... sp = 3033ba00
Called from 1005cb74, fp=30033c20, args=0 60760b14 20 10418440 0 0
Called from 1005cc90, fp=30033c80, args=60098aa0 600992c0 60098ac0
40000000 60099328 8c2421a
Called from 10026a48, fp=30033ce0, args=60098aa0 60098ab4 10418440
10418440 d 0
Called from 1005cc48, fp=0, args=60098aa0 0 0 0 0 0
```

This kind of problem is always a risk when installing kernel-loadable modules. However, Solaris does provide some tools to determine which modules are at fault. To examine the cause of the IPFilter problem, use the following steps:

1. Create the system crash directory, and enable the *savecore* facility in the system startup file (*/etc/init.d/sysetup*).

2. Wait for a crash, and then let the system reboot.

3. Enter the crash directory and analyze the crash file with the `iscda.sh` script available from SunSolve (**http://sunsolve1.sun.com.au/sunsolve/us/iscda.html**).

4. Identify the offending command that caused the kernel panic. If it is IPFilter, download and test the most recent version.

Fortunately, there is a very active discussion group on IPFilter, with searchable archives available at **http://false.net/ipfilter/**. The firewall mailing list is also good for more general discussion of firewall-related issues, and the contents are available at **http://www.greatcircle.com/firewalls/**. If you are more interested in commercial firewall products, check out the comparisons with freeware at **http://www.fortified.com/ fwcklist.html/**.

Configuring the SunScreen Firewall

The best system for users who are new to Solaris is Sun's own SunScreen firewall (**http://www.sun.com/software/securenet/lite/download.html**). It comes in both a free and commercial edition, with the latter being more than adequate for protecting small networks. It is available for both Solaris Intel and Solaris Sparc. The current release version is 3.1, which supports gigabit Ethernet, SNMP management, and direct editing of security policy tables. However, it does not currently support IPv6. The firewall may be administered locally or remotely by using a secure session.

Several important limitations are placed on the Lite version of SunScreen:

- It is designed to work with a system that is already acting as a router (if it wasn't, why would you want SunScreen anyway?).

- It does not operate in the special "stealth" mode employed by the commercial edition.

- It does not support any of the High Availability features of the commercial version.

- It does not support more than two network interfaces. However, because most routers have only two interfaces, this should not be an issue for small networks.

- It does not provide support for proxying.

SunScreen can be operated in either GUI mode, through a standard Web browser such as Netscape, or by directly editing the system's configuration files. It is easy to install using the Web Start wizard, which is provided with the installation package.

To install the software, you need to run the */opt/SUNWicg/SunScreen/bin/ss_install* script. You need to configure several options for SunScreen to operate as desired:

- Routing or stealth mode operation

- Local or remote administration

- Restrictive, secure, or permissive security level

- Support for DNS resolution

After choosing the appropriate option for your system, the following message will be displayed:

```
--Adding interfaces & interface addresses
--Initialize 'vars' databases
--Initialize 'authuser' & 'proxyuser' databases
--Initialize 'logmacro' database
--Applying edits
--Activating configuration
loading skip keystore.
Successfully initialized certificate database in /etc/skip/certdb
starting skip key manager daemon.
Configuration activated successfully on cassowary.
Reboot the machine now for changes to take effect.
```

After rebooting the system, the firewall software will be loaded into the kernel, and you will then need to add rules to the firewall by using your browser to set the appropriate administration options. Figure 20-5 shows the browser starting on port 3852 on the localhost.

When first installed, the SunScreen username and password will be *admin* and *admin*. You need to enter these in the Admin User and Password fields. After clicking the Login button, the SunScreen Information page is displayed, as shown in Figure 20-6. There are several options available at this point. You can view firewall logs and connection statistics. However, most users will want to create a set of security policies immediately upon starting the firewall service.

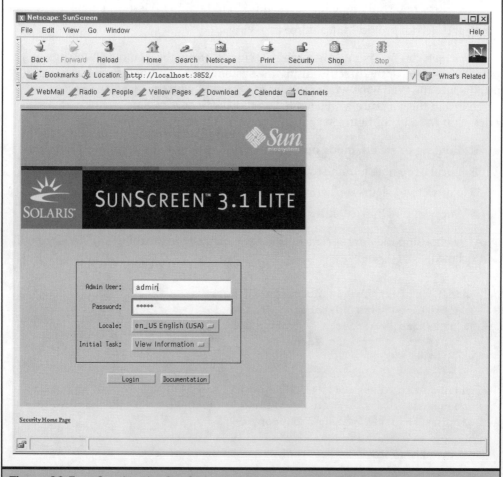

Figure 20-5. *Starting the SunScreen administrative interface*

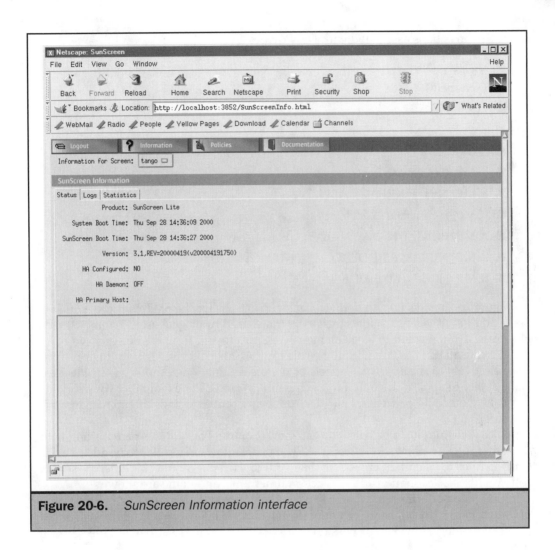

Figure 20-6. *SunScreen Information interface*

Security policies are based on rules that either ALLOW or DENY a packet to be transmitted from a source to a destination address. Or, you may specify an address class by using wildcards. The main actions associated with ALLOW rules are listed here:

- LOG_NONE
- LOG_SUMMARY
- LOG_DETAIL
- SNMP_NONE
- SNMP

The main actions associated with DENY rules are as follows:

- LOG_NONE
- LOG_SUMMARY
- LOG_DETAIL
- SNMP_NONE
- SNMP
- ICMP_NONE
- ICMP_NET_UNREACHABLE
- ICMP_HOST_UNREACHABLE
- ICMP_PORT_UNREACHABLE
- ICMP_NET_FORBIDDEN
- ICMP_HOST_FORBIDDEN

Figure 20-7 shows how to define a rule with actions for the SMTP service, which is operated by *sendmail*. This allows mail to be transferred from local users to remote hosts. However, if you wanted to block all mail being sent to and from the network, you could create a DENY action within the rule for the SMTP service. You could apply the rule selectively to specific local subnets or remote destinations. Another useful feature is the ability to apply rules only for specific time periods. For example, if you worked in a bank, you could prevent all e-mails from being sent externally after 5 P.M. and before 9 A.M.

Once you enter the new rule, you can view it on the Policy Rules panel, along with any other rules, as shown in Figure 20-8. The panel allows new rules to be added and existing rules to be edited, moved, or deleted. For each packet filtering rule, the service, source address, destination address, action timeframe, and name are shown.

SunScreen performs more than just packet filtering—you can use it to set up a virtual private network (VPN), and you can perform advanced network address translation (NAT) functions. However, discussion of these advanced topics is beyond the scope of this book.

Examples

The following examples demonstrate how to manage network interfaces, routers, and firewalls.

Viewing Router Status

For both routing and multihomed hosts, you can check the status of all network interfaces by using the `netstat -i` command:

```
# netstat -i
Name  Mtu   Net/Dest      Address      Ipkts    Ierrs  Opkts    Oerrs Collis Queue
lo0   8232  loopback      localhost    199875   0      199875   0     0      0
hme0  1500  203.17.65.0   department.gov 16970779 623190 19543549 0   0      0
hme1  1500  10.17.65.0    internal.gov 68674644 54543  65673376 0            0
```

In this example, *mtu* is the maximum transfer rate, which is much higher for the loopback address than the network interface (as would be expected), and the number of *Ipkts* (inbound packets) and *Opkts* (outbound packets) is equivalent for *lo0* (as one would hope). The loopback interface significantly increases the efficiency of a host that transmits packets to itself: in this example, there is an almost sixfold increase in the *mtu* for the *lo0* interface over either of the standard network interfaces. The primary network interface *hme0* is connected to the 203.17.65.0 network, and transmitted a large number of packets in and out since booting (16,970,779 and 19,543,549), respectively. There have been a number of inbound errors (623,190), but no outbound errors or collisions. Examining how these figures change over time can indicate potential problems in network topology that *may* need to be addressed. For example, if you are testing a Web

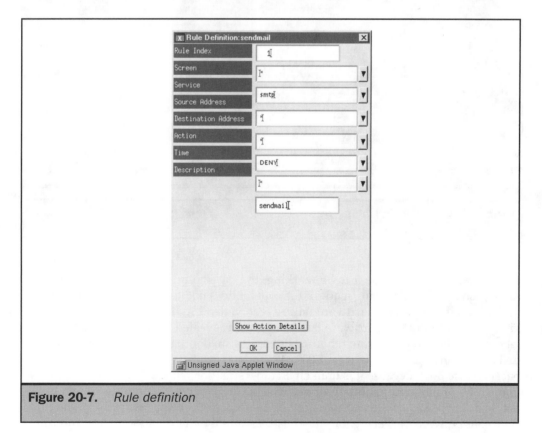

Figure 20-7. *Rule definition*

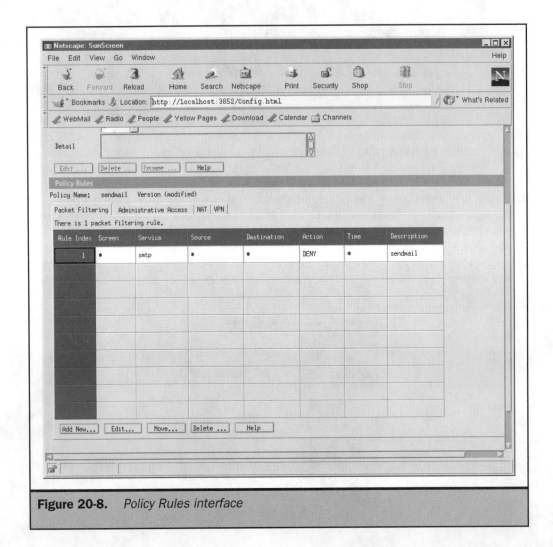

Figure 20-8. Policy Rules interface

server, and it doesn't appear to be working, the *Ipkts* count can reveal whether the connections are actually being made. If the counter does not increase as expected, it may indicate an intermediate hardware failure (e.g., a dead hub). Another example of identifying intermittent hardware failure might be revealed by a large number of inbound packets, representing requests, but only a small number of outbound packets. In the following example, there are 1,000,847 inbound packets, but only 30,159 outbound packets since boot. Because it is unlikely in most situations that a 33:1 imbalance exists in the ratio of inbound to outbound packets, the *hme0* network interface should be checked. There are also many collisions being experienced by the *hme0* interface. Collisions between packets render them useless, and the figure reported here indicates a significant loss of bandwidth. If the interface is working as expected, it can also be worthwhile to investigate other causes arising from software (e.g., incorrect configuration of a packet filter):

```
server# netstat -i
Name Mtu   Net/Dest     Address      Ipkts   Ierrs Opkts Oerrs Collis Queue
lo0  8232  loopback     localhost    7513    0     7513  0     0      0
hme0 1500  204.17.64.0  1000847 5    30159   0     3979  0
```

netstat –s also allows these per-interface statistics to be viewed on a per-protocol basis, which can be very useful in determining potential problems with routing, especially if the router is packet filtering. The following example shows output from the netstat –s command, which displays the per-protocol statistics for the UDP, TCP, and ICMP protocols:

```
# netstat -s
UDP
        udpInDatagrams      =502856      udpInErrors      =     0
        udpOutDatagrams     =459357
```

The output from netstat –s begins with the UDP statistics, including the number of datagrams received and the number transmitted. The In/Out ratio is fairly even at 1.09, and the networking appears to be working well: no UDP errors were detected (i.e., *udpInErrors=0*),

```
TCP     tcpRtoAlgorithm     =      4    tcpRtoMin         =    200
        tcpRtoMax           =240000     tcpMaxConn        =     -1
        tcpActiveOpens      =  33786    tcpPassiveOpens   =  12296
        tcpAttemptFails     =    324    tcpEstabResets    =    909
        tcpCurrEstab        =    384    tcpOutSegs        =19158723
        tcpOutDataSegs      =13666668   tcpOutDataBytes   =981537148
        tcpRetransSegs      =  33038    tcpRetransBytes   =41629885
        tcpOutAck           =5490764    tcpOutAckDelayed  =462511
        tcpOutUrg           =     51    tcpOutWinUpdate   =    456
        tcpOutWinProbe      =    290    tcpOutControl     =  92218
        tcpOutRsts          =   1455    tcpOutFastRetrans =  18954
        tcpInSegs           =15617893
        tcpInAckSegs        =9161810    tcpInAckBytes     =981315052
        tcpInDupAck         =4559921    tcpInAckUnsent    =      0
        tcpInInorderSegs    =5741788    tcpInInorderBytes =1120389303
        tcpInUnorderSegs    =  25045    tcpInUnorderBytes =16972517
        tcpInDupSegs        =4390218    tcpInDupBytes     =4889714
        tcpInPartDupSegs    =    375    tcpInPartDupBytes =130424
        tcpInPastWinSegs    =     17    tcpInPastWinBytes =1808990872
        tcpInWinProbe       =    162    tcpInWinUpdate    =    270
        tcpInClosed         =    313    tcpRttNoUpdate    =  28077
        tcpRttUpdate        =9096791    tcpTimRetrans     =  18098
```

```
tcpTimRetransDrop    =      26     tcpTimKeepalive         =    509
tcpTimKeepaliveProbe=      76      tcpTimKeepaliveDrop     =      1
tcpListenDrop        =       0     tcpListenDropQ0         =      0
tcpHalfOpenDrop      =       0
```

The TCP statistics were more mixed: there were 324 *tcpAttemptFails,* but given that there were 33,786 *tcpActiveOpens* at the time netstat was run, this is quite reasonable. The ratio of *tcpInInorderSegs* to *tcpInUnorderSegs* (i.e., received in order versus not received in order) was 229:1, which is not uncommon.

```
IP      ipForwarding        =       2     ipDefaultTTL       =    255
        ipInReceives        =16081438     ipInHdrErrors      =      8
        ipInAddrErrors      =       0     ipInCksumErrs      =      1
        ipForwDatagrams     =       0     ipForwProhibits    =      2
        ipInUnknownProtos   =     274     ipInDiscards       =      0
        ipInDelivers        =16146712     ipOutRequests      =19560145
        ipOutDiscards       =       0     ipOutNoRoutes      =      0
        ipReasmTimeout      =      60     ipReasmReqds       =      0
        ipReasmOKs          =       0     ipReasmFails       =      0
        ipReasmDuplicates   =       0     ipReasmPartDups    =      0
        ipFragOKs           =    7780     ipFragFails        =      0
        ipFragCreates       =   40837     ipRoutingDiscards  =      0
        tcpInErrs           =     291     udpNoPorts         =144065
        udpInCksumErrs      =       2     udpInOverflows     =      0
        rawipInOverflows    =       0
```

There are some IP errors, but they were quite minor: there were eight *ipInHdrErrors,* but only one *ipInCksumErrs* and two *udpInCksumErrs.*

```
ICMP    icmpInMsgs          =   17469     icmpInErrors       =      0
        icmpInCksumErrs     =       0     icmpInUnknowns     =      0
        icmpInDestUnreachs  =    2343     icmpInTimeExcds    =     26
        icmpInParmProbs     =       0     icmpInSrcQuenchs   =      0
        icmpInRedirects     =      19     icmpInBadRedirects =     19
        icmpInEchos         =    9580     icmpInEchoReps     =   5226
        icmpInTimestamps    =       0     icmpInTimestampReps =     0
        icmpInAddrMasks     =       0     icmpInAddrMaskReps =      0
        icmpInFragNeeded    =       0     icmpOutMsgs        =  11693
        icmpOutDrops        =  140883     icmpOutErrors      =      0
        icmpOutDestUnreachs =    2113     icmpOutTimeExcds   =      0
        icmpOutParmProbs    =       0     icmpOutSrcQuenchs  =      0
        icmpOutRedirects    =       0     icmpOutEchos       =      0
        icmpOutEchoReps     =    9580     icmpOutTimestamps  =      0
        icmpOutTimestampReps=       0     icmpOutAddrMasks   =      0
        icmpOutAddrMaskReps =       0     icmpOutFragNeeded  =      0
        icmpInOverflows     =       0
```

On the ICMP front, *icmpOutErrors* and *icmpInErrors* are both zero, although there were 2,113 *icmpOutDestUnreachs*, indicating that at some point, a network connection was not able to be made when requested. You can check this with the `traceroute` utility described in this chapter. It also is often useful to run a `cron` job to extract these figures to a file, and then to write a Perl script to compare the values of concern. This is because errors could possibly be masked by integers being "wrapped around" and starting at zero, after they reach values that are greater than the maximum available for a machine's architecture. However, this should not be a problem for the new 64-bit kernels available with Solaris 7, 8, and 9.

Command Reference

The following commands can be used to manage the network and associated devices.

traceroute

If the process of finding a route is difficult to conceptualize, Solaris provides the *traceroute* tool, to literally display the route taken by a packet between two hosts. The *traceroute* utility measures the time taken to reach each intermediate host from source to destination. If an intermediate host cannot be reached in a specified time period (usually the *ttl* "time to live" field), an error message is reported. A maximum number of hops (usually 30) is specified to prevent *traceroute* from looping infinitely if an operational route cannot be found. *traceroute* is also very useful for determining network points of failure due to misconfiguration and hardware problems. Here is an example of a *traceroute* between a host on the AT&T network and a host on the Sun network:

```
$ traceroute www.sun.com
Tracing route to wwwwseast.usec.sun.com [192.9.49.30]
over a maximum of 30 hops:
  1    184 ms    142 ms    138 ms   202.10.4.131
  2    147 ms    144 ms    138 ms   202.10.4.129
  3    150 ms    142 ms    144 ms   202.10.1.73
  4    150 ms    144 ms    141 ms   atm11.optus.net.au [202.139.32.17]
  5    148 ms    143 ms    139 ms   202.139.1.197
  6    490 ms    489 ms    474 ms   hssi9-0-0.sf1.optus.net.au [192.65.89.246]
  7    526 ms    480 ms    485 ms   g-sfd-br.gn.cwix.net [207.124.109.57]
  8    494 ms    482 ms    485 ms   core7.SanFrancisco.cw.net [204.70.10.9]
  9    483 ms    489 ms    484 ms   c2.SanFrancisco.cw.net [204.70.9.132]
 10    557 ms    552 ms    561 ms   xcore3.Boston.cw.net [204.70.150.81]
 11    566 ms    572 ms    554 ms   sun.Boston.cw.net [204.70.179.102]
 12    577 ms    574 ms    558 ms   wwwwseast.usec.sun.com [192.9.49.30]
Trace complete.
```

NETWORKING

ndd

ndd is used to set parameters for network protocols, including TCP, IP, UDP, and ARP. You can use it to modify the parameters associated with IP forwarding and routing. For example, let's look at the set of configurable parameters for TCP transmission:

```
# ndd /dev/tcp \?
?                               (read only)
tcp_close_wait_interval         (read and write)
tcp_conn_req_max_q              (read and write)
tcp_conn_req_max_q0             (read and write)
tcp_conn_req_min                (read and write)
tcp_conn_grace_period           (read and write)
tcp_cwnd_max                    (read and write)
tcp_debug                       (read and write)
tcp_smallest_nonpriv_port       (read and write)
tcp_ip_abort_cinterval          (read and write)
tcp_ip_abort_linterval          (read and write)
tcp_ip_abort_interval           (read and write)
tcp_ip_notify_cinterval         (read and write)
tcp_ip_notify_interval          (read and write)
tcp_ip_ttl                      (read and write)
tcp_keepalive_interval          (read and write)
tcp_maxpsz_multiplier           (read and write)
tcp_mss_def                     (read and write)
tcp_mss_max                     (read and write)
tcp_mss_min                     (read and write)
tcp_naglim_def                  (read and write)
tcp_rexmit_interval_initial     (read and write)
tcp_rexmit_interval_max         (read and write)
tcp_rexmit_interval_min         (read and write)
tcp_wroff_xtra                  (read and write)
tcp_deferred_ack_interval       (read and write)
tcp_snd_lowat_fraction          (read and write)
tcp_sth_rcv_hiwat               (read and write)
tcp_sth_rcv_lowat               (read and write)
tcp_dupack_fast_retransmit      (read and write)
tcp_ignore_path_mtu             (read and write)
tcp_rcv_push_wait               (read and write)
tcp_smallest_anon_port          (read and write)
tcp_largest_anon_port           (read and write)
```

```
tcp_xmit_hiwat                       (read and write)
tcp_xmit_lowat                       (read and write)
tcp_recv_hiwat                       (read and write)
tcp_recv_hiwat_minmss                (read and write)
tcp_fin_wait_2_flush_interval        (read and write)
tcp_co_min                           (read and write)
tcp_max_buf                          (read and write)
tcp_zero_win_probesize               (read and write)
tcp_strong_iss                       (read and write)
tcp_rtt_updates                      (read and write)
tcp_wscale_always                    (read and write)
tcp_tstamp_always                    (read and write)
tcp_tstamp_if_wscale                 (read and write)
tcp_rexmit_interval_extra            (read and write)
tcp_deferred_acks_max                (read and write)
tcp_slow_start_after_idle            (read and write)
tcp_slow_start_initial               (read and write)
tcp_co_timer_interval                (read and write)
tcp_extra_priv_ports                 (read only)
tcp_extra_priv_ports_add             (write only)
tcp_extra_priv_ports_del             (write only)
tcp_status                           (read only)
tcp_bind_hash                        (read only)
tcp_listen_hash                      (read only)
tcp_conn_hash                        (read only)
tcp_queue_hash                       (read only)
tcp_host_param                       (read and write)
tcp_1948_phrase                      (write only)
```

You can also set parameters for IP as well as TCP. For example, if the parameter *ip_forwarding* has a value of two (the default), it will only perform routing when two or more interfaces are active. However, if this parameter is set to zero, *ip_forwarding* will never be performed (i.e., to ensure that multihoming is enabled rather than routing). You can set this by using the following command:

```
# ndd -set /dev/ip ip_forwarding 0
```

Administrators should be aware that modifying ndd parameters for a specific purpose could interfere with other TCP services provided by the server. Proceed with caution!

NETWORKING

Chapter 21

System Logging, Accounting, and Tuning

A well-managed system needs to be continuously monitored for security, accounting, and performance purposes. Solaris 9 provides several built-in mechanisms for accounting for resource usage, which you can then further use with an automated billing procedure. This is very useful for Internet Service Providers and shared-use systems that must account for the resources utilized by users or groups. In addition, you can easily detect inappropriate usage of resources by unauthorized individuals, and you can limit utilization by enforcing quotas.

Key Concepts

In the following sections, we examine how to enable system logging, monitoring, and accounting.

System Logging

Syslog is a centralized logging facility that provides different classes of events that are logged to a log file, as well as providing an alerting service for certain events. Because *syslogd* is configurable by root, it is very flexible in its operations. Multiple log files can exist for each daemon whose activity is being logged, or a single log file can be created. The *syslog* service is controlled by the configuration file */etc/syslog.conf*, which is read at boot time, or whenever the *syslog* daemon receives a HUP signal. This file defines the facility levels or system source of logged messages and conditions. Priority levels are also assigned to system events recorded in the system log, while an action field defines what action is taken when a particular class of event is encountered. These events can range from normal system usage, such as FTP connections and remote shells, to system crashes.

The source facilities defined by Solaris are for the kernel (*kern*), authentication (*auth*), daemons (*daemon*), mail system (*mail*), print spooling (*lp*), and user processes (*user*). Priority levels are classified as system emergencies (*emerg*), errors requiring immediate attention (*attn*), critical errors (*crit*), messages (*info*), debugging output (*debug*), and other errors (*err*). These priority levels are defined for individual systems and architectures in <sys/syslog.h>. It is easy to see how logging applications, such as TCP wrappers, can take advantage of the different error levels and source facilities provided by *syslogd*.

On the Solaris platform, the *syslog* daemon depends on the *m4* macro processor being present. *m4* is typically installed with the software developer packages, and it is usually located in */usr/ccs/bin/m4*. This version has been installed by default since Solaris 2.4. Users should note that the *syslogd* supplied by Sun has been error-prone in previous releases. With early Solaris 2.*x* versions, the *syslog* daemon left behind zombie processes when alerting logged-in users (e.g., notifying root of an *emerg*). If *syslogd* does not work, check that *m4* exists and is in the path for root, and/or run the *syslogd* program interactively by invoking it with a *–d* parameter.

Quotas

Resource management is one of the administrator's key responsibilities, particularly where the availability of a service is the organization's primary source of income (or recognition). For example, if an application server requires 10MB of free disk space for internal caching of objects retrieved from a database, performance on the client side will suffer if this space is not available because a user decided to dump his collection of MP3 music files onto the system hard drive. If external users cannot access a service because of internal resource allocation problems, they are unlikely to continue using your service. There is also a possibility that a rogue user (or competitor) may attempt to disrupt your service by attempting any number of well-known exploits to reduce your provision of service to clients. In this section, we examine resource management strategies that are flexible enough to meet the needs of casual users, but which limit the potential for accidental or malicious resource misuse.

System Accounting

Solaris provides a centralized auditing service known as *system accounting*. This service is very useful for accounting for the various tasks that your system may be involved in—you can use it to monitor resource usage, troubleshoot system failures, isolate bottlenecks in the system, and assist in system security. In addition, system accounting acts as a real accounting service, and you can use it for billing in the commercial world. In this section, we review the major components of system accounting, including several applications and scripts that are responsible for preparing daily reports on connections, process, and disk load, and usage statements for users. Once you enable the appropriate script in */etc/init.d*, system accounting does not typically involve administrator intervention.

Performance

Measuring performance is a necessary task to determine whether current utilization levels require a system to be upgraded, and/or whether user applications and system services are executing as quickly and efficiently as possible. Solaris provides a wide variety of tools to tune and monitor the operation of individual devices and core system elements, and other tools which can be applied to improve performance. These tools work with the kernel, disk, memory, network, compilers, applications, and system services. An alternative to the tools provided with Solaris is to use the SymbEL tools developed by Adrian Cockroft and Richard Pettit (**www.sun.com/sun-on-net/performance/se3**), which are fully described in their book, *Sun Performance and Tuning*, published by Sun Microsystems Press, 1998. In this chapter, we examine how to use some of the standard Solaris tools to monitor performance, identify performance issues and bottlenecks, and implement new settings.

Procedures

The following procedures are commonly used to manage log files, quotas, and accounting.

NETWORKING

Examining Log Files

Log files are fairly straightforward in their contents, and you can stipulate what events are recorded by instructions in the *syslog.conf* file. Records of mail messages can be useful for billing purposes and for detecting the bulk sending of unsolicited commercial e-mail (spam). The system log will record the details supplied by *sendmail*: a message-id, when a message is sent or received, a destination, and a delivery result, which is typically "delivered" or "deferred." Connections are usually deferred when a connection to a site is down. *Sendmail* will usually try to redeliver failed deliveries in four-hour intervals.

When using TCP wrappers, connections to supported Internet daemons are also logged. For example, an FTP connection to a server will result in the connection time and date being recorded, along with the hostname of the client. A similar result is achieved for telnet connections.

A delivered mail message is recorded as

```
Feb 20 14:07:05 server sendmail[238]: AA00238:
 message-id=<bulk.11403.19990219175554@sun.com>
Feb 20 14:07:05 server sendmail[238]: AA00238:
 from=<sun-developers-l@sun.com>,
size=1551, class=0, received from gateway.site.com (172.16.1.1)
Feb 20 14:07:06 server sendmail[243]: AA00238:
 to=<pwatters@mail.site.com>,
 delay=00:00:01, stat=Sent, mailer=local
```

whereas a deferred mail message is recorded differently:

```
Feb 21 07:11:10 server sendmail[855]: AA00855: message
-id=<Pine.SOL.3.96.990220200723.5291A-100000@oracle.com>
Feb 21 07:11:10 server sendmail[855]: AA00855: from=<support@oracle.com>,
 size=1290, class=0, received from gateway.site.com (172.16.1.1)
Feb 21 07:12:25 server sendmail[857]: AA00855: to=pwatters@mail.site.com,
 delay=00:01:16, stat=Deferred: Connection timed out during user open with
 mail.site.com, mailer=TCP
```

A FTP connection is recorded in a single line,

```
Feb 20 14:35:00 server in.ftpd[277]: connect from workstation.site.com
```

in the same way that a telnet connection is recorded:

```
Feb 20 14:35:31 server in.telnetd[279]: connect from workstation.site.com
```

Implementing Quotas

Solaris provides a number of tools to enforce policies on disk and resource usage, based around the idea of quotas, or a prespecified allocation of disk space for each user and file system. Thus, a single user can have disk space allocated on different slices, and file systems can have quotas either enabled or disabled (they are disabled by default). Although many organizations disable disk quotas for fear of reducing productivity by placing unnecessary restrictions on the development staff, there are often some very good reasons for implementing quotas on specific slices. For example, if an open file area, like an anonymous FTP "incoming" directory, is located on the same partition as normal user data, a denial-of-service attack could be initiated by a rogue user who decides to fill the incoming directory with large files, until all free space is consumed. Or, a CGI application that writes data to a user's home directory (for example, a guestbook) can also fall victim to a denial-of-service attack: a malicious script could be written to enter a million fake entries into the address book, thereby filling the partition to capacity. The result in both of these cases is loss of service and loss of system control. It is therefore important that networked systems have appropriate checks and balances in place to ensure that such situations are avoided.

Quotas are also critical to ensure fair resource sharing among developers. Otherwise, a developer who decides to back up his PC drive to his home directory on a server, completely filling the partition, could thereby prevent other users from writing data.

In addition to security concerns, enforcing quotas is also optimal from an administrative point of view: It forces users to rationalize their own storage requirements so that material that is not being used can be moved offline or deleted. This saves administrators from having to make such decisions for users (who may be dismayed at the results if the administrator has to move things in a hurry!).

One simple policy is to enforce disk quotas on all public file systems that have network access. Increasing quotas for all users is easy, therefore the policy can be flexible. In addition, quotas can be hard or soft: *Hard* quotas strictly enforce incursions into unallocated territory, whereas *soft* quotas provide a buffer for temporary violations of a quota, and the users are given warning before enforcement begins. Depending on the security level at which your organization operates (for example, C2 standards for military organizations), a quota policy may already be available for you to implement.

A total limit on the amount of disk space available to users can be specified using quotas for each user individually. Let's take the user *pwatters* on *server* as an example. You may allot this user, a Java developer, a quota of 10MB for development work on the */staff* file system. To set up this quota, you need to undertake the following steps:

1. Edit the */etc/vfstab* file as root, and add the *rq* flag to the *mount* options field for the */staff* file system. This enables quotas for the file system.

2. Change directory to */staff*, and create a file called *quotas*.

3. Set permissions on */staff/quotas* to be read and write for root only.

4. Edit user quotas for user *pwatters* on file system */staff* by using the edquota command, and entering the number of inodes and 1KB blocks that will be available to user *pwatters*. For example, enter the following:

   fs /staff blocks (soft = 10000, hard = 11000) inodes (soft = 0, hard = 0)

5. Check the settings that you have created by using the quota command.

6. Enable the quota for user *pwatters* by using the quotaon command.

You can implement these steps by entering the following:

```
# vi /etc/vfstab
# cd /staff
 # touch quotas
 # chmod u+rw quotas
 # edquota pwatters
 # quota -v pwatters
 # quotaon /staff
```

When you verify the quotas using `quota -v`,

```
# quota -v pwatters
```

the output should look like the following:

```
Disk quotas for pwatters (uid 1001):
Filesystem     usage  quota  limit     timeleft  files  quota
/staff             0  10000  11000            0      0      0
```

You can see that a soft limit of 10MB and a hard limit of 11MB was entered for user *pwatters*. If halfway through the development project, this user requests more space, you could adjust the quota by using the `edquota` command again. To check quotas for all users, use the `repquota` command:

```
# repquota /staff

Block limits
User              used   soft    hard
jsmith      --    2048   4096    8192
pwatters    --     131  10000   20000
qjones      --   65536  90000  100000
llee        --    4096   8192   10000
```

If a user attempts to exceed his or her quota during an interactive session, unless you've set up a warning to be issued under those circumstances, the first indication that the user will have will often come in the form of a "file system full" or "write failed" message. After checking the amount of free space on the partition where their home disk is located, many users are at a loss to explain why they can no longer edit files or send e-mail!

Collecting Accounting Data

Collecting data for accounting is simple: Create a startup script (*/etc/rc2.d/S22acct*) in order to begin collecting data soon after the system enters multi-user mode, and optionally, create a kill script (*/etc/rc0.d/K22acct*) to turn off data collection cleanly before the system shuts down. As per standard System V practice, you should create a single script in */etc/init.d* (e.g., */etc/init.d/accounting*) and link it symbolically to both of those filenames, thus ensuring that both a *start* and a *stop* parameter can be interpreted by the script. When accounting is enabled, details of processes, storage, and user activity are recorded in specially created log files, which are then processed daily by the */usr/lib/acct/runacct* program. The output from *runacct* is also processed by */usr/lib/acct/prdaily* (which generates the reports described in the next section). There is also a separate monthly billing program called */usr/lib/acct/monacct*, which is executed monthly and generates accounts for individual users.

The accounting file startup and shutdown script should look like this:

```
parameter=$1
case $parameter in
'start')
        echo "Initializing process accounting"
           /usr/lib/acct/startup
           ;;
'stop')
           echo "Halting process accounting"
           /usr/lib/acct/shutacct
           ;;
esac
```

When called with the *start* parameter, this script executes another script, */usr/lib/acct/startup*, which is responsible for executing the */usr/lib/acct/acctwtmp* program, which sets up record-writing utilities in the */var/adm/wtmp* file. It then starts a script called *turnacct*, which is called with the name of the file in which the kernel records the process accounting details (usually named */var/adm/pacct.*). Finally, the startup section of the script removes all the temporary files associated with previous accounting activities.

Collecting Performance Data

The following applications are commonly used to measure system performance:

iostat	Collects data about input/output operations for CPUs, disks, terminals, and tapes from the command line
vmstat	Collects data on virtual memory performance from the command line and prints a summary

| *mpstat* | Breaks down CPU usage per operation type |
| *sar* | Runs through `cron` or the command line to collect statistics on disk, tape, CPU, buffering, input/output, system calls, interprocess communication, and many other variables |

The following sections examine how each of these commands is used.

iostat

The kernel maintains low-level counters to measure various operations, which you can access by using *iostat*. When you first execute it, *iostat* reports statistics gathered since booting. Subsequently, the difference between the first report and the current state is reported for all statistics. Thus, when you run it at regular intervals (such as each minute), you can obtain high-resolution samples for establishing system performance within a specific epoch by using *iostat*. This can be very useful for gaining an accurate picture of how system resources are allocated.

To display statistics disk usage statistics, the following command produces ten reports over epochs of 60 seconds:

```
# iostat -x 60 10
device r/s w/s kr/s kw/s wait actv svc_ t %w %b
sd0     0.2 0.4 12.2 9.0  1.0  2.0  38.6   0  1
. . .
device r/s w/s kr/s kw/s wait actv svc_t %w %b
sd0     0.3 0.3 12.5 8.0  2.0  1.0  33.2   0  1
. . .
```

Let's review what each column indicates for the disk device:

device	Shows the device name (*sd1* indicates a disk)
r/s	Displays the number of disk reads per second
w/s	Prints the number of disk writes per second
kr/s	Shows the total amount of data read per second (in kilobytes)
kw/s	Displays the total amount of data written per second (in kilobytes)
wait	Prints the mean number of waiting transactions
actv	Shows the mean number of transactions being processed
svc_t	Displays the mean period for service in milliseconds
%w	Prints the percentage of time spent waiting
%b	Shows the percentage of time that the disk is working

To display statistics for the CPU at second intervals 20 times, you could use the following command:

```
# iostat -c 1 20
```

The output would display four columns, showing user time, system time, I/O wait, and idle time, respectively, in percentage terms.

vmstat

One of the greatest performance issues in system tuning is virtual memory capacity and performance. Obviously, if your server is using large amounts of swap, running off a slow disk, the time to perform various operations will increase. One application that reports on the current state of virtual memory is the vmstat command, which displays a large collection of statistics concerning virtual memory performance. As you can see from the following display, the virtual memory report on the server is not encouraging: 1,346,736,431 total address translation faults were recorded, as well as 38,736,546 major faults, 1,346,736,431 minor faults, and 332,163,181 copy-on-write faults. This suggests that more virtual memory is required to support operations, or at least the disk on which the swap partition is placed should be upgraded to 10,000 RPM:

```
# vmstat -s
        253 swap ins
    237 swap outs
    253 pages swapped in
 705684 pages swapped out
1346736431 total address trans. faults taken
 56389345 page ins
 23909231 page outs
152308597 pages paged in
 83982504 pages paged out
 26682276 total reclaims
 26199677 reclaims from free list
        0 micro (hat) faults
1346736431 minor (as) faults
 38736546 major faults
332163181 copy-on-write faults
316702360 zero fill page faults
 99616426 pages examined by the clock daemon
      782 revolutions of the clock hand
126834545 pages freed by the clock daemon
 14771875 forks
  3824010 vforks
 29303326 execs
```

```
160142153 cpu context switches
2072002374 device interrupts
3735561061 traps
2081699655 system calls
1167634213 total name lookups (cache hits 70%)
 46612294 toolong
964665958 user    cpu
399229996 system cpu
1343911025 idle    cpu
227505892 wait    cpu
```

mpstat

Another factor influencing performance is the system load—obviously, on a system that runs a large number of processes and consistently has a load of greater than 1.0 cannot be relied upon to give adequate performance in times of need. You can use the mpstat command to examine a number of system parameters, including the system load, over a number of regular intervals. Many administrators take several hundred samples using *mpstat* and compute an average system load for specific times of the day when a peak load is expected (e.g., at 9 A.M.). This can greatly assist in capacity planning of CPUs to support expanding operations. Fortunately, SPARC hardware architectures support large numbers of CPUs, so it's not difficult to scale up to meet the demand.

The output from *mpstat* contains several columns, which measure the following parameters:

- Context switches
- Cross-calls between CPUs
- Idle percentage of CPU time
- Interrupts
- Minor and major faults
- Sys percentage of CPU time
- Thread migrations
- User percentage of CPU time

For the server output shown next, the proportion of system time consumed is well below 100 percent—the peak value is 57 percent for only one of the CPUs in this dual-processor system. Sustained values of *sys* at or near the 100-percent level indicate that you should add more CPUs to the system:

```
# mpstat 5
CPU minf mjf xcal intr ithr  csw icsw migr smtx  srw syscl  usr sys  wt idl
  0   46   1  250   39  260  162   94   35  104    0    75   31  14   8  47
  1   45   1   84  100  139  140   92   35  102    0    14   35  13   7  45
```

```
CPU minf mjf xcal intr ithr  csw icsw migr smtx  srw syscl  usr sys  wt idl
  0  141   3  397  591  448  539  233   38  111    0 26914   64  35   1   0
  1  119   0 1136  426  136  390  165   40  132    0 21371   67  33   0   0
CPU minf mjf xcal intr ithr  csw icsw migr smtx  srw syscl  usr sys  wt idl
  0    0   0  317  303  183  367  163   28   63    0  1110   94   6   0   0
  1    0   0    4  371  100  340  148   27   86    0 56271   43  57   0   0
```

sar

The sar command is the most versatile method for collecting system performance data. From the command line, it produces a number of snapshots of current system activity over a specified number of time intervals. Or, if you don't specify an interval, the current day's data extracted from sar's regular execution by cron is used. For example, to display a summary of disk activity for the current day, you can use the following command:

```
# sar -d
SunOS 5.9 sun4u    01/25/02
09:54:33   device   %busy   avque   r+w/s   blk/s   avwait   avserv
              sd01      27     5.8       6       8     21.6     28.6
              sd03      17     2.4       4       7     14.2     21.2
              sd05      13     1.7       3       6      9.3     18.3
              sd06      35     6.9       8      10     25.7     31.8
```

In this example, you can see that several disk devices are shown with varying percentages of busy time, mean number of transaction requests in the queue, mean number of disk reads and writes per second, mean number of disk blocks written per second, mean time for waiting in the queue, and mean time for service in the queue.

When a new disk, memory, or CPU is added to the system, you should take a baseline sar report to determine the effect on performance. For example, after adding an 128MB RAM on the system, you should be able to quantify the effect on mean system performance by comparing sar output before and after the event during a typical day's workload.

Examples

The following examples show how to manage log files, quotas, and accounting.

Logging Disk Usage

For auditing purposes, many sites generate a *df* report at midnight or during a change of administrator shifts, to record a snapshot of the system. In addition, if disk space is becoming an issue, and extra volumes need to be justified in a systems budget, it is useful to be able to estimate how rapidly disk space is being consumed by users. Using the cron utility, you can set up and schedule a script using crontab to check disk space at different time periods and to mail this information to the administrator (or even post it to a Web site, if system administration is centrally managed).

A simple script to monitor disk space usage and mail the results to the system administrator (*root@server*) looks like this:

```
#!/bin/csh -f
df | mailx -s "Disk Space Usage" root@localhost
```

As an example, if this script were named */usr/local/bin/monitor_usage.csh*, and executable permissions were set for the *nobody* user, you could create the following crontab entry for the *nobody* user to run at midnight every night of the week:

```
0 0 * * * /usr/local/bin/monitor_usage.csh
```

Or, you could make the script more general so that users could specify another user who would be mailed:

```
#!/bin/csh -f
df | mailx -s "Disk Space Usage" $1
```

The crontab entry would then look like this:

```
0 0 * * * /usr/local/bin/monitor_usage.csh remote_user@client
```

The results of the disk usage report would now be sent to the user *remote_user@client* instead of *root@localhost*.

You can find further information on the cron utility and submitting cron jobs in Chapter 13.

Another way of obtaining disk space usage information with more directory-by-directory detail is by using the */usr/bin/du* command. This command prints the sum of the sizes of every file in the current directory and performs the same task recursively for any subdirectories. The size is calculated by adding together all of the file sizes in the directory, where the size for each file is rounded up to the next 512-byte block. For example, taking a du of the */etc* directory looks like this:

```
# du /etc

14      ./default
7       ./cron.d
6       ./dfs
8       ./dhcp
```

```
201      ./fs/hsfs
681      ./fs/nfs
1        ./fs/proc
209      ./fs/ufs
1093     ./fs

...
2429     .
```

Thus, */etc* and all its subdirectories contain a total of 2,429KB of data. Of course, this kind of output is fairly verbose and probably not much use in its current form. If you were only interested in *recording* the directory sizes in order to collect data for auditing and usage analysis, you could write a short Perl script to collect the data, as follows:

```perl
#!/usr/local/bin/perl
# directorysize.pl: reads in directory size for current directory
# and prints results to standard output
@du = `du`;
for (@du)
{
($sizes,$directories)=split /\s+/, $_;
print "$sizes\n";
}
```

If you saved this script as *directorysize.pl* in the */usr/local/bin/directory* and set the executable permissions, it would produce a list of directory sizes as output, like the following:

```
# cd /etc
 # /usr/local/bin/directorysize.pl

28
14
12
16
402
1362
2
418
2186
...
```

Because you are interested in usage management, you might want to modify the script to display the total amount of space occupied by a directory and its subdirectories, as well as the average amount of space occupied. The latter is very important when evaluating caching or investigating load balancing issues:

```perl
#!/usr/local/bin/perl
# directorysize.pl: reads in directory size for current directory
# and prints the sum and average disk space used to standard output
$sum=0;
$count=0;
@ps = `du -o`;
for (@ps)
{
  ($sizes,$directories)=split /\s+/, $_;
  $sum=$sum+$sizes;
  $count=$count+1;
}
print "Total Space: $sum K\n";
print "Average Space: $count K\n";
```

Note that du -o was used as the command so that the space occupied by subdirectories is not added to the total for the top-level directory. The output from the command for */etc* now looks like this:

```
# cd /etc
 # /usr/local/bin/directorysize.pl
Total Space: 4832 K
Average Space: 70 K
```

Again, you could set up a cron job to mail this information to an administrator at midnight every night. To do this, first create a new shell script to call the Perl script, which is made more flexible by passing the directory to be measured, and the user to which the mail will be sent as arguments:

```csh
#!/bin/csh -f
cd $1
/usr/local/bin/directorysize.pl | mailx -s "Directory Space Usage" $2
```

If you save this script to */usr/local/bin/checkdirectoryusage.csh* and set the executable permission, you could then schedule a disk space check of a cache file system. You could include a second command that sends a report for the */disks/junior_developers* file system, which is remotely mounted from *client*, to the team leader on *server*:

```
0 0 * * * /usr/local/bin/checkdirectoryusage.csh /cache squid@server
1 0 * * * /usr/local/bin/checkdirectoryusage.csh /disks/junior_developers
team_leader@server
```

NETWORKING

Note	*Tools may already be available on Solaris to perform some of these tasks more directly. For example, du –s will return the sum of directory sizes automatically. However, the purpose of this section has been to demonstrate how to customize and develop your own scripts for file system management.*

Generating Accounting Reports

Once you have enabled data collection, generating reports is a simple matter of setting up a cron job for a nonprivileged user (usually *adm*), typically at a time of low system load. In the following example, accounting runs are performed at 6 A.M.:

```
0 6 * * * /usr/lib/acct/runacct 2> /var/adm/acct/nite/fd2log
```

Accounting runs involve several discrete stages, which are executed in the following order:

SETUP	Prepares accounting files for running the report
WTMPFIX	Checks the soundness of the *wtmpx* file and repairs it, if necessary
CONNECT	Gathers data for user connect time
PROCESS	Gathers data for process usage
MERGE	Integrates the connection and process data
FEES	Gathers fee information and applies to connection and process data
DISK	Gathers data on disk usage and integrates with fee, connection, and process data
MERGETACCT	Integrates accounting data for the past 24 hours (*daytacct*) with the total accounting data (*/var/adm/acct/sum/tacct*)
CMS	Generates command summaries
CLEANUP	Removes transient data and cleans up before terminating

After each stage of *runacct* has been successfully completed, the *statefile* (*/var/adm/acct/nite/statefile*) is overwritten with the name of that stage. Thus, if the accounting is disrupted for any reason, it can be easily resumed by rereading the *statefile*. On 23 January, if the *statefile* contained *FEES* but terminated during *DISK*, you could restart the accounting run for the day by using the following command:

```
# runacct 2301 DISK >> /var/adm/acct/nite/fd2log
```

Once the daily run has been completed, the *lastdate* file is updated with the current date in *ddmm* format, where *dd* is the day and *mm* is the month of the last run. In addition, you can review a number of files manually to obtain usage summaries. For example, the daily report is stored in a file called *rprtddmm*, where *dd* is the day and *mm* is the month of the run. This contains the *cms* and *lastlogin* data, as well as a connection usage summary:

```
Jan 26 02:05 2002  DAILY REPORT FOR johnson Page 1
from Fri Jan 25 02:05:23 2002
to   Sat Jan 26 02:05:54 2002


TOTAL DURATION IS 46 MINUTES
LINE          MINUTES  PERCENT  # SESS  # ON  # OFF
/dev/pts/1    0        0        0       0     0
pts/1         46       0        8       8     8
TOTALS        46       --       8       8     8
```

Here, you can see that the total connection time for the previous day was 46 minutes.

Login Logging

The *loginlog* file contains a list of the last login dates for all local users. Some system accounts appear as never having logged in, which is expected:

```
00-00-00   adm
00-00-00   bin
00-00-00   daemon
00-00-00   listen
00-00-00   lp
00-00-00   noaccess
00-00-00   nobody
00-00-00   nuucp
00-00-00   smtp
00-00-00   sys
02-01-20   root
02-01-26   pwatters
```

You should check the *loginlog* file for access to system accounts, which should never be accessed, and for unexpected usage of user accounts.

Command Summaries

A typical command summary (*cms*) statement generated by the *runacct* program is shown in Table 21-1.

COMMAND NAME	NUMBER CMDS	TOTAL KCORE MIN	TOTAL CPU MIN	TOTAL REALMIN	MEAN SIZE-K	MEAN CPU-MIN	HOG FACTOR	CHARS TRNSFRD	BLOCKS READ
TOTALS	1034	1843.03	0.46	546.88	4049.14	0.00	0.00	107141376	982
Pine	5	1426.41	0.11	177.47	13477.87	0.02	0.00	72782400	237
sendmail	171	176.44	0.09	4.73	1873.71	0.00	0.02	14895311	306
sh	107	31.15	0.04	0.29	881.70	0.00	0.12	58380	0
Uudemon	114	27.91	0.02	0.10	1154.92	0.00	0.24	67765	8
in.ftpd	1	23.20	0.02	0.69	1435.05	0.02	0.02	6422528	7
mail.loc	13	19.69	0.02	0.06	1193.21	0.00	0.27	11973498	57
tcsh	4	13.61	0.01	179.98	1361.33	0.00	0.00	153040	1
uuxqt	48	11.01	0.01	0.08	1159.30	0.00	0.13	35568	0
Uusched	48	10.99	0.01	0.09	1014.52	0.00	0.13	36096	180
popper	9	7.84	0.01	1.55	1205.74	0.00	0.00	155107	32
sed	58	7.63	0.01	0.02	618.38	0.00	0.58	44907	2
date	34	7.26	0.01	0.01	821.74	0.00	0.72	26348	1
rm	36	5.68	0.01	0.02	681.44	0.00	0.45	0	8
Acctcms	4	4.92	0.01	0.01	953.03	0.00	0.97	125984	1
in.telne	4	4.85	0.00	180.03	1076.74	0.00	0.00	55744	0
cp	42	4.47	0.01	0.02	525.65	0.00	0.36	14434	60
Ckpacct	24	4.23	0.00	0.09	907.14	0.00	0.05	49200	0
awk	26	4.01	0.01	0.02	616.82	0.00	0.36	950	0
chmod	37	3.69	0.01	0.01	553.60	0.00	0.55	0	0
cat	22	3.58	0.00	0.01	825.54	0.00	0.55	1540	2
Acctprc	1	2.98	0.00	0.00	744.00	0.00	0.96	46152	0

Table 21-1.   A Typical Command Summary (cms) Statement

NETWORKING

Once you know what each column in this report represents, it becomes obvious that in this example, reading, sending, and receiving mail are the main uses of this server, on a daily basis at least, while the *runacct* command, which actually performs the accounting, was one of the least used programs. Here is an explanation of the columns in the preceding report:

- **COMMAND NAME**   Shows the command as executed. This can lead to some ambiguity, because different commands could have the same filename. In addition, any shell or Perl scripts executed would be displayed under the shell and Perl interpreter respectively, rather than showing up as a process on their own.

- **NUMBER CMNDS**   Displays the number of times that the command named under COMMAND NAME was executed during the accounting period.

- **TOTAL KCOREMIN**   Shows the cumulative sum of memory segments (in kilobytes) used by the process identified under COMMAND NAME per minute of execution time.

- **TOTAL CPU-MIN**   Prints the accumulated processing time for the program named under COMMAND NAME.

- **TOTAL REAL-MIN**   Shows the actual time in minutes that the program named in COMMAND NAME consumed during the accounting period.

- **MEAN SIZE-K**   Indicates the average of the cumulative sum of consumed memory segments (TOTAL KCOREMIN) over the set of invocations denoted by NUMBER CMDS.

- **MEAN CPU-MIN**   The average CPU time computed from the quotient of NUMBER CMDS divided by TOTAL CPU-MIN.

- **HOG FACTOR**   The amount of CPU time divided by actual elapsed time. This ratio indicates the degree to which a system is available compared to its use. The hog factor is often used as a metric to determine overall load levels for a system, and it is useful for planning upgrades and expansion.

- **CHARS TRNSFD**   Displays the sum of the characters transferred by system calls.

- **BLOCKS READ**   Shows the number of physical block reads and writes that the program named under COMMAND NAME accounted for.

Often, the values of these parameters are confusing. For example, let's compare the characteristics of *pine*, which is a mail client, and *sendmail*, which is a mail transport agent. *pine* was executed only five times, but accounted for 1426.41 KCOREMIN, while *sendmail* was executed 171 times with a KCOREMIN of 176.44. The explanation for this apparent anomaly is that users probably log in once in the morning and leave their pine mail client running all day. The users sent an average of 34.2 messages during this day, many of which contained attachments, thus accounting for the high CPU overhead.

monacct

When examined over a number of days, accounting figures provide a useful means of understanding how processes are making use of the system's resources. When examined in isolation, however, they can sometimes misrepresent the dominant processes that the machine is used for. This is a well-known aspect of statistical sampling: Before you can make any valid generalizations about a phenomenon, your observations must be repeated and sampled randomly. Thus, it is useful to compare the day-to-day variation of a system's resource use with the monthly figures that are generated by */usr/lib/acct/monacct*. Compare these daily values with the previous month's values generated by *monacct* in Table 21-2.

As you can see in Table 21-2, the individual day's figures were misleading. In fact, spread over a whole month, the *netscape* program tended to use more resources than the *pine* mail client, being invoked 1,538 times, and using 163985.79 KCOREMIN, compared to 165 invocations and 43839.27 KCOREMIN for *pine*. Clearly, it is very useful to examine monthly averages for a more reliable, strategic overview of system activity, while daily summaries are useful for making tactical decisions about active processes.

Charging Fees Using Accounting

In the previous section, we looked at the output for *monacct*, which is the monthly accounting program. To enable *monacct*, you need to create a `cron` job for the *adm* account, which is similar to the entry for the `runacct` command in the previous section:

```
0 5 1 * * /usr/lib/acct/monacct
```

In addition to computing per-process statistics, *monacct* also computes usage information on a per-user basis, which you can use to bill customers according to the number of CPU minutes they used. Examine the user reports in Table 21-3 for the same month that was reviewed in the previous section.

COMMAND NAME	NUMBER CMDS	TOTAL KCOREMIN	TOTAL CPU MIN	TOTAL REALMIN	MEAN SIZE-K	MEAN CPU-MIN	HOG FACTOR	CHARS TRNSFRD	BLOCKS READ
TOTALS	513833	529119.94	262.83	632612.94	2013.17	0.00	0.00	8955614208	138299
nscp	1538	163985.79	6.77	59865.58	24233.18	0.00	0.00	4744854	720
Installp	110508	58676.62	33.65	197.77	1743.57	0.00	0.17	27303024	139
Sed	122726	45704.45	40.87	98.07	1118.16	0.00	0.42	20044188	171
Pine	165	43839.27	3.88	1594.97	11304.12	0.02	0.00	157816160	4675
Project	13	37654.92	22.76	22.79	1654.41	1.75	1.00	6187332	106
ll-ar	4	24347.44	26.49	50.37	919.24	6.62	0.53	201642	5
nawk	75544	21678.96	24.46	40.21	886.40	0.00	0.61	61351684	135
predict	289	16808.70	13.59	13.74	1236.66	0.05	0.99	38996306	293
Sqpe	17	15078.86	4.15	10.30	3636.67	0.24	0.40	90547712	889
Grep	71963	13042.15	18.69	26.47	697.69	0.00	0.71	377825714	3
Pkgparam	24578	11360.71	9.11	9.68	1246.38	0.00	0.94	102325648	0
false_ne	7	10399.85	2.12	2.13	4899.81	0.30	1.00	212530	5
pkgremov	89	10073.67	8.95	22.70	1125.88	0.10	0.39	1129787392	18845
pkginsta	125	7163.67	4.75	38.21	1508.46	0.04	0.12	1912983552	4077
tee	8622	3237.38	2.03	2.30	1592.24	0.00	0.88	2134692	0
ls	8825	3133.31	2.59	3.31	1209.06	0.00	0.78	2038136	215

Table 21-2. *Monthly Account Summary*

UID	LOGIN NAME	CPU (MINS) PRIME	KCORE-MINS NPRIME	CONNECT (MINS) PRIME	DISK NPRIME	# OF PRIME	# OF NPRIME	# DISK BLOCKS	FEE PROCS	SESS	SAMPLES
TOTAL	233	30	363969	158762	1061	1005	11830502	513833	134	45	0
0	root	157	4	180984	3881	546	0	1858608	444602	3	3
1	daemon	0	0	0	0	0	0	6	0	0	3
2	bin	0	0	0	0	0	0	5759280	0	0	3
3	sys	0	0	114	89	0	0	18	51	0	3
4	adm	1	7	618	4856	0	0	15136	20005	0	3
5	uucp	1	4	1371	3557	0	0	5088	22036	0	3
10	pwatters	65	6	104572	15758	197	88	2026666	1842	68	3
12	llee	0	0	0	0	0	0	12	0	0	3
71	lp	0	0	0	26	0	0	13822	134	0	3
108	jsmith	0	0	0	0	0	0	318	0	0	3
436	dbrown	0	0	0	0	0	0	48	0	0	3
1001	bjones	0	0	16	9	0	2	78	21	2	3
1002	ledwards	0	0	130	21	0	0	34	102	0	3
1003	tgonzale	0	0	0	0	0	0	40896	0	0	3
1012	ljung	5	10	74282	130564	318	915	2110492	3521	61	3
60001	nobody	3	0	1883	0	0	0	0	21519	0	0

Table 21-3.   Charging Fees Using Accounting

Of the nonsystem users, obviously *pwatters* is going to have a large bill this month, with 65 prime CPU minutes consumed. Billing could also proceed on the basis of KCOREMINS utilized; *pwatters*, in this case, used 104572 KCOREMINS. How an organization bills its users is probably already well-established, but even if users are not billed for cash payment, examining how the system is used is very valuable for planning expansion and for identifying rogue processes that reduce the availability of a system for legitimate processes.

Performance Tuning

In previous sections, we've examined how to use tools such as *sar*, *vmstat*, and *iostat* to measure system performance before and after key events such as adding new RAM or CPUs or upgrading disks to faster speeds. In addition to these hardware changes, it is possible to increase the performance of an existing system by tuning the kernel. This could involve switching from a 32-bit to a 64-bit kernel, if supported by hardware, and setting appropriate parameters for shared memory, semaphores, and message queues in */etc/system*. However, note that the Solaris 9 kernel is self-tuning to some extent for normal operations. Once database servers with special requirements are installed, or many users must be supported on a single system, it may be necessary to tweak some parameters and reboot.

If a system is slow, the process list is the first place to look, as described in Chapter 13. One of the reasons that so much space is devoted to process management in this book is that it is often user processes, rather than system CPU time, that adversely impact system performance. The only time that kernel tuning will really assist occurs when shared memory and other parameters need to be adjusted for database applications, or where system time for processes far exceeds the user time. This can generally be established by using the `time` command. We examine some commonly modified parameters in the */etc/system* file shortly, which you can use to improve system performance. After you make changes to */etc/system*, you need to reboot the system. You need to take caution: If a syntax error is detected in */etc/system*, the system may not be able to be booted.

The first step in tuning the kernel is generally to set the maximum number of processes permitted per user to a sensible value. This is a hard limit that prevents individual users from circumventing limits imposed by quotas and nice values set by the super-user. To insert a maximum of 100 processes per user, you need to make the following entry in */etc/system*:

```
set maxuprc=100
```

If you are running a database server, your manual will no doubt supply minimum requirements for shared memory for the server. Shared memory is memory that can be locked but can be shared between processes, thereby reducing overhead for memory allocation. You can set the following parameters to determine how shared memory is allocated:

shmmax	The peak shared memory amount
shmmin	The smallest shared memory amount
shmmni	The largest number of concurrent identifiers permitted
shmseg	The quantity of segments permitted for each process
semmap	The initial quantity of entries in the semaphore map
semmni	The largest number of semaphore sets permitted
semmns	The total number of semaphores permitted
semmsl	The largest number of semaphores in each semaphore set

The following example entry for */etc/system* allocates 128MB of shared memory and sets other parameters appropriately:

```
set shmsys:shminfo_shmmax=134217728
set shmsys:shminfo_shmmin=100
set shmsys:shminfo_shmmni=100
set shmsys:shminfo_shmseg=100
set semsys:seminfo_semmap=125
set semsys:seminfo_semmni=250
set semsys:seminfo_semmns=250
```

Command Reference

The following commands are commonly used to manage log files, quotas, and accounting.

The syslog.conf *File*

The file */etc/syslog.conf* contains information used by the system log daemon, *syslogd*, to forward a system message to appropriate log files and/or users. *syslogd* preprocesses this file through *m4* to obtain the correct information for certain log files, defining LOGHOST if the address of "loghost" is the same as one of the addresses of the host that is running *syslogd*.

The default *syslogd* configuration is not optimal for all installations. Many configuration decisions depend on the degree to which the system administrator wishes to be alerted immediately should an alert or emergency occur, or whether it is sufficient for all auth notices to be logged, and a `cron` job run every night to filter the results for a review in the morning. For noncommercial installations, the latter is probably a reasonable approach. A `crontab` entry like the following.

```
0 1 * * * cat /var/adm/messages | grep auth | mail root
```

will send the root user a mail message at 1 A.M. every morning with all authentication messages.

A basic *syslog.conf* should contain provision for sending emergency notices to all users, as well as alters to the root user, and other nonprivileged administrator accounts. Errors, kernel notices, and authentication notices probably need to be displayed on the system console. It is generally sufficient to log daemon notices, alerts, and all other authentication information to the system log file, unless the administrator is watching for cracking attempts, as shown here:

```
*.alert                                             root,pwatters
*.emerg                                             *
*.err;kern.notice;auth.notice                       /dev/console
daemon.notice                          /var/adm/messages
auth.none;kern.err;daemon.err;mail.crit;*.alert    /var/adm/messages
auth.info                                          /var/adm/authlog
```

The
Complete
Reference

Chapter 22

Device Management

One of the most important but most challenging roles of a system administrator is device management. Devices, in this context, can be defined as both physical and logical entities that together constitute a hardware system. Although some operating systems hide device configuration details from all users (even administrators!) in proprietary binary formats, Solaris device configuration is easy to use, with configuration information stored in special files, known as *device files*. In addition to providing the technical background on how device files operate, and how device drivers can be installed, this chapter provides practical advice on installing standard devices, such as new hard drives, as well as more modern media, like CD-Rs and Zip drives.

Solaris 9 now supports the dynamic reconfiguration of many system devices on some SPARC platforms, particularly in the medium-level server range (e.g., E450) and above. This allows administrators to remove faulty hardware components and replace them, without having to power down a system, and perform a reconfiguration boot, which is necessary for older systems. This is particularly significant for systems that have high redundancy of system components to guarantee uptime under all but the most critical of circumstances.

Key Concepts

The following key concepts are central to understanding devices.

Device Files

Device files are special files that represent devices in Solaris 9. Device files reside in the */dev* directory, and its subdirectories (such as */dev/dsk*), while the */devices* directory is a tree that completely characterizes the hardware layout of the system in the file system namespace. Although it may seem initially confusing that separate directories exist for devices and for system hardware, the difference between the two systems will become apparent in the discussion that follows. Solaris 9 refers to both physical and logical devices in three separate ways, with physical device names, physical device files, and logical device names. Physical device names are easily identified because they are long strings that provide all details relevant to the physical installation of the device. Every physical device has a physical name. For example, an SBUS could have the name */sbus@1f,0*, while a disk device might have the name */sbus@1f,0/SUNW,fas@2,8800000/sd@1,0*. Physical device names are usually displayed at boot time and when using selected applications that access hardware directly, such as *format*. On the other hand, physical device files, which are located in the */devices* directory, comprise an instance name that is an abbreviation for a physical device name, which can be interpreted by the kernel. For example, the SBUS */sbus@1f,0* might be referred to as *sbus*, and a device disk */sbus@1f,0/SUNW,fas@2,8800000/sd@1,0* might be referred to as *sd1*. The mapping of instance names to physical devices is not hard-wired: the */etc/path_to_inst* file always contains these details, keeping them consistent between boots. For an Ultra 2, this file looks like this:

```
"/sbus@1f,0" 0 "sbus"
"/sbus@1f,0/sbusmem@2,0" 2 "sbusmem"
"/sbus@1f,0/sbusmem@3,0" 3 "sbusmem"
"/sbus@1f,0/sbusmem@0,0" 0 "sbusmem"
"/sbus@1f,0/sbusmem@1,0" 1 "sbusmem"
"/sbus@1f,0/SUNW,fas@2,8800000" 1 "fas"
"/sbus@1f,0/SUNW,fas@2,8800000/ses@f,0" 1 "ses"
"/sbus@1f,0/SUNW,fas@2,8800000/sd@1,0" 16 "sd"
"/sbus@1f,0/SUNW,fas@2,8800000/sd@0,0" 15 "sd"
"/sbus@1f,0/SUNW,fas@2,8800000/sd@3,0" 18 "sd"
"/sbus@1f,0/SUNW,fas@2,8800000/sd@2,0" 17 "sd"
"/sbus@1f,0/SUNW,fas@2,8800000/sd@5,0" 20 "sd"
"/sbus@1f,0/SUNW,fas@2,8800000/sd@4,0" 19 "sd"
"/sbus@1f,0/SUNW,fas@2,8800000/sd@6,0" 21 "sd"
"/sbus@1f,0/SUNW,fas@2,8800000/sd@9,0" 23 "sd"
"/sbus@1f,0/SUNW,fas@2,8800000/sd@8,0" 22 "sd"
"/sbus@1f,0/SUNW,fas@2,8800000/sd@a,0" 24 "sd"
"/sbus@1f,0/sbusmem@f,0" 15 "sbusmem"
"/sbus@1f,0/sbusmem@d,0" 13 "sbusmem"
"/sbus@1f,0/sbusmem@e,0" 14 "sbusmem"
"/sbus@1f,0/cgthree@1,0" 0 "cgthree"
"/sbus@1f,0/SUNW,hme@e,8c00000" 0 "hme"
"/sbus@1f,0/zs@f,1000000" 1 "zs"
"/sbus@1f,0/zs@f,1100000" 0 "zs"
"/sbus@1f,0/SUNW,bpp@e,c800000" 0 "bpp"
"/sbus@1f,0/lebuffer@0,40000" 0 "lebuffer"
"/sbus@1f,0/lebuffer@0,40000/le@0,60000" 0 "le"
"/sbus@1f,0/SUNW,hme@2,8c00000" 1 "hme"
"/sbus@1f,0/SUNW,fdtwo@f,1400000" 0 "fd"
"/options" 0 "options"
"/pseudo" 0 "pseudo"
```

/dev and /devices Directories

In addition to physical devices, Solaris 9 also needs to refer to logical devices. For example, physical disks may be divided into many different slices, so the physical disk device will need to be referred to using a logical name. Logical device files in the /dev directory are symbolically linked to physical device names in the /devices directory. Most user applications will refer to logical device names. A typical listing of */dev* directory has numerous entries that look like this:

```
arp         ptys0       ptyyb       rsd3a       sd3e        ttyu2
audio       ptys1       ptyyc       rsd3b       sd3f        ttyu3
audioctl    ptys2       ptyyd       rsd3c       sd3g        ttyu4
bd.off      ptys3       ptyye       rsd3d       sd3h        ttyu5
be          ptys4       ptyyf       rsd3e       skip_key    ttyu6
bpp0        ptys5       ptyz0       rsd3f       sound/      ttyu7
...
```

Many of these device filenames are self-explanatory:

■ */dev/console* represents the console device–error and status messages are usually written to the console by daemons and applications using the syslog service (described in Chapter 16). */dev/console* typically corresponds to the monitor in text mode, however, the console is also represented logically in windowing systems, such as OpenWindows, where the command `server% cmdtool -C` brings up a console window.

■ */dev/hme* is the network interface device file.

■ */dev/dsk* contains device files for disk slices.

■ */dev/tty*n and */dev/pty*n are the *n* terminal and *n* pseudo-terminal devices attached to the system.

■ */dev/null* is the end point of discarded output; many applications pipe their output.

The `drvconfig` command creates the */devices* directory tree, which is a logical representation of the physical layout of devices attached to the system, and pseudo-drivers. `drvconfig` is executed automatically after a reconfiguration boot. It reads file permission information for new nodes in the tree from */etc/minor_perm*, which contains entries like this,

```
sd:* 0666 httpd staff
```

where *sd* is the node name for a disk device, *0666* is the default file permission, *httpd* is the owner, and *staff* is the group.

Storage Devices

Solaris 9 supports many different kinds of mass-storage devices, including SCSI hard drives (and IDE drives on the x86 platform), reading and writing standard and rewriteable CD-ROMs, Iomega Zip and Jaz drives, tape drives, DVD-ROM, and floppy disks. Hard drives are the most common kinds of storage devices found on a Solaris 9 system, ranging from individual drives used to create system and user file systems, to highly redundant, server-based RAID systems. These RAID configurations can comprise a set of internal disks, managed through software (such as DiskSuite), or high-speed, external arrays, like the A1000, which include dedicated RAM for write-caching. Because disk writing is one of the slowest operations in any modern server system, this greatly increases overall operational speed.

Hard drives have faced stiff competition in recent years, with new media such as Iomega's Zip and Jaz drives providing removable media for both random and sequential file access. This makes them ideal media for archival backups, competing with the traditional magnetic tape drives. The latter have largely been replaced in modern systems by the digital DAT tape system, which has high reliability and data throughput rates (especially the DDS-3 standard).

In this section, we look at the issues surrounding the installation and configuration of storage devices for Solaris 9, providing practical advice for installing a wide range of hardware.

Hard Drives

When formatted for operation with Solaris 9, hard disks are logically divided into one or more "slices" (or partitions) on which a single file system resides. File systems contain sets of files that are hierarchically organized around a number of directories. Solaris 9 contains a number of predefined directories that often form the top level of a file system hierarchy. Many of these directories lie one level below the *root directory*, often denoted by "/", which exists on the primary system disk of any Solaris 9 system. In addition to a primary disk, many Solaris 9 systems will have additional disks that provide storage space for user and daemon files. Each file system has a mount point that is usually created in the top level of the root file system. For example, the */export* file system is obviously mounted in the top level of "/". The mount point is created by using the `mkdir` command:

```
# mkdir /export
```

In contrast, the */export/home* file system, which usually holds the home directories of users and user files, is mounted in the top level of the */export* file system. Thus, the mount point is created by using the following command:

```
# mkdir /export/home
```

A single logical file system can be created on a single slice, but cannot exist on more than one slice, unless there is an extra level of abstraction between the logical and physical file systems (for example, a virtual disk is created using DiskSuite, which spans many physical disks). A physical disk can also contain more than one slice. On SPARC architecture systems, eight slices can be used, numbered zero through seven. On Intel architecture systems, however, ten slices are available, numbered zero through nine.

The actual assignment of logical file systems to physical slices is a matter of discretion for the individual administrator, and although there are customary assignments recommended by Sun and other hardware vendors, a specific site policy, or an application's requirements, might necessitate the development of a local policy. For example, database servers often make quite specific requirements about the allocation of disk slices to improve performance. However, with modern high-performance RAID systems, these recommendations are often redundant. Because many organizations will have many different kinds of systems deployed, it is useful to maintain compatibility between systems as much as possible.

Figure 22-1 shows the typical file system layout for a SPARC architecture system following customary disk slice allocations. Slice 0 holds the root partition, while Slice 1 is allocated to swap space. For systems with changing virtual memory requirements, it might be better to use a swap file on the file system, rather than allocating an entire slice for swap. Slice 2 often refers to the entire disk, while */export* on Slice 3 traditionally holds older versions of the operating system, which are used by client systems with lower performance (for example, Classic or LX systems that use the trivial FTP daemon *tftpd* to download their operating system upon boot). These systems may also use Slice 4 as exported swap space. Export may also be used for file sharing using the networked file system, NFS. Slice 5 holds the */opt* file system, which is the default location under Solaris 9 for local packages installed using the pkgadd command. Under earlier versions of Solaris, the */usr/local* file system held local packages, and this convention is still used by many sites. The system package file system */usr* is usually located on Slice 6, while */export/home* usually contains user home directories on Slice 7. Again, earlier systems located user home directories under */home*, but because */home* is reserved by the automounter program, some contention can be expected.

Figure 22-2 shows the typical file system layout for an Intel architecture system following customary disk slice allocations. Slice 0 again holds the root partition, while

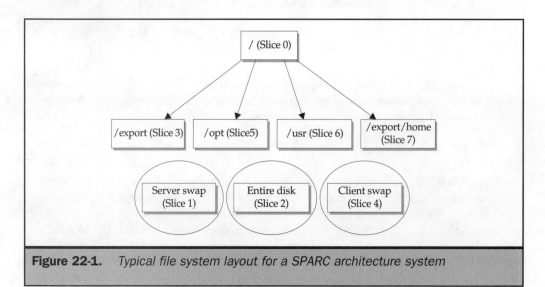

Figure 22-1. *Typical file system layout for a SPARC architecture system*

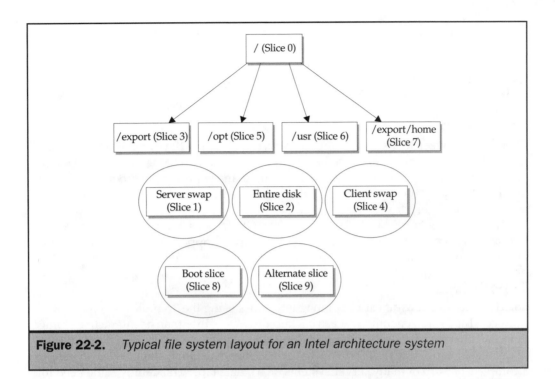

Figure 22-2.   *Typical file system layout for an Intel architecture system*

Slice 1 is also allocated to swap space. Slice 2 continues to refer to the entire disk, while */export* on Slice 3 again holds older versions of the operating system, which are used by client systems, and Slice 4 contains exported swap space for these clients. The local package file system */opt* is still located on Slice 5, and the system package file system */usr* is again located on Slice 6. Slice 7 contains the user home directories on */export/home*. However, the two extra slices serve very different purposes: Boot information for Solaris 9 is located on Slice 8 and is known as the *boot slice*, whereas Slice 9 provides space for alternative disk blocks and is known as the *alternative slice*.

CD-ROMs

A popular format of read-only mass storage on many servers is the compact disc read-only memory (CD-ROM). Although earlier releases of Solaris worked best with Sun-branded CD-ROM drives, as of Solaris 2.6, Solaris 9 fully supports all SCSI-2 CD-ROMs. For systems running older versions of Solaris, it may still be possible to use a third-party drive, but the drive must support 512 byte sectors (the Sun standard). A second Sun default to be aware of is that CD-ROMs must usually have the SCSI target ID of 6, although this limitation has again been overcome in later releases of the kernel. However, a number of third-party applications with "auto detect" functions may still expect to see the CD-ROM drive at SCSI ID 6.

NETWORKING

A number of different CD formats are also supported with the `mount` command, which is used to attach CDs to the file system. It is common to use the mount point */cdrom* for the primary CD-ROM device in Solaris 9 systems, although it is possible to use a different mount point for mounting the device by using a command-line argument to `mount`.

Zip and Jaz Drives

There are two ways to install Zip and Jaz drives: by treating the drive as a SCSI disk, in which case format data needs to be added to the system to recognize it, or by using Andy Polyakov's ziptool, which will format and manage protection modes supported by Zip 100 and Jaz 1GB/2GB drives. Both of these techniques will support only SCSI and not parallel port drives.

Treating the Zip 100 SCSI drive or the Jaz 1GB drive as a normal SCSI device is the easiest approach, because there is built-in Solaris 9 support for these SCSI devices. However, only standard, non-write-protected disks can be used.

Tape Drives

Solaris 9 supports a wide variety of magnetic tapes using the "remote magtape" (*rmt*) protocol. Tapes are generally used as backup devices, rather than as interactive storage devices. What they lack in availability, they definitely make up for in storage capacity: Many digital audio tape (DAT) drives have capacities of 24GB, making it easy to perform a complete backup of many server systems on a single tape. This removes the need for late-night monitoring by operations staff to insert new tapes when full, as many administrators will have experienced in the past.

Device files for tape drives are found in the */dev/rmt* directory. They are numbered sequentially from 0, so default drives will generally be available as */dev/rmt/0*.

To back up to a remote drive, use the command `ufsdump`, which is an incremental file system dumping program. For example, to create a full backup of the */dev/rdsk/c0t1d0s1* file system to the tape system */dev/rmt/0*, simply use the command:

```
# ufsdump 0 /dev/rmt/0 /dev/rdsk/c0t1d0s1
```

This command specifies a level zero (i.e., complete) dump of the file system, specifying the target drive and data source as */dev/rmt/0* and */dev/rdsk/c0t1d0s1*, respectively.

Floppy Disks

Floppy disk drives (1.44MB capacity) are standard on both SPARC and Intel architecture systems. In addition, by using the Volume Manager, detecting and mounting floppy disks is straightforward. Insert the target disk into the drive, and use this command:

```
# volcheck
```

This will check all volumes that are managed by volume management and will mount any valid file system which is found. The mount point for the floppy drive is determined by the settings in */etc/vfstab*:

```
fd    -    /dev/fd    fd    -    no    -
```

Refer to the section on entering disk information into the virtual file system database for more details on configuring the */etc/vfstab* file. A very useful feature of `volcheck` is to automatically check for new volumes; for example,

```
# volcheck -i 60 -t 3600 /dev/diskette0 &
```

works in the background to check every minute if a floppy is in the drive. However, this polling takes place only for one hour unless renewed.

CD-ROMs *and DVD-ROMs*

CD-ROMs are supported directly by the operating system in SPARC architectures and do not require any special configuration, other than the usual process of initializing the system for a reconfiguration reboot, powering down the system, attaching the CD-ROM device to the SCSI bus, and powering on the system. It is not necessary to use `format` or `newfs` to read the files on the CD-ROM, nor is it usually necessary to manually mount the file system, because the volume manager (`vold`) is usually enabled on server systems. `vold` is covered in detail in Chapter 8.

A common problem for Solaris 9 x86 users is that there are few tested and supported CD-ROM brands for installing the operating system (although most fully compliant ATA/ATAPI CD-ROMs should work). The older Sound Blaster IDE interface for CD-ROMs does not appear to be suitable, although support may be included in a later release (the Alternate Status register is apparently not implemented on the main integrated circuit for the controller board). It is always best to check the current Hardware Compatibility List (HCL) from the Sun site.

Many recent SPARC and Intel systems come installed with a DVD-ROM drive. Although the drive cannot be used yet to play movies, it can be effectively used as a mass storage device, with a capacity equal to several individual CD-ROMs. Future releases of Solaris may include a DVD player and support for the newer DVD-RAM technology.

CD-Rs and CD-RWs

Solaris 9 supports both reading and writing CD-ROMs. In addition to the CD-R (CD-Readable) format, Solaris 9 also supports CD-RW (CD-ReWritable), previously known as CD-Erasable. It is a new optical disc specification created by the industry organization OSTA (**www.osta.org**). You can hook up many SCSI CD-R and CD-RW devices to a SPARC system or SCSI device ID 6, and they will function as normal CD-ROM drives. Although the technical ability to support any SCSI-based device is a given for the operating system, a potentially limiting factor for nonstandard hardware is finding software to adequately support it. Luckily, many different open source and commercial editions of CD-recording software are available for the Solaris 9 platform. To obtain support for both Solaris 1.*x* and 2.*x*, the best application is *cdrecord* by Jörg Schilling, which you can download from **ftp://ftp.fokus.gmd.de/pub/ unix/ cdrecord/**. It is freeware, and it makes use of the real-time scheduler in Solaris 9. It also compiles on the Solaris 9 x86 platform, and can create both music and data discs. Although it has a rather clunky command-line interface, it has more features than some of the commercial systems, including the ability to simulate a recording for test purposes (-*dummy* option); using a single CD for multiple recording sessions (-*multi* option); manually fixing the disk, if you want to view data from an open session on a normal CD-ROM (-*fix* option); and setting the recording speed factor (-*speed* option). If you prefer a commercial system, GEAR for UNIX is also available (**http://www.gearcdr.com/ html/products/gear/unix/index.html**), as well as Creative Digital Research's CDR Publisher (**http://www.cdr1.com/**), which is available through Sun's Catalyst program. For more general information about the CD recording process, see Andy McFadden's very comprehensive FAQ at **http://www.fadden.com/cdrfaq/**.

Procedures

The following procedures demonstrate how to manage system devices.

Adding Devices

In many cases, adding new devices to a Solaris 9 system is straightforward, because most devices connect to the SCSI bus, which is a standard interface. The steps involved are usually preparing the system for a reconfiguration boot, powering down the system, connecting the hardware device, noting the SCSI device number, powering on the system, and using the `format` command, if necessary, to create a file system. In this section, we examine the procedure for adding disks to both SPARC and Intel architecture machines and highlight potential problems which may occur.

Hard Drives

Hard disk installation and configuration on Solaris 9 is often more complicated than other UNIX systems. However, this complexity is required to support the sophisticated hardware operations typically undertaken by Solaris 9 systems. For example, Linux refers to hard disks using a simple BSD-style scheme: */dev/hdn* are the IDE hard disks on a system, and */dev/sdn* are the SCSI hard disks on a system, where *n* refers to the hard disk number. A system with two IDE hard disks and two SCSI hard disks will therefore have the following device files configured:

```
/dev/hda
/dev/hdb
/dev/sda
/dev/sdb
```

Partitions created on each drive are also sequentially numbered: if */dev/hda* is the boot disk, it may contain several partitions on the disk, reflecting the basic UNIX system directories:

```
/dev/hda1 (/ partition)
/dev/hda2 (/usr)
/dev/hda3 (/var)
/dev/hda4 (swap)
```

Instead of simply referring to the disk type, disk number and partition number, the device filename for each partition ("slice") on a Solaris 9 disk contains four identifiers: controller (*c*), target (*t*), disk (*d*), and slice (*s*). Thus, the device file,

```
/dev/dsk/c0t3d0s0
```

identifies slice 0 of disk 0, controller 0 at SCSI target ID 3. To complicate matters further, disk device files exist in both the */dev/dsk* and */dev/rdsk* directories, which correspond to block device and raw device entries, respectively. Raw and block devices refer to the same physical partition, but are used in different contexts: Using raw devices allows only operations of small amounts of data, whereas a buffer can be used with a block device to increase the data read size. It is not always clear whether to use a block or raw device interface, however, low-level system commands (like the `fsck` command, which performs disk maintenance) typically use raw device interfaces, whereas commands that operate on the entire disk (such as `df`, which reports disk usage) will most likely use block devices.

To install a new hard drive on a Solaris 9 system, just follow these steps:

1. Prepare the system for a reconfiguration boot by issuing the command:

   ```
   server# touch /reconfigure
   ```

2. Synchronize disk data and power down the system using the commands:

   ```
   server# sync; sync; sync; shutdown
   ```

3. Switch off power to the system and attach the new hard disk to the external SCSI chain, or install it internally into an appropriate disk bay.

4. Check that the SCSI device ID does not conflict with any existing SCSI devices. If a conflict exists, simply change the ID using the switch.

NETWORKING

5. Power on the system and use the `boot` command to load the kernel, if the OpenBoot monitor appears:

```
ok boot
```

The next step, assuming that you have decided which partitions you want to create on your drive using the information supplied earlier, is to run the `format` program. In addition to creating slices, format also displays information about existing disks and slices and can be used to repair a faulty disk. When format is invoked without a command-line argument,

```
# format
```

it displays the current disks and asks the Administrator to enter the number of the disk to format. Selecting a disk for formatting at this point is nondestructive, so even if you make a mistake, you can always exit the format program without damaging data. For example, on a SPARC-20 system with three 1.05G SCSI disks, *format* opens with this screen:

```
Searching for disks...done
AVAILABLE DISK SELECTIONS:
0. c0t1d0 <SUN1.05 cyl 2036 alt 2 hd 14 sec 72>
/iommu@f,e0000000/sbus@f,e0001000/espdma@f,400000/esp@f,800000/
sd@1,0
1. c0t2d0 <SUN1.05 cyl 2036 alt 2 hd 14 sec 72>
/iommu@f,e0000000/sbus@f,e0001000/espdma@f,400000/esp@f,800000/
sd@2,0
2. c0t3d0 <SUN1.05 cyl 2036 alt 2 hd 14 sec 72>
/iommu@f,e0000000/sbus@f,e0001000/espdma@f,400000/esp@f,800000/
sd@3,0
Specify disk (enter its number):
```

It is also possible to pass a command-line option to *format*, comprising the disk (or disks) to be formatted; for example:

```
# format /dev/rdsk/c0t2d0
```

After selecting the appropriate disk, the message

```
[disk formatted]
```

will appear if the disk has previously been formatted. This is an important message, because it is a common mistake to misidentify a target disk from the available selection of both formatted and unformatted disks. The menu looks like this:

```
FORMAT MENU:
        disk       - select a disk
        type       - select (define) a disk type
        partition  - select (define) a partition table
        current    - describe the current disk
        format     - format and analyze the disk
        fdisk      - run the fdisk program
        repair     - repair a defective sector
        show       - translate a disk address
        label      - write label to the disk
        analyze    - surface analysis
        defect     - defect list management
        backup     - search for backup labels
        verify     - read and display labels
        save       - save new disk/partition definitions
        volname    - set 8-character volume name
        !<cmd>     - execute <cmd>, then return
        quit
format>
```

If the disk has not been formatted, the first step is to prepare the disk to contain slices and file systems by formatting the disk by issuing the command format:

```
format> format
Ready to format. Formatting cannot be interrupted
and takes 15 minutes (estimated). Continue? yes
```

The purpose of formatting is to identify defective blocks and mark them as bad, and generally to verify that the disk is operational from a hardware perspective. Once this has been completed, new slices can be created and sized by using the *partition* option at the main menu:

```
format> partition
```

In this case, we want to create a new Slice 5 on disk 0 at target 3, which will be used to store user files when mounted as */export/home*, and corresponding to block device

NETWORKING

/dev/dsk/c0t3d0s5. After determining the maximum amount of space available, enter that size in gigabytes (in this case, 1.05GB) when requested to do so by the `format` program for Slice 5 (enter 0 for the other slices). If the disk is not labeled, you will also be prompted to enter a label, which contains details of the disk's current slices, which is useful for recovering data. This is an important step, because the operating system will not be able to find any newly created slices, unless the volume is labeled. To view the disk label, use the `prtvtoc` command. Here's the output from the primary drive in an x86 system:

```
# prtvtoc /dev/dsk/c0d0s2
* /dev/dsk/c0d0s2 partition map
*
* Dimensions:
*     512 bytes/sector
*      63 sectors/track
*     255 tracks/cylinder
*   16065 sectors/cylinder
*    1020 cylinders
*    1018 accessible cylinders
*
* Flags:
*    1: unmountable
*   10: read-only
*
*                      First     Sector     Last
* Partition  Tag  Flags Sector    Count     Sector  Mount Directory
        0     2   00    48195    160650    208844   /
        1     7   00   208845     64260    273104   /var
        2     5   00        0  16354170  16354169
        3     3   01   273105    321300    594404
        6     4   00   594405   1317330   1911734   /usr
        7     8   00  1911735  14442435  16354169   /export/home
        8     1   01        0     16065     16064
        9     9   01    16065     32130     48194
```

The disk label contains a full partition table, which can be printed for each disk by using the `print` command:

```
format> print
```

For the 1.05GB disk, the partition table will look like this:

```
Part Tag Flag Cylinders Size Blocks
```

```
0 root wm 0 0 (0/0/0) 0
1 swap wu 0 0 (0/0/0) 0
2 backup wm 0 - 3732 (3732/0/0) 2089920
3 unassigned wm 0 0 (0/0/0) 0
4 unassigned wm 0 0 (0/0/0) 0
5 home wm 0 - 3732 1075MB (3732/0/0) 2089920
6 usr wm 0 0 (0/0/0) 0
7 unassigned wm 0 0 (0/0/0) 0
```

After saving the changes to the disk's partition table, exit the format program and create a new UFS file system on the target slice by using the newfs command:

```
# newfs /dev/rdsk/c0t3d0s5
```

After a new file system is constructed, it is ready to be mounted. First a mount point is created:

```
# mkdir /export/home
```

followed by the appropriate mount command:

```
# mount /dev/dsk/c0t3d0s5 /export/home
```

At this point, the disk is available to the system for the current session. However, if you want the disk to be available after reboot, you need to create an entry in the virtual file systems table, which is created from /etc/vfstab file. An entry like this,

```
/dev/dsk/c0t3d0s5 /dev/rdsk/c0t3d0s5 /export/home ufs 2 yes -
```

contains details of the slice's block and raw devices, the mount point, the file system type, instructions for fsck, and most importantly, a flag to force mount at boot.

For an x86 system, the output of format looks slightly different, given the differences in the way that devices are denoted:

```
AVAILABLE DISK SELECTIONS:
     0. c0d0 <DEFAULT cyl 1018 alt 2 hd 255 sec 63>
```

```
            /pci@0,0/pci-ide@7,1/ata@0/cmdk@0,0
Specify disk (enter its number):
```

The partition table is similar to that for the SPARC architecture systems:

```
partition> print
Current partition table (original):
Total disk cylinders available: 1018 + 2 (reserved cylinders)

Part        Tag   Flag     Cylinders        Size          Blocks
  0        root    wm       3 -    12      78.44MB    (10/0/0)     160650
  1         var    wm      13 -    16      31.38MB    (4/0/0)       64260
  2      backup    wm       0 -  1017       7.80GB    (1018/0/0) 16354170
  3        swap    wu      17 -    36     156.88MB    (20/0/0)     321300
  4  unassigned    wm       0                   0     (0/0/0)           0
  5  unassigned    wm       0                   0     (0/0/0)           0
  6         usr    wm      37 -   118     643.23MB    (82/0/0)    1317330
  7        home    wm     119 -  1017       6.89GB    (899/0/0)  14442435
  8        boot    wu       0 -     0       7.84MB    (1/0/0)       16065
  9  alternates    wu       1 -     2      15.69MB    (2/0/0)       32130
```

Installing a Zip/Jaz Drive

The steps for installation are similar for both the Zip and Jaz drives:

1. Set the SCSI ID switch to any ID that is not reserved.

2. Attach the Zip or Jaz drive to your SCSI adapter or chain and ensure that it has power.

3. Create a device entry in */etc/format.dat* by editing the file and inserting the following for a Zip drive:

```
disk_type="Zip 100"\
                    :ctlr=SCSI\
                    :ncyl=2406:acyl=2:pcyl=2408:nhead=2\
                    :nsect=40:rpm=3600:bpt=20480
        partition="Zip 100"\
                    :disk="Zip 100":ctlr=SCSI\
                    :2=0,192480
                    :2=0,1159168
```

For a Jaz drive, enter the following information in */etc/format.dat*:

```
disk_type="Jaz 1GB"\
                    :ctlr=SCSI\
                    :ncyl=1018:acyl=2:pcyl=1020:nhead=64\
                    :nsect=32:rpm=3600:bpt=16384
```

```
                  partition="Jaz 1GB"\
                            :disk="Jaz 1GB":ctlr=SCSI\
                            :2=0,2084864
```

4. Perform a reconfiguration boot by typing

```
ok boot -r
```

at the OpenBoot prompt, or by using these commands from a super-user shell:

```
server# touch /reconfigure
server# sync; sync; init 6
```

The drive should now be visible to the system. To actually use the drive to mount a volume, insert a Zip or Jaz disk into the drive prior to booting the system. After booting, run the `format` program:

```
# format
```

5. Assuming that the *sd* number for your drive is 3, select this *sd* as the disk to be formatted. Create the appropriate partition using the *partition* option, then create an appropriate label for the volume and quit the format program. Next, create a new file system on the drive by using the `newfs` command, for example:

```
# newfs -v /dev/sd3c
```

6. After creating the file system, you can mount it by typing

```
# mount /dev/sd3c /mount_point
```

where */mount_point* is something self documenting (such as */zip* or */jaz*). You need to create this before mounting by typing the following:

```
# mkdir /zip
```

or

```
# mkdir /jaz
```

An alternate and more flexible approach is to use the ziptool program, which is available at **http://fy.chalmers.se/~appro/ziptool.html**. Ziptool supports all Zip and Jaz drive protection modes, permits unconditional low-level formatting of protected disks, disk labeling, and volume management for Solaris 2.6 and greater. The program has to be executed with root privileges regardless of the access permissions set on SCSI disk device driver's entries in */devices*. Consequently, if you want to let all users use it, you must install it as *set-root-uid*:

```
# /usr/ucb/install -m 04755 -o root ziptool /usr/local/bin
```

However, you should note that running *setuid* programs has security implications.

NETWORKING

After downloading and unpacking the sources, you can compile the program by using this:

```
# gcc -o ziptool ziptool.c -lvolmgt
```

Of course, you will need to ensure that the path to *libvolmgt.a* is in your *LD_LIBRARY_PATH* (usually */lib*),

```
ziptool device command
```

where *device* must be the full name of a raw SCSI disk file, such as */dev/rsdk/c0t5d0s2*, and *command* is one or more of the following:

rw	Unlocks the Zip disk temporarily
RW	Unlocks the Zip disk permanently
ro	Puts the Zip disk into read-only mode
RO	Puts the Zip disk into a read-only mode that is password protected
WR(*)	Protects the disk by restricting reading and writing unless a password is entered
eject	Ejects the current Zip disk
noeject	Stops the Zip disk being ejected

You can find further information on installing Jaz and Zip drives on the Iomega support Web site:

```
http://www.iomega.com/support/documents/4019.html
http://www.iomega.com/support/documents/2019.html
```

Examples

The following examples demonstrate how to manage devices.

Checking for Devices

Obtaining a listing of devices attached to a Solaris 9 system is the best way to begin examining this import issue. In Solaris 9, you can easily obtain system configuration information, including device information, by using the "print configuration" command,

```
# prtconf
```

on any SPARC or Intel architecture system. On an Ultra 5 workstation, the system configuration looks like this:

```
SUNW,Ultra-5_10
    packages (driver not attached)
        terminal-emulator (driver not attached)
        deblocker (driver not attached)
        obp-tftp (driver not attached)
        disk-label (driver not attached)
        SUNW,builtin-drivers (driver not attached)
        sun-keyboard (driver not attached)
        ufs-file-system (driver not attached)
    chosen (driver not attached)
    openprom (driver not attached)
        client-services (driver not attached)
    options, instance #0
    aliases (driver not attached)
    memory (driver not attached)
    virtual-memory (driver not attached)
    pci, instance #0
        pci, instance #0
            ebus, instance #0
                auxio (driver not attached)
                power (driver not attached)
                SUNW,pll (driver not attached)
                se, instance #0
                su, instance #0
                su, instance #1
                ecpp (driver not attached)
                fdthree (driver not attached)
                eeprom (driver not attached)
                flashprom (driver not attached)
                SUNW,CS4231, instance #0
            network, instance #0
            SUNW,m64B, instance #0
            ide, instance #0
                disk (driver not attached)
```

```
                    cdrom (driver not attached)
                    dad, instance #0
                    atapicd, instance #2
          pci, instance #1
              pci, instance #0
                  pci108e,1000 (driver not attached)
                  SUNW,hme, instance #1
                  SUNW,isptwo, instance #0
                      sd (driver not attached)
                      st (driver not attached)
          SUNW,UltraSPARC-IIi (driver not attached)
          pseudo, instance #0
```

Never panic about the message that a driver is "not attached" to a particular device. Because device drivers are loaded only on demand in Solaris 9, only those devices that are actively being used will have their drivers loaded. When a device is no longer being used, the device driver is unloaded from memory. This is a very efficient memory management strategy that optimizes the use of physical RAM by deallocating memory for devices when they are no longer required. In the case of the Ultra 5, we can see that devices like the PCI bus and the IDE disk drives have attached device drivers, and they were being used while *prtconf* was running.

For an x86 system, the devices found are quite different:

```
System Configuration: Sun Microsystems i86pc
Memory size: 128 Megabytes
System Peripherals (Software Nodes):
i86pc
    +boot (driver not attached)
        memory (driver not attached)
    aliases (driver not attached)
    chosen (driver not attached)
    i86pc-memory (driver not attached)
    i86pc-mmu (driver not attached)
    openprom (driver not attached)
    options, instance #0
    packages (driver not attached)
    delayed-writes (driver not attached)
    itu-props (driver not attached)
    isa, instance #0
        motherboard (driver not attached)
        asy, instance #0
        lp (driver not attached)
        asy, instance #1
        fdc, instance #0
            fd, instance #0
```

```
        fd, instance #1 (driver not attached)
    kd (driver not attached)
    bios (driver not attached)
    bios (driver not attached)
    pnpCTL,0041 (driver not attached)
    pnpCTL,7002 (driver not attached)
    kd, instance #0
    chanmux, instance #0
pci, instance #0
    pci8086,1237 (driver not attached)
    pci8086,7000 (driver not attached)
    pci-ide, instance #0
        ata, instance #0
            cmdk, instance #0
            sd, instance #1
    pci10ec,8029 (driver not attached)
    pci5333,8901 (driver not attached)
used-resources (driver not attached)
objmgr, instance #0
pseudo, instance #0
```

At Boot Time

The *OpenBoot* monitor has the ability to diagnose hardware errors on system devices before booting the kernel. This can be particularly useful for identifying bus connectivity issues, such as unterminated SCSI chains, but also some basic functional issues, such as whether devices are responding. Issuing the command

```
ok reset
```

will also force a self-test of the system.

Just after booting, it is also useful to review the system boot messages, which you can retrieve by using the dmesg command, or by examining the */var/log/messages* file. This displays a list of all devices that were successfully attached at boot time, and it also displays any error messages that were detected. Let's look at the dmesg output for a SPARC Ultra architecture system:

```
# dmesg
Jan 17 13:06
cpu0: SUNW,UltraSPARC-IIi (upaid 0 impl 0x12 ver 0x12 clock 270 MHz)
SunOS Release 5.9 Version Generic_103640-19
[UNIX(R) System V Release 4.0]
Copyright (c) 1983-2002, Sun Microsystems, Inc.
mem = 131072K (0x8000000)
avail mem = 127852544
Ethernet address = 8:0:20:90:b3:23
```

```
root nexus = Sun Ultra 5/10 UPA/PCI (UltraSPARC-IIi 270MHz)
pci0 at root: UPA 0x1f 0x0
PCI-device: pci@1,1, simba #0
PCI-device: pci@1, simba #1
dad0 at pci1095,6460 target 0 lun 0
dad0 is /pci@1f,0/pci@1,1/ide@3/dad@0,0
        <Seagate Medalist 34342A cyl 8892 alt 2 hd 15 sec 63>
root on /pci@1f,0/pci@1,1/ide@3/disk@0,0:a fstype ufs
su0 at ebus0: offset 14,3083f8
su0 is /pci@1f,0/pci@1,1/ebus@1/su@14,3083f8
su1 at ebus0: offset 14,3062f8
su1 is /pci@1f,0/pci@1,1/ebus@1/su@14,3062f8
keyboard is </pci@1f,0/pci@1,1/ebus@1/su@14,3083f8>
  major <37> minor <0>
mouse is </pci@1f,0/pci@1,1/ebus@1/su@14,3062f8>
  major <37> minor <1>
stdin is </pci@1f,0/pci@1,1/ebus@1/su@14,3083f8>
  major <37> minor <0>
SUNW,m64B0 is /pci@1f,0/pci@1,1/SUNW,m64B@2
m64#0: 1280x1024, 2M mappable, rev 4754.9a
stdout is </pci@1f,0/pci@1,1/SUNW,m64B@2> major <8> minor <0>
boot cpu (0) initialization complete - online
se0 at ebus0: offset 14,400000
se0 is /pci@1f,0/pci@1,1/ebus@1/se@14,400000
SUNW,hme0: CheerIO 2.0 (Rev Id = c1) Found
SUNW,hme0 is /pci@1f,0/pci@1,1/network@1,1
SUNW,hme1: Local Ethernet address = 8:0:20:93:b0:65
pci1011,240: SUNW,hme1
SUNW,hme1 is /pci@1f,0/pci@1/pci@1/SUNW,hme@0,1
dump on /dev/dsk/c0t0d0s1 size 131328K
SUNW,hme0: Using Internal Transceiver
SUNW,hme0: 10 Mbps half-duplex Link Up
pcmcia: no PCMCIA adapters found
```

dmesg first performs a memory test, sets the Ethernet address for the network interface, and then initializes the PCI bus. Setting the Ethernet address is critical on SPARC systems, because the Ethernet interfaces will have the same address stored in PROM. An IDE disk is then recognized and mapped into a physical device, and the appropriate partitions are activated. The standard input devices (keyboard and mouse) are then activated, and the boot sequence is largely complete. However, the output is slightly different for the x86 system:

```
Jan 17 08:32
SunOS Release 5.9 Version Generic [UNIX(R) System V Release 4.0]
Copyright (c) 1983-2002, Sun Microsystems, Inc.
mem = 130688K (0x7fa0000)
```

```
avail mem = 114434048
root nexus = i86pc
isa0 at root
pci0 at root: space 0 offset 0
        IDE device at targ 0, lun 0 lastlun 0x0
        model ST310230A, stat 50, err 0
                cfg 0xc5a, cyl 16383, hd 16, sec/trk 63
                mult1 0x8010, mult2 0x110, dwcap 0x0, cap 0x2f00
                piomode 0x200, dmamode 0x200, advpiomode 0x3
                minpio 240, minpioflow 120
                valid 0x7, dwdma 0x407, majver 0x1e
ata_set_feature: (0x66,0x0) failed
        ATAPI device at targ 1, lun 0 lastlun 0x0
        model CD-912E/ATK, stat 50, err 0
                cfg 0x85a0, cyl 0, hd 0, sec/trk 0
                mult1 0x0, mult2 0x0, dwcap 0x0, cap 0xb00
                piomode 0x200, dmamode 0x200, advpiomode 0x1
                minpio 209, minpioflow 180
                valid 0x2, dwdma 0x203, majver 0x0
PCI-device: ata@0, ata0
ata0 is /pci@0,0/pci-ide@7,1/ata@0
Disk0:  <Vendor 'Gen-ATA ' Product 'ST310230A        '>
cmdk0 at ata0 target 0 lun 0
cmdk0 is /pci@0,0/pci-ide@7,1/ata@0/cmdk@0,0
root on /pci@0,0/pci-ide@7,1/ide@0/cmdk@0,0:a fstype ufs
ISA-device: asy0
asy0 is /isa/asy@1,3f8
ISA-device: asy1
asy1 is /isa/asy@1,2f8
Number of console virtual screens = 13
cpu 0 initialization complete - online
dump on /dev/dsk/c0d0s3 size 156 MB
```

While the System Is Up

If you are working remotely on a server system, and you are unsure of the system
architecture, the command

```
# arch -k
```

returns *sun4u* on the Ultra 5 system, but *sun4m* on a SPARC 10 system. For a complete
view of a system's device configuration, you may also want to try the sysdef command,

which displays more detailed information concerning pseudo-devices, kernel loadable modules, and parameters. Here's the `sysdef` output for an x86 server:

```
# sysdef
# sysdef
*
* Hostid
*
  0ae61183
*
* i86pc Configuration
*
*
* Devices
*
+boot (driver not attached)
        memory (driver not attached)
aliases (driver not attached)
chosen (driver not attached)
i86pc-memory (driver not attached)
i86pc-mmu (driver not attached)
openprom (driver not attached)
options, instance #0
packages (driver not attached)
delayed-writes (driver not attached)
itu-props (driver not attached)
...
*
* System Configuration
*
  swap files
swapfile            dev  swaplo blocks    free
/dev/dsk/c0d0s3     102,3      8 321288 321288
```

The key sections in the `sysdef` output are details of all devices, such as the PCI bus, and pseudo-devices for each loadable object path (including */kernel* and */usr/kernel*). Loadable objects are also identified, along with swap and virtual memory settings. Although the output may seem verbose, the information provided for each device can prove to be very useful in tracking down hardware errors, or missing loadable objects.

Command Reference

The following commands can be used to manage system devices.

format

The `format` command displays the following options:

disk	Nominates a disk to format
type	Specifies a disk type
partition	Specifies a partition table
current	Specifies the current disk
format	Formats the current disk
fdisk	Executes the `fdisk` program against the current disk
repair	Repairs a faulty sector on the current disk
show	Translates a disk address
label	Writes a disk label
analyze	Analyzes errors
defect	Lists problems
backup	Examines backup labels
Verify	Verifies labels
save	Saves new partition data
volname	Sets a volume name
!<cmd>	Runs command in a shell
quit	Exits application

The Complete Reference

Solaris 9

Chapter 23

Modems and Internet Access

The service access facility (SAF) is a port management system that manages requests and responses for access to system ports. In this case, a port is defined as the physical connection between a peripheral device and the system. For example, most systems have one or more serial ports that allow for sequential data transmission effectively down a single line. In contrast, a parallel port allows for several lines of data to be transmitted bidirectionally. The SAF system is designed to allow requests to be made to the system from peripheral devices through ports, and to ensure that these requests are appropriately serviced by the relevant port monitor.

Modems, which allow Solaris 9 systems to connect to the Internet over a phone line, require SAF to operate through system serial ports. Thus, it's important to understand how to configure ports, port monitors, and listeners in preparation for making an Internet connection using a modem. Note that most Solaris systems are never accessed through a modem; however, if a system's only network card has died, and the console is physically inaccessible, a modem can be a lifesaver.

The Point-to-Point Protocol (PPP) daemon is commonly used to set up modem access to an Internet Service Provider (ISP). PPP supports TCP/IP and offers the Challenge Handshake Authentication Protocol (CHAP), adding a higher level of security than is usually found on modem links. The PPP daemon relies on the chat program to perform dial-up and handle connections. In this chapter, we'll examine how to set up PPP for Internet connections.

Key Concepts

The following key concepts are required to understand how Solaris supports modems and Internet access.

Port Monitors

Central to the idea of providing services through serial ports is the port monitor, which continuously monitors the serial ports for requests to login. The port monitor doesn't process the communication parameters directly, but accepts requests and passes them to the operating system. Solaris 9 uses the ttymon port monitor, which allows multiple concurrent getty requests from serial devices.

To configure the port for a terminal, start up admintool and enter the user mode, which can be either Basic, More, or Expert. In most cases, Basic setup will be useful for most circumstances. admintool allows the configuration of most parameters for the port, including the baud rate for communications, default terminal type, flow control, and carrier detection. The values entered here should match those on the matching VT-100 terminal. Once the settings have been saved, it is possible to check the validity of the settings by using the pmadm command:

```
# pmadm -l -s ttyb
```

The Service Access Facility (SAF)

The process that initiates the service access facility is known as the service access controller (*/usr/lib/saf/sac*). It is started when the system enters run-level 2, 3, or 4, as shown in this */etc/inittab* entry:

```
sc:234:respawn:/usr/lib/saf/sac -t 300
```

Here, the respawn entry indicates that if a process is not running when it should be, it should be respawned. For example, if a system changes from run-level 2 to run-level 3, *sac* should be running. If it is not present, it will be restarted.

When *sac* is started, it reads the script */etc/saf/_safconfig*, which contains any local configurations tailored for the system. Next, the standard configuration file */etc/saf/_sactab* is read and *sac* spawns a separate child process for each of the port monitors it supports (ttymon and listen). A sample *_sactab* is shown below:

```
# VERSION=1
zsmon:ttymon::0:/usr/lib/saf/ttymon #
```

Each of these monitors also reads it own configuration file: the files */etc/saf/ttymon/ _config* and */etc/saf/listen/_config* are used to configure the ttymon and listen port monitors, respectively. A sample *_config* file is shown below:

```
# VERSION=1
ttya:u:root:reserved:reserved:reserved:/dev/term/a:I::
    /usr/bin/login::9600:ldterm, ttcompat:ttya login\: ::tvi925:y:#
```

The point of this hierarchical configuration file structure is that values read from */etc/saf/_safconfig* and */etc/saf/_sactab* by *sac* are inherited by the spawned port monitor processes, which then have the ability to configure their own operations. This hierarchy is shown in Figure 23-1.

The SAF has two types of port monitors: the terminal port monitor (ttymon) and the network port monitor (listen). For example, the ttymon port monitor for the console is started in run-levels 2, 3, and 4, through an /etc/inittab entry like the following:

```
co:234:respawn:/usr/lib/saf/ttymon -g -h -p
    "`uname -n` console login: " -T vt100 -d
    /dev/console -l console -m ldterm,ttcompat
```

The ttymon process is active when a monitor is connected to a server, such as a dumb terminal, rather than a graphics monitor.

NETWORKING

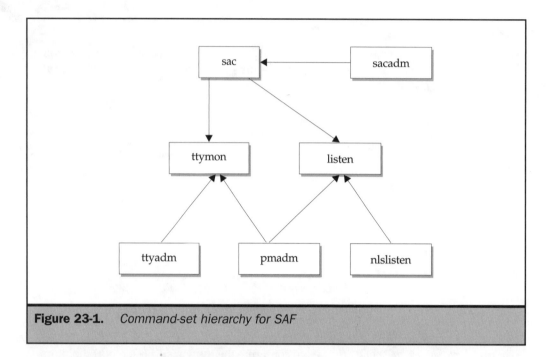

Figure 23-1.   *Command-set hierarchy for SAF*

Point to Point Protocol (PPP)

PPP is the most commonly used protocol for connecting modems over a phone line (or uncommonly over a normal serial line) to support TCP/IP. It replaces the earlier Serial Line Interface Protocol (SLIP), which did not provide any level of security or authentication for serial line services. The Solaris 9 implementation of PPP is based on the ANU version (**ftp://cs.anu.edu.au/pub/software/ppp**). PPP provides reliable access to the Internet because it includes error correction and the ability to auto-detect some network parameters automatically. All of the parameters for the PPP daemon (pppd) are stored in */etc/ppp/options*. Alternatively, for options that are specific to each serial port, a new configuration file can be created (such as */etc/ppp/options.cua.a* for the serial port */dev/cua/a*). This is useful where two modems are connected to the two standard serial interfaces on a SPARC system, which are connected to two separate modems that in turn dial completely different ISPs—the lesson for high availability is to be prepared for the worst case scenario. Supporting network operations through a 56K modem is going to be challenging—but not impossible—in an emergency. Figure 23-2 shows a PPP configuration with high availability in mind.

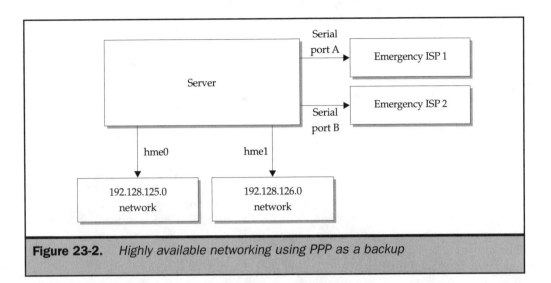

Figure 23-2.   *Highly available networking using PPP as a backup*

Procedures

The following procedures are commonly used to setup modems and Internet access.

Setting Up Port Listeners

The listen port monitor is managed by the `nlslisten` and `nlsadmin` commands. In contrast to ttymon, the listen port monitor manages network ports and connections by listening for requests to access services and daemons. The listen monitor uses the Transport Layer Interface (TLI) and STREAMS to implement OSI-compliant network service layers. Specific networks ports are assigned to the listen monitor, and child processes are spawned to handle each client request. One of the key features of listen is that it can provide services that are not managed by inetd—since all daemons can be accessed through a listen service. This is an important feature for the different users accessing services on a Solaris system. For example, a network connection could serve Web traffic, while a dial-in connection could cater to telnet or SSH access.

The `nlsadmin` command is used to set up transport providers for STREAMS-compatible network services. In order to configure a TLI listener database, the `nlsadmin` command can be used to configure the listener. First, the TCP/IP database is created:

```
# nlsadmin -i tcp
```

Next, set the local hexadecimal address:

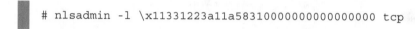

```
# nlsadmin -l \x11331223a11a58310000000000000000 tcp
```

All services that need to be run will then need to be entered into the TLI listener database.

Adding a Serial Port

Like any modern server system, Solaris 9 supports the connection of simple external devices through both a serial (RS-232-C or RS-423) and a parallel port. The two most common uses for serial devices on a Sparc system are connecting a VT-100 terminal or equivalent to operate as the system console if no graphics device is installed, and as a modem, enabling dial-up Internet access using the Point-to-Point Protocol (PPP). The former is a common practice in many server rooms, where the expense of a monitor and video card can be eliminated by using a VT-100 terminal as the console because many Sparc machines require a display device to boot at all. On x86 systems, there are many more devices available that often only have drivers available for other operating systems. Sun and other third-party hardware vendors are slowly making releases available for these devices through the Solaris Developer Connection. If you need to obtain an updated copy of the Solaris Device Configuration Assistant, and any updated device drivers for supported external devices, these are currently available to be downloaded at **http://soldc.sun.com/support/drivers/boot.html**.

Solaris 9 has a graphical user interface (GUI) for serial device configuration, provided through the admintool program (shown in Figure 23-3). admintool is generally used for system administration tasks, like adding users and groups, but it also has facilities for configuring parallel devices (like printers) and serial devices (like modems). It contains templates for configuring standard modem and terminal devices, and supports multiple ports.

Adding a Modem

Solaris 9 works best with external Hayes-compatible modems, which are also supported by other operating systems such as Microsoft Windows. However, modems that require specific operating system support (such as so-called "WinModems") will not work with Solaris 9. In addition, internal modem cards are generally not supported by Solaris 9. While older modems tend to use external (but sometimes internal!) DIP switches, modern modems can be configured using software to set most of their key operational parameters.

Modem access can be configured to allow inbound-only, outbound-only, and bi-directional access, which allows traffic in both directions, using a similar scheme. In the following example, we'll consider the scenario of dial-out-only access. The modem

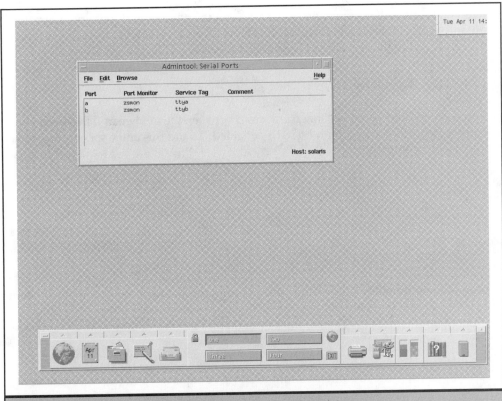

Figure 23-3. *Managing serial devices using admintool*

should be connected to one of the system's serial ports (A or B) and switched on. The A and B serial ports map to the devices */dev/cua/a and /dev/cua/b*, respectively.

To test the modem, use the `tip` command:

```
# tip hardwire
```

where hardwire should be defined in */etc/remote*. The hardwire entry should be similar to this entry:

```
hardwire:\
        :dv=/dev/cua/a:br#19200:el=^C^S^Q^U^D:ie=%$:oe=^D:
```

where 19,200 bps is the connection speed between the modem and the serial port. In addition, /etc/remote should have a connection string associated with each modem that's connected to the system. For example, the string

```
cual:dv=/dev/cua/a:p8:br#19200
```

specifies that 19,200 bps is the connection speed between the modem and the serial port, with 8-bit transmission and with no parity enabled. To use this entry specifically, you would use the command

```
# tip cua1
```

If the message

```
connected
```

appears on your terminal, the system is able to communicate successfully with the modem. For Hayes-compatible modems, command strings can be entered directly like this:

```
ATE1V1
```

If you see "ok," the modem is communicating as expected and can be configured to run PPP.

Setting Up PPP

The first step in configuring PPP is to insert appropriate configuration information in /etc/ppp/options. The following options are the most commonly used:

- *<tty_name>*   The name of the terminal device to use for communication
- *<speed>*   The speed at which to transmit data
- *auth*   Specifies that authentication is required (noauth specifies that no authentication is required)
- *callback*   Requests a callback from the remote server. Useful for saving on long distance charges!
- *connect* or *init*   Specifies the chat script to configure line communications
- *mru*   Sets a Maximum Receive Unit (MRU) value, which specifies a limit on the packet size transmitted by the server

■ *mtu* Sets a Maximum Transmit Unit (MTU) value, which specifies a limit on the packet size transmitted by the client

Other options may be required, especially for authentication, but using these options is generally sufficient to make a connection.

Examples

The following examples demonstrate how to set up modems and Internet access.

Using ttymon

The ttymon port monitor is managed by the `ttyadm` command. ttymon is designed to monitor requests from ports to allow remote access to the system. The ttymon monitor operates continually, spawning child processes when appropriate in order to service requests, which are sequentially numbered (for example, ttymon1, ttymon2, and so forth). The most common request for terminals is probably for an interactive login; thus, */usr/bin/login* is requested. The `sacadm` command can be used to list all current ttymon processes:

```
# sacadm -l
PMTAG     PMTYPE    FLGS   RCNT   STATUS    COMMAND
ttymon1   ttymon    -      2      ENABLED   /usr/lib/saf/ttymon #ttymon1
ttymon2   ttymon    -      2      ENABLED   /usr/lib/saf/ttymon #ttymon2
ttymon3   ttymon    -      2      ENABLED   /usr/lib/saf/ttymon #ttymon3
```

In order to view the services currently being provided through a particular monitor, you can use the `pmadm` command for each monitor process:

```
# pmadm -l -p ttymon2
PMTAG     PMTYPE    SVCTAG      FLGS     ID       <PMSPECIFIC>
ttymon2   ttymon    11          u        root     /dev/term/11
   -   -   /usr/bin/login - 9600 - login:   -tvi925
ttymon2   ttymon    12          u        root     /dev/term/12
   -   -   /usr/bin/login - 9600 - login:   -tvi925
ttymon2   ttymon    13          u        root     /dev/term/13
   -   -   /usr/bin/login - 9600 - login:   -tvi925
ttymon2   ttymon    14          u        root     /dev/term/14
   -   -   /usr/bin/login - 9600 - login:   -tvi925
```

Here, we can see that ports */dev/term/11* through */dev/term/14* are being serviced using the login service.

Connecting to an ISP

Once the */etc/options/ppp* file has been set up, a connection can then be made from the command line. For example, to connect using a 56K modem using the chat script emergency1.chat, the following command will establish a connection without authentication:

```
# pppd connect 'chat -f emergency1.chat' /dev/cua/a 57600 noauth
```

 # Command Reference

The following commands can be used to support modem services and Internet access.

pmadm

The port monitors are managed by the pmadm command. Port services can be managed by using the following commands:

pmadm -a	Adds a port monitor service.
pmadm -d	Disarms a port monitor service.
pmadm -e	Enables a port monitor service.
pmadm -r	Removes a port monitor service.

sacadm

The sacadm command is used to manage port monitors. The following functions are available:

sacadm -a	Attaches a new port monitor.
sacadm -e	Arms a port monitor.
sacadm -d	Disarms a port monitor.
sacadm -s	Initializes a port monitor.
sacadm -k	Kills a port monitor.
sacadm -l	Lists port monitor details.
sacadm -r	Deletes a port monitor.

tip

`tip` is a command that acts like a terminal. It can be used, for example, to access remote systems directly through a serial port, where one system acts as the console for the other. Below, we'll use the `tip` command to connect a Solaris 9 system to a modem. Before proceeding, however, we'll examine some of the key features of `tip` in its own right.

`tip` uses the */etc/remote* file to enable it to make connections through the serial port. For example, if you have a profile setup in */etc/remote*, it's possible to fire up a terminal session immediately by using the command

```
# tip -profile
```

where *profile* is the name of the profile that you've set up with all the settings that the port requires to operate. `tip` also uses initialization settings in the *.tiprc* file to specify its operational parameters.

The following shows the most commonly used `tip` commands:

Command	Description
~.	Exits the session.
~c	Changes directory.
~!	Spawns a shell.
~>	Sends a local file.
~<	Receives a remote file.
~p	Sends a local file.
~t	Receives a remote file.
~C	Allows a local application to connect to a remote system.
~#	Issues a `break` command.
~s	Defines a variable.
~^z	Suspends tip.

The
Complete
Reference

Part VI

Services and Directories

Chapter 24

Network File System (NFS)

In this chapter, we examine Sun's Network File System (NFS), which is a distributed file system architecture based on the Remote Procedure Call (RPC) protocol. RPC is a standard method of allocating and managing shared resources between Solaris systems. Although NFS is similar to Samba in concept, supporting transparent file system sharing between systems, NFS features high data throughput because of dedicated support in the Solaris kernel, and support for both NFS 2 and 3 clients.

NFS was one of the first distributed network applications to ever be successfully deployed on local area networks. It allows users to mount volumes of other systems connected to the network, with the same ability to change permissions, delete and create files, and apply security measures as any other locally mounted file system. One of the great advantages of NFS is its efficient use of network bandwidth, by using RPC (remote procedure) calls. In Solaris 9, the NFS concept has been extended to the Internet, with the new WebNFS providing file system access through a URL similar to that used for Web pages. In this section, we will examine the theory behind distributed file systems, and examine how they can best be established in practice.

Prior to Solaris 2.5, NFS 2 was deployed, which used the unreliable UDP protocol for data transfer, hence NFS 2's poor reputation for data integrity. However, the more modern NFS 3 protocol, based around TCP, is now implemented in all new Solaris releases. NFS 3 allows a NFS server to cache NFS client requests in RAM, speeding up disk writing operations and the overall speed of NFS transactions. In addition, Solaris 2.6 and onwards provide support for a new type of NFS called WebNFS. The WebNFS protocol allows file systems to be shared across the Internet, as an alternative to traditional Internet file-sharing techniques, like FTP. In addition, initial testing has shown that Sun's WebNFS server has greater bandwidth than a traditional Web server, meaning that it might one day replace the Hypertext Transfer Protocol (HTTP) as the Web standard for transferring data.

In this chapter, the reader will learn how to set up and install an NFS server and an NFS client, and how to export file systems. In addition, we examine how to set up the automounter so that a user's home directory across all machines on an intranet is automatically shared and available, irrespective of their login host.

Key Concepts

The following concepts are required knowledge for installing and managing NFS.

NFS Architectures

A Solaris 9 system can share any of its file systems with other systems, making them available for remote mounting. NFS considers the system that shares the file system to be a server, and the system that remotely mounts the file system as a client. When an NFS client mounts a remote file system, it is connected to a mount point on the local file system, which means it appears to local users as just another file system. For example, a system called *carolina* may make its mail directory */var/mail* available for

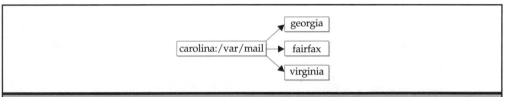

Figure 24-1. *NFS server* carolina *exports its mail directory to NFS clients* georgia, fairfax, *and* virginia, *using the same mount point as the exported file system.*

remote mounting by NFS clients. This would allow users on machines like *georgia, virginia,* and *fairfax* to read their mail stored on *carolina* to be read locally from their own machines, without their having to explicitly log in to *carolina*. This means that a single mail server that acts as an NFS server can serve all NFS clients on a local area network with mail. Figure 24-1 shows this configuration.

However, one important aspect of NFS is the ability to export file systems and mount them on a remote mount point that is different from the original shared directory. For example, the NFS server *carolina* may also export its Sun AnswerBook files (from the directory */opt/answerbook*) to the clients *virginia, georgia,* and *fairfax*. However, *virginia* mounts these files in the */usr/local/www/htdocs* directory, as it publishes them via the World Wide Web, while *georgia* mounts them in */opt/doc/answerbook*. The client *fairfax* mounts them in */opt/answerbook,* just like they are exported from *carolina*. The point is that the remote mount point can be completely different from the actual directory exported by an NFS server. This configuration is shown in Figure 24-2.

Remote Procedure Calls (RPC)

NFS makes use of Remote Procedure Call (RPC) technology, which makes it easy for systems to make requests for remote execution of procedures on server systems. RPC is currently supported across a number of different operating systems, including Solaris, Linux, and Microsoft Windows. The purpose of RPC is to abstract the connection details and methods required to access procedures across networks—that is, the client and server programs do not need to implement separate networking code, as a simple

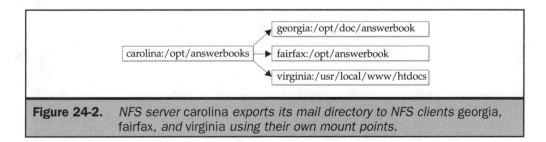

Figure 24-2. *NFS server* carolina *exports its mail directory to NFS clients* georgia, fairfax, *and* virginia *using their own mount points.*

API is provided for finding services through a service called the *portmapper* (or *rpcbind*). The portmapper should be running on both the client and server for NFS to operate correctly. The portmapper is registered with both UDP and TCP 111, since requests may be generated for or received using NFS 2 or NFS 3, respectively.

Automounter

The automounter is a program that automatically mounts NFS file systems when they are accessed and then unmounts them when they are no longer needed. It allows you to use special files, known as *automounter maps*, which contain information about the servers, the pathname to the NFS file system on the server, the local pathname, and the mount options. By using the automounter, you don't have to update the entries in */etc/vfstab* on every client by hand, every time you make a change to the NFS servers.

Normally, only `root` can mount file systems, so when users need to mount an NFS file system, they need to find the system administrator. The main problem is that once users are finished with a file system, they rarely tell the system administrator— even if they did, manually mounting and unmounting resources at the request of users would create an administrative burden that is not scalable. In addition, if the NFS server containing that file system ever crashed, you may be left with one or more hanging processes. This can easily increase your workload if you are responsible for maintaining an NFS server. The automounter can solve both of these problems, because it automatically mounts an NFS file system when a user references a file in that file system, and it will automatically unmount the NFS file system if it is not referenced for more than five minutes.

The automounter is a RPC daemon that services requests from clients to mount and unmount remote volumes using NFS. During installation, a set of server-side maps are created that list the file systems to be automatically mounted. Typically, these file systems include shared user home directories (under */home*), and network-wide mail directories (*/var/mail*).

Procedures

The following procedures are commonly used for installing and managing NFS.

Configuring a NFS Server

If you installed the NFS server during installation, a startup script will have been created in */etc/init.d*, called *nfs.server*. Thus, the NFS server can be started manually by typing the command

```
# /etc/init.d/nfs.server start
```

This command will start at least two daemons: the NFS server (*/usr/lib/nfs/nfsd*) and the mount daemon (*/usr/lib/nfs/mountd*). The `nfsd` is responsible for answering access requests from clients for shared volumes on the server, while the mountd is responsible for providing information about mounted file systems.

To check whether or not the NFS server has started correctly, it is possible to examine the process list for nfsd and mountd by using the following commands:

```
# ps -eaf | grep nfsd
    root 19961    1  0    Aug 31 ?    0:09 /usr/lib/nfs/nfsd -a 16
# ps -eaf | grep mountd
    root   370    1  0    May 16 ?    2:49 /usr/lib/nfs/mountd
```

In this case, both the nfsd and mountd are operating correctly. In order to stop the NFS server, the following command may be used:

```
# /etc/init.d/nfs.server stop
```

There are some optional services started by the NFS server startup script, including daemons that support diskless booting (the Reverse Address Resolution Protocol daemon, */usr/sbin/in.rarpd*, and the boot parameter server, */usr/sbin/rpc.bootparamd*). In addition, a separate daemon for x86 boot support (*/usr/sbin/rpld*), using the Network Booting RPL (Remote Program Load) protocol, may also be started. You only need to configure these services if you wish to provide diskless booting for local clients; otherwise, they can be safely commented from the */etc/init.d/nfs.server* script.

Sharing File Systems

To actually share file systems and directories, you can use the share command. For example, if you want to share the */var/mail* directory from *carolina* to *georgia*, you could use the command

```
# share -F nfs -o rw=georgia /var/mail
```

In this example, "-F nfs" stands for "a file system of type NFS." Of course, we really want to share the volume to *virginia* and *fairfax* as well, so we would probably use the command

```
# share -F nfs -o rw=georgia,virginia,fairfax /var/mail
```

The */var/mail* volume is shared to these clients because users on these systems need to read and write their e-mail. However, if we need to share a CD-ROM volume, we obviously need to share it read-only:

```
# share -F nfs -o ro /cdrom
```

Normally, the volumes to be shared are identified in the */etc/dfs/dfstab* file. One of the really innovative features of NFS is that a system that shares volumes to other systems can actually remotely mount shared volumes from its own clients. For example, while *carolina* might share the volume */cdrom* to *georgia*, *fairfax*, and *virginia*, and *virginia* might share the */staff* directory, which contains home directories, to *carolina*, *georgia*, and *fairfax*, using the command

```
# share -F nfs -o rw=georgia,carolina,fairfax /staff
```

File systems can be unshared using the `unshare` command. For example, if we are going to change a CD-ROM on *carolina* that is shared to clients using NFS, it might be wise to unmount it first:

```
# unshare -F nfs /cdrom
```

To unshare all volumes that are currently being shared from a NFS server, the following command can be used:

```
# unshareall
```

The command `dfmounts` shows the local resources shared through the networked file system are currently mounted by specific clients:

```
# dfmounts
RESOURCE   SERVER PATHNAME                 CLIENTS
   -           carolina /cdrom             virginia,georgia
   -           carolina /var/mail          fairfax,virginia,georgia
   -           carolina /opt/answerbook    fairfax
```

However, `dfmounts` does not provide information about the permissions with which directories and file systems are shared, nor does it show those shared resources that have no clients currently using them. To display this information, we need to use the `share` command with no arguments. On *virginia*, this looks like this,

```
# share
/staff rw=georgia,fairfax,carolina  "staff"
```

while on *carolina*, the volumes are different:

```
# share
 -              /cdrom   ro=georgia,fairfax,carolina "cdrom"
 -              /var/mail  rw=georgia,fairfax,carolina "mail"
```

Conversely, as a client, you want to determine which volumes are available for you to mount from NFS servers. This can be achieved by using the `dfshares` command. For example, to view the mounts available from the server *virginia*, executed on *carolina*, the following output would be displayed:

```
# dfshares -F nfs virginia
RESOURCE                   SERVER        ACCESS      TRANSPORT
virginia:/staff            virginia      -           -
```

Installing a NFS Client

In order to access file systems being shared from an NFS server, a separate NFS client must be operating on the client system. There are two main daemon processes that must be running in order to use the `mount` command to access shared volumes: the NFS lock daemon (*/usr/lib/nfs/lockd*) and the NFS stat daemon (*/usr/lib/nfs/statd*). The *lockd* manages file sharing and locking at the user level, while the *statd* is used for file recovery after connection outage.

If NFS was installed during the initial system setup, a file called *nfs.client* should have been created in */etc/init.d*. In order to run the NFS client, the following command needs to be executed:

```
# /etc/init.d/nfs.client start
```

Just like the NFS server, you can verify that the NFS daemons have started correctly by using the following commands:

```
# ps -eaf | grep statd
  daemon   211    1  0   May 16 ?        0:04 /usr/lib/nfs/statd
# ps -eaf | grep lockd
    root   213    1  0   May 16 ?        0:03 /usr/lib/nfs/lockd
```

If these two daemons are not active, then the NFS client will not run. The next step is for the client to consult the */etc/vfstab file*, which lists both the UFS and NFS file systems that need to be mounted, and attempts to mount the latter if they are available by using the `mountall` command.

In order to stop the NFS client once it is operating, the following command may be used:

```
# /etc/init.d/nfs.client stop
```

The NFS server is usually started automatically during run-level 3.

Configuring a CacheFS File System

In general terms, a cache is a place where important material can be placed so that it can be quickly retrieved. The location of the cache may be quite different from the normal storage location for the specified material. For example, field commanders in the army may store ammunitions in local caches so that their forces can obtain their required materials quickly, in case of war. These ammunitions would normally be stored securely well away from the battlefield, but must be "highly available" when required. The state of the battlefield may make it difficult to access outside sources of ammunition during live fire, so a sizable cache of arms is always wise.

This analogy can be easily extended to client/server scenarios, where an unreliable or slow data link may give rise to performance issues. A cache, in this case, can be created to locally store commonly used files, rather than retrieving them each time they are requested from a server. The cache approach has the advantage of speeding up client access to data. However, it has the disadvantage of data asynchronization, where a file is modified on the server after it has been stored in the cache. Thus, if a local file retrieved from the cache is modified before being sent back to the server, any modifications performed on the server's copy of the file would be overwritten. Conversely, cached data may be out-of-date by the time it is retrieved by the local client, meaning that important decisions could be taken on inaccurate information.

Many Internet client/server systems involved in the exchange of data across a HTTP link use a cache to store data. This data is never modified and sent back to the server, so overwriting server-side data is never an issue. Small ISPs with limited bandwidth often use caches to store files that are commonly retrieved from a server. For example, if the ISP has 1,000 customers who routinely download the front page of the *Sydney Morning Herald* each morning, it makes sense to download the file once from the *Sydney Morning Herald* Web site, and store it locally for the other 999 users to retrieve. Since the front page may only change from day to day, the page will always be current, as long as the cache purges the front-page file at the end of each day. The daily amount of data to be downloaded from the *Sydney Morning Herald* Web site has been reduced by 99.9 percent, which can significantly boost the ISP's performance in downloading other noncached files from the Internet, as well as reduce the overall cost of data throughput.

Solaris provides a cache file system (CacheFS) that is designed to improve NFS client/server performance across slow or unreliable networks. The principles underlying CacheFS are exactly the same as the two examples above: locally stored files that are frequently requested can be retrieved by users on the client system without having to download them again from the server. This approach minimizes the number of connections required between an NFS client and server to retrieve the same amount of data in a manner that is invisible to users on the client system. In fact, users will notice that their files are retrieved more quickly than before the cache was introduced.

CacheFS seamlessly integrates with existing NFS installations, with only simple modifications to mount command parameters and */etc/vfstab* entries required to make use of the facility. The first task in configuring a cache is to create a mount point and a cache on a client system. If a number of NFS servers are to be used with the cache, it makes sense to create individual caches underneath the same top-level mount point. Many sites use the mount point */cache* to store individual caches. In this example, we'll assume that a file system from the NFS server *yorktown* will be cached on the local client system *midway*, so the commands to create a cache on *midway* are

```
# mkdir /cache
# cfsadmin -c /cache/yorktown
```

Here, we've used the `cfsadmin` command to create the cache once the mount point */cache* has been created. Now, let's examine how we would force the cache to be used for all accesses from *midway* to *yorktown* for the remote file system */staff*, which is also mounted locally on */staff*:

```
# mount -F cachefs -o backfstype=nfs,cachedir=/cache/yorktown \
  yorktown:/staff /staff
```

Once the *yorktown:/staff* file system has been mounted in this way, users on *midway* will not notice any difference in operation, except that file access to */staff* will be much quicker.

It is possible to check the status of the cache by using the `cachefsstat` command. In order to verify that */cache/yorktown* is operating correctly, the following command would be used:

```
# cachefsstat /cache/yorktown
```

Alternatively, the `cfsadmin` command can be used:

```
# cfsadmin -l /cache/yorktown
cfsadmin: list cache FS information
maxblocks 80%
minblocks 0%
threshblocks 75%
maxfiles 80%
minfiles 0%
threshfiles 75%
maxfilesize 12MB
yorktown:_staff:_staff
```

Note the last line, which is the current cache ID. You will need to remember the cache ID if you ever want to delete the cache. If a cache needs to be deleted, the cfsadmin command can be used with the *–d* option:

```
# umount /staff
# cfsadmin -d yorktown:_staff:_staff /cache/yorktown
```

Here, we've unmounted the */staff* volume on *merlin* locally before attempting to remove the cache by providing its ID along with its mount point.

Enabling the Automounter

The automount command installs autofs mount points, and associates an automount map with each mount point. This requires that the automount daemon be running (automountd). When the automount daemon is initialized on the server, no exported directories are mounted by the clients: these are only mounted when a remote user attempts to access a file on the directory from a client. The connection eventually times out, in which case the exported directory is unmounted by the client. Automounter maps usually work with a network information service, like NIS+, to manage shared volumes, meaning that a single home directory for individual users can be provided on request from a single server, no matter which client machine they log in to. Connection and reconnection is handled by the automount daemon. If automount starts up and has nothing to mount or unmount, this is reported (and is quite normal):

```
# automount
automount: no mounts
automount: no unmounts
```

Automounter Maps

The behavior of the automounter is determined by a set of files called automounter maps. There are two main types of maps: indirect and direct. An indirect map is useful when you are mounting several file systems that will share a common pathname prefix. As we will see shortly, an indirect map can be used to manage the directory tree in */home*. A direct map is used to mount file systems where each mount point does not share a common prefix with other mount points in the map. In this section, we will look at examples of each of these types of maps. An additional map, called the *master map*, is used by the automounter to determine the names of the files corresponding to the direct and indirect maps.

Indirect Maps

The most common type of automounter maps are indirect maps, which correspond to "regularly" named file systems like */home* or */usr* directory trees. Regularly named file systems share the same directory prefix. For example, the directories */home/jdoe* and */home/sdoe* are regularly named directories in the */home* directory tree.

Normally, indirect maps are stored in the */etc* directory, and are named with the convention *auto_directory*, where *directory* is the name of the directory prefix (without slashes) that the indirect map is responsible for. As an example, the indirect map responsible for the */home* directory is usually named *auto_home*. An indirect map is made up of a series of entries in the following format:

```
directory     options     host:filesystem
```

Here *directory* is the relative pathname of a directory that will be appended to the name of the directory that is corresponding to this indirect map as specified in the master map file. (The master map is covered later in this section.) For *options*, you can use any of the mount options covered earlier in this chapter. To specify options, you will need to prefix the first option with a dash (–). If you do not need any extra options, you can omit the options entirely. The final entry in the map contains the location of the NFS file system.

Here is an example of the indirect map that is responsible for the directories in */home*:

```
# /etc/auto_home - home directory map for automounter
jdoe         orem:/store/home/jdoe
sdoe         orem:/store/home/sdoe
kdoe -bg srv-ss10:/home/kdoe
```

Here, the entries for *jdoe*, *sdoe*, and *kdoe* correspond to the directories */home/jdoe*, */home/sdoe*, and */home/kdoe*, respectively. The first two entries indicate that the automounter should mount the directories */home/jdoe* and */home/sdoe* from the NFS server *orem*, while the last one specifies that the directory */home/kdoe* should be mounted from the NFS server *srv-ss10*. The last entry also demonstrates the use of options.

Now that we have taken a look at an indirect map, let's walk through what happens when you access a file on an NFS file system that is handled by the automounter. For example, consider the following command that accesses the file */home/jdoe/docs/book/ch17.doc*:

```
$ more /home/jdoe/docs/book/ch17.doc
```

Because the directory */home/jdoe* is automounted, the following steps are used by the automounter to allow you to access the file:

1. The automounter looks at the pathname and determines that the directory */home* is controlled by the indirect map *auto_home*.

2. The automounter looks at the rest of the pathname for a corresponding entry in the *auto_home* map. In this case, it finds the matching entry, *jdoe*.

3. Once a matching entry has been found, the automounter checks to see if the directory */home/jdoe* is already mounted. If the directory is already mounted, you can directly access the file; otherwise, the automounter mounts this directory and then allows you to access the file.

Direct Maps

When you use an indirect map, the automounter takes complete control of the directory corresponding to the indirect map. This means that no user, not even `root`, can create entries in a directory corresponding to an indirect map. For this reason, directories specified in an indirect map cannot be automounted on top of an existing directory. In this case, you need a special type of map known as a direct map. A direct map allows you to mix automounter mount points and normal directories in the same directory tree. The directories specified in a direct map have "nonregular" mount points, which simply means that they do not share a common prefix. A common use for direct maps is to allow for directories in the */usr* directory tree to be automounted.

The direct map is normally stored in the file */etc/auto_direct*. The format of this file is similar to the format of the indirect maps:

```
directory      options      host:filesystem
```

Here, *directory* is the absolute pathname of a directory. For *options*, you can use any of the mount options covered earlier in this chapter. To specify options, you will need to prefix the first option with a dash (–). If you do not need any extra options, you can omit the options entirely. The final entry in the map contains the location of the NFS file system. Here is an example of the direct map that is responsible for some of the directories in */usr*:

```
# /etc/auto_direct - Direct Automount map
/usr/pubsw/man   orem:/internal/opt/man
/usr/doc         orem:/internal/httpd/htdocs
```

When any files in the directories */usr/pubsw/man* or */usr/doc* are accessed, the automounter will automatically handle the mounting of these directories.

Master Maps

When the automounter first starts, it reads the file */etc/auto_master* to determine where to find the direct and indirect map files. The *auto_master* file is known as the master map. Its consists of lines whose format is as follows:

```
directory      map
```

Here, *directory* is the name of the directory that corresponds to the indirect map. For a direct map, this entry is /–. The *map* is the name of the map file in the */etc* directory corresponding to the *directory* given in the first column. The following example shows a master map file for the direct and indirect maps given earlier in this section:

```
# Master map for automounter
/home           auto_home
/-              auto_direct
```

Other entries can also be made in the master map. For example, to share a common directory for mail between a number of clients and a mail server, we would enter the following definition:

```
/-                 /etc/auto_mail
```

This creates a share called "auto_mail" that makes mail on a single server accessible to all client machines upon request. Automounter permits two kinds of shares, which can be defined by direct and indirect maps: a *direct map* is a set of arbitrary mount points that are listed together, while an *indirect map* mounts everything under a specific directory. For example, *auto_home* mounts user directories and all subdirectories underneath them. If an automounted share is available on the server, you should see its details being displayed in the */etc/mnttab* file:

```
burbank:/var/mail   /var/mail   nfs   nosuid,dev=2bc0012   951071258
```

Continuing with the example of *auto_mail*, as defined in the master map, a file */etc/auto_mail* would have to contain the following entry:

```
# cat /etc/auto_mail
  /var/mail       burbank:/var/mail
```

This ensures that the *burbank* server knows where to find the */var/mail* directory physically, and that automount can mount the shared volume at will. Sometimes, the network load caused by mounting and unmounting home directories can lead to an increase in I/O load and reduce the effective bandwidth of a network. For this reason, only volumes that need to be shared should be shared. Alternatively, the timeout parameter for automount can be modified to extend its latency for mounting and unmounting directories.

Automount and NIS+

A common problem with *auto_home* is that systems in a NIS+ environment may create user accounts on a file system mounted as */home*. This means that if *auto_home* is active, as defined by */etc/auto_master*, then after rebooting the shared home directories are mounted on */home*, and when the local */home* attempts to mount the same point, it fails. This is one of the most frequently asked questions about Solaris 8, as the convention was different for earlier Solaris systems, which used local */home* directories. The recommended practice is now to create home directories under */export/home*, on the local file system if required, or to use *auto_home* in a NIS+ environment. However, if you wish to disable this feature altogether, and stick with a local */home*, then simply remove *+auto_master* from the master map (*/etc/auto_master*).

Starting and Stopping the Automounter

Starting and stopping the automounter is normally handled by your system at boot and shutdown time, but you will have to start and stop the automounter manually if you make changes to any of its map files.

The automount daemon is typically started from */etc/init.d/autofs* during the multi-user startup, with a command like this:

```
# /etc/init.d/autofs start
```

This should start the automounter. You can confirm that it started correctly by using the following command:

```
# /bin/ps -ef | grep automountd
```

The output should look like the following:

```
root 21642    1  0 11:27:29 ?       0:00 /usr/lib/autofs/automountd
```

If you receive no output, the automounter has not started correctly. In that case, you should run the startup script again.

Stopping the NFS client is similar to starting it:

```
# /etc/init.d/autofs stop
```

The stop script usually stops the automounter, but you can confirm this using the command:

```
# /bin/ps -ef | grep automountd
```

This is the same command that is used to check to see if the automounter is running, except that once you stop it, this command should not produce any output. If you do see some output and it contains a `grep` command, you can ignore those lines. Any other output indicates that the automounter has not stopped, in which case you should execute the NFS client stop command again.

If you receive a message similar to

```
/home: busy
```

you will need to determine if anyone is logged on to the system and is using files from */home*. If you cannot determine this, you can use the following command to get a list of all of the mounted directories in the directory that caused the error message (in this case, */home*):

```
$ df -k -F nfs
/home/jdoe
```

Just replace */home* with the name of the directory that produced the error message. In this case, only one directory, */home/jdoe*, was automounted. Once you have a list of these directories, try unmounting each one with the `umount` command. When you receive an error message, you will know which directory contains the files that are in use. You can ask the user to finish with those files, and then proceed to stop the automounter.

Examples

The following examples provide some real-world cases for installing and managing NFS.

Checking Portmapper Status

If you're having trouble starting the NFS daemon, it's often an *rpc* problem. In order to determine whether an *rpc* portmapper is running, you may use the `rpcinfo` command:

```
# rpcinfo -p
   program vers proto   port  service
    100000    4   tcp    111  rpcbind
    100000    3   tcp    111  rpcbind
    100000    2   tcp    111  rpcbind
    100000    4   udp    111  rpcbind
    100000    3   udp    111  rpcbind
    100000    2   udp    111  rpcbind
    100007    3   udp  32774  ypbind
    100007    2   udp  32774  ypbind
```

```
100007    1    udp    32774    ypbind
100007    3    tcp    32771    ypbind
100007    2    tcp    32771    ypbind
100007    1    tcp    32771    ypbind
100011    1    udp    32785    rquotad
100024    1    udp    32789    status
100024    1    tcp    32775    status
100021    1    udp     4045    nlockmgr
100021    2    udp     4045    nlockmgr
100021    3    udp     4045    nlockmgr
100021    4    udp     4045    nlockmgr
100068    2    udp    32809
100068    3    udp    32809
100068    4    udp    32809
100068    5    udp    32809
100083    1    tcp    32795
100021    1    tcp     4045    nlockmgr
100021    2    tcp     4045    nlockmgr
100021    3    tcp     4045    nlockmgr
100021    4    tcp     4045    nlockmgr
100005    1    udp    32859    mountd
100005    2    udp    32859    mountd
100005    3    udp    32859    mountd
100005    1    tcp    32813    mountd
100005    2    tcp    32813    mountd
100005    3    tcp    32813    mountd
100026    1    udp    32866    bootparam
100026    1    tcp    32815    bootparam
```

In this example, both the *mountd* and *nfsd* are running, along with several other services, so the NFS daemon should have no problems executing. However, the RPL service is not active, so x86 clients would not be able to use the local server as a boot server.

Mounting Remote File Systems

On the client side, if we want to mount a volume that has been shared from an NFS server, we use the mount command. For example, if we want to mount the exported CD-ROM from *carolina* on the NFS client *virginia*, we would use the command

```
# mount -F nfs -o ro carolina:/cdrom /cdrom
```

Like the */etc/dfs/dfstab* files, which records a list of volumes to be exported, the */etc/vfstab* file can contain entries for NFS volumes to be mounted from remote servers. For example, on the machine *fairfax*, if we wanted the */var/mail* volume on *carolina* to be mounted locally as */var/mail*, we would enter the following line in */etc/vfstab*:

```
carolina:/var/mail  -  /var/mail  nfs  -  yes  rw
```

This line can be interpreted as a request to mount */var/mail* from *carolina* read/write on the local mount point */var/mail* as an NFS volume that should be mounted at boot time. If you make changes to the */etc/vfstab* file on *virginia*, and you want to mount the */var/mail* partition, you can use the command

```
# mount /var/mail
```

which will attempt to mount the remote */var/mail* directory from the server *carolina*. Alternatively, you can use the command

```
# mountall
```

which will mount all partitions that are listed in */etc/vfstab*, but which have not yet been mounted. This should identify and mount all available partitions.

File systems can be unmounted by using the umount command. For example, if the */cdrom* file system on *carolina* is mounted on *virginia* as */cdrom*, then the command

```
# umount /cdrom
```

will unmount the mounted NFS volume. Alternatively, the unmountall command can be used, which unmounts all currently mounted NFS volumes. For example, the command

```
# umountall -F nfs
```

unmounts all volumes that are currently mounted through NFS.

When a remote volume is mounted on a local client, it should be visible to the system just like a normal disk, and so commands like df, which displays disk slice information, will display results for all mounted disk volumes:

```
# df -k
carolina:/cdrom  412456 341700  70756    83%   /cdrom
carolina:/var/mail  4194304 343234  3851070   8%   /var/mail
carolina:/opt/answerbook  2097152 1345634  750618 64%   /opt/answerbook
```

Enhancing Security

So far, we've examined NFS without considering the security implications of sharing a file system to clients. In a local intranet environment, with protection from a firewall, some administrators implement open NFS sharing, where client lists are not supplied to share commands to limit access to server volumes. The problem with this approach is spoofing: an external system may be able to "pretend" to be part of your local network, thereby gaining access to globally shared NFS volumes. Given that NFS authentication is usually based on mappings of usernames on the client to server, if a spoofed system contains equivalent user accounts to those found on the server, then unauthorized clients will be able to read and write data at will. This is why it's critical to only share volumes to specific client systems, using the appropriate "read-write" or "read-only" designation.

The other key parameter for the share command sec specifies the type of authentication required to access server volumes. By default, the "sys" level is used, whereby usernames and groups are mapped between client and server. Thus, the user *lynda* on the client will have the same access permissions as *lynda* on the server. However, other alternatives are available, depending on the relative risks involved in data loss. If sensitive data is being shared by an NFS server, it may be wise to implement a more sophisticated authentication method, including one based on DES public key cryptography (the "dh" level, standing for Diffie-Hellman), or the Kerberos 4 authentication method (the "krb4" level). If a volume is exported with the *dh* or krb4 authentication levels, then all clients must use the method specified to access data on the volume specified. To support the *dh* or *krb4* authentication levels, secure RPC must be running. User keys can be updated by using the chkey command.

Performance

NFS performance is determined by a number of factors, including the following:

- Server CPU speed, and number of server CPUs
- Server physical RAM and virtual RAM
- Server disk speed
- Server system load
- Server CacheFS capacity
- Server network interfaces
- Number of clients
- Speed of local network
- Domain Name Lookup Cache (DNLC) speed

Many sites develop NFS services incrementally—as the number of users grows, so does the number of CPUs, memory, network interfaces, and faster disks allocated to improving NFS performance. In addition, a number of software methods, including the CacheFS and DNLC settings, can be modified to improve data throughput.

One of the best methods for determining how NFS is performing, from both a client and server perspective, is to use the `nfsstat` command to gather performance statistics over a period of weeks or months. In particular, counting the number of calls and bad calls can show the proportion of successful to unsuccessful requests, respectively, to the server. To run `nfsstat` on the server, the following command is used:

```
# nfsstat -s
...
Server nfs:
calls badcalls
575637455 3433
...
```

Here, we can see that the proportion of bad calls to the total number of calls is 3433 ÷ 575637455, which is much less than 1 percent. After gathering statistics for each interval, the counters can be reset to zero by using the following command:

```
# nfsstat -z
```

Command Reference

The following commands are commonly used to install and manage NFS.

share

The following table shows the most common options for the `share` command:

Parameter	Description
anon=username	Sets the username of unknown users to *username*
log	Starts NFS logging
nosuid	Prevents applications from executing as *set-uid*
nosub	Prevents client access to subdirectories of exported server volumes
ro	Prevents writing to an exported file system
root	Allows remote access by remote root users as the local root user
rw	Permits reading and writing to an exported file system
sec	Specifies the authentication level (*sys*, *dh*, or *krb4*)

mount

The main options available for mounting NFS file systems are shown here:

Option	Description
ro	Mounts a file system's read-only permissions
rw	Mounts a file system's read/write permissions
hard	No timeouts permitted—the client will repeatedly attempt to make a connection
soft	Timeouts permitted—the client will attempt a connection, and give an error message if connection fails
bg	Attempts to mount a remote file system in the background if connection fails

Chapter 25

Sendmail

lectronic mail was one of the first applications to be widely adopted across the Internet, and despite changes in technology and a shift towards information delivery via the World Wide Web (WWW), "e-mail" has managed to hold its ground. E-mail has undergone many changes in recent years: instead of plaintext messages being sent from command-line clients (or mail user agents, MUAs), there are many different mail protocols for remote clients to retrieve their mail from a centralized server (e.g., POP, IMAP), as well as multimedia content being supported through MIME extensions.

Although desktop clients are technically capable of running mail servers, most organizations still prefer to run a single main mail server, running a mail transport agent (MTA), such as the traditional Sendmail daemon or a newer replacement (e.g., qmail). This is because server systems such as Solaris have high uptime and better security features than the average desktop client, and because the security of mail services can be managed centrally. For example, if a security problem is revealed in Sendmail, then a patch can be freely downloaded from SunSolve and applied to the server with minimal disruption to users. If everyone ran their own mail server, new security problems could take weeks (if not months) per incident to rectify in a large organization.

In this chapter, we will examine the background to understanding how e-mail is addressed and delivered, and examine the configuration of the popular Sendmail mail transport agent. Finally, we will shift the focus to the client side, examining local and remote mail user agents that make use of the POP and IMAP protocols to retrieve their mail from a dedicated mail server.

Key Concepts

The following concepts are required knowledge for configuring and managing e-mail services.

Understanding E-Mail Protocols

Transferring electronic mail between servers on the Internet is largely conducted using the Simple Mail Transfer Protocol, or SMTP. The advantage of using SMTP is that mail transfer can be initiated by a local third-party mail user agent, such as elm or pine, or it can be performed manually by a user using Telnet. This makes installing Sendmail somewhat easier because all mail commands can be tested interactively by a human operator, and the response to each command can be evaluated appropriately.

If your users are not logged in through a shell on the local mail server, it will be necessary for you to provide a means by which they can send and retrieve mail through the server by using a remote mail client. There are two protocols that support this: the Post Office Protocol (POP), which is the oldest client/server mail transfer protocol and only supports offline mail reading, and IMAP (the Internet Message Access Protocol), which supports both offline and online mail reading. The choice between the two will often come down to which mail user agents your users are comfortable with, and which protocol their favorite client supports. However, there can be other considerations like authentication, authorization, and security that would sway an administrator to stipulate that IMAP be used over POP, even for offline mail reading. It should be noted that POP is generally easier to install and configure than IMAP.

SMTP

SMTP, the Simple Mail Transfer Protocol, allows servers to exchange mail with each other on a message-by-message basis. Standardized since the publication of RFC 821, SMTP has become the dominant Internet mail transfer protocol at the expense of earlier transfer methods, such as the ancient UUCP (UNIX-to-UNIX copy program), and the X.400 protocol, which is still popular with intranet and LAN-based e-mail. SMTP allows Sendmail and other mail transport agents, such as qmail, to accept connections on port 25, and "speak" to each other in a language that is interpretable by humans. In fact, as we will see later, it is actually possible for an administrator to manually test Sendmail by telnetting to port 25 and issuing SMTP commands directly. This is very useful for troubleshooting and testing existing configurations. Unfortunately, SMTP is almost too "simple," because it can be used by malicious users to forge many e-mail headers so as to make an e-mail appear to come from another user.

SMTP supports a sender-receiver model of host-host e-mail transactions: a host, such as *mail.companyA.com*, may wish to transfer a message to *mail.companyB.com*. The server mail.companyA.com first makes a connection to port 25, which mail.companyB.com acknowledges. Then, mail.companyA.com identifies the sender of the message, and again, mail.companyB.com acknowledges. Next, mail.companyA.com states the recipient of the message, and again, mail.companyB.com acknowledges. If the local user exists, or is listed in the */etc/aliases* database, the acknowledgement is in the affirmative. However, if no local user can be matched to the intended recipient, the acknowledgement is in the negative. If a user is found, the message is transmitted from mail.companyA.com to mail.companyB.com, and the latter acknowledges receipt (with a receipt number). Then mail.companyA.com requests a disconnection, and mail.companyB.com complies. Mail is held on the MTA until the RECV command to retrieve the message is sent by the MUA. This transaction is shown in Figure 25-1.

This kind of transaction is conducted millions of times every day on mail servers around the world, and is very fast. In the example, each of the acknowledgements from mail.companyB.com is associated with a three-digit numeric code: for example, a successful command from mail.companyA.com is always acknowledged with a code "250" from mail.companyB.com. Alternatively, if a user is not local, the code "551" is returned.

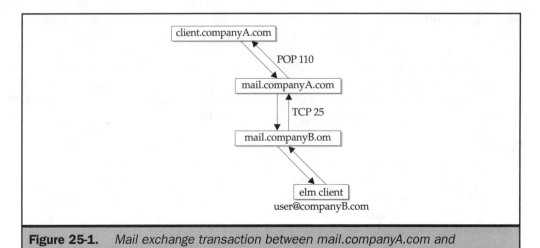

Figure 25-1. *Mail exchange transaction between mail.companyA.com and mail.companyB.com*

There are a number of standard SMTP commands:

HELO   Identifies the mail sending host to the mail receiving host

MAIL   Identifies the remote user who is sending the mail to the mail receiving host

RCPT   Indicates the local user to whom the mail is to be delivered

DATA   Precedes the body of the mail message

VRFY   Checks that a particular local user is known to the mail system

EXPN   Expands local mailing lists

QUIT   Terminates a session

In addition to the standard SMTP commands presented here, RFC 1869 proposed extensions to SMTP called ESMTP. ESMTP allows developers to extend the services currently provided by SMTP. MTAs, which support ESMTP commands, will attempt to greet each other with the EHLO command. If ESMTP is supported, a list of implemented commands on the remote server is returned—for example, as in the following:

```
$ telnet server.companyB.com 25
Trying 192.68.232.45...
Connected to server.companyB.com.
Escape character is '^]'.
```

```
220 server.companyB.com ESMTP Sendmail 8.9.1a/8.9.1;
Fri, 18 Feb 2002 13:05:14 +1100 (EST)
EHLO server.companyA.com
250-server.companyB.com Hello pwatters@server.companyA.com
[192.68.231.64], pleased to meet you
250-EXPN
250-VERB
250-8BITMIME
250-SIZE
250-DSN
250-ONEX
250-ETRN
250-XUSR
250 HELP
```

One example of an ESMTP command is Delivery Status Notification (DSN), which was proposed in RFC 1891 and reports on the status of remote mail deliveries to local users.

POP

Many users today do not log in directly to an interactive shell on a mail server, and run a local mail client like mailx or elm—instead, they are able to use a GUI-based mail reading client that runs locally on their PC, contacting the mail server directly to retrieve and send their mail. One of the most popular client/server protocols that facilitates this kind of mail delivery is the Post Office Protocol (POP), as proposed in RFC 1725. POP supports offline mail delivery to remote clients when mail addressed to a user account is delivered via a centralized mail server. POP supports many useful features, including the ability to retain copies of e-mail on the server and transmitting a copy to the client. This can be very useful for auditing and backup purposes, as a client machine may have to be reinstalled, or it may crash, in which case all the user's mail (including unread mail) might be lost. Reliability of service is still one of the main arguments for using a centralized mail server.

To retrieve mail from a POP server, a client machine makes a TCP connection to port 110. The client then greets the server and receives an acknowledgement, and then the session continues until it is terminated. During this time, a user may be authenticated. If a user is successfully authenticated, they may begin conducting transactions in the form of retrieving messages until the QUIT command is received by the server, at which point the session is terminated. Errors are indicated by status codes like "-ERR" for negative responses and "+OK" for positive responses. POP is deliberately SMTP-like in its command set and operation, making it easier for administrators to apply their skills to configuring both kinds of systems.

One of the drawbacks of POP is its lack of security: Although users are authenticated using their username and password on the mail server, this exchange is not encrypted, so anyone "snooping" the network might be able to retrieve this username and password. This would allow a rogue user to log into the mail server as the mail user—perhaps without the mail user realizing this for a long time, because they themselves never log in directly to the mail server. Since telnet and ftp use exactly the same method of authentication, it's certainly no worse than the standard networking toolset.

To obtain a free POP server for Solaris, download the freeware Qpopper server from Qualcomm at **http://www.eudora.com/qpopper/index.html**. Alternatively, Netra systems are supplied with the SUNWipop package, which provides a POP service for that platform. Qualcomm also has a free POP mail user agent called Eudora that is very popular in educational institutions and is available for both Macintosh and Windows platforms. Figure 25-2 shows the main user screen from Eudora: users can retrieve their mail from a remote server and display it ordered by date, sender, and subject. In addition, files from the local Macintosh or Windows file system can be sent as attachments by using the MIME extensions. Software like Eudora makes it easy for Macintosh or Windows users to have the convenience of local file access and GUI-based interfaces, while retaining the security and reliability of the Solaris server platform. However, it should be noted that browsers such as Netscape and other command-line MUAs (such as elm or pine) may be more appropriate for some environments than Eudora.

IMAP

The Internet Message Access Protocol (IMAP), proposed in RFC 2060, is intended to be a replacement for the POP protocol. While IMAP can perform offline processing, it is primarily intended for remote clients to retain some of the features of online processing enjoyed by MUAs like mailx and elm. A remote MUA using IMAP has the ability to perform more sophisticated transactions than a POP-based client: while POP caters to requests like retrieving all new messages on the server and passing them to the client, IMAP supports requests for just headers, just message bodies, or both. In addition, a search can be made for messages matching a particular criterion; for example, a request could be made to find all messages received by a particular user, or all messages received on a particular day. Although a POP-based MUA can perform these operations on its local copy of mail messages, IMAP can perform these operations remotely on the server. In addition, server-side messages can be marked with different flags indicating whether they have been replied to. Again, this reflects the kind of functionality often supplied by server-side MUAs like mailx or elm, but allows these operations to be performed by remote, easy-to-use GUI interfaces. Even if IMAP users want to store their files locally, like a POP-based service, this is also supported—but significantly, there is a synchronization feature whereby the local mailbox contents can be regularly matched with the mailbox on the server. This ensures that no data corruption occurs due to errors on the client machine.

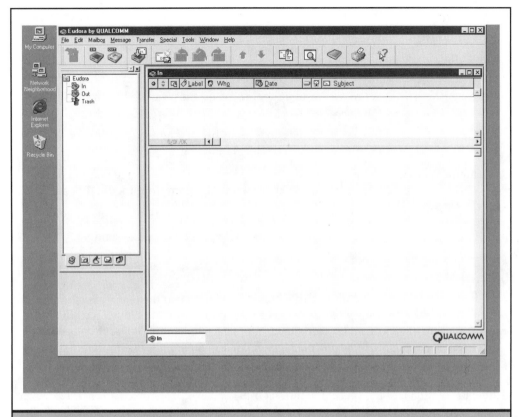

Figure 25-2.   *The POP-based Eudora client for Microsoft Windows, which receives
mail from a centralized and secure Solaris mail server*

In summary, POP and IMAP offer significantly different functions, and the use of
either protocol depends on the mail user agents that are supported and the needs of the
users. Many mail clients only support POP, and it may be that your organization keeps
with the POP platform because of this reason alone, even though IMAP offers many
more features.

Mail Headers

When a mail message is delivered into a user's mailbox, it contains a history of its
delivery process in the headers, which precede the message body. These headers
include the following:

From   Records the mail sending user, and the date and time at which
                        the mail was received.

Received	Provides details of how the mail was received by the MTA on the mail server, including the remote computer's name, MTA name, and identification.
Date	Indicates the time and date at which the message was received.
Message-Id	A unique number generated by the sending host that identifies the message.
To	Indicates the user to whom the message was addressed—usually a user on the local machine.
Content-Type	Indicates the MIME type in which the message was encoded. This is usually text, but could contain multimedia types as well.
Content-Length	The number of lines making up the body of the message.
Subject	Subject of the mail message as entered by the sender.

Sendmail

Now that we have reviewed how mail is transferred between the client and the server, we now turn our attention to server-server mail communications. Mail exchange between servers is performed by using mail transport agents (MTAs), such as Sendmail, which implement the SMTP protocol. Sendmail is the most popular mail transport agent for Solaris and many other UNIX systems, even though newer systems such as qmail make it easier to configure an MTA. In this section, we cannot cover all material relating to Sendmail, as it is one of the most complex Solaris programs to master. However, we provide sufficient detail so that most administrators working in a standard environment will be able to configure and test their mail transfer environment.

Sendmail is the standard mail transport agent that is supported by default under Solaris, although it is certainly possible to install an alternative third-party MTA like qmail (see **http://www.qmail.org/** for details). Solaris 9 supports Sendmail 8.

In most Solaris installations, the Sendmail MTA relies on a single configuration file (*sendmail.cf*), which contains sets of rules, to determine how e-mail is to be sent from the local host to any arbitrary remote host, and which mailer is to be used (e.g., for local versus remote delivery). The rules are used to choose the mechanism by which each message is delivered, while mail addresses are often rewritten to ensure correct delivery. For example, a mail message sent from a server command line may not include the fully qualified domain name in the Reply To field. This would mean that a remote user would not be able to reply to a message sent to them. The Sendmail MTA ensures that the "virtual envelopes" that contain e-mail messages are addressed correctly by inserting headers, where appropriate, to identify senders and recipients.

Although Sendmail is highly customizable, it is also difficult to configure and test, because a single error in the rules can produce unexpected results. Sendmail reads and processes every rule in *sendmail.cf*, so in order to speed up the process, the rules are written in a "computer friendly" format. Unfortunately, like assembly language, computer-friendly rules are rarely human friendly! In this section, we will review the configuration of Sendmail and highlight some of the security issues that continue to surround its deployment. Fortunately, the public version of Sendmail allows you to use simple configuration rules to generate a *sendmail.cf* file, which is easier than working directly on the *sendmail.cf* file.

Procedures

The following procedures are commonly used for configuring and managing e-mail services.

Configuring Sendmail (sendmail.cf)

The *sendmail.cf* file consists of single-line commands, which can range from rules and macros to options and headers. Some of these commands must appear only once if they specify a directive that affects the interpretation of rules (there can, however, be many rules in a *sendmail.cf* file). The main kinds of commands in a *sendmail.cf* file are listed here:

- **C** Specifies a class that can contain more than item. For instance,
  C{MAILCLIENTS} mars venus pluto
  specifies an array that contains a list of mail clients (*mars*, *venus*, and *pluto*).

- **D** Specifies a macro. For example,
  DR mail.companyA.com
  specifies a macro named *R* whose content is *mail.companyA.com*.

- **E** Specifies an environment variable. As a security measure, Sendmail does not use environment information passed to it, preferring to use values specified in the *sendmail.cf* file. To set the location of a Java Virtual Machine (VM), which may be used to support some mail-related applications, use the variable specification *EJVM=/usr/local/java/bin/java*.

- **H** Specifies a header, such as the "Received:" header. These definitions can be very complex because of the inclusion of multipart MIME messages.

- **M** Specifies the mail delivery agent. For instance,
  Mlocal, P=/bin/mail
  specifies that */bin/mail* is the mail delivery agent, which is usually the case under Solaris.

- **O** Specifies an option. For example, setting
  O SendMimeErrors=True
  enables the sending of MIME-encapsulated error messages.

- **P** Sets message precedence. For example, first class mail is set with a precedence of zero (*Pfirst-class=0*), while junk mail is set with a precedence of *–100 (Pjunk=-100)*.

- **R** Specifies a rule. For example, the rule
  `R$- $@ $1 @ ${Mydomain} Rewrite address`
  appends the FQDN defined by the macro *${Mydomain}* to a username.

- **S** Indicates the start of a ruleset, which can either be specified as a number (e.g., *S2* for ruleset 2) or with a label (e.g., *SDomainRules* for the DomainRules ruleset).

There are six kinds of system-defined rulesets contained in the *sendmail.cf* file:

- **S0** Handles basic address parsing. For example, if a user address is not specified, an error message "user address required" is returned.

- **S1** Processes the e-mail sender's address.

- **S2** Processes the e-mail recipient's address.

- **S3** Derives a canonical name, and initiates the rewriting rules. For example, invalid addresses are checked (e.g., those with colons), and any angle brackets <> are stripped from the address.

- **S4** Performs the final output post rewriting, including conversion of expanded addresses like *pwatters%mail @companyA.com* to *pwatters@mail.companyA.com*.

- **S5** The final rewriting ruleset that occurs after all aliases, defined in */etc/aliases*, have been expanded.

User-defined rulesets can occupy S6 and above. For example, ruleset 33 is defined in Solaris to support Sun's RemoteMode. A typical Sendmail rule takes the form

```
Rlhs   rhs   description
```

where *R* indicates that the line is a rule, *lhs* is the left-hand side of the rule, *rhs* is the right-hand side of the rule, and *description* is a comment that is useful for humans to interpret what action the rule performs. The left-hand side is a specification for matching a particular mail header, and the right-hand side specifies the action to be taken if a match is found for the rule.

Just as lex, yacc, and JavaCC can be used for specifying actions based on matched tokens, so does the Sendmail parser. When the *sendmail.cf* file is parsed by Sendmail, it recognizes several specifiers on the left-hand side:

$-	Matches a single token
$*	Matches any number of tokens, including zero tokens

$+   Matches any number of tokens greater than zero

$=character   Matches any token equal to character

If any rule stated using these specifiers finds a match, then one or more actions may be performed by one or more right-hand side specifiers:

$@   Rewrite and return

$>integer   Rewrite using the ruleset specified by integer

$#   Deliver through the specified mailer

$character and $integer   Actions can be performed on variables defined on the left-hand side

As an example, we examine a rule that adds a fully qualified domain name onto a mail server username, where a message is destined for external delivery. In this case, *$h (host)* is set to *mail* and *$d (domain)* is set to *companyA.com*. Thus, a rule to match a username with no FQDN specified would be

```
R$+        $@$1<@$h.$d>   Add a FQDN to username
```

Thus, any valid Solaris username like *pwatters* will have *mail*, "." and *companyA.com* appended to it for external delivery, giving

```
paul<@mail.companyA.com>
```

A more complex rule for a more complex organization that has multiple internal networks might have a second level in the FQDN above the company name (for example, the mail server for the *sales* department of *companyA.com* would have the FQDN *mail.sales.companyA.com*). In this case, we define *$o (organization-level)*, set *$o* to *sales*, and change the rule to

```
R$+  $@$1<@$h.$o.$d>   Add a FQDN to username, including organization level
```

Hence, any valid Solaris username like *neil* will have *mail*, ".", *sales*,"." and *companyA.com* appended to it for external delivery, giving

```
neil<@mail.sales.companyA.com>
```

Thus, the combination of rules, macros, and options can successfully create and resolve most e-mail addresses. If all of the rule writing and option setting seems daunting to a first-time Sendmail administrator, it is possible to use GUI-based configuration tools to ease the burden. One of the easiest ways to run and configure Sendmail is to use Webmin, which is freely available at **http://www.webmin.com/ webmin/**. Webmin is a Web-based interface for system administration for Solaris, including Sendmail. Using any browser that supports tables and forms, you can make use of the "Sendmail configuration" module, which allows administrators to manage Sendmail aliases, masquerading, address rewriting, and other features. Webmin can also use SSL to secure connections between your Web browser and the Webmin server, which is especially useful for remote administration. Figure 25-3 shows the Webmin interface, and the options it supports for configuring Sendmail.

m4 Configuration

When generated by m4 macros, administrators should never need to directly edit the *sendmail.cf* file. The m4 macro language can be used to create a *sendmail.cf* file by making use of a set of pre-defined macros which have been developed for use with Sendmail. In order to create a *sendmail.cf* file using m4 macros, a text file containing a list of macros to run, as well as the appropriate parameter values for your site need to

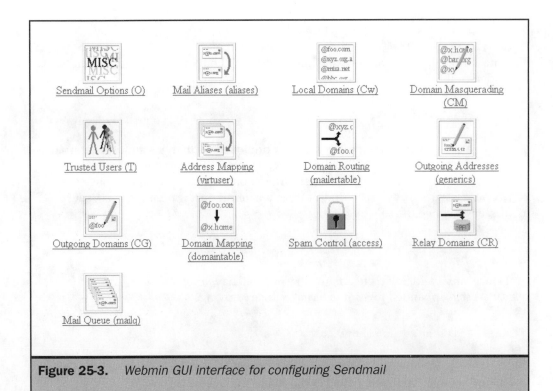

Figure 25-3. *Webmin GUI interface for configuring Sendmail*

be created in a text file, typically called *sendmail.mc*. Once this file has been installed into the *cf/cf* subdirectory underneath the main Sendmail directory, then the following command can be used from that directory to build a new *sendmail.cf* file:

```
# cp /etc/sendmail.cf /etc/sendmail.orig
# m4 ../m4/cf.m4 sendmail.mc > /etc/sendmail.cf
```

The first command backs up the current production *sendmail.cf* file, while the next command builds a new production *sendmail.cf* file. Once Sendmail has been started, by using the command defined in the previous section, Sendmail will be running with the new configuration.

Let's take a closer look at the macros and parameters which can be used to configure Sendmail, before examining a sample *sendmail.mc* file.

Macros

The following macros are defined for use with *sendmail.mc*:

DOMAIN	Used to define common elements for mail servers with the same domain name
EXPOSED_USER	Prevents domain masquerading for specific users
FEATURE	Enable a specific Sendmail feature
MAILER	Specifies the mail delivery program to use on the server (local, smtp, or procmail)
MASQUERADE_AS	Inserts an effective domain on all outgoing e-mail rather than the real domain
OSTYPE	Defines the host operating system type

Features

Once the basic domain and operating system parameters have been generated, the next step is to enable specific Sendmail features by using the FEATURE macro. One instance of FEATURE is required for every feature that is to be enabled. Commonly used features include the following:

accept_unqualified_senders	Accepts messages for delivery from users with e-mail addresses that do not have a fully qualified domain name
accept_unresolvable_domains	Accepts messages for delivery from users with e-mail addresses whose fully qualified domain name is not resolvable

access_db	Enables a database of senders and domains to be maintained from whom mail is automatically bounced or rejected
always_add_domain	Inserts domain onto all e-mails sent through Sendmail, even those which are being delivered to local users
blacklist_recipients	Defines a list of recipients who are not allowed to receive e-mail
domaintable	Substitutes a new domain name for a previous domain name
mailertable	Allows a different mail server to be associated with each virtual domain supported
nullclient	Allows local Sendmail instances to forward all messages to a single outbound Sendmail server for delivery
promiscuous_relay	Allows relaying of mail from any site through the local server. This should never be used because of the risk that SPAM merchants will find your server and use it to relay SPAM, thereby obscuring its true origin
redirect	Redirects messages destined for users who no longer exist on the system. Requires a corresponding entry in /etc/aliases with the name of the former user and his/her new e-mail address
relay_based_on_mx	Uses the MX record defined in DNS to determine if the local Sendmail server is the correct server to relay messages from other servers
relay_entire_domain	Permits all hosts within the local domain to route e-mail through the local Sendmail server
smrsh	A functionally limited shell that can be used to restrict system access by the Sendmail daemon
use_ct_file	Prevents users from changing their username part of their e-mail addresses on outbound e-mails
use_cw_file	Contains a list of all DNS aliases for the mail server

virtusertable	Supports routing of e-mail for user accounts with the same username that actually belong to different virtual domains. Thus, *joe@domainone.com* is not confused with *joe@domaintwo.com*, even though both domains use the same Sendmail instance.

Parameters

Specific parameters can be set for Sendmail's operation with the m4 `define` command. Although most of the values set by default within Sendmail will be satisfactory for normal use, you may occasionally need to change a value. Sendmail defines a very large number of parameters; however, we'll only examine some of the most commonly modified parameters:

confDOMAIN_NAME	If your DNS server is unreliable, then you might want to set the default domain name here.
confLOG_LEVEL	This specifies the logging level for Sendmail from 0 (minimal) to 13 (everything).
confMAILER_NAME	The alias used for returning messages and other automatically generated mails sent by the system. This is generally set to MAILER-DAEMON, which is typically aliased to root. So, it's possible to just set the value to root.
confMAX_MESSAGE_SIZE	The maximum size, in bytes, of any message that is accepted for delivery. Although large attachments are common these days, an upper limit of a few megabytes should be set to prevent a denial of service attack.
confSMTP_LOGIN_MSG	Replaces the standard Sendmail version banner with a local (usually nondescript) message. Can be useful in preventing would-be crackers from attempting an exploit that is specific to your version of Sendmail.

Sample sendmail.mc File

Here, we define a sample *sendmail.mc* file, which contains some of the parameters, features, and macros that we've just discussed:

```
OSTYPE('solaris2')
define('confDOMAIN_NAME', 'cassowary.net')
```

```
define('confLOG_LEVEL', '13')
define('confMAILER_NAME', 'root')
define('confMAX_MESSAGE_SIZE', '1048576')
define('confSMTP_LOGIN_MSG', 'No Name Mail Server')
FEATURE('smrsh','/usr/sbin/smrsh')
FEATURE(redirect)
FEATURE(always_add_domain)
FEATURE(blacklist_recipients)
FEATURE('access_db')
```

There are more extensive examples for many different configuration files supplied with the Sendmail source. In particular, Eric Allman's excellent README file should be read by anyone who is seriously contemplating extensive Sendmail configuration.

Running Sendmail

Sendmail is started as a daemon process from scripts that are usually activated during multi-user startup (*/etc/rc2*). To stop Sendmail manually, use the command:

```
/etc/init.d/sendmail stop
```

In order to start Sendmail, use the command:

```
/etc/init.d/sendmail start
```

Troubleshooting

Since Sendmail can be a difficult program to configure, Sendmail also includes some provisions for troubleshooting. For example, the command

```
# sendmail -bt
```

causes Sendmail to execute in address-testing mode, which is very useful for testing rulesets interactively before including them in a production system. Keep in mind that ruleset 3 is no longer invoked automatically in address-testing mode. Thus, to test the address,

```
Paul.Watters.1996@pem.cam.ac.uk
```

you should use the test string,

```
"3,0 Paul.Watters.1996@pem.cam.ac.uk"
```

instead of just using

```
"0 Paul.Watters.1996@pem.cam.ac.uk"!
```

Here is a complete example:

```
ADDRESS TEST MODE (ruleset 3 NOT automatically invoked)
Enter <ruleset> <address>
> 0 Paul.Watters.1996@pem.cam.ac.uk
rewrite: ruleset   0   input: Paul . Watters . 1996 @ pem . cam . ac . uk
rewrite: ruleset 199   input: Paul . Watters . 1996 @ pem . cam . ac . uk
rewrite: ruleset 199 returns: Paul . Watters . 1996 @ pem . cam . ac . uk
rewrite: ruleset  98   input: Paul . Watters . 1996 @ pem . cam . ac . uk
rewrite: ruleset  98 returns: Paul . Watters . 1996 @ pem . cam . ac . uk
rewrite: ruleset 198   input: Paul . Watters . 1996 @ pem . cam . ac . uk
rewrite: ruleset 198 returns: $# local $: Paul . Watters .
    1996 @ pem . cam . ac . uk
rewrite: ruleset   0 returns: $# local $: Paul . Watters .
    1996 @ pem . cam . ac . uk
> 0,3 Paul.Watters.1996@pem.cam.ac.uk
rewrite: ruleset   0   input: Paul . Watters . 1996 @ pem . cam . ac . uk
rewrite: ruleset 199   input: Paul . Watters . 1996 @ pem . cam . ac . uk
rewrite: ruleset 199 returns: Paul . Watters . 1996 @ pem . cam . ac . uk
rewrite: ruleset  98   input: Paul . Watters . 1996 @ pem . cam . ac . uk
rewrite: ruleset  98 returns: Paul . Watters . 1996 @ pem . cam . ac . uk
rewrite: ruleset 198   input: Paul . Watters . 1996 @ pem . cam . ac . uk
rewrite: ruleset 198 returns: $# local $: Paul . Watters .
    1996 @ pem . cam . ac . uk
rewrite: ruleset   0 returns: $# local $: Paul . Watters .
    1996 @ pem . cam . ac . uk
rewrite: ruleset   3   input: $# local $: Paul . Watters .
    1996 @ pem . cam . ac . uk
rewrite: ruleset   3 returns: $# local $: Paul . Watters .
    1996 @ pem . cam . ac . uk
```

In addition to Sendmail-based troubleshooting, the mailx MUA has a *–v* (verbose) switch, which tracks the process of mail delivery directly after mail has been sent. For example, if a message is sent from *user@companyA.com* to *user@companyB.com*, from the machine *client.companyA.com*, the process of delivery is displayed to the sender:

```
client% mailx -v user@companyB.com
Subject: Hello
Hi user@companyB.com. This is a test.
```

```
^D
EOT
client% user@companyB.com... Connecting to mailhost (mail)...
220 mail.serverB.com ESMTP Sendmail 8.9.1a/8.9.1; Sat, 19 Feb 2002
  12:13:22 +1100 (EST)
>>> HELO mail.companyA.com
250 mail.serverB.com Hello mail.companyA.com (moppet.companyA.com),
  pleased to meet you
>>> MAIL From:<user@companyA.com>
250 <user@companyA.com>... Sender ok
>>> RCPT To:<user@companyB.com>
250 <user@companyA.com>... Recipient ok
>>> DATA
354 Enter mail, end with "." on a line by itself
>>> Hi user@companyB.com. This is a test.
>>>.
250 Ok
>>> QUIT
221 mail.companyB.com closing connection
user@companyB.com... Sent (Ok)
```

In the above example, the local mail server (*mail.companyA.com*) contacts the remote mail server (*mail.companyB.com*) and delivers the mail correctly to the user. Used in this way, mailx can provide immediately useful hints for users and administrators to identify delivery problems with particular user addresses or remote network problems.

Since e-mail is a key Internet service, and since Sendmail is the most widely deployed MTA, it is often associated with security warnings and issues. This has led some developers to develop alternative MTA systems like qmail, while many organizations worldwide devote the appropriate resources to tracking down and solving bugs in Sendmail. If you are a Sendmail administrator, it pays to watch the headlines at sites like the Sendmail Consortium (**http://www.sendmail.org/**).

For example, Sendmail has been shown to suffer from the "buffer overflow" problem that allows remote users to execute arbitrary commands on a server running Sendmail. This is a common problem for UNIX applications written in the C language, but only if proper bounds checking on array sizes is not correctly implemented. In the case of Sendmail, very long MIME headers could be used to launch an attack—a patch is available that allows Sendmail to detect and deny messages that might be associated with such an attack. If you need to apply the patch, it is available at **ftp://ftp.sendmail .org/pub/ sendmail/sendmail.8.9.1a.patch**.

Examples

The following examples provide some real-world cases for configuring and managing e-mail services.

An Example SMTP Transaction

In this section, we will walk through an actual SMTP session so that you can see how straightforward the procedure is. For example, it is possible to initiate message transfer from a client machine to a user on *server.companyB.com* by using the following commands:

```
client% telnet mail.serverB.com 25
Trying 192.68.232.41...
Connected to mail.serverB.com.
Escape character is '^]'.
220 mail.serverB.com ESMTP Sendmail 8.9.1a/8.9.1; Fri, 18 Feb 2000
   10:25:59 +1100 (EST)
```

If you now type

```
help
```

you will receive a list of SMTP commands that can be used to transfer mail interactively:

```
214-This is Sendmail version 8.9.1a
214-Topics:
214-     HELO      EHLO      MAIL      RCPT      DATA
214-     RSET      NOOP      QUIT      HELP      VRFY
214-     EXPN      VERB      ETRN      DSN
214-For more info use "HELP <topic>".
214-To report bugs in the implementation send email to
214-     sendmail-bugs@sendmail.org.
214-For local information send email to Postmaster at your site.
214 End of HELP info
```

To actually send a message, you can use a combination of the HELO, MAIL, RCPT, and QUIT commands. HELO introduces the hostname that you are connecting from:

```
HELO client.companyB.com
250 server.companyB.com Hello client.companyB.com [192.68.232.45],
   pleased to meet you
```

Next, you need to specify a sender using the MAIL command:

```
MAIL FROM: <pwatters@companyB.com>
250 <pwatters@companyB.com>... Sender ok
```

A recipient for the mail should then be specified by the RCPT command:

```
RCPT TO: <postmaster@server.companyB.com>
250 <postmaster@server.companyB.com>... Recipient ok
```

After transmitting the sender and recipient information, it's then time to actually send the body of the message by using the DATA command:

```
DATA
354 Enter mail, end with "." on a line by itself
Hello,
My mail client is not working so I had to send this message
  manually - can you help?
Thanks.
.
250 KAA11543 Message accepted for delivery
```

After the message has been accepted for delivery, you can then terminate the session by using the QUIT command:

```
QUIT
221 server.company.com closing connection
Connection closed by foreign host.
```

The message has now been successfully transmitted.

Mail Headers

These headers are useful in understanding how mail is transferred. For example, if a message is sent from a mail client on the local server to another user on the local server, the headers are easy to interpret:

```
From pwatters@companyA.com Fri Feb 18 13:31 EST 2000
Received: (from pwatters@localhost)
        by mail.companyA.com (8.9.1a/8.9.1) id NAA17837
        for pwatters; Fri, 18 Feb 2000 13:31:34 +1100 (EST)
```

```
Date: Fri, 18 Feb 2000 13:31:34 +1100 (EST)
From: WATTERS Paul Andrew <pwatters@companyA.com>
Message-Id: <200002180231.NAA17837@mail.companyA.com>
To: pwatters@companyA.com
Subject: Testing Local Delivery
Content-Type: text
Content-Length: 5
This is a test of local delivery.
```

These headers can be interpreted thus: the local user *pwatters@localhost* sent
the remote user *pwatters@companyA.com* a five-line message, encoded as text,
on the subject of "Testing Local Delivery." The message had an ID of
200002180231.NAA17837@mail.CompanyA.com, and was serviced by the Sendmail
MTA version 8.9.1a/8.9.1. If mail is forwarded from another host, the headers
become more complicated but follow the same general principles.

Using the Multipurpose Internet Mail Extensions (MIME)

As we saw in the previous example concerning mail headers, there was a "Content-Type"
that was text, but it could have conceivably been any kind of digital medium thanks to
the Multipurpose Internet Mail Extensions (MIME), as proposed in RFC 2045. MIME
is very useful for sending multimedia files through e-mail, without having to worry
about the specifics of encoding. Since many multimedia files are binary, and e-mail
message bodies are transmitted as text, MIME suggests that these files be encoded as
text, and sent as a normal message. In addition, MIME supports the notion of multipart
messages—that is, a single e-mail message may contain more than one encoded file.
This is very useful for sending a number of documents to another user—it is not
necessary to overburden Sendmail by sending a new message for each document
(recall that Sendmail processes e-mail messages one at a time). MIME also provides
supports for languages that are encoded in ASCII but need to be displayed in another
script (e.g., Japanese kanji).

MIME defines how a Content-Type header can be used to specify a particular
character set or other nontextual data type for an e-mail message. For example, the
e-mail header

```
Content-Type: text/plain; charset=us-ascii
```

indicates that the message consists of plaintext in the US-ASCII character set. MIME
also specifies how to encode data when necessary. MIME also stipulates that it is the
responsibility of the receiving user to interpret the encoded information, in order to

correctly display an encoded message in a form that will be understood by the user. Here is an example of a MIME-encoded message:

```
This is a multi-part message in MIME format.
------=_NextPart_000_01A6_01BF7314.FF804600
Content-Type: text/plain;
        charset="iso-8859-1"
Content-Transfer-Encoding: 7bit
Joe,
Just confirmed the latest sales figures.
See the attached report.
Jane
------=_NextPart_000_01A6_01BF7314.FF804600
Content-Type: application/msword;
        name="report.doc"
Content-Disposition: attachment;
        filename="report.doc"
Content-Transfer-Encoding: base64
0M8R4KGxGuEAAAAAAAAAAAAAAAAAAAAPgADAP7/CQAGAAAAAAAAAAAAAAC
EAAAmwAAAAEAAAD+////AAAAAJcAAACYAAA//////////////////////
//////////////////////////////////////////////////////////
//////////////////////////////////////////////////////////
//////////////////////////////////////////////////////////
//////////////////////////////////////////////////////////
//////////////////////////////////////////////////////////
//////////////////////////////////////////////////////////
```

After the headers are printed, indicating the number and type of attachments, the actual encoded data is printed (which is what all the forward slashes represent, in case you were wondering!). When you run metamail on this file, since it contains MIME encoded data, the user is prompted to save any detected attachments:

```
This message contains data in an unrecognized format, application/msword,
which can either be viewed as text or written to a file.
What do you want to do with the application/msword data?
1 -- See it as text
2 -- Write it to a file
3 -- Just skip it
```

At this point, the user enters **2**, and they are then prompted to save the file:

```
Please enter the name of a file to which the data should be written
(Default: report.doc) >
```

The data is then saved to the file specified. MIME is thus very useful for encoding data from several binary files into a portable format that can be transmitted as an e-mail message.

Using Mail Clients

Mail clients can be local or remote. Local clients have online access to many Solaris commands, including .forward and vacation, while remote clients are GUI-based and are often easier to use. Remote clients can use either the IMAP or POP protocol to communicate with the server-based MTA, as reviewed earlier in the chapter. In this section, we will introduce a popular local client (elm) and an equally popular remote client (Netscape mail), and examine how each client is configured.

Local Clients (elm)

Although Solaris is supplied with the mailx program—a local user agent developed by the University of California at Berkeley—many sites choose to install the elm MUA, which was originally developed by HP. elm is now freeware, and supports many advanced features such as MIME and DSN. elm is highly configurable, and can operate in beginner, intermediate, and advanced user mode. elm can be started with the command

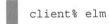

```
client% elm
```

The user interface for elm is shown in Figure 20-4. Using elm, users can issue most commands by typing a single letter from the main menu:

	Pipes the displayed message through a user-defined command.
!	Executes a shell process.
?	Obtain help for elm commands.
<n>	Set current message number to n.
/pattern	Search for pattern "pattern" in message.
a	Create alias for sender of the current message in the address book.
b	Bounce the current message to a user to make it appear as if it hasn't been delivered.
c	Change to a folder other than the inbox.
d	Delete the current message from the inbox.
f	Forward the current message to another user.
m	Create a new mail message.

o	Set options for skill level and general elm options (saved in *elmrc*).
p	Print current message.
q	Exit elm and save changes to inbox.
s	Save current message to a specific folder.
u	Undelete a message marked for deletion.
x	Exit without saving changes to inbox.

By default, elm uses the vi editor to edit messages, but if this is too daunting it is possible to set the editor to emacs or pico by editing the defaults in the elmrc configuration file. By convention, it is normal to include a signature at the bottom of every message, containing contact details. This is usually kept in ~/.signature. A typical signature file might contain the following:

```
--
Paul A. Watters
Principal Consultant, Cassowary Computing Pty Ltd
Sydney NSW Australia
Paul.Watters.1996@pem.cam.ac.uk
```

This allows readers of your messages to quickly identify you and your role in the organization you represent. Since you may already be known to local users, elm actually has the ability to automatically attach a different signature to messages addressed to either local or remote users. This is but one of the many features that has ensured elm's continued success in the age of GUI-based remote clients.

Remote Clients (Netscape Mail)

GUI-based mail clients, operating on a remote PC, have become commonplace in offices where mail is centralized on a Solaris server, but where a desktop system is used to read mail. Popular choices for reading e-mail remotely include the Netscape mail client and the Eudora mail client, both of which are freely available from **http://www.netscape.com/** and **http://www.eudora.com/**, respectively. Both Eudora and Netscape use POP to retrieve their mail from a remote POP server. In this section, we review the configuration of the POP-based Netscape mail client, as this is more complicated than a local client like elm that reads mail directly from the spooler.

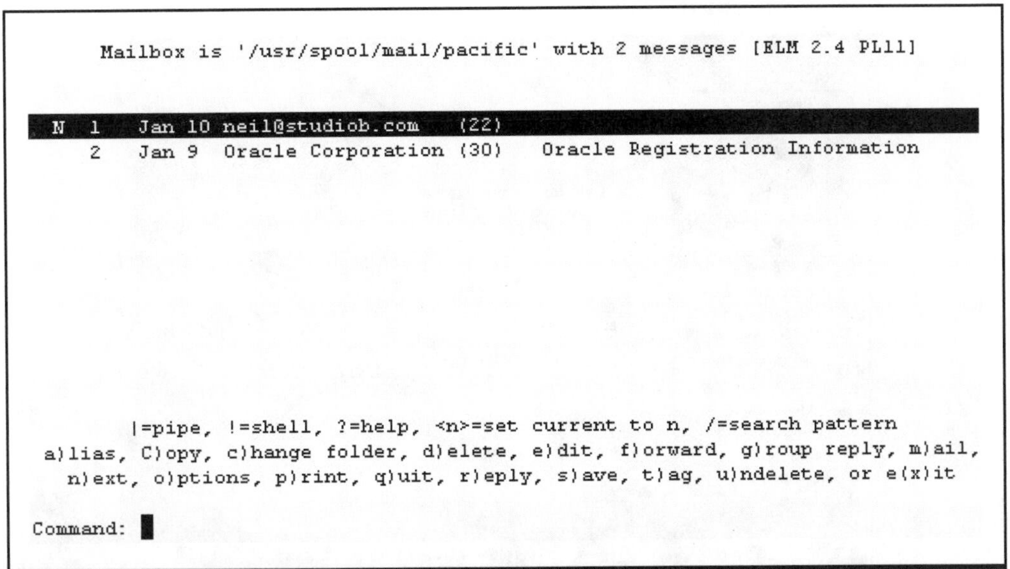

```
       Mailbox is '/usr/spool/mail/pacific' with 2 messages [ELM 2.4 PL11]


 N  1     Jan 10  neil@studiob.com     (22)
    2     Jan 9   Oracle Corporation (30)   Oracle Registration Information
```

```
          |=pipe, !=shell, ?=help, <n>=set current to n, /=search pattern
    a)lias, C)opy, c)hange folder, d)elete, e)dit, f)orward, g)roup reply, m)ail,
     n)ext, o)ptions, p)rint, q)uit, r)eply, s)ave, t)ag, u)ndelete, or e(x)it

  Command:  █
```

Figure 25-4.   *The elm mail user agent*

The first step after installing the Netscape mail software is to set the user preferences. In the Preferences pop-up, there is a section called "Mail & Newsgroups," as shown in Figure 25-5. Here, the user needs to set up basic information about their contact details: their full name, their e-mail address, their Reply-To address (if it is different from their e-mail address), their organization, and the location of their signature file on the local file system. This enables e-mails that are sent from the client to be identified easily.

The next step is to configure the POP settings. In Figure 25-6, we can see the General preferences tab. The POP server name is recorded here, along with the server type (in this case, POP-3). The remote username is also recorded, along with an instruction to remember the remote password, and to automatically check for and retrieve mail every ten minutes. The POP tab contains an option to leave the mail on the server, as well as storing it on the local file system.

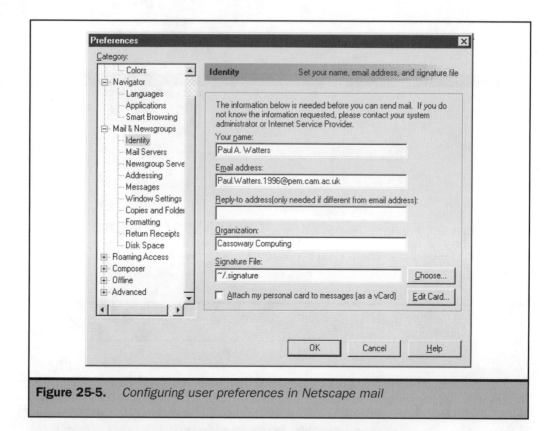

Figure 25-5. *Configuring user preferences in Netscape mail*

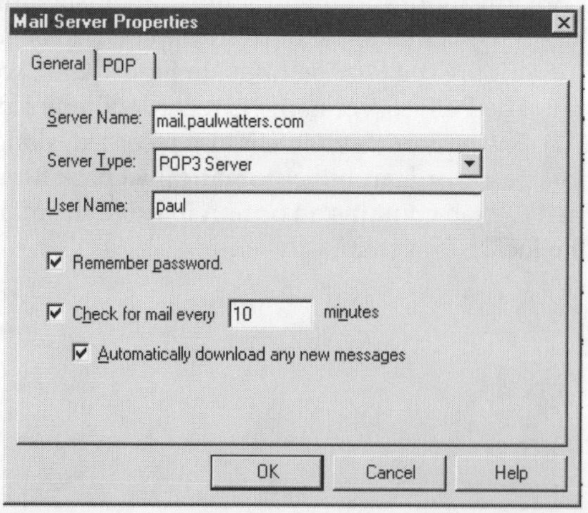

Figure 25-6. *Configuring POP settings in the Netscape mail client*

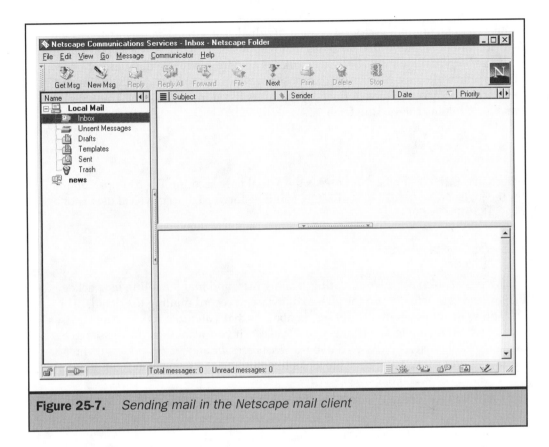

Figure 25-7. *Sending mail in the Netscape mail client*

When the Netscape mail client is started, the user interface is shown, similar to that
in Figure 25-7. On the left-hand pane, the different supported mailboxes are shown:
inbox, unsent mail, draft e-mails, templates, sent mail, and a trash folder. In addition,
messages can be ordered by subject, sender, date, or priority level.

Command Reference

Alias

E-mail addresses typically correspond to a local Solaris user: for example, for the user
account *pwatters* on host *mail.companyA.com*, the e-mail address would naturally be
pwatters@mail.companyA.com. However, there are many situations in which mail needs
to be addressed to a user who may not have a user account as such. In addition, there
are often aliases required by application programs and daemons as administrative

contacts that should not go to a specific individual, but should be forwarded to the user account of an individual who has that responsibility at a particular point in time. To cover both of these cases, Solaris maintains an administrative database of e-mail aliases, which allows a user for the purposes of Sendmail to be logically different from actual Solaris users (as defined by the users listed in */etc/passwd*). The */etc/aliases* database contains rules of the form

```
alias: user
```

where *alias* is the user alias, and *user* is the actual user account. For example, all mail for the logical user MAILER-DAEMON could be forwarded to physical user root by using the alias as follows:

```
MAILER-DAEMON: root
```

Aliases are also useful for creating mailing lists, and many mailing list packages like majordomo actually use the aliases database to record mailing list details. The only tip to remember with the aliases database is that you must run the "newaliases" command after making any changes to */etc/aliases* if you want the new aliases to be available; otherwise, the aliases database (*/etc/aliases.dir* and */etc/aliases/pag*) won't be up-to-date. A sample */etc/aliases* file looks like this:

```
# Following alias is required by the mail protocol, RFC 822
# Set it to the address of a HUMAN who deals with
# this system's mail problems.
Postmaster: root
# Alias for mailer daemon; returned messages from our MAILER-DAEMON
# should be routed to our local Postmaster.
MAILER-DAEMON: postmaster
# Aliases to handle mail to programs or files, eg news or vacation
nobody: /dev/null
# To be specified in as sender in USENET postings (anti-UCE trap)
spam: /dev/null
# Alias for staff distribution list, members specified here:
staff:  pwatters,neil@indiana,maya@sydney,greg@sydney,lori@sydney
# Alias for a person, so they can receive mail by several names:
paul:   pwatters
root:   maya@sydney
help:   greg@sydney
helpdesk:  help
support:  neil@indiana
abuse:   spam
```

The Complete Reference

Solaris 9

Chapter 26

DNS

Although Solaris 9 has its own naming service, known as the Network Information Service (NIS), support is also provided for DNS, which maps IP addresses to hostnames. Every computer that is connected to the Internet must have an IP address, which identifies it uniquely within the network. For example, 192.18.97.241 is the IP address of the Web server at Sun. IP addresses are hard for humans to remember, and don't adequately describe the network on which a host resides. Thus, by examining the Fully Qualified Domain Name (FQDN) of 192.18.97.241—*www.sun.com*—it's immediately obvious that the host "www" lies within the "sun.com" domain. The mapping between human-friendly domain names and machine-friendly IP addresses is performed by a distributed naming service, known as the Domain Name Service (DNS). In this chapter, we examine how DNS servers manage records of network addresses, and how this information can be accessed by Solaris applications. In addition, we examine how to build and configure the latest version of the Berkeley Internet Daemon (BIND) from source, if security issues leave your existing Berkeley Internet Daemon (BIND) service vulnerable to attack.

Key Concepts

The following key concepts are central to understanding the role of DNS as a naming service.

Overview of DNS

The Domain Name Service (DNS) is a distributed database that maps human friendly fully qualified hostnames, like *paulwatters.com*, to a numeric IP address like *209.67.50.203*. In the early days of the Internet, a single file was distributed to various hosts (called the HOSTS.TXT file), which contained an address to hostname mapping for known hosts. Administrators would periodically upload a list of any new hosts added to their networks, after which they would download the latest version of the file. However, as the Internet grew, maintaining this text database became impossible. A new system for mapping addresses to names was proposed in RFC 882 and 883, based around information about local networks being sourced from designated servers for each network. It should be noted that Solaris retains a variant of the HOSTS.TXT file in the form of the */etc/hosts* file, which is typically used to map IP addresses to domain names for the localhost, as well as key network servers such as the local domain name server. This is very useful in situations where the DNS server is not responding, while the system is being booted. The */etc/hosts* file is consulted by some applications, such as the *syslog* daemon (*syslogd*) to determine which host (the "loghost") should be used for system logging. A typical */etc/hosts* file looks like this:

```
127.0.0.1          localhost
204.168.14.23      bryce          bryce.paulwatters.com       loghost
204.168.14.24      wasatch        wasatch.paulwatters.com
```

Of course, only key servers and the localhost should be defined in the */etc/hosts* file—otherwise, any change in IP address for that server will not be reflected in the value resolved from */etc/hosts*.

DNS works on a simple client/server principle: If you know the name of a DNS server for a particular network, you will be able to retrieve the IP address of any host within that network. For example, if I know that the name server for the domain paulwatters.com is dns20.register.com, I can contact dns20.register.com to retrieve the address for any host within the paulwatters.com domain (including *www.paulwatters.com*, or *209.67.50.203*). Of course, this leads us to a classic "chicken and egg" problem—how would we know, in the first instance, that the DNS server dns20.register.com was authoritative for paulwatters.com? The answer is that, in the same way that the addresses of all hosts under paulwatters.com are managed by its DNS server, the address of the DNS server is managed by the next server along the chain—in this case, the DNS server for the ".com" domain.

There are many such top-level domains now in existence, including the traditional *.edu* (educational organizations), *.com* (commercial organizations), and *.net* (network) top-level domains. Most countries now have their own top-level domains, including *.au* (Australia), *.ck* (Cook Islands), and *.ph* (Philippines). Underneath each top-level domain is a number of second-level domains; for example, Australia has *.com.au* (Australian commercial organizations), *.edu.au* (Australian educational organizations), and *.asn.au* (Australian nonprofit associations). The organizations that manage each top-level and second-level domain can also be quite different: While Network Solutions Inc. (**http://www.nsi.com/**) is responsible for the wholesale allocation of domain names for the *.com* top-level domain, the *.com.au* second-level domain is managed by Melbourne IT (**http://www.melbourneit.com.au/**).

As an example, let's look at how the hostname www.finance.saltlake.com is resolved: the client resolver needs to determine which DNS server is authoritative for *.com* domains, followed by the DNS server that is authoritative for *saltlake.com* domains, potentially followed by the DNS server that is authoritative for the *finance.saltlake.com* domain, if all mappings for *saltlake.com* are not stored on a single server. The *.com* resolution is taken care of by the list of root servers provided by the Whois database (**ftp://ftp.rs.internic.net/domain/named.root**):

```
>>> Last update of whois database: Mon, 9 Oct 2000 09:43:11 EDT <<<
The Registry database contains ONLY .COM, .NET, .ORG, .EDU domains and
Registrars.
ftp://ftp.rs.internic.net/domain/named.root
;       This file holds the information on root name servers needed to
;       initialize cache of Internet domain name servers
;       (e.g. reference this file in the "cache  .  <file>"
;       configuration file of BIND domain name servers).
;
;       This file is made available by InterNIC registration services
```

```
;             under anonymous FTP as
;                 file                  /domain/named.root
;                 on server             FTP.RS.INTERNIC.NET
;             -OR- under Gopher at      RS.INTERNIC.NET
;                 under menu            InterNIC Registration Services (NSI)
;                     submenu           InterNIC Registration Archives
;                 file                  named.root
;
;             last update:    Aug 22, 1997
;             related version of root zone:    1997082200
.                             3600000  IN  NS    A.ROOT-SERVERS.NET.
A.ROOT-SERVERS.NET.           3600000      A     198.41.0.4
.                             3600000      NS    B.ROOT-SERVERS.NET.
B.ROOT-SERVERS.NET.           3600000      A     128.9.0.107
.                             3600000      NS    C.ROOT-SERVERS.NET.
C.ROOT-SERVERS.NET.           3600000      A     192.33.4.12
.                             3600000      NS    D.ROOT-SERVERS.NET.
D.ROOT-SERVERS.NET.           3600000      A     128.8.10.90
.                             3600000      NS    E.ROOT-SERVERS.NET.
E.ROOT-SERVERS.NET.           3600000      A     192.203.230.10
.                             3600000      NS    F.ROOT-SERVERS.NET.
F.ROOT-SERVERS.NET.           3600000      A     192.5.5.241
.                             3600000      NS    G.ROOT-SERVERS.NET.
G.ROOT-SERVERS.NET.           3600000      A     192.112.36.4
.                             3600000      NS    H.ROOT-SERVERS.NET.
H.ROOT-SERVERS.NET.           3600000      A     128.63.2.53
.                             3600000      NS    I.ROOT-SERVERS.NET.
I.ROOT-SERVERS.NET.           3600000      A     192.36.148.17
.                             3600000      NS    J.ROOT-SERVERS.NET.
J.ROOT-SERVERS.NET.           3600000      A     198.41.0.10
.                             3600000      NS    K.ROOT-SERVERS.NET.
K.ROOT-SERVERS.NET.           3600000      A     193.0.14.129
.                             3600000      NS    L.ROOT-SERVERS.NET.
L.ROOT-SERVERS.NET.           3600000      A     198.32.64.12
.                             3600000      NS    M.ROOT-SERVERS.NET.
M.ROOT-SERVERS.NET.           3600000      A     202.12.27.33
```

The *named.root* file shown above can be used by servers to resolve IP addresses for root DNS servers if they do not run a local DNS server. After obtaining an IP address for a root server for the *.com* domain, a query is then made to the DNS server authoritative for *saltlake.com* for the address *www.finance.saltlake.com*. Two possible scenarios can occur at this point: either the DNS server that is authoritative for the entire saltlake.com domain can resolve the address, or the query is passed to a DNS server for the finance. saltlake.com domain, if the root server has delegated authority to another server. In the latter situation, the saltlake.com DNS server does not know the IP address for any hosts within the finance.saltlake.com domain, except for address of the DNS server. DNS is therefore a very flexible system for managing the mapping of domain names to IP addresses.

The software that carries out the client request for, and server resolution of, IP addresses is the Berkeley Internet Daemon (BIND). Although most vendors, including Sun, ship their own customized version of BIND, it is possible to download, compile, configure, and install your own version of BIND (available for download from **http://www.isc.org/**).

Examples

The following examples demonstrate how to install and configure DNS client tools and the DNS server.

DNS Client Tools

Configuring a DNS client in Solaris is very easy, and can be accomplished in a few easy steps. First, you must have installed the Berkeley Internet Daemon (BIND) package during system installation to use the DNS client tools. Secondly, you must configure the name service switch (*/etc/nsswitch.conf*) to consult DNS for domain name resolution, in addition to checking the */etc/hosts* file and/or NIS/NIS+ maps or tables for hostnames. The following line must appear in */etc/nsswitch.conf* for DNS to work correctly:

```
/etc/nsswitch.conf hosts:  dns [NOTFOUND=return] files
```

If you have NIS+ running, the line would look like this:

```
/etc/nsswitch.conf hosts:  dns nisplus nis [NOTFOUND=return] files
```

Next, the name of the local domain should be entered into the file */etc/defaultdomain*. For example, the */etc/defaultdomain* file for the host *www.paulwatters.com* should have the following entry:

```
paulwatters.com
```

Finally, the */etc/resolv.conf* file needs to contain the name of the local domain, as well as the IP addresses of the local primary DNS server, as well as a secondary (off-site) DNS server. This means that even if your local DNS server goes down, you can rely on the secondary to provide up-to-date information about external hosts, relying on data within the */etc/hosts* file to resolve local addresses. In the following example, we demonstrate how the */etc/resolv.conf* file might look for the host *www.finance.saltlake.com*:

```
domain finance.saltlake.com
domain saltlake.com
nameserver 204.168.12.1
nameserver 204.168.12.16
nameserver 64.58.24.1
```

Here, there are two domains to which the host belongs: the subdomain finance. saltlake.com, as well as the domain saltlake.com. Thus, there are two primary DNS servers listed within the local domain (204.168.12.1 and 204.168.12.16). In addition, an external secondary is also listed, corresponding to *ns.utahisp.com*, or 64.58.24.1.

Once the client resolver is configured in this way, we can use a number of tools to test whether DNS is working, and also to further examine how IP addresses are resolved. The most important tool for performing DNS resolutions is *nslookup*, which can be used in a simple command-line mode to look up fully qualified domain names from IP addresses, and vice versa. However, *nslookup* also features an interactive mode that is very useful for retrieving name server characteristics for a particular domain, and to determine which DNS servers are authoritative for a specific host or network.

Let's look at a simple example—if we wanted to determine the IP address of the host *www.paulwatters.com*, using a client on the host *provo.cassowary.net*, we would use the following command:

```
$ nslookup www.paulwatters.com
```

The following response would be returned:

```
Server:   provo.cassowary.net
Address:  206.68.216.16

Name:     paulwatters.com
Address:  209.67.50.203
Aliases:  www.paulwatters.com
```

This means that the primary DNS server for the local (*cassowary.net*) domain is *provo.cassowary.net* (206.68.216.16). This server then makes a connection through to the DNS server, which is authoritative for the domain paulwatters.com (*dns19.hostsave.com*). This server then returns the canonical (actual) name for the host (*paulwatters.com*), as well as the alias name (*www.paulwatters.com*), as well as the desired IP address. If we reversed the process, and instead supplied the IP address 209.67.50.203 on the command line, we would be able to perform a reverse lookup on that address, which would resolve to the domain name *paulwatters.com*.

If you want to verify that your DNS server is returning the correct IP address, or if you want to verify an address directly yourself, then running *nslookup* in interactive mode allows you to set the name of the DNS server to use for all lookups. For example, if we wanted to resolve the domain name for the Web server of the University of Sydney, we could use the following command:

```
$ nslookup www.usyd.edu.au
```

The following response would then be returned:

```
Server:   provo.cassowary.net
Address:  206.68.216.16

Name: solo.ucc.usyd.edu.au
Address:  129.78.64.2
Aliases:  www.usyd.edu.au
```

However, we could verify that this IP address was indeed correct by setting our DNS server to be the DNS server that was authoritative for the *ucc.usyd.edu.au* domain:

```
$ nslookup
Default Server:  provo.cassowary.net
Address:  206.68.216.16
```

Here, we enter the name of the DNS server that is authoritative for the target domain:

```
> server metro.ucc.su.oz.au
Default Server:  metro.ucc.su.oz.au
Address:  129.78.64.2
```

Next, we enter the name of the host to resolve:

```
> www.usyd.edu.au
Server:  metro.ucc.su.oz.au
Address:  129.78.64.2
```

And the IP address is returned correctly:

```
Name:     solo.ucc.usyd.edu.au
Address:  129.78.64.24
Aliases:  www.usyd.edu.au
```

If you wanted to determine some of the key characteristics of the DNS entry for *www.usyd.edu.au*, such as the DNS server that is authoritative for the host, and the mail address of the administrator who is responsible for the host, it is possible to retrieve the Start of Authority (SOA) record through *nslookup*:

```
$ nslookup
Default Server:  provo.cassowary.net
Address:  206.68.216.16

> server metro.ucc.su.oz.au
Default Server:  metro.ucc.su.oz.au
Address:  129.78.64.2
> set q=soa
> www.usyd.edu.au
Server:  metro.ucc.su.oz.au
Address:  129.78.64.2

www.usyd.edu.au canonical name = solo.ucc.usyd.edu.au
ucc.usyd.edu.au
        origin = metro.ucc.usyd.edu.au
        mail addr = root.metro.ucc.usyd.edu.au
        serial = 316
        refresh = 3600 (1 hour)
        retry   = 1800 (30 mins)
        expire  = 36000 (10 hours)
        minimum ttl = 43200 (12 hours)
```

This SOA record indicates the following:

- The canonical name of *www.usyd.edu.au* is *solo.ucc.usyd.edu.au*.
- The origin of the DNS record is *metro.ucc.usyd.edu.au* (and this server is authoritative for the host *solo.ucc.usyd.edu.au*).
- The serial number for the current record is *316*. Next time a change is made to the record, the serial number should be incremented.
- The refresh rate is *1* hour.
- The retry rate in *30* minutes.
- The expiry rate is *10* hours.
- The TTL is *12* hours.

We further examine the meaning of each field below, when we discuss how to create DNS records for the server. The use of *nslookup* to determine which servers are authoritative for a particular query is not limited to individual hosts—in fact, the authoritative servers for entire networks can be determined by using *nslookup*. For example, if we wanted to determine which servers were authoritative for the Cook Islands top-level domain (*.ck*), we would use the following command:

```
$ nslookup
> set type=ns
> ck.
Server:  provo.cassowary.net
Address:  206.68.216.16

Non-authoritative answer:
ck        nameserver = DOWNSTAGE.MCS.VUW.AC.NZ
ck        nameserver = NS1.WAIKATO.AC.NZ
ck        nameserver = PARAU.OYSTER.NET.ck
ck        nameserver = POIPARAU.OYSTER.NET.ck
ck        nameserver = CIRCA.MCS.VUW.AC.NZ

Authoritative answers can be found from:
DOWNSTAGE.MCS.VUW.AC.NZ internet address = 130.195.6.10
NS1.WAIKATO.AC.NZ       internet address = 140.200.128.13
PARAU.OYSTER.NET.ck     internet address = 202.65.32.128
POIPARAU.OYSTER.NET.ck  internet address = 202.65.32.127
CIRCA.MCS.VUW.AC.NZ     internet address = 130.195.5.12
```

Some servers that are authoritative for the top-level domains of the Cook Islands are located in New Zealand. This geographic separation may seem strange, but it makes sense if you've ever lived through a tropical storm in Rarotonga—if the power to the OYSTER.NET.ck network was disrupted, hostnames could still be resolved through the backup servers at WAIKATO.AC.NZ.

It's also possible to obtain a list of all the networks and hosts within a particular top-level domain by using the `ls` command—but be warned, the output can be verbose:

```
$ nslookup
> set type=ns
> ls ck.
[DOWNSTAGE.MCS.VUW.AC.NZ]
 ck.                          server = parau.oyster.net.ck
 parau.oyster.net             202.65.32.128
 ck.                          server = poiparau.oyster.net.ck
 poiparau.oyster.net          202.65.32.127
 ck.                          server = downstage.mcs.vuw.ac.nz
```

```
ck.                        server = circa.mcs.vuw.ac.nz
sda.org                    server = parau.oyster.net.ck
parau.oyster.net           202.65.32.128
sda.org                    server = poiparau.oyster.net.ck
```

The final tool that is often useful for resolving hostnames is the `whois` command. This uses InterNIC servers to perform all of the resolutions for you, and includes useful information, like the registrar of the domain name (useful when making complaints about SPAM or harassment on the net!). Here's the `whois` entry for *paulwatters.com*:

```
$ whois paulwatters

Whois Server Version 1.3

Domain names in the .com, .net, and .org domains can now be
registered with many different competing registrars. Go to
http://www.internic.net for detailed information.

    Domain Name: PAULWATTERS.COM
    Registrar: REGISTER.COM, INC.
    Whois Server: whois.register.com
    Referral URL: www.register.com
    Name Server: DNS19.REGISTER.COM
    Name Server: DNS20.REGISTER.COM
    Updated Date: 30-may-2000
```

Procedures

The following procedures show how to configure a DNS server.

Configuring a DNS Server

Now that we've examined DNS from a client viewpoint, and explored concepts like SOAs, IP-to-address mapping, and address-to-IP mapping, it should be obvious what kind of services a DNS server needs to provide to clients. In addition, DNS servers need to be able to support both primary and secondary services as described earlier.

The Berkeley Internet Daemon (BIND) is the most commonly used DNS server for Solaris. It is supplied in a package that is generally installed during initial system configuration. Its main configuration file is */etc/named.conf*, for BIND 8 supplied with Solaris 8. BIND 4 and earlier used a configuration file called */etc/named.boot*; however, these versions are no longer supported by the ISC, and administrators running BIND 4 should upgrade to BIND 9 (as described in the next section).

The */etc/named.conf* file is responsible for controlling the behavior of the DNS servers and provides the following keywords, which are used to define operational statements:

acl   Defines an access control list that determines which clients can use the server.

include   Reads an external file that contains statements in the same format as */etc/named.conf*. This is very useful when your configuration file becomes very large, as different sections can be divided into logically related files.

logging   Determines which activities of the server are logged in the logfile specified by the statement.

options   Defines local server operational characteristics.

server   Defines operational characteristics of other servers.

zone   Creates local DNS zones.

Let's examine a sample statement involving each of these keywords.

acl

If we want to define an access control list for all hosts on the local network (10.24.58.*), we would insert this statement:

```
acl local_network {
10.24.58/24
};
```

Here, *24* indicates the netmask 255.255.255.0 in prefix notation. Now, if our router was the host 10.24.58.32, and we wanted to prevent any access to the DNS server from that address, we would amend the above statement to the following:

```
acl local_network {
!10.24.58.32; 10.24.58/24
};
```

Note that the negation of a specific address from a subnet that is also permitted must precede the definition of that subnet in the statement.

include

A little later, we'll examine how to configure DNS zones. Since these definitions can be very long for large networks, administrators often place them in a separate file so that they can be managed separately from ACL definitions and system options. Thus, to include all of the zone definitions from the file */var/named/zones.conf*, we would insert the following statement into the */etc/named.conf* file:

```
include "/var/named/zones.conf"
```

options

The options section sets key parameters that affect the run-time behavior of the BIND server. Typically, these are the directories in which the zone databases are stored, and the file in which the process ID of the named process is stored. The following example gives the standard options for BIND 8:

```
options {
directory "/var/named";
pid-file "/var/named/pid";
}
```

server

The server statement defines characteristics of remote name servers. There are two main options that can be set with a server statement: whether or not a remote server is known to transmit incorrect information, and whether or not the remote server can answer multiple queries during a single request. A sample server statement would look like this:

```
server 10.24.58.32
{
    bogus yes;
    transfer-format many-answers;
}
```

zone

A zone must be created for each network or subdomain that your DNS server manages. Zones can either be created as primary or secondary, depending on which server is authoritative for a particular domain. Entries for IP-to-name and name-to-IP mappings must also be included to correctly resolve both IP address and domain names. For the domain *cassowary.net*, the following zone entries would need to be created:

```
zone "cassowary.net"
{
    type master;
```

```
        file "cassowary.net.db";
}
zone "58.24.10.in-addr.arpa"
{

        type master;
        file "cassowary.net.rev";
}
```

In this case, the two zone files */var/named/cassowary.net.db* and */var/named/cassowary. net.rev* need to be populated with host information. A sample */var/named/cassowary.net.db* file would contain SOA entries like this:

```
@       IN      SOA     cassowary.net.        root.cassowary.net.       (
        2000011103      ;serial number
        10800           ;refresh every three hours
        1800            ;retry every 30 mins
        1209600         ;Two week expiry
        604800)         ;Minimum one week expiry
        IN      NS      ns.cassowary.net.
        IN      MX      10      firewall.cassowary.net.
        firewall        IN      A       10.24.58.1       ;firewall
        emu             IN      A       10.24.58.2       ;webserver
        quoll           IN      A       10.24.58.3       ;webserver
        tazdevil        IN      A       10.24.58.4       ;kerberos
        security        IN      CNAME   tazdevil
```

A sample */var/named/cassowary.net.rev* file would contain SOA entries like this:

```
@       IN      SOA     58.24.10.in-addr.arpa.       root.cassowary.net.      (
        2000011103      ;serial number
        10800           ;refresh every three hours
        1800            ;retry every 30 mins
        1209600         ;Two week expiry
        604800)         ;Minimum one week expiry
        IN      NS      ns.cassowary.net.
1       IN      PTR     firewall.cassowary.net.
2       IN      PTR     emu.cassowary.net.
3       IN      PTR     quoll.cassowary.net.
4       IN      PTR     tazdevil.cassowary.net.
```

Each host within the domain must have an IP-to-domain as well as a domain-to-IP mapping. Once a change is made to the zone file, the serial number should be incremented as appropriate. Note that in addition to address (A) and pointer (PTR) records for IP address and domain names, it is also possible to identify hosts as mail exchangers (MX), and by canonical names (CNAME). The former is required to define which host is responsible for handling mail within a domain, while the latter is used to create aliases for specific machines (thus, the tazdevil Kerberos server is also known as *security.cassowary.net*).

The
Complete
Reference

Solaris 9

Chapter 27

Network Information Service (NIS/NIS+)

In Chapter 26, we looked at the Domain Name Service (DNS), which allows hosts around the Internet to be easily and consistently identified by user-friendly names, rather than computer-friendly IP addresses. However, while DNS is a very common network information service, it is not the version of the Network Information Service (NIS), which was popular with Solaris 1. However, NIS is the only kind of service available. Solaris 9 supports NIS+, which is an improved /NIS+ will eventually be deprecated in favor of the Lightweight Directory Access Protocol (LDAP), which is an industry standard. LDAP is covered in Chapter 28.

NIS+ is comprised of a centralized repository of information about hosts, networks, services, and protocols on a local area network. This information is physically stored in a set of maps that are intended to replace the network configuration files usually stored in a server's /etc directory. The set of all maps on a NIS+ network is known as a namespace, supporting large networks of up to 10,000 hosts where responsibilities can be delegated to local servers. NIS+ improves upon the standard NIS by allowing enhancements to authentication processes, combined with sophisticated resource authorization. This allows NIS+ namespaces to exist over public networks like the Internet without risk of data loss or interception, with the caveat that NIS+ relies on the relatively weak DES encryption algorithm.

In this chapter, we will examine the processing of setting up a NIS+ server and highlight the differences between NIS+ and NIS, and between NIS+ and other naming services like DNS. In fact, many sites will choose to run DNS alongside NIS+, which is also possible. In addition, we will review the role and configuration of primary and slave servers, and walk through the installation of NIS+ using the script method.

Key Concepts

The following concepts are required knowledge for installing and running NIS/NIS+.

Managing Resources

NIS+ is a Solaris network information service whose primary focus is the management of users, hosts, networks, services, and protocols. NIS+ does not replace DNS, which is still required for host addressing and identification. However, NIS+ namespaces can be constructed to parallel the host designations assigned through DNS, to simplify operations, and to make the integration of both services more seamless. NIS+ gives networks more than just DNS: namespaces are used as centralized repositories of shared network information that can be used to more effectively manage large networks. However, many organizations choose not to use NIS+ because it has some overlap with DNS, and because of the extra administrative burden involved in installing and configuring NIS+ primary and slave servers. However, if you use the NIS+ scripts to install and configure namespaces, instead of using NIS+ commands directly, NIS+ can be much easier to configure.

NIS revolves around the idea of maps: a map is generally a database with two columns, of which one is a primary key that is used to retrieve an associated value.

This associative nature makes the storage and retrieval of group, mail, passwords, and Ethernet information fast for small networks, but can rapidly become difficult to manage (not to mention slow) for large networks. NIS+, in contrast, uses tables, of which 16 are defined by the system. Tables store information like server addresses, time zones, and networks services. In this section, we review the most commonly used types of NIS maps and NIS+ tables.

First, however, we present a conceptual overview of how NIS+ could be used to better manage an organization's network data. Let's imagine that we're setting up a Solaris network for an imaginary college called Panther College, which has a DNS domain of *panther.edu*. Panther has two teaching divisions: an undergraduate school (*undergrad.panther.edu*) and a graduate school (*graduate.panther.edu*). *panther.edu* has a Class C network (*192.12.1.0*), as do each of the undergraduate (*192.12.2.0*) and graduate schools (*192.12.3.0*). Each of these networks can have up to 255 hosts, which more than adequately covers the staff members in both teaching divisions. To support DNS, there may be a campus-wide DNS server *ns.panther.edu* at *192.12.1.16*, while the *undergrad.panther.edu* network has its own DNS servers at *ns.undergrad.panther.edu* (*192.12.1.16*) and *ns.graduate.panther.edu* (*192.12.2.16*). This is a fairly standard setup for a medium-sized network like a college campus, and is demonstrated in Figure 27-1.

The NIS+ domains for Panther College can exactly mirror the DNS configuration, as shown in Figure 27-2. However, some differences in naming are immediately apparent: while DNS uses lowercase names by convention, which do not terminate in a period, the NIS+ convention is to name write elements in a domain, beginning with capital letters and terminating with a period.

In addition, the second-level domain identified in DNS as panther.edu would be the "root domain" in an NIS+ network, and the third-level domains undergrad.panther.edu and graduate.panther.edu would be described as "nonroot domains." Each of these domains would be associated with a server, in which case the existing DNS servers would double up as NIS+ servers. In fact, in normal NIS+ usage, each of the three domains at Panther College would require two servers: a master server and at least one replica or slave server. This ensures that if the master server is disrupted or experiences hardware failure,

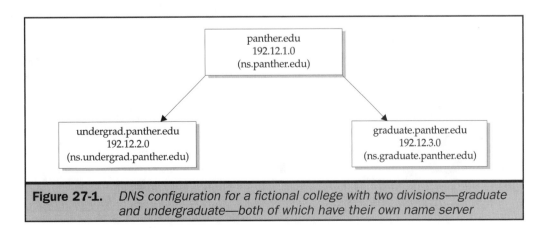

Figure 27-1. *DNS configuration for a fictional college with two divisions—graduate and undergraduate—both of which have their own name server*

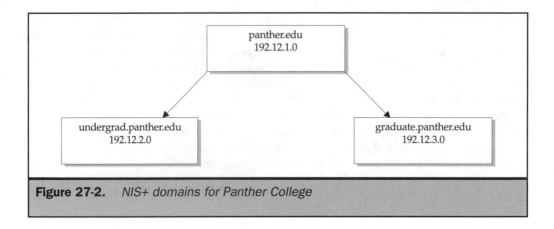

Figure 27-2. NIS+ domains for Panther College

the replica server holds copies of network service information and service continues. The expanded NIS+ domains for Panther College, with a master and slave server each (called Master and Replica), are shown in Figure 27-3.

In addition to domains and servers, NIS+ also caters to clients. Each client is associated with a specific server and domain. For example, a client in the chemistry lab in the graduate school (*Curie.Graduate.Panther.Edu.*) would be served by *Master.Graduate.Panther.Edu.*, and

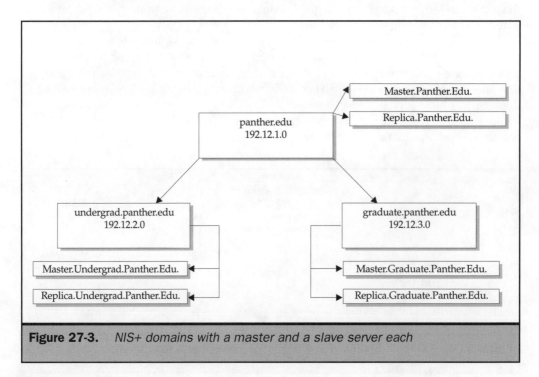

Figure 27-3. NIS+ domains with a master and a slave server each

would be part of the *Graduate.Panther.Edu.* domain. Alternatively, a history professor in the undergraduate school with a computer named *FDR.Undergrad.Panther.Edu* would be served by *Master.Undergrad.Panther.Edu.*, and would be part of the *Undergrad.Panther.Edu.* domain. Figure 27-4 shows the hierarchy of control for the *FDR.Undergrad.Panther.Edu.* client. When each client is installed, a directory cache is created, which enables the client to locate other hosts and services via the appropriate server.

So far, we have mentioned only one of the many kinds of namespace components: the domain. However, there are many other components that exist in the namespace, including group objects, directory objects, and table objects. We will examine these important features of the namespace in the following sections. In addition, we review the specific configuration of NIS maps and NIS+ tables.

It is worth mentioning at this point that one of the main reasons that organizations choose to implement NIS+ is the improved security that accompanies the system. For example, NIS+ tables are not directly editable, unlike their normal Solaris counterparts in the */etc* directory. Requests to change or even access information in the namespace can only take place once a user has been authenticated. In addition to authentication, each user must be authorized to access a particular resource. This doubly protects sensitive and organizational data in a networked environment. The main authentication exchange takes place when either a user presents their credentials or a host presents its credentials, in the form of an unencrypted LOCAL form or a more secure DES-encrypted exchange. The former is used for testing, while the latter is always used for deployment. After authentication, authorization for the requested resource is checked. Access rights can always be examined by using the `niscat` command, which is discussed later in this chapter.

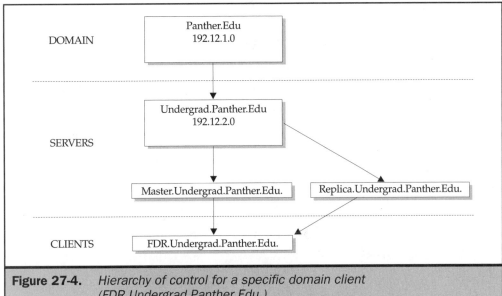

Figure 27-4.   *Hierarchy of control for a specific domain client (FDR.Undergrad.Panther.Edu.)*

NIS Maps

As we mentioned above, NIS uses a series of maps to encode data about the network structure. Many of these are in a form that can be accessed through an address key (having a "byaddr" suffix) or through a name (with a "byname" suffix). Whenever a client needs to find information about a particular host, service, group, network, or netgroup, it can be retrieved by consulting the appropriate map as defined in the namespace. The main system maps are listed in this table:

bootparams	Contains a list of diskless clients for a domain
ethers.byaddr	Contains a list of the Ethernet addresses of all hosts in the domain, and their hostnames
ethers.byname	Contains a list of the hostnames of all hosts in the domain, and their Ethernet addresses
group.bygid	Contains a list of groups that are indexed by group ID (gid)
group.byname	Contains a list of groups that are indexed by group name
hosts.byaddr	Contains a list of the addresses of all hosts in the domain, and their hostnames
hosts.byname	Contains a list of the hostnames of all hosts in the domain, and their addresses
mail.aliases	Contains a list of mail aliases within the namespace, indexed by name
mail.byaddr	Contains a list of mail aliases within the namespace, indexed by address
netgroup	Contains netgroup information, indexed by group name
netgroup.byhost	Contains netgroup information, indexed by hostname
netgroup.byuser	Contains netgroup information, indexed by username
netid.byname	Contains the netname of hosts and users
netmasks.byaddr	Defines the netmasks defined in the domain namespace
networks.byaddr	Defines the networks in the domain namespace, sorted by address
networks.byname	Defines the networks in the domain namespace, sorted by name
passwd.byname	Defines the password database, sorted by username
passwd.byuid	Defines the password database, sorted by user ID
protocols.byname	Defines the network protocols used in the domain, sorted by name

protocols.bynumber	Defines the network protocols used in the domain, sorted by number
publickey.byname	Contains public keys for RPC
rpc.bynumber	Contains RPC details indexed by number
services.byname	Defines all available Internet services by name
ypservers	Contains a list of all NIS servers available

As we can see, there are many similarities in name and function between the NIS maps and the */etc* system files they are intended to replace. However, both the */etc* files and NIS maps perform poorly under heavy loads when the number of hosts defined in a specific namespace exceeds several hundred. In this case, it is much more appropriate to bypass NIS and */etc*, and move directly to a NIS+ installation where a single table (such as Ethers) replaces the dual lookup system used by NIS (such as ethers.byname and ethers.byaddr).

NIS+ Tables

Namespace information in NIS+ is stored in tables, which are based around a centralized administration model (even though particular functions can be delegated to specific servers). NIS+ is similar to DNS because it arranges hosts and resources hierarchically into domains, it has inbuilt redundancy with master and slave servers, and it can store much more information about a network than just its hosts. However, since each host in a domain has many different characteristics and user details that must be recorded and stored centrally, updating these details can be time-consuming, and issues like contention in the recording of user and host data often arise. However, NIS+ namespaces can be updated incrementally, as changes occur, so that the entire database does not need to be updated immediately. Changes are entered into a master domain server, and are then propagated through time to the rest of the domain. This process is governed by a time-to-live setting similar to that used for DNS.

- **Hosts** The Hosts table lists all of the hosts in a particular domain, matching their IP address with a hostname and an optional nickname. For example, if the host *maria* had an alias called *bruny*, and had the IP address *192.34.54.3*, then the entry in the Hosts table would look like this:
  ```
  192.34.54.3 maria bruny
  ```

- **Bootparams** The Bootparams tables contains the necessary information to boot and configure any diskless clients in the domain. It contains entries for server-based dump and swap, as well as a root directory, for each client. For example, if there is a diskless client called *pembroke*, and it is configured by the server *downing*, the Bootparams table would contain the following entry:
  ```
  pembroke root=downing:/export/root/pembroke \
  swap=downing:/export/swap/pembroke \
  dump=downing:/export/dump/pembroke
  ```

Thus, each diskless client will have its own Bootparams entry and resources available on the server.

■ **Passwd**   The Passwd table stores all the standard user information expected on Solaris hosts, including username, encrypted password, user ID, group ID, user's real name, their home directory, and their login shell. A typical entry may look like this: `pwatters:8dfjh4h.rj:101:10:Paul A.` `Watters:/home/pwatters:/bin/tcsh:10905:-1:-1:-1:-1::0`

In addition to the standard details, there is extra information that specifies how often a password must be changed, or how many days until it must next be changed. This significantly increases the functionality of NIS+ over standard Solaris password authorization.

■ **Group**   The Group table consists of a group name, group password, group ID number, and member list, and stores information about the three kinds of groups accessible by NIS+ clients: Solaris groups (such as "staff"), NIS+ groups, and netgroups.

■ **Netgroups**   The Netgroup table defines a group of hosts and users that are authorized to perform specific operations on one or more other hosts within a group. The table format contains entries that identify the name of the group, as well as its members. For small organizations, everyone belongs to a single group, perhaps called *everyone*:
`everyone paulwatters.com`

■ **Mail Aliases**   The Mail Aliases table replicates the functionality of the old */etc/aliases* file for the local mail transport agent (MTA), which is typically Sendmail. An Aliases table can store an alias for a specific user, or it can be used to construct a mailing list. For example, if the user bounty wanted to receive mail as *endeavour*, the Mail Aliases entry would look like this:
`endeavour:bounty`

However, if an advertising company had a local mailing list for *newclients*, these messages could be distributed nationally to local offices by using an alias like this:
`newclients:layton,miami,oakton,sanfran`

■ **Timezone**   This defines the local time zone, which will affect all system settings and applications, such as Sendmail. For example, the entry `hartog` `Australia/NSW` allows the host *hartog* to be identified as belonging to the New South Wales time zone in Australia. In addition, time zones can be specified on a host-by-host basis. This allows systems that exist in different time zones to belong to the same domain. For example, a SPARCstation in Sydney can belong to the same domain as an Ultra in San Francisco. The Timezone table consists of entries that relate a time zone to a specific host.

■ **Networks** This contains details of the local networks and their IP addresses. For example, if a Class B network 192.12.0.0 was known on the Internet as *brunswick*, but had an alias of *essendon*, it would be entered into the Networks table as
```
brunswick 192.12.0.0 essendon
```

■ **Netmasks** The Netmasks table specifies the netmasks for all local Class A, Class B, and Class C networks. For example, if the network 192.12.34.0 has a netmask of 255.255.255.0, the entry would look like this:
```
192.12.34.0 255.255.255.0
```

■ **Ethers** The Ethers table contains entries that associate a hostname with a specific hardware address. For example, if the host *freycinet* has an Ethernet address of *00:ff:a1:b3:c4:6c*, the Ethers table entry would look like this:
```
00:ff:a1:b3:c4:6c freycinet
```

■ **Services** This contains a list of the IP services that are available through both TCP and UDP. For example, the HTTP service provided by many Web servers, such as Apache, is usually available through TCP port 80. This would be defined in the Services table as
```
http 80/tcp
```

■ **Protocols** This defines the protocols available to the network. A necessary entry for Internet use would be the Internet Protocol (IP),
```
ip 0 IP
```
which identifies *ip* as protocol number zero, which also has the alias IP.

■ **RPC** This defines the RPC programs available to the network. An entry consists of a name, a program number, and an alias. For example, `rpcbind` is also known as `portmap`, `sunrpc`, and the `portmapper`. The entry for `rpcbind` looks like this:
```
rpcbind 100000 portmap sunrpc portmapper
```

■ **Auto_Home** This table is an automounter map that facilitates the mounting of a home directory for any user in the local domain. It is commonly used to share a common home directory for a user who has accounts on multiple machines. It is also the cause of some consternation among administrators who attempt to create their user's home directories under */home*, but who don't use the automounter! The Auto_Home table has two columns: a common username that is consistent across all machines in a domain, and a physical location for the user's shared home directory. For example, the home directory of user pwatters might be located physically on the server *winston*, in the directory */u1/export/pwatters*. In this case, the entry in Auto_Home would be
```
pwatters winston:/u1/export/pwatters
```

■ **Auto_Master** The Auto_Master maps the physical mount points of all of the NFS automounter maps in a particular domain to a name. For example, it can be used to map user home directories to */home* or */staff* using Auto_Home, with either of the following mount points, respectively:
```
/home auto_home
/staff auto_home
```

Procedures

The following procedures are commonly used for installing and running NIS/NIS+. In this section, we will walk through a configuration session with NIS+, focusing on using a script-based installation, which makes using NIS+ much easier. The main tasks involved in setting up NIS+ involve domain, master server, slave server, and user configuration. These tasks can only be performed once a network has been designed along the lines discussed in previous sections.

Whether or not you are setting up a root or a nonroot domain, the basic process is the same: after initializing a master server and creating the appropriate administrative groups, the NIS+ tables are populated, and clients and servers can then be installed. In the case of a root domain, these servers can then act as master servers for lower-level domains. In this section, we review the process of setting up a master server, populating the NIS+ tables, configuring clients and servers, and setting up other domains.

Setting Up a Root Domain

The first step in creating a NIS+ namespace is to create the root master server for the new domain. Continuing with the example for the *Panther.Edu.* domain, we create the root master server for *Panther.Edu* by using the `nisserver` command. The server will be known in DNS as *ns.panther.edu*. This command is used for most server configuration operations. In this case, we use the command:

```
ns.panther.edu# nisserver -r -d Panther.Edu.
```

This creates a root domain master server without backward compatibility with NIS. In order to enable NIS support, you need to use the command:

```
ns.panther.edu# nisserver -Y -r -d Panther.Edu.
```

Populating Tables

After creating the master root server for the Panther.Edu. domain on ns.panther.edu, the next step is to populate the NIS+ tables. To achieve this, we need to use the `nispopulate` command:

```
ns.panther.edu# nispopulate -F -p /nis+files -d Panther.Edu.
```

This populates all the tables for the Panther.Edu. domain, and stores the information on the master server. Again, if you need to support NIS, you need to include the *–Y* option:

```
ns.panther.edu# nispopulate -Y -F -p /nis+files -d Panther.Edu.
```

In order to administer the NIS+ namespace, we need to add administrators to the admin group. We can achieve this by using the `nisgrpadmin` command. In the Panther.Edu. example, imagine we have two administrators, *michael* and *adonis*. In order to add these administrators, use this command:

```
ns.panther.edu# nisgrpadm -a admin.Panther.Edu. michael.Panther.Edu.
adonis.Panther.Edu.
```

If you are satisfied with the configuration, then it is best to checkpoint the configuration and transfer the domain configuration information to disk copies of the tables. This can be achieved by using the `nisping` command:

```
ns.panther.edu# nisping -C Panther.Edu.
```

Now that we have successfully created the root domain, we can create clients that will act as master and slave servers for the two subdomains in the *Panther.Edu.* root domain: *Graduate.Panther.Edu.* and *Undergrad.Panther.Edu.*

Setting Up Clients

To create master servers for the nonroot domain Undergrad.Panther.Edu., we first need to set up the client within a domain by using the `nisclient` command. For the host client1.panther.edu, which will become the master server for the nonroot domain, the command is

```
client1.panther.edu# nisclient -i -d Panther.Edu. -h Ns.Panther.Edu
```

In order to actually set up clients user within the domain, we can use also use the `nisclient` command, when executed from a nonprivileged user's shell:

```
client1.panther.edu% nisclient -u
```

If this was for the user *maya*, then *maya* would now be able to access the namespace. Next, we need to turn the client host we have initialized into a nonroot domain master server.

Setting Up Servers

After the root server is created, most organizations will want to create new master servers for each of the subdomains that form the domain. For example, in the Panther.Edu. domain, there are two subdomains: Undergrad.Panther.Edu. and Graduate.Panther.Edu. In this case, two clients must be created from the root master server and then converted to be servers. Initially, these are root server replicas, but their designation then changes to a nonroot master server for each of the subdomains. Replica servers for the subdomain master servers can also be enabled.

In the following example, we designate two client machines whose DNS names are client1.panther.edu and client2.panther.edu (recall that the master server for the root domain is ns.panther.edu). These two clients will actually become the master and slave servers for the subdomain Undergrad.Panther.Edu. To begin the server creation process, an approach similar to that used to create the master server for the root domain is followed. First, we need to start the rpc daemon on the client machine, which will become the master server for the nonroot domain:

```
client1.panther.edu# rpc.nisd
```

Next, we need to convert the client1 server to a root replica server in the first instance. This ensures that the subdomain inherits the appropriate settings from the top-level domain:

```
ns.panther.edu# nisserver -R -d Panther.Edu. -h client1.panther.edu
```

After replicating the settings from the root master server, the new nonroot master server is ready to begin serving the new subdomain. In this case, the root master server (ns.panther.edu) must delegate this authority explicitly to the master of Undergrad.Panther.Edu., which is client1.panther.edu:

```
ns.panther.edu# nisserver -M -d Undergrad.Panther.Edu. \
   -h client1.panther.edu
```

Following the same routine we outlined for the root master server, we must now populate the tables of the new subdomain server client1.panther.edu:

```
client1.panther.edu# nispopulate -F -p /nis+files \
   -d Undergrad.Panther.Edu.
```

Finally, having created a new master server for the new subdomain, we have to create a replica server to ensure service reliability in the event of failure:

```
client1.panther.edu# nisclient -R -d Undergrad.Panther.Edu. \
   -h client2.panther.edu
```

The process of installing a server for the Undergrad.Panther.Edu. subdomain would need to be adapted to create the other subdomain (Graduate.Panther.Edu.), but the general process of setting up a client, converting it to a replica server, and populating the tables, would be very similar to this domain. Now that we have investigated how to create subdomains, the next section covers the day-to-day usage of NIS+, and the most commonly used commands that access tables, groups, and objects in the namespace.

Examples

The following examples provide some real-world cases for installing and running NIS/ NIS+, using the name service switch. You might be wondering—in a mixed network information service environment comprising NIS maps, NIS+ tables, and DNS servers— how name services are selected to resolve particular requests. The answer provided in Solaris 2.x is the name service switch, whose configuration is specified in the file */etc/nsswitch.conf*. Non-NIS+ users who performed Solaris 1 to Solaris 9 upgrades will recognize *nsswitch.conf* as the pesky file that apparently appeared to prevent DNS from working; however, the name service switch is very useful because it enables the administrator to configure which name service handles specific kinds of requests. It is also possible to specify more than one kind of service for every kind of request; thus, if a request fails on the default service, it can be applied to a different service. For example, to resolve hostnames, many sites will have at least some local hostnames statically hardwired into the */etc/hosts* database. In addition, many sites connected to the Internet will use the DNS for resolving hostnames. Where does this leave the relative sophistication of NIS+ namespaces, or the legacy of NIS maps? The answer is that files, DNS, NIS, and NIS+ can be configured to be selected as the first, second, third, and fourth choices as the default name service for resolving hosts in */etc/nsswitch.conf*. For example, the line

```
hosts: files dns nisplus nis
```

indicates that the */etc/hosts* file should be consulted first, and if a match cannot be found for a hostname, try DNS second. If DNS fails to resolve, then NIS+ should be tried. As a last resort, NIS map resolution can be attempted. This is a useful setup for a network that makes great use of the Internet, and relies less on NIS+ and NIS. Of course, many NIS+ advocates would suggest using the line,

```
hosts: nisplus nis files dns
```

since this ensures that NIS+ is always selected over the */etc/hosts* database or DNS.

In addition to host resolution, *nsswitch.conf* also allows the configuration of 14 other options, which roughly correspond to the contents of the NIS+ tables and/or the NIS maps. A NIS+ oriented *nsswitch.conf* file would look like this:

```
passwd:     files nisplus
group:      files nisplus
hosts:      nisplus dns [NOTFOUND=return] files
```

```
services:     nisplus [NOTFOUND=return] files
networks:     nisplus [NOTFOUND=return] files
protocols:    nisplus [NOTFOUND=return] files
rpc:          nisplus [NOTFOUND=return] files
ethers:       nisplus [NOTFOUND=return] files
netmasks:     nisplus [NOTFOUND=return] files
bootparams:   nisplus [NOTFOUND=return] files
publickey:    nisplus
netgroup:     nisplus
automount: nisplus files
aliases: nisplus files
sendmailvars: nisplus files
```

In most of these situations, NIS+ is consulted before the files, except for the password and group information. In addition, DNS is listed as a host resolution method after NIS+. However, it would also be possible to implement a bare-bones system, which only relies on files for most resource information and DNS for name resolution:

```
passwd:       files
group:        files
hosts:        dns [NOTFOUND=return] files
networks:     files
protocols:    files
rpc:          files
ethers:       files
netmasks:     files
bootparams:   files
publickey:    files
netgroup:     files
automount:    files
aliases:      files
services:     files
sendmailvars:   files
```

Before any other services may be installed, NIS+ requires that the master server for the root domain be created. The master server will primarily be responsible for the management of the NIS+ namespace. For example, for the Panther.Edu. domain, the DNS server (*ns.panther.edu*) will also be used for NIS+. This means that the nisserver script can be executed on the DNS server system (*ns.panther.edu*) in order to initialize the master server for the root domain:

```
ns.panther.edu# nisserver -r -d Panther.Edu.
This script sets up this machine "ns" as an NIS+
```

```
root master server for domain Panther.Edu..

Domain name            : Panther.Edu.
NIS+ group             : admin.Panther.Edu.
NIS (YP) compatibility : OFF
Security level         : 2=DES

Is this information correct? (type 'y' to accept, 'n' to change) y
This script will set up your machine as a root master server for
domain Panther.Edu. without NIS compatibility at security level 2.

Use "nisclient -r" to restore your current network service environment.

Do you want to continue? (type 'y' to continue, 'n' to exit this script)

setting up domain information "Panther.Edu." ...

setting up switch information ...

running nisinit ...
This machine is in the "Panther.Edu." NIS+ domain.
Setting up root server .

starting root server at security level 0 to create credentials...

running nissetup to create standard directories and tables ...

running nissetup to create standard directories and tables ...
org_dir.Panther.Edu. created
groups_dir.Panther.Edu. created
passwd.org_dir.Panther.Edu. created
group.org_dir.Panther.Edu. created
auto_master.org_dir.Panther.Edu. created
auto_home.org_dir.Panther.Edu. created
bootparams.org_dir.Panther.Edu. created
cred.org_dir.Panther.Edu. created
ethers.org_dir.Panther.Edu. created
hosts.org_dir.Panther.Edu. created
ipnodes.org_dir.Panther.Edu. created
mail_aliases.org_dir.Panther.Edu. created
sendmailvars.org_dir.Panther.Edu. created
netmasks.org_dir.Panther.Edu. created
netgroup.org_dir.Panther.Edu. created
networks.org_dir.Panther.Edu. created
protocols.org_dir.Panther.Edu. created
rpc.org_dir.Panther.Edu. created
services.org_dir.Panther.Edu. created
timezone.org_dir.Panther.Edu. created
client_info.org_dir.Panther.Edu. created
```

```
auth_attr.org_dir.Panther.Edu. created
exec_attr.org_dir.Panther.Edu. created
prof_attr.org_dir.Panther.Edu. created
user_attr.org_dir.Panther.Edu. created
audit_user.org_dir.Panther.Edu. created

adding credential for ns.Panther.Edu...
Enter login password:
creating NIS+ administration group: admin.Panther.Edu. ...
adding principal ns.Panther.Edu. to admin.Panther.Edu. ...

restarting NIS+ root master server at security level 2 ...
starting NIS+ password daemon ...
starting NIS+ cache manager ...

This system is now configured as a root server for domain Panther.Edu.

You can now populate the standard NIS+ tables by using the
nispopulate script or /usr/lib/nis/nisaddent command.
```

That's all that's required for NIS+ support. However, in order to enable support for NIS clients within the domain, you would need to use the following command instead:

```
ns.panther.edu# nisserver -Y -r -d Panther.Edu.
```

Command Reference

Having reviewed the configuration of NIS+, and the main tables that are used to define a NIS+ domain, we now examine how to use NIS+ effectively to manage hosts and resources within a domain. As we have seen, many different objects can be managed and identified within a NIS+ domain, and there are several commands that are used to access them. In this section, we examine commands, such as nisdefault, which displays the NIS+ settings for the local client system, as well as nischmod, which is used to set access rights on NIS+ objects. In addition, the nisls command is reviewed, which can be used for object lookups and queries. Finally, we will examine the niscat command, which displays the contents of table entries, and can be used to examine NIS+ objects in detail.

nisdefaults

The current settings for a local client system and the active user can be displayed by using the nisdefaults command. The nisdefaults command is commonly used when attempting to troubleshoot an error, such as a user's credentials not being

correctly authenticated from the Passwd table. As an example, let's examine the
nisdefaults for the host *comorin* when executed by the user *walter*:

```
comorin$ nisdefaults
Principal Name  : walter.develop.panther.edu.
Domain Name     : develop.panther.edu.
Host Name       : comorin.develop.panther.edu.
Group Name      : develop
Access Rights   : ----rmcdr---r---
Time to live    : 11:00:00
Search Path     : develop.panther.edu. panther.edu.
```

The output of the nisdefaults command can be interpreted in the following way:

- The principal user is *walter*, who belongs to the NIS+ domain *develop.panther.edu*.

- The primary domain name is *develop.panther.edu*.

- The hostname of the local system is *comorin.develop.panther.edu*.

- The user *walter*'s primary group is *develop*.

- The time-to-live setting is *11* hours.

- The client's access rights within the domain are stated.

- The search path starts with the current nonroot domain (*develop.panther.edu*),
  followed by the root domain (*panther.edu*).

The access rights stated for the user in this example are outlined in more detail in
the next section.

nischmod

Every user has a set of access rights for accessing objects within the network. The
notation for setting and accessing object permissions is very similar to that used for
Solaris file systems. The following permissions may be set on any object, or may be
defined as the default settings for a particular client:

c	Sets create permission
d	Sets delete permission
m	Sets modify permission
r	Sets read permission

This `nischmod` command is used to set permissions on objects within the domain. The following operands are used to specify access rights for specific classes of users:

a	All (all authenticated and unauthenticated users)
g	Group
n	Nobody (all unauthenticated users)
o	Object owner
w	World (all authenticated users)

There are two operators that can be used to set and remove permissions:

+	Sets a permission
-	Removes a permission

Some examples of how permissions strings are constructed will clarify how these operators and operands are combined for use with the `nichmod` command. The following command removes all modify (*m*) and create (*c*) access rights on the Passwd table for all unauthenticated (*n*) users:

```
moorea# nischmod n-cm passwd.org_dir
```

Even unauthenticated users require read (*r*) access to the Passwd table for authentication, which can be granted with the following command:

```
moorea# nischmod n+r passwd.org_dir
```

To grant modify and create access rights to the current user (in this case, root) and his or her primary group on the same table, we would use the command:

```
moorea# nischmod og+cm passwd.org_dir
```

NIS+ permission strings are easy to remember, but hard to combine into single commands where some permissions are granted while others are removed, unlike the octal codes used to specify absolute permissions on Solaris file systems. However, it is possible to combine permissions strings by using a comma to separate individual strings. The following complex string is an example of how it is possible to set permissions within a single string, but equally shows how challenging it is to interpret:

```
moorea# nischmod o=rmcd,g=rmc,w=rm,n=r hosts.org_dir
```

This command grants the following permissions to four different categories of users:

owner	Read, modify, create, and delete
group	Read, modify, and create
world	Read and modify
nobody	Read only

nisls

The `nisls` command is used as a lookup and query command that can provide views on NIS+ directories and tables. For example, to view all of the NIS+ directories that have been populated within the local namespace, we can use the `nisls` command:

```
moorea# nisls
develop.panther.edu.:
org_dir
groups_dir
```

There are two directory object types listed here: the *org_dir*, which lists all of the tables that have been set up within the namespace, while the *groups_dir* stores details of all NIS+ groups. We can view a list of tables by using the `nisls` command once again on the *org_dir* directory:

```
moorea# nisls org_dir
org_dir.sales.panther.edu.:
auto_home
auto_master
bootparams
client_info
cred
ethers
group
hosts
mail_aliases
netgroup
netmasks
networks
passwd
protocols
rpc
sendmailvars
services
timezone
```

A large number of tables have been populated for this domain. The *groups* directory contains the admin group we created earlier, which lists all of the administrators, as well as several other groups that are based on distinct organizational units within the current domain:

```
moorea# nisls groups_dir
groups_dir.sales.panther.edu.:
admin
adverts
legal
media
```

niscat

The `niscat` command is used to retrieve the contents of objects within the domain—primarily the data contained within NIS+ tables. For example, all hosts listed within the domain can be listed by using the following command:

```
moorea$ niscat -h hosts.org_dir
moorea.panther.edu moorea 10.58.64.16
borabora.panther.edu borabora 10.58.64.17
tahiti.panther.edu tahiti 10.58.64.18
orana.panther.edu orana 10.58.64.19
```

Alternatively, we can use the `niscat` command to examine the contents of the Passwd table:

```
moorea$ niscat passwd.org_dir
moppet:*LK*:1001:1:moppet:/staff/moppet:/bin/tcsh:10910:-1:-1:-1:-1::0
miki:*LK*:1002:1:miki:/staff/miki:/bin/bash:10920:-1:-1:-1:-1::0
maya:*LK*:1003:1:maya:/staff/maya:/bin/sh:10930:-1:-1:-1:-1::0
paul:*LK*:1004:1:paul:/staff/paul:/bin/csh:10940:-1:-1:-1:-1::0
```

Next, we can examine which groups these users belong to by using the `niscat` command once again:

```
moorea$ niscat group.org_dir
root::0:root
staff::1:moppet,miki,maya,paul
bin::2:root,bin,daemon
sys:*:3:root,bin,sys,adm
adm::4:root,adm,daemon
uucp::5:root,uucp
mail::6:root
```

All of the hosts that form part of the local domain can be examined based on their Ethernet address, which is extracted from the Ethers table, as shown in the following example:

```
moorea$ niscat ethers.org_dir
1:4a:16:2f:13:b2 moorea.panther.edu.
1:02:1e:f4:61:2e borabora.panther.edu.
f4:61:2e:1:4a:16 tahiti.panther.edu.
2f:13:b2:1:02:1e orana.panther.edu.
```

To get an idea of the services that are offered to these hosts, we can examine the Services table:

```
moorea$ niscat services.org_dir
tcpmux tcpmux tcp 1
echo echo tcp 7
echo echo udp 7
discard discard tcp 9
discard sink tcp 9
discard null tcp 9
discard discard udp 9
discard sink udp 9
discard null udp 9
systat systat tcp 11
systat users tcp 11
daytime daytime tcp 13
daytime daytime udp 13
```

Every other table that is defined within the domain may be viewed by using the niscat command in this way.

Chapter 28

Lightweight Directory Access Protocol

Lightweight Directory Access Protocol (LDAP) is a "white-pages" type of service that is similar to the older X.500 standard for managing organization-wide directory information, for which it originally acted as a front end. X.500 was based on the "heavyweight" Directory Access Protocol (DAP), while LDAP, as a "lightweight" protocol, sits directly on top of TCP/IP. Operations on LDAP servers, such as iPlanet Directory Server (iDS), are of two kinds: data management operations, in which records are inserted, updated or deleted; and queries, in which authentication and identification tokens are retrieved from the organization's database. In theory, LDAP allows for a lot of different types of data about individuals and groups to be stored—including sounds, images, and text.

In Solaris 8, only an LDAP client was supplied with the operating environment release, making it less attractive to use than Network Information Service (NIS/NIS+), because a separate LDAP server had to be purchased and installed. However, Solaris 9 has integrated the iDS into its core architecture, which means that LDAP servers and clients can be installed and configured directly after and during installation, respectively. iDS is a key component of the iPlanet software suite that provides centralized authentication and authorization services for other iPlanet applications, and for third-party applications. For example, access to the Internet mediated through the iPlanet Proxy Server can be gained only by being an attribute of a group defined within the local iDS database, demonstrating the key role that iDS plays in supporting enterprise applications. Alternatively, access to scheduling and event notification facilities through the iPlanet Calendar Server can be provided only to users who are authenticated through the iDS database. Many Solaris applications can use LDAP for authentication and authorization.

iDS does not use a proprietary protocol for storing user and group data, or for communicating with clients; instead, iDS uses the LDAP standard for authenticating users. This is an open standard, which means that a Solaris-based LDAP server can authenticate some Microsoft Windows clients. In addition, it means that iDS can act as a drop-in replacement for any other LDAP-compliant server, enabling you to standardize directory services across a single platform. Alternatively, multiple server types from different vendors can be combined to form an integrated solution. For example, you might choose to use iDS in mission-critical applications because of its clustering and high availability features, which might be overkill in other situations. It is also possible to use the LDAP client software supplied with Solaris to connect to a LDAP server running on a different platform.

Two of the key benefits in switching from NIS/NIS+ are the ease of replication and the assurance of high availability. While NIS/NIS+ architecture is based on the idea of a primary server, which is backed up by some slaves, LDAP servers can be replicated across subnets and domains to servers known as *replicas*, increasing the number of servers available for authoritative lookups and reducing the burden on any one server.

In addition, updates occur rapidly between LDAP servers, rather than relying on uploads of all data between primary and slave servers in a NIS/NIS+ architecture.

Although LDAP has many features, and the iDS implementation implements all the most important operations defined in the protocol, LDAP has a number of limitations. It does not have an interface defined to store data in a relational database, nor does it store data internally in a relational way. Although queries can be performed on the directory, they are not "actioned" by using a query language (like SQL). LDAP is better designed for a reference data environment, where the types of lookups are well-defined and data updates are infrequent.

LDAP's power lies in its flexibility for storing and managing names and data. While schema elements are predefined, such as users and organizations, other elements can be added as necessary. In addition, developers can write client programs that can easily access the directory and retrieve authoritative data. Because most networked applications perform some kind of authentication, a single, centralized source of authentication data can be accessed, reducing administrative overhead.

In this chapter, we examine how to configure LDAP servers and how to configure a wide range of client services.

Key Concepts

Because LDAP is a directory service, its basic data element is known as an *entry*. Like a phone book entry, a number of attributes are associated with each entry in the directory when it's regarded as an object. For example, a phone directory object has a surname, first name, address, and phone number, which together comprise a single entry when instantiated. The overall organization of entries in a LDAP directory is defined by a schema, which consists of a ruleset that determines what attributes can be associated with different object types. Although it is possible to define your own schemas and data models, all LDAP servers support a standard schema that promotes interoperability and is the basis for the LDAP standard, as proposed in RFC 2307. Alternatively, your application can extend the standard schema with some additional object attributes, although these may not be accessible by other servers.

LDAP is used in Solaris 9 as a naming service that is compatible with existing NIS and NIS+ services. This allows integration at the present time, but it also suggests future deprecation of the NIS and NIS+ services. iDS contains a set of objects and their attributes that are able to store all the data contained within NIS/NIS+ maps and tables. Additional schema data must also be stored within the LDAP directory to support client operations.

The directory structure for LDAP is arranged hierarchically, from a single top node within the Directory Information Tree (DIT), to as many levels of abstraction as are required to support an organization's directory requirements. The tree structure might, for example, be based on purely geographical information with the top node representing a country, or it might be based on organizational lines, with the top node corresponding to a company name. All entries within the tree can be identified by their Distinguished Name (DN), and each attribute of the entry can be described as a Relative Distinguished Name (RDN). Figure 28-1 shows an example DIT, with all of the common elements found therein.

At the first level, the country *c* is defined as *US*, so the DN would simply be *c=US*. At the second level, the organization *o* is defined as *cassowary.net*, so the DN is defined as *dc=cassowary, dc=net, c=US*, where *dc* represents the Domain Component (DC). On the third level, the organizational unit *ou* is defined as *Engineering*, so the DN is defined as *ou=Engineering, dc=cassowary, dc=net, c=US*. On the fourth level, an individual user is identified by a Common Name (CN) of *Paul Watters*, and a corresponding UID of *paul*. Thus, the DN is *uid=paul, ou=Engineering, dc=cassowary, dc=net, c=US*. Thus, it is possible to clearly distinguish individuals belonging to organizations and departments in specific countries from each other, by simply using a DN, if the DIT is defined at a fine-grained level, and assuming that no two users in the same department have exactly the same name.

iDS stores all data in LDIF files. This standard is used by all LDAP directory servers and many messaging systems to store user and group data. Thus, it is possible to export an LDIF file with an organization's data from a previous version of iDS, and import it here. Alternatively, third-party products may be able to export LDIF files that can also

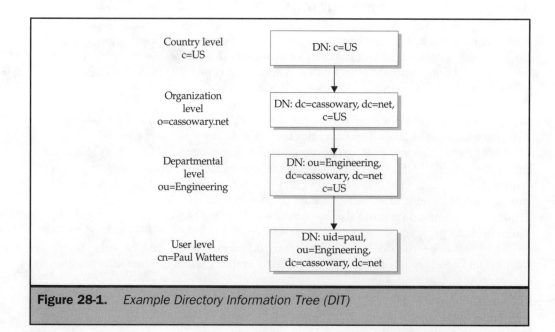

Figure 28-1.   *Example Directory Information Tree (DIT)*

be read into iDS to initialize the directory structure. Let's look at an example entry in an LDIF file for the directory entry defined above:

```
dn: cn=Paul Watters, o=cassowary.net, c=US
cn: Paul Watters
sn: Watters
mail: paul@cassowary.net
objectClass: people
```

As you can see, the LDIF file structure simply reflects the attributes that are defined within the directory, written sequentially to the file immediately following the DN.

Procedures

The following procedures can be used to install and configure an LDAP server.

Configuring iDS

Configuring iDS is a two-stage process: the first stage involves installing and configuring the server to run iDS, and the second stage involves setting up iDS to support LDAP clients (as described in the next section). To begin the process of configuring the server to run iDS, the *directoryserver* program must be executed:

```
# /usr/sbin/directoryserver setup
```

You can either install the iDS or the standalone iPlanet Console. After selecting iDS, you are presented with three installation options: *express*, which presents few opportunities for customization but is very fast; *typical*, which offers some configuration before installation; and *custom*, which offers maximum flexibility but is the slowest installation method.

Three packages comprise the iDS installation:

- Server Core Components, which make up all the common objects used by iDS
- iPlanet Directory Suite, which contains the management console and the iDS software
- Administration Server, which contains packages for system administration and directory management

After selecting the appropriate packages to install, you need to indicate whether the current installation will store configuration information or whether this will be stored in another server. If data will be stored in another server, the hostname, port number, username, and password must all be entered so that the correct target iDS installation for configuration can be identified.

Following the selection of the configuration iDS target, you need to indicate whether the current installation will store user and group information, or whether this information will be stored in another server. Again, if data will be stored in another server, the hostname, port number, Distinguished Name (DN), password, and suffix must all be entered so that the correct target iDS installation for user and group data can be identified.

Next, the new iDS server must be set up, with a unique server identifier, a port number that is not used by any other application, and the appropriate suffix for the local installation. The default port number for LDAP is 389, while LDAP over SSL typically runs on port 636.

The administrator ID and password for the local iDS installation must be selected and entered next. This ID and password are also used for managing the local LDAP server using the management console. Since the administrator ID and password can be used to gain access to the iDS server and modify user and group data without restriction, it's important that these credentials are chosen carefully to avoid easy guessing by rogue users.

The Administration domain must be entered next. Since iDS can manage multiple domains simultaneously from a single server, it's important that domain data is kept functionally and physically separate. Typically, the Administration domain name matches the Internet domain name. However, each server located underneath a top-level domain needs to have a separate Administration domain. For example, if two separate iDS servers are running in the *cassowary.net* domain, one for engineering and another for sales, the Administration domains could be *engineering.cassowary.net* and *sales.cassowary.net*, respectively.

The Directory Manager's password for the local iDS installation must be selected and entered next. Since the Directory Manager ID and password can be used to gain access to the iDS server and modify user and group data with few restrictions, it's important that these credentials are chosen carefully to avoid dictionary-based cracking.

The Administration Server for iDS is used to manage all aspects of the LDAP service. The Administration Server runs as a Web server, meaning that any HTML browser can be used to view and configure all current settings for the iDS server. A port must be chosen to access the iDS Administration Server. The URL for the Administration Server is then given by appending the port number with a colon to the hostname. For example, the URL **http://ldap.cassowary.net:38575/** suggests a LDAP server running on port 38575 of the host *ldap.cassowary.net*.

Supporting LDAP Clients

To configure iDS to provide services to clients, the `ixdsconfig` command is used. The service configuration can be either entered manually on the command-line or supplied from an external file when the *–i* option is passed. Alternatively, a configuration file from one system (generated by passing the *–o* option) can also be read in from an external file. If multiple iDS instances are installed, configuration information from the first installation can be used by subsequent installations. idsconfig can be started with the following command:

```
# /usr/lib/ldap/idsconfig
```

The following output shows a sample idsconfig session for *sales.cassowary.net*. In the first section, you are required to review the basic configuration of the directory service, including the port number and directory manager DN (and its password):

```
Enter the port number for iDS (h=help): [389]
Enter the directory manager DN: [cn=Directory Manager]
Enter passwd for cn=Directory Manager :
Enter the domainname to be served (h=help): [sales.cassowary.net]
```

Next, you need to review the directory and server details, including the base DN, profile name, and list of servers:

```
Enter LDAP BaseDN (h=help): [dc=sales,dc=cassowary,dc=net]
Enter the profile name (h=help): [default]
Are you sure you want to overwrite profile cn=default? y
Default server list (h=help): [192.64.18.1]
Preferred server list (h=help):
Choose desired search scope (one, sub, h=help): [one]
```

Security choices must be made next, including the credential level and authentication method:

```
The following are the supported credential levels:
1 anonymous
2 proxy
3 proxy anonymous
Choose Credential level [h=help]: [1] 1
The following are the supported Authentication Methods:
1 none
2 simple
3 sasl/DIGEST-MD5
4 tls:simple
5 tls:sals/DIGEST-MD5
Choose Authentication Method (h=help): [1] 2
```

```
Current authenticationMethod: simple
Do you want to add another Authentication Method? N
```

After reviewing the server configuration, you need to configure client access. This includes setting timeouts for profile and directory access, password formats, and time and size limits:

```
Do you want the clients to follow referrals (y/n/h)? [n] n
Do you want to modify the server timelimit value (y/n/h)? [n] n
Do you want to modify the server sizelimit value (y/n/h)? [n] n
Do you want to store passwd's in "crypt" format (y/n/h)? [n] y
Do you want to setup a Service Authentication Methods (y/n/h)? [n] n
Search time limit in seconds (h=help): [60]
Profile Time To Live in seconds (h=help): [3600]
Bind time limit in seconds (h=help): [10] 2
Do you wish to setup Service Search Descriptors (y/n/h)? [n] n
```

Finally, you are presented with a configuration summary before any actions are performed by `idsconfig`:

```
Summary of Configuration
1 Domain to serve : sales.cassowary.net
2 BaseDN to setup : dc=sales,dc=cassowary,dc=net
3 Profile name to create : default
4 Default Server List : 192.64.18.1
5 Preferred Server List :
6 Default Search Scope : one
7 Credential Level : anonymous
8 Authenication Method : simple
9 Enable Follow Referrals : FALSE
10 iDS Time Limit :
11 iDS Size Limit :
12 Enable crypt passwd storage : 1
13 Service Auth Method pam_ldap :
14 Service Auth Method keyserv :
15 Service Auth Method passwd-cmd :
16 Search Time Limit : 30
17 Profile Time to Live : 43200
18 Bind Limit : 2
19 Service Search Descriptors Menu
```

Creating LDAP Entries

The `ldapaddent` command is used to create entries in the LDAP container for all the standard system databases stored in files under the */etc* directory. All of the following Solaris databases (with the corresponding *ou*) can be transferred into LDAP by this method:

- aliases (*ou=Aliases*)
- bootparams (*ou=Ethers*)
- ethers (requires bootparams database to be installed first) (*ou=Ethers*)
- group (*ou=Group*)
- hosts (*ou=Hosts*)
- netgroup (*ou=Netgroup*)
- netmasks (requires networks database to be installed first) (*ou=Networks*)
- networks (*ou=Networks*)
- passwd (*ou=People*)
- shadow (requires passwd database to be installed first) (*ou=People*)
- protocols (*ou=Protocols*)
- publickey (*ou=Hosts*)
- rpc (*ou=Rpc*)
- services (*ou=Services*)

A simple script can be created to automate the process of adding each of these databases to LDAP when the bindDN password is supplied on the command-line:

```
#!/bin/sh
ldapaddent -D "cn=directory manager" -w $1 -f /etc/aliases aliases
ldapaddent -D "cn=directory manager" -w $1 -f /etc/bootparams bootparams
ldapaddent -D "cn=directory manager" -w $1 -f /etc/ethers ethers
ldapaddent -D "cn=directory manager" -w $1 -f /etc/group group
ldapaddent -D "cn=directory manager" -w $1 -f /etc/hosts hosts
ldapaddent -D "cn=directory manager" -w $1 -f /etc/netgroup netgroup
ldapaddent -D "cn=directory manager" -w $1 -f /etc/networks networks
ldapaddent -D "cn=directory manager" -w $1 -f /etc/netmasks netmasks
ldapaddent -D "cn=directory manager" -w $1 -f /etc/passwd passwd
ldapaddent -D "cn=directory manager" -w $1 -f /etc/shadow shadow
ldapaddent -D "cn=directory manager" -w $1 -f /etc/protocols protocols
ldapaddent -D "cn=directory manager" -w $1 -f /etc/publickey publickey
ldapaddent -D "cn=directory manager" -w $1 -f /etc/rpc rpc
ldapaddent -D "cn=directory manager" -w $1 -f /etc/services services
```

This script can be used on all client systems that will use LDAP.

Starting a Client

The *ldapclient* program can be used for several purposes, including starting LDAP client services on client systems and reviewing the LDAP cache. To initialize a client, the address of the LDAP server where its profile is stored must be supplied on the command line. The LDAP cache manager (*ldap_cachemgr*) is responsible for ensuring that the correct configuration data is returned to a client upon initialization, especially if changes have been made to the profile. One of the following subcommands must be supplied on the command line to specify the behavior of ldapclient:

`genprofile`	Creates an LDIF format configuration file that can be exported to another system or imported at some future time
`init`	Initializes a LDAP client from a LDAP server using a profile
`list`	Prints a list of entries stored in the client cache to standard output
`manual`	Initializes a LDAP client from a LDAP server using parameters specified on the command line
`mod`	Permits the modification of parameter values after initialization has been completed
`uninit`	Uninitializes a LDAP client from a LDAP server

The following parameters can be modified by using the `ldapclient mod` command or passed directly for manual initialization using the `ldapclient manual` command:

attributeMap	Used to modify the default schema for a specific service.
authenticationMethod	Stipulates the authentication method to be used (*none, simple, sasl/CRAM-MD5, sasl/DIGEST-MD5, tls:simple, tls:sasl/CRAM-MD5,* or *tls:sasl/DIGEST-MD5*). *None* means no security at all, while *simple* means that a password is sent in the clear and is vulnerable to interception. The other methods use a message digest algorithm to enhance security.
bindTimeLimit	The maximum number of seconds allowed for a bind operation to be performed.
certificatePath	The full path to the certificate database.
credentialLevel	The type of credential required for authentication (either *anonymous* or *proxy*).

defaultSearchBase	The *baseDN* for searching.
defaultSearchScope	Determines the scope for searching on the client side.
domainName	Fully-qualified domain name.
followReferrals	Determines whether the referral setting is used.
objectclassMap	Designates a different schema.
preferredServerList	Lists a set of alternative LDAP servers to be contacted prior to the default.
profileName	Determines the name of the client profile.
profileTTL	Refresh epoch for the client cache to obtain new information from the server.
proxyDN	The DN for the proxy server.
proxyPassword	The password for the proxy server.
searchTimeLimit	Restricts the amount of time for each LDAP search.
serviceAuthentication Method	Determines the authentication method for the *passwd-cmd*, *keyserv*, and *pam_ldap* services.
serviceCredentialLevel	The type of credential required for service authentication (either *anonymous* or *proxy*). *Proxy* access for clients can occur only if a *proxy* account has previously been created in the directory, and the *proxyDN* and *proxyPassword* attributes have been defined. *Anonymous* is not recommended, since it provides no security at all.
serviceSearchDescriptor	Allows a different *baseDN* to be specified on a per-service basis.

Let's look at some different examples of how LDAP clients can be initialized by using `ldapclient`. In the first example, the LDAP server *192.64.18.1* will be used to initialize the local client by using the `init` subcommand:

```
# ldapclient init 192.64.18.1
```

No additional parameters are necessary. However, a manual installation is much more complex, as all nondefault parameters must be specified. Sometimes, only a single parameter will differ from the default; for example, if simple authentication

was required, instead of no authentication (the default), the following command
would be used:

```
# ldapclient manual -a authenticationMethod=simple \
-a defaultServerList=192.64.18.1
```

Alternatively, if a higher level search base needed to be specified, the following
command could be used:

```
# ldapclient manual -a authenticationMethod=simple \
-a defaultSearchBase=dc=cassowary,dc=net \
-a defaultServerList=192.64.18.1
```

To generate an LDIF format configuration file, we would use the `genprofile`
subcommand and redirect the output to a file (*/tmp/default.ldif*):

```
# ldapclient genprofile -a profileName=default \
-a defaultSearchBase=dc=cassowary,dc=net \
-a defaultServerList=192.64.18.1 \
> /tmp/default.ldif
```

Using the LDAP-NIS+ Interface

The `nisldapmaptest` command is used to operate on data stored within LDAP by
using a NIS+ interface. This is particularly important when testing to see that NIS+
and LDAP services are correctly integrated. It can also be useful for experienced NIS+
administrators who want to add, delete, or modify LDAP records by using a familiar
NIS+ interface. Several options can be passed to the `nisldapmaptest` command,
including the following:

–d	Enables deletion of data
–r	Updates data or adds new data
–s	Searches for existing data
–t	The name of the target NIS+ object

Let's look at some examples of `nisldapmaptest` that can be used. First, we will
examine how to determine whether a user entry (*pwatters*) exists in the password table:

```
# nisldapmaptest -t passwd.org_dir name=pwatters
```

Any of the following tables can be queried in this way:

auto_home	auto_master	bootparams	client_info	cred	ethers
group	hosts	mail_aliases	netgroup	netmasks	networks
passwd	protocols	rpc	sendmailvars	services	timezone

For example, to obtain a list of hosts stored in the *hosts* table, we would use the following command:

```
# nisldapmaptest -t hosts.org_dir
```

If a host was found in the table that was no longer valid, it could be deleted using the following command:

```
# nisldapmaptest -d -t hosts.org_dir name=oldhost
```

Worked Example

In this example, we will demonstrate how to manage iDS by using the console. Once the iDS server has been installed, you should be able to start the console using this command:

```
# directoryserver startconsole
```

The appropriate admin port number and hostname will be displayed on the login window, as shown here:

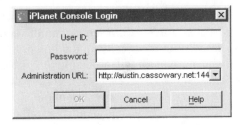

In this case, *14462* is the admin port for the LDAP server that was specified during install. The administration user ID and corresponding password must be entered to bring up the main administration window.

The main iDS console is then displayed, as shown in Figure 28-2, with two tabs that are used to separate the two main functions of the console: Servers and Applications,

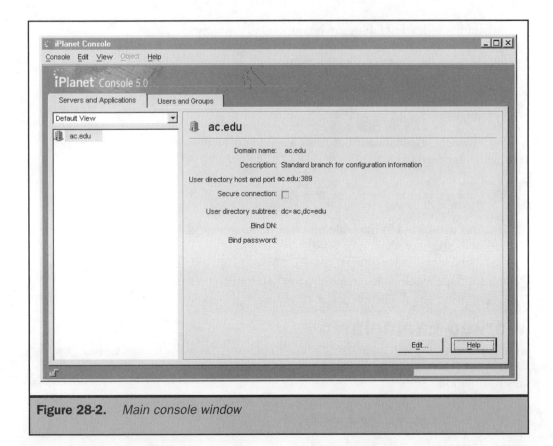

Figure 28-2.   *Main console window*

and Users and Groups. The Servers and Applications tab has two separate panes: The first pane, on the left, is a hierarchical object list of all servers and their respective databases that have been configured for the network. The local server group is displayed, along with entries for the local administration server and the actual directory server. By selecting the icon associated with the localhost, the hostname, description, physical location, platform, and operating system will be displayed. Selecting the server group icon displays the group name, description, and installation path.

The second pane, on the right, shows the domain name, description, port number, and user directory structure for the iDS server. In addition, the DN and password are displayed, as well as an option to encrypt connections to the server. It is possible to edit these details by clicking the Edit button.

By selecting the Directory Server icon in the Servers and Applications tab, a list of configured items for the local server is displayed, as shown in Figure 28-3. For example, the server name, description, installation date, product name, vendor name,

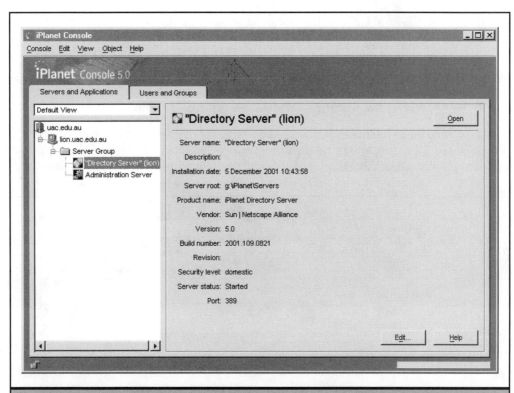

Figure 28-3.   *Main Directory Server window*

version number, build number, revision level, security level, server status, and port are all displayed. It is possible to edit all of these entries by clicking the Edit button.

By double-clicking the directory server icon, a new window is displayed, as shown in Figure 28-4, which is used to configure the directory server's operation. Four panes are available, each with a number of different operations. The Tasks pane defines nine different operations:

- Start directory server, which initializes the local iDS server and launches it.
- Stop directory server, which shuts down all local services and stops the iDS processes.
- Restart directory, which shuts down all local services, stops the iDS processes, initializes the local iDS server, and relaunches it.
- Back up the local ids database.

- Restore the local iDS database from a backup.
- Manage certificates for security.
- Log into iDS as a different user.
- Import a new iDS database from a different system.
- Export an existing local iDS database to a different system.

The Configuration pane contains a hierarchical list of objects associated with the iDS database, including tables, replication features, the database schema, logs, and optional plug-ins. In addition, a set of tabs allows various options to be configured.

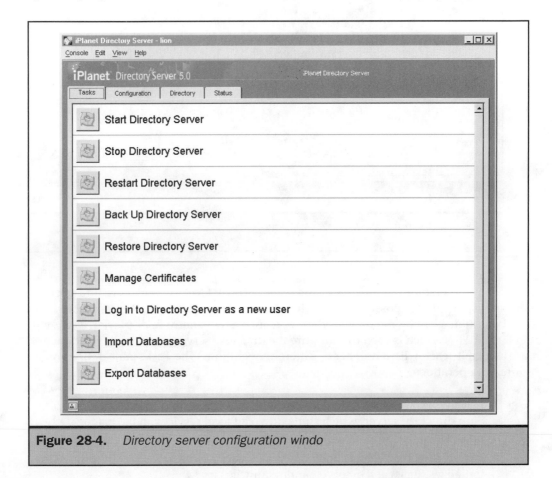

Figure 28-4. *Directory server configuration windo*

The Settings subpane allows the unencrypted port, encrypted port, and referrals to be set, as shown here:

Settings	Performance	Encryption	SNMP	Manager

Network Settings

Port: `389`

Encrypted port: `636`

Referrals to: ` `

☐ Make entire server read-only

☑ Track entry modification times

☑ Enable schema checking

In addition, the server can be set up as read-only, and entry modification times can be tracked along with various schema checks.

The Performance subpane sets limits on the size of the directory, a time limit for access, and an idle timeout, as shown here:

Settings	Performance	Encryption

Size limit: `2000`   entries

Time limit: `3600`   seconds

Idle timeout: `0`   seconds

These settings will need to be modified for local use, but are set at *2000* entries, *one hour* and *zero*, respectively.

The Encryption subpane has two main tasks: setting options for server security and for client authentication, as shown in Figure 28-5. On the server side, access can be granted using SSL, thereby protecting authentication tokens from interception by a third party. In this case, RSA options need to be set, including the name of the security device (by default, *internal/software-based*), the certificate location, and the cipher. On the client side, authentication can be disallowed, allowed, or required, depending on the application's requirements. In addition, using SSL can be made mandatory within the iPlanet console.

ENTERPRISE

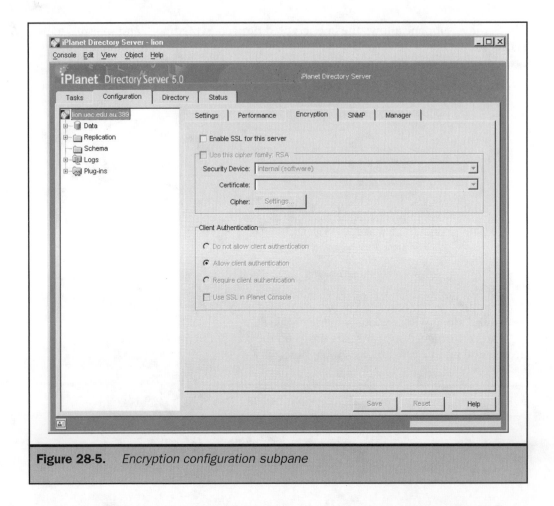

Figure 28-5. *Encryption configuration subpane*

The SNMP subpane shown next provides an interface to the Simple Network Management Protocol (SNMP), allowing service status to be remotely monitored by a third-party SNMP monitoring product.

Settings	Performance	Encryption	SNMP	Manager

☑ Enable statistics collection

┌─ Descriptive Properties ─────────────────────────┐

Description: [   ]

Organization: [   ]

Location: [   ]

Contact: [   ]

└──┘

Start SNMP	Stop SNMP	Restart SNMP

When alarm events are triggered because of run-time errors, administration staff can be notified by pager, phone, or e-mail, and appropriate action can be taken to rectify the problem. Descriptive properties, including the organization, location, and support contact, can be entered from the SNMP subpane, which also includes three buttons that allow the service to be started, stopped, and/or restarted.

The Manager subpane, shown next, sets several options for the Directory Manager role.

Settings	Performance	Encryption	SNMP	Manager

Directory Manager DN: [cn=Directory Manager   ]

Manager password encryption: [Salted Secure Hashing Algorithm (SSHA) ▼]

New password: [*******************]

Confirm password: [*******************]

This includes the Distinguished Name of the Directory Manager, the algorithm used to encrypt the Directory Manager's password (by default, the Secure Salted Hashing Algorithm, or SSHA), and the Directory Manager's password. It's also possible to enter a new password into the New Password field and confirm it in the Confirm Password field.

The administration server can be configured by double-clicking the administration server icon in the Servers and Applications tab, as shown next, which is used to configure the directory server's operation.

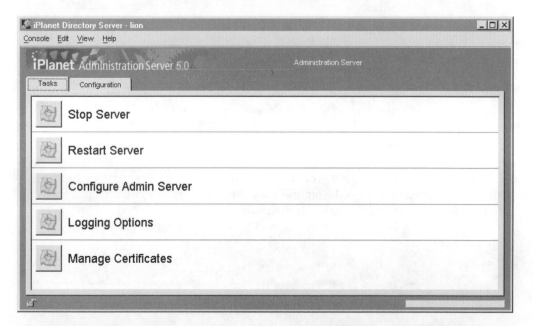

Four panes are available, each with a number of different operations. The Tasks pane defines five different operations:

- Start/stop the directory server, which initializes the local iDS server and launches it.

- Restart the directory server, which shuts down all local services, stops the iDS processes, initializes the local iDS server, and relaunches it.

- Configure the local administration server.

- Set up local logging options.

- Manage certificates for security.

The console provides an interface for querying the directory, as well as adding new entries at the user, group, and organizational unit levels. The search facility allows a search string to be entered as a full or partial username, group name, or organizational unit. For example, to find the user "Paul Watters" in the directory, you could search on

"Paul" or "Watters." The searching interface and the result of a search on "Watters" (no matches were found in the directory) is shown here:

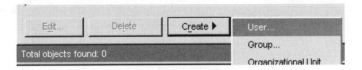

If a match had been found, the name, user ID, e-mail address, and phone number would have been displayed. In addition, each entry found as the result of a search can be modified by selecting the Edit button.

If an entry is not found, it can be easily created by clicking on the Create button, located at the bottom of the screen, as shown here:

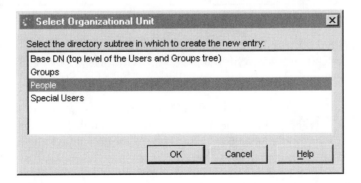

A drop-down list of all possible entry types will appear, including users, groups, and organizational units.

After choosing to create a new user, group, or organizational unit, you need to indicate the directory subtree under which the entry will appear, as shown here,

from among four options: the Base Distinguished Name (the top level of the directory), Groups, Users, and Special Users.

A new user can be created by using the Create User window shown in Figure 28-6. The user's first name, last name, common name, user ID, password, e-mail address,

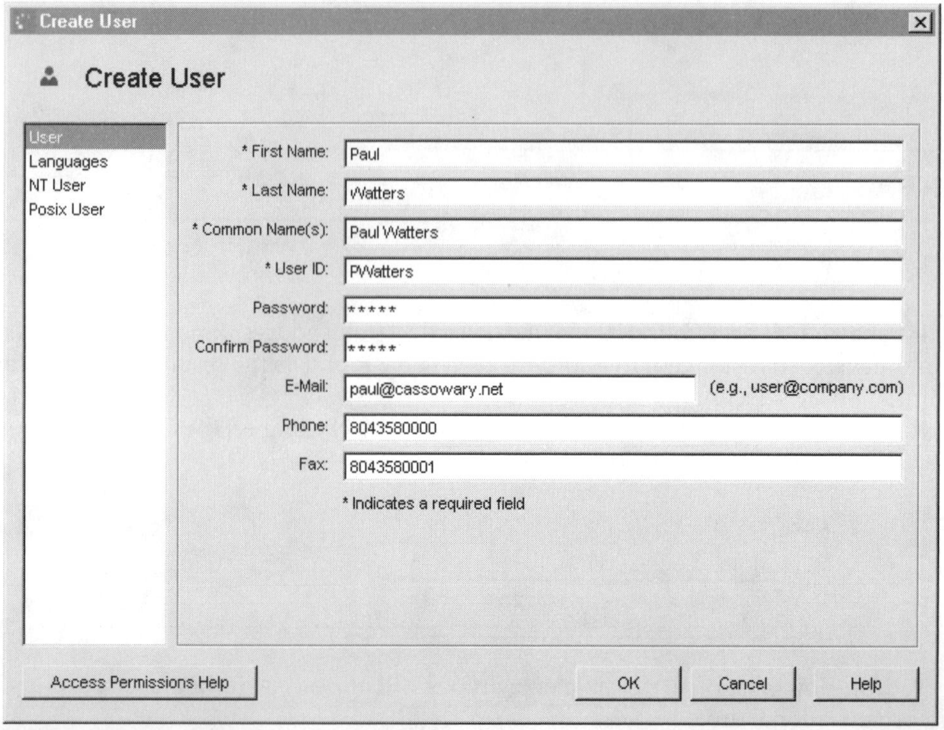

Figure 28-6. *Creating a new user*

phone number, and fax number can be entered into their respective fields. In addition, a target language can be entered for the user, and Windows NT or POSIX-specific user data can be stored. Since this iDS installation is based on Solaris, POSIX should be selected.

After the user's details have been entered, it should be possible to return to the user search screen, enter in the name of the user whose details have been stored, and retrieve the user's complete record, as shown next. Once retrieved, the user's details can be modified or the record can be deleted.

| Servers and Applications | Users and Groups | | |

Enter name of User, Group, or Organizational Unit to search for:

Paul Watters

Search   Advanced...

Search Results:

Name	User ID	E-Mail	Phone
Paul Watters	PWatters	paul@cassowary.net	8043580000

A key user characteristic is group membership. Thus, once a number of users have been created in a directory, it makes sense to create a group in which to store them, rather than entering them at the top level of the directory. Defining a new group requires a group name as well as a group description. These can be entered into the Create Group window shown in Figure 28-7. The languages required to be used by group members can also be entered by selecting Languages from the left-hand pane.

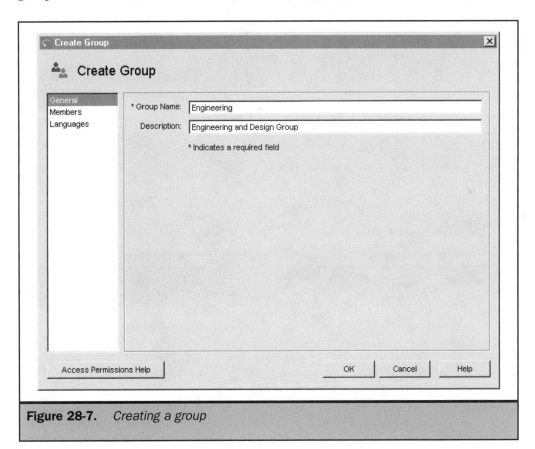

Figure 28-7.   *Creating a group*

After a group has been defined, members can be added individually by selecting Members from the left pane, as shown in Figure 28-8, and clicking the Add button. Alternatively, group members, once created using this screen, can be easily removed by clicking the Remove button.

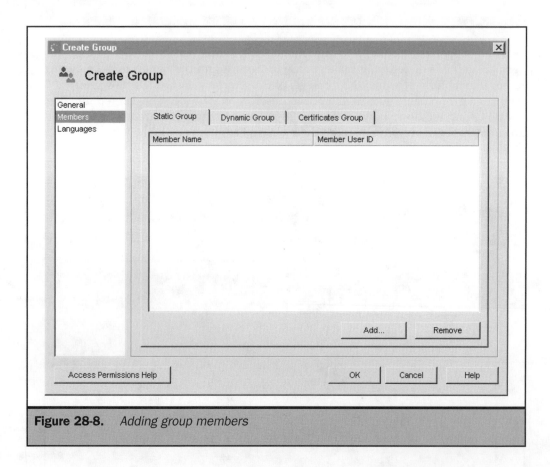

Figure 28-8.   *Adding group members*

After members have been added to groups, it's possible to search on a user and group basis, rather than just a user basis, as shown here:

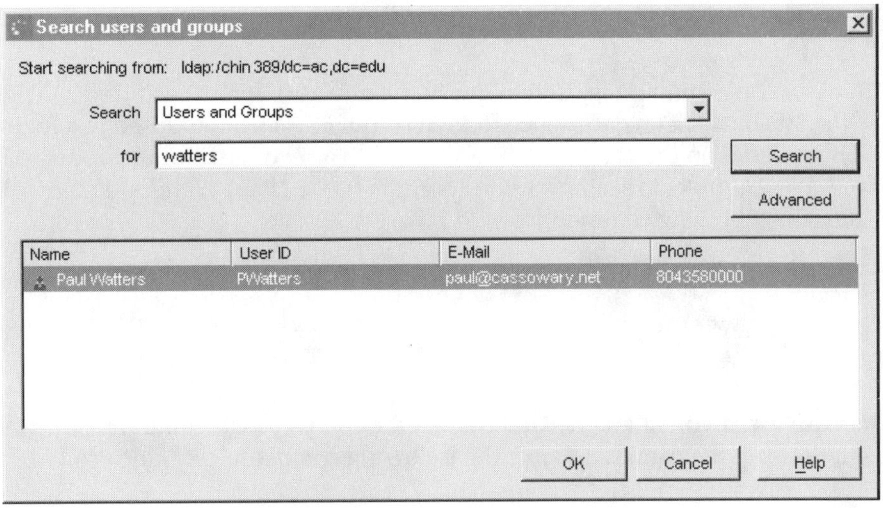

The search string can be either a group name or a username. After group members have been selected on the basis of the search term, their details are displayed sorted by name, with user ID, e-mail address, and phone number appearing.

At the top level, it's possible for you to define a new organizational unit. The unit's entry can contain the unit's name, description, phone number, fax number, alias, and full address, as shown in Figure 28-9. In addition, the language support required for the organizational can be defined by selecting Languages from the left pane.

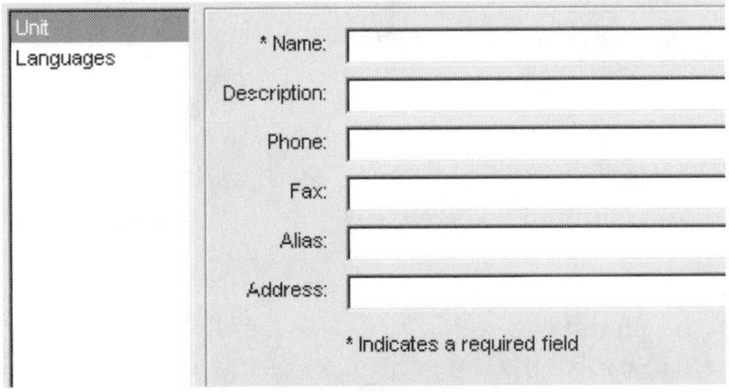

Figure 28-9. *Creating an organizational unit*

Command Reference

The following commands can be used in conjunction with the LDAP server.

ldapsearch

The ldapsearch command is used to query the directory for a specific entry and to display the attributes of an entry once located. A query string composed of a logical condition is passed on the command line along with a set of attributes that are to be displayed. For example, to search for the common name "Paul Watters" and display the results, the following command would be used:

```
$ ldapsearch -u "cn=Paul Watters" cn
cn=Paul A Watters, ou=Engineering, o=cassowary.net, c=US
cn=Paul Watters
```

Alternatively, if you knew the UID of the user you were searching for, and you wanted to look up the common name, the following command could be used:

```
$ ldapsearch -u -t "uid=paul" cn
cn=Paul A Watters, ou=Engineering, o=cassowary.net, c=US
cn=Paul Watters
```

It's possible to perform a wider area search than just looking for a single individual. For example, to print a description of all organizations below the country "US" in the directory information tree, the following command would be used:

```
$ ldapsearch -L -b "c=US" description
dn: o=cassowary.net, c=US
description: Cassowary Computing Pty Ltd
```

ldapmodify

The ldapmodify command is used to create, read, update, or delete entries in the directory. An ldapadd command is used to create new directory entries. However, this command is equivalent to invoking ldapmodify with the –a (add) option. In addition, while it is possible to enter data using standard input, most users will perform actions based on data stored in a file. (After all, if you make a mistake when typing and you have to cancel the data entry, all of the input will be lost.)

If we want to create a new entry for Moppet Watters in the directory, the following data should be inserted into a file called *newdata.txt*:

```
dn: cn=Moppet Watters, o=cassowary.net, c=US
objectClass: person
cn: Mopster Watters
sn: Watters
title: Mascot
mail: moppet@cassowary.net
uid: moppet
```

To insert this data into the directory, the following command would be used:

```
# ldapmodify -a -f newdata.txt
```

To delete this entry from the directory, we would first insert the following data into *delentry.txt*:

```
dn: cn=Moppet Watters, o=cassowary.net, c=US
changetype=delete
```

We could then delete the entry from the directory by using this command:

```
# ldapmodify -f delentry.txt
```

The Complete Reference

Solaris 9

## Chapter 29

Samba

One of the most commonly used file and print sharing protocols is the Session Message Block (SMB) protocol, developed by Microsoft, and used extensively in Windows systems. SMB allows file systems and printers to be shared with a number of remote clients, with full access rights. For example, in a Windows NT domain, printing access rights to networked printers may be granted, but read-only may be provided to a shared CD-ROM on the server. It is also possible to mount remotely exported file systems as virtual local drives, making it easy to integrate centralized data storage with local data management systems (such as databases). Fortunately, Solaris supports SMB networking through the Samba suite of programs, which even includes a NetBIOS name service. In this chapter, we examine how you can use Samba to share Solaris 9 file systems and printers to any client that supports SMB networking, including Windows, Linux, and MacOS clients. This means that you can use Solaris 9 as a reliable, centralized file server, replacing unreliable servers running other operating systems. Although Samba had to be installed as a third-party package in previous versions of Solaris, Solaris 9 includes Samba 2.2.0. In this chapter, you will learn how to export file systems, share printers, and share file systems between Samba servers.

Key Concepts

The key concepts of Samba are discussed next.

Samba Server

Samba is a package that makes it easy to bring the Windows and Solaris networking environments closer together. Although both Windows and Solaris support standard TCP/IP networking, both Microsoft and Sun have tended to develop their own versions of file system and printer sharing. Microsoft's Explorer program, shown in Figure 29-1, is used to create combined views of all local and remote file systems within a domain. The example given shows two local drives (C and D), a local CD-ROM drive, as well as the computer Tiger, as shown in the Network Neighborhood. If the entry for Tiger was expanded, several shared disks could potentially be mounted, if access rights were granted to the local user for the remote volumes, through Security Access Manager. In addition, printers attached to Tiger could also be accessed, and print jobs could be managed using the printer control panel.

Figure 29-2 shows how easy it is to share file systems using Windows: You simply right-click on the drive you want to share in the Explorer window, select Sharing, and define the authentication procedures and access rights for the shared volume.

In contrast, Sun developed the Network File System (NFS) protocol, which also allows file systems and printers to be shared to other clients. There are even Windows-based NFS clients that allow Windows clients to access Solaris NFS shares. However, the

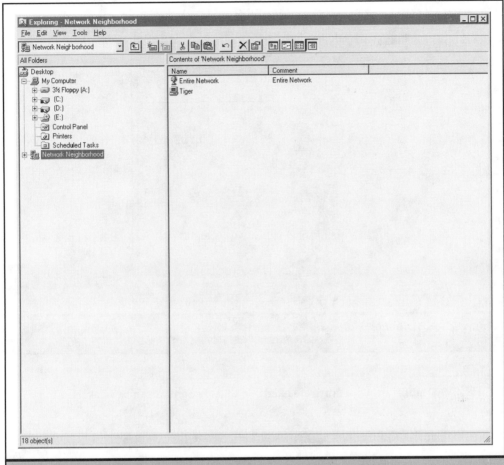

Figure 29-1.   *Viewing the Network Neighborhood in Microsoft Windows*

choice between using NFS and Samba in a heterogeneous network may be one of cost
(PC-NFS costs money, Samba is free), but is more likely a question of numbers: Would
you rather install NFS client software on hundreds of Windows systems that already
have SMB support, or would you prefer to install a single SMB-compliant server (like
Samba)? Using Samba as a centralized Windows server reduces the need to buy extra
server licenses for file and print servers, because these functions could be provided by
a Solaris Intel or Solaris SPARC system running Samba. Samba also runs on Linux systems.

Figure 29-2. *Sharing a drive in Microsoft Windows*

This illustration shows a concrete example of how Samba can be useful on the (Microsoft Windows) client side:

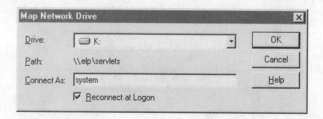

A remote file system (**elp****servlets**) being exported using Samba running on Solaris allows a Microsoft Windows user to map a local drive letter (K) to that file system. As far as the Windows client is concerned, the Solaris Samba volume is equivalent to a file system being shared from Windows NT Server or equivalent.

There are two main services that you must run in order to use Samba: the *nmbd* NetBIOS name lookup service and the *smbd* Samba daemon. The NetBIOS service is necessary to "find" local Windows clients and all SMB servers within the local domain. The *smbd* daemon takes care of the actual file and print sharing operations. A new process is created for every client that connects to the *smbd*, although only one *nmbd* is ever created.

NetBIOS Naming

Before file systems may be exported using the Samba daemon, you need to locate the client and server systems by using the NetBIOS name lookup protocol. The *nmbd* service runs on port 137 on Solaris, and it carries out the same functions as NetBIOS naming under Microsoft Windows. *nmbd* is a server that understands and can reply to NetBIOS over IP name service requests. It also participates in the browsing protocols that make up the Windows Network Neighborhood view. In addition, you can use *nmbd* as a WINS (Windows Internet Name Server) server for resolution of hostnames. You can best gain an insight into how this operates by looking at some of the Windows NT commands that you can use to browse SMB shares and compare these with the equivalent Linux commands that perform the same tasks.

In order to view a list of client systems that are currently accessing a Windows NT server, you would use the command:

```
C:\WINNT\SYSTEM32>nbtstat -s
```

The following output would then be displayed:

```
               NetBIOS Connection Table

Local Name     State       In/Out  Remote Host        Input   Output
---------------------------------------------------------------------
SYDNEY <00>    Connected   Out     HUNTER    <20>     101KB   15KB
SYDNEY <00>    Connected   Out     MELBOURNE   <20>   1MB     100MB
SYDNEY <00>    Connected   Out     WGONG     <20>     203KB   205KB
```

This output states that the server called SYDNEY is serving the remote systems HUNTER, MELBOURNE, and WGONG. You can examine how much data has been uploaded and downloaded to and from the server by looking at the input/output column. In the case of HUNTER, the input is greater than the output, whereas for MELBOURNE, the output greatly exceeds the input, which would be expected of a file serving system. In contrast, WGONG has approximately similar levels of input and output.

In order to view all of the hosts available for connections within a specific Windows NT domain, you can use the net view command:

```
C:\WINNT\SYSTEM32>net view
```

This produces output similar to the following:

```
Server Name           Remark

------------------------------------------------------
```

```
\\HUNTER      Regional Server
\\SYDNEY      Capital Server
\\WGONG       Regional Server
\\BRISBANE    Capital Server
\\BATHURST    Web Server
\\ORANGE      Web Server
\\DINGO       Kerberos Server
\\DINGBAT     Anonymous FTP Server
The command completed successfully.
```

Here, you can see that a number of systems are available within the local EASTAUS domain. There are several file servers for capital cities and regional cities, as well as two Web servers, a Kerberos server, and an anonymous FTP server. These kinds of systems would typically be found in a modern network, and all would potentially require remote file access to other systems. For example, the two Web servers might require access to some files on the anonymous FTP server; this access could be provided by Samba.

Solaris systems don't have the net view command. However, Samba does provide a number of tools, such as *nmblookup*, which you can use to list all of the systems within a specific domain. For example, to display all of the systems within the EASTAUS domain, you would use the command:

```
$ nmblookup EASTAUS
Added interface ip=62.12.48.43 bcast=62.12.48.255 nmask=255.255.255.0
Sending queries to 62.12.48.255
Got a positive name query response from 62.12.48.39 (62.12.48.39)
Got a positive name query response from 62.12.48.41 (62.12.48.41)
Got a positive name query response from 62.12.48.42 (62.12.48.42)
Got a positive name query response from 62.12.48.43 (62.12.48.43)
Got a positive name query response from 62.12.48.50 (62.12.48.50)
Got a positive name query response from 62.12.48.57 (62.12.48.57)
Got a positive name query response from 62.12.48.58 (62.12.48.58)
```

Remember that any of these hosts could be Samba servers running on Linux or Solaris, as well as Microsoft Windows servers and clients using native SMB networking. You can start the *nmbd* daemon with the following command:

```
# /usr/local/samba/bin/nmbd -D
```

The –D option specifies that the NetBIOS name service daemon should run as a standalone daemon, rather than as a service through the Internet super daemon *inetd*.

Samba Clients

There are a number of ways to make a client connection to a Samba server. If you are using an NT Workstation system or similar, the Solaris Samba server should simply appear as a normal NT Server, with individual file systems listed as shares (as determined by the *smb.conf* program). In addition, Solaris file systems may be mapped as local NT drives. This makes Solaris Samba an ideal solution for servicing multiple NT Workstation systems as a reliable file server.

Linux users can use the `smbmount` command to mount shared Solaris file systems. In order to mount the answerbook share on the Solaris Samba server SYDNEY, for example, the following command would be issued from a Linux system:

```
# smbmount //SYDNEY/answerbook /usr/local/answerbook
```

This would mount the remote answerbook share onto the local file system on the mount point */usr/local/answerbook*. Of course, the mount point would need to be created prior to mounting by using this command:

```
# mkdir -p /usr/local/answerbook
```

To unmount the share once it is no longer required, the following command would be used:

```
# umount /usr/local/answerbook
```

Solaris users who wish to access remote Samba shares (from Solaris, NT, or Linux servers) typically use the *smbclient* program, which runs from the command line and has a simple command-set that is similar to that used by FTP. *smbclient* provides a very useful and compact way to upload, download, and delete files on a remote server. In order to make an initial connection, you would use a command of the form

```
# smbclient -L system
```

where *system* is the name of the remote Samba server. To determine which shares were available on the server SYDNEY, use the command:

```
# smbclient -L SYDNEY
Added interface ip=62.12.48.43 bcast=62.12.48.43 nmask=255.255.255.0
Domain=[EASTAUS] OS=[Unix] Server=[Samba 2.0.6]
```

```
Sharename       Type        Comment
---------       ----        -------
answerbook      Disk        Sun Answerbooks
homes           Disk        User Home Directories
IPC$            IPC         IPC Service (Samba 2.0.6)

Server                  Comment
---------               -------
SYDNEY                  Samba 2.0.6

Workgroup               Master
---------               -------
EASTAUS                 WGONG
```

In order to make a connection to the share *//SYDNEY/answerbook*, use this command:

```
# smbclient //SYDNEY/answerbook
```

You would then be able to use one of the commands listed in Table 29-1 to list directory contents, change working directories, and upload and download files.

Accessing a remote printer using Samba is slightly different: You must supply the *–P* option to the *smbclient* command in order to identify that target share as a printer. For example, to mount the printer called *hp* on the Samba server SYDNEY, you would use the command:

```
$ smbclient -P //SYDNEY/hp
```

Command	Action
cd *<dir>*	Change working directory
dir *<dir>*	Display directory contents
get *<file>*	Retrieve a single file from the server
ls *<dir>*	Display directory contents
mget *<files>*	Retrieve multiple files from the server
mput *<files>*	Store multiple files on the server
put *<file>*	Store a single file on the server

Table 29-1.   *Basic* smbclient *Commands*

You may then print a local file (such as *address_book.txt*) by using a command such as the following:

```
smb:\> print address_book.txt
```

You can then use the standard printing tools to examine print queues to determine whether the print job was successfully completed.

Procedures

Configuring the Samba daemon and troubleshooting are discussed next.

Configuring the Samba Daemon

You can start the *smbd* server with this command:

```
# /usr/local/samba/bin/smbd -D
```

Again, the *–D* option specifies that the NetBIOS name service daemon should run as a standalone daemon, rather than as a service through the Internet super daemon *inetd*. The Samba daemon has a special configuration file called *smb.conf*. It is usually stored in the */usr/local/samba/lib* directory. The smb.conf can either be very short or very long, depending on the extent to which your local system requires customization and how many file systems need to be exported. A sample *smb.conf* file is shown here:

```
[global]
workgroup = EASTAUS
netbios name = SYDNEY
server string = Solaris Samba Server V2.0.6
interfaces = 62.12.48.43
security = SHARE
log file = /usr/local/samba/log/log.%m
max log size = 500
socket options = TCP_NODELAY SO_RCVBUF=4096 SO_SNDBUF=4096
dns proxy = Yes
guest account = guest
hosts allow = localhost, 62.12.48.43/255.255.255.0

[printers]
comment = SYDNEY HP Printer
path = /var/spool/hp
```

```
print ok = Yes
browseable = Yes

 [homes]
comment = User Home Directories
read only = No
browseable = Yes

 [answerbook]
comment = Sun Answerbook Docs
path = /usr/answerbook/
guest ok = Yes
```

The global section defines several key parameters that affect the operation of *smbd*, including the name of the workgroup (EASTAUS), the name of the local server (SYDNEY), the server string that identifies the system (Solaris Samba Server V2.0.6), the primary network interface IP address (*62.12.48.43*), the security level (standard share level), the path to the Samba log file (*/usr/local/samba/log*), TCP transmission parameters (such as send and receive buffer sizes in bytes), and the name of the guest account (*guest*). Next, the local *hp* printer is specified as a share in the printers section. In addition, two different file systems are shared: the homes file system shares the local home directory for each user on the system, while the answerbook file system shares the local copy of Sun's answerbooks. Although NFS provides the automounter service through NFS that makes it easy for users to retrieve files from a single home directory on a server, the homes facility on Samba can be just as versatile. Although most of the settings in *smb.conf* are easy to interpret, you can find the complete Samba manual online at the Samba site (**http://www.samba.org/**).

One of the nice features of Samba is the configuration script–checking program *testparm*. The *testparm* program will alert you to any configuration errors prior to starting a Samba service. In addition, *testparm* prints out ALL of the Samba parameters associated with the system in general, and for each share, not just those that were explicitly declared in the *smb.conf* file:

```
$ testparm
Load smb config files from /usr/local/samba/lib/smb.conf
Processing section "[printers]"
Processing section "[homes]"
Processing section "[answerbook]"
Loaded services file OK.
WARNING: You have some share names that are longer than 8 chars
These may give errors while browsing or may not be accessible
```

```
to some older clients
Press enter to see a dump of your service definitions
# Global parameters
[global]
        workgroup = EASTAUS
        netbios name =
        netbios aliases =
        server string = Samba 2.0.6
        interfaces =
        bind interfaces only = No
        security = USER
        encrypt passwords = Yes
        update encrypted = No
        allow trusted domains = Yes
        hosts equiv =
        min passwd length = 5
        map to guest = Never
        null passwords = No
        password server =
[printers]
comment = SYDNEY HP Printer
path = /var/spool/hp
print ok = Yes
browseable = Yes

  [homes]
comment = User Home Directories
read only = No
browseable = Yes

  [answerbook]
comment = Sun Answerbook Docs
path = /usr/answerbook/
guest ok = Yes
```

Samba Daemon Status

After the Samba server has been started on port 139, it is easy to keep track of the
server status by using the smbstatus command:

```
$ smbstatus
```

This will return a list of all current clients accessing data through the local Samba system:

```
Samba version 2.0.6
Service      uid      gid      pid     machine
-------------------------------------------------
answerbook   root     root     344     MELBOURNE   Wed Nov 1 10:45:00 2000
homes        root     root     345     MELBOURNE   Wed Nov 1 10:45:30 2000
homes        julian   staff    1023    HUNTER Thu Nov 2 00:15:34 2000
answerbook   steve    staff    2333    WGONG Wed Nov 1 10:45:30 2000
```

In addition to the share name being accessed, the UID, GID, and PID of the *smbd* process associated with the client are shown along with the client system name and the date the connection was established. For example, the root user from the system MELBOURNE opened the answerbook and the root home directory on Wednesday, November 1, 2000, at 10:45 A.M.

The `smbstatus` command also displays details of actual files being opened by the users who have established a connection to the local Samba server. This can be very useful when trying to determine why a file on the local server file system can't be modified—a remote user may have placed a lock on it, which will not be released until the user has closed the file:

```
Locked files:
Pid     DenyMode    R/W      Oplock   Name
-------------------------------------------------
345     DENY_NONE   RDWR     NONE     /root/data.txt   Wed Nov 1 10:51:34 2000
345     DENY_NONE   RDONLY   NONE     /root/db.txt     Wed Nov 1 10:56:21 2000
1023    DENY_NONE   RDWR     NONE     /home/julian/address_book.txt
   Thu Nov 2 00:20:34 2000
```

The details of all currently locked files are displayed. Along with the PID of the Samba daemon spawned for each client process, the read/write status and the full path to the locked file is displayed, along with the time and date that the file was first opened.

Finally, *smbstatus* displays some useful statistics regarding shared memory usage, which can be useful when trying to size the amount of RAM required by a departmental server or similar system that services a large number of Samba clients:

```
Share mode memory usage (bytes):
   2096928(99%) free + 112(0%) used + 112(0%) overhead = 2097152(100%) total
```

In this situation, almost all of the allocated memory is free, meaning that many more Samba clients may be serviced.

Troubleshooting

Samba problems can be difficult to isolate, because you have to deal with both Microsoft Windows and Solaris issues and their integration. For example, Windows and Solaris use completely different authentication systems, particularly with respect to encrypted passwords. Thus, you will need to choose whether to enable Windows-style authentication in *smb.conf* for password encryption or modify the Windows registry to transmit passwords in the clear. If you suspect a password-related problem, you can disable the use of passwords for authentication by entering the string "NOPASSWORDXXXXXXXXXXXXXXXXXXXX." By temporarily removing the password on the Solaris side, you can determine whether an authentication issue is password-related. However, allowing logins to Solaris without passwords is a very bad idea on production systems or those connected to the Internet, so it would be wise to create a special account with */bin/false* as the shell, which you must remove after testing.

In the first instance, the Samba daemons can be restarted. This can assist if the daemon has "hung," because of a name conflict, timeout, or some other reason. In addition, the daemons must be restarted every time a change is made to the *smb.conf* file.

Examples

The following examples show how Samba works in action.

Samba GUI Interfaces

If manually configuring Samba by using the *smb.conf* file is a bit daunting, you can use several third-party GUI interfaces to automate the process of creating a *smb.conf* through a browser. One of the most popular tools is the Samba Web Administration Tool (SWAT) tool, which runs as a service through the Internet super daemon (*inetd*) on port 901. It can be administered locally, through a browser running on Solaris, or remotely, through a browser running on Microsoft Windows. The current Samba source distribution will build SWAT by default, however, a number of configuration changes need to be made in order to enable the SWAT service. If you're unsure about how to edit the *inetd.conf* file or restart the *inetd* service, you should refer to Chapter 12.

The first step is to map the SWAT service name to the required TCP port (901), by adding the following line to the */etc/services* files:

```
swat    901/tcp
```

The following line then needs to be added to the */etc/inetd.conf* file:

```
swat    stream  tcp  nowait  root  /usr/local/samba-2.0.5/bin/swat  swat
```

For the changes to take effect, you must restart the *inetd* service by using the following steps:

```
# ps -eaf | grep inetd
    root   200     1  0   Nov 1 ?        01:25 /usr/sbin/inetd -s
```

The PID of inetd is *200*, so the command to restart the service with the modified *inetd.conf* file is

```
kill -1 200
```

After opening a browser, you can then access the SWAT interface by using the URL **http://SYDNEY:901/**, as shown in Figure 29-3.

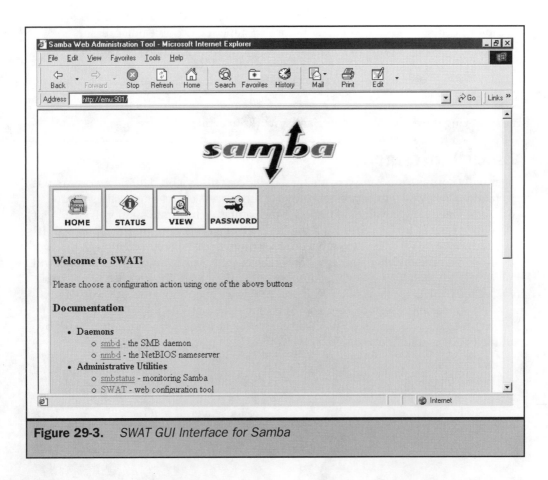

Figure 29-3.   *SWAT GUI Interface for Samba*

NT Authentication

In order to allow users to be authenticated from an NT domain and access Samba shares, the following lines should be inserted into *smb.conf*:

```
encrypt passwords = yes
security = server
password server = "pdc"
```

In this example, the server name *pdc* corresponds to the NetBIOS name of the PDC.

The Complete Reference

Solaris 9

Part VII

Enterprise

The Complete Reference

Chapter 30

Advanced Security

ecurity is a key concern for Solaria administrators. Although we discussed security procedures in Chapter 9, there are a number of advanced security issues that Solaris administrators confront in their daily lives. In this chapter, we review some higher level material, such as security levels and definitions, before reviewing some sample security advanced procedures.

Key Concepts

The following key concepts are central to understanding Solaris security architectures.

Security Architecture

In Chapter 9, we examined the essential features of Solaris security, including the need to protect individual files, as well as entire systems, from unauthorized access. In addition, we examined how both files and systems can be protected from remote access tools. However, we need to place these individual actions within a context that logically covers all aspects of security, typically known as levels. A level is an extra "step" that must be breached in order to obtain access to data.

In terms of physical security, a bank provides an excellent analogy. Breaking into a bank's front counter and teller area is as easy as walking through the door, because these doors are publicly accessible. However, providing this level of access sometimes opens doors deeper inside the building. For example, the private banking area, which may normally be accessed only by staff and identified private banking customers, may allow access using a smart card. If a smart card is stolen from a staff member, it could be used to enter the secure area, because the staff member's credentials would be authenticated. Entering this level would not necessarily provide access to the vault: Super-user privileges would be required. However, a thorough physical search of the private banking area might yield the key required for entry. Or, a brute force attack on the safe's combination might be used to guess the correct combination. Having accessed the vault, if readily negotiated currency or bullion is contained therein, an intruder could easily steal them. However, if the vault contained checks that needed to be counter-signed, the intruder may not be able to make use of the contents. The lesson here is simple: Banks provide public services that open up pathways straight to the cash. Banks know that any or all of the physical security layers may be breached. That's why the storage of negotiable securities is always minimized, because any system designed by humans can be broken by humans, with enough time and patience. The only sensible strategy is to make sure that external layers are as difficult to breach as possible and to ensure that security experts are immediately notified of breaches.

Similarly, public file areas, such as FTP and WWW servers, are publicly accessible areas on computer systems that sometimes provide entry to a different level in the system. An easily guessed or stolen password may provide user-level (but unprivileged) access to the system. A brute force attack against the local password database might even yield the super-user password. Accessing a local database might contain the target records of interest. However, instead of storing the data plaintext within tables, data may have been written using a stream cipher, making it potentially very difficult to obtain the data. However, because 40-bit ciphers have been broken in the past, obtaining the encrypted data might eventually lead to its dissemination. Again, a key strategy is ensuring that data is secure by as many external layers as possible, and also that the data itself is difficult to negotiate.

Increasing the number of levels of security typically leads to a decrease in system ease-of-use. For example, setting a password for accessing a printer requires users to remember and enter a password when challenged. Whether printer access needs this level of security will depend on organizational requirements. For a printer that prints on plain paper, no password may be needed. However, for a printer that prints on bonded paper with an official company letterhead, a password should be used to protect the printer, and optionally, a copy of the file being sent to the printer may need to be stored securely for auditing purposes.

For government and military systems, a number of security specifications and policy documents are available, which detail the steps necessary to secure Solaris systems in "top secret" installations. The U.S. Department of Defense, for example, publishes the "Orange Book," formally known as the "Trusted Computer System Evaluation Criteria" specification. This book describes systems that it has evaluated in terms of different protection levels, from weakest to strongest, including the following:

- **Class D**   Systems that do not pass any tests and are therefore untrusted. No sensitive data should be stored on Class D systems.

- **Class C1**   Systems that require authentication based on a user model.

- **Class C2**   Systems that provide auditing and logging on a per-user basis, ensuring that file accesses and related operations can always be traced to the initiating user.

- **Class B1**   Requires security labeling for all files. Labels range from "top secret" to "unclassified."

- **Class B2**   Separates normal system administration duties from security activities, which are performed by a separate security officer. This level requires covert channels for data communications and verified testing of an installation's security procedures.

- **Class B3**   Requires that a standalone request monitor be available to authenticate all requests for file and resource access. In addition, the request monitor must be secured and all of its operations logged.

- **Class A1**   A formally tested and verified installation of a Class B3 system.

All of the strategies that we discuss in this chapter are focused on increasing the number of layers through which a potential cracker (or disgruntled staff member) must pass to obtain the data that they are illegally trying to access. Reducing the threat of remote access exploits and protecting data are key components of this strategy.

ENTERPRISE

Physical Security

It may seem obvious, but if an intruder can physically access your system, then he or she may be able to take control of your system without the root password, bypassing all of the software-based controls that normally limit such activity. How is this possible you might ask? If the intruder has access to a bootable CD-ROM drive and a bootable CD-ROM (of Solaris, Linux, or any other operating system that can mount UFS drives), it's trivial to enter the following command at the OpenBoot prompt and start the system without a password:

```
ok boot cdrom
```

Once the system has booted from the CD-ROM drive, a number of options are available to the intruder:

- FTP any file on the system to a remote system.
- Copy any file on the system to a mass storage device (such as a DAT tape).
- Format all of the drives on the system.
- Launch a distributed denial of service attack against other networks, which you will be blamed for.

Of course, the possibilities are endless, but the result is the same. You may ask why compromising a system in this way is so easy. One good reason is that if you forget your root password, you can boot from the CD-ROM, mount the boot disk, and manually edit the shadow password file.

This requirement doesn't really excuse poor security, and the OpenBoot monitor provides some options to secure the system. There are three security levels available:

- **None**   Surprisingly, this is the default. No password is required to execute any of the commands in OpenBoot. This is convenient but dangerous, for the reasons outlined earlier.

- **Command**   This level needs a password to be entered for all commands except boot and go. Thus, details of the SCSI bus and network traffic can't be observed by the casual browser. But an intruder could still boot from the CD-ROM.

- **Full**   This level requires a password for every command except go, including the boot command. Thus, even if the system is interrupted and rebooted using the boot command, only the default boot device will be available through go.

To set the security level, use the eeprom command. To set the command level, use the following command:

```
# eeprom security-mode=command
```

Or, to set the command level, use the following command:

```
# eeprom security-mode=full
```

The password for the command and full security levels must be set by using the eeprom command:

```
# eeprom security-password
Changing PROM password:
New password:
Retype new password:
```

Note that if the root password and the full level password are lost, there is no way to recover the system by software means. You will need to order a new PROM from Sun.

Trusted Solaris

Trusted Solaris implements much stricter controls over UNIX than the standard releases, and it is capable of meeting B1 level security by default. It is designed for organizations that handle military grade or commercially sensitive data. In addition to the mandatory use of Role-Based Access Control (as reviewed in Chapter 12), Trusted Solaris actually has no super-user at all: no single user is permitted to have control over every aspect of system service. This decentralization of authority is necessary in situations where consensus and/or authorization is required to carry out specific activities. For example, a system administrator installing a new Web server might inadvertently interfere with the operations of an existing service. For a server that's handling sensitive production data, the results could be catastrophic. Once a system has been installed in production, it's crucial to define a set of roles that specifies what operations need to be performed by a particular individual. For example, the role of managing a firewall is unrelated to the database administration role, so the two roles should be separated, rather than being run from a single super-user account. In addition, access to files is restricted by special access control lists, which define file contents from "unclassified" up to "top secret." Access to data that is labeled as more secret requires a higher level of authentication and authorization than unclassified data.

Four roles are defined by default under Trusted Solaris for system management purposes: the *security officer* manages all aspects of security on the system, such as auditing, logging, and password management; the *system manager* performs all system management tasks that are not related to security, except for installing new software; the *root account* is used for installing new software; and the *oper account* is used for performing backups. New roles can be created for other tasks, such as database and Web server administration, where necessary.

Some aspects of a Trusted Solaris installation already form part of a standard Solaris installation. For example, Trusted Solaris requires that centralized authentication be performed across an encrypted channel using NIS+. This feature is also available on Solaris, although many sites are now moving to LDAP-based authentication.

Procedures

The following procedures explain IP ports, firewalls, and filters in Solaris.

Disabling IP Ports

The first step in network security is to prevent unauthorized entry by disabling access to specific IP ports, as defined by individual entries in the services database. This action prevents specific services from operating, even if the *inetd* attempts to accept a connection for a service because it is still defined in */etc/inetd.conf*. In this section, we examine how to disable specific services from *inetd*, in conjunction with the services database.

The following services are typically enabled in */etc/services*, and configured in */etc/inetd.conf*. Most sites will want to disable them and install more secure equivalents. For example, the *ftp* and *telnet* services may be replaced by the encrypted secure *copy* and *secure shell* programs, respectively. To disable the *ftp, telnet, shell, login, exec, comsat, talk, uucp,* and *finger* services, you would "comment out" their entries in */etc/inetd.conf* by inserting a hash character (#) at the first character position of the line that defines the service. The following configuration enables the *ftp, telnet, shell, login, exec, comsat, talk, uucp,* and *finger* services in */etc/inetd.conf*:

```
ftp      stream  tcp   nowait   root     /usr/sbin/in.ftpd      in.ftpd -l
telnet   stream  tcp   nowait   root     /usr/sbin/in.telnetd   in.telnetd
shell    stream  tcp   nowait   root     /usr/sbin/in.rshd      in.rshd
login    stream  tcp   nowait   root     /usr/sbin/in.rlogind   in.rlogind
exec     stream  tcp   nowait   root     /usr/sbin/in.rexecd    in.rexecd
comsat   dgram   udp   wait     root     /usr/sbin/in.comsat    in.comsat
talk     dgram   udp   wait     root     /usr/sbin/in.talkd     in.talkd
uucp     stream  tcp   nowait   root     /usr/sbin/in.uucpd     in.uucpd
finger   stream  tcp   nowait   nobody   /usr/sbin/in.fingerd   in.fingerd
```

The following configuration disables the *ftp, telnet, shell, login, exec, comsat, talk, uucp,* and *finger* services in */etc/inetd.conf*:

```
#ftp      stream  tcp   nowait   root     /usr/sbin/in.ftpd      in.ftpd -l
#telnet   stream  tcp   nowait   root     /usr/sbin/in.telnetd   in.telnetd
#shell    stream  tcp   nowait   root     /usr/sbin/in.rshd      in.rshd
#login    stream  tcp   nowait   root     /usr/sbin/in.rlogind   in.rlogind
#exec     stream  tcp   nowait   root     /usr/sbin/in.rexecd    in.rexecd
#comsat   dgram   udp   wait     root     /usr/sbin/in.comsat    in.comsat
#talk     dgram   udp   wait     root     /usr/sbin/in.talkd     in.talkd
#uucp     stream  tcp   nowait   root     /usr/sbin/in.uucpd     in.uucpd
#finger   stream  tcp   nowait   nobody   /usr/sbin/in.fingerd   in.fingerd
```

Similarly, the following configuration enables the *ftp*, *telnet*, *shell*, *login*, *exec*, *comsat*, *talk*, *uucp*, and *finger* services in */etc/services*:

```
ftp              21/tcp
telnet           23/tcp
shell            514/tcp          cmd
login            513/tcp
exec             512/tcp
biff             512/udp          comsat
talk             517/udp
uucp             540/tcp          uucpd
finger  stream  tcp      nowait  nobody  /usr/sbin/in.fingerd   in.fingerd
```

Similarly, the following configuration disables the *ftp*, *telnet*, *shell*, *login*, *exec*, *comsat*, *talk*, *uucp*, and *finger* services in */etc/services*:

```
#ftp             21/tcp
#telnet          23/tcp
#shell           514/tcp          cmd
#login           513/tcp
#exec            512/tcp
#biff            512/udp          comsat
#talk            517/udp
#uucp            540/tcp          uucpd
#finger  stream  tcp      nowait  nobody  /usr/sbin/in.fingerd   in.fingerd
```

Firewalls

The basic idea behind many firewall products is to "filter" the IP packets that arrive at a router and selectively permit them to be processed by the kernel and passed through the router or explicitly rejected. This is useful for allowing external users to send mail on port 25, to retrieve Web pages on port 80, or conversely to prevent secure shell access on port 22. Similarly, IP packets that arrive from behind a firewall may also be blocked on specific ports. This allows local users to ping external hosts or establish an FTP connection to a remote archive, while preventing them from using services that are not sanctioned. Firewall systems are also available for both Microsoft Windows and Linux systems; while the former tend to be GUI-oriented, such as Checkpoint's Firewall-1 (**http://www.checkpoint.com/**), Linux firewalls are typically configured from the command line. An example is the IP Filter program, available from **http://cheops.anu.edu.au/ ~avalon/ip-filter.html**, which works with both Solaris and Linux.

SunScreen

The best system for users who are new to Solaris is Sun's own SunScreen firewall (**http://www.sun.com/software/securenet/lite/download.html**). It comes in both a free and commercial edition, with the latter more than adequate for protecting small networks. It is available for both Solaris Intel and Solaris Sparc. The current release version is 3.1, which supports gigabit Ethernet, SNMP management, and direct editing of security policy tables. However, it does not currently support IPv6. The firewall may be administered locally or remotely by using a secure session.

There are several important limitations which are placed on the Lite version of SunScreen:

- It is designed to work with a system that is already acting as a router.

- It does not operate in the special "stealth" mode employed by the commercial edition.

- It does not support any of the High Availability features of the commercial version.

- It does not support more than two network interfaces, which can be a limitation for a "three-legged" firewall architecture (External, Internal, and DMZ).

- It does not provide support for proxying.

SunScreen can be operated in either GUI mode, through a standard Web browser such as Netscape or by directly editing the system's configuration files. It is easy to install using the Web Start wizard, which is provided with the installation package.

To install the software, you need to run the */opt/SUNWicg/SunScreen/bin/ss_install* script. You need to configure several options for SunScreen to operate as desired:

- Routing or stealth mode operation

- Local or remote administration

- Restrictive, secure, or permissive security level

- Support for DNS resolution

After choosing the appropriate option for your system, the following message will be displayed:

```
--Adding interfaces & interface addresses
--Initialize 'vars' databases
--Initialize 'authuser' & 'proxyuser' databases
--Initialize 'logmacro' database
--Applying edits
--Activating configuration
loading skip keystore.
Successfully initialized certificate database in /etc/skip/certdb
starting skip key manager daemon.
Configuration activated successfully on okami.
Reboot the machine now for changes to take effect.
```

After rebooting the system, the firewall software will be loaded into the kernel, and you will then need to add rules to the firewall by using your browser to set the appropriate administration options. Figure 30-1 shows the browser starting on port 3852 on the localhost.

When first installed, the SunScreen username and password will be "admin" and "admin," respectively. These should be entered into the Admin User and Password fields. After clicking the Login button, the SunScreen Information page is displayed, as shown in Figure 30-2. Several options are available at this point: You can view firewall

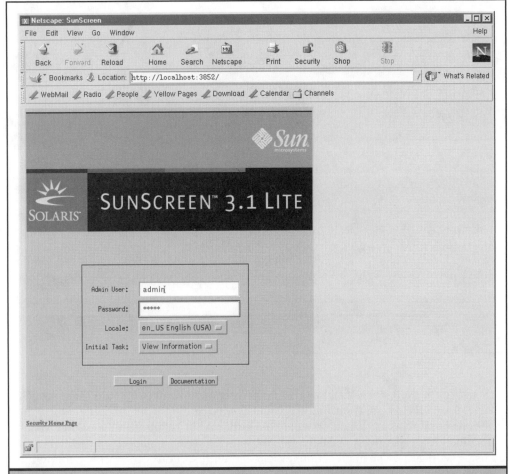

Figure 30-1. *Starting the SunScreen administrative interface*

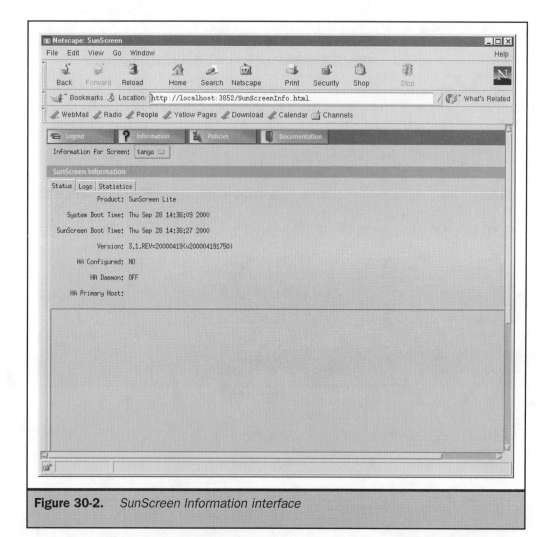

Figure 30-2. *SunScreen Information interface*

logs and connection statistics. However, most users will want to create a set of security policies immediately upon starting the firewall service.

Security policies are based on rules that either ALLOW or DENY a packet to be transmitted from a source to a destination address. Or, you may specify an address class by using wildcards. The main actions associated with ALLOW rules are the following:

LOG_NONE   LOG_SUMMARY   LOG_DETAIL

SNMP_NONE   SNMP

The main actions associated with DENY rules are the following:

LOG_NONE	LOG_SUMMARY	LOG_DETAIL
SNMP_NONE	SNMP	ICMP_NONE
ICMP_NET_ UNREACHABLE	ICMP_HOST_ UNREACHABLE	ICMP_PORT_ UNREACHABLE
ICMP_NET_ FORBIDDEN	ICMP_HOST_ FORBIDDEN	

Figure 30-3 shows how to define a rule with actions for the SMTP service, which is operated by *sendmail*. This allows mail to be transferred from local users to remote hosts. However, if you wanted to block all mail being sent to and from your network,

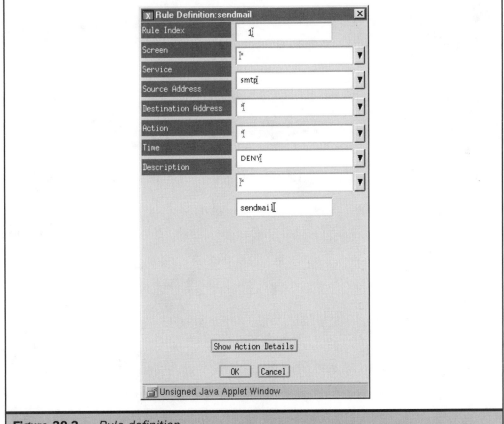

Figure 30-3.   *Rule definition*

you could create a DENY action within the rule for the SMTP service. The rule could be applied selectively to specific local subnets or remote destinations. Another useful feature is the ability to apply rules only for specific time periods. For example, if you worked in a bank, you could prevent all e-mails from being sent externally after 5 P.M. and before 9 A.M.

Once you have entered the new rule, you can view it on the Policy Rules panel, along with any other rules, as shown in Figure 30-4. The panel allows you to add new rules and edit, move, or delete existing rules. For each packet filtering rule, the service, source address, destination address, action timeframe, and name are shown.

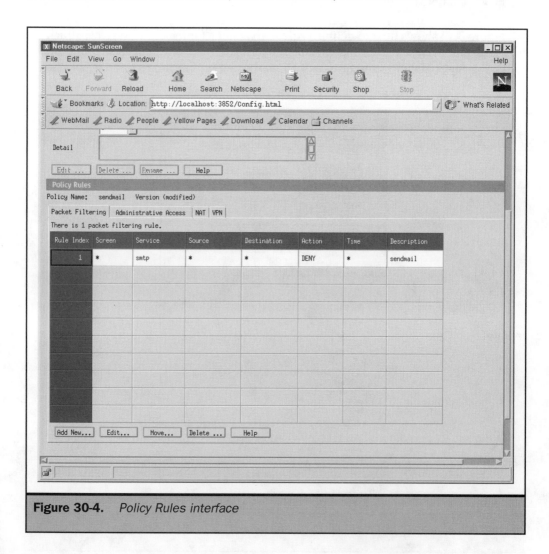

Figure 30-4. *Policy Rules interface*

SunScreen performs more than just packet filtering—it can be used to set up a virtual private network (VPN), and it can perform advanced network address translation (NAT) functions. Discussion of these topics is beyond the scope of this book, however, *Virtual Private Networks* by Scott, Wolfe, and Erwin (published by O'Reilly) discusses these issues in depth.

IP Filter

IPFilter is a popular freeware packet filtering package for Solaris, which is a kernel-loadable module that is attached at boot time. This makes IPFilter very secure, because it cannot be tampered with by user applications. However, as you will see shortly, there are also problems with this approach because loading unstable modules into the kernel can cause a Solaris system to crash. Instability in kernel modules is not restricted to IPFilter; however, by using the methods outlined in this section, you can isolate the offending command that may have caused the kernel to panic. The IPFilter distribution is available from **http://coombs.anu.edu.au/~avalon/**.

The first step in creating an IPFilter configuration file is to consult with users and managers to determine a list of acceptable services. Many companies will already have an acceptable use policy that will govern which ports should be available and what permissions should be given for user-initiated services. After a list of incoming and outgoing port requirements is determined, it is best to write a rule that first denies all packets, and then to write rules that explicitly allow the services you have identified. It is also important to enable allowed services in both directions. For example, it is usually necessary for users to both receive and send electronic mail, so you need to include an inbound and outbound rule for *sendmail* (port 25).

IPFilter rules are processed in the order that they are specified in the configuration file. Every rule is processed, which means that more general rules (such as blocking all connections) should precede specific rules (such as allowing bidirectional *sendmail* connections) in the configuration file. If you have a very complicated configuration, you can also specify that processing terminate at any point in the file, if a condition is met, by using the `quick` keyword. Other important keywords include `block`, `to`, and `from` to construct rules for limiting packet transmission. The `block` command blocks packets from a particular source to a particular destination. The `from` command specifies the source of these packets, whereas the `to` command specifies the destination of these packets. The following example prevents any packets from the Class B network 178.222.0.0:

```
block in quick from 178.222.0.0/16 to any
```

The `pass` command allows packets to pass the firewall. For example, the rule

```
pass in all
```

allows all packets to pass. Because routers by definition have more than two interfaces, you can also specify a network interface to which a specific rule applies. For example, the rule

```
block in quick on hme2 all
```

prevents all transmissions on the hme2 interface. You can mix an interface specification with a normal rule, so that one interface accepts traffic from one Class C network (178.222.1.0), but another interface may accept traffic only from a different Class C network (178.221.2.0):

```
block in quick on hme2 from 178.222.1.0/24 to any
block in quick on hme1 from 178.222.2.0/24 to any
```

All of the examples so far have focused on inbound traffic using the in command. As mentioned earlier, you can also restrict outbound traffic in the same way by using the out command. The following example prevents traffic from the internal, nonroutable network (10.222.1.0) to pass through:

```
block out quick on hme0 from 10.222.1.0/24 to any
```

This rule would be applied only to organizations who didn't want employees using the Internet. Perhaps it could be combined with a cron job, which would reconfigure the firewall to allow access during lunchtime and after work. You can also limit particular protocols so that TCP applications (such as SSH) would be allowed, but UDP applications (like some streamed audio applications) would be banned, by specifying proto udp in the rule:

```
block in quick on hme0 proto udp from 10.222.1.0/24 to any
```

The most complicated rule comes in the form of a port-by-port specification of what is allowed and disallowed on a protocol-by-protocol basis. For example, the following rule blocks all Web server requests from the internal network from reaching their destination:

```
block in quick on hme0 proto tcp from any to 10.222.1.0/24 port = 80
```

This would allow Telnet and FTP connections to proceed freely, because TCP is restricted only on port 80.

Although this technology is very comprehensive and is very useful in placing very specific restrictions on network transmission, there are some drawbacks with configuring firewalls in general, and IPFilter in particular. Because firewall configuration involves writing rules, the syntax of the commonly used rule languages is often difficult to understand, thus packet filters can be difficult to configure correctly. Once you've created a configuration, there is also no testbed provided that determines whether your configuration is satisfactory. There may be contention between one or more rules that is incorrectly resolved. Also, packet filtering packages may contain bugs, which means that administrators should not just rely on them to protect their network. Other measures, like disabling unrequired services in */etc/services* and commenting out all unwanted daemons in */etc/inetd.conf*, go a long way to protecting a system. Bugs are more serious in IPFilter because it is a kernel-loadable module. Thus, instead of an application-level filtering program crashing and dumping core, IPFilter will sometimes crash the kernel and cause a panic. Be aware that some versions of IPFilter will cause panics on Solaris kernels, while others work happily. The output from a crash looks like this:

```
BAD TRAP: cpu=1 type=0x31 rp=0x3b103003 addr=0xe1 mmu_fsr=0x0
BAD TRAP occurred in module "ipf" due to an illegal access to a user
address.
sched: trap type = 0x31
addr=0x1e
pid=0, pc=0x60bc8607, sp=0x33ba0300, tstate=0x1e02f000, context=0x0
g1-g7: 1c, 13578104, 0, 0, 0, 0, 333e8000
Begin traceback... sp = 3033ba00
Called from 1005cb74, fp=30033c20, args=0 60760b14 20 10418440 0 0
Called from 1005cc90, fp=30033c80, args=60098aa0 600992c0 60098ac0
40000000 60099328 8c2421a
Called from 10026a48, fp=30033ce0, args=60098aa0 60098ab4 10418440
10418440 d 0
Called from 1005cc48, fp=0, args=60098aa0 0 0 0 0 0
```

This kind of problem is always a risk when installing kernel-loadable modules, and it may occur with any module. However, Solaris does provide some tools to determine which modules are at fault. To examine the cause of the IPFilter problem, you can follow these steps:

1. Create the system crash directory, and enable the "savecore" facility in the system startup file (*/etc/init.d/sysetup*).

2. Wait for a crash, and then let the system reboot.

3. Enter the crash directory, and analyze the crash file with the `iscda.sh` script available from SunSolve.

4. Identify the offending command that caused the kernel panic. If it is IPFilter, download and test the most recent version.

Fortunately, you can find a very active discussion group on IPFilter, with searchable archives available at **http://false.net/ipfilter/**. The firewall mailing list is also good for more general discussion of firewall-related issues, and the contents are available at **http://www.greatcircle.com/firewalls/**. If you are more interested in commercial firewall products, check out the comparisons with freeware at **http://www.fortified.com/ fwcklist.html/**.

Examples

The following examples demonstrate how to secure Solaris.

Encryption

One of the potential weaknesses of Solaris and other UNIX systems is that the super-user is able to read the data of all users on the system. This means that if the system administrator account is breached, all data on the system can potentially be accessed by an intruder. In this context, individual users must ensure that they can protect the contents of their data, if not the representation of the data. This is where file encryption plays a major role: Users can store a form of their files on the file system, which are readable by the super-user, but whose contents cannot be easily discerned. This is because the file contents have been passed through a cipher, which uses a mathematical function to scramble them, while ensuring that the contents can be successfully decrypted. The simplest encryption schemes are symmetric—that is, a key is used to encrypt the data, and the same key is used to decrypt the data. While most keys take the form of passwords, it's also possible to engage biometric devices, which perform iris scans and capture thumbprints, to extract and apply a key.

Symmetric Key Cryptography

The `crypt` command is a symmetric key encryption system. It accepts a key supplied on the command line, which is used to encrypt data supplied from standard input, and then it pipes the data through a stream cipher to produce encrypted data on standard output. For example, if a set of medical records are stored in the file *medical.txt*, and the encrypted records are to be stored in the file *medical.crypt*, using the key *8rgbfde4f*, the following command could be used:

```
$ crypt 8rgbfde4f < medical.txt > medical.crypt
```

The contents of *medical.crypt* would then contain binary data that can be viewed on screen by using this command:

```
$ strings medical.crypt
84jh$&;4-=+-45fsfg5HGhfdk
```

The original file *medical.txt* could then be deleted, and only a user who has both read access to the *medical.crypt file* and the key *8rgbfde4f* would be able to decrypt the contents of the file and obtain the original data. The `crypt` command is used to decrypt the data using the same format as encryption.

Be aware that if you supply the key on the command line, and if the encryption takes a significant amount of time, the command string will be visible to all users by using the `ps` command. Thus, unless the command is being performed in a script, it's best to omit the key from the command line, in which case you will be prompted for it. In scripts, the key can be set as an environment variable prior to the use of the `crypt` command and then unset after the command has completed.

Note that the `crypt` algorithm is one of the least secure available. It is vulnerable to brute force cracking attacks, which is why it is not frequently used. A number of other symmetric key encryption programs can be used in place of `crypt`, such as the 56-bit Data Encryption Standard (DES), or its more secure variant, Triple DES, which uses three keys. No matter what symmetric key algorithm is used to encrypt the data, there is always the possibility that it may be decrypted by a cryptanalysis method. This typically involves matching known portions of the text to be decrypted to the encrypted text, and applying brute force methods to find a match. For example, if all letters sent on company letterhead contained the company name, that name could be successfully used as a starting point for cryptanalysis. However, if the target data cannot be easily guessed, cryptanalysis becomes much harder. One way of making cryptanalysis more difficult is to repeat the encryption process several times, each time substituting the encrypted file for the plaintext file. Thus, a triple encryption strategy (to some extent emulating Triple DES, which uses three 56-bit keys) would involve the following commands, assuming that the keys *8rgbfde4f*, *df454rfx*, and *4gfdg56* were used:

```
$ crypt 8rgbfde4f < medical.txt > medical.crypt.3
$ crypt df454rfx < medical.crypt.3 > medical.crypt.2
$ crypt 4gfdg56< medical.crypt.2 > medical.crypt
$ rm medical.txt medical.crypt.3 medical.crypt.2
```

In each case, the contents of two previously encrypted files would need to be guessed before the original file could be decrypted. Given that encryption potentially takes a long time to perform, a faster method of scrambling the data can be used: a file compression program. In addition to reducing encryption time and file size, the contents of a compressed file are scrambled for all intents and purposes. Using several different compression algorithms on a file before encryption makes it very difficult to decrypt:

```
$ gzip medical.txt
$ compress medical.txt.gz
$ pack medical.txt.gz.Z
$ crypt 8rgbfde4f < medical.txt.gz.Z.z > medical.crypt
```

Asymmetric Key Cryptography

One major limitation of symmetric key cryptography is that the same key is required to encrypt and decrypt data. This is fine for protecting individual files from unauthorized users, but many data protection scenarios require multiple users, and in many cases, parties amongst which trust has never been established, to be involved. For example, if a manager in New York needed to exchange sales data with a manager in Buffalo, and this data required encryption, both managers could simply share the key required to decrypt the data. However, this approach has two problems: First, users tend to apply the same password and key to multiple purposes, meaning that one manager might be able to access the other manager's files; second, what if more than two managers were involved? Clearly, passing a password around a user group of 1,000 users is tantamount to having no security at all! A system is required that allows individual users to encrypt data using one key, and for the file to be decrypted using a separate key for each user.

Asymmetric encryption allows separate keys to be used for encrypting and decrypting data. How is this possible? Basically, every user is assigned a private key, which they never release to anyone else, and a public key, which is supplied to other users who need to send the user encrypted data. For example, the New York manager would have a private key stored on a floppy disk, locked in a safe, as would the Buffalo manager. Both would also exchange their public keys via e-mail, or another offline method such as floppy disk, verifying that the keys were genuine by using a key "fingerprints" check over the telephone. To encrypt a file for the Buffalo manager, the New York manager would need to use both the Buffalo manager's public key and his own private key. Conversely, the Buffalo manager would need to use her private key and the New York manager's public key to encrypt a file for him. Remember that if you exchange public keys via e-mail, and have no other method of verifying who is on the other end of the line, then you're ripe for a "man in the middle attack," because the person you think you are exchanging data with could be an intermediary. For example, imagine if Joe substitutes his key in place of his manager's, and manages to place his machine between a manager's machine and an external router. Now Joe is able to pretend to be his manager, issuing his own public key with his manager's name for which he actually has the corresponding private key.

The most important feature (or limitation, depending on your requirements) of asymmetric key cryptography is that obtaining the private key used to encrypt data is not sufficient to decrypt that data: Only the private key of the individual whose public key was used for signing can be used for this purpose. This can be very important in situations where data may be compromised in a specific location. For example, an embassy in a foreign country under threat of attack may decide to encrypt all data using the public key of an officer in the State Department in Washington, send it via e-mail, and then delete the on-site originals. Even if the encrypted data and the embassy's private key were obtained by force, they could not be used to decrypt the data.

Of course, asymmetry implies that if you lose your original data accidentally, you must rely on the public key holder's private key to decrypt the data. However, at least one avenue of recourse is available, unlike symmetric key cryptography, where a lost key almost certainly means lost data.

Public Key Cryptography

One of the most commonly used "public key" systems that uses asymmetric keys is the Pretty Good Privacy (PGP) application (**http://www.pgp.com/**). PGP is available for a wide variety of operating systems, making it very popular among PC and UNIX users, because data can be exchanged without conversion. PGP works both on the command line, to facilitate secure storage of files, and as a plug-in to e-mail programs, allowing messages to be exchanged securely. This ensures that intermediate mail servers and routers cannot intercept the decrypted contents of transmitted messages, even if they can intercept packets containing the encrypted data.

In order to use PGP, each user needs to generate his or her own public/private key pair. This can be performed by using the following command:

```
$ pgp -kg
```

The following prompt will be displayed:

```
Choose the type of your public key:
  1)  DSS/Diffie-Hellman - New algorithm for 5.0 (default)
  2)  RSA
Choose 1 or 2:
```

The public key format that you choose will determine what types of block ciphers can be used to encrypt your data. The DSS/Diffie-Hellman algorithm allows Triple DES, CAST, or IDEA, while RSA keys will work only with IDEA, so most users will want to select the DSS/Diffie-Hellman algorithm.

Next, you will need to select the key size:

```
Pick your public/private keypair key size:
(Sizes are Diffie-Hellman/DSS; Read the user's guide for more information)
  1)   768/768  bits- Commercial grade, probably not currently breakable
  2)  1024/1024 bits- High commercial grade, secure for many years
  3)  2048/1024 bits- "Military" grade, secure for
   foreseeable future(default)
  4)  3072/1024 bits- Archival grade, slow, highest security
Choose 1, 2, 3 or 4, or enter desired number of Diffie-Hellman bits
(768 - 4096):
```

Keep in mind that although a large key provides greater security, it also slows down operations significantly because it is CPU-intensive. Thus, if your needs are really commercial rather than military, you should use the 768- or 1024-bit key. Military users should certainly select the largest key size available (currently 4096 bits).

Next, you will need to enter a user ID. This should be recognizable by your intended recipients. For example, a programmer called Yayoi Rei from Rei Corporation would have a user ID of Yayoi Rei <yayoi@rei.com>. Even in countries where the family name is usually written first, the expectation for the keyserver is that the family name will appear last, followed by an e-mail address:

```
You need a user ID for your public key.  The desired form for this
user ID is your FULL name, followed by your E-mail address enclosed in
<angle brackets>, if you have an E-mail address.  For example:
  Joe Smith <user@domain.com>
Enter a user ID for your public key:
```

If you wish your key to be valid for a specific time period, you can enter its validity in days. Or, if the key is intended to be permanent, you can enter zero days:

```
Enter the validity period of your key in days from 0 - 999
0 is forever (and the default):
```

You will need a password to be associated with the private key for future use, and you will need to enter it twice for verification:

```
You need a pass phrase to protect your private key(s).
Your pass phrase can be any sentence or phrase and may have many
words, spaces, punctuation, or any other printable characters.
Enter pass phrase:
Enter again, for confirmation:
```

Finally, a number of random numbers needs to be generated from the intervals between random keypresses on your keyboard. Try to insert some variation in the key press latency to ensure security:

```
We need to generate 595 random bits.  This is done by measuring the
time intervals between your keystrokes.  Please enter some random text
on your keyboard until you hear the beep:
```

Once the keypair has been created, you can list all of the keys on your local keyring by using the following command:

```
$ pgp -kl
```

```
Type Bits KeyID       Created     Expires    Algorithm     Use
sec+ 768 0x71849810 2002-01-07 ---------- DSS           Sign & Encrypt
sub  768 0x78697B9D 2002-01-07 ---------- Diffie-Hellman
uid  Yayoi Rei <yayoi@rei.com>
1 matching key found
```

The keypair is now available for use. In order to generate a copy of your public key for your correspondents and colleagues to use, you will need to extract this from your key ring as follows:

```
$pgp -x Yayoi
-----BEGIN PGP PUBLIC KEY BLOCK-----
mQFCBDw5+oURAwDBKeBtW+0PdDvCC7KO1/gUAF9X//uGRhbPkg6m83QzaA7pr6T+
QAVQE4q74NXFCakX8GzmhzHtA2/Hoe/yfpfHGHMhJRZHZIWQWTS6W+r5wHYRSObm
NNNTeJ4C+3/klbEAoP/Mjlim4eMkfvYwNmifTUvak5zRAv48SrXOHmVI+5Mukx8Z
1T7txut60VeYd34QvidwtUbbL7p2IVVa3fGW/gsuo7whb1aW//+5Z/+4wxbaqnu6
WxT5vFObm1sJ7E20OW3SDLxdVjeTlYbzTUfNwbN/KHoUzMsC/2EZ3aDB6mGZuDPL
0SMT8sOoxlbpPouuBxnF/sbcxgOVKkGZDS5XrhodUbp2RUflwFSMyqjbmoqITnNq
xzpSXEhT0odwjjq3YeHj1icBaiy9xB/j0CBXe3QQKAXk5bXMEbQZWWF5b2kgUmVp
IDx5YXlvaUByZWkuY29tPokASwQQEQIACwUCPDn6hQQLAwECAAoJEHCOVqNxhJgQ
riMAn18a5kKYaepNk8BEksMJOTbRgDQmAKC0JD6wvYfo5zmziGr7TAv+uFWN5LkA
zQQ8OfqHEAMA6zd3dxeMkyKJmust3S3IrKvQzMLlMoRuQdb+N2momBYDF1+slo8k
EMK8F/Vrun+HdhJW+hWivgZRhTMe9fm6OL7PDYESkwuQsMizqAJJ1JF0yhbfTwE5
GjdVPcUMyPyTAAICAwCgdBO1XyiPbwdQtjxq+8CZ7uchASvJXsU28OFqbLzNcAW2
Q64lWSs6qr2HNfgf+ikG8S8eVWVKEBgm6md9trr6CK25SYEu4oB3o1f45X4daa/n
iNytKUglPPOJMK/rhJOJAD8DBRg8OfqHcI5Wo3GEmBARAs3mAJ0ZPQjmlYyNsMDY
ZVbR9/q2xQl8gACgkqVCNYR40mPIaxrd5Cw9ZrHqlkQ=
=Gsmt
-----END PGP PUBLIC KEY BLOCK-----
```

To encrypt a file using standard, symmetric encryption, you simply pass the *–c* option on the command line along with the name of the file that you want to encrypt. This provides Solaris users with an alternative to crypt, where a more secure encryption algorithm is desired:

```
$ pgp -c secret.doc
You need a passphrase to encrypt the file
Enter pass phrase:
Enter same passphrase again
Enter pass phrase:
Creating output file secret.pgp
```

After entering a password to protect the data in *secret.doc*, the encrypted file *secret.pgp* is created. In order to sign the file for another user, the *–e* option needs to be passed, along with the name of user from your keyring who will have the power to decrypt your data:

```
$ pgp -e Henry secret.doc
   4096 bits, Key ID 76857743, Created 2002-01-07
   "Henry Bolingbroke <henry@bolingbroke.co.uk>"
Creating output file secret.pgp
```

The file can then be transmitted to Henry by UUencoding it, sending it as an e-mail attachment, or by directly generating the file in ASCII format:

```
$ pgp -ea Henry secret.doc
```

Security Auditing

After installing a new Solaris system and applying the local security policy, a security audit must be undertaken to ensure that no known vulnerabilities exist in the system, particularly threats posed by remote access. As we have examined earlier in this chapter, there are a number of strategies, such as switching off ports, that should be adopted prior to releasing a system into production and making it accessible through the Internet. A security audit should first examine what services are being offered and determine an action plan based on services which should be disabled. In addition, monitoring and logging solutions should be installed for services that are sanctioned so that it is possible at all times to determine what activity is occurring on any service. For example, a denial of service attack may involve hitting a specific port (such as port 80, the Web server port) with a large number of packets, aimed at reducing overall performance of the Web server and the host system. If you don't have logs of all this activity, it will be difficult to determine why your system performance is slow and/or where any potential attacks have originated— that's why TCP wrappers are so important. The final phase of a security audit involves comparing the current list of services running on the system to the security bulletins which are released by the Computer Emergency Response Team (CERT) (**http://www.cert.org/**) and similar computer security groups. After determining the versions of software running on your system, you should determine which packages require patching and/or upgrading in order to eliminate the risks from known vulnerabilities.

SAINT

Running a security audit and implementing solutions based on the audit can be a time-consuming task. Fortunately, a number of tools are available that can significantly reduce the amount of time required to conduct security audits and cross-check existing applications with known security holes. One of these programs is called SAINT, which is freely available from World Wide Digital Security at **http://www.wwdsi.com/saint/**.

SAINT, currently in version 3.0, is the Security Administrator's Integrated Network Tool, and is based in part on an earlier auditing tool known as SATAN. Both SATAN and SAINT have the ability to scan all of your system services and identify potential and/or known vulnerabilities. These are classified according to their risk: Some items may be critical, requiring immediate attention, whereas other items may come in the form of suggestions rather than requirements. For example, while many local services are vulnerable to a buffer overflow, where the fixed boundaries on an array are deliberately overwritten by a remote client to "crash" the system, other issues, such as the use of "r" remote access commands, may be risky but acceptable in suitably protected local area networks. Thus, SAINT is not prescriptive in all cases, and suggested actions are always to be performed at the discretion of the local administrator.

Some administrators are concerned that using programs such as SAINT actually contribute to cracking and system break-ins, because they provide a ready-made toolkit that can be used to identify system weaknesses in preparation for a break-in. However, if sites devote the necessary resources to monitoring system usage and identifying potential security threats, the risk posed by SAINT is minimal (particularly if its "suggestions" are acted upon). Indeed, World Wide Digital Security actually offers a Web version of SAINT (called WebSAINT) as the basis for security consulting. For a fee, they will conduct a comprehensive security audit of your network, from the perspective of a remote (rather than a local) user. This can be very useful when attempting to identify potential weaknesses in your front-line systems, such as routers, gateways, and Web servers.

In this section, we examine how to install and configure the SAINT program and how to run an audit on a newly installed Solaris 9 system. This will reveal many of the common issues that arise when Solaris is installed out of the box. Most of these issues are covered by CERT advisories. Sun often releases patches very soon after a CERT vulnerability is discovered on shipped Solaris products. For example, a patch is available for a well-known vulnerability existing in the Berkeley Internet Daemon (BIND) package, which matches IP addresses with fully-qualified domain names (**http://www.cert.org/advisories/CA-99-14-bind.html**). However, some CERT advisories are of a more general nature, because no specific code fix will solve the problem. One example is the identification of a distributed denial of service system known as *Stacheldraht*, which combines the processing power and network resources of a group of systems (that are geographically distributed), and can prevent Web servers from serving pages to clients (**http://www.cert.org/advisories/CA-2000-01.html**). CERT releases advisories on a regular basis, so it's advisable to keep up-to-date with all current security issues by reading their news.

One of the great strengths of the SAINT system is that it has an extensive catalog of CERT advisories and in-depth explanations of what each CERT advisory means for the local system. Every SAINT vulnerability is associated with a CVE number that matches descriptions of each security issue from the Common Vulnerabilities and Exposures database (**http://cve.mitre.org/**). Each identified vulnerability will contain a hyperlink back to the CVE database so that information displayed about every issue is updated directly from the source. New patches and bug fixes are also listed.

SAINT has the ability to identify security issues for the following services:

- **Domain Name Service (DNS)**   Responsible for mapping the fully-qualified domain name of Internet hosts to a machine-friendly IP address. In particular, the Berkeley Internet Daemon (BIND), commonly used for DNS resolution, is susceptible to vulnerabilities.

- **File Transfer Program (FTP)**   Allows remote users to retrieve files from the local file system; has historically been associated with serious daemon buffer overflow problems.

- **Internet Message Access Protocol (IMAP)**   Supports advanced e-mail exchange facilities between mail clients and mail servers; also has buffer overflow issues, which have previously allowed remote users to execute privileged commands arbitrarily on the mail server.

- **Network File System (NFS) service**   Shares disk partitions to remote client systems; is often misconfigured to provide world read access to all shared volumes, when this access should be granted only to specific users.

- **Network Information Service (NIS)**   A distributed network service that shares maps of users, groups, and passwords between hosts to minimize administrative overheads; can be compromised if a rogue user can detect the NIS service operating.

- **Sendmail Mail Transport Agent (MTA)**   Once allowed Solaris commands to be embedded within e-mails, which were executed without authentication on the server side.

SAINT works by systematically scanning ports for services that have well-known exploits, and then reporting these exploits back to the user. In addition, it runs a large number of password checks for default passwords on system accounts, or accounts that often have no passwords. SAINT checks all of the services and exploits that it knows about, and the database of known exploits grows with each new release. SAINT also tests the susceptibility of your system to denial of service attacks, where a large number of large sized packets are directed to a specific port on your system. This tactic is typically used against Web servers, where some high-profile cases in recent years have highlighted the inherent weakness of networked systems that allow traffic on specific ports without some kind of regulation. Many of the system daemons checked by SAINT will have a so-called "buffer overflow" problem, where a system may be crashed because memory is overwritten with arbitrary values outside the declared size of an array. Without appropriate bounds checking, passing a GET request to a Web server of 1025 bytes when the array size is 1024 would clearly result in unpredictable behavior, because the C language does not prevent a program from doing this. Because Solaris daemons are typically written in C, a number have been fixed in recent years to prevent this problem from occurring (but you may be surprised at just how often new weaknesses are exposed).

You can download the latest release of SAINT from **http://www.wwdsi.com/saint/**. To run SAINT, you will need to install the GNU C compiler or use the Sun C compiler. The Perl interpreter and Netscape Web browser supplied with Solaris 8 are also required. After using *make* to build the SAINT binary, you can start SAINT by typing this command:

```
# ./saint
```

This starts up the Netscape Web browser, with the URL shown in Figure 30-5.

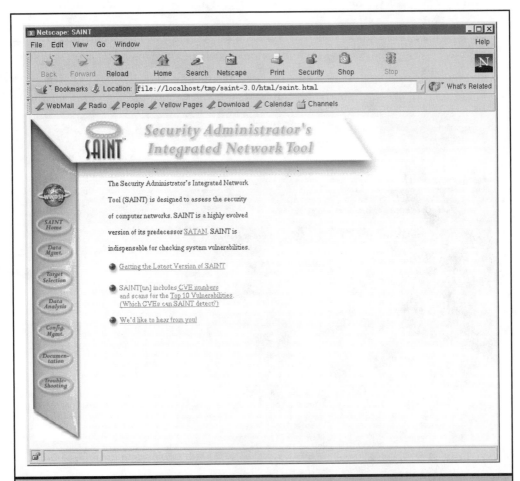

Figure 30-5.   *Security Administrator's Integrated Network Tool*

SAINT has several pages, including data management, target selection, data analysis, and configuration management. You can visit these pages sequentially to conduct your audit. The data management page, shown in Figure 30-6, allows you to create a new SAINT database in which to store the results of your current audit. Or, you may open an existing SAINT database if you have created one previously, and/or you can merge data from other SAINT scans.

Next, you will need to use the target selection page to identify the host system that you wish to scan using SAINT, as shown in Figure 30-7. Here, you need to enter the fully-qualified domain name of the host that you wish to scan. Or, if you have a large number of hosts to scan, it may be more useful to create a file containing a list of

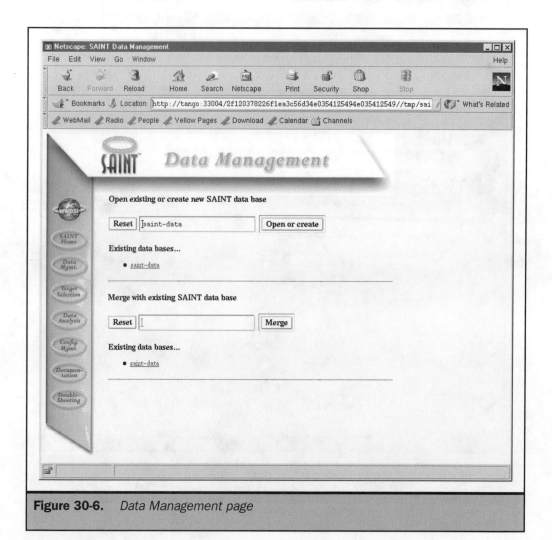

Figure 30-6.   *Data Management page*

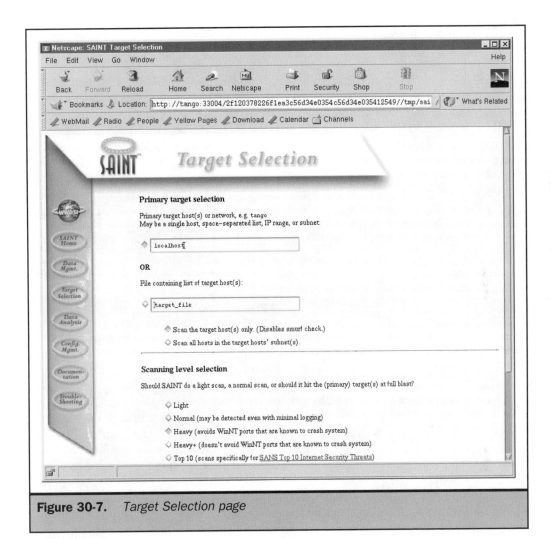

Figure 30-7.   *Target Selection page*

hosts. This file could then be used by a system behind the firewall to identify locally-visible weaknesses, and used by a system external to the firewall to reveal any threats visible to the outside world. You may also elect to scan all hosts in the local area network, which should only be performed out of hours, because it places a heavy load on network bandwidth.

You also need to select a scanning level option, which includes the following:

- **Light scanning**   Difficult to detect
- **Normal scanning**   Easy to detect

- **Heavy scanning**   Won't crash Windows NT targets
- **Heavy+ scanning**   May well crash Windows NT targets

There is a final option that just checks the "top ten" security flaws, as identified by the report at **http://www.sans.org/topten.htm**. These flaws include BIND weaknesses, vulnerable CGI programs, Remote Procedure Call (RPC) weaknesses, Sendmail buffer overflow, mountd, UNIX NFS exports, User IDs, especially root/administrator with no passwords, IMAP and POP buffer overflow vulnerabilities, and SNMP community strings set to 'public' and 'private.'

Always remember that attempting to break into a computer system is a criminal offense in many jurisdictions: You should obtain written authorization from the owner of your system before embarking on a security-related exercise of this kind; otherwise, it may be misconstrued as a real attack.

Once the target selection is complete, the data collection process begins by executing a number of scripts on the server and reporting the results through the Web browser. Data is collected by testing many different Solaris services, including *ping*, *finger*, *RPC*, *login*, *rsh*, *sendmail*, *tooltalk*, *snmp*, and *rstatd*.

SAINT uses several different modules to probe vulnerabilities in the system, including *tcpscan*, *udpscan*, and *ddos*, which scan for TCP and UDP denial of service issues, respectively. In addition, a number of well-known username and password combinations are also attempted in order to break into an account—you would imagine that root/root would never be used as a username and password combination, but it does happen.

Once all of the data has been collected, the results of the scan are then displayed on the reporting and analysis page, as shown in Figure 30-8. It is possible to list vulnerabilities by their danger level, by the type of vulnerability, or by the number of vulnerabilities in a specific category. Most administrators will want to deal with the most dangerous vulnerabilities, so the first option should be selected. In addition, it is possible to view information about the target system by class of service, the type of system, domain name, subnet, and by its hostname.

Vulnerabilities are listed in terms of danger level: critical problems, areas of concern, and potential problems, as shown in Figure 30-9. For the local host *okami*, which was a standard Solaris install out-of-the-box, two critical problems were identified, both associated with gaining root access via buffer overflow:

- The CDE-based Calendar Manager service may be vulnerable to a buffer overflow attack, as identified in CVE 1999-0320 and 1999-0696. The Calendar Manager is used to manage appointments and other date/time–based functions.

- The remote administration daemon (*sadmind*) may be vulnerable to a buffer overflow attack, as described in CVE 1999-0977. The remote administration daemon is used to manage system administration activities across a number of different hosts.

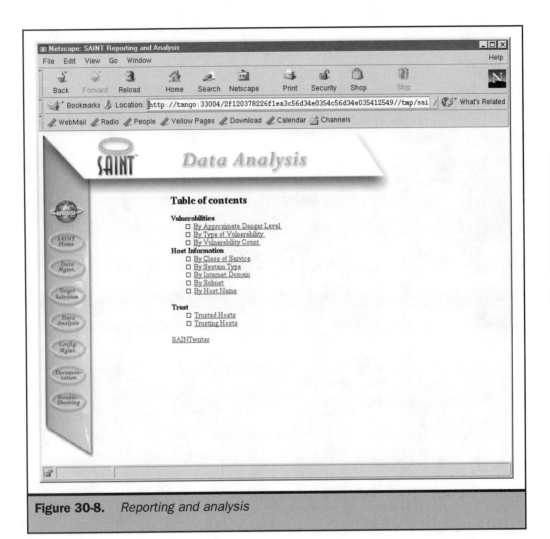

Figure 30-8. *Reporting and analysis*

There were also two areas of concern identified, with information gathering vulnerabilities exposed:

■ The finger daemon returned personal information about users that could be used to stage an attack. For example, the home directory, full name, and project was displayed (CVE 1999-0612).

■ The remote users list daemon was active, providing a list of users on the system to any remote user (CVE 1999-0626). Like the finger daemon, information gathered from the ruserd could be used to stage an attack.

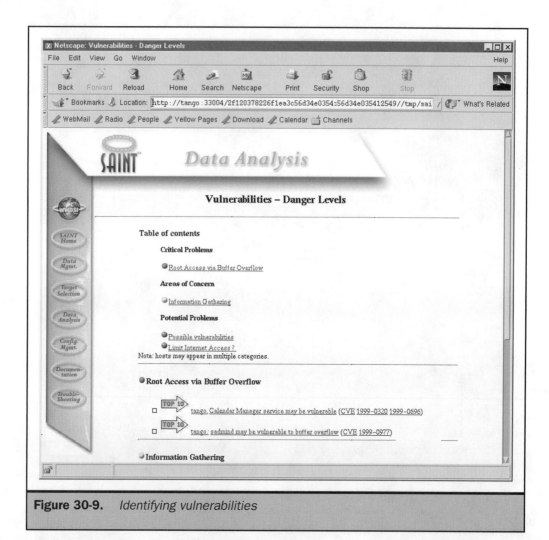

Figure 30-9. *Identifying vulnerabilities*

Two possible vulnerabilities were identified:

■ The *chargen* program is vulnerable to UDP flooding used in denial of service attacks, such as Fraggle (CVE 1999-0103).

■ The *sendmail* server allows mail relaying, which may be used by remote users to forward mail using the server. This makes it easy for companies promoting spam to make it appear as if their mail originated from your server.

Six recommendations were made to limit Internet access, including stopping all of the "r" services. These make it easy for a remote user to execute commands on the local system, such as spawning a shell or obtaining information about system load, but have been used in the past to break into systems. In addition, some *sendmail* commands (such as EXPN and VRFY) are allowed by the *sendmail* configuration: This allows remote users to obtain a list of all users on the current system, which is often the first step to obtaining their passwords.

If you are concerned that a rogue user may be using SAINT against your network, you may download and run one of the many SAINT-detecting programs, such as Courtney (**http://ciac.llnl.gov/ciac/ToolsUnixNetMon.html#Courtney**). Courtney monitors TCP traffic to determine whether or not a single remote machine is systematically scanning the ports within a specified time frame. Obviously, this program is useful for detecting all kinds of port scanning.

Command Reference

The following commands can be used to secure Solaris.

aset

The Automated Security Enhancement Tool (*aset*) is supplied by Sun as a multilevel system for investigating system weaknesses. In addition to reporting on potential vulnerabilities, *aset* can actually fix problems that are identified. There are three distinct operational levels (*low*, *medium*, and *high*) for *aset*:

- **Low level**   Undertakes a number of checks and reports any vulnerabilities found. No remedial action is performed.

- **Med level**   Undertakes a moderate number of checks and reports any vulnerabilities found. Restricts system access to some services and files.

- **High level**   Undertakes a wide range of checks and reports any vulnerabilities found. Implements a restrictive security policy by enforcing pessimistic access permissions.

Low level reports are recommended to be run as a weekly `cron` job, allowing administrators to determine if newly installed applications, services, or patches have compromised system security. In contrast, a medium level *aset* run should be performed on all newly installed systems that lie behind a firewall. For all systems that are directly connected to the Internet, such as Web and proxy servers, a high level *aset* run should be performed directly after installation. This will ensure that many of the default system permissions that are assigned to system files are reduced to an appropriate scope. It is possible to modify the *asetenv* file to change the actions that are performed when *aset* is executed. The individual tasks performed by *aset* include the following:

tune	Checks all file permissions
cklist	Validates system directories and file permissions
usrgrp	Checks user accounts and groups for integrity
sysconf	Verifies the system files stored in /etc
env	Parses environment variables stored in configuration files
eeprom	Checks the security level of the OpenBoot PROM monitor
firewall	Determines whether the system is secure enough to operate as a packet filter

TCP Wrappers

Logging access information can reveal whether an organization's networks have an authentication problem. In addition, specific instances of unauthorized access to various resources can be collated, and using statistical methods, can be assessed for regular patterns of abuse. Monitoring of log files can also be used by applications to accept or reject connections, based on historical data contained in centralized logging mechanisms provided under Solaris, such as the *syslogd* system logging daemon.

One reason why access monitoring is not often discussed is that implementations of the standard UNIX network daemons that are spawned by the Internet super server *inetd* (discussed earlier) do not have a provision to write directly to a syslog file. Later Internet service daemons, such as the Apache Web server, run as standalone services not requiring *inetd*, but have enhanced logging facilities that are used to track Web site usage.

Wietse Venema's TCP Wrappers are a popular method of enabling daemons launched from *inetd* to log their accepted and rejected connections, because the wrapper programs that are installed for each service do not require alterations to existing binary software distributions or to existing configuration files. You can download TCP Wrappers in source form from **ftp://ftp.porcupine.org/pub/security/index.html**.

In their simplest form, TCP wrappers are used for monitoring only, but they could be used to build better applications that can reject connections on the basis of failed connections. For example, a flood of requests to log in using *rsh* from an untrusted host could be terminated after three failed attempts from a single host. TCP wrappers work by compiling a replacement daemon that points to the "real" daemon file, often located in a subdirectory below the daemon wrappers. The wrappers log the date and time of a service request, with a client hostname and whether the request was rejected or accepted. The current version of TCP Wrappers supports the SVR4 (System V Release 4) TLI network programming interface under Solaris, which has equivalent functionality to the Berkeley socket programming interface. In addition, the latest release supports access control and detection of host address or hostname spoofing. The latter is particularly important in the context of authentication services that provide access to services based on IP subnet ranges or specific hostnames in a local area network; if these are spoofed, and access is granted to a rogue client, the entire security infrastructure has failed. It is critical to detect and reject any unauthorized connections at any early stage, and TCP wrappers are an integral part of this mechanism.

When writing access information to *syslog*, the output looks like this:

```
Nov 18 11:00:52 server in.telnetd[1493]: connect from client.site.com
Nov 18 11:25:03 server in.telnetd[1510]: connect from workstation.site.com
Nov 18 11:25:22 server in.telnetd[1511]: connect from client.site.com
Nov 18 12:16:30 server in.ftpd[1556]: connect from workstation.site.com
```

These entries indicate that between 11:00 A.M. and 1:00 P.M. on November 18th, clients connected using Telnet from *client.site.com* and *workstation.site.com*. In addition, there was an FTP connection from *workstation.site.com*. Although we've only examined wrappers for *in.ftpd* and *in.telnetd*, wrappers can be compiled for most services launched from *inetd*, including *finger*, *talk*, *tftp* (trivial FTP), and *rsh* (remote shell).

ENTERPRISE

The Complete Reference

Chapter 31

Application Development and Debugging

A lthough most system administrators are not application developers, there are many situations where a Perl script or small C program, making use of system calls, can be used fruitfully. A key challenge of system management involves the automation of as many mundane, repetitive tasks as possible. Although shell scripting can be useful in this context, sometimes complete programs are required. In this chapter, we examine how to develop, compile, and execute C applications, and we look at how to create and run Perl programs.

Programming Languages

There are many ways to develop software for Solaris, all of which depend on the internal representation of data and executable code. At the most basic level, all data and instructions are encoded as binary data—quite literally, sets of 1's and 0's which represent data words. For example, a processor with an 8-bit word length means that integers between 0 and 255 can be directly addressed by the CPU, without any kind of intermediate translation. Most Intel CPUs today have a word length of 32 bits, while UltraSPARC processors have a 64-bit word length, making it easier (and faster) to directly process large numbers. This ability is very important in scientific applications, like processing data from human genomes, or in database applications, where transactions of financial data associated with many billions of dollars are performed constantly.

In the early days of computing, a new "higher level" programming interface was developed, called assembly language. By using assembly language to write programs, instead of directly writing binary code, developers were able to use an interface that was one level of abstraction away from the hardware. They could use English-like statements and identifiers to move and address blocks of memory, for example. This increased productivity and decreased production time. However, anyone who has ever written an assembler language program would recognize that it was still far from easy. In addition, a different assembly language existed for every processor in existence, meaning that skills developed for a Z80 processor were completely different to those for a 2650 CPU. This made it difficult for programmers to transfer their skills to other systems.

A third level of abstraction was realized by early application development languages like C, in which the original UNIX kernel and later Solaris kernels were written. Although C can contain in-line assembly language, it was designed to be independent of the CPU on which its compiled instructions were executing. A compiler translated the English-like instructions written into binary code for a specific CPU, but the actual C source code was highly portable: As long as the program was written to conform to the ANSI standard for C, and as long as a compiler existed for the target platform, the source of a C application could be copied to that platform, compiled, and executed. C++ was a language based around C that had object-oriented data structures, improving design processes and making implementation of complex software easier.

However, this ideal was far from the reality: Differences in C and C++ compilers across vendors made it very difficult to maintain compatibility, particularly with the rise of graphical user interfaces (GUIs). GUIs not only had to deal with creating binary code for different CPU types, but also for the broad spectrum of display devices on the market, which had little in common with each other. Particularly in the 1980s and early 1990s, it became fashionable to ditch cross-platform products like C to focus specifically on application development for a particular platform. For example, Microsoft developers used Visual Basic to create applications that would only run on the Microsoft Windows or MS-DOS platforms, and UNIX developers wrote applications for the X11 environment that were not necessarily designed to be cross-platform. Although these applications worked well for their target environments, it also meant that markets for software were constrained by the development platform. Many excellent desktop products never made it to UNIX, and several well-known data processing systems were unable to run on Windows.

This situation seemed to reflect the frustration felt when development was performed using assembler: Different codebases were required for the same product on different platforms, and a separate development team was required for each platform. It was often very difficult to synchronize these efforts in any realistic way—so, an application with the same version number in Microsoft Windows might have completely different functionality than an equivalent product for the MacOS. One solution to this problem was to begin looking at what went wrong with C and other third-generation languages that promised cross-platform runtime abilities. A solution was required to ensure that source distributions could be copied to a target platform and executed with little or no modification. One possibility was the Perl programming environment: Here, developers created Perl source, which could then be copied to any machine with a Perl interpreter, and it would be parsed and compiled just prior to execution. However, Perl (at that stage) was not object-oriented, and it did not have support for graphical environments.

On the other hand, the Java programming language (which grew out of the Oak project) promised full cross-platform graphical environment, which was based around the idea of a "virtual machine." If programmers focused on writing applications based around an API (Application Programming Interface) for the virtual machine, it should execute on any platform for which there was a Java virtual machine that met the specifications developed by Sun Microsystems, the creators of Java. Java also featured single-process multithreading, which is very important in applications like Web servers, because traditional Web servers create a new process for each client connection, while a Java Web server runs in a single process, and creates internal threads for each client to execute in. This is much more memory- and CPU-efficient than creating and destroying processes for each client in high transaction volume environments.

Unlike Perl, Java applications were compiled on the development platform into an intermediate bytecode format, which could then be executed on any target platform. This reduced the runtime compilation overhead associated with Perl. Unfortunately, some vendors decided to innovate and create their own extensions to the Java VM, which has created some uncertainty about the future of the Java language. In addition, Sun Microsystems has refused to hand the control of Java over to an independent body so that an ANSI standard could be created, for example. Even with these caveats, however, Java is being rapidly adopted worldwide as the platform in which to deploy networked applications.

Perl Programming

Perl stands for the Practical Extraction and Reporting Language, and was originally developed by Larry Wall. One of the things that developers really like about Perl is how quickly it is possible to write a full-blown application literally within a few minutes. When teamed up with the Common Gateway Interface (CGI) provided by Web servers such as Apache, Perl provides an easy way to write applications that can be executed on a server when requested by a client. This means that HTML pages can be generated dynamically by a Perl application and streamed to a client. Coupled with Perl's database access libraries (known as the Perl Database Interface, or DBI), Perl can be used to create multitiered applications, which is especially useful for system management applications.

To create a Perl application, simply follow these five steps:

1. Create a text file by using the *vi* editor or *pico* editor.

2. Give the file executable permissions, by using the `chmod` command.

3. Instruct the shell to execute the Perl interpreter by including a directive in the first line of the script.

4. Write the Perl code.

5. Run the application.

As an example, let's create a Perl program that simply prints a line of text to the screen (for example, the string "Hello World!"). First, create a file called *helloworld.pl* by using the command `touch`:

```
$ touch helloworld.pl
```

Next, set the permissions on the file to be executable:

```
$ chmod +x helloworld.pl
```

Next, edit the file like this:

```
$ vi helloworld.pl
```

and insert a directive to the shell to execute the Perl interpreter contained in the */usr/bin* directory (it may also be installed in */usr/local/bin*):

```
#!/usr/bin/perl
```

Next, insert the Perl code that actually constitutes the program:

```
print "Hello World\n";
```

Finally, save the file in the current directory and execute it on the command line:

```
$ ./helloworld.pl
Hello World!
```

Like most programming languages, Perl uses variables to store values that can change over time. These are represented as names with the $ symbol preceding them. So, if you developed a program that printed the balance of a checking account, you might create and assign values to variables with names like *$date*, *$transaction*, *$amount*, and *$balance*. You can use variables to store just about any kind of information, including simple messages. A revision of the "Hello World" program code using a variable to store the message you want to print out would look like this:

```
#!/usr/bin/perl
$message="Hello World!";
print $message, "\n";
```

When you run this program, you get exactly the same output as before:

```
$ ./helloworld.pl
Hello World!
```

This is because the comma symbol here acts to concatenate the string contained in the *$message* variable, and the `newline` command contained between the quotes directly after the comma symbol. Variables in Perl do not just contain strings; they can also store numeric values, and Perl has a series of operators that you can use to perform arithmetic operations on variables. For example, you may want to perform a simple addition:

```
#!/usr/bin/perl
$val1=10;
$val2=20;
print $val1, " + ", $val2, " = ", $val1+$val2, "\n";
```

This program assigns the value of 10 to the variable *$val1*, and the value of 20 to the variable *$val2*. It then prints the addition expression that is going to be evaluated, and then actually performs the addition of *$val1* and *$val2* by using the "+" operator. Here's the result, which is unsurprising:

```
$ ./addition.pl
10 + 20 = 30
```

ENTERPRISE

Other operators for Perl include the following:

-	Subtraction operator
*	Multiplication operator
/	Division operator
==	Equivalence operator
!=	Non-equivalence operator
<	Less-than operator, also called *le*
>	Greater-than operator, also called *gt*
<=	Less-than or equal-to operator, also known as *le*
>=	Greater-than or equal-to operator, also known as *ge*

So far, we've only seen the special escape character *n*, which comes from C, and means "newline character." It's also possible to use other escape characters from C, such as *t*, which is the tab escape character. Let's have a look at the results of combining the tab escape character to produce tabulated output, and then examine other arithmetic operators from Perl:

```
#!/usr/bin/perl
$val1=10;
$val2=20;
print $val1, " + ", $val2, " =\t", $val1+$val2, "\n";
print $val1, " - ", $val2, " =\t", $val1-$val2, "\n";
print $val1, " * ", $val2, " =\t", $val1*$val2, "\n";
print $val1, " / ", $val2, " =\t", $val1/$val2, "\n";
```

Once again, the results are as expected, with the result column being separated from the expression by a tab character:

```
$ ./operators.pl
10 + 20 =        30
10 - 20 =        -10
10 * 20 =        200
10 / 20 =        0.5
```

Other escape characters commonly used in Perl include the following:

\a	Terminal bell
\b	Backspace
\f	Form-feed
\r	Return
\\	Insert "\" as a character literal
\"	Inserts " as a character literal

In many cases, applications require that some kind of decision be taken on the basis of the current value of a specific variable. One way of making this decision is to use an *if/else* construct: This separates two blocks of code, one that is executed if a statement is true, and one that is executed if a statement is false. For example, imagine that you want to test whether a particular file exists. There are many reasons why you would want to do this. If a password file does not exist, for example, you might want to notify the system administrator, or if a shadowed password file does not exist, you might want to suggest that one be created for improved security. You can perform a file test by creating an expression using the *–e* operator, which tests for existence. Thus, an expression like this,

```
(-e /etc/passwd)
```

when evaluated, will return true if the file */etc/passwd* exists, and will return false if the file does not exist. Other file operators used in Perl include the following:

–B	Tests if the file contains binary data
–d	Tests if the file is a directory entry
–T	Tests if the file contains text data
–w	Tests if the file is writeable

To test for the existence of both the password file and the shadowed password file, you can create a program like this:

```
#!/usr/bin/perl
$passwdfile="/etc/passwd";
$shadowfile="/etc/shadow";
if (-e $passwdfile)
{
        print "Found standard Solaris password file\n";
```

```
}
else
{
        print "No standard Solaris password file found\n";

if (-e $shadowfile)
{
        print "Found shadow password file - good security move!\n";
}
else
{
        print "No shadow password file found!\n";

}
```

When executing the file on a Solaris 9 system, you should see output like this:

```
$ ./checkpasswords.pl
Found standard Solaris password file
Found shadow password file - good security move!
```

This kind of check could be added as a `cron` job for the root user, meaning that it could be executed on a regular basis as part of a security check. If any errors were detected, instead of writing a message to standard output, a mail message could be sent to the system administrator. Of course, password files are not the only kinds of files that might be included as part of a security check. Imagine the situation where a Trojan horse or virus has deleted one of the major shells or changed their permissions to render them inoperable. Thus, it is not adequate to just check for the existence of a file. You may also need to check other characteristics, such as being executable (–x), being readable (–r), and having file size greater than zero (–s). Imagine that you want to check the status of the default Bourne Again shell (*/bin/bash*): You can define a valid shell state as existing, being readable, being executable, and having a file size greater than zero, where logical AND is represented by the operator *&&*. If the shell does not have these attributes, you can generate a warning message. A simple program to achieve this could look like this:

```
#!/usr/bin/perl
$shell="/bin/bash";
if (-e $shell && -x $shell && -r $shell && -s $shell)
{
        print "Valid shell found\n";
```

```
}
else
{
        print "No valid shell found\n";
}
```

When executed, the program prints the following message:

```
$ ./checkbash.pl
Valid shell found
```

Other logical operators commonly used in Perl include the following:

		Logical OR
!	Logical NOT
|	Bitwise OR
^	Bitwise XOR

Of course, there is more than one shell to be found on Solaris systems, and users are free to choose any one of them for their default login. You can modify the shell checking program to verify the attributes of each of these shells by using an array that contains the name of each shell, rather than just creating a single scalar variable (e.g., *$shell* in the previous example). If you create an array called *@shell* that stores the names of all shells on the system, you can just iterate through the list using the `foreach` command, as shown in this program:

```
#!/usr/bin/perl
@shells=("/bin/sh", "/bin/csh", "/bin/sh", "/bin/tcsh", "/bin/zsh");
foreach $i (@shells)
{
        if (-e $i && -x $i && -r $i && -s $i)
        {
                print "Valid shell: ".$i."\n";
        }
        else
        {
                print "Invalid shell: ".$i."\n";
        }
}
```

When you execute the program on a Solaris system, you might see output like this:

```
Valid shell: /bin/sh
Valid shell: /bin/csh
Valid shell: /bin/sh
Valid shell: /bin/tcsh
Invalid shell: /bin/zsh
```

Oops—you can see that the first four shells check out okay, but a problem occurs with the */bin/zsh* shell. This means that a system administrator should check if there is a problem. Again, this could be achieved by creating a `cron` job that runs once per day, which e-mails the administrator if a problem is detected. However, it may be much more useful to actually run this application through a Web browser, which is possible by using the Common Gateway Interface (CGI). There are few modifications necessary to convert a Perl program to use the CGI: You simply need to print out a content-type header and then continue to print output as usual. For example, the earlier program could be restated in CGI terms as follows:

```perl
#!/usr/bin/perl
print "Content-type: text/html\n\n";
@shells=("/bin/sh", "/bin/csh", "/bin/sh", "/bin/tcsh", "/bin/zsh");
foreach $i (@shells)
{
        if (-e $i && -x $i && -r $i && -s $i)
        {
                print "<b>Valid shell:</b> ".$i."<br>\n";
        }
        else
        {
                print "<b>Invalid shell:</b> ".$i."<br>\n";
        }
}
```

C Programming

Most Solaris developers use the GNU C (*gcc*) or C++ (g++) compiler for their development work, because unlike many vendor-supplied compilers in the UNIX world, *gcc* is 100 percent ANSI-compliant. It is available for Solaris, Linux, and Microsoft Windows, meaning that applications can be relatively easily ported between different platforms with some modifications. In addition, g++ brings object-oriented data structures and methods to the world of Solaris. The GNU C compiler development project now falls under the broader banner of the "GNU Compiler Collection," which aims to integrate the existing GNU development environments (including Fortran, Pascal, and so on) into a single development suite. C is the language in which the Solaris kernel and many other applications are written, including many of the applications in the GNU suite, such as flex and bison. You can find more information about the GNU Compiler Collection project at **http://www.gnu.org/software/gcc/**.

As we mentioned earlier, C is a language that requires a compiler to convert a source file, containing legal C language statements, into binary code that is suitable for execution. Because C applications require no runtime interpretation at all (like Java or Perl), C is often the language of choice where fast performance is required. However, it is also true that writing C programs reduces the level of abstraction between the developer and the system, thereby making it easier for mistakes with programming constructs such as pointers to locations of data elements in memory, for example. A common problem that we examined in Chapter 7 involved "buffer overflow," which results from a C program overwriting the bounds of a fixed-size array. C will not prevent you from making these kinds of mistakes, because the compiler assumes that you know what you are doing. Java is much better suited to catching runtime exceptions such as these. Indeed, you can define customized exception handling in Java, which can be modified to suit the application at hand. For example, if your application is mission critical, it may not be appropriate to terminate a service just because unexpected input is encountered. The application might instead shift into a failsafe mode and e-mail the system administrator for attention.

A C application can consist of up to five different components:

- **Source files**   Usually have .c extensions and contain the C language instructions necessary to execute the application

- **Any local "include" files**   Define application-wide constants and declarations that are related to user library functions

- **System-wide header files**   Define all of the declarations related to system library functions

- **Local libraries**   Contain precompiled functions and components that can be called from a user application

- **System libraries**   Precompiled functions and components that are required to operate the Solaris kernel, and which form the basis for system functions

When compiling a C program, you may need to define particular paths and directories where system or user-supplied libraries can be located by the linker, which is responsible for combining local object files to form an executable. An application can either be statically linked, in which case all components are combined to form a single executable, or dynamically linked, in which case libraries are loaded from their own separate files at runtime. For example, the shell environment variable *LD_LIBRARY_PATH* is usually set to */lib*, which is the directory that contains the majority of system libraries under Solaris. Many C developers use a local library directory to store user-developed application libraries, so it's often useful to replace the default *LD_LIBRARY_PATH* with a replacement like this:

```
$ USER_LIBRARY_PATH=/staff/pwatters/lib; export USER_LIBRARY_PATH
$ SYS_LIBRARY_PATH=/lib; export SYS_LIBRARY_PATH
$ LD_LIBRARY_PATH=$USER_LIBRARY_PATH:$ SYS_LIBRARY_PATH;
  export LD_LIBRARY_PATH
```

Using gcc

Creating and compiling a simple C program is straightforward: Simply call the compiler with the command gcc, supply the source file name, and optionally an executable filename (the default is *a.out*), and press RETURN. For example, let's create a file called *helloworld.c* with the following contents:

```
#include <stdio.h>
main()
{
     printf("Hello World!\n");
}
```

This is about the simplest program possible in C, and it is similar to the "Hello World" Perl program shown earlier. The standard input/output header file is "included" in the compilation process to ensure that the correct libraries that support functions like printf are dynamically linked. To compile this program, simply type

```
$ gcc helloworld.c -o helloworld
```

This produces an executable called *helloworld*. If all goes well, no error messages will be printed. To execute the program, you simply need to type this command:

```
$ ./helloworld
Hello World!
```

Let's take a slightly more complicated example and revisit one of the Perl programs from earlier in the chapter to see how it could be implemented in C. This program implements the C arithmetic operators to print out the result of a set of simple operations:

```
#include <stdio.h>
main()
```

```
{
    int val1=10;
    int val2=20;
printf("%i + %i = %i\n", val1, val2, (val1+val2));
printf("%i - %i = %i\n", val1, val2, (val1-val2));
printf("%i * %i = %i\n", val1, val2, (val1*val2));
printf("%i / %i = %i\n", val1, val2, (val1/val2));
}
```

If you save this program in a file called *operators.c*, you can compile it with the command:

```
$ gcc operators.c -o operators
```

You can now execute the program with the following command:

```
$ ./operators
10 + 20 = 30
10 - 20 = -10
10 * 20 = 200
10 / 20 = 0
```

Oops! 10 divided by 20 is not zero: Let's revisit the program. Although Perl allows all variables to be simply defined by the $ operator, C requires that explicit types be declared for all variables, and for the results of all operations performed on variables (even simple arithmetic operations!). Thus, it would be more appropriate (and correct) to continue to define integer variables as integers, but floating point variables, or operations that return floating point values, should be explicitly cast as floating point types. So, the preceding application could be rewritten as follows:

```
#include <stdio.h>
main()
{
    int val1=10;
    int val2=20;
printf("%i + %i = %i\n", val1, val2, (val1+val2));
printf("%i - %i = %i\n", val1, val2, (val1-val2));
printf("%i * %i = %i\n", val1, val2, (val1*val2));
printf("%i / %i = %2.2f\n", val1, val2, (float)(val1/val2));
}
```

You can now execute the modified program and obtain the correct results:

```
$ ./operators
10 + 20 = 30
10 - 20 = -10
10 * 20 = 200
10 / 20 = 0.5
```

When you create programs that have a lot of iterative operations, or which are intended for a production environment, you can enable an optimization mode in *gcc* by using the *–O* or *–O2* option. Because code is generated by default to contain debugging information, you can remove it by specifying the optimization option. In addition, you can specify many other tweaks and tricks individually or in combination. You can utilize spare CPU registers for arithmetic operations, for example. However, keep in mind for large programs that turning on optimization can slow down compilation time considerably; thus, you should only enable optimization just prior to production.

System Calls, Libraries, and Include Files

In the example presented in the previous section, we made use of only one function (`printf`) contained within a single system library, whose functions are all prefaced in the *file stdio.h*. It is a typical C convention to include constants and interface definitions for precompiled libraries in header files. As you've probably guessed, there are many more system libraries than the single one we have examined so far. In addition, it is possible (and often desirable) to create and distribute your own libraries, which can also make use of header files.

Although you can write your own functions and libraries, you can speed up application development time considerably by reusing many of the components that come presupplied with Solaris. In particular, you must use system calls in order to access system and kernel functions. These can be important when building server-side software, although they are less important for graphical or GUI-based applications. However, note that system calls, when directly accessing data within the kernel, can cause buffer overflows if you don't correctly preprocess arguments. For example, if the length of a string passed to a system call has a maximum length of 1024 bytes, but a 1025-byte string is passed, a kernel panic is possible if the executing user has privileges (real or effective).

Solaris provides manual pages for all system calls and functions in the third group of man pages. These provide invaluable information about function and library interfaces, including the number of required parameters, return types, and other dependencies. In this section, we walk through the development of a simple application (a horse race winner predictor) that makes use of two system calls (*rand()* and *srand()*). The aim of the program is to randomly select a winning horse from a variable sized field of horses—although this may seem like a trivial example, it is a simple application whose development touches upon the basic elements of constructing a C program.

The first step in developing the application is to investigate the system calls and functions that will be used to generate the random numbers. You can start by reading the Solaris documentation, where you'll find that the *rand()* function is an ANSI-compliant suitable method to use. Through man, you can check the required parameters to pass to *rand()*, the name of the include file that defines the interface, and any information that is relevant to calling the function. For example, you can display the man page for *rand()* by typing this command:

```
$ man 3 rand
```

The man page for *rand()* identifies the system header file as *<stdlib.h>*, so all programs that use the *rand()* function must "include" the relevant include file, by specifying this header file in the C source:

```
#include <stdlib.h>
```

The man page for *rand()* specifies that the return type of the *rand()* function is an integer (*int*), and it doesn't require any parameters to be passed in order to return a randomly generated number (*void*). The man page also states that the *rand()* function returns a pseudo-random integer, lying on the interval between 0 and *RAND_MAX*. By convention, nonchanging numerical values such as *RAND_MAX* are defined as constants and cannot be modified by a program.

A second important requirement for generating random numbers is also displayed on the man page: A seeding function must be called by any program before calling the *rand()* function. This is because random number generation by digital computers is only pseudo-random—it generates a series of potentially predictable numbers, using a linear congruential algorithm. Although it is possible to guess a random sequence if you know the seed value, the trick is to use a seed number that changes constantly—retrieving the second or millisecond value from a time-of-day system call is a popular choice. The man page for *rand()* states that the *srand* function takes an unsigned integer argument, representing the seed, and does not return a value. However, if a seed is not supplied, the default value of one is used.

Let's have a look at how to put all of these requirements together to form a program that uses random numbers. Our example here is a program that guesses a winning horse number from a field of horses in a race:

```
#include <stdio.h>
#include <stdlib.h>
main(int argc, char *argv[])
{
  int numberOfHorses, horsePicked, seed;
```

```
printf("Horses 1.0\n");
printf("This program picks a winning horse \n");
if (argc != 3)
{
  printf("usage: horses number_of_horses seed\n");
  exit(1);
}
numberOfHorses=atoi(argv[1]);
seed=atoi(argv[2]);
if (numberOfHorses>24)
{
  printf("Sorry - the maximum number of horses is 24\n");
  exit(1);
}
else
{
  printf("Number of horses: %i\n", numberOfHorses);
}
srand(seed);
horsePicked=1+(int)((float)numberOfHorses*rand()/(RAND_MAX+1.0));
printf("Horse number %i shall win the race\n",horsePicked);
}
```

The program begins by including the header files for the standard input/output and standard C libraries. Next, we declare the *main()* function, which is the exclusive entry point into the program. We pass two parameters to the main function: an integer called *argc* and a pointer to an array of characters called *argv*. These two functions are used to enumerate and pass in command-line parameters, respectively. Because we want to pass in two variables (the *number_of_horses* in a race and the random number seed), then *argc* should equal 3 (the extra parameter is the name of the program, in this case, *horses*).

Next, we will declare some internal variables representing the number of horses (*numberOfHorses*), the horse selected (*horsePicked*), and the random number seed (*seed*). After a banner is printed, the number of command-line arguments is checked. If it is not equal to 3, the application terminates. Checking the bounds of arguments prevents any nasty problems arising later on (including overwriting the boundary of an array— a situation that we examine later with respect to the GNU debugger, *gdb*). Next, we check that the number of horses is not greater than a typical field—say, 24 horses. If the parameter passed on the command line is greater than 24, the program exits with a value of 1—the exit value of a program can be checked by a shell script, for example, to determine whether an application has failed.

If all the parameters have been passed to the application, as expected, the main body of the program can be executed. The random number generator is seeded with the variable called *seed*, and the winning horse number is then randomly selected by using the formula supplied—the *numberOfHorses* multiplied by the number returned by the *rand()* function, scaled appropriately by the *RAND_MAX* constant. Finally, the number of the winning horse is printed on standard output.

This line-by-line explanation may seem long-winded, and it certainly won't teach you to be a C programmer. However, it does introduce the essential elements of a C program and highlights the evaluation of logical expressions at all points in an application in order to carry out some specified task. Although the number and type of system calls on a Solaris system is very large (several hundred, in fact), they can all be accessed using the general approach used in developing this small application.

In order to compile the program using *gcc*, use the following command:

```
$ gcc horses.c -o horses -lm
```

This command string compiles the source file *horses.c* to produce the executable file *horses*, and forces the math library to be linked so that any mathematical functions can be accessed at runtime. If an application uses system calls, and the appropriate libraries are not linked in, the application will fail when executed. Let's see what happens when we execute the horses program with a field of 12 horses and a seed value of 769:

```
$ ./horses 12 769
Horses 1.0
This program picks a winning horse from a dynamic field size
Number of horses: 12
Horse number 7 shall win the race
```

Our program suggests that horse number 7 shall win the horse race. However, if we supply a new random number seed, we may receive a completely different prediction:

```
$ ./horses 12 768
Horses 1.0
This program picks a winning horse from a dynamic field size
Number of horses: 12
Horse number 3 shall win the race
```

We really shouldn't be basing our bets using the results computed by the program. In any case, we definitely don't want to take a bet on a field with many horses running, otherwise the odds of guessing the correct horse are way too high:

```
$ ./horses 1000
Horses 1.0
This program picks a winning horse from a dynamic field size
Sorry - the maximum number of horses allowed in a race is 24
```

The random number generator used in this demonstration is not really suitable for production use, you should consult the "bible" of numerical computing, which is *Numerical Recipes*. The source code, and many book chapters, are now freely available on-line at **http://nr.harvard.edu/nr/nronline.html**.

High Level Input/Output

Solaris applications make extensive use of standard input and standard output streams, so that they can be executed on the command line. For example, the *cat* program displays the contents of files, which can then be piped through a filter (like *more* or *grep*) on the command line. Many Solaris scripts combine a number of small utilities to create complex applications. Understanding input and output streams is critical to developing utilities that can interoperate with existing Solaris applications.

The specific functions for operating on standard input and standard output are defined in the *<stdio.h>* header file. The most commonly used input and output routines are these:

- **fgetc**   Reads a single character from a file
- **fgets**   Reads a string from a file
- **getchar**   Reads in a single character from standard input

Other supported input/output functions, such as *getc*, are less commonly used, because they may be equivalent to another function, or may simply not be applicable to a wide range of situations.

Let's look at a simple example of a program that uses the *fgetc* routine to read all characters from a file, character by character, using the `fgetc` command:

```
#include <stdio.h>
main(int argc, char *argv[])
{
    FILE *fp;
    int character;

    if ((fp=fopen(argv[1],"r"))==NULL)
```

```
        {
                fprintf(stderr, "Cannot open file %s for input\n",
                        argv[1]);
                exit(1);
        }
        do
        {
                character=fgetc(fp);
                if (character!=EOF)
                {
                        printf("%c",character);
                }
        } while (character!=EOF);
        fclose(fp);
}
```

This program acts very much like the *cat* utility, because it requires the name of a file to be passed on the command line. The program begins by reading in the *<stdio.h>* header file, which determines the scope for resolving all input/output routines contained in the program (in this case, *fgetc*). After the main function is declared with the number of arguments to be passed from the command line (*argc*), and the arguments themselves (**argv[]*), a file opening function is called (*fopen*). In contrast to the low-level file handling discussed later, *fopen* can open an input stream for reading, writing, and appending by using the FILE type. In this example, a file handle (*fp*) is declared, and it is opened for reading by the fopen command, using the "r" (read-only) attribute. If the file cannot be opened for reading, an appropriate error message is printed to standard error. Finally, a *do...while* loop is constructed so that every character in the named file is printed to standard output, until the condition that the read character is not the end-of-file (EOF) character has been violated. After the file is closed using the *fclose()* function, the program ends, having successfully printed the entire contents of the named file to the screen.

A related example comes from the *fgets* function, which reads in strings of a predetermined buffer size from a named file. In the following example, we read all data from the named file by using *fgets*, rather than *fgetc*, as the former reduces the overall number of input operations by a factor proportional to the size of the buffer. Thus, a buffer size of eight characters requires eight times fewer read operations for *fgets* than the equivalent *fgetc* operation:

```
#include <stdio.h>
main(int argc, char *argv[])
{
        FILE *fp;
        char *buf;
```

```
        int size=8;
        if ((fp=fopen(argv[1],"r"))==NULL)
        {
                fprintf(stderr, "Cannot open file %s for input\n",
                        argv[1]);
                exit(1);
        }
        do
        {

                buf=fgets(buf, size, fp);
                if (buf!=NULL)
                {
                        printf("%s",buf);
                }
        } while (buf!=NULL);
        fclose(fp);
}
```

In this example, a pointer to a file handle (*fp*) is declared, as well as a pointer to a string of characters (*buf*). In addition, a buffer size of eight is allocated. After a file open operation is performed by *fopen*, and the appropriate error handling is implemented through *stderr*, a *do...while* loop is implemented, which contains the decision logic of the program. This reads a buffer of size eight from the file *fp*, and stores the contents in the character array *buf*. The *printf* function is then used to display the contents of the buffer as a string. The loop continues until a NULL is returned from *fgets* read. After the file is closed using the *fclose()* function, the program ends, having successfully printed the entire contents of the named file to the screen.

One of the most common problems associated with standard input/output libraries is boundary violations. These typically occur when the size of an input stream exceeds what has been declared in the application. If no appropriate boundary checking is performed on the size of the input before it is processed, unexpected behavior can occur, usually in the form of a segmentation violation. Let's examine how this can occur:

```
#include <stdio.h>
#define MAX_SIZE 16

main()
{
    int character=0, i=0, j=0;
    char buf1[MAX_SIZE];
    do
    {
        character=getchar();
```

```
            if (character!=EOF)
            {
                    buf1[i]=character;
                    i++;
            }
    } while (character!=EOF);
    do
    {
            printf("%c", buf1[j]);
            j++;
    } while (j<i);
}
```

This program reads in a set of characters from standard input, stores them in a character array of static size (defined by *MAX_SIZE*), and then prints out the characters individually to standard output. If the application was executed, and the characters 1234567 were typed in, they would be dutifully printed to standard output. However, if the characters 12345678901234567890 were typed in, the message "Segmentation fault (core dumped)" would appear (along with a very large core file!). If this application was running as root, or any other privileged user, the unpredictable behavior of the program may have serious security implications, as well as potentially violating the integrity of kernel and user memory.

To remove the problem, we simply need to add an appropriate boundary checking condition to the input routine. In this case, we simply check that the number of characters being read does not exceed the number specified by *MAX_SIZE*. We don't need to do the same check when printing the characters to standard output, because we know that there will never be an inappropriate number of characters stored in the character buffer in the first place:

```
#include <stdio.h>
#define MAX_SIZE 16

main()
{
    int character=0, i=0, j=0;
    char buf1[MAX_SIZE];
    do
    {
            character=getchar();
            if (character!=EOF)
            {
```

```
                buf1[i]=character;
                i++;
        }
    } while ((character!=EOF)&&(i<MAX_SIZE));
    do
    {
        printf("%c", buf1[j]);
        j++;
    } while (j<i);
}
```

If the application was executed now, and the characters 1234567 were typed in, they would be dutifully printed to standard output. If the characters 12345678901234567890 were typed in, however, only 1234567890123456 would be displayed, and no core file would be dumped. A core file is an image of memory dumped when a process terminates abnormally. Because some applications can consume many megabytes of RAM, it is possible that core files can become very large and waste valuable disk space. If you don't intend to use core files for debugging, you can safely remove them.

Regardless of whether standard input, or another stream is used (such as a file), it is critical to check that boundaries have not been overwritten, especially where arrays and pointers are concerned.

We've so far looked at some simple cases involving text files. However, more complex applications that use structs to create database-like records usually require faster read/write access provided by binary data streams. Using a binary stream makes it impossible to use *cat* or *grep* to examine the contents of a file, but it does allow a valuable abstraction from files on a character-by-character basis. Complex data structures can be easily serialized and written to a binary file.

In the following example program, we define a struct called *dbRecord*, which contains some of the user data typically stored in the password file (*/etc/passwd*). Many applications use this data for authentication purposes. Imagine that we were going to write a new improved version of */etc/passwd* that used a binary data format rather than the existing cumbersome (and slow) text format. We'd need an administrative interface to allow new records to be easily added, because they could no longer be added by manually editing the */etc/passwd* file. Let's have a look at how this could be achieved:

```
#include <stdio.h>

void printMenu();
char getInput();
void enterData(FILE *fp);
```

```
struct dbRecord
{
    int uid;
    int gid;
    char username[8];
    char homeDirectory[64];
    char shell[64];
    char comment[64];
};

main(int argc, char *argv[])
{
    FILE *dbFile;
    char menuChoice;
    if ((dbFile=fopen(argv[1],"a+"))==NULL)
    {
        fprintf(stderr, "Cannot open database file %s\n",
                argv[1]);
        exit(1);
    }
    do
    {
        printMenu();
        menuChoice=getInput();
        switch (menuChoice)
        {
            case 'e':
                enterData(dbFile);
                break;
            case 'q':
                printf("Session terminated\n");
    fclose(dbFile);
exit(1);
                break;
        }
    } while (menuChoice!='q');
}

void printMenu()
{
    printf("Database Main Menu\n");
    printf("------------------\n");
```

ENTERPRISE

```
        printf("(e)nter new dbRecord\n");
        printf("(q)uit\n");
}

char getInput()
{
        char answer;
        printf("\nYour Choice: ");
        answer=getchar();
        return answer;
}

void enterData(FILE *fp)
{
        struct dbRecord user;
        printf("Data Entry\n");
        printf("----------\n\n");
        printf("Enter UID: ");
        scanf("%i",&user.uid);
        printf("Enter GID: ");
        scanf("%i",&user.gid);
        printf("Enter username: ");
        scanf("%s",user.username);
        printf("Enter full name: ");
        scanf("%s",user.comment);
        printf("Enter shell: ");
        scanf("%s",user.shell);
        printf("Enter home directory: ");
        scanf("%s",user.homeDirectory);
        fwrite((char *)&user, sizeof(struct dbRecord), 1, fp);
}
```

Let's walk through the code, and see how we've implemented the data structures and decision procedures required to implement the password database administration interface. We start by declaring three functions: *printMenu()*, *getInput()I*, and *enterData(FILE *fp)*. These will be used to print the application menu to standard output, process user menu selections, and solicit user data, respectively. Next, we define a struct called *dbRecord*, which resembles the user record type employed by the */etc/passwd* file. This struct contains the following variables:

int uid	Stores the user's ID
int gid	Stores the user's primary group ID
char username[8]	Defines the login for the user
char homeDirectory[64]	Stores the full path to the user's home directory
char shell[64]	Contains the full path to the user's default shell
char comment[64]	Stores the user's full name and optionally a description of some kind

Next, we introduce the main body of the program, beginning with the declaration of a file handle *dbFile*. This is file in which user data will be stored using a binary format, and its name is retrieved from *argv[1]* (i.e., passed on the command line). After the file is opened for appending and reading, as signified by the permission string *a+*, a *do...while* loop is constructed. The loop iterates until *menuChoice*, as entered by the user after the menu is printed, is *q*. In practice, this condition is never reached, because the *q* is caught by the *switch* statement, and the case *q* immediately exits from the program. If the case *e* is encountered, the function *enterData(FILE *fp)* is called. This function proceeds by asking the user to enter all data elements that are defined for *dbRecord*. Each entry is read in by using the *scanf* function. Once the data has been collected, a record is written to the specified file by using the *fwrite()* function.

Let's see how a data operation performs in practice:

```
$ ./database database.txt
Database Main Menu
------------------
(e)nter new record
(q)uit

Your Choice:
```

After selecting *e*, the Data Entry menu is displayed, and a new record can be inserted:

```
Data Entry----------
Enter UID: 1001
Enter GID: 100
Enter username: pwatters
Enter full name: Paul
Enter shell: /bin/sh
Enter home directory: /home/paul
```

After the record has been inserted, the main menu is displayed once again. Further records can be inserted, or you can simply quit the application:

```
Database Main Menu
------------------
  (e)nter new record
  (q)uit

Your Choice:q
Session terminated
```

Here, we started the database application by passing the filename *database.txt*, which is to contain the user data entered through the application. After the welcome banner is printed, we enter *e* to go to the data entry screen. Here, we enter data for the user *pwatters*, including UID *1001*, GID *100*, full name *Paul*, shell */bin/sh*, and home directory */home/paul*. After all of the data has been accepted and the entry written to the database file, we are returned to the main menu.

Low Level Input/Output

The *open()* system call is used to open a file using a low-level call. The file remains open until closed with a *close()* system call. When the *open()* system call is called, a file descriptor is returned, which is a unique integer that distinguishes the current open file from other opened files. A pool of available file descriptor integers is maintained, and the next integer in the queue is selected. Recall that there are three file descriptors that are defined by the low-level interface: standard input (*0*), standard output (*1*), and standard error (*2*).

The named file is always opened at its beginning, so subsequent operations are operating sequentially on the data contained in the file. The *open()* function opens the file named in the string pathname, with the permissions specified by primary flags. These flags include these:

- **O_RDONLY**   Opens the file read-only
- **O_WRONLY**   Opens the file write-only
- **O_RDWR**   Opens the file read/write

In addition, the following secondary flags may be bitwise-OR'ed with the secondary flags to extend the functionality of the *open()* call:

- **O_CREAT**   Creates the file on the file system if it does not already exist
- **O_EXCL**   The reverse of *O_CREAT*: if a file already exists, the call will fail
- **O_NOCTTY**   Prevents the process being overtaken by a terminal (tty) device that is specified by pathname

- **O_TRUNC**   Allows a file to be truncated
- **O_APPEND**   Allows data to be appended to the end of a file
- **O_NONBLOCK**   Prevents waiting
- **O_SYNC**   Enforces synchronous input/output
- **O_NOFOLLOW**   Prevents the opening of a file if it is a symbolic link
- **O_DIRECTORY**   Fails if the named file is not a directory
- **O_LARGEFILE**   Allows large files, whose sizes cannot be addressed (in 32-bit systems), to be opened

The *open()* function always returns an integer, which is the file descriptor (if positive), or an error (if negative). The errors associated with *open()*, which are set by *errno*, include *EEXIST, EISDIR, EACCESS, ENAMETOOLONG, ENOENT, ENOTDIR, ENODEV, EROFS, ETXTBSY, EFAULT, ELOOP, ENOSPC, ENOMEM, EMFILE,* and *ENFILE*.

Two operations are supported by low-level input/output: reading (with the *read()* function) and writing (with the *write()* function). The main difference between high- and low-level reading and writing functions is that the latter require you to specify your own buffer size, and the type of data being read and written is not assumed.

The *read()* call has the form

```
ssize_t read(int fd, void *buf, size_t count)
```

where *fd* is a file descriptor, *buf* is a pointer to a (variable-sized) buffer, and *count* is the number of bytes to be read from the file. If the call is successful, the number of bytes read successfully is returned. If the call fails, one of the following codes will be returned by *errno*: *EINTR, EAGAIN, EIO, EISDIR, EBADF, EINVAL,* and *EFAULT*. These are defined and described at the end of this chapter.

The *write()* call has the form

```
ssize_t write(int fd, void *buf, size_t count)
```

where *fd* is a file descriptor, *buf* is a pointer to a (variable-sized) buffer, and *count* is the number of bytes to be written to the file. If the call is successful, the number of bytes written successfully is returned. If the call fails, one of the following codes will be returned by *errno*: *EINTR, EAGAIN, EIO, EISDIR, EBADF, EINVAL, EPIPE,* and *EFAULT*. These are defined and described at the end of this chapter.

A file opened with *open()* can be closed with *close(int fd)*, where *fd* is the file descriptor.

Let's examine how these low-level calls can be used in practice. We revisit the user database application and modify the file operations to use low-level rather than high-level routines.

The first thing to notice is that we've added in several different header files, including *sys/types.h*, *sys/stat.h*, *unistd.h*, and *fcntl.h*. These are all necessary to support low-level I/O. Next, we've changed the declaration of the *enterData()* function from a pointer to type FILE to a single integer. This is the integer that contains the file descriptor. This means we must also change the *fopen()* request to an *open()* call. This specifies the name of the file to be opened, along with three OR'ed flags: *O_RDWR*, *O_CREAT*, and *O_APPEND*. This ensures that the database file will be opened read/write, will be created if it doesn't already exist, and will be opened for appending. In addition, note that the error checking condition has now changed: Instead of checking to see whether the return value of *fopen()* is NULL, we now simply check to see whether the returned integer value from *open()* is positive (success) or negative (failure).

Finally, the *write()* call is similar to the original: A file descriptor is passed, using the instantiation of *dbRecord* (user), where each record is written individually (i.e., the size of the buffer being written is defined by the record size). The modified file listing is given here:

```c
#include <stdio.h>
#include <sys/types.h>
#include <sys/stat.h>
#include <unistd.h>
#include <fcntl.h>

void printMenu();
char getInput();
void enterData(int fd);

struct dbRecord
{
    int uid;
    int gid;
    char username[8];
    char homeDirectory[64];
    char shell[64];
    char comment[64];
};

main(int argc, char *argv[])
{
    int fd;
    char menuChoice;
    if ((fd=open(argv[1],O_RDWR|O_CREAT|O_APPEND))<0)
    {
```

```
            fprintf(stderr, "Cannot open database file %s\n",
                    argv[1]);
            exit(1);
        }
    do
    {
            printMenu();
            menuChoice=getInput();
            switch (menuChoice)
            {
                case 'e':
                    enterData(fd);
                    break;
                case 'q':
                    printf("Session terminated\n");
                    exit(1);
                    break;
            }
    } while (menuChoice!='q');
    close(fd);
}

void printMenu()
{
    printf("Database Main Menu\n");
    printf("------------------\n");
    printf("(e)nter new dbRecord\n");
    printf("(q)uit\n");
}

char getInput()
{
    char answer;
    printf("\nYour Choice: ");
    answer=getchar();
    return answer;
}

void enterData(int fd)
{
    struct dbRecord user;
    printf("Data Entry\n");
```

```
        printf("----------\n\n");
        printf("Enter UID: ");
        scanf("%i",&user.uid);
        printf("Enter GID: ");
        scanf("%i",&user.gid);
        printf("Enter username: ");
        scanf("%s",user.username);
        printf("Enter full name: ");
        scanf("%s",user.comment);
        printf("Enter shell: ");
        scanf("%s",user.shell);
        printf("Enter home directory: ");
        scanf("%s",user.homeDirectory);
        write(fd, (char *)&user, sizeof(struct dbRecord));
}
```

Performance Optimization and Debugging

If you write your own programs, or if you compile those written by others, speed of execution and size of executables are often major considerations. For example, if you are writing a program that attempts to solve differential equations or perform highly complex numerical operations, you will obviously want to optimize for speed of execution. Or, if you're a Java applet developer, your codebase must be downloaded to remote Web browser clients before it can be executed, so you'd definitely be more interested in optimizing for executable size rather than speed. Any kind of optimization performed on source code during compilation will almost certainly increase compilation time, so this needs to be factored into plans for code optimization during early phases of development.

The Solaris development environment and the GNU compilers provide several ways in which you can monitor and enhance performance. The best way to evaluate application performance is to time the application. You can use the time command to measure the actual time taken to execute the application; it breaks this down into user and system components. Let's run the time command on the compiler command used earlier to build the *horses* program from source:

```
$ time gcc horses.c -o horses -lm
real    0m0.547s
user    0m0.450s
sys     0m0.100s
```

The total time taken to compile the command was 0.547 seconds ("real time"), made up of approximately 0.45 seconds of user time, and 0.1 seconds of system time. In this context, user time is the number of seconds that the CPU spent processing instructions in user mode, while system time is the number of seconds the kernel was running on the CPU. It is also possible to measure the execution time of the application itself:

```
$ time ./horses
real    0m0.031s
user    0m0.020s
sys     0m0.000s
```

Here, we can see that the execution time of the application is many times faster than the compilation process: the real time used was 0.031 seconds, of which the user component was 0.02 seconds, and the system component was negligible. However, let's examine how long it actually took to compile the program:

```
$ time gcc -O2 horses.c -o horses -lm
real    0m0.895s
user    0m0.740s
sys     0m0.150s
```

The compilation time of 0.895 seconds was around 50 percent longer than an unoptimized compile. However, the execution time of the optimized program was less than half that required by the unoptimized program:

```
$ time ./horses
real    0m0.014s
user    0m0.010s
sys     0m0.010s
```

Using optimization can also have an effect on the size of a binary—a faster application is usually larger in executable size, as loops are unrolled and external functions are moved in-line. In addition, producing debugging and profiling data for later examination using the GNU debugger (*gdb*) also increases the application binary size. For example, if we compile the horses program using the standard options, we can examine the size of executable by using the `ls` command:

```
$ gcc horses.c -o horses -lm
$ ls -l horses
-rwxr-xr-x   1 root      root           11533 Jul 18 19:37 horses
```

ENTERPRISE

However, when we specify debugging information to be included in the binary, we can use the *–pg* option with *gcc*—this also produces a much larger binary, as we can see using ls:

```
$ gcc -pg horses.c -o horses -lm
$ ls -l horses
-rwxr-xr-x   1 root      root        21215 Jul 18 19:37 horses
```

In this case, the object file contains the executable code as well as the types associated with all functions and variables in the program. In addition, the mapping between line numbers in the source, and memory addresses in the object code, is retained, making the executable almost twice as large as a binary with no debugging information.

When we write C programs, we're often faced with the difficult task of debugging an application that produces unexpected behavior. Integrated Develop Environments (IDEs) are generally quite good at picking up syntax errors, but they cannot always diagnose what will occur at runtime, because of differences in environment, system load, virtual memory and system library availability, and so on. That's where the *gdb* really comes into its own.

Let's examine a simple program that declares an array of integers, assigns a value to the first and last elements of the array, and then prints it out:

```c
#include <stdio.h>

main()
{
        int i[10];
        i[0]=1;
    printf("%i \n",i[0]);
        i[9]=1;
        printf("%i \n",i[9]);
}
```

If we compile and run the program, we would expect to see the output:

```
$ ./array_test
1
1
```

However, a common problem with C programming is overwriting the boundaries of an array. You would think that having declared the array to have ten elements, that only ten elements would be addressable—accessing elements outside this range should cause a compile error. However, in our ten-element array declared in the preceding code example, most compilers will allow us to address the eleventh, twelfth, or thirteenth element, even though they don't "exist." In fact, if we modify our program to write to the twelfth element of the array, we will get a runtime error:

```
#include <stdio.h>
main()
{
        int i[10];
        i[0]=1;
        printf("%i \n",i[0]);
        i[11]=1;
        printf("%i \n",i[11]);
}
```

Let's see what happens when we run the program:

```
$ ./array_test
1
Segmentation fault
```

Although we can write off such errors easily by going back to the source and checking for programming errors, this can be a long and tedious process in large applications. In addition, it may not always be clear why a segmentation fault (or any other memory access violation error) is occurring at all. In these cases, it can be useful to get a snapshot of memory contents associated with a specific program, by using the GNU debugger (*gdb*). This can help determine the circumstances under which a program crashed and pinpoint any offending commands or variable values that were invalid at the time of execution. In addition, the specific values of variables in your programs can be "watched" while stepping through line-by-line execution of the program. This also gives developers an indication of where an error occurs in the source. It's even possible to pass new values of variables to the application while it is running to "fix" any problems in real time. You can find the *gdb* manual online at **http://www.cis.ohio-state.edu/htbin/info/info/gdb.info**.

The main commands used in a *gdb* session are shown in Table 31-1.

We can use the *gdb* to trace the error in our application:

```
$ gdb array_test
GNU gdb 4.17.0.11 with Solaris/x86 hardware watchpoint and FPU support
Copyright 1998 Free Software Foundation, Inc.
GDB is free software, covered by the
GNU General Public License, and you are
```

```
welcome to change it and/or distribute copies
of it under certain conditions.
Type "show copying" to see the conditions.
There is absolutely no warranty for GDB.  Type "show warranty" for details.
This GDB was configured as "i386-Solaris"...
(gdb)
```

Command	Action
break	Sets a breakpoint at a specific point in a program prior to stepping. Breakpoints can be set on functions and source line numbers.
clear	Clears breakpoints specified for functions and line numbers in source files
continue	Continues execution of a program after a breakpoint has been met, until the next breakpoint
delete	Deletes breakpoints by breakpoint number
display	Displays the value of an expression every time program execution is halted
finish	Continues execution of a program after a breakpoint until the program has completed
info	Prints details of breakpoints and watchpoints set during a *gdb* session
lisxt	Displays specific lines of source code
next	Continues execution of a program to the next source line, if step mode has been set
print	Displays the value of an expression
run	Begins executes of a program under *gdb*
step	Steps through code line-by-line so that the effect of individual statements and expressions in the source can be evaluated
watch	Halts execution if the value of a variable is modified

Table 31-1. *Basic GNU Debugger (gdb) Commands*

First, we read in the content's executable file:

```
(gdb) file array_test
Reading symbols from array_test...done.
```

Next, we attempt to re-create the error, by executing the program within *gdb*:

```
(gdb) run
Starting program: /tmp/array_test
1

Program received signal SIGSEGV, Segmentation fault.
0x1 in ?? ()
```

This is the same point that the application failed when executed within the shell. Because we have received a segmentation violation, we need to determine the circumstances under which it arose. When the *main()* function is called, details about the function call are generated, including the location of the call in the source file, its arguments (if any), and details of any local variables. This set of information is known as the *stack frame*, and all stack frames are stored in memory in a *call stack*. We can use the bt command to display trace of the current call stack, with one line displayed for each stack frame. In our application, we had only a single function (the *main()* function), so only a single line is displayed:

```
(gdb) bt
#0   0x1 in ?? ()
```

At any point of execution, you can generate a list of the variables used in an application by using the list command:

```
(gdb) list 'array_test.c'
There are 365 possibilities.  Do you really
wish to see them all? (y or n)
                                __DTOR_LIST__
Letext                          __EH_FRAME_BEGIN__
_CS_LFS64_CFLAGS                __FRAME_END__
_CS_LFS64_LDFLAGS               __bb
_CS_LFS64_LIBS                  __blkcnt64_t
_CS_LFS64_LINTFLAGS             __blkcnt_t
_CS_LFS_CFLAGS                  __bss_start
```

ENTERPRISE

```
_CS_LFS_LDFLAGS                      __caddr_t
_CS_LFS_LIBS                         __clock_t
_CS_LFS_LINTFLAGS                    __compar_fn_t
_CS_PATH                             __daddr_t
_CS_XBS5_ILP32_OFF32_CFLAGS          __data_start
_CS_XBS5_ILP32_OFF32_LDFLAGS         __deregister_frame_info
_CS_XBS5_ILP32_OFF32_LIBS            __dev_t
_CS_XBS5_ILP32_OFF32_LINTFLAGS       __do_global_ctors_aux
_CS_XBS5_ILP32_OFFBIG_CFLAGS         __do_global_dtors_aux
_CS_XBS5_ILP32_OFFBIG_LDFLAGS        __fd_mask
_CS_XBS5_ILP32_OFFBIG_LIBS           __fd_set
_CS_XBS5_ILP32_OFFBIG_LINTFLAGS      __fsblkcnt64_t
_CS_XBS5_LP64_OFF64_CFLAGS           __fsblkcnt_t
_CS_XBS5_LP64_OFF64_LDFLAGS          __fsfilcnt64_t
```

You can also retrieve and set the values of these variables. More usefully, you can extract the values of the CPU registers by using the info all-registers command:

```
(gdb) info all-registers
     eax:          0x3              3
     ecx:          0x0              0
     edx:          0x2              2
     ebx: 0x400f6618      1074751000
     esp: 0xbffff874     -1073743756
     ebp: 0xbffff8a8     -1073743704
     esi: 0x4000aa20      1073785376
     edi: 0xbffff8d4     -1073743660
     eip:          0x1              1
  eflags:      0x10282 IOPL: 0; flags: SF IF RF
orig_eax: 0xffffffff             -1
      cs:         0x23             35
      ss:         0x2b             43
      ds:         0x2b             43
      es:         0x2b             43
      fs:          0x0              0
      gs:          0x0              0
     st0: 0x3fff8000000000000000   Empty Normal 1
     st1: 0x00000000000000000000   Empty Zero   0
     st2: 0x3fff8000000000000000   Empty Normal 1
     st3: 0x00000000000000000000   Empty Zero   0
     st4: 0x00000000000000000000   Empty Zero   0
```

Setting a breakpoint for a function is easy when using the `break` command. In the case of our test program, we have only a single function (*main()*), so this will be reached almost as soon as the program is executed. Better symbolic information, including the code and line numbers concerned, can be obtained by compiling the application with the –*g* option. We can set a breakpoint on *main()* by using the following command:

```
(gdb) break main
Breakpoint 1 at 0x8048536
```

Next, we need to run the program again, and it will be halted once the declared breakpoint has been reached:

```
(gdb) run
Starting program: /tmp/array_test

Breakpoint 1, 0x8048536 in main ()
(gdb)
```

At this point, we can examine the values of all declared variables, and set watches appropriately. One issue when stepping through applications using *gdb* is referring to source files that are not in your path:

```
(gdb) s
Single stepping until exit from function main,
which has no line number information.
printf (format=0x80485d0 "%i \n") at printf.c:30
printf.c:30: No such file or directory.
```

Fortunately, you can obtain the source for many Solaris libraries, so it is often feasible to debug to the level of the standard input/output libraries and similar.

The Complete Reference

Solaris 9

Chapter 32

Enterprise Services

ome Solaris services are specifically designed to be implemented in the enterprise, rather than on individual systems. These services are able to leverage resources across networks and different systems to reduce administrative overhead and to ensure that applications can scale appropriately and are secure. In this chapter, we review several key enterprise technologies that are either bundled with Solaris or that can be downloaded as options from the Solaris Web site (**http://www.sun.com/solaris**).

Resource Manager

For workstations, resource allocation is usually not an issue, because only a small number of applications are generally running at any one time. Of these applications, the common desktop environment (CDE) and X11 may consume the largest amount of CPU time, particularly if the workspace is fully utilized. However, servers have diverse needs with respect to resource management, particularly in a shared hosting environment, where time and process priority are billable items. Being able to specify which processes have priority over others is a key requirement for servers running hundreds of different processes for potentially hundreds of different customers.

The concept of process priority is built into the kernel: if processes belong to the time sharing (TS) priority class, they may be assigned a priority value (PRI) that determines the order in which their operations are executed on the CPU. The scheduler is responsible for allocating resources to different processes according to priority values. Non-privileged users can only decrease the priority associated with their processes, while the super-user can actually increase the priority associated with any user's processes.

One way to appreciate this is to use *ps* to display the process list in the scheduler format. This includes two extra columns in the *ps* output: the priority class memberships and the process priority values:

```
$ ps -c
  PID  CLS PRI TTY         TIME CMD
 6667   TS  45 pts/8      0:00 sh
 6675   TS  35 pts/8      0:00 httpd
```

In this example, the httpd command and the Bourne shell (sh) are both members of the Time Sharing class, meaning that a priority value may be assigned to their respective processes. In this example, the sh process has a higher priority value than the httpd process, and thus has greater access to the system's resources.

An unprivileged user can reduce any of the processes he or she owns by reducing the priority granted to the *ps* process using the nice command. The following example reduces the priority for sh, potentially increasing the amount of CPU available for the httpd process:

```
$ nice -30 sh
```

This would reduce the priority for the sh process to *15*, well below the priority
for httpd at *35*. Alternatively, the super-user may directly increase the priority of a
process, also by using the command, by specifying a negative increment, which when
subtracted from the process priority actually increases it (that is, subtracting a negative
integer is equivalent to addition). The following example would increase the process
priority for the httpd command from *35* to *55*:

```
# nice --20 ps
```

However, nice solves only part of the problem of resource allocation, because normal
users still have unbounded access to execute as many applications as they wish, unless
the super-user continually monitors their activity, reducing priority values when necessary.
In a multiprocessor system, it may be possible to run an "honor system" in which
individuals or groups agree to use only a specific CPU for their work, by using the
pbind command. pbind forces a process and its children to use only a specific CPU.
For example, if a httpd process was started, and it had a PID of 2234, it could be
bound to CPU 1 using the following command:

```
$ pbind -b 1 2234
process id 2234: was 1, now 1
```

Again, by using the pbind command, a super-user can bind (or unbind) any process
from a specific CPU if resources are being drained. But this still requires monitoring
and oversight from a system administrator. Another alternative is to create a processor
set using the psrset command, which binds a process to a single CPU or to a group
of CPUs. This limits the maximum CPU usage by a specific process to whatever it can
obtain from the CPU (or CPUs) to which it is bound. The problem here is that a system
has limited resources, so if a process does not use all the CPU allocated to it, resources
are being wasted as the CPU sits idling.

What is required is a policy-based mechanism for ensuring that individual users
and applications never exceed a pre-allocated quota of CPU resource, much like disk
quotas specify exactly how much disk space a user can utilize. The Resource Manager
provides this functionality by implementing a fine-grained resource access policy that
limits the resources that can be utilized by different users. It allows CPU usage to be
allocated on a per-user basis and allows virtual memory consumption to be limited on
both a user and process basis. In addition, the total number of processes spawned by
a user, the number of concurrent log ins, and their total connection time can be limited.
This allows complete control over an individual user's access to the system as well as
to their individual processes. For example, a numerical scientist might have free access

to the system except when running the MATLAB (**www.mathworks.com**) application, where the MATLAB process might be limited to how much CPU and virtual memory can be consumed.

The simplest method of allocating CPU resources is to divide up the available CPU among the existing users, according to organizational priorities. For example, a Web server for an online catalogue may have three main accounts whose access to resources needs to be limited: the oracle account, responsible for running the Oracle database; the apache user, responsible for running the Apache Web server; and the jdk user, responsible for executing the Java Virtual Machine (JVM) for the Apache Tomcat servlet runner. To prevent large numbers of httpd clients from causing a resource drain on the database, or from thread lock in the JVM causing the same problem, you must limit the maximum CPU usage of the httpd and Java processes by setting limits on the amount of CPU that the apache and jdk users can use.

Since the Resource Manager allows for the hierarchical allocation of resources to groups of users and processes (known as *sgroups*), all allocations must descend from the root *sgroup*. In our example, only the root *sgroup* will be used, so we first associate the oracle, apache, and jdk users as descendants of the root *sgroup*, by using the limadm command:

```
# limadm set sgroup=root oracle
# limadm set sgroup=root apache
# limadm set sgroup=root jdk
```

If the allocation of CPU to the oracle, apache, and jdk groups was 50 percent, 25 percent, and 25 percent, respectively, the following commands would set the share of each user appropriately:

```
# limadm set cpu.shares=50 oracle
# limadm set cpu.shares=25 apache
# limadm set cpu.shares=25 jdk
```

To check the status of the resources being used by the oracle user, we could use the liminfo command:

```
# liminfo -c oracle
Login name:      oracle       Uid (Real,Eff):  1024 (-,-)
Sgroup (uid)     root(0)      Gid (Real,Eff):  10(-,-)

Shares:          50           Myshares:        1
Share:           50 %         E-share:         0 %
Usage:           0            Accrued usage:   0

Mem usage:       0 B          Term usage:      0s
```

```
Mem limit:        0 B          Term accrue:     0s
Proc mem limit:  0 B          Term limit:      0s
Mem accrue:       0 B.s

Processes:        2            Current logins:  1
Process limit:    0
```

More complex *sgroup*s can be created for a system, based on organizational units. For example, the Sales division may require 25 percent of the CPU in a system, while the Finance division may be entitled to 75 percent. Individual *sgroup*s must be created for each of these divisions underneath root, and then individual users who are members of the divisions must be associated with the correct *sgroup*.

JumpStart

JumpStart is a client/server system for installing Solaris systems on a local area network using a standard operating environment (SOE). This removes the need to configure each installation individually on every host on a subnet. This greatly reduces the administrative burden on sysadmins, as most client systems use exactly the same settings, particularly within the same organizational unit.

JumpStart has three roles that are filled by different systems on the network:

- An install server, which provides all of the data and services required to install the system
- A boot server, which uses the Reverse Address Resolution Protocol (RARP) daemon to boot client systems that have not been installed
- An install client, which is the target system for installation

Boot Servers

A boot server provides a copy of the operating system to be installed on a target host. After the target host has been booted using the *network* and *install* options (see the next section), a kernel is downloaded to the target host from an install server and booted locally. After the system has been loaded, the operating system is downloaded from the boot server. The rules for downloading and installing specific files are located in the *rules.ok* file. Individual systems can have their own entries in the rules file, or generic rules can be inserted. After loading the system from the boot server, the install client executes a post-installation script and will then be ready for use.

Installing Servers

The install server uses RARP to listen for requests to install the system from target
hosts. When such a request is received, a mini-root system is downloaded from the
install server to the target host.

To set up an install server, you need to perform the following tasks:

```
# mkdir -p /export/install /export/config
# cp -r /cdrom/sol_9_sparc/s0/Solaris_2.9/Misc/jumpstart_sample/ \
  * /export/config
# /cdrom/sol_9_sparc/s0/Solaris_2.9/Tools ./setup_install_server \
  /export/install
```

This assumes that */export/install* has sufficient space to store the installation files and
that the JumpStart configuration data, such as the rules file, will be stored in */export/config*.
Here is a sample *host_class* file, which is referred to in rules, that specifies the UFS disk
layout for all boot clients:

```
install_type initial_install
system_type standalone
partitioning explicit
filesys c1t2d0s0 512 /
filesys c1t2d0s3 2048 /usr
filesys c1t2d0s4 256 /var
filesys c0t3d1s0 1024 swap
filesys c0t3d1s1 free /export
cluster SUNWCall
```

Here, you can see that the standard layout allocated 512MB to /, 2048MB to */usr*,
256MB to */var*, 1024MB to swap, and all free space to */export*. In addition, the cluster
SUNWCall is to be installed.

When the *rules* file has been customized, its contents must be verified by using
the check command. After the check command parses the *rules* file and validates
its contents, a *rules.ok* file is created.

Boot Clients

To set up a boot client, the target system must be shut down to init level 0 by using
the init 0 command or equivalent. Next, the system needs to be booted by using the
following command from the OK prompt:

```
boot net - install
```

At this point, a broadcast is made on the local subnet to locate an install server. When an install server is located, a mini-root system is downloaded to the target system. When the kernel is loaded from the mini-root system, the operating system is then downloaded from the boot server.

```
Resetting ...
SPARCstation 20 MP (2 X SuperSPARC-II)
ROM Rev. 2.28, 256 MB memory installed, Serial #345665.
Ethernet address 8:0:19:6b:22:a2, Host ID: 49348a3.
Initializing Memory |
Boot device: /iommu/sbus/ledma@f,400010/le@f,c00000 File and args: -
hostname: paul.cassowary.net
domainname: cassowary.net
root server: installserv
root directory: /solaris_2.9/export/exec/kvm/sparc.sun
Copyright (c) 1983-2001, Sun Microsystems, Inc.
The system is coming up. Please wait.
```

When the system has started, you'll see individual clusters being installed:

```
Selecting cluster: SUNWCXall
Total software size: 324.55 MB
Preparing system to install Solaris. Please wait.
Setting up disk c1t2d0:
Creating Solaris disk label (VTOC)
Creating and checking UFS file systems:
- Creating / (c1t2d0)
- Creating /var (c1t2d0)
- Creating /scratch (c1t2d0)
- Creating /opt (c1t2d0)
- Creating /usr (c1t2d0)
- Creating /staff (c1t2d0)
Beginning Solaris package installation...
SUNWcsu.....done. 321.23 MB remaining.
SUNWcsr.....done. 277.34 MB remaining.
SUNWcsd.....done. 312.23 MB remaining.
```

sysidcfg

When installing JumpStart on a large number of clients, installation can be expedited by using a *sysidcfg* file that defines a number of standard parameters for installation. The *sysidcfg* file can contain configuration entries for the properties shown in Table 32-1.

Property	*sysidcfg* Parameter
Date and time	*timeserver*
DHCP	*dhcp*
Domain name	*domain_name*
Graphics card	*display*
Hostname	*hostname*
IP address	*ip_address*
IPv6	*protocol_ipv6*
Keyboard language	*keyboard*
Monitor type	*monitor*
DNS, LDAP or NIS/NIS+ name server	*name_server*
DNS, LDAP or NIS/NIS+ name service	*name_service*
DNS domains to search	*search*
LDAP profile	*profile*
Netmask	*netmask*
Network interface	*network_interface*
Pointing device	*pointer*
Root password	*root_password*
Security policy	*security_policy*
Kerberos administration server	*admin_server*
Kerberos KDC	*kdc*
Kerberos realm	*default_realm*
Terminal type	*terminal*
Time zone	*timezone*

Table 32-1. *Configurable sysidcfg Properties*

The following is a sample *sysidcfg* file:

```
system_locale=en_US
timezone=US/Eastern
timeserver=localhost
network_interface=le0 {netmask=255.255.255.0 protocol_ipv6=yes}
security_policy=NONE
terminal=dtterm
name_service=NONE
root_password=f7438:;H2ef
```

Apache Web Server

Apache is a multiprocess Web server that is supplied with the Solaris 9 distribution. It is used by the majority of Web servers in the world to serve HTTP (insecure) and HTTPS (secure) content. Apache also performs a number of different tasks, including the following:

- Providing a Common Gateway Interface (CGI) to grant client access to server-side processes and applications. CGI applications can be written in C, C++, Perl, Bourne shell, or the language of your choice.

- Supporting the hosting of multiple sites on a single server, where each site is associated with a unique fully-qualified domain name. Thus, a single Solaris system in an Internet service provider (ISP) environment can host multiple Web sites, such as **www.java-support.com**, **www.paulwatters.com**, and so on, using a single instance of Apache.

- Securing the transmission of credit card details and other sensitive data by supporting the Secure Socket Layer (SSL). This allows for key-based encryption of the HTTP protocol (called HTTPS), with key sizes of up to 128 bits.

- A fully-featured proxy/cache server, which provides an extra level of protection for clients behind a firewall, and also keeps a copy of the most commonly retrieved documents from the WWW.

- Customized access, agent, and error logs that can be used for marketing and reporting purposes.

- The main Apache configuration file is *httpd.conf*, which contains three sections:

  - The global environment section sets key server information, such as the root directory for the Apache installation, and several process management settings, such as the number of concurrent requests permitted per server process.

■ The main server configuration section sets runtime parameters for the server, including the port on which the server listens, the server name, the root directory for the HTML documents and images that comprise the site, and the server authorization configuration if required.

■ The virtual hosts configuration section configures the Apache server to run servers for multiple domains. Many of the configuration options that are set for the main server can also be customized for each of the virtual servers.

We will now examine the configuration options in each of these sections in detail.

Global Environment Configuration

The following options are commonly set in the global environment configuration section:

```
ServerType standalone
ServerRoot "/opt/apache1.3"
PidFile /opt/apache1.3/logs/httpd.pid
ScoreBoardFile /opt/apache1.3/logs/apache_status
Timeout 300
KeepAlive On
MaxKeepAliveRequests 100
KeepAliveTimeout 15
MaxRequestsPerChild 0
LoadModule auth_module        modules/mod_auth.so
```

The server configuration shown here does not run as a service of the Internet super daemon (*inetd*); rather, Apache runs as a standalone daemon. This gives Apache more flexibility in its configuration, as well as performance better than running through *inetd*. Because Apache is able to service more than one client through a single process (using the KeepAlive facility), no production system should ever use the *inetd* mode.

The ServerRoot for the Apache installation is set to */opt/apache1.3* in this installation. All the key files required by Apache are located below this directory root, such as the lock file, the scoreboard file, and the file that records the process identifier (PID) of the current Apache process.

Each of the clients that connect to the server has an expiry date, in the form of a timeout. In this configuration, the timeout is set to 300 seconds (5 minutes). This is the period of inactivity after which a client is deemed to have timed out. Requests are kept alive, with up to 100 requests. There is no limit to the number of requests allowed per child process.

Main Server Configuration

The following options are commonly set in the main server configuration:

```
Port 80
ServerAdmin paul@paulwatters.com
ServerName www.paulwatters.com
DocumentRoot "/opt/apache1.3/htdocs"
<Directory/>
    Options FollowSymLinks
    AllowOverride None
</Directory>
<Directory "/opt/apache1.3/htdocs">
    Options Indexes FollowSymLinks MultiViews
    AllowOverride None
    Order allow,deny
    Allow from all
</Directory>
UserDir "/opt/apache1.3/users/"
DirectoryIndex index.html
AccessFileName .htaccess
<Files .htaccess>
    Order allow,deny
    Deny from all
</Files>
```

The parameters in this section determine the main run-time characteristics of the Apache server. The first parameter is the port on which the Apache server will run. If the server is being executed by an unprivileged user, this must be set at port 1024 or higher. However, if a privileged user like root is executing the process, any unreserved port may be used. (You can check the services database, */etc/services*, for ports allocated to specific services.) By default, port 80 is used.

Next, some details about the server are entered, including the hostname of the system to be displayed in all URLs and a contact e-mail address for the server. This address is usually displayed on all error and CGI misconfiguration pages. The root directory for all HTML and other content for the Web site must also be supplied. This allows for both absolute and relative URLs to be constructed and interpreted by the server. In this case, the *htdocs* subdirectory beneath the main Apache directory is used. Thus, the file *index.html* in this directory will be the default page displayed when no specific page is specified in the URL. Several options can be specified for the *htdocs* directory, including whether or not the server should ignore symbolic links to directories that do not reside under the *htdocs* subdirectory. This is useful when you have files available on CD-ROMs and other file systems that do not need to be copied onto a hard drive, and are simply to be served through the Worldwide Web.

Apache has a simple user authentication system that is similar to the Solaris password database (*/etc/passwd*), in that it makes use of encrypted passwords but does not make use of the Solaris password database. This means that a separate list of users and passwords must be maintained. Thus, when a password-protected page is requested by a user, a username and matching password must be entered using a dialog box. Any directory that appears under the main *htdocs* directory can be password protected using this mechanism.

Next, the various Multipurpose Internet Mail Extensions (MIME) types that can be processed by the server are defined in a separate file called *mime.types*. Let's look at some examples of the MIME types defined for the server:

```
application/mac-binhex40        hqx
application/msword              doc
application/x-csh               csh
```

You can see the file types defined here for many popular applications, including compression utilities (Macintosh BinHex, *application/mac-binhex40*, with the extension *hqx*), word processing documents (Microsoft Word, *application/msword*, with the extension *doc*), and C shell scripts (*application/x-csh*, with the extension *csh*).

The next section deals with logfile formats, as shown here:

```
HostnameLookups Off
ErrorLog /opt/apache1.3/logs/error.log
LogLevel warn
LogFormat "%h %l %u %t \"%r\" %>s %b \"%{Referer}i\"
   \"%{User-Agent}i\"" combined
LogFormat "%h %l %u %t \"%r\" %>s %b" common
LogFormat "%{Referer}i -> %U" referer
LogFormat "%{User-agent}i" agent
CustomLog /opt/apache1.3/logs/access.log common
CustomLog /opt/apache1.3/logs/access.log combined
```

The first directive switches off hostname lookups on clients before logging their activity. Because performing a reverse DNS lookup on every client making a connection is a CPU- and bandwidth-intensive task, many sites prefer to switch off the hostname lookups. However, if you need to gather marketing statistics on where your clients are connecting from (for example, by geographical region or by second-level domain type), you may need to switch on hostname lookups. In addition, an error log is specified as a separate entity to the access log. A typical set of access log entries looks like this:

```
192.64.32.12 - - [06/Jan/2002:20:55:36 +1000]
  "GET /cgi-bin/printenv HTTP/1.1" 200 1024
192.64.32.12 - - [06/Jan/2002:20:56:07 +1000]
  "GET /cgi-bin/Search.cgi?term=solaris&type=simple HTTP/1.1" 200 85527
192.64.32.12 - - [06/Jan/2002:20:58:44 +1000]
  "GET /index.html HTTP/1.1" 200 94151
192.64.32.12 - - [06/Jan/2002:20:59:58 +1000]
  "GET /pdf/secret.pdf HTTP/1.1" 403 29
```

The first example shows that the client *192.64.32.12* accessed the CGI application *printenv* on January 6, 2002, at 8:55 P.M. The result code for the transaction was 200, which indicates a successful transfer. The *printenv* script comes standard with Apache, and it displays the current environment variables being passed from the client. The output is useful for debugging, and it looks like this:

```
DOCUMENT_ROOT="/usr/local/apache-1.3.12/htdocs"
GATEWAY_INTERFACE="CGI/1.1"
HTTP_ACCEPT="image/gif, image/x-xbitmap, image/jpeg, image/pjpeg, */*"
HTTP_ACCEPT_ENCODING="gzip, deflate"
HTTP_ACCEPT_LANGUAGE="en-au"
HTTP_CONNECTION="Keep-Alive"
HTTP_HOST="www"
HTTP_USER_AGENT="Mozilla/4.75 (X11; I; SunOS 5.8 i86pc; Nav)"
PATH="/usr/sbin:/usr/bin:/bin:/usr/ucb:/usr/local/bin "
QUERY_STRING=""
REMOTE_ADDR="209.67.50.55"
REMOTE_PORT="3399"
REQUEST_METHOD="GET"
REQUEST_URI="/cgi-bin/printenv"
SCRIPT_FILENAME="/usr/local/apache/cgi-bin/printenv"
SCRIPT_NAME="/cgi-bin/printenv"
SERVER_ADDR="209.67.50.203"
SERVER_ADMIN="paul@paulwatters.com"
SERVER_NAME="www.paulwatters.com"
SERVER_PORT="80"
SERVER_PROTOCOL="HTTP/1.1"
SERVER_SIGNATURE="Apache/1.3.12 Server at
  www.paulwatters.com Port 80\n"
SERVER_SOFTWARE="Apache/1.3.12 (Unix)" TZ="Australia/NSW"
```

The second example from the log shows that a client running from the same system successfully executed the CGI program *Search.cgi*, passing two *GET* parameters: a search term of *'solaris'* and a search type of *'simple'*. The size of the generated response page was 85,527 bytes. The third example shows a plain HTML page being successfully retrieved, with a response code of 200 and a file size of 94,151 bytes.

The fourth example demonstrates one of the many HTTP error codes being returned, instead of the 200 success code. In this case, a request to retrieve the file */pdf/secret.pdf* is denied with a 403 code being returned to the browser. This code would be returned if the file permissions set on the */pdf/secret.pdf* file did not grant read access to the user executing Apache (for example, nobody).

Virtual Hosts Configuration

The following options are commonly set in the main server configuration:

```
<VirtualHost www.cassowary.net>
    ServerAdmin webmaster@paulwatters.com
    DocumentRoot /opt/apache1.3/htdocs/www.cassowary.net
    ServerName www.cassowary.net
    ErrorLog /opt/apache1.3/logs/www.cassowary.net-error_log
    CustomLog /opt/apache1.3/logs/www.cassowary.net-access_log common
</VirtualHost>
```

Here, a single virtual host (called *www.cassowary.net*) is defined, in addition to the default host for the Apache Web server. Virtual host support allows administrators to keep separate logs for errors and access, as well as a completely separate document root to the default server. This makes it easy to maintain multiple virtual servers on a single physical machine.

Starting Apache

Apache is bundled with a control script (*apachectl*) that can be used to start, stop, and report on the status of the server. To obtain help on the *apachectl* script, the following command is used:

```
$ /opt/apache1.3/apachectl help
usage: /opt/apache1.3/apachectl
 (start|stop|restart|fullstatus|status|graceful|configtest|help)

start      - start httpd
stop       - stop httpd
restart    - restart httpd if running by sending a SIGHUP or start if
             not running
fullstatus - dump a full status screen; requires lynx
  and mod_status enabled
status     - dump a short status screen; requires lynx
  and mod_status enabled
```

```
graceful   - do a graceful restart by sending a SIGUSR1
  or start if not running
configtest - do a configuration syntax test
help       - this screen
```

To start Apache, you issue the following command from the same directory:

```
$ /opt/apache1.3/apachectl start
```

To stop the service, the following command may be used from the same directory:

```
$ /opt/apache1.3/apachectl stop
```

If you change the Apache configuration file, and you need to restart the service so that the server is updated, you can use the following command from the same directory:

```
$ /opt/apache1.3/apachectl restart
```

After Apache is running on port 80, clients will be able to begin requesting HTML pages and other content. However, in recent times, Apache has grown to be more than a simple Web server.

Running Servlets

Many organizations now run Java servlets to provide access to back-end information systems through a Web interface, as discussed in Chapter 2. Apache provides support for servlets through another project known as Apache Tomcat. However, Tomcat does not support the complete Java 2 Enterprise Edition (J2EE) specification as an application server, so its use is limited to applications that do not use Enterprise Java Beans (EJBs) or other enterprise-level services, such as messaging. Commercial application servers, such as JRun from Macromedia, can be configured to work with Apache. Requests for servlets are passed from Apache to the application server on the back end, where they are executed within a JVM.

One of the easiest ways to evaluate servlet technology is to download the Java Servlet Development Kit (JSDK), which is freely available from Sun's Java Web site (**java.sun.com/products/servlet**). The classes included with this reference implementation (such as *javax.servlet.**) can be used with the supplied standalone server (known as *servletrunner*) or can be called using a servlet-enabled Web server. Actually, most Web servers do not yet have in-built support for Java. Typically, a third-party servlet engine must be installed, such as Macromedia's JRun service manager. In addition to performance and reliability benefits, JRun also supports Java Server Pages and other J2EE technologies, which have the ability to include servlet code in-line with HTML pages (a Java version of server-side includes, with many enhancements).

Three basic steps are involved in configuring Apache and JRun to work with Solaris: Compiling the JRun connector proxy source within the Apache source tree, and activating the JRun module (*mod_jrun*); configuring Apache to recognize servlets; and configuring individual servlets within the JRun service manager. Let's look at what each step involves.

Compiling a Connector

The JRun service manager will operate with several different Web servers, including Apache. However, a different connector proxy interface is required for each type of Web server. The source for these connectors is located under the *JRUN_HOME* source tree in the *connectors* subdirectory. The connector source is copied across to a *src/modules/JRun* directory under the *Apache* source tree, and Apache is recompiled with a command like this:

```
$ ./configure --prefix=/opt/apache \
        --activate-module=src/modules/jrun/libjrun.a
```

The activate-module directive should lead to this message being displayed during the Apache build:

```
+ activated JRun module (modules/jrun/libjrun.a)
```

Configuring Apache

After the JRun-enabled version of Apache has been installed, the *httpd.conf* file can be edited to include directives for handling servlets using *mod_jrun*:

```
# JRun Settings
<IfModule mod_jrun.c>
JRunConfig Verbose false
JRunConfig ProxyHost 127.0.0.1
JRunConfig ProxyPort 8081
JRunConfig Timeout 180
JRunConfig Mappings "/opt/jrun-2.2.1/2.2/jsm
-default/services/jse/properties/rules.properties"
</IfModule>
```

Configuring JRun

The *rules.properties* file in the JRun tree contains directives for handling various URLs. An example *rules.properties* file would look like this:

```
*.jrun=invoker
/servlet/=invoker
```

This means that URLs for files with the extension *.JRun* or those that reside under the directory *servlet* will execute a servlet. For example, the servlet *SearchFoo* on the server *www.bar.com* could be executed by this URL:

```
www.bar.com/servlet/SearchFoo
```

The properties that govern the execution of servlets can be found in (unsurprisingly) properties files. After servlets have been loaded into the appropriate *servlets* directory defined in *servlets.properties*, the JRun service manager can be started with a command like this:

```
java com.livesoftware.jrun.service.ServiceManager .
```

Performance Tuning

In the future, when servlet runners and Web servers are fully integrated, performance tuning might be a little less the black art that it currently is. However, the tuning of Apache and JRun is not too difficult (and there's an excellent mailing list archive on the Macromedia site with more than 500 Solaris=related JRun articles). The most important rule with JRun is to "think big": in other words, plan for the peak load periods that your servlets will have to cope with, keeping in mind that the number of processes will be reduced greatly compared to CGI, as outlined earlier.

In the *session.properties* file, for example, we can set the *session.inavalidationinterval* and *session.invalidationtime* to be quite large (for example, 180,000 for 3 minutes). A corresponding value can be set in Apache's *httpd.conf* for the *Timeout* parameter. These values will vary depending on hardware capacity and available network bandwidth. More importantly, several parameters in both *httpd.conf* and the JRun *session.properties* file must be consistent with each other; otherwise, concurrency overflow will arise. In this case, the values for JRun must exceed those given for Apache. For example, the *MaxClients 150* parameter in *httpd.conf* must be lower than the *endpoint.main.max.threads* and *endpoint.main.active.threads* defined in *session.properties*; otherwise, a dreaded error message will be displayed to users:

```
Too many concurrent users. Please try again later.
```

A Sample Servlet

Now that we've examined how to implement a scalable servlet and Web server solution, let's take a quick peek inside a servlet: here's a simple variation on a theme for "Hello World," servlet-style:

```
import java.io.*;
import javax.servlet.*;
import javax.servlet.http.*;

public class ServletHelloWorld extends HttpServlet
{
public void doGet (
    HttpServletRequest      rq,
    HttpServletResponse       rs
    ) throws ServletException, IOException
    {
    PrintWriter out;
rs.setContentType("text/html");
    out = rs.getWriter();
    out.println("<B>Hello, World!</B>");
    out.close();
    }
}
```

Although this servlet does not meet some of the current standards for HTML (like *HEAD* and *BODY* elements), it prints a simple greeting by extending *HttpServlet* and overloading the *doGet()* method (only *HttpServletResponse* is used in this servlet, however). After setting the content type to be HTML, *PrintWriter* is activated to produce some simple HTML output that is produced upon every request to the servlet passed by the Web server. Servlets (and Java programs in general) are much more complex than the simple example presented here, but the same principles of inheritance and overloading can result in complex applications being constructed from relatively few lines of code.

Index

INTERNATIONAL CONTACT INFORMATION

AUSTRALIA
McGraw-Hill Book Company Australia Pty. Ltd.
TEL +61-2-9417-9899
FAX +61-2-9417-5687
http://www.mcgraw-hill.com.au
books-it_sydney@mcgraw-hill.com

CANADA
McGraw-Hill Ryerson Ltd.
TEL +905-430-5000
FAX +905-430-5020
http://www.mcgrawhill.ca

GREECE, MIDDLE EAST, NORTHERN AFRICA
McGraw-Hill Hellas
TEL +30-1-656-0990-3-4
FAX +30-1-654-5525

MEXICO (Also serving Latin America)
McGraw-Hill Interamericana Editores S.A. de C.V.
TEL +525-117-1583
FAX +525-117-1589
http://www.mcgraw-hill.com.mx
fernando_castellanos@mcgraw-hill.com

SINGAPORE (Serving Asia)
McGraw-Hill Book Company
TEL +65-863-1580
FAX +65-862-3354
http://www.mcgraw-hill.com.sg
mghasia@mcgraw-hill.com

SOUTH AFRICA
McGraw-Hill South Africa
TEL +27-11-622-7512
FAX +27-11-622-9045
robyn_swanepoel@mcgraw-hill.com

UNITED KINGDOM & EUROPE (Excluding Southern Europe)
McGraw-Hill Education Europe
TEL +44-1-628-502500
FAX +44-1-628-770224
http://www.mcgraw-hill.co.uk
computing_neurope@mcgraw-hill.com

ALL OTHER INQUIRIES Contact:
Osborne/McGraw-Hill
TEL +1-510-549-6600
FAX +1-510-883-7600
http://www.osborne.com
omg_international@mcgraw-hill.com